ARCHITECTURAL DRAWING
AND LIGHT CONSTRUCTION

FOURTH EDITION

ARCHITECTURAL DRAWING
AND LIGHT CONSTRUCTION

EDWARD J. MULLER

JAMES G. FAUSETT

PRENTICE HALL CAREER & TECHNOLOGY
Englewood Cliffs, New Jersey 07632

Library of Congress Cataloging-in-Publication Data

Muller, Edward John, 1916–
   Architectural drawing and light construction / Edward J. Muller,
James G. Fausett. — 3rd ed.
      p.   cm.
   Includes index.
   ISBN 0-13-045477-X
   1. Architectural drawing.   2. Building—Equipment and supplies—
Drawings.   3. Computer-aided design.   I. Fausett, James G.
II. Title.
NA2700.M8   1993
720′.28′4—dc20   92-35686
                                                          CIP

Editorial/production supervision: Eileen M. O'Sullivan
Acquisitions Editor: Robert Koehler
Cover Design: Marianne Frasco
Manufacturing buyer: Ed O'Dougherty
Prepress buyer: Ilene Levy Sanford
Editorial Assistant: Mark Cohen
Page layout: Laura Ierardi
Interior design: Circa 86
Poster insert (Designer): Ruta Kysilewskyj

©1993, 1985, 1976, 1967 by Prentice-Hall, Inc.
A Simon & Schuster Company
Englewood Cliffs, New Jersey 07632

Printed in the United States of America
10 9 8 7 6 5 4 3 2

ISBN 0-13-045477-X

ISBN 0-13-045501-6 {IEC}

Prentice-Hall International (UK) Limited, *London*
Prentice-Hall of Australia Pty. Limited, *Sydney*
Prentice-Hall Canada Inc., *Toronto*
Prentice-Hall Hispanoamericana, S.A., *Mexico*
Prentice-Hall of India Private Limited, *New Delhi*
Prentice-Hall of Japan, Inc., *Tokyo*
Simon & Schuster Asia Pte. Ltd., *Singapore*
Editora Prentice-Hall do Brasil, Ltda., *Rio de Janeiro*

CONTENTS

2 Lettering   24

3 Basic Technical Drawing   42

4 Axonometric and Oblique Pictorial Drawings   64

5 Freehand Sketching   84

6   Basic Residential Planning   106

7   Light Construction Principles   150

8   Structural Member Selection   222

13 Perspective Drawings, Shades, and Shadows   374

14 Presentation Drawings and Rendering   416

15 Drawing a Small Commercial Building   446

PREFACES

First Edition

This book is intended for the student who likes to draw and who is interested in architectural construction. Although not exhaustive in the many categories of architecture, this work is meant to introduce the important, fundamental areas dealing with the drawing of small buildings. It assumes that the starting point is at the drawing board, and that the first requirement is learning the "graphic language."

The first five chapters are devoted to the mechanics of representing graphic ideas on paper—to be learned in their proper order. Architectural lettering, drafting, geometry, conventional projection principles, and methods of showing sections must be understood before original construction representations are attempted. Some technical schools require a prerequisite of elementary technical drawing before architectural drawing courses are taken. The basic material is included in the book mainly for those students who have not been exposed to technical drawing, for those who may need it for review, or for those who may use the book for home study. The material selected for the introductory work and exercises is architectural in nature, however, rather than mechanical, keeping it within the realm of the title.

Each step is progressive, and simplified procedures are used to develop the principal building representations. The wide variety of detail drawings will provide excellent exercises, not only for developing drafting skill, but for learning construction background information.

Considerable work on freehand sketching is included. Ability to sketch must be given emphasis in drawing courses. Most architectural ideas start with a sketch, and technical discussions are limited unless sketches are used to supplement verbal descriptions. Freehand lettering rather than mechanical lettering is used throughout the material to maintain a consistent architectural appearance. Skill in lettering can be acquired by duplicating plates directly from the text.

The author has tried to bring together written information needed by the student to understand construction problems and examples of good drafting techniques to show him how they are drawn. Where practical, application is made to new products and materials available to the dynamic construction industry. To add variation to the student's work and to make the book more adaptable to classroom use, supplementary exercises are given at the end of appropriate chapters. Additional architectural data are to be found in the Appendices.

Principles of perspective drawing, shades and shadows, rendering, as well as model building, also are included for the purpose of completing the necessary background experience now required in architectural drawing.

In acknowledging the assistance afforded in the preparation of this book, the author wishes to express his sincere gratitude to the following people and organizations: to H. Alan Dale, Jr., A.I.A., of Dale & Smith, Architects, for his invaluable council and the generous contribution of Figs. 12–32, 13–29, 13–30, 14–5, 14–6, 14–7, 14–8, 14–9, 14–10, 14–11; to my colleagues—Dean George L. Carroll for his relentless help with the manuscript; to Robert W. Hays and Ted R. McClure for their help; to Chester R. Orvold, L. A., Wilton W. Vaugn, P.E., Robert L. Myatt, P.E., Charles T. Holldady, P.E., Turner M. Sullivan, P.E., also colleagues, for their assistance; to Seiss Wagner and Charles Stormes for their work on many of the drawings; to Julia Parker for her dedicated library research; to Bob Carter for photos (Figs. 1–1, 1–2, 1–3); to Prentice-Hall, Inc., for permission to adapt Fig. 2–8 from Warren J. Luzadder, *Fundamentals of Engineering Drawing*, 5th Ed.; to Keuffel & Esser Co., for Fig. 2–21; to Master Plan Service, Inc. for Figs. 4–18, 12–29, 12–51, 12–54, 13–4, 13–5, 13–6; to Summer-White & Associates for Figs. 6–6, 6–7, 6–8, 10–15, 12–31; to Aeck Associates Inc., Architects for Fig. 5–29; to General Electric Company for Fig. 6–36; to Lumber Dealers Research Council, Inc. for the material for Figs. 6–45, 6–46, 6–47; to Brown & Wright Associates, Registered Architects for Figs. 8–30, 8–31; to Anderson Corporation for Fig. 9–11; to Curtis Companies, Incorporated for Fig. 9–15; to Glide Corporation, division of Aluminum Extrusion Co., for Fig. 9–16; to The Donley Brothers Company for Fig. 9–20; to General Aniline & Film Corporation for Fig. 8–35; to American Radiator & Standard Sanitary Corporation for Figs. 11–21, 11–29; to Rolscreen Company for Figs. 12–5, 13–17; to Bob Allen for material on professional perspective; to Hugh Stubbins, F.A.I.A., for Fig. 13–2; to Paul Lyons for Fig. 13–3; to Ed Moulthrop of Robert & Co. Associates, Architects & Engineers for Figs. 13–1, 13–2, 13–14, 13–15; to Stevens & Wilkinson, Architects for Fig. 15–1; to Larry Cuba for photos (Figs. 15–2, 15–3, 15–5, 15–6, 15–11, 15–12); to Sholtz Homes, Inc. for many of the chapter-opening drawings; to National Warm Air Heating and Air Conditioning Association for permission to reproduce Worksheet Form J-1 (Appendix G); to Sara Howard for the final typing of the manuscript; to the others who may have been overlooked; and especially to my wife, Colette, for her indulgence and help in so many ways.

Second Edition

Since the original edition was published in 1967, hundreds of schools throughout the country and abroad have found the book effectual in their drawing, architectural, and construction courses. Almost all levels of instruction in a wide variety of applications have shown favorable responses to the material and its presentation. Home study programs as well have found it readily adaptable, which, needless to say, has been gratifying to the author.

Therefore, much of the first edition has been retained, and suggestions by the many users have been added wherever possible to make the second edition even more applicable.

New lumber sizes have required some updating, many illustrations have been added, new material on basic drawing, lettering, sketching, residential site planning, roofs, insulation, metric conversion, perspective drawing, reflections, and others have been in-

cluded. An entirely new chapter on careers in construction, an expanded glossary, and a set of residential working drawings also have been added. You will notice other refinements throughout the book that will make the new edition a most valuable tool for classroom or homestudy instruction as well as a handy reference for the many areas of architectural drawing and building construction.

Acknowledgment is gratefully made to the following, and others who may have been overlooked, for their generous help in furnishing photos or material for this edition: to Keuffel & Esser Company for Fig. 2–21; to Cheshire-Bladwin, Architects, for Figs. 5–42, 5–43; to Pella Windows and Doors for Fig. 6–58; to Brown Brothers for Fig. 6–60, 6–62; to Hedrich-Blessing, Architectural Photographers, for Figs. 6–51, 6–52, 6–53, 6–54, 6–55, 6–56, 6–57, 6–59; to John Jobson, student, for Fig. 6–63; to Bob Carter Photos for Figs. 6–64; 6–65, 17–1, 17–3, 17–5, 17–6; to Western Wood Products Association for Figs. 7–54; to California Redwood Association for Fig. 7–59; to American Plywood Association and Southern Forest Products Association for the material in Fig. 8–32; to Mr. Klok and U.S. Gypsum Company for Fig. 12–27; to Grayson Evans, student, for Fig. 13–7; to Ed Moulthrop, architect, for Figs. 13–15, 13–21; to Robers Sussenback, student, for Fig. 13–28; to W. Roy Reese, Jr. & Associates for Fig. 14–4; to Ken Sargent, student, for Chapter 15 opening drawing; to Frank Vella for Fig. 17–2; to National Forest Products Association for Appendix E, Plank-and-Beam Design Data; to Charles H. Stormes for Appendix I, Residential Working Drawings; and finally to Rosalie Herion and her coworkers in the Prentice-Hall College Editorial-Production Department for their diligent care in putting it all together.

Third Edition

In keeping with the intent of the previous editions, the third edition is intended to update material and be even more helpful to the student of architectural drawing and technology. A new chapter on selecting structural members for light framing has been added. A completely new set of working drawings for a Solar Home designed by TVA has been included, and more extensive material on passive solar design considerations in home construction will be found in this edition; the many new illustrations should strengthen student interpretation and underscore this important area of modern energy-efficient housing.

More information on inking, lettering, axonometric drawing, construction details, new materials, pictorial drawing, specifications, and construction terms has also been added to bring together the most helpful information available for architecturally oriented students.

Acknowledgements are in order to my former colleagues; James G. Faucett, who is a practicing architect, for his help in reviewing the previous edition; Mr. Robert L. Myatt, Jr., P.E., for his help in reviewing the new Chapter 8; Mr. James W. C. McKay, Jr., also a practicing architect, for his drafting of the Solar Home working drawings.

To Mr. Tony Ames, Architect—Atlanta—for Figs. 4–17A, B, & C; to Koh-I-Noor Rapidograph, Inc., for Fig. 1–22; and to any others who may have been overlooked. May I also say many thanks to the Prentice-Hall College Editorial-Production Department again for their splendid cooperation as always.

EDWARD J. MULLER
Atlanta, Georgia

Fourth Edition

For a quarter of a century *Architectural Drawing and Light Construction* has been the premier textbook selected by educators and students of architectural drawing and technology in North America. The fourth edition continues this fine tradition by reflecting current trends in drafting equipment, drawing techniques, environmental planning, construction materials and details, architectural delineation, writing specifications and CAD.

State-of-the-art drafting instruments and drawing mediums are presented. The chapter on lettering has been revised to include modern style lettering and lettering devices used by the drafting profession. Methods for developing axonometric, isometric, dimetric, trimetric and oblique pictorial drawings are explained. Residential planning has been expanded to include site and program analysis. Light frame structural systems including floor trusses, roof trusses, truss joists, space frames and cable structure are illustrated. The latest building materials and systems of enclosing space in residences and small commercial buildings are discussed. A new set of detailed working drawings for a commercial building has been adopted. Updated architectural presentations and renderings with an explanation of delineation mediums are illustrated. Not only has the chapter on writing specifications been revised, but also the automated systems used to develop construction specifications are discussed. A new introductory chapter to CAD has been written to offer the student, who has mastered architectural drawing skills, the insight to pursue computer drafting and design. Creative and challenging drawing exercises at the end of the chapters have been expanded.

The authors have endeavored to offer the most comprehensive textbook devoted to architectural drawing and the principles of light construction in print today.

In sincere appreciation the authors wish to acknowledge the following individuals and organizations for the exemplary contributions to the fourth edition: Paul M. Black, A.I.A. for writing the CAD chapter; James N. Davis, C.S.I. for revising, Writing Specifications; Robert Boehmig, P.E. for updating, Structural Member Selection; Kenneth Beckworth, P.E., William E. Owen, P.E. and James W. Phillips, P.E. for reviewing, Residential Mechanical and Electrical Systems; James W. C. McKay, Jr., Professor, for reviewing, Perspective Drawings, Shades and Shadows and for Figs. 13–57 through 13–60; Edward T. White, Professor, for perfecting the site analysis and space adjacency analysis that are referenced in Chapter 6; David Surface, Architect, for updating architectural lettering throughout the book; James Currier, A.I.A. for assistance with building codes; Christopher Crossman, student, for providing the artwork for the cover of the book; James W. Mise, student, for providing the artwork for the title page for the book; Frank Betz, residential designer, for renderings for the opening pages of Chapters 1, 3, 5, 12, and Fig. 6–50, 6–54, 6–67A, 6–67B and 13–56; W. D. Farmer, A.I.B.D., for renderings for the opening pages of Chapters 2, 4, 6, 7, 8, 10, 11, 13, 16, 17, 18, and Fig. 14–17B; James Zirkel, C.E.O., Home Design Services for renderings for the opening pages of Chapters 9 and 15; Donald A. Gardner, A.I.A., for a rendering for the opening page of Chapter 14; Craig Headrick, student, for Fig. 4–1; Thomas Smith, for Figs. 5–38, 5–47, 5–48, 14–1A, 14–1B, 14–4A, 14–4B, 14–4C, 16–2; Steve Lewis, for Figs. 5–29, 5–49; Lucian L. Tatum III, student, for Figs. 5–40, 5–42, 5–43; Robin K. Ammons, for Figs. 6–18, 6–44; Frank F. Venning, Architect, Fig. 6–86; Western Pennsylvania Conservancy for Fig. 6–45; Monticello, Thomas Jefferson Memorial Foundation for Fig. 6–46; William E. Chegwidden, A.I.A., for Figs. 3–3, 5–50, 13–30, 14–29A, 14–29B, 14–29C, 14–29D, 16–5; George W. Evans for Fig. 14–2; Dimitri A. Parein, student, for Fig. 14–3; Stephen S. Fuller for Figs. 14–5A, 14–5B, 14–5C; Christopher Holley, student, for Fig. 14–6; Mark M. Freeman for Fig. 14–7; Hugh H. Westberry for Figs. 14–8, 14–21B, 14–21C, 14–27, 14–28; Dan Harmon for Figs. 14–30A, 14–30B; Ray Elliott for Fig. 14–30C; James Cagle for Fig. 14–31; Don R. Dorsey, A.I.A. for Figs. 15–4 through 15–25; Wesley W. Taylor for Figs. 16–11A, 16–11B, 16–11C.

For special contributions the authors are indebted to Cecily Merchant for typing and Angela Fausett for reviewing the manuscript. May we also recognize Robert Koehler, Eileen O'Sullivan and others of the Prentice-Hall Editorial Production Department for their high level of professionalism in publishing the fourth edition.

EDWARD J. MULLER
JAMES G. FAUSETT

Reviewers

Earl Faulkner
ITT Technical Institute

Robert Hudson
St. Petersburg Junior College

Murray Kinnich
Milwaukee Area Technical College
Milwaukee, WI

Fred Brasfield
Tarrant County Junior College
Fort Worth, TX

Michael Davis
Henry Ford Community College

James Merrigan
Brookdale Community College

Carmine Ruocca
Jefferson State College

Olga Szokolay
Norwalk State Technical College

Bill Cantrell
Texas Tech University

Murray Cohen
New York Institute of Technology

Dennis Niewig
Ranken Technical Institute

Bob Vezzuto
California State University-Long Beach

The authors especially wish to thank the following people for their in-depth assistance:

Stephen Brasgalla
Broward Community College

James Lesslie
Central Piedmont Community College

Tom Madigan
Northern Virginia Community College

Brian Matthews
Wake Technical Community College

James Patton
Purdue University

ARCHITECTURAL DRAWING
AND LIGHT CONSTRUCTION

DRAFTING EQUIPMENT AND ITS USES

FRANK BETZ

"Man is a tool-using animal . . . without tools he is nothing, with tools he is all."

—*THOMAS CARLYLE*

The first consideration in the mastery of the mechanics of drafting is, naturally, the selection of the proper equipment. Many instruments are available at drafting supply stores, so many, in fact, that it would be bewildering for a beginning student to select appropriate and proper equipment without getting a few words of preliminary advice. Comparatively few pieces of equipment are necessary if carefully chosen. In selecting any of the instruments, the first advice is—buy the best quality you can afford. Second, purchase only equipment produced by reputable manufacturers; you will then be assured of accuracy and good design. Many instruments and pieces of equipment are continually being improved and redesigned to aid the drafter. Third, good equipment deserves proper care and treatment; do not abuse it or use it for any purpose other than the purpose for which it was designed.

To get the most from equipment, the aspiring architectural drafter must develop enough skill to have complete control of his or her instruments. This comes with *practice*, deliberate and well-directed practice, which develops good work habits and eventually leads to the attainment of speed. Early training in drawing places particular emphasis on accuracy and skill until correct work habits are formed; speed will develop gradually with experience.

1.1 A List of Necessary Equipment

The following list is the recommended minimum equipment for student use. Refer to Fig. 1-1 of basic equipment, which illustrates each piece listed below. Although some of the equipment is identical to that used in engineering drawing, it is nevertheless specifically appropriate for architectural drawing:

1. Drawing board (24″ × 36″) (32″ × 48″)
2. T square or parallel bar (36″–48″)
3. 30°–60° plastic triangle (14″)
4. 45° plastic triangle (10″)
5. 12″ architect's scale, triangular
6. Two mechanical pencils, several 3H, 2H, H, F and non-print leads
7. Pencil pointer, either sandpaper or mechanical pointer
8. Erasers, 1 Pink Pearl, 1 Artgum, 1 white plastic, 1 kneaded
9. Roll of drafting tape
10. Erasing shield

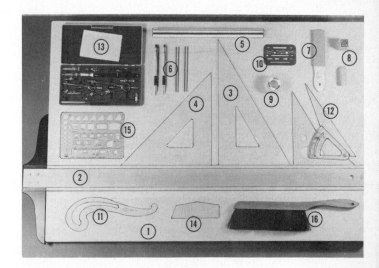

FIGURE 1-1 Basic drafting equipment.

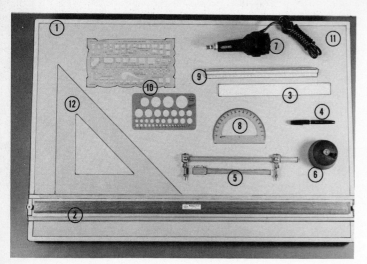

Figure 1-2 Supplementary drafting equipment.

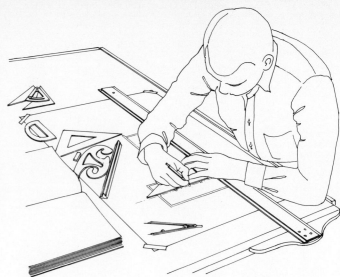

Figure 1-3 Using the drafting equipment on the drawing table.

11. Irregular curve or French curve
12. Adjustable triangle (a small size is sufficient)
13. Small set of case instruments
14. Lettering guide
15. Architectural template ($\frac{1}{4}'' = 1'\text{-}0''$) (select one with circles)
16. Dusting brush
17. Tracing paper

The following list of supplemental equipment (Fig. 1-2) will be useful for advanced students or drafters working in architectural offices:

1. Large drawing table ($38'' \times 72''$), drafting stool ($30''$)
2. Parallel bar ($60''$)
3. Flat architect's scale, 4-bevel
4. Technical drafting pen, India ink
5. Beam compass
6. Mechanical pencil pointer
7. Electric eraser
8. Protractor, semicircular
9. Civil engineer's scale
10. Additional architectural templates
11. Vinyl plastic pad for drawing surface
12. Large 45° plastic triangle ($14''$)
13. Plastic drafting leads, E-1, E-2, E-3
14. Mylar drafting film
15. Drafting lamp

1.2 Drawing Boards and Tables

The drawing board or table should be large enough to accommodate the anticipated drawing sheet sizes. Architectural drawings may be $24''$ to $48''$ long by $24''$ to $36''$ wide, thus requiring large boards; beginning work can usually be placed on a $24''$ by $36''$ board. The board should have a perfectly smooth surface and be rigid enough to prevent warping and bending. The edges that guide the T square must be straight and true. Students often rely on portable drawing boards for beginning work. Boards made of seasoned basswood or clear white pine, laminated or constructed to prevent warping, are relatively light and easily transported (Fig. 1-3). The drawing surface of a wood board should be protected with a paper or vinyl pad. An inclined board with a 10° or 15° slope from the horizontal is a desirable position for drafting. Portable boards with collapsible supports under the corners are available.

A flush solid core wood door $2'\text{-}6''$ or $3'\text{-}0''$ wide by $6'\text{-}8''$ or $7''\text{-}0''$ long supported on legs or cabinets is a popular choice for a drawing board (Fig. 1-4). Care should be taken to select a door that is not warped and has one smooth surface. A $42''$ to $60''$ parallel bar and surface cover should be placed near the center of the door to allow space for instruments at the sides.

Although some drafters use a drafting chair and a board height of $28''$ to $30''$ at the lower edge, most prefer a drafting stool and a board height of $36''$ to $40''$ at the lower edge. It is desirable to select or construct a drafting board or table that can be adjusted in height and slope. The drafter occasionally moves from a seated position to a standing position to alleviate fatigue.

Many types of drafting boards and tables are marketed today. Some are constructed of melamine-covered particle board with lightweight tubular steel legs; these boards are more suitable for the occasional drafter. Elaborate tables are available with sturdy wood or vinyl-laminated metal tops. These tables have adjustable slopes and heights. Most have metal edges to prevent warping and provide an easy sliding edge for the T square.

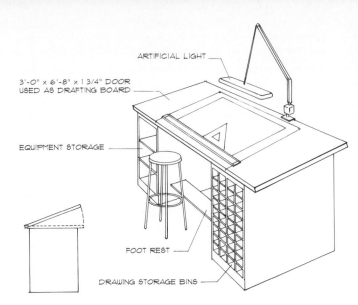

Figure 1-4 An economical table can be made from a flush door.

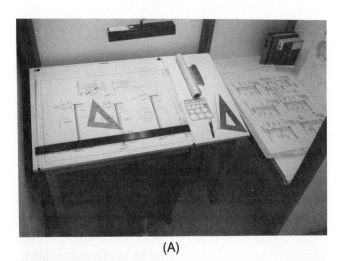

(A)

(B)

Figure 1-5 (A) Student's drafting space. (B) Professional's drafting work station.

A simple metal drafting stool with a wood or metal seat 27″ to 28″ high is frequently used by the beginning drafter. The swivel chair, 17″ to 18″ high, and the swivel stool, 27″ to 28″ high, on casters are used by the professional drafter. Most of these are designed with a foot rest and have upholstered seats and backs that are adjustable.

Drafting work stations are common in the professional workplace and in some schools. These work stations consist of a drafting table, CADD monitor, keyboard, digitizer pad, layout table, file drawers, equipment storage cabinets, shelving, and a drafting chair (Fig. 1-5).

1.3 Board Covers and Drafting Surfaces

The surface of the board is very important if good drafting techniques are to be attained. It is never desirable to draft on an unprotected wood drawing board unless the drafting medium is an illustration board or a very heavyweight paper. Sharp pencil leads etch the wood surface. Paper underlays are satisfactory if they have a slightly spongy effect; however, paper usually will retain grooves from line work, occasionally necessitating replacing the paper pads. Plastic-coated tinted paper with or without a ⅛″ vertical and horizontal grid is available for an underlayment. The grid serves as guidelines for tracing paper overlays. The resilient sheet-vinyl pad is the most desirable board cover. Available in light tint, this product is durable and provides an excellent drafting surface. All drawing board covers should be installed with care. Paper covers are usually wrapped around the edges of the drawing board and taped or tacked to the back surface. Vinyl pads simply lay on the drafting surface and can be stabilized with double-face tape or tacks at the edges. Vinyls tend to expand and contract with temperature change. The use of glues and mastics to attach papers or vinyl pads should be avoided. Glues can dissolve the vinyl pad and produce irregular surfaces under paper and pad covers that make drafting difficult. Board covers should lay perfectly flat.

1.4 T Squares

The standard, fixed-head T square is frequently used by the beginning drafter to draw horizontal lines. Select a T square that is rigidly attached at the head and has perfectly straight edges on the blade. The most satisfactory T squares have wood or high-quality plastic heads and blades (Fig. 1-1). The blades should have transparent plastic edges so that the drafter can see the drawing below the edges. Avoid using T squares longer than the drawing board or greater than 42″ in length as they become unwieldy and less accurate. Only the top edge of the blade is used; it is referred to as the working edge.

A right-handed drafter should hold the head of the T square firmly against the left edge of the board with the left hand; the left-handed drafter should reverse the procedure. To draw a horizontal line, the right-handed drafter should position the T square with the left hand on the T square head and then slide the left hand over the top surface of the blade and hold it with a slight pressure so that the T square will not move until the line is drawn. Keep the pencil point against the top edge of the blade and lean it slightly, approximately 80° from the drafting surface, in the direction the line is advancing (Fig. 1-6). The pencil should maintain the same slope and pressure in relation to the T square throughout the entire length of the line; otherwise, a variable-width line will result. The pencil should be revolved slowly when the line is drawn so that the point will wear evenly and last longer. Allow the pencil point to contact the edge of the T square before drawing the line; this provides accuracy. The practice of putting pressure on the beginning and end of each line should be developed early. Avoid going back and forth over a line.

1.5 Parallel Bars and Drafting Machines

Many drafters save time by using the parallel bar, which is always kept parallel by braided wires attached to the board at the corners and running on pulleys through the bar (Fig. 1-2). Hardwood or hard plastic parallel bars with edges of clear plastic in lengths of 36″, 42″, 48″, 54″, 60″, 72″, 84″, and 96″ are standard. Some are adapted with small ball-bearing rollers underneath the bars to minimize direct contact with the drawing surface and to facilitate sliding the bar up and down the board. Parallel bars with a raised blade above the edges are desirable because the blade serves as a finger grip and allows the drafter to grasp the bar easily. A setscrew and compression plate at the top of the drawing table held tight against the braided wire keeps the bar parallel. The drafter can adjust the bar by loosening the setscrew, sliding the bar to the stops at the bottom edge of the drawing table, and then tightening the setscrew against the compression plate.

Drafting machines are more popular with the engineering drafter than the architectural drafter. The drafting machine is a mechanical device that is attached to the top edge of the drafting table and has a pair of pinned arms with an elbow, a head with a protractor, and both vertical and horizontal scales (Fig. 1-7). The drafter can move the drafting machine horizontally, vertically, and diagonally across the drafting surface. It is a convenient device for drawing sloping lines. The protractor on the head can be set at any angle, and bars can be interchanged with different scales. The length of lines drawn at any one position is limited to the length of the scale, which is approximately 18″ long.

Track drafting machines are designed with a fixed horizontal track at the top edge of the drawing board and a movable vertical track attached to the horizontal

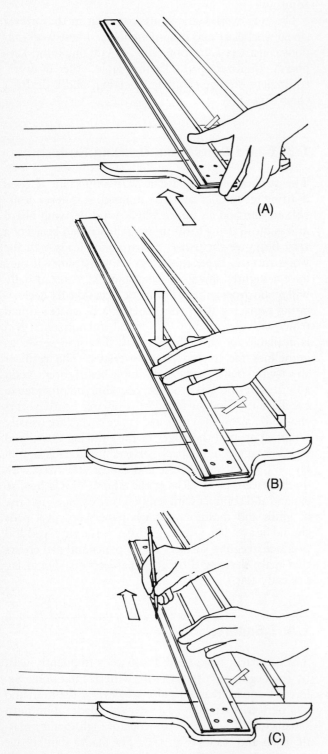

(A)

(B)

(C)

Figure 1-6 Drawing horizontal lines with the T square. (A) Placing T square in position on board; (B) holding T square with slight pressure; (C) drawing horizontal line. (Left-handed drafters would use opposite side of board.)

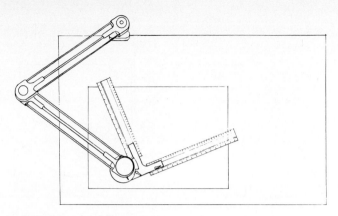

FIGURE 1-7 Arm-style drafting machine.

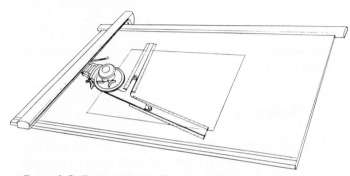

FIGURE 1-8 Track-style drafting machine.

track (Fig. 1-8). The protractor head is mounted on the vertical track. Two scales can be attached to the head. Track drafting machines offer versatility and accuracy. Both the arm-style and track machines are fabricated from metals and hard plastics. Wide varieties of clear acrylic and metal scales ranging in length from 12″ to 18″ are available for the drafting machine.

1.6 Pencils, Leads, and Pointers

Traditional wooden pencils are hexagonal in shape and are available in 17 degrees of hardness, which are indicated by letters and numbers near the end of the pencil (Fig. 1-9). Sharpen the wooden pencil with a pen knife or pencil pointer by removing the wood from the end opposite the hardness symbol until approximately ³⁄₈″ of lead is exposed (Fig. 1-10). A cone point or chisel point can be achieved by revolving the lead over a sandpaper pad (Fig. 1-11).

Lead holders or mechanical pencils manufactured from metals and hard plastics hold sticks of lead and are popular tools of the drafter (Fig. 1-12). These pencils have a knurled surface at the finger area. Lead is held by a spring chuck and can be quickly released for sharpening or removal by pressing the cap. Lead holders ac-

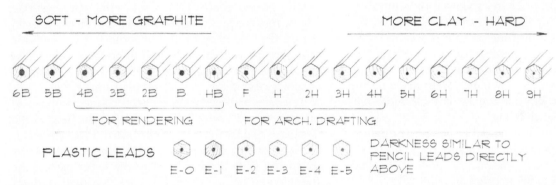

FIGURE 1-9 Pencil hardness chart.

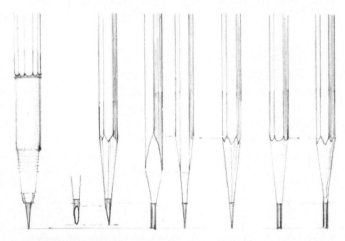

FIGURE 1-10 Sharpening drafting pencils.

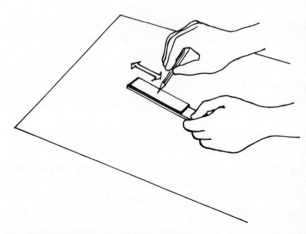

FIGURE 1-11 Pointing the wood pencil with a sandpaper pad. (Do not sharpen over drawings.)

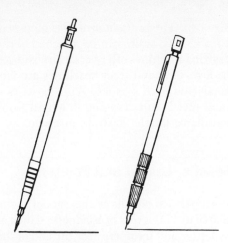

FIGURE 1-12 Lead holder and mechanical pencil.

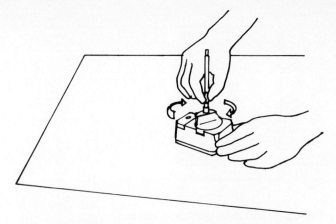

FIGURE 1-13 Pointing the lead with a mechanical lead pointer.

commodate 2-mm-diameter lead, and mechanical pencils hold 0.5, 0.7, and 0.9 mm sizes. Leads in varying degrees of hardness are available for both the lead holders and mechanical pencils.

Graphite-clay leads are used predominantly with papers and illustration boards. The majority of architectural drafting can be accomplished with 2H, H, and F leads. Plastic leads in 6 degrees of hardness are available for drafting on film and are produced in 2, 0.5, 0.7, and 0.9 mm sizes. The degree of hardness of plastic leads is designated by a letter followed by a number, such as E-0, E-1, or E-2. The softest is E-0 and the hardest is E-5. Most drafting on film is accomplished using E-1, E-2, and E-3 plastic leads. NON-PRINT or NON-PHOTO pencils and leads are used for making guidelines and notes on drawings. Marks made by the blue-colored leads will not appear on most reproductions of the original drawing.

A sharp lead point is essential to good line quality. Leads can be sharpened on sandpaper pads; however, most drafters use a mechanical lead pointer. Several models of mechanical pointers are available (Fig. 1-13). Some pointers are small and must be held in the hand and revolved to create a point. A weighted metal pointer that can be located at random on the drawing table uses a circular sandpaper insert to create a sharp point. Another style of lead pointer clips to the edge of the drafting table. Lead dust collects inside each pointer and must be removed periodically. Both graphite lead and plastic lead can be sharpened using the same style of pointer.

The main consideration in choosing a lead is the sharpness of lines and its opaqueness for reproduction. Softer leads wear faster and require repointing, whereas hard leads may groove or cut the paper. Different drafters produce various line weights with the same leads; experience will lead the individual to the correct lead to use for the desired lines. Remember that the pressure used by the drafter, the texture of the paper, atmospheric conditions, the accuracy required, and the opaqueness needed for reproduction should all be considered when selecting a lead.

1.7 Triangles

Relatively large triangles are needed for architectural drawings; a 10″ 45° triangle and a 14″ 30°–60° triangle are satisfactory for the work covered in this book (Fig. 1-1). Triangles should be made of heavy, transparent acrylic plastic about 0.06″ thick with true, accurate edges. Inside edges should be beveled to facilitate picking up the triangle with the fingernails. Lucite plastic triangles are available in tinted fluorescent colors that transmit light through their edges, thus reducing shadows near the edges of the instrument.

Triangles are used to draw vertical lines or diagonal lines at 30°, 45°, or 60°. First, position the head of the T square against the edge of the board. Place the triangle with one of its legs against the upper edge of the T square; slide the left hand to the lower part of the triangle and blade of the T square. Maintain a slight pressure on the instruments until a line is drawn upward along the vertical edge of the triangle (Fig. 1-14).

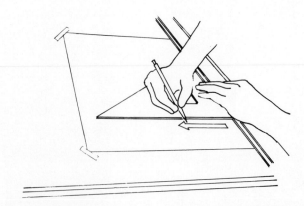

FIGURE 1-14 Drawing vertical lines with triangle. (Reverse for left-handed drafters.)

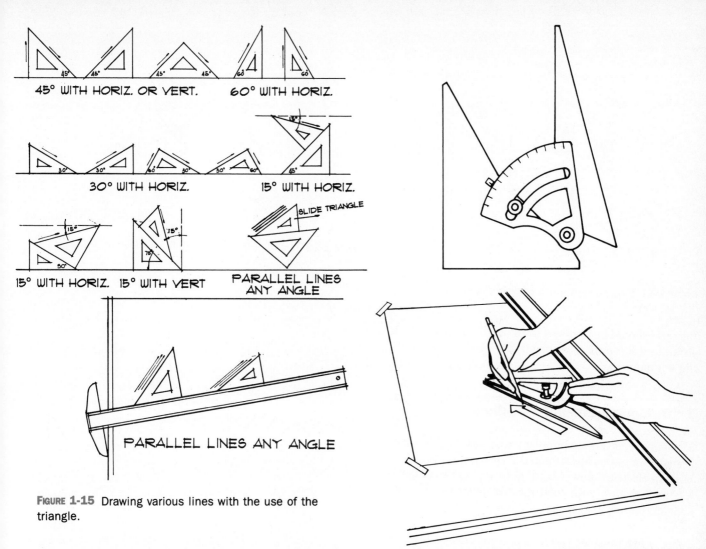

FIGURE 1-15 Drawing various lines with the use of the triangle.

FIGURE 1-16 Drawing lines with the adjustable triangle.

The left-handed drafter should hold the T square blade and the triangle with the right hand and draw vertical lines upward, away from the body. The vertical ruling edge of the triangle should be placed so that the vertical line will be drawn along the edge closest to the head of the T square. Refrain from pulling the pencil down along the vertical side of the triangle. If long vertical or diagonal lines are required, stop the line short of the end of the triangle, and slide the triangle and T square up so that the line can be continued. Various angles and parallel lines can be drawn with triangles and a T square (Fig. 1-15).

1.8 Adjustable Triangles

The adjustable triangle is used to draw diagonal lines at angles other than 30°, 45°, or 60°. It has a protractor scale adjustment from 0° to 45° from the horizontal or base line. The outer protractor scale indicates angles from 0° to 45° from the longer base, while the inner scale indicates angles from 45° to 90° from the shorter base (Fig. 1-16). Some adjustable triangles have scales that indicate roof slopes and stair risers. The triangle

can be adjusted by loosening or tightening a setscrew, which also serves as a convenient lifting handle. A small adjustable triangle with a 6″ to 8″ leg is most useful.

1.9 Erasers

Even the most advanced drafters must erase occasionally; excessive erasing should be avoided. Selecting the proper eraser for a specific lead type that will not damage or discolor the surface of the paper or film is important. Block erasers such as artgum, soft pink, or white plastic are effective in removing graphic pencil or plastic lead from tracing paper and film. Paper-wrapped, pencil-shaped erasers can be reshaped by peeling the paper from the end of the eraser. Pencil-type eraser holders are available for soft pink or white plastic eraser sticks (Fig. 1-17). Block or stick erasers in pastel tints such as blue, yellow, or green and imbibed with an erasing fluid are suitable for erasing ink on film and some selected papers. A residue left from the eras-

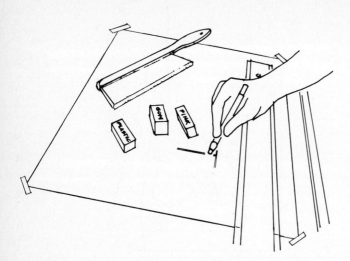

FIGURE 1-17 Erasing with a holder-type eraser.

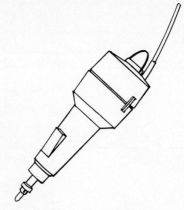

FIGURE 1-18 Electric erasing machine.

ing fluid should be removed from the film or paper with a standard soft pink or white plastic eraser before drafting commences.

1.10 Electric Erasing Machines

Mechanical erasers are popular with drafters. These are available in numerous sizes and styles (Fig. 1-18). Most have an electrical power cord; however, some are cordless and operate with rechargeable batteries. All mechanical erasers use replacable eraser sticks that are held securely on the end of the shaft with a screw-type collet. Care must be taken to prevent erasing holes in papers and films when using the mechanical erasers.

Drafters frequently clean a drawing during and after the drawing process. Some drafters use an artgum eraser for removing guidelines and smudges. Others prefer a dry cleaning pad, which is a small cloth bag filled with a granular eraser dust. Placing too much pressure on the eraser or dry cleaning pad can result in the removal of important lines.

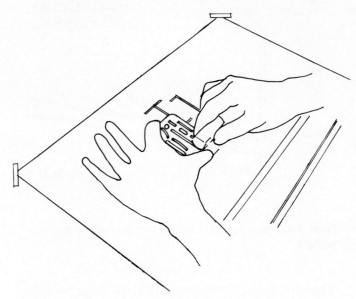

FIGURE 1-19 Using the erasing shield.

1.11 Erasing Shield

The erasing shield is a thin, metal instrument with holes of various shapes. To erase with the shield, select the opening that best fits the line or area to be eradicated and hold the erasing shield down firmly on the drawing. Then rub the line with the appropriate eraser (Fig. 1-19). Not only is it handy when eradicating small lines in confined areas without disturbing the lines, but it also can save time in other situations. For example, thin columns in front of a brick elevation view can be erased from the wall symbol line work much faster than starting and stopping the brickwork on each side of the column.

1.12 Protractor

Odd angles, other than those drawn with a 45° triangle, a 30°–60° triangle, or a combination of both, can be laid out with the protractor. It is a semicircular plastic instrument with degree calibrations marked off along its curved edge and a center or apex identified in the center of its straight side. The two reversed scales along the curvature of the protractor allow angles to be laid out in either direction from the horizontal. More expensive protractors have ruling bars attached to the pivot point or apex for easier angle layout. Many drafters use the calibrated adjustable triangle instead of a protractor when odd angle layout is required (Fig. 1-20).

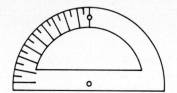

FIGURE 1-20 Protractor.

FIGURE 1-21 Irregular curves.

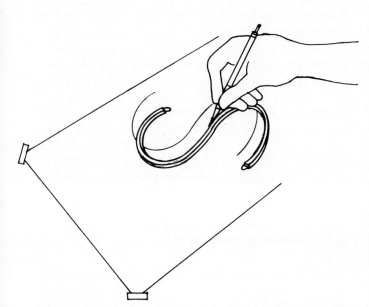

FIGURE 1-22 Adjustable curve.

1.13 Irregular Curves

Regular curves, that is, true circles and arcs, are drawn with a compass or circle template, but often it is necessary to draw irregular curves—those with nonuniform curvature. Many clear acrylic curves are manufactured. Experience has shown that the most useful irregular curve is one that has a number of small curvatures, as well as a few long, slightly curved edges (Fig. 1-21).

To draw an irregular curved line, first plot the points accurately through which the curve should pass and then select the edge on the irregular curve that will coincide with the most points on the paper. Intersecting lines on a curve should be continuous. If considerable curved work is involved and the curvatures are not too small, an adjustable curve will save time and result in neater lines. This instrument is made of a flexible metal core covered with a rubber or metal ruling edge (Fig. 1-22). It can be bent to the desired curvature before the line is drawn. Long, accurate curves often require the use of a flexible spline curve that is held in place on the drawing with metal weights. Ship curves or highway curves are convenient instruments for drawing long, smooth, uninterrupted lines.

1.14 The Architect's Scale

Most measurements on architectural drawings are made with the architect's scale. Scales are made of wood, plastic, or wood laminated with plastic. Sharp edges and distinct, machine-divided markings on the scale are necessary for accurate measurements. Scales are usually flat or triangular in shape and are available in 6″, 12″, and 18″ lengths, with the triangular-shape 12″ length being the most popular. The edges of all scales are beveled (see Fig. 1-23). Scales are fully divided or open divided. Fully divided scales have each

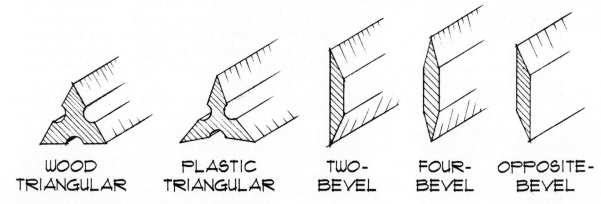

WOOD TRIANGULAR   PLASTIC TRIANGULAR   TWO-BEVEL   FOUR-BEVEL   OPPOSITE-BEVEL

FIGURE 1-23 Sectional shapes of drafting scales.

main unit throughout the entire scale fully subdivided. Open-divided scales have the main units undivided and a fully subdivided extra unit placed at the zero end of the scale; the architect's scale that is calibrated in feet and inches is open divided. Listed below are the 11 scales found on the triangular architect's scale:

Full scale—$^1/_{16}$" graduations
$^1/_8$" = 1'-0"
$^1/_4$" = 1'-0" (one-forty-eighth size)
$^3/_8$" = 1'-0"
$^3/_4$" = 1'-0"
$^1/_2$" = 1'-0" (one-twenty-fourth size)
1" = 1'-0" (one-twelfth size)
$1^1/_2$" = 1'-0" (one-eighth size)
3" = 1'-0" (one quarter size)
$^3/_{32}$" = 1'-0"
$^3/_{16}$" = 1'-0"

Two different scales are combined on each face except the full-size scale, which is fully divided into sixteenths. The combined scales are compatible; one is twice as large as the other, and their zero points and extra subdivided units are on opposite ends of the scale. The extra unit near the end of the scale is subdivided into twelfths of a foot or inches, as well as fractions of inches on the larger scales.

Accuracy in using the scale when preparing drawings is extremely important. To measure correctly with the scale, select the proper scaling edge and place it on the drawing with the edge parallel and slightly below the line to be measured (see Fig. 1-24). First, count from zero the full number of feet in the dimension, and using a sharp pencil make a dash with a non-print pencil at right angles to the scale; then count the inches (if the dimension has both feet and inches) from the same zero

in the opposite direction on the scale and mark the other limit of the dimension (refer to Fig. 1-25). Laying out fractional parts of an inch at smaller scales will require interpolation between the calibrations. To avoid accumulative errors, a series of dimensions should be marked off, if possible, without moving the scale. Unequal dimensions should be added and then marked off consecutively from the original reference point. Always check the total length of the line to ensure that no accumulative error has resulted.

1.15 Civil Engineer's Scale

Occasionally, a civil engineer's scale is needed by architectural drafters for drawing plot plans, land measurement, and stress diagrams. Civil engineer's scales are always fully divided and can be obtained in any of the flat or triangular types (see Fig. 1-23). Scales found on the triangular type are 1" = 10', 1" = 20', 1" = 30', 1" = 40', 1" = 50', and 1" = 60'. Land measurement is always recorded in feet and decimal parts of a foot, rather than in inches. Therefore, the inch unit on the 1" = 10' scale would have 10 divisions, and the inch unit on the 1" = 20' scale would have 20 divisions, each representing feet throughout the other scales. If a scale of 1" = 100' were needed, the 1" = 10' scale could be used by merely letting each inch represent 100' instead of 10'. This method applies to other scales as well.

1.16 Drafting Templates

Templates are made of thin plastic with various sized or scaled openings cut in the sheet. Many symbols used on architectural drawings can be found on templates. Circles, squares, rectangles, triangles, ovals, hexagons, arrows, door swings, furniture, plumbing fixtures, and electrical symbols are a few of the items that are available in template form. Architectural templates are available in scales of $^1/_8$" = 1', $^1/_4$" = 1', and $^1/_2$" = 1' (Fig. 1-26). In using the template, first, select the proper-size symbol and hold it firmly over the drawing in the correct location; then, using a conical point, draw a sharp, clear line around the opening in the template. To draw a circle with a template, lay out vertical and horizontal center lines on the drawing where the circle is to be drawn; then superimpose the correct circle opening over the center line. To draw an arc, lay out the tangent lines on the drawing first; then place the correct-size circle on the paper so that the quadrant lines coincide with the tangent lines. Allowance must be made for the width of the pencil line in placing the opening in the correct position on the drawing.

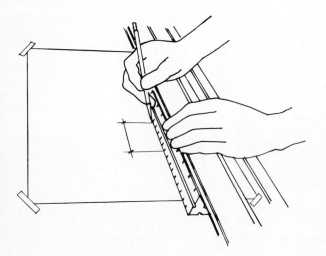

FIGURE 1-24 Using the triangular architect's scale.

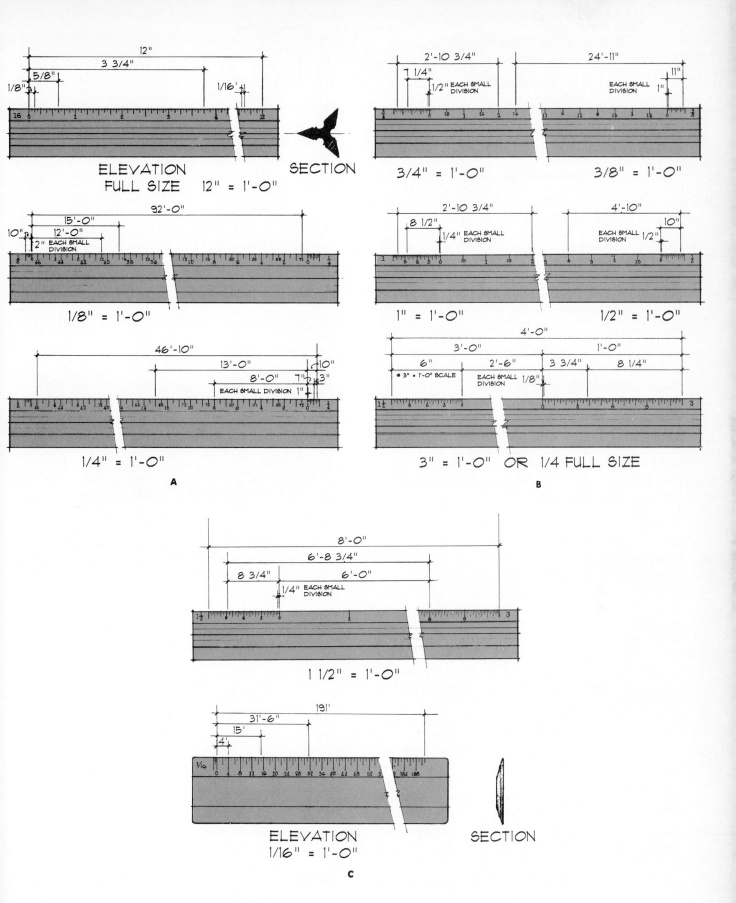

FIGURE 1-25 Measurements with various architectural scales.

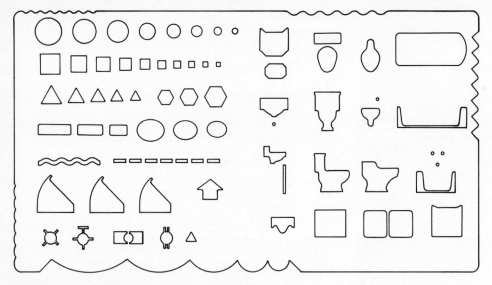

FIGURE 1-26 Architectural drafting templates.

1.17 Case Instruments

A set of good quality case instruments consisting of a compass, dividers, ruling pen, lead holder, needle points, and a screwdriver are the main items needed in architectural drafting. Quality instruments are carefully finished and have well-fitted components without play or tolerance in their joints or threaded parts (see Fig. 1-27).

The compass is the most frequently used instrument and is available in three basic types of different sizes. The friction compass is adjustable at its hinged joints. The center wheel and side wheel compasses can be accurately set by revolving a thumb wheel on a threaded bar that passes through both legs of the instrument (Fig. 1-28). The 6″ large bow compass is the most versatile. When drawing a circle with the bow compass, hold it with the thumb and forefinger and lean it slightly in the direction of travel as it is twirled between the fingers. The needle end of the compass should be slightly longer than the pencil lead-point end. Sharpen the compass lead point with the sandpaper pad by forming a single outside bevel on the lead (Fig. 1-29). A ruling pen attachment can be inserted in place of the pencil lead attachment. By removing the pencil lead or inking attachment and inserting a needle point, the compass can be used as a divider. Some large bow compass sets are equipped with beam lengthening bars, if circles up to 26″ diameter are needed. For still larger circles, the standard beam compass may be used with a rigid metal beam and beam extensions; these have adjustable needle points, pencil lead, and inking attachments.

A ruling pen is used for drawing various-width lines (Fig. 1-30). Using a dropper, insert ¼″ of ink between

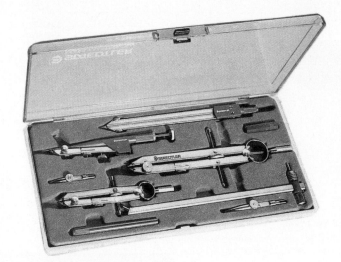

FIGURE 1-27 Case instruments.

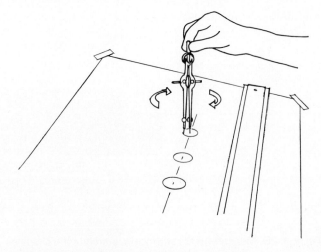

FIGURE 1-28 Drawing an arc with the compass.

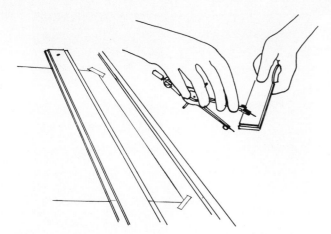

FIGURE 1-29 Sharpening compass lead point with sandpaper pad.

FIGURE 1-30 Ruling pen, Swedish border pen, technical drafting pen, and black drawing ink.

the nibs of the pen and wipe the outer surface of the nibs clean before using it. Never dip the pen into the ink bottle. The width of the line can be varied by revolving an adjustment screw that passes through the nibs. Always clean the ruling pen after using it. Technical drafting pens with various-size points are now more popular than the ruling pens.

1.18 Drafting Brush

A drafting brush (shown in Fig. 1-1) should be a part of every drafter's equipment. It will quickly remove eraser, dust, and graphite particles from the drawing without smudging the linework. One should not dust a drawing with the hands or blow on the drawing. Students can use an inexpensive 3″ paint brush on small drawings as a substitute, but the regular drafting brush

will save time on larger drawings. A clean cloth in the drafting kit is indispensable for wiping instruments and minor cleaning jobs.

1.19 Drafting Tape and Dots

Drafting tape, 5/8″ or 3/4″ wide, and drafting dots, 7/8″ in diameter, provide a convenient method for securing drawings to the board. Tape can be purchased in 10- to 60-yard rolls; some rolls come in packages with handy tear-off cutting edges. Drafting dots are attached to a coated paper tape and are boxed in units of 500. The round dots pop up from the paper tape as the tape is pulled from the storage box. Small pieces of drafting tape or dots are placed at the corners of the drawing to attach it to the board. The tape or dots can be removed without leaving marks or gum residue on the drawing.

1.20 Drawing Papers and Film

Although architectural drafting work can be done on good quality, opaque white paper, most work is done on tracing paper and films. A desirable paper or film should be durable, have a medium grain or tooth, and erase well. Many types of tracing paper are marketed. It is important to know the characteristics and quality of various papers. Thin, transparent tracing paper should be used for sketching and lettering; heavier grades of tracing paper should be used for drafting. Rolls of thin white or light-yellow tracing paper are available in widths of 10½″ to 48″ and 50-yard lengths. A similar, thin tracing paper is available in sketching pads. The drafter uses the thin paper for preliminary sketches and overlays.

When executing more permanent drawings that will be reproduced a high grade of tracing paper should be used. The better quality tracing papers are made from 100 percent rag stock. Vellums are rag stock tracing papers that have been made transparent with a synthetic resin. Before drafting on a tracing paper, hold the paper in front of a light and read the watermark on the paper. The drafting side of the paper is the side on which the watermark is legible.

Drafting films developed from polyesters have many advantages over tracing papers. Films are durable, transparent, and waterproof and resist deterioration. A single-matte, 3-mil-thick Mylar® is the most popular film for architectural drafting. The drawing side of this film has a special coating or matte that gives the surface a grain or tooth. A double-matte Mylar can be drawn on either side.

Graphite lead and ink are suitable for tracing papers. Plastic lead and ink are best for Mylars. Although ink may be difficult to erase on tracing paper, it can be easily erased on film using a white plastic eraser or an eraser imbibed with erasing fluid. The paper or film surface should be perfectly clean before inking. Oil from fingertips often inhibits ink from adhering to the drafting surface; it can be removed by using a soft eraser. No pounce or powders should be used on film, since they interfere with the chemical bond and clog the tip of the pen.

Heavier quality tracing papers and films are available in rolls of widths of 24″, 30″, 36″, and 42″ in 20- and 60-yard lengths. These materials are also available in standard cut sheet sizes, which are listed below for both architects and engineers.

| Sheet designations | Actual dimensions (″) | |
	Architects	Engineers
A	9″ × 12″	8½″ × 11″
B	12″ × 18″	11″ × 17″
C	18″ × 24″	17″ × 22″
D	24″ × 36″	22″ × 34″
E	30″ × 42″	28″ × 40″

Drafting papers and films are available with a non-reproducible grid printed on the surface. Most of the grids are based on 1/16″, 1/8″, 1/4″, 1/2″, and 1″ divisions and are a light blue or light green color. The grid coordinates offer the drafter a convenient reference and eliminate the use of the architects scale for measuring every line.

1.21 Technical Drafting Pens

Most ink drafting is done with technical pens. These pens are fabricated from hard plastics and have either standard steel, tungsten carbide, or jewel points. The tungsten carbide and jewel points last longer and are suitable for use on films (Fig. 1-31). Technical drafting pens are available in a variety of point sizes. The following chart indicates the designated sizes.

Point size	Line thickness (mm)	Point size	Line thickness (mm)
000000	0.13	2½	0.7
0000	0.18	3	0.8
000	0.25	3½	1.0
00	0.30	4	1.1
0	0.35	5	1.2
1	0.45	6	1.4
2	0.50	7	2.0

FIGURE 1-31 Technical drafting pen.

The care and use of pens are of the utmost importance. The pen has a clear plastic reservoir, which should be filled with black India ink or specialized inks from a squeeze bottle, dropper, or syringe. Use fresh ink; ink stored for long periods of time tends to separate. Avoid filling or shaking the pen over the drawing. Always have a cloth handy to wipe the pen after filling. Do not drop the pens as the points are fragile and can be easily damaged. When not in use, pens must be sealed with their airtight caps to prevent the ink from drying in the pen. If the pens are not to be used for longer periods, ink should be removed and the pen flushed with water. When storing pens, all ink should be removed and the pen cleaned with a special cleaning fluid and syringe. No moisture or cleaning fluid should be left in the pen when it is stored. When ink has dried in the pen, it may be necessary to soak the pen in a pen cleaner or clean it with an electronic pen cleaner. The pen can be disassembled for cleaning and repairs, but since the inner parts damage easily, this should be a last resort.

Most architectural drafting can be accomplished using the 00, 0, 1, 2, and 3 point sizes. These pens are available in a five-pen set. Pens can be purchased individually, and replacement parts can be obtained for most pens.

Technical drafting pens are a valuable asset to the drafter. Hold the pen against the T square, parallel bar, or triangle with a slight tilt, using little pressure so that the ink will not flow under the edges of the instruments. This takes practice. Some triangles and templates have special edges and are known as inking instruments. Elevating a standard triangle slightly above the drawing surface may help the beginning drafter.

Capillary cartridge pens with disposable ink cartridges are available and are similar to the technical drafting pens previously described. These pens are available in a wide variety of point sizes and eliminate the chore of manually filling the pen from the ink bottle.

Disposable drafting pens with fine to broad points are also available. These pens have felt-tip points and are discarded when the ink supply is depleted. Standard India ink is not used in the disposable drafting pens. The ink in these pens may vary in color or may not be suitable on some tracing papers or Mylar.

When properly cared for, technical drafting pens can provide years of good service. Purchase the correct pens for the medium on which the drafting is to be done.

1.22 Optional Equipment

An aid for reducing or enlarging a drawing is the proportional dividers, which is a two-legged, metal instrument with needle points at each end, a ratio marked on the legs, and a sliding pivot. To use the dividers, move the legs together and set the sliding pivot to the desired ratio mark or setting on the leg and tighten the screw (Fig. 1-32). When the legs are spread, the relative distance between the two needle points at one end and the two needle points at the other end will always be in the same indication ratio. For example, when the dividers are set to a 3 : 1 ratio, the distance between the two long needles will always be three times greater than the distance between the two short points. This instrument can be used to divide a line or circle into equal parts or it can be used to change meters to feet.

Drawings or tracings should be rolled, never folded. A fiberboard or plastic tube 3″ in diameter and 24″, 30″, or 36″ long with a slip-on or screw-on cap is available for storing or transporting work.

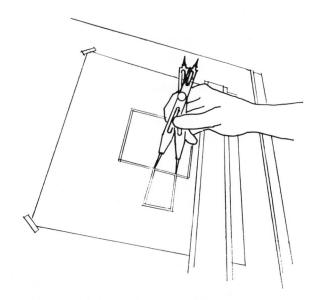

FIGURE 1-32 Using the proportional dividers.

Paper shears or a knife with interchangeable blades should be used for cutting papers and films. Never cut on an unprotected drawing table surface or against the plastic edges of drawing instruments. Metal straightedges are available and should be used for cutting straight lines. Cutting against plastic instruments can make nicks and gouges which will render them unusable for drafting.

Transparent mending tapes ¾″ wide by 5 to 36 yards long can be used to repair torn sheets. Mending kits are available for papers and films with transparent patches and heating tools that weld the patch.

1.23 Lighting and Light Fixtures

Adequate lighting on the drafting table is very important. Natural north light or soft light of the proper intensity from the upper left is the most effective for right-handed drafters, and vice versa for left-handed drafters. Direct sunlight should never fall on the drafting board; it is too intense.

Most drafting boards are illuminated with artificial lighting from a fluorescent source ranging from 60 to 100 footcandles. Drafting lamps with an adjustable, floating arm holding either fluorescent or incandescent lamps, or a combination of both, can be clamped to the drafting board. Some models have illuminated magnifiers attached for small detail work. Daylight, bright white, and soft white lamps are available. Choose lamps or combine lamps that give soft illumination without glare or confusing shadows and make sure the level of intensity is proper.

1.24 Reproduction of Drawings

The majority of all architectural working drawings are made on either tracing paper, vellum, or film for the sole purpose of making economical reproductions. Drawings have little value unless they can be satisfactorily reproduced. Sets of the prints (often referred to as *blueline prints*) must be furnished to contract bidders, estimators, subcontractors, workers, and others who are concerned with the construction of the proposed building; the original drawings are retained by the architectural or engineering office. Several types of reproduction equipment are in use for making prints; each type requires the original tracing to have opaque and distinct linework and lettering in order to produce legible copies. Some architectural offices have their own print-making equipment; others send their tracings to local blueprinting companies, which charge a nominal square-foot fee for the service.

Diazo Prints Commonly known as Ozalid prints, are produced on paper coated on one side with light-sensi-

FIGURE 1-33 A floor model machine for reproducing working drawings.

tive diazo chemicals. The sensitive paper, with the tracing above it in direct contact, is fed into a print machine (Fig. 1-33) and exposed to ultraviolet light for a controlled amount of time. The pencil or ink lines of the tracing prevent exposure of the chemical directly below, while the translucent areas are completely exposed. After the exposure, the sensitized paper only is again fed into a dry developer, utilizing ammonia vapors, which turn the background of the print white and the lines either blue, black, or sepia, depending on which type of paper has been selected. Dry development does not shrink the paper and change the scale of the drawing. The white background of prints also allows changes or notes to be added, if necessary, directly on the paper with ordinary pencils.

Blueprints This process was used extensively for many years as the conventional method of producing prints of all types of technical drawings. The blue nature of the prints gave rise to the once common term blueprints. These prints are made by exposing sensitized paper and tracing paper, in direct contact, in a blueprint machine. They are exposed to ultraviolet light for a controlled amount of time (the sun could also be used as a light source). The exposure is followed by a fixing bath of potassium bichromate and water, followed by a bath of clear water, which turns the background of the sensitized paper dark blue and the line-work white. After the baths, the print must be dried. Both blueprints and diazo prints will gradually deteriorate in color if continually left in open sunlight.

Photographic Reproduction processes of various types are available today. Photostats can be made from

an original drawing by using a large, specially designed camera that produces enlargements or reductions from the original work. This direct print process delivers a negative with white lines and a dark background. By photostating the print, a positive image with dark lines and a light background results. A number of high-quality reproduction methods using a film negative made from the original drawing are available. Projection prints from a photographic negative can be reproduced on matte paper, glossy paper, vellum and Mylar (Cronoflex™). These excellent quality prints can be enlarged or reduced in scale with accuracy and are very durable. Microfilm negatives can be made from original drawings using a microfilm processing camera that prepares film ready for use within a few seconds. The negative is usually mounted on a standard-size aperture or data card and systematically filed for future retrieval. A microfilm enlarger reader-printer with a display screen is used to review the images as well as reproduce print copies of various sizes from the negative. Microfilming is an excellent means of storing drawings, thus eliminating the need to retain cumbersome original tracings.

Contact Prints the same size of the original drawing can be reproduced on autopositive paper or autopositive Mylar (Cronoflex). This process simply means that if the original is a positive the print will also be positive. Prints made in a contact printer or vacuum frame by exposure to high-intensity lights will have most of the background present in the original filtered out. The duplicate in most cases is sharper than the original.

Photocopy Reproductions are gaining popularity. A number of high-speed electronic copiers are manufactured today that reproduce images from an original drawing onto paper, vellum, and various films. Some copiers have the capability of enlarging or reducing the size of the drawing from the original scale. Original work on paper, film, and illustration board can be reproduced on most photocopy machines.

In choosing the right reproduction process, it is important to know what the finished product will be. For architectural working drawings that are used for bidding and construction, diazo prints the same size as the original tracings are the most suitable and cost-effective reproductions. When only a few copies of a drawing are needed and enlargements or reductions are necessary, the photocopy process is desirable. Where high quality and durability are essential, photographic reproductions would be best. Cost and the sizes of prints vary greatly among the types of reproduction alternatives. It is always wise to consult professional printers who offer guidance in selecting the proper reproduction method for the desired results.

1.25 Using Drafting Equipment to Draw Lines

Understanding line quality and line types is the first fundamental of technical drafting. Lines on drawings are similar to print types in a newspaper. A successful newspaper will capture ones attention by using bold print to emphasize major features, medium weight print for supporting captions and fine print to tell the story. A successful drawing will contain bold lines that outline primary objects, medium weight lines that depict secondary elements and fine lines that depict details. Line quality can be controlled by the drafter. Pencil lines may vary in both value and width depending on the type and sharpness of the lead and the pressure placed on the pencil. Hard leads tend to produce fine, lighter lines. Soft leads tend to produce bold, darker lines (see Fig. 1-34). Inked lines are generally of the same value and vary only in width depending on the size of the pen selected (see Fig. 1-35). Drafters describe a line using the term weight, such as a light weight line, a medium weight line and a heavy weight line.

The drafter should be familiar with the various types of lines that are commonly shown on architectural drawings (see Fig. 1-36). The primary lines which define the major object in a drawing are heavy weight lines that are drawn dark and wide (see Fig. 1-37). Hidden lines that depict features that are concealed from the viewer are dashed medium weight lines (see Fig. 1-38). Center lines drawn as alternating long and short dashes are light weight lines (see Fig. 1-39). Extension lines that depict the extremities of a dimension

FIGURE 1-34 Pencil lines.

FIGURE 1-35 Ink lines.

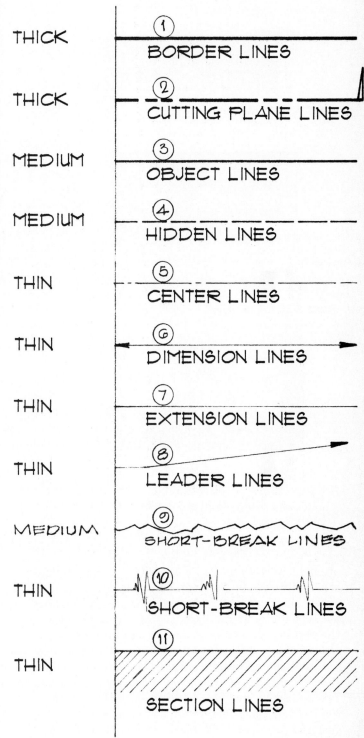

FIGURE 1-36 Types of lines on architectural drawings.

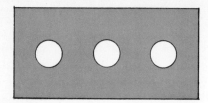

Figure 1-37 Object lines.

Figure 1-38 Hidden lines.

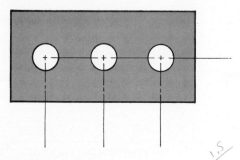

Figure 1-39 Center lines.

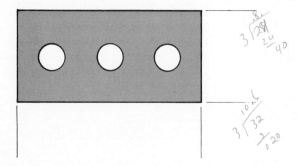

Figure 1-40 Extension lines.

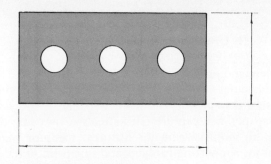

Figure 1-41 Dimension lines.

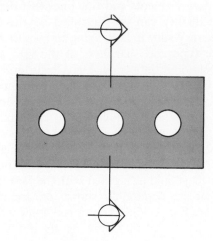

Figure 1-42 Cutting plane lines.

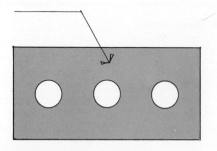

Figure 1-43 Break lines.

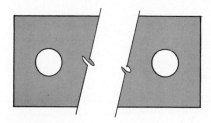

Figure 1-44 Leader lines.

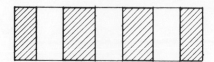

Figure 1-45 Section lines or poché.

are light weight lines (see Fig. 1-40). Dimension lines are light weight lines that are terminated by an arrow, dot or diagonal line (see Fig. 1-41). Cutting plane lines are very heavy weight lines with an arrow pointing in the direction the section is viewed (see Fig. 1-42). Break lines are light weight lines that are interrupted at intervals with zigzag lines (see Fig. 1-43). Leader lines are light weight lines with an arrow at one end connecting a note to a detail (see Fig. 1-44). Section lines or poché are light weight lines which symbolize a specific building material (see Fig. 1-45). The beginning drafter should study architectural drawings to become familiar with all types of lines. One should practice drawing lines of various types in order to improve drafting skills.

E X E R C I S E S

IN THE USE OF INSTRUMENTS

The following problems should be drawn accurately in pencil using your drawing instruments. They should be drawn lightly with a 3H pencil, and then carefully retraced with an H pencil. Construction lines need not be erased if they are light and hardly visible. Keep the pencil *sharp* and bear down slightly at the beginning and end of each line. Once you have mastered the use of the pencil and drawing instruments, you may trace the exercises using technical drafting pens and India ink.

1. Parquet flooring (Fig. 1-46). Draw a 3″ square. Divide the top and side into three equal parts and draw in the nine squares. Complete the figure by drawing the horizontal and vertical lines as indicated.

2. Geometric shape (Fig. 1-47). Using the scale 1″ = 1′-0″, draw a square with 1′-2″ sides, a circle 1′-6″ in diameter, a rectangle 8″ × 1′-9″, an equilateral triangle with 1′-5″ sides, a parallelogram 9″ × 1′-7″ using a 30°–60° triangle; a trapezoid with the longest side 2′-3½″ and a vertical height of 11″ using a 45° triangle.

3. Wood double-hung window (Fig. 1-48). Using the scale 1″ = 1′-0″, draw the rectangle 2′-8″ × 4′-2″. Divide the height in two and draw the 1⅛″ sash rail in the center of the height. Draw the inside of both sash according to the dimensions shown. Complete the drawing by dividing the inside of the sash in half vertically and in thirds horizontally. Show the muntins with close, sharp lines.

4. Sill detail (Fig. 1-49). Using the scale 1½″ = 1′-0″, draw the footing as shown. Locate the 8″ block and 4″ brick veneer wall in the center of the footing; make a cavity in the block 5″ wide, mortar joints ½″.

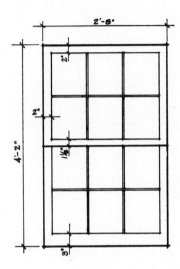

FIGURE 1-48

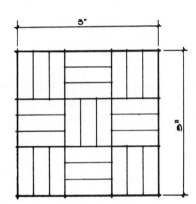

FIGURE 1-46

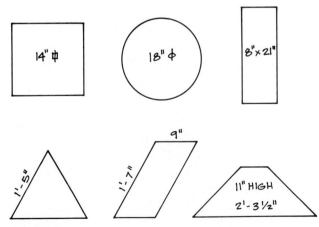

FIGURE 1-47

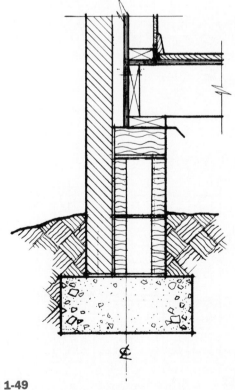

FIGURE 1-49

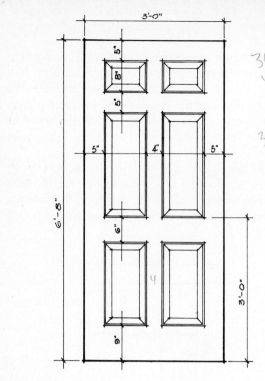

FIGURE 1-50

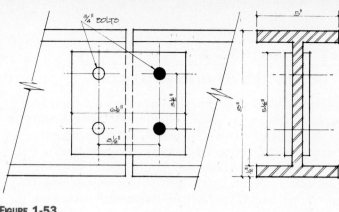

FIGURE 1-53

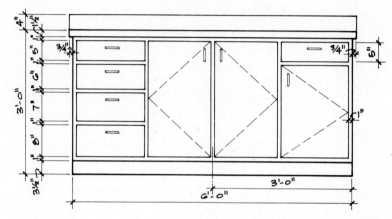

FIGURE 1-54

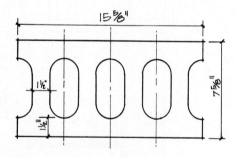

FIGURE 1-51

FIGURE 1-52

5. Six-panel colonial wood door (Fig. 1-50). Using the scale 1″ = 1′-0″, draw the rectangle 3′-0″ × 6′-8″. Draw the outside lines of the panels as shown by the dimensions; show the panel bevels 1¹/₂″ wide.

6. Concrete block—top view (Fig. 1-51). Using the scale 3″ = 1′-0″, draw the 8″ × 16″ rectangular shape. Divide the 16″ length into four equal parts and draw vertical center lines for the cavities. Make the webs 1¹/₂″ thick at their thinnest points.

7. Pigeonholes (Fig. 1-52). Using the scale ³/₄″ = 1′-0″, draw 9″ squares with 2″ spaces between the squares; place a 6″ square in the upper right of each 9″ square. Connect the lower-left corners of each square using a 45° triangle.

8. Wide-flange beam detail (Fig. 1-53). Using the scale 3″ = 1′-0″, lay out the height of both views using the dimensions shown; block in both views and transfer sizes to the other with the T square. Make bolts symmetrical on the plate.

9. Kitchen cabinet elevation (Fig. 1-54). Using the scale 1″ = 1′-0″, draw the base rectangle 3′-0″ × 6′-0″;

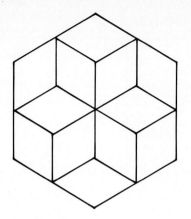

FIGURE 1-55

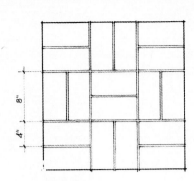

FIGURE 1-56

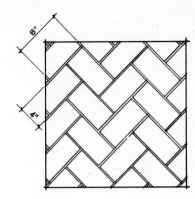

FIGURE 1-57

add the 4″ backsplash; the pair of centered doors are 1′-4″ × 2′-5″; a 1″ space surrounds all doors and drawers. Draw all lines very lightly, erase lines between features, darken lines where required, and indicate ¼″ diameter × 3″ pulls placed 1½″ from edge of door and drawers. Dashed lines indicate door swings.

10.   Cubes (Fig. 1-55). Using the scale 3″ = 1′-0″, draw a hexagon with 9″ sides; using a 30° angle, place three 4½″ cubes inside the hexagon shape.

11.   Basket weave brick pattern (Fig. 1-56). Using the scale 1½″ = 1′-0″, lay out a 2′-0″ × 2′-0″ square with light lines. Divide the height and width into thirds and lightly draw the nine squares. Allow ½″ mortar joints between the brick, and lay out the alternate brick as indicated. Erase the original layout lines and darken the lines around each brick.

12.   Herringbone brick pattern (Fig. 1-57). Using the scale 1½″ = 1′-0″, lay out a 2′-0″ × 2′-0″ square with light lines. With the 45° triangle, draw the diagonals. From the diagonals, lay out 4″ squares and fill the entire space. Then lay out the ½″ mortar joints ¼″ on each side of the 4″ square lines. Erase the proper construction lines and darken the lines surrounding each brick as indicated.

13.   Arch and pediment (Fig. 1-58). Using the scale ⅜″ = 1′-0″, draw three 4″ risers and two 12″ treads; four columns are 8″ diameter with 2½″ high by 12″ diameter capitals and bases; pediment has 45° slope.

14.   Handicapped symbol (Fig. 1-59). Using the scale 1″ = 1′-0″, draw a circle 2′-3″ in diameter for the wheel of the chair and a 7″ diameter circle for the head; the upper body is 10° off vertical, the leg is drawn with a 30°–60° triangle, and all lines are 3″ thick.

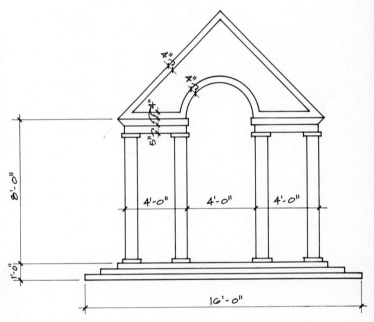

FIGURE 1-58

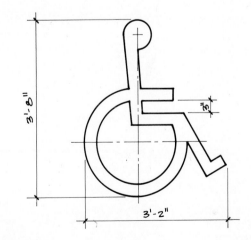

FIGURE 1-59

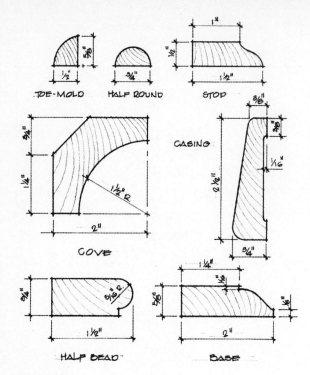

FIGURE 1-60

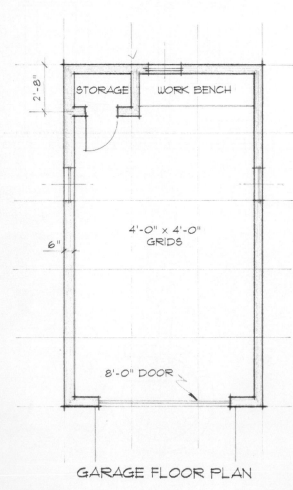

GARAGE FLOOR PLAN

FIGURE 1-61

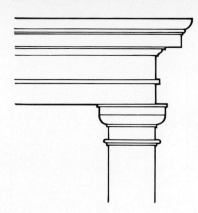

FIGURE 1-62

15. Wood trim profiles (Fig. 1-60). Using the 12″ scale, draw the figures as shown full size. Keep the pencil sharp and let the intersection of lines run over at the corners. Draw the end-grain symbol of the wood freehand.

16. Garage plan (Fig. 1-61). Using the scale ¼″ = 1′-0″, draw the 4′-0″ × 4′-0″ grid lines lightly. Lay out the 6″ wide walls on the inside of the 12′-0″ and 20′-0″ grid lines. Center the doors and make the small door and windows 2′-0″ wide. Fill the walls with a gray tone.

17. Tuscan column entablature (Fig. 1-62). Using the scale 1″ = 1′-0″, draw the column shaft D (diameter) = 12″, cornice = ¾D, frieze = ½D, architrave = ½D, capital = ¾D, and eave = ¾D.

REVIEW QUESTIONS

1. Why are quality drafting instruments important for good work?

2. Why is the drawing board slightly inclined?

3. For what purpose is a pad used under tracing paper?

4. Do left-handed drafters place the triangles on the T square in the same manner as right-handed drafters? If so, why?

5. What is the advantage of transparent equipment such as triangles?

6. Why are drawing pencils often hexagonal in shape?

7. Is the 2H lead harder than the 2B?

8.   For what purpose is the pencil turned between the fingers when drawing a line?

9.   Why is the adjustable triangle time saving?

10.   What is the difference between the architect's scale and the civil engineer's scale?

11.   List the necessary qualities of suitable tracing paper.

12.   What are the most ideal lighting conditions for drafting?

13.   What is a parallel bar and why is it preferred over a T square?

14.   What is the most suitable type of lead for drafting on films?

15.   What are templates and where are they used?

16.   How are drafting papers or films attached to the drawing surface?

17.   What is an adjustable triangle and how is it used?

18.   What is the difference between the arm drafting machine and the track drafting machine?

19.   Draw a line 3″ long and measure the line with the scale $3/4″ = 1'\text{-}0″$. What is the length of the line?

20.   Draw a line $4^{1}/_{2}″$ long and measure the line with the scale $1/4″ = 1'\ 0″$. What is the length of the line?

LETTERING

W. D. Farmer, AIBD

"Practice is the best of all instructors."

—Publitius Syrus

2

Legible lettering on a drawing fulfills an important requirement. Information that cannot be revealed by graphic shapes and lines alone must be included in the form of notes, titles, dimensions, and identifications to make the drawing informative and complete. The lettering can either enhance the drawing by making it simple to interpret and pleasant to look at or ruin an otherwise good drawing by making it difficult to read and unsightly in appearance.

2.1 Lettering Skill

Skill in freehand lettering adds style and individuality to a drafter's work. Even though the various mechanical devices available aid in producing the uniform technical lettering required in some offices, freehand lettering is generally preferred on architectural drawings and should be an important phase of training. In fact, many employers evaluate drafting skill in direct relation to lettering skill. If the student learns the basic letter forms (Fig. 2-1) and gives deliberate application to their mastery during early practice, he or she will soon be able to do a creditable job of lettering. Anyone who can write can learn to letter. After considerable experience, every drafter's freehand lettering acquires an individuality—much the same as his or her handwriting—which is soon identifiable and which contributes favorably to good technique in architectural drawing.

Lettering is also occasionally incorporated into the design of structures. Inscriptions, plaques, signs, and other applications comprising well-designed letter forms in the architectural aspects of the building often fall upon drafters for their execution. Therefore, the basic styles of alphabets and their various characteristics should be of particular interest to you.

2.2 Alphabet Classifications

By closely observing the alphabets and typefaces in use by the modern commercial world, you will notice that each fits one of the following basic letter classifications (see Fig. 2-1).

FIGURE 2-1 Basic alphabet types. All lettering can be classified under one of these types.

Roman Perfected by the Greeks and Romans and modernized during the eighteenth century by typefounders, this alphabet imparts a feeling of grace and dignity and is considered our most beautiful typeface. The classic example can be found on the column of Trajan in Rome. Thick- and thin-width strokes and serifs are the distinguishing features. Serifs are the spurs or "boots" forming the ends of the strokes, which can be used on gothic letters as well as roman. Although the lettering found on old Roman stonework is light-

FIGURE 2-2 (A) Uppercase and lowercase letters. (B) The vertical, single-stroke technical alphabet, showing proportion and sequence of strokes. Master this basic alphabet before trying the architectural variations.

face, modern roman lettering has a bolder characteristic. Extensive modifications of this beautiful alphabet are in wide use today.

Gothic   This basic alphabet has been in use for many years as a commercial, block-type letter, which is comparatively simple to execute and easy to read. Its distinguishing characteristic is the uniformity in width of all strokes. Its modifications include inclined, the addition of serifs, rounded, squared, boldface, and lightface. The gothic alphabet is the base from which our single-stroke technical lettering has evolved.

Script   This completely different basic alphabet is cursive in character and resembles handwriting. Interconnected lowercase letters are used within words; capital letters, of course, are used only at word or sentence beginnings, a practice not required of roman or gothic letters. The free-flowing, continuous strokes produce a delicate and personal temperament, making this alphabet popular for many commercial trademarks. Modifications of either vertical or inclined scripts range from very thin lines to bold or thick-and-thin varieties of many modern interpretations.

Text   Sometimes referred to as Old English, this alphabet was first used by central European monks for recording religious manuscripts before the advent of the printing press. The strokes of different width are due to the fact that a flat quill pen was employed. It is similar to script in that lowercase letters must be used throughout the words, with the use of capitals restricted to word beginnings only. Text is difficult to read and draw.

The term *italics* is generally given to typefaces having inclined, lightface, and curved characteristics. It is not given a separate grouping because all the above-mentioned letter types can be made in the italic form.

2.3 Uppercase and Lowercase Letters

Nearly all alphabets have both uppercase (capitals) and smaller, more rounded lowercase letters. The height of the lowercase body is usually two-thirds the height of its capitals, with ascenders extending to the capital line and descenders dropping the same amount below (see Fig. 2-2A). If a great deal of copy or an unusually large note is necessary on a drawing, lowercase letters will be found to require less space, and they are usually more readable. Yet capitals are used for the majority of the lettering done on architectural drawings. Because of the universal acceptance and popularity of capitals, the material in this chapter will mainly consider their various characteristics.

2.4 Basic Lettering Practice

The vertical, single-stroke gothic alphabet shown in Fig. 2-2B is the basic style used by drafters for most of the lettering found on technical drawings. Because of its legibility and simplicity of execution, it has been universally accepted as a standardized alphabet. Lettering on architectural drawings is known for its freedom of style and individuality, yet no style can be developed that is easily read unless the student thoroughly learns the basic alphabet. The architectural variations should not be attempted until the rudiments of letter construction are accomplished. (For a beginning lettering exercise, it is suggested that a sheet of tracing paper or Mylar film be fastened over Fig. 2-2B and a direct duplication of the basic characters be made.)

Select an H or 2H drafting lead or E-1 or E-2 plastic lead for lettering and keep the point medium sharp at all times. Figure 2-3 shows the proper method of holding the pencil. A comfortable, natural posture is the most desirable. Be sure the entire forearm rests on the flat table surface; this position allows for more stability than trying to letter over instruments or equipment on the drawing table. Rotate the pencil continually between strokes to maintain a uniform pencil point. A point that is too sharp is difficult to control—it will either break or create grooves in the paper if a desirable, firm pressure is applied. A pencil that becomes too dull, on the other hand, produces ragged and awkward strokes (see Fig. 2-4). As a preliminary exercise, try a few of the practice

Figure 2-3 Holding the pencil for lettering.

AVOID LETTING THE PENCIL GET **TOO DULL**

Figure 2-4 Maintain a medium-sharp point to avoid variations in stroke width.

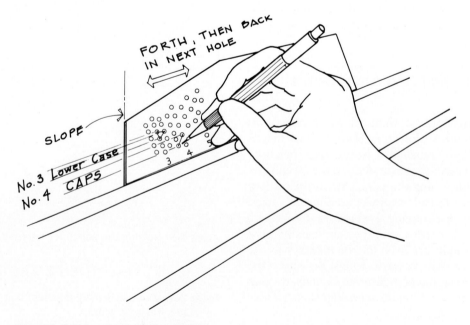

FIGURE 2-5 Preliminary practice strokes.

strokes shown in Fig. 2-5 before starting the actual letter forms.

2.5 Guidelines

All lettering is done with the aid of penciled guidelines. Even experienced drafters carefully draw horizontal guidelines for their lettering. It is nearly impossible to maintain straight lettering without guidelines—use them like the experts do. See Fig. 2-6 for the method of drawing uniform guidelines with one type of plastic lettering guide. Until you have developed skill in *vertical* lettering strokes, use vertical guidelines also; after you have attained confidence, dispense with the vertical guidelines—but never with the horizontal ones. In pencil lettering, the guidelines are always left on the drawing; therefore, care should be taken in placing the lines neatly on the paper with a sharp pencil or a nonprint pencil. Architectural drafters give more prominence to their horizontal guidelines and make no effort to minimize them; in fact, they usually draw guidelines well beyond the intended extremities of the actual letters. Only on inked lettering are the lines erased. (see Fig. 2-7).

One of the available lettering guides or triangles (Braddock, Ames) will aid in maintaining uniform let-

ter heights. *To draw lines with the guide*, a sharp pencil is inserted into the proper countersunk hole and the guide is pulled along the top edge of the parallel bar; then the pencil is inserted into a lower hole to form the height of the letters and returned along the parallel bar blade. A series of uniform guidelines can be easily drawn in this manner. Holes in the guide are grouped for capitals and lowercase; the numbers below each group indicate the height of the caps in thirty-seconds of an inch. For example, holes in the No. 4 row would lay out lines for capitals $4/32''$ or $1/8''$ high.

2.6 Height of Letters on Working Drawings

Generally, small lettering carefully fitted into open spaces on a drawing is more legible than larger letters crowded into insufficient spaces. For the sake of readability, never allow lettering to touch any of the drawing linework. On work drawn to the $1/4'' = 1'-0''$ scale, $3/16''$ high lettering can be used for minor titles such as room names on floor plans, and $1/8''$ lettering can be used for small notes. On smaller drawings, the minor titles can be made $1/8''$ high and the small notes $3/32''$ high. Slight variations are permissible, depending on the layout and the preference of the drafter, but if lettering is kept small and neat, a more professional appearance will result. Beginning lettering exercises should be done with letter heights of $1/4''$ or $3/8''$ until correct letter forms have been mastered. The distance between sets of guidelines for long notes should be spaced the same as the height of the letters; that is, if the letters are $3/32''$ high, the vertical space between each line should be

FIGURE 2-6 Using the lettering guide.

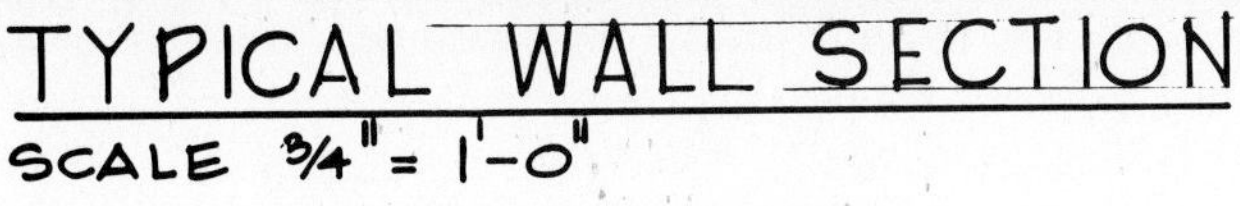

TYPICAL WALL SECTION
SCALE ¾" = 1'-0"

FIGURE 2-7 Using guidelines for lettering.

³/₃₂″, which will prevent a crowded appearance. A short note having only several lines of lettering can be made with the rows of letters slightly closer together and still be satisfactory.

2.7 Letter Proportion

After studying the basic letter forms in Fig. 2-2B with the suggested sequence and direction of strokes, you will notice evidence of different letter widths relative to the basic rectangular shape. These definite letter widths are identified with each character and should be maintained if the lettering is to be legible and harmonious. Not only do widths vary from the single line of the letter I to the widest character, the W, but all alphabets as a whole can be distorted, if necessary, in general width (see Fig. 2-8). The narrower distortion is called *compressed* lettering, and the wider is called *extended*. In either method the letters vary in width, yet retain the relative basic characteristics. Condensed lettering occasionally becomes necessary in confined areas on drawings, yet it is more difficult to read than standard or extended letters. Extended lettering is appropriate when a word or title must identify a large area or a group of drawings. Remember that visual unity is attained when condensing or extending has been consistent and the recognizable silhouette or design of the individual letter has not been altered.

The effect of *visual gravity* is evident in correct letter construction. If the horizontal center bar of the letters B, E, F, and H is placed at midheight, it will appear to be below center. This effect is called visual gravity, and all lines, especially horizontal, are influenced by it when observing a graphic figure. Lines on a page have optical weight. To counteract visual gravity, notice that the central horizontal stroke of the above-mentioned letters is placed slightly above center. Even the upper portions of the B, S, 3, and 8 are reduced in size to gain stability. Each character is a well-designed form in itself, and you should not attempt to improve or alter an accepted letter form. Put more grace in the letter M by extending the center "V" portion to the bottom guide line, rather than terminating it above the line. Keep the W vertical by making the third stroke parallel with the first and the fourth stroke parallel with the second. Both "V's" in the W are narrower than the regular letter A or V. Make circular letters full height, or even slightly larger than the space between the guidelines, with smooth, curving strokes. If vertical lettering is used, make the vertical strokes perfectly vertical. Check

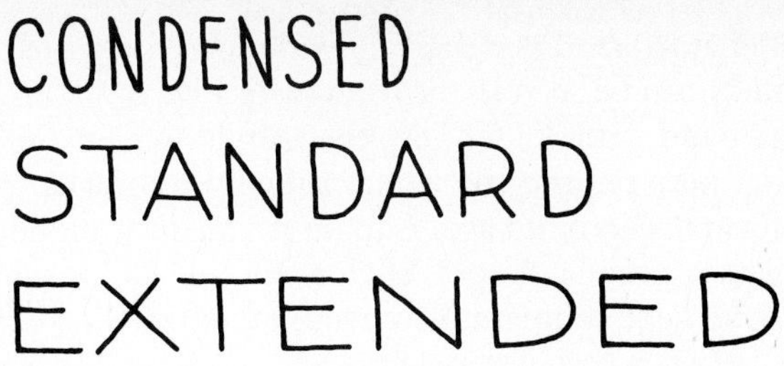

CONDENSED
STANDARD
EXTENDED

FIGURE 2-8 Condensed and extended lettering.

your work occasionally with a triangle—strokes that may appear to be perfectly vertical may nevertheless be slightly inclined.

2.8 Lettering Technique

The beginning and ending of each stroke are important—emphasize them with a slight pressure of the pencil to bring the strokes to sharp and cleancut terminations. Eliminate careless gaps in lettering by carefully intersecting the strokes. Make each stroke definite and firm; going over a stroke twice ruins the appearance of the letter. To gain positive pencil control, pull strokes toward you when lettering rather than away from you. Develop perfection of the letters before attempting speed. *There is no substitute for diligent practice.* Concentrate on letter forms before you concern yourself with spacing.

2.9 Spacing of Letters and Words

Because each letter has a different profile and width, the spacing of characters within each word becomes a visual problem rather than one of mechanical measurement between letters. The spaces between letters should be nearly identical in *area* if the word is to appear uniform in *tone*. This can be done only by eye or by optical judgment (see Fig. 2-9). Notice that the letters of the lower line are incorrectly spaced when they are equidistant from each other. Letters with vertical adjacent sides or edges must be kept well apart to allow a similar amount of space between very irregular adja-

LETTER SPACING
VISUAL — *Good*
LETTER SPACING
MECHANICAL — *Poor*

FIGURE 2-9 Spacing of letters.

cent characters. The relatively wide space between the I and N can be seen in the top row of Fig. 2-9. On the other hand, an LT, AT, or other similar offset combination may require the letters actually to overlap if a uniform background area is to be attained throughout. Adjacent circular shapes, such as OO or DC, usually must be kept comparatively close together. The exact area between each letter cannot always be made identical, yet the general area should appear somewhat uniform. Good spacing can be evaluated by squinting the eye and observing the gray tone throughout the lettering; if the tone appears spotty or varies too much, it is poorly spaced. Beginning students tend to compress individual letters and space them too far apart. Poor spacing often results in awkward appearance or difficult legibility.

Spaces between words should be adequate to make word divisions obvious. A good rule of thumb would be to make the space between words about twice the area between letters within the words, since spacing is a variable problem. If letters are tightly spaced, words can be put rather close together. If a group of words must be spread over a wide space, the space between each word must be sufficient to give the words identity and make the note readable. Too much space between words, however, produces a disconnected, spastic effect.

2.10 Inclined Lettering

Occasionally, to produce contrast or variety on drawings, inclined lettering can be used. Although vertical lettering is used primarily, inclined letters, if used appropriately for minor notes, will often add more expression to the lettering. Figure 2-26 shows an architectural, inclined alphabet; the sequence and direction of strokes are similar to the vertical alphabet. To keep the incline uniform, random guidelines can be lightly drawn, using the $67\frac{1}{2}°$ inclined edge of the lettering guide. This is the American Standard slope of 2 to 5 for inclined letters.

2.11 Lettering With a Triangle

Some experienced drafters, who have developed unusual speed in lettering, use their triangle for drawing all vertical strokes (see Fig. 2-10). They simply slide the triangle along the T square with their left hand as they letter; when a vertical stroke is needed, they quickly set the triangle into place and draw perfectly vertical strokes with the edge. All the other strokes are made freehand, and a personalized lettering style results. The system is used mainly with the alphabet shown in Fig. 2-27. Using the triangle to make vertical strokes is especially helpful with letters $\frac{3}{8}''$ high or higher.

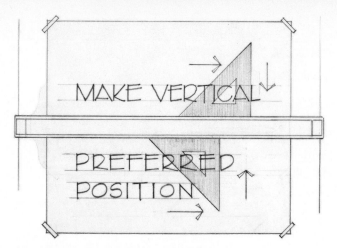

Figure 2-10 Making vertical lettering with the use of a triangle.

2.12 Lettering Titles

More skill in composition and spacing is demanded in designing titles with larger lettering. Defects that may go unnoticed in the small notes of a drawing frequently become obvious in larger titles. The size of a title should be consistent with the importance it carries—titles of similar magnitude should be similar in size. Select the guideline heights after establishing title magnitudes so that the titles will have the correct importance throughout the drawing. Often titles can be given more importance by the use of extended lettering or by using a thicker stroke with the pencil. Underlining also provides a means of emphasis (see Fig. 2-11).

Another important consideration is the finished silhouette formed by the title; if a number of words are used, care should be given to the general shape of the completed title, especially if the words must be put on two or three lines (see Fig. 2-12). Allow sufficient surrounding space to avoid a crowded appearance. Be sure

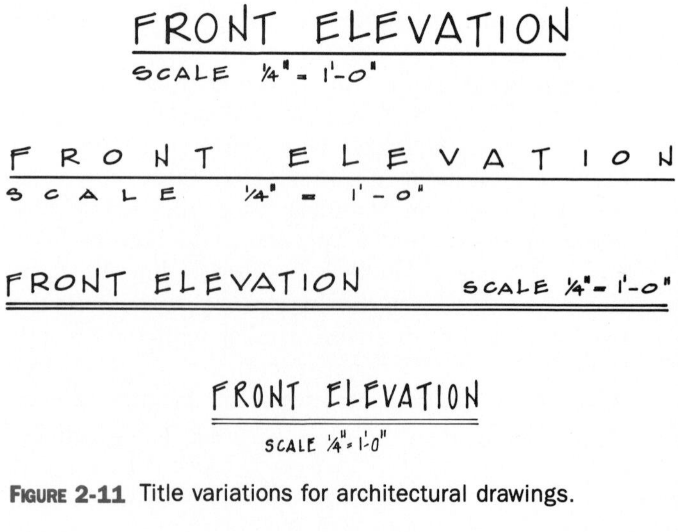

FRONT ELEVATION
SCALE ¼" = 1'-0"

F R O N T E L E V A T I O N
S C A L E ¼" = 1'-0"

FRONT ELEVATION SCALE ¼"= 1'-0"

FRONT ELEVATION
SCALE ¼"= 1'-0"

Figure 2-11 Title variations for architectural drawings.

FIGURE 2-12 Arrangements of lettering blocks.

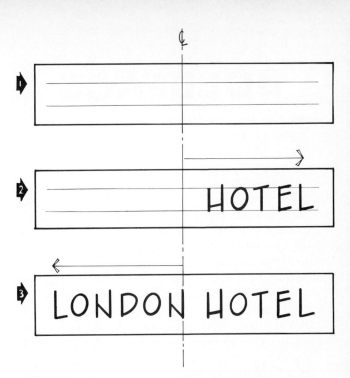

FIGURE 2-13 Steps in laying out a symmetrical title within a title block.

it is close enough to the view or detail it identifies to ensure positive association. Titles can be easily misinterpreted if they are placed midway between two views. If a title must identify two views, position it to indicate an obvious relationship to both views. Extended lettering with spread spacing must be used if a title is to ramble over a wide area. If possible, place a title directly below the view or detail, rather than above or at the side of the view or detail. A reader will search below a drawing for its title when reading prints, and consistent relationships between title sizes and their placement will make drawings easier to interpret.

2.13 Symmetrical Titles

Occasionally, a title must be *justified*, or centered within a given space. This presents the problem of spacing and layout to make the end of a line fall at a predetermined point. For example, lettering that must be put into title blocks appears more pleasing if it is centrally located (see Fig. 2-23). Several methods can be used to determine the title's length and control its symmetry. One method is to count the number of letters (include the space between words as one letter width) to find its exact center. Then, after the guidelines and a vertical center line have been drawn in the desired space, the title can be put in by starting with the middle letter, or space, on the center line. Complete the last half of the line; then, working from the center letter toward the beginning, complete the first half of the title (see Fig. 2-13). Differences in letter widths are usually compensated for by similar-size letters on both sides of the center. If more wide letters, especially W or M, happen

to fall on one side, adjustments can be made to allow for them. Another method that may be preferred by some drafters is first to lay out the required title on a separate slip of paper. The length is measured, and its center is indicated with a mark. This mark establishes symmetry and is centered directly above the space to be titled. The final title can be duplicated below with the spacing taken from the preliminary layout. These methods are only suggestions for fitting titles into given spaces; each individual may find various methods for arriving at the desired result.

2.14 Laying Out Large Titles

To be graceful in appearance, large letters usually require the use of instruments for making both straight and curved strokes. Unless one is very accomplished in lettering art, freehand letters over an inch or so in height are difficult to make. After guidelines of the proper height are laid out, begin by constructing the letter forms lightly in pencil first, working over the construction until spacing and proportion have been perfected (from an established alphabet). Then, using a triangle and T square for straight lines and a compass and irregular curve for curved lines, carefully finish each letter in a mechanical technique. The freehand construction can be erased as soon as the settings for the instruments have been established. Width of lines should be uniform, and tangencies between curves and

LIGHTFACE
BOLDFACE

FIGURE 2-14 Use a thick point to give important titles a boldface characteristic.

ABCDEFGHIJKLMN
OPQRSTUVWXYZ&
1234567890
abcdefghijklm
nopqrstuvwxy

FIGURE 2-15 Helvetica light alphabet.

ABCDEFGHIJKL
MNOPQRSTUV
WXYZ12345678

FIGURE 2-16 Single-stroke alphabet with serifs.

straight lines should be neat and unbroken. When straight lines are tangent to an arc (as in the U or B) the arc should be drawn first and the tangent lines attached to it. This method is much simpler than joining an arc to existing straight lines. If roman lettering is used, be sure that the correct inclined strokes are thick and the established thickness is uniform on both straight and curved strokes.

Avoid mixing freehand and mechanical lines on the same lettering. If instruments are used, make all the lines with instruments.

If a freehand technique is desired on a large title (often on display drawings), construct all letters lightly with instruments after they have been spaced and proportioned by sketching. Then go over the mechanical lines freehand, using neat, deliberate pencil lines. The mechanical guides will maintain straightness and form, and the freehand finish will soften the appearance.

The Helvetica typeface (Figs. 2-15 and 2-29) is now most widely used for architectural applications throughout this country and Europe. The simple, clean-cut lines of the alphabet make it easy to read and universally adaptable. Study the alphabet carefully and consider it when beauty and ease of reading are important.

2.15 Lettering With Ink

The student should devote some practice to ink lettering, since ink is often the medium used for presentation drawings. Also, if the lettering on working drawings is expected to reproduce very clearly, drafters may do the lettering in ink. Small, freehand lettering and titles can be effectively done with the use of a technical drafting pen, such as shown in Fig. 2-2A. Many point sizes are available, and regardless of the pressure applied, the width of the line will always remain uniform. Usually, lightface freehand ink lettering is more readable than boldface. Observe the comparison in Fig. 2-14. Care should be taken in selecting the proper-size point according to the height of the letters.

When inking large, precise titles, the ruling pen and ink compass should be used. The accurate layout of each letter should first be done in pencil, centers for circles and arcs should be perfectly plotted, and all ink lines should be done with ruling edges. Handling inking instruments requires more skill and experience than

pencil work. If single-stroke lettering is used, care must be taken in adjusting the instruments to ensure identical widths from ruling pens and compasses (see Fig. 2-16). Waterproof, black India ink should be used for all inkwork.

An example of one of the many pressure-sensitive alphabets suitable for major titles is shown in Fig. 2-17. Many sizes and styles are available at drafting and art supply stores. If a title is to be put on tracing paper, a grid sheet placed below the tracing will facilitate its layout.

2.16 Lettering Devices and Machines

Several types of lettering sets are available for making uniform technical letters in ink or pencil. Although they produce lettering stiff in appearance, they are sometimes used in offices when uniformity is essential. The most widely accepted type is the *Leroy*® device shown in Fig. 2-18. It consists of a scriber with changeable points and different-size template guides. Either vertical or inclined lettering can be made with each template by adjusting the scriber. The template controls the shape of each letter form, but the drafter must space the characters by sliding the template back and forth along the edge of the parallel bar. Many special Leroy templates are available for other than standard lettering.

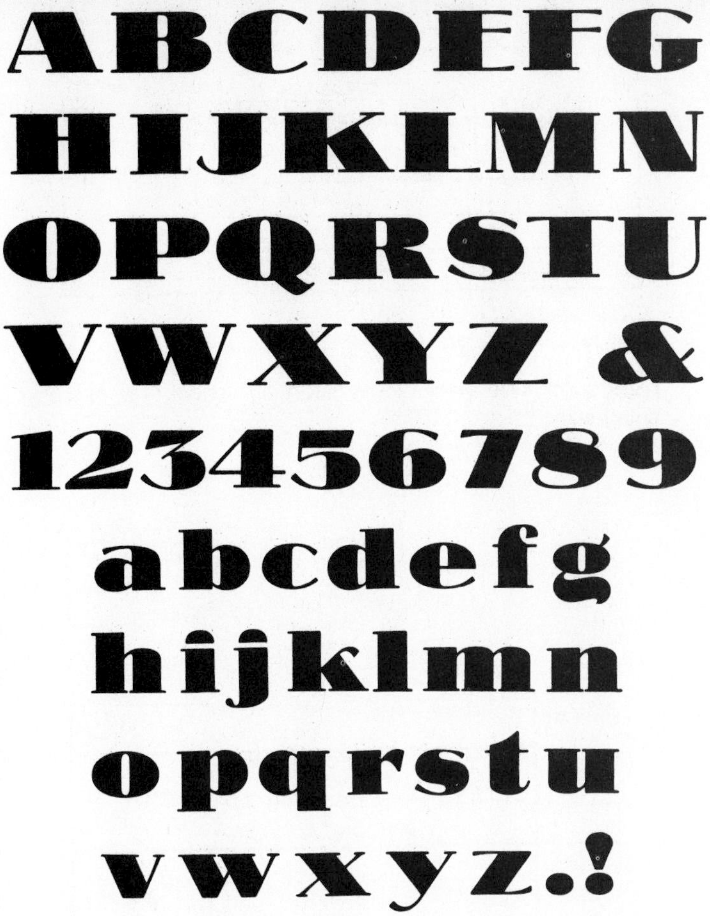

ABCDEFG
HIJKLMN
OPQRSTU
VWXYZ &
123456789
abcdefg
hijklmn
opqrstu
vwxyz.!

FIGURE 2-17 Boldface alphabets. Various sizes and styles on pressure-sensitive paper are available for students and drafters, and the lettering is easily applied to drawings.

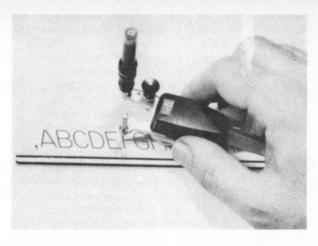

FIGURE 2-18 Leroy lettering device, used for uniform mechanical lettering.

LETTERING MACHINE
ABC

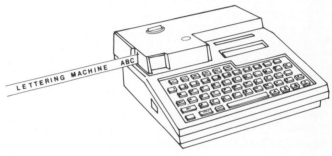

FIGURE 2-19 Lettering machine.

Lettering machines are available that produce consistent letters on the drawing or on a medium suitable for transfer to the drawing. These machines vary in type and each functions differently.

The *Kroy®* machine allows the drafter to select a size and style of letter from a series of fonts. The drafter then manually operates the machine, which prints out letters on a plastic adhesive-backed tape. The tape is applied to the drawing (Fig. 2-19).

Computerized lettering machines with a keyboard are attached to the arm of a drafting machine. The drafter selects a cassette with appropriate lettering fonts and types the letters onto a small display. A high-performance scriber, which holds drafting leads or technical drafting pens, plots letters and symbols directly on the original tracing. This process creates uniform, readable letters (Fig. 2-20).

Word processors are used as lettering machines. Lettering is typed on the keyboard and monitored on a screen. A laser printer transfers the lettering to a plastic sheet known as a *sticky-back*. By removing a thin film from the rear of the sticky-back, the sheet becomes

COMPUTERIZED LETT
MACHINES
SCRIBER

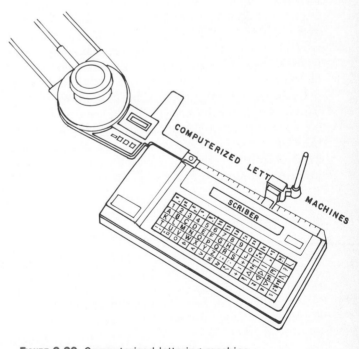

FIGURE 2-20 Computerized lettering machine.

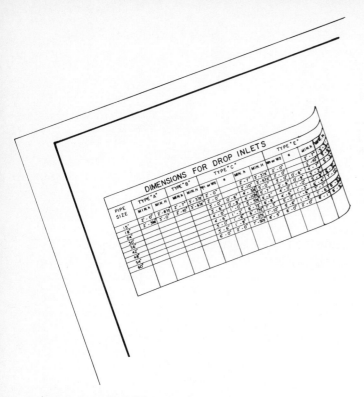

Figure 2-21 Sticky-back transfer.

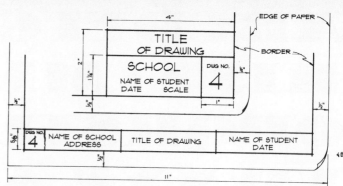

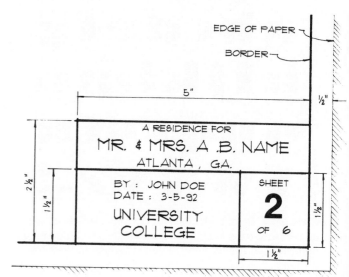

Figure 2-22 Title blocks satisfactory for school drawings of small size.

ready for mounting on the original drawing. This method of lettering is desirable when notes are extensive and speed is essential (Fig. 2-21).

2.17 Notes

Most of the hand-lettering done by the drafter is in the form of general notes on drawings. These notes play an important role in depicting specific information about a detail. Notes must be clearly lettered, concise, and readable. Since architectural drawings become legal instruments in construction contracts, the importance of accurate lettering cannot be over-emphasized.

Uniformly spaced guidelines should be drawn with a hard lead or non-print pencil before notes are lettered. Notes are blocked or justified at the left. Most notes are brief and can be expressed on one or two lines of lettering. Leader lines with arrows relate the note to a certain item shown on the drawing (Fig. 10-3).

2.18 Title Blocks

Each sheet of a set of drawings requires identification, usually in the form of a title block placed in the lower-right corner of the sheet. Various types and sizes of blocks can be used. School projects need to have only simple title blocks; architectural offices often require more complex ones. Several examples are shown in Figs. 2-22 and 2-23. Many offices have sheets with

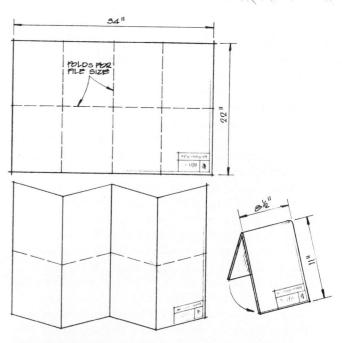

Figure 2-23 (A) Title block for a set of architectural working drawings; (B) folding a print to file size so that the title block is exposed.

borders and title blocks preprinted, ready for drafting use; others have title block stamps, called hand stamps, made up that can be quickly imprinted on each sheet before the drafting is started; others use *appliqué* preprinted title blocks of transparent plastic that will adhere to tracing paper and reproduce effectively. The use of either type conserves drafting time.

Information in title blocks varies, but a completed title block usually contains the following data:

1. Name and location of the structure
2. Name and location of the owner or client
3. Name and address of the architect
4. Date drawing is made
5. Date of revisions of drawing, if any
6. Initials of the drafter
7. Initials or signature of the checker
8. Architect's or engineer's seal
9. Identification number of sheet

2.19 Laying Out Similar Title Blocks on Continuous Sheets

A very convenient method for laying out similar title blocks on a number of sheets in a set is as follows: First, carefully lay out the required block on a small piece of paper. Then simply slip the layout under each sheet of tracing paper as it is needed and duplicate the block. Most of the lettering can be accurately spaced on the original layout, and considerable time will be saved in duplicating the linework. Keep the lettering symmetrical within the block for the most pleasing appearance. To aid in quick observation, sheet numbers are usually made very bold and placed in the lower right of the block.

2.20 Developing an Architectural Style

The architectural alphabets (Figs. 2-24 to 2-28) are included as suggested letter styles for the student. Each sample has been taken from competent drafter's work and represents accepted lettering currently being used on working drawings. It is recommended that the most appropriate styles be duplicated carefully and tried experimentally on several drawings. A few trials will indicate whether they satisfy the personal taste of the student and whether they can be drawn easily and rapidly. The one style that seems to be the most satisfactory should be studied in detail and practiced until every character can be done automatically. Uniformity in appearance should be attained, even in different sizes. Refinement should be a continual process until a polished style develops that can be proudly put on drawings.

If the need arises, one or two of the other alphabets can be used as alternates, for emphasis or de-emphasis. Regardless of the alphabet selected, avoid extreme modifications—flairs with no meaning or awkward curves that only result in faulty letter structure. Straightforward and uncomplicated lettering will be found to be the most acceptable.

Condensed No. 1 (Fig. 2-24) is extremely condensed and gains its distinction from the spread spacing between the letters. Each character is made as condensed as possible without destroying its recognizable features. Spacing must be uniform, and word divisions must be obvious for readability. The letter S is made with one reverse-curve stroke. Other letters are also made with fewer strokes than are required for similar basic letters. Ends of strokes are made with prominent points, thus giving the appearance of slight serifs.

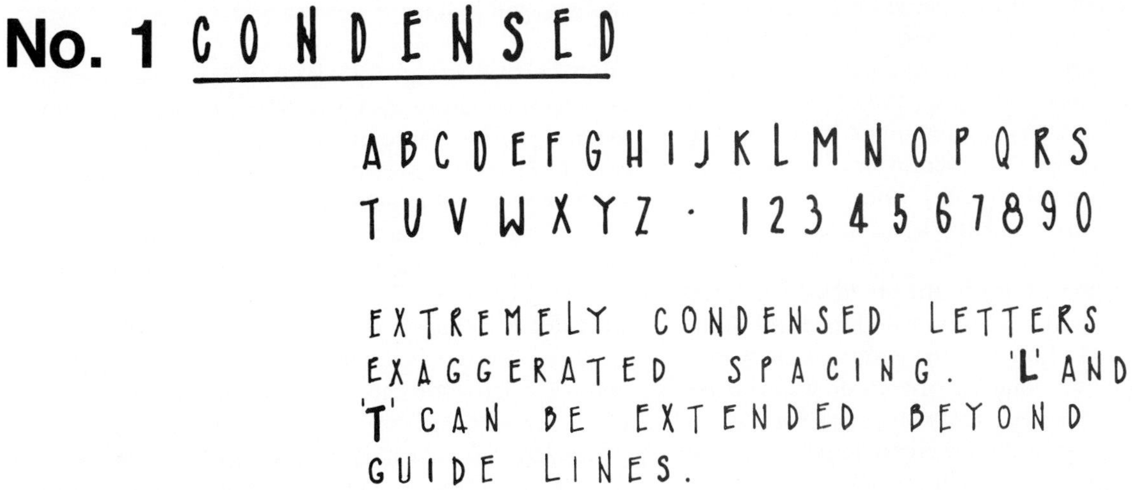

FIGURE 2-24 Condensed lettering.

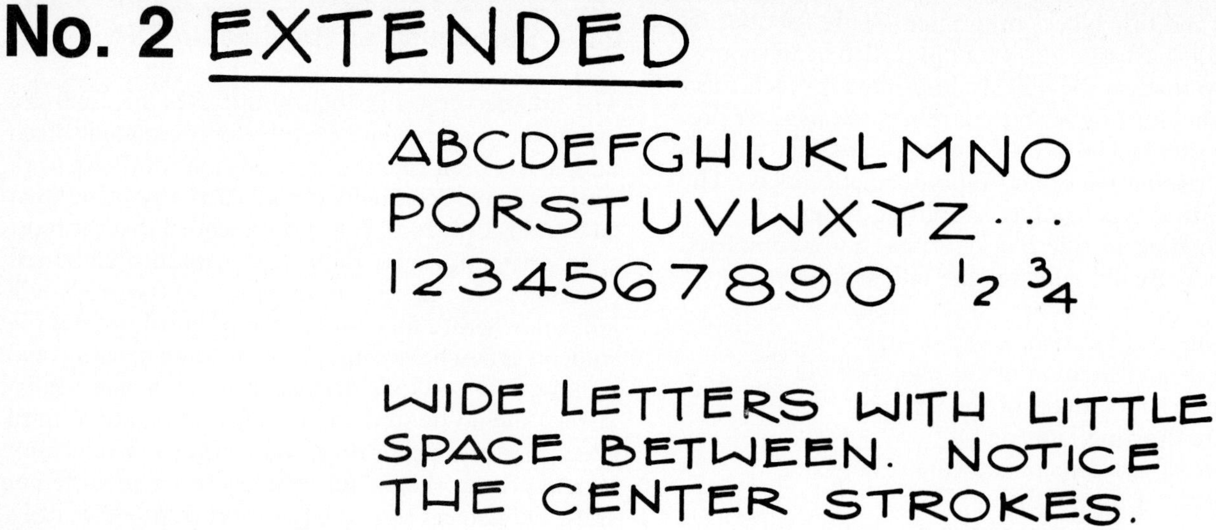

No. 2 <u>EXTENDED</u>

ABCDEFGHIJKLMNO
PORSTUVWXYZ...
1234567890 $\frac{1}{2}$ $\frac{3}{4}$

WIDE LETTERS WITH LITTLE
SPACE BETWEEN. NOTICE
THE CENTER STROKES.

FIGURE 2-25 Extended lettering.

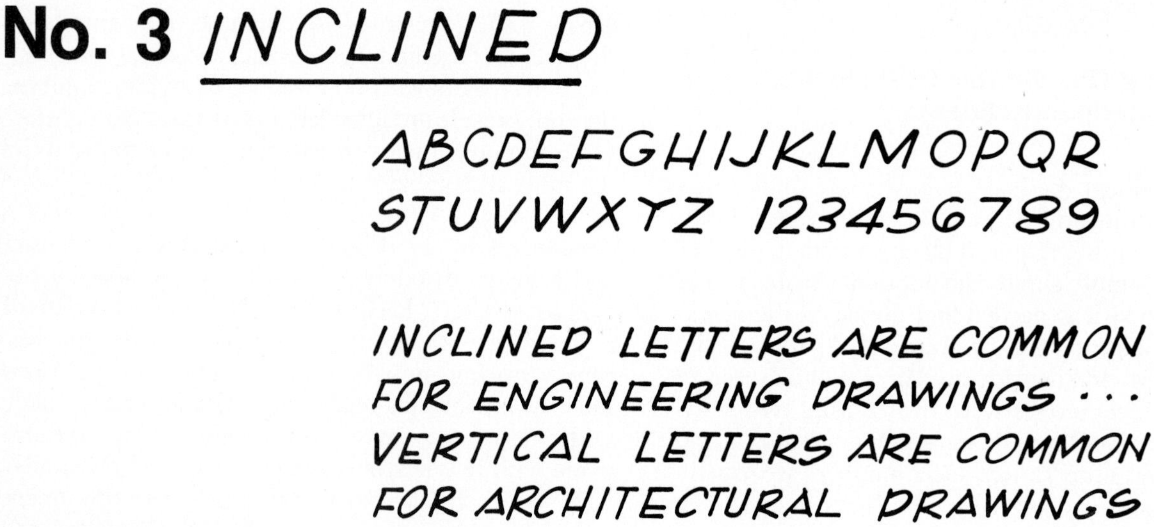

No. 3 <u>*INCLINED*</u>

*ABCDEFGHIJKLMOPQR
STUVWXYZ 123456789*

*INCLINED LETTERS ARE COMMON
FOR ENGINEERING DRAWINGS...
VERTICAL LETTERS ARE COMMON
FOR ARCHITECTURAL DRAWINGS*

FIGURE 2-26 Inclined lettering.

Extended No. 2 (Fig. 2-25) is an extended style with very little space between each letter—the opposite of condensed No. 1. It is widely used and represents the practice of extending each letter. Each word should appear as a tight unit; otherwise, use of the alphabet would require an extensive amount of space on the drawing. It is very readable, even in small sizes. If the low middle bar is used on the E and F, similar low strokes should be used on the H, K, R, and so on.

Inclined No. 3 (Fig. 2-26) is the standard, inclined technical alphabet with a few minor architectural variations. Many drafters find inclined letters easier to execute. Every student should be able to do a lowercase alphabet well for occasional minor notes (see Fig. 2-2A). To attain proficiency in the lowercase letters, practice making a graceful, inclined ellipse, which forms the basic shape for many of the characters; very little space

should be used between the letters in each word. Use inclined guide lines if necessary.

Triangle No. 4 (Fig. 2-27) is an alphabet used by many architectural drafters. Use a small triangle for all the vertical strokes. Place the T square above the lettering area and use the lower horizontal edge for guiding the triangle so that the instruments will not interfere with your hand. The other strokes are quickly made freehand. Keep the letters in each word close together.

Bold No. 5 (Fig. 2-28) is a highly stylized free-form alphabet created by using a technical inking pen or marker. Such letters are effective additions to architectural drawings where freehand graphics are used. These letters are formed casually with a broad-tip pen or marker. A fine-tip pen or marker is used to outline each letter.

No. 4 TRIANGLE...

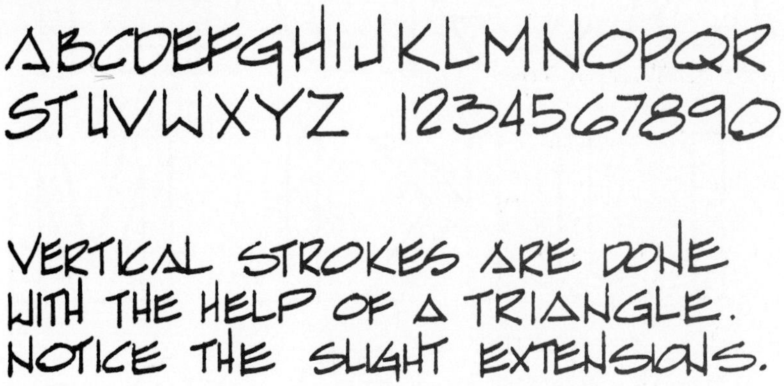

ABCDEFGHIJKLMNOPQR
STUVWXYZ 1234567890

VERTICAL STROKES ARE DONE
WITH THE HELP OF A TRIANGLE.
NOTICE THE SLIGHT EXTENSIONS.

FIGURE 2-27 Triangle lettering.

No. 5 BOLD

ABCDEFGHI
JKLMNOPQR
STUVWXYZ
123456789

abcdefghijklmn
opqrstuvwxyz

Bold free-style letters
are appropriate for
preliminary drawings

FIGURE 2-28 Bold free-form lettering.

Alphabets for Large Titles (Figs. 2-29, 2-30.) are used for major titles on drawings, for numerals in title blocks, or for identification letters, which find incidental use on working drawings. Several styles are included to allow latitude in choice and appropriateness. The large letters can be traced directly from the book onto tracing paper if they are suitable in size and style. Boldface lettering when placed adjacent to very small, lightface lettering creates interesting contrast in the composition of titles for display drawings.

ABCDEFG
HIJKLMN
OPQRSTU
VWXYZ.&
123456789
abcdefghi
jklmnopqr
stuvwxyz!

FIGURE 2-29 Helvetica Outline Medium alphabet, a popular architectural typeface for major titles. Place tracing paper over the characters that are needed and trace with pencil or ink. Fill in centers if a bolder title is appropriate.

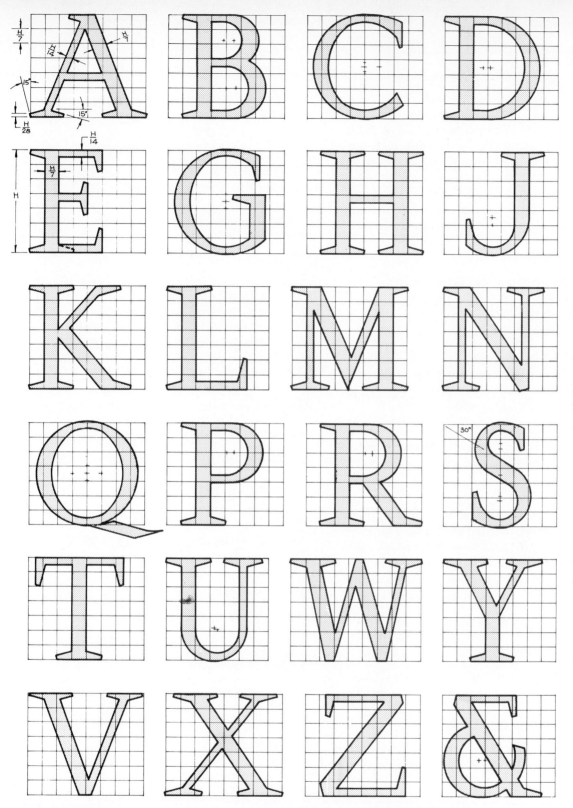

Figure 2-30 A modified roman alphabet suitable for major titles on drawings. Notice that this alphabet can be quickly drawn with a compass and an adjustable triangle set at 15°. Heights of the letters (H) may vary according to the need, but the proportions shown should be maintained.

1. On 8½″ × 11″ drawing paper, lay out a ½″ border and the 2″ by 4″ title block shown in Fig. 2-22. Using guidelines ⅜″ high and ½″ between each set, draw four each of the basic lettering strokes shown in Fig. 2-5 in the first set. On the next two rows, letter the complete basic single-stroke alphabet twice, centering each row. On the fifth row, letter two sets of the numerals. In the space below the numerals, lay out ¼″ guidelines ¼″ apart and, centered both vertically and horizontally, letter the following:

**GOOD LETTERING MUST BE
MADE EASY TO READ BEFORE
ANY ATTEMPT IS MADE TO
DO IT RAPIDLY.**

2. On similar drawing paper, with border and title block as in Exercise 1, lay out similar guidelines and letter the same copy in inclined capitals (see Fig. 2-26). Use inclined guidelines lightly drawn.

3. On similar paper, also prepared with the border and title block as in Exercise 1, duplicate the architectural lettering and layout of Fig. 2-25.

4. On similar paper, again with border and title block as in the previous exercises, lay out and center the title ROMAN, in large roman letters 1¼″ high (Fig. 2-30). Allow a 1½″ space from the top border. One inch below the title lay out ½″ guidelines, ⅜″ between each set. Letter the condensed architectural alphabet in Fig. 2-24, with all rows of lettering symmetrical. Keep the numerals on a separate line. Use instruments for the title only.

5. Repeat Exercise 4 using the word GOTHIC for the title and the lettering from Fig. 2-29.

6. On similar paper, with the border and title block of Exercise 1, make your own layout, using large, instrument-drawn roman letters for the title and an architectural alphabet of your own choice.

7. Draw guidelines for ³⁄₃₂″ high lettering and letter the following exercises using one of the architectural alphabets:

**WELD VERTICAL LEG TO SIDE OF COLUMN
UNDERCUT ALL DOORS WHERE AIR
PASSAGE IS REQUIRED
SEE DETAIL SHEET S-4
THIS PORTION OF WALL TO BE PIERCED
BRICK (SEE FRONT ELEV.)
SHADED AREA IN PLAN INDICATES
FURRED CEILINGS**

**PROVIDE WEEP HOLES EVERY 4′-0″
TURN DOWN REINF. 3″ FROM EDGE
SET THRESHOLD IN ELASTIC
BEDDING MASTIC**

8. On 8½″ × 11″ drawing paper lay out a ½″ border and the title block shown in Fig. 2-22. Using guidelines ³⁄₁₆″ high and ¼″ between each set, fill the sheet with lettered dimensions showing feet, inches, and fractions of an inch, such as 2′-0″, 7′-4″, and 15′-8½″, using the strokes shown for numbers in Fig. 2-25.

9. On similar drawing paper, with border and title block as in Exercise 8, lay out guidelines ¼″ high for sheet titles and ⅛″ high for scales, with ³⁄₁₆″ space between sheet titles and scales. Underscore sheet titles. Using the lettering style from Fig. 2-27, neatly arrange and letter all the sheet titles shown below on the 8½″ × 11″ paper. We suggest that ½″ space be maintained between titles vertically and ¾″ horizontally.

Site Plan	Foundation Plan
Scale 1″ = 20′–0″	Scale 1/8″ = 1′–0″
Floor Framing Plan	Roof Framing Plan
Scale 1/8″ = 1′–0″	Scale 1/8″ = 1′–0″
North Elevation	East Elevation
Scale 1/4″ = 1′–0″	Scale 1/4″ = 1′–0″
West Elevation	Transverse Section
Scale 1/4″ = 1′–0″	Scale 3/8″ = 1′–0″
Longitudinal Section	Typical Wall Section
Scale 3/8″ = 1′–0″	Scale 3/4″ = 1′–0″
Interior Elevation	Cabinet Details
Scale 1/2″ = 1′–0″	Scale 1-1/2″ = 1′–0″
South Elevation	Floor Plan
Scale 1/4″ = 1′–0″	Scale 1/4″ = 1′–0″

10. On similar drawing paper, with border and title block as in Exercise 8, lay out guidelines ⅝″ high, with 1″ between each set. Using a broad-tip and fine-tip felt pen and the bold style illustrated in Fig. 2-28, letter the titles listed below.

**SITE ANALYSIS
ZONE DIAGRAM
LOCATION MAP
AXONOMETRIC**

1. What are the distinguishing characteristics of the roman alphabet?

2. Why has the gothic alphabet been the most adaptable to technical lettering?

3. What are serifs?

4. Describe in your own words the meaning of *lowercase* lettering.

5. Which letter is the widest in the alphabet?

6. Why are guide lines needed for lettering on working drawings?

7. What is meant by a *boldface* alphabet?

8. List several methods of giving titles emphasis.

9. What is meant by *architectural style* in lettering?

10. Where is the title block usually placed on a working drawing?

11. Which of the five styles of lettering illustrated in this chapter would be most appropriate for notes on an architectural working drawing? (See Figs. 2-24 to 2-28).

12. What are lettering devices?

13. What are transfer letters and where are they used?

14. Why are letters not spaced equally apart in each word?

15. When would it be appropriate to use the bold freehand letters that are executed with broad- and fine-tip felt pens?

16. How much space should be allowed between each word when lettering?

17. Architects generally use vertical stroke letters. What type of strokes are commonly used by engineers?

18. What height letters would be appropriate for the title NORTH ELEVATION on architectural working drawings: $1/16''$, $1/4''$, $3/4''$, or $1''$ high?

19. When would it be appropriate to use an extended lettering style?

20. What is the best method for developing perfection in lettering?

BASIC TECHNICAL DRAWING

"Geometry . . . is the only science that it hath pleased God to bestow upon mankind."

—Thomas Hobbes

3

A knowledge of multiview drawings or orthographic projections, sectioning, auxiliary views and geometric construction is basic training needed for a solid foundation in architectural drawing. Each of these fundamentals is of equal importance; each is discussed here for the benefit of those students who may not possess the necessary background, and for those who may need an accelerated review. Further study of architectural drawing assumes that these essential concepts have been mastered. The knowledge of multiview or orthographic drawings serves as a conventional and universally accepted method of representing three-dimensional objects in a two-dimensional way on architectural drawings. Sections are necessary to show information about construction that is normally hidden on exterior views. Auxiliary projections illustrate how views that lie on other than orthogonal planes are drawn. Applied geometric construction provides methods for arriving at general graphic lines and shapes that form most elements of architectural design.

3.1 Multiview Two-Dimensional Drawings

We live in a three-dimensional world, but in most instances we use two-dimensional drawings to represent the three-dimensional objects around us. We are familiar with the terms top, bottom and side as we use them to describe a three-dimensional object. In essence we are using multiviews to communicate in a three-dimensional language. One cannot visualize an object in three dimensions if only the top is graphically represented; the sides and possibly the bottom must also be drawn (Fig. 3-1). Thus a number of multiview drawings must be assembled to create the total effect which could be accomplished by one singleview drawing (Fig. 3-2).

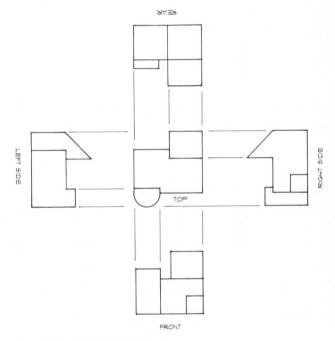

FIGURE 3-1 Multiview drawings.

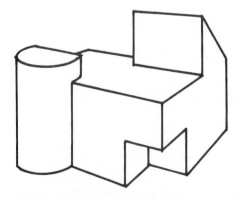

FIGURE 3-2 Singleview drawing.

FIGURE 3-3 Pictorial singleview drawing of a building.

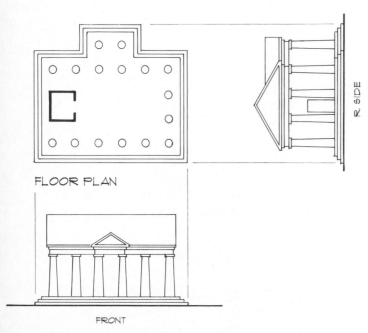

FLOOR PLAN

R. SIDE

FRONT

FIGURE 3-4 Orthographic projections.

The representation of a three-dimensional object such as a building on a flat piece of drawing paper is a fundamental and important consideration of the drafter. A pictorial, singleview, representation would be the most realistic in appearance; (Fig. 3-3) yet from the standpoint of an accurate graphic description for technical use, multiview drawings known as orthographic projections are commonly used. ("Ortho" means "perpendicular" or "at right angles.") Over the years orthographic projections have proved to be the clearest method for showing true shapes, relationship of features and necessary dimensions of an object (Fig. 3-4).

A multiview drawing, or orthographic drawing requires as many related views as necessary to reveal all necessary information about an object. Some objects, such as simple gaskets for example, require only one view, since the slight thickness can better be shown by a note rather than by graphic methods. On the other hand, if a more complex object, such as a building is drawn, often four or five views might be needed. Graphic experience, together with knowledge of construction, provides the architectural drafter with the means to determine the number and type of views necessary to accurately represent a structure on paper.

3.1.1 Principles of Projection: The Glass Box

For the simplest method of understanding this graphic language, let us think of an object, such as the basic house shown in Fig. 3-5, as being enclosed by transparent picture planes, or actually a glass box. Notice that

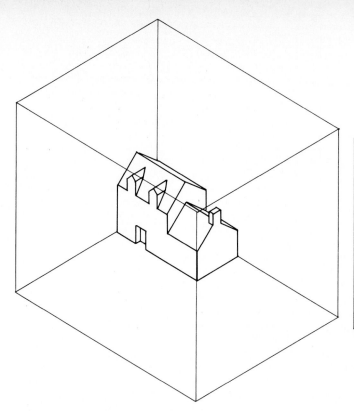

FIGURE 3-5 The glass box.

the sides of the house are parallel to the glass planes, and if we viewed each side through each transparent plane, a true-shape image of the side would result.

The inclined surfaces of the roof are not parallel to the upper horizontal glass plane; therefore, they do not appear in their true shape. The ridges of the roof, on the other hand, appear as full-length lines on the top view because they are parallel to the top picture plane. The profile of the gable roof, which is not evident on the top view, appears in true shape on the end views. Theoretically, the surfaces of the house that are perpendicular to the transparent planes and lines formed by the intersections of inclined surfaces are brought to the projection planes with parallel projectors. And the images created by these projectors on the planes are known as an *orthographic projection*.

3.1.2 The Relationship of Views

If the glass box is then opened, using theoretical hinges as shown in Fig. 3-6, an orthographic multiview drawing is formed on a flat plane. If required, six views of the house could be extended to the planes of the box (Fig. 3-7); however, six views would seldom be necessary. After opening the box, you will notice that the top view is directly over the front view, the right-side view is directly to the right of the front, the left-side view is directly to the left of the front, and so on. This alignment of views allows features of the house to be clarified

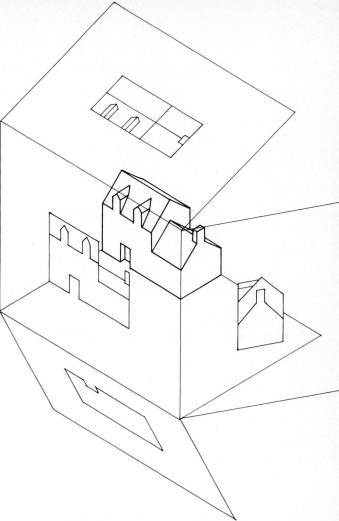

FIGURE 3-6 Opening the box to form a flat plane.

by cross-observation of more than one view. Only two dimensions (height and width) can be shown on each orthographic view; thus, by aligning the views an accurate, three-dimensional description can be obtained from the combined views.

3.1.3 Third-Angle Projection

It is conventional, for most engineering drawings in this country, to use the front view (the principal view), the top view, and the right-side view. Usually, these three views will give a complete graphic description of the object. (If important information is located on the left side, this view is substituted for the right-side view.) Ordinarily, the left-end view of the house would only duplicate the information shown on the right end, and the left-end view also has the disadvantage of showing part of the roof as hidden surfaces. The same is generally true of the rear or bottom views; they only dupli-

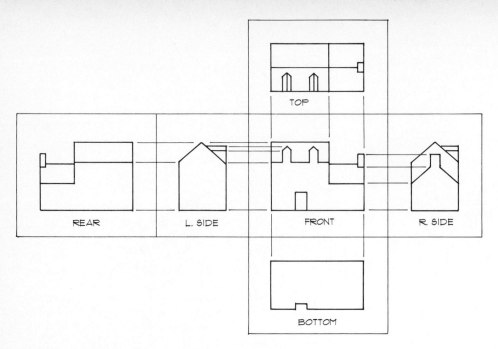

FIGURE 3-7 The relationship of orthographic views.

TOP

REAR   L. SIDE   FRONT   R. SIDE

BOTTOM

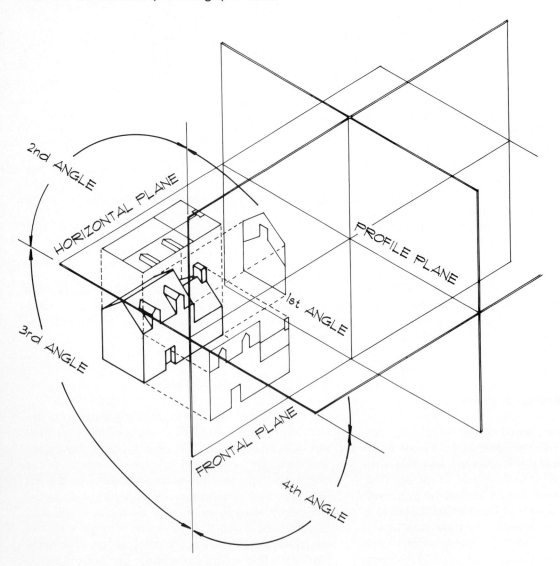

2nd ANGLE

HORIZONTAL PLANE

PROFILE PLANE

1st ANGLE

3rd ANGLE

FRONTAL PLANE

4th ANGLE

FIGURE 3-8 Third-angle projection planes.

cate information and are therefore unnecessary. As long as all information is shown, a minimum number of views is used. The three conventional views (front, top, and right side) are produced by placing the object within the third octant of the transparent plane assembly shown in Fig. 3-8. The top view is projected to the horizontal plane, the front view is projected to the frontal plane, and the right-side view is projected to the profile plane. This method of projection and relationship of views is called *third-angle projection* and is universally used for technical drawings throughout the United States and Canada.

3.1.4 Hidden Surfaces

Often surfaces and features on orthographic views are hidden from the observer. If these features contribute necessary information, they are represented by dashed (hidden) lines. In Fig. 3-7 the hidden roof surfaces are shown as dashed lines on the left-side view since they are behind the higher portion of the object. Dashed lines should be carefully made by the drafter. Uniform dashes should be used, very little space is left between each dash, and the ends of each dash should be made prominent (see Fig. 9-6).

3.1.5 Architectural Views

In architectural drawing, orthographic views that are projected to vertical planes, such as the front, side, and rear views, are called *elevations*. Views that are projected to horizontal planes and observed from the top (or bottom) are called *plans*. Hereafter, this terminology will be used when referring to the different architectural views.

Another variation in architectural work is the placement of the different elevations and plans on paper. As previously mentioned, when drawing the orthographic views of a small object, the views must be related for proper cross-reference. Because the elevations and plans of a building are often comparatively large, it becomes difficult to place them all on the paper in definite orthographic relationship. For convenience, the plan and the elevations are frequently put on separate sheets. Such an arrangement allows the drafter to draw each view large enough to facilitate reading and interpretation. However, each plan and elevation must be properly identified so that all views can be related in the reader's mind. Elevations should be shown horizontally and, if space permits, the right elevation should be to the right of the front and the left elevation to the left of the front. Avoid an elevation "on end" on the paper—it would not appear in a natural position. Otherwise, the elevations are true orthographic projections with few, if any, hidden surfaces or features shown.

Top views of buildings are limited mainly to roof framing plans showing the layout of complex roof structural members. Occasionally, a roof plan is necessary to show skylight, drains, and other important information on commercial buildings. Top views of houses would be largely for the purpose of developing different roof intersections and overhang treatments during planning stages. It is seldom necessary to draw a top view of a house showing only the roof surface.

The main drawing of a set of working drawings, the *floor plan*, is actually a horizontal section view of the building as seen from above. The cutting plane (see Fig. 3-9A&B) is theoretical and passes through important

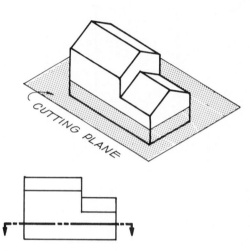

FIGURE 3-9 (A) The imaginary cutting plane of a first-floor plan.

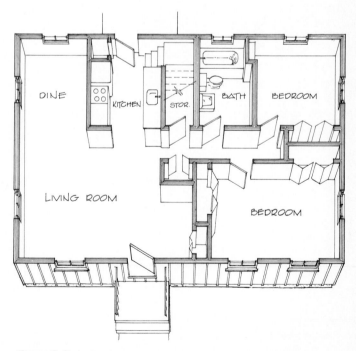

FIGURE 3-9 (B) The first-floor plan is shown as though the upper part of the house is cut away to reveal the layout of rooms.

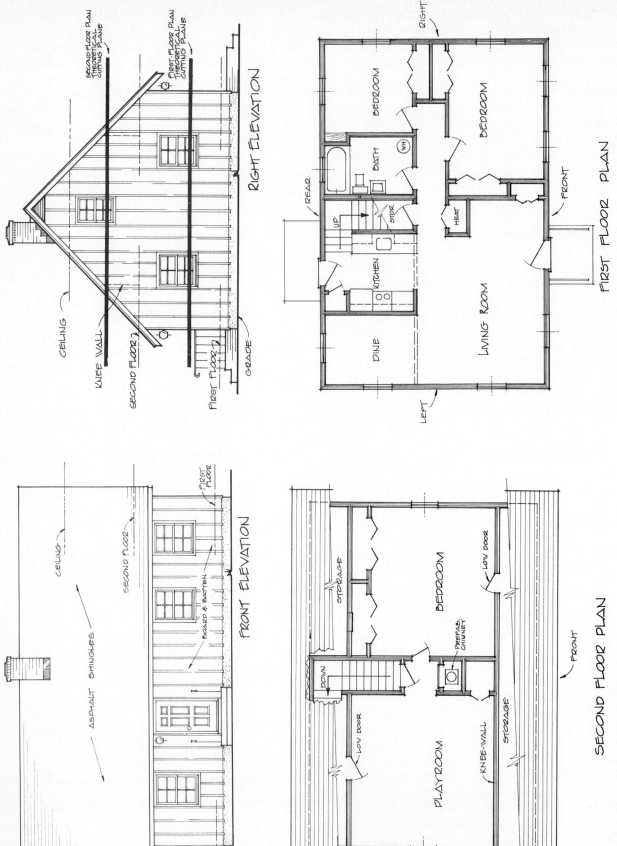

FIGURE 3-10 Architectural views of a small house.

vertical features such as doors, windows, walls, stairs, and fireplaces, to show their location and size within the building (also see Fig. 3-10). To do this, the cut must often have offsets to pass through features that might be located high or low on the walls. Yet, the offsets are not shown on the plan. This conventional method of floor plan representation will be seen after studying a number of the floor plans shown throughout the book. Floor plans will be considered further under Working Drawings in Chapter 11.

Other architectural views of only portions of a building, such as structural members and small sections, come under the broad, general heading of *details* and will be discussed throughout later chapters.

3.2 Sectioning

A *section* is defined as an imaginary cut made through an object, or a combination of objects, with the material in front of the cut removed. A view of this cut or plane, then, becomes a direct method of revealing important internal information about the object. Usually, sections are drawn through walls, floors, windows, doors, structural members, cornices, fireplaces, stairs, footings, trim moldings, cabinet work, special construction, and the like.

3.2.1 Importance of Architectural Sections

When looking at the elevation of a building, only the exterior materials and features are visible. If dashed lines were used to indicate the many hidden materials, their shapes, and their interrelationships, the resulting hodgepodge of lines would make the drawing impossible to read (see Fig. 3-11). A simple method must be used, therefore, to show clearly each important feature of interior construction on working drawings for the benefit of builders and workers. Sections are drawn mainly for this structural purpose, although occasionally a simplified section is used on design drawings. On typical architectural working drawings, drafters seldom employ the use of hidden lines to the extent that they are employed on many engineering drawings. Rather, the architectural drafter uses a series of sections taken through strategic points of the construction throughout the building and arranges them for easy reference to the other views. Different types of sections are used, and each has an appropriate application, determined by the drafter, to show necessary information simply and comprehensibly. Often, for clarity in dimensioning, sections are drawn at a larger scale than the view from which they are taken.

3.2.2 Indicating the Cutting Plane

Unless the plane of the section is obvious, a *cutting-plane line* should be used to identify the imaginary cut on the related drawing (see Fig. 3-12). Cutting planes are usually represented by a heavy dash and double-dot line; usually, arrows are placed at the ends of the line to indicate the direction of observation revealed by the section view. If the section is identical when looking in either direction, the arrows would be unnecessary.

As previously mentioned, floor plans are actually horizontal sections, and no cutting plane is conventionally needed to identify them (see Fig. 3-9). This is understandable if we think of the floor plan as a means for showing information about only one floor level; as long as the theoretical cut is somewhere through that floor level, there is no reason for showing a cutting-plane line on an elevation view (see Fig. 3-10). Even if the cut is offset in some parts of the building to encom-

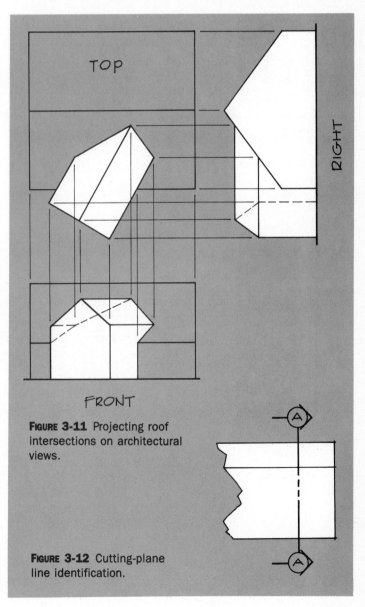

FIGURE 3-11 Projecting roof intersections on architectural views.

FIGURE 3-12 Cutting-plane line identification.

pass features found at different heights in the walls, no cutting plane is needed since the elevation views show the correct heights of such features.

Also, typical wall sections, showing uniform construction throughout major exterior walls, require no cutting planes for identification.

On drawings having two or more cutting planes and section views, each section must be related to the proper cutting plane; usually letters, such as A-A or B-B, are used for this identification (see Fig. 3-12). Complex drawings having section views on several sheets must have letter identifications as well as sheet identification to relate the view correctly. Figure 10-6 shows a satisfactory method for relating numerous sections to their cutting planes when views must be arranged on different sheets. The small circles can be quickly drawn with a circle template (see Fig. 3-12).

3.2.3 Sectioning Conventions

The section must distinctly show the outline of all solid materials that have been cut and also the voids or spaces that may fall between the materials. Occasionally, features lying beyond the cutting plane must also be shown for clarity (see Fig. 3-13). These features are brought to the plane of the section by perpendicular projectors, very much like the features of an object are brought to the projection plane of an orthographic projection drawing. Usually, hidden features are not shown on section views; dashed lines only confuse sectioned details. On some views, however, it is necessary to violate true projection for added clarity; features such as holes, ribs, and spokes, which do not fall on the cutting plane of a symmetrical object, are revolved to the cutting plane and then projected to the section view (Fig. 3-14). It is also conventional practice not to section bolts, screws, rivets, shafts, rods, and the like, which may fall in the plane of the section. They are more clearly shown unsectioned (see Fig. 3-15).

3.2.4 Crosshatching Sections

Other than the above-mentioned conventions, the materials that are cut must be crosshatched (symbol line tone) with the proper material symbol. (See Fig. 9-11 for the various standard sectioning symbols used on

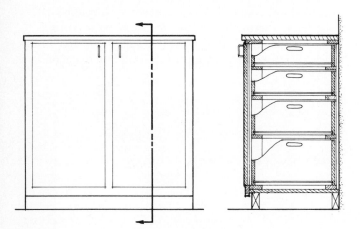

FIGURE 3-13 Section showing features beyond cutting plane.

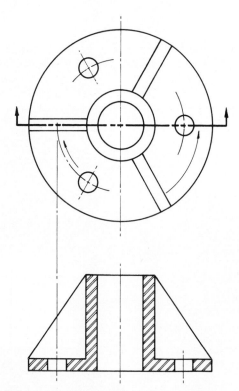

FIGURE 3-14 Conventional symmetry in sections.

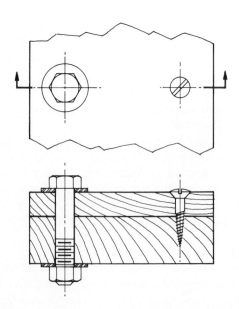

FIGURE 3-15 Fasteners on the cutting plane are not cut.

50 Basic technical drawing

construction drawings.) Adjacent materials are cross-hatched in different directions for easier identification; the 45° triangle can be used for the majority of the linework; and to conserve time, the spacing of cross-hatch lines should be done by eye—experience will develop uniformity of tone. Small, sectioned pieces should have darker tones; larger surfaces can be lighter. Wood structural members are merely indicated with diagonals drawn with instruments; others, such as finish lumber and concrete, are executed freehand. Thin members, such as sheet metal, building paper, or gaskets, are filled-in solid black—usually only a heavy line. If the same member is revealed in several places in a section view or in different sections, the crosshatch technique should always be identical. Important profile lines of a section should be made prominent.

Many architects use a technique called *poché* to make sectioned areas of a drawing appear more prominent, especially on display drawings. The term means to shade, color, or otherwise darken the value of an area to provide contrast.

3.2.5 Full Sections

A full section shows an object or a building *cut entirely across* so that the resulting view is completely "in section." The cutting plane can be a straight plane (see Fig. 3-13), or it can be offset to pass through features it may have missed if it were a straight, nonoffset plane (see Fig. 3-14). An offset does not show on the section view, as the change in plane is purely imaginary and is meant to gather as many features as necessary to make the section inclusive and complete. Sections can be either horizontal or vertical. Although drawings showing horizontal section views through a building are in reality one of the types of sections, it is customary to call these *plans*, whereas drawings showing vertical section views are commonly referred to as *section details*. This is the usual method of showing cuts through walls and is the most predominant way of showing sections in architectural drawings. A vertical section, if completely taken through the narrower width of a building, is called a *transverse section;* taken through the long dimension of a building, it is called a *longitudinal section* (see Chapter 15). Either type is usually informative and often reveals construction detail that is difficult to show with other drawing procedures.

3.2.6 Half-sections

Instead of the cutting plane passing entirely through the object, as in the full section, the cutting plane in a half-section goes only to the center and gives the appearance of having the front quadrant removed (see Fig. 3-16). On symmetrically shaped objects, half-sections

conveniently show both the interior and the exterior in only one view. Because of symmetry, some objects do not warrant a full section. When drawing a half-section, the hidden features on the uncut half of a symmetrical object need not be shown with dashed lines, since they would merely duplicate the features of the section. Notice that a center line separates the interior and exterior portions of the half-section view.

3.2.7 Broken-out Sections

A broken-out section is a convenient method of showing important interior features that can be given sufficient description in a small area of an exterior view. Usually, the removal of only a small portion of exterior material will not affect the appearance of a view, and the flexibility of a broken-out section allows it to be placed where important exterior features need not be removed (see Fig. 3-16). Irregular break lines indicative of the material removed are used to show the limits of the sectioned area.

3.2.8 Revolved Sections

The cross-sectional shapes of I beams, wood moldings, irregular shaped structural members, and the like, can

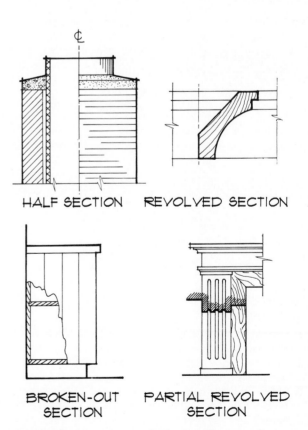

HALF SECTION   REVOLVED SECTION

BROKEN-OUT SECTION   PARTIAL REVOLVED SECTION

FIGURE 3-16 Various types of minor sections used on drawings.

be effectively shown by the use of revolved sections. Each is drawn by assuming a cutting plane perpendicular to the axis of the member, as shown in Fig. 3-16, which has been revolved through a 90° arc to the frontal plane and superimposed directly on the elevation view of the member. Lines of the elevation view that may underlay the section should be removed before the crosshatch lines are applied.

3.2.9 Revolved Partial Sections

Occasionally, elevations of traditional fireplaces, exterior door trim, molded woodwork, and the like, requiring only information about their exterior profiles, can conveniently employ a revolved partial section (see Fig. 3-16). Using a bold line, only the profile is drawn directly over the elevation. (Notice that the offsets in the profile coincide with the lines on the elevation that represent the offsets.) Short crosshatch lines may be drawn along the material side of the heavy profile line for more emphasis. This method of sectioning clearly shows the projection and contour of the elevation surface without the need for a separate view (see Fig. 3-17).

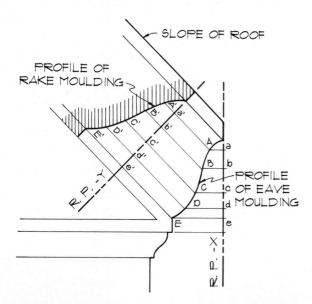

FIGURE 3-17 Plotting the profile of a rake molding (partial revolved section).

1. Lay out profile of horizontal molding and slope of roof with side view.
2. Draw reference plane X (RP-X) vertically and RP-Y perpendicularly to roof slope.
3. Establish arbitrary points A, B, C, and D. Transfer distances A-a, B-b, and so on, to RP-Y on the projection lines.
4. Connect points A′, B′, C′, and so on, with an irregular curve to form the profile of the rake mold.

3.2.10 Removed Sections

Removed sections are similar to revolved sections; instead of being superimposed on the exterior view, they are removed to a convenient position near the view from which they are taken, and a cutting-plane line is used to show their origin. Identification letters (Section 3.3.2) relate the cutting planes to their sections; several methods can be used (refer to Fig. 10-6). The advantage of the removed section over the revolved section is the possibility of enlargement, if necessary. Small details can be shown and dimensioned more easily at larger scales. If a series of sections relating to a main view is drawn, each section should be arranged in a logical manner and located, if possible, near its cutting plane. Whenever workable, a removed section should be drawn in its natural projected position. Sections difficult to orient will create complications in interpreting a drawing.

3.2.11 Pictorial Sections

Sometimes a pictorial section becomes the most effective method of showing structural assemblies or other construction features that are awkward to explain with orthographic views alone (see Figs. 4-19 to 4-21). Pictorial sections are discussed in Chapter 4.

3.3 Auxiliary Views

As previously mentioned under orthographic projection, the principal surfaces of a rectangular object, such as our miniature building, are shown in true shape when their features are observed from the surface in a perpendicular manner. That is, the surfaces, or elevations, appear in true shape if their projection planes are parallel to each surface. However, when the sloping roof appears on the front and rear elevations, the view of the roof is not a true shape because the surfaces are inclined to the front and rear projection planes (see Fig. 3-7). The top view also shows the roof surfaces distorted because of their inclination to the horizontal projection plane (see Fig. 3-18). Usually, inclined roof surfaces do not require true-shape representation; therefore, principal elevations are adequate. But suppose we have a building with a wing, or part of an elevation, extending in a nonparallel direction from the other elevations. In contemporary architecture, many buildings have oblique wings or nonparallel sides, cabinets are designed at angles other than right angles, and structural members have elevations and surfaces that are sometimes inclined to the principal planes. These inclined surfaces would appear distorted on the principal views or elevations. Occasionally, several important surfaces are inclined and often must be shown in true shape on working drawings (see Fig. 3-19). To reveal the true shape of an inclined surface, an *auxiliary view* is necessary.

This is done by assuming an auxiliary plane *parallel* to the inclined surface; the features of the surface are then projected to the auxiliary plane with parallel projectors that are perpendicular to the surface. The direction of observation also becomes perpendicular to the inclined surface and the auxiliary plane. In most respects, an auxiliary view is similar to an orthographic view, except that the plane to which it is projected is *inclined* from the principal orthographic planes of projection. It is also convenient to think of the auxiliary plane as being hinged to the (profile) plane from which it is developed. *Reference planes*, one of which appears as a line on a principal view and the other as a line parallel to the auxiliary projection plane, are assumed to facilitate the construction of the auxiliary view. An auxiliary view, then, is a view projected to any plane *other than* one of the six orthographic planes and has been projected from a surface that is parallel to the auxiliary plane.

3.3.1 To Draw an Auxiliary View of an Irregular Object

The step-by-step construction shown in Fig. 3-20A,B is meant to simplify the procedure for developing a typical auxiliary view.

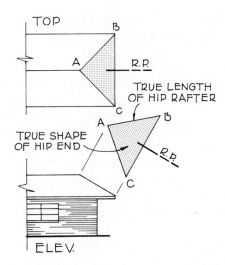

FIGURE 3-18 Drawing the true length of a hip rafter.

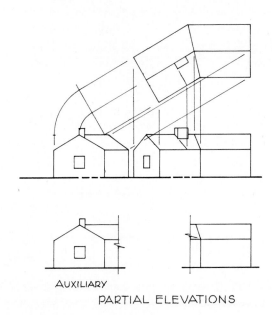

FIGURE 3-19 Auxiliary elevation views.

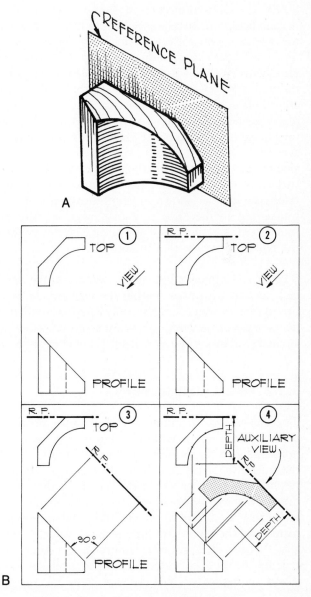

FIGURE 3-20 Steps in drawing an auxiliary view.

STEP 1.   Draw two views of the object, one showing the profile of the auxiliary surface and one showing the top and depth characteristics. Indicate the direction from which the auxiliary is to be taken.

STEP 2.   Assume a reference line on the top view, from which depths of the auxiliary are taken. A reference plane is established in back of this object for convenience, and it will show as a line on both the top view and the auxiliary view. (On symmetrical objects, the reference plane is best established on the center line.) Draw the reference line (a heavy dash and double-dot line) on the top view.

STEP 3.   Draw the auxiliary reference line parallel to the inclined surface of the front view. Be sure it is located far enough away from the front view to allow enough space for the auxiliary view.

STEP 4.   Draw projection lines from the front view perpendicular to the reference line, as shown. Transfer the measurements of the various necessary points of the top view to the corresponding features of the auxiliary view, with the dividers or by measurement. Notice that the auxiliary view will form between the auxiliary reference plane and the front view, because the reference plane has been assumed to be in back of the object on the top view. Irregular or curved surfaces can be plotted accurately by projecting as many points as needed along the curved surface of the top view to the inclined surface of the profile view and then to the auxiliary reference line as shown. Depth measurements are transferred in the same way that other features are transferred. Use an irregular plastic curve to connect the plotted points with a smooth line.

STEP 5.   Connect all the proper points on the auxiliary surface with lines, noting the visibility of each. Strengthen the lines. Usually, only a partial auxiliary is necessary, but the complete object as viewed from the auxiliary plane can be drawn for graphic experience.

3.3.2 Partial Auxiliary Views

The drafter will encounter auxiliary views mainly in drawing elevations of buildings whose exterior walls are nonparallel to the principal planes (see Fig. 3-19). If these elevations have important information and need to be shown in true shape, a partial auxiliary elevation is drawn. If the complete elevation is drawn on the auxiliary plane, a portion of the elevation will appear distorted and therefore have little pictorial value. Generally, this distorted portion is not drawn; the same holds true for the inclined surface in the principal elevation. The termination between the true shape and the dis-

torted shape in either elevation is shown with a conventional break line.

To draw a *partial auxiliary elevation*, assume an observation direction perpendicular to the auxiliary surface. (The projection plane then becomes parallel to the auxiliary surface, as previously mentioned.) It is preferable to draw the auxiliary view in a natural, horizontal position, rather than in its projection position. Show all features, such as windows and doors, in true shape and size and all horizontal dimensions in true length. These features can be projected from the plan view, which has been fastened above the drawing and inverted in a position to make the auxiliary wall horizontal. Take the heights from the other main elevations, or assume a horizontal reference plane at the ground line of the other elevations, and transfer the heights with the dividers or by measurement.

3.3.3 Inclined Oblique Auxiliary Views (Secondary Auxiliary Views)

If an inclined surface cannot be seen as a line in any of the six principal views and is not perpendicular to any of the six principal planes, its true shape must be constructed by the use of a secondary auxiliary, rather than a direct-projection method. Such views are rarely required, yet the drafter should be able to develop inclined oblique surfaces, principally to determine the true length of structural members that may have to be placed in an inclined oblique position within a building.

A convenient method is shown in Fig. 3-21. *To con-*

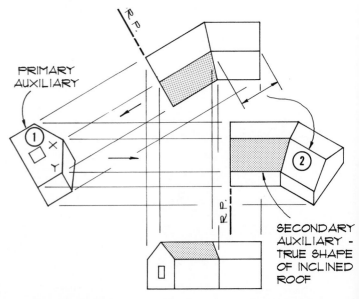

FIGURE 3-21 Drawing the true shape of an inclined oblique plane (secondary auxiliary).

struct *the true shape* of the shaded portion of the roof, first, draw a primary auxiliary (1) projected from the top view. This auxiliary view is needed first because it shows the *edge view* of the shaded roof; the required surface is represented as a line (X-Y). It must be remembered that auxiliary views of inclined surfaces are projected from views that show the inclined surface as a line. From the primary auxiliary view, construct parallel projectors that are perpendicular to the edge view line X-Y; these projectors form the true width of the shaded surface. For convenience, place the reference plane on the end of the oblique wing of the top view, and on the secondary auxiliary view draw it parallel to line X-Y of the primary auxiliary. Transfer the true lengths of the shaded surface on the top view to the second auxiliary view (2). Connect all visible points of intersection. The entire house can be drawn by projecting all points from the primary auxiliary view and by transferring lengths of all points from the reference line of the top view to the corresponding projection lines of the second auxiliary.

3.4 Geometric Construction

For centuries the architect has relied on the principles of plane and solid geometry to design two and three dimensional elements in the built environment. Most structures are composed of squares, rectangles, triangles, circles, arcs, polygons, pyramids, cones, cylinders and so on (Figs. 5-31 and 5-39). It is essential that the drafter become proficient in geometric constructions. Such knowledge will enable the drafter to bisect lines and angles, divide lines into equal parts, draw arcs and circles, construct regular and irregular polygons

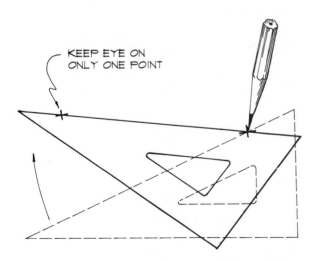

KEEP EYE ON ONLY ONE POINT

Figure 3-22 Convenient method of drawing a line through two points.

and the like. Once these skills are mastered the drafter should be able to develop plans, elevations, sections, details and pictorial drawings with greater ease.

The parallel bar, triangles, compass, and irregular curve are the tools required for beginning geometric construction exercises. To gain accuracy in drafting, use a well-sharpened 3H or 4H pencil. Often the locations of center points from which arcs or circles are drawn become the important steps in the construction. Place these carefully.

3.4.1 To Draw a Line through Two Points (Fig. 3-22)

After the two points have been established, hold the pencil firmly on either point and pivot the triangle edge against the anchored pencil until the other point is aligned. Draw a line between the two points with the pencil. The triangle should be held firmly during this exercise.

3.4.2 To Divide a Line into Equal Divisions

First Method (Fig. 3-23A) Given line AB to be divided into, for example, five equal parts, draw line BC at any convenient angle and, along it, measure or step off five equal divisions. Any suitable increment can be measured with the scale or stepped off with the dividers. Connect point A with the fifth point on line BC and transfer the remaining points to line AB with parallel connectors.

Alternate Method (Fig. 3-23B) Draw a perpendicular from line AB as shown and place the scale between point B and the perpendicular. If five divisions are required, select five divisions on the scale and pivot it from point B and the perpendicular until the end of the five divisions coincides with point B and the other with the perpendicular. (Slightly larger divisions on the scale must be used than the intended divisions on line AB.) Indicate the remaining divisions along the scale, and transfer them with perpendiculars to line AB. Any number of divisions can be made, and considerable latitude in choice of increment size on the scale can be employed. However, the smaller the angle between the line to be divided and the edge of the scale, the more accurate the divisions will be.

Division by Trial and Error Many drafters merely step off the divisions with the use of the dividers, if the number of divisions is not excessive. Several trials usually result in an accurate division.

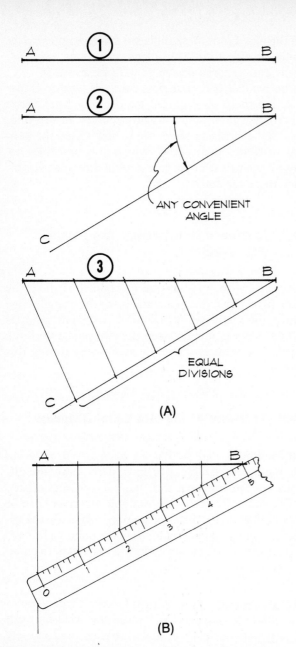

(A)

(B)

FIGURE 3-23 (A) Dividing a line into equal divisions (first method); (B) dividing a line into equal divisions (alternate method).

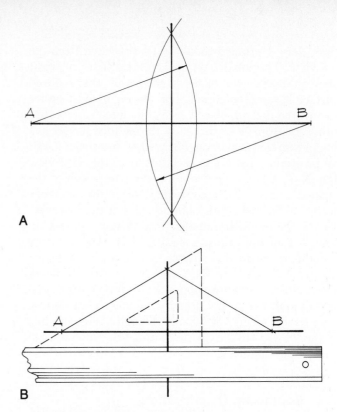

A

B

FIGURE 3-24 (A) Bisecting a line with a perpendicular bisector; (B) bisecting a line with a triangle.

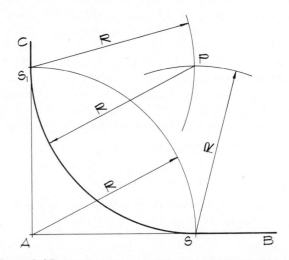

FIGURE 3-25 Drawing an arc tangent to a right angle.

3.4.3 To Bisect a Line with a Perpendicular Bisector

With the Compass (Fig. 3-24A) Given line AB, with the compass set larger than half the length of the line, draw the same arc from both ends. A line passing through both intersections of the arcs will divide line AB with a perpendicular bisector.

With the T Square and Triangle (Fig. 3-24B) Given line AB, from both ends draw equal angles, as shown,

with the triangle. A perpendicular from line AB passing through the intersection of angular lines will bisect line AB with a perpendicular bisector.

3.4.4 To Draw an Arc Tangent to the Lines of a Right Angle (Fig. 3-25)

Given right angle CAB, with its center at corner A, draw the arc with given radius R, intersecting AB at S and AC at S_1. Then, using points S and S_1 as centers, construct arcs of the same radius. Their intersection at

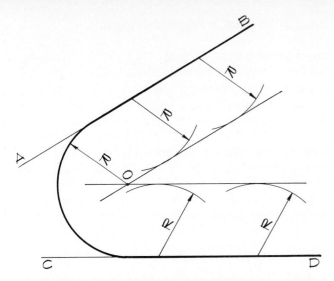

FIGURE 3-26 An arc tangent to two straight lines (the arc center must be equidistant from both lines).

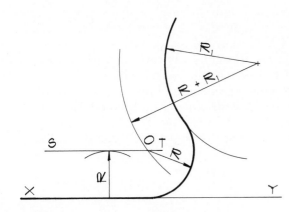

FIGURE 3-27 Drawing an arc tangent to a circle and straight line.

P forms the center for the given radius arc R, which will be tangent to the lines of the right angle.

3.4.5 To Draw an Arc Tangent to Two Straight Lines That Are Not Perpendicular (Fig. 3-26)

Given lines AB and CD forming an acute angle as shown (use the same procedure for lines forming an obtuse angle), set the compass for the given radius and draw arcs R at random points on each line. The intersection O is located by drawing light lines through the extremities of the arcs. The lines will be parallel to the given lines AB and CD and be equidistant.

3.4.6 To Draw an Arc of Any Radius R Tangent to a Given Circle and a Straight Line (Fig. 3-27)

Let R_1 be the radius of the given circle or arc and XY be the given line. Draw line ST parallel to XY at R dis-

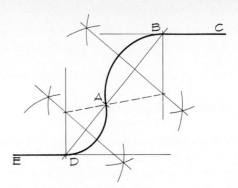

FIGURE 3-28 Drawing an ogee curve.

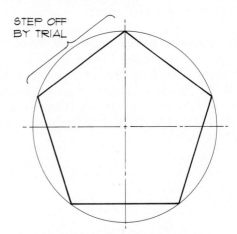

FIGURE 3-29 Drawing a regular pentagon.

tance away as shown. Using P as the center and the sum $R_1 + R$ as the radius, construct an arc intersecting line ST at point O. The arc of R radius drawn from point O will be tangent to the given circle and line XY.

3.4.7 To Draw an Ogee or Reverse Curve (Fig. 3-28)

Given two parallel lines BC and ED, connect B and D with a line and upon it indicate the reversal point A. (The placement of point A is arbitrary, depending on the desired nature of the ogee curve.) Erect perpendiculars from line BC at B and line ED at D. Construct perpendicular bisectors BA and AD. The intersections of the bisectors and the previous perpendiculars are the centers for the required arcs. Set the compass at the required radii, established graphically by the perpendiculars. A line intersecting both centers of the arcs will pass through point A, revealing the accuracy of the construction and the tangent point of the two arcs.

3.4.8 To Draw a Regular Pentagon (Fig. 3-29)

Given the size of the circle within which the pentagon is to be inscribed, draw the circle and divide its circumference into five equal parts by trials with the dividers, and connect the points. The points on the circle can also be located with the protractor: step off five 72° angles (360° ÷ 5).

3.4.9 To Draw a Regular Hexagon

When the Distance across Flats Is Given (Fig. 3-30A) The flats are the parallel sides. A hexagon can be dimensioned either across its parallel sides or across its corners. Construct a circle with a diameter of the given distance across flats. Circumscribe a hexagon around the circle that is tangent to the center of each side using the 30°–60° triangle and T square.

When the Distance across Corners Is Given (Fig. 3-30B) Construct center lines and draw a circle of the diameter required across corners of the hexagon. Using the 30°–60° triangle and T square, inscribe the hexagon within the circle starting at an intersection of one center line and the circle. The radius of the given circle will be the length of each side.

3.4.10 To Draw a Regular Octagon

Construction around a Circle (Fig. 3-31A) Given the distance across flats (between parallel sides), draw center lines and construct a circle of the given diameter. Using a 45° triangle and a T square, draw the sides of the octagon tangent to the circle as indicated.

Construction within a Square (Fig. 3-31B) Draw a square with sides equal to the required distance across flats. Draw diagonals and, using half the length of the diagonal as a radius and the corners of the square as centers, draw the arcs as shown. Connect the intersections of the arcs and sides to form the octagon.

3.4.11 To Construct a Regular Polygon with Any Number of Sides (Fig. 3-32)

Given the length of one side and, for example, let seven sides be required. From any point A, draw the semicircle CDB using AB as the radius. By trial with the dividers, divide the semicircle into seven equal parts. AD will become the second side. Bisect side AB and AD with perpendicular bisectors to locate point O, which will be the center of the polygon. Draw the circle through points A, B, and D. The remaining vertices can be located by stepping off chord AB along the remainder of the circle, or by extending lines A3, A4, and so on, to the circle.

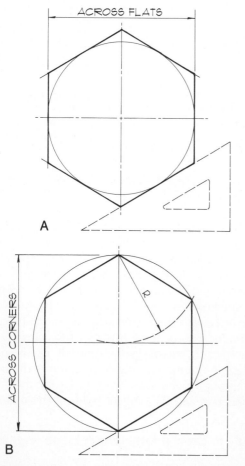

FIGURE 3-30 (A) Drawing a hexagon with distance across flats given; (B) drawing a hexagon with distance across corners given.

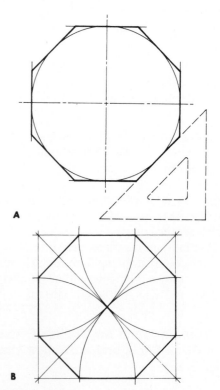

FIGURE 3-31 (A) Drawing an octagon with a circle; (B) drawing an octagon with a square.

3.4.12 To Draw an Ellipse by the Concentric-Circle Method (Fig. 3-33)

Given the major axis AB and the perpendicular minor axis CD, draw concentric circles of both diameters from point O. Divide each quadrant into an arbitrary number of angular dimensions; the example shows four divisions in each quadrant that have been conveniently laid out with the triangles—more accuracy can be obtained by more divisions. From the intersections of the division lines and the outer circumference, draw vertical lines parallel to CD. From the intersections of the angular division lines and the inner circle, draw horizontal lines parallel to AB as indicated. The intersections of these perpendicular construction lines produce points from which the ellipse can be constructed. Completion is achieved by smoothly connecting the points with the use of the irregular curve. If all the points in one quadrant of the ellipse can be aligned with one setting of the irregular curve, the other quadrants can be completed by merely marking the curve and tipping it over for the remaining curved lines. Elliptical arches can be quickly drawn with the foregoing construction.

3.4.13 To Draw an Ellipse by the Parallelogram Method (Fig. 3-34)

Given the major axis AB and minor axis DE. From the axes draw a rectangle or parallelogram with sides equal to the axes. Divide AO and AC into equal number of parts. Draw light lines from point E through the AO divisions and from point D through the AC divisions. Intersections of similar numbered lines will create points along the ellipse. Complete the remaining three quadrants by the same procedure and draw the ellipse with an irregular curve.

3.4.14 To Draw an Approximate Ellipse by the Four-Center Method (Fig. 3-35)

Given the axes AB and CD. Connect points A and D with a diagonal line. With AO as the radius, draw the

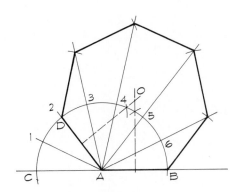

FIGURE 3-32 Drawing a polygon.

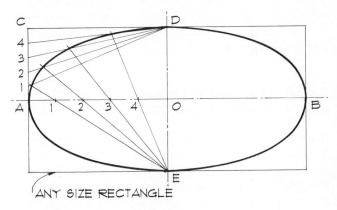

FIGURE 3-34 Parallelogram ellipse.

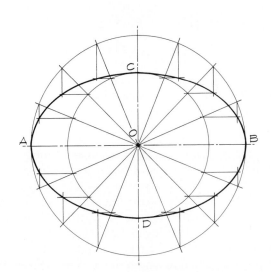

FIGURE 3-33 Drawing an ellipse (concentric circle method).

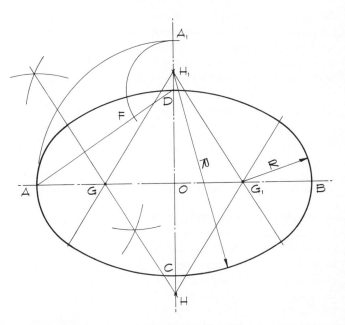

FIGURE 3-35 Four-center approximate ellipse.

arc AA_1 using O as the center. With DA_1 as the radius, draw the arc FA_1 using D as the center. Bisect line AF with a perpendicular bisector as shown; this locates points G and H, which become the centers for the required arcs. Points G_1 and H_1 are located equidistant from O as points G and H, respectively. The distance GO equals OG_1 and HO equals OH_1. Draw the radius AG arc from points G and G_1 and the radius HD arc from points H and H_1 to complete the ellipse. Notice that an ellipse drawn by the four-center method is not as graceful as the previous ellipses.

3.4.15 To Draw a Parabola within a Rectangle (Fig. 3-36)

Given a rectangle CDEF. Usually, these are the given dimensions, indicating the width and depth (or span and rise) of the needed parabola. Divide AC and CD into the same number of parts as shown. The intersections of like-numbered lines become points on the parabola. Notice that one set of lines is parallel and the other radiating. Connect the points with the use of an irregular curve. The parabola is finding use in various contemporary structures.

3.4.16 To Enlarge or Reduce an Irregular Drawing (Fig. 3-37)

If a drawing is to be enlarged, first lay out a uniform grid field over the figure as shown. Use a grid size convenient for enlargement. For example, if a drawing is to be enlarged, say, five times or 500 percent, then it would be appropriate to select a spacing for the grid lines of the smaller field that could be conveniently increased five times for the larger grid. Next, lay out a larger, compatible grid field, using the same number of grid lines as the smaller field. For convenience, number the corresponding grid spaces in both fields as shown. The detail within each small grid space can then be enlarged within the corresponding larger grid block. Complete one block at a time until the entire figure is enlarged. *To reduce the size of a drawing,* the opposite procedure is used; the detail is taken from the large grid field and reduced to the corresponding smaller one.

3.4.17 Esthetic Proportions through Geometry

A number of interesting geometric proportioning methods have appeared from time to time in the history of architecture and art. Some have withstood the test of time and should be accepted for their esthetic worth, even by modern standards. Not only do they provide the student of drawing with valuable construction exercise, but they indicate an application of geometry to the esthetics of structures.

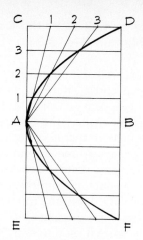

FIGURE 3-36 Drawing a parabola within a rectangle (use equal increments).

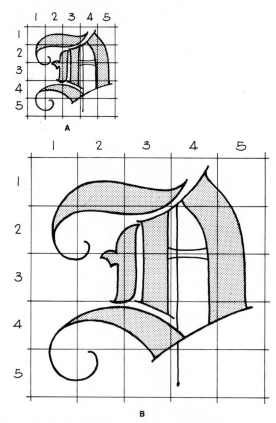

FIGURE 3-37 Enlarging or reducing a figure.

The Golden Section—originally a Greek method of dividing lines and form into pleasing proportions (Fig. 3-38A). Mathematically, its ratio may be expressed as follows: $(\sqrt{5} + 1\ )/2 = 1.618$. The ratio of one division to the other, then, can be stated as 1/1.618. Given line AE, to be divided according to the Golden Section, first bisect the line at point C. Erect a perpendicular to line AE at point E, equal in length to CE. On the hypotenuse (AD) of the triangle, locate point B so that BD

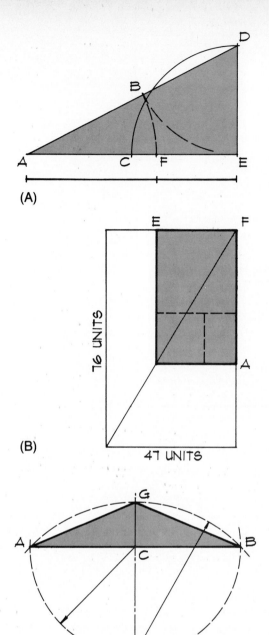

(A)

(B)

76 UNITS

47 UNITS

(C)

FIGURE 3-38 (A) The Golden Section; (B) the Golden Rectangle, made from the Section proportions; (C) the classic pediment triangle (Vignola).

interest, the short side of the rectangle can be laid out within it to form a square, and the remaining space will always be another Golden Rectangle (see dashed line).

Construction of the Basic Triangle for a Classic Pediment (Vignola) (Fig. 3-38C) Given width of the base AB, bisect line AB with a center line intersecting it at C. With AC (one-half of AB) as the radius, construct the semicircle AEB. With the radius EB, construct the arc AGB from point E. Connect points AG and GB.

GEOMETRIC CONSTRUCTION

On 8½″ × 11″ paper, lay out a ½″ border and divide into nine equal spaces similar to Fig. 3-39. With the following information, complete the exercises as shown.

1. Construct a 1″ arc tangent to the given right angle.

2. Find the center of the given circle using chord perpendicular bisectors.

3. Construct a ¾″ arc tangent to the given arc and straight line.

4. Divide line AB into five equal divisions.

5. Construct a ⅞″ arc tangent to the given circle arcs.

6. With the compass, bisect the given angle.

7. Construct a hexagon 1½″ across corners.

8. Construct a 1⅜″ octagon.

9. Construct an ogee curve from point A to point B, passing through point E (EB = 2AE). The line passing through A is parallel to the line passing through B.

ORTHOGRAPHIC PROJECTION

Study the pictorial drawings in Fig. 3-40 and develop the orthographic views of each problem. The exercises are meant to provide you with experience in understanding projection principles and upon completion should be examined by your instructor to ensure proper interpretation.

equals DE. On the original line AE, locate point F so that AF equals AB. F divides AE according to the proportions of the Golden Section.

The Golden Rectangle (Fig. 3-38B) The Golden Section provides the stable proportions for the Golden Rectangle. The long side of the rectangle is in proportion to the short side as AF is to FE in Fig. 3-38A. For convenience in drawing a predetermined size of the rectangle, the numerical proportion 76-47 units will provide a satisfactory method of scaling. As a matter of

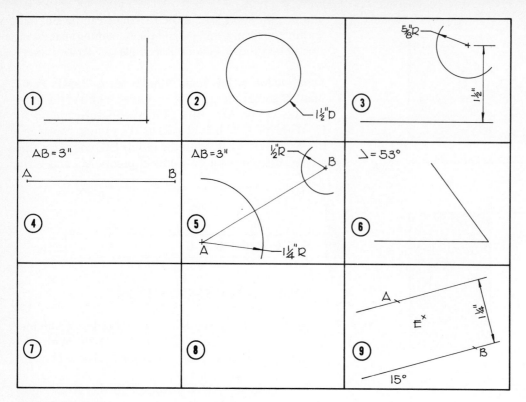

Figure 3-39 Exercises in geometric construction.

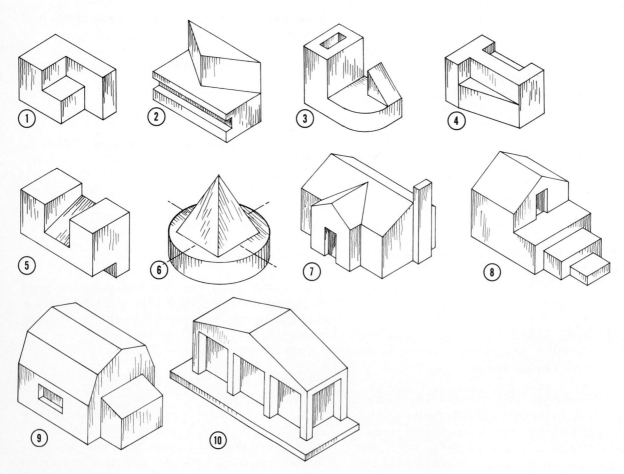

Figure 3-40 Exercises in orthographic projection drawing. With the use of dividers, double or triple each exercise.

SECTIONING

On 8½″ × 11″ paper draw the following exercises:

1. Draw a full section of Fig. 4-19 (double size). With the use of dividers, take the dimensions directly from the figure in the book.

2. Draw a half-section of Fig. 4-20 (double size).

3. Draw a longitudinal and transverse section of Fig. 4-35. Scale: 6″ = 1′-0″. Hatch sections with the steel symbol.

4. Draw the orthographic section of Fig. 4-17. Take dimensions directly from the figure.

5. Draw a footing and box sill section detail of a wood frame building; see Chapter 10. Scale: ¾″ = 1′-0″.

AUXILIARY VIEWS

1. Construct the true shape of the end of the hip roof shown in Fig. 3-18 (surface ABC). Select a convenient scale to fit your paper.

2. Construct the true shape of 45° miter cut from wood profiles (Fig. 3-41):
   a. 1¼″ dowel
   b. 2″ × 2″ molding
   c. 3″ × 3″ ogee molding

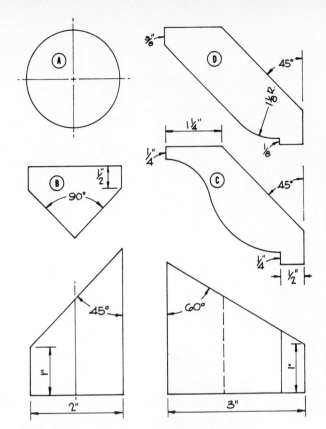

FIGURE 3-41 Exercises in auxiliary projection.

REVIEW QUESTIONS

1. Describe the term *orthographic projection*.

2. What is a *frontal* plane?

3. Why do drawings of many objects require more than one orthographic view?

4. Which orthographic view is considered the major view?

5. How are hidden surfaces shown on an orthographic view?

6. Why are orthographic views of a building often drawn in an unrelated position on working drawings?

7. What is the *cutting plane* of a section?

8. Why are cutting planes sometimes offset rather than straight planes?

9. Why are hidden lines seldom used in section views?

10. What is the advantage of a partial section?

11. Why are auxiliary surfaces projected to planes that are parallel to the surfaces?

12. How are numerous sections identified as to their position on the major view?

13. Describe a *transverse section*.

14. Describe a *longitudinal section*.

15. Define the term *poché*.

16. How many orthographic views can be made from a cube?

17. What two views of a house could be revealed if a horizontal cutting plane passes midway between the floor and ceiling and completely bisects the house?

18. Why is it important to draw a vertical wall section from the footing to the roof of a house?

19. Why are pictorial sections used?

20. What is the *Golden Section?*

AXONOMETRIC AND OBLIQUE PICTORIAL DRAWINGS

W. D. Farmer

"Step after step the ladder is ascended."
—George Herbert

4

Pictorial or paraline drawings enable the drafter to create singleview images which represent three dimensional space. Since we view the objects and the space that surround us in a three dimensional way, it becomes easier for us to comprehend our three dimensional environment when pictorial drawings are used (Fig. 4-1). The drafter has the option to choose the three dimensional view that he or she wishes to draw from a family of pictorial techniques.

Axonometric and oblique drawings are pictorial in nature, yet they are compatible with orthographic drawings in that three sides are shown and the principal lines of each side or plane are measured directly. As mentioned previously, orthographic views have certain advantages, but they also have limitations: two or three isolated views are required to present the information clearly (Fig. 4-2A). This information must be shown only on the orthographic planes; visualizing their features makes training in technical graphics a prerequisite. Even trained persons find that orthographic views are not always entirely adequate for representing construction in the best way. A pictorial drawing, on the other hand, is easy to interpret by the average person because three surfaces are combined into one realistic view. To represent an object pictorially so that the height, width, and depth can be observed in one composite representation, the object is turned to make three sides visible (axonometric); or the top and side are

FIGURE 4-1 Pictorial drawing.

65

shown by projecting oblique lines from a frontal ortho-graphic view (oblique). An example of each is shown in Fig. 4-2B. The sides of an object on either type of drawing are represented with parallel lines, conveniently executed with parallel bar and triangles and are sometimes collectively termed *paraline* drawings.

Because these pictorial views are easy to draw with instruments, they become suitable for use on working drawings and are satisfactory for occasional design drawings. They are also handy for quick freehand sketches (see Chapter 5)—for analyzing construction details or for graphic communication between co-workers. Drafters should, therefore, be able to draw and interpret the conventional pictorial drawings covered in this chapter. Other types of technical-pictorial drawings have been devised; however, they are more time consuming and they do not find application in architectural work. Axonometric and oblique drawings, used intelligently, will be found entirely adequate for presenting supplementary construction information whenever needed.

4.1 Axonometric Drawings

An *axonometric* is an accurately scaled drawing that depicts an object that has been rotated on its axes and inclined from a regular parallel position to give it a three-dimensional appearance. The word is derived from the Greek term *axon*, meaning axis, and the French term *metrique*, pertaining to measurement. Three systems of the family of axonometrics are commonly used: isometric, dimetric, and trimetric. (Some other variations of axonometrics will be described later in this chapter.) Graphically, the three axes x, y, and z are used to create the illusion of three-dimensional space on a two-dimensional plane (see Fig. 4-3). A characteristic of axonometric axes (assuming that the y axis is vertical) is that neither the angle formed between the x and y axes nor the angle formed between the y and z axes may be drawn at 90°, although each of these referenced angles could represent 90° in space (see Fig. 4-4).

Isometric When the rotation and inclination of the planes result in a drawing with three equally divided angles about a center point, the principal of construction is known as *isometric* (the prefix *iso*, from the Greek word *isos*, means equal). The axes may be turned in several different positions, but the most pleasing and generally the most convenient position shows one axis vertical and the other two 30° above the horizontal. The

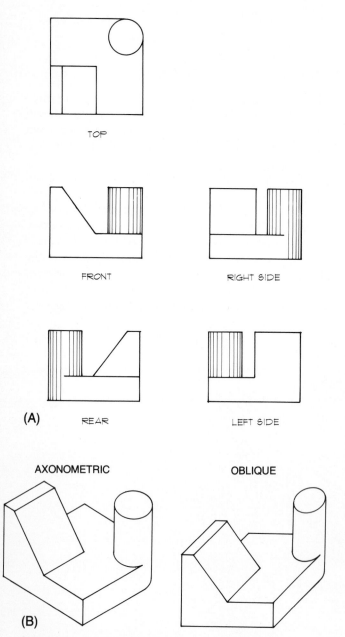

TOP

FRONT   RIGHT SIDE

(A)   REAR   LEFT SIDE

AXONOMETRIC   OBLIQUE

(B)

FIGURE 4-2 (A) Orthographic views. (B) Comparison of axonometric and oblique pictorial drawings.

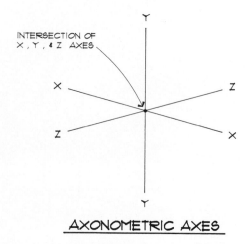

INTERSECTION OF
X, Y, & Z AXES

Y

X   Z

Z   X

Y

AXONOMETRIC AXES

FIGURE 4-3 Axonometric axes.

three angles created by the intersection of the *x*, *y*, and *z* axes are all equal, measuring 120° each (Fig. 4-5). In Fig. 4-6, the concrete masonary unit (C.M.U.) with equal exterior dimensions clearly shows the uniformity of the angles and sides. Regardless of the position of the axes, the three faces of the C.M.U. are equally fore-shortened; intersecting surfaces produce 120° angles (Fig. 4-7), and similar intersections of the surfaces produce parallel lines. Because the lines that recede from the viewer must be foreshortened in a true perspective, which makes them difficult to measure, the drafter merely uses scaled lengths for convenience and speed. For example, if the actual size of the C.M.U. in Fig. 4-8 is 8″ × 8″ × 8″, then the lines representing the surfaces are scaled to the same measurement. No allowance is made for foreshortening, but all measurements must be made on the axes lines. The front, top, and side view of the block are given equal importance, and they can be easily drawn with the 30°–60° triangle. If it becomes

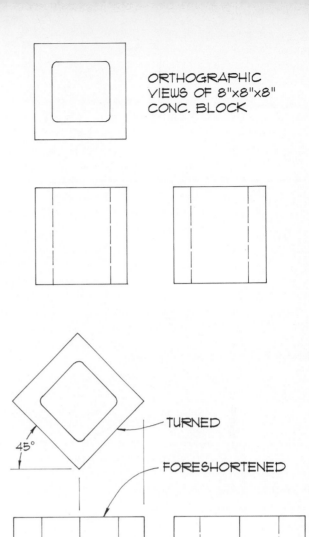

ORTHOGRAPHIC VIEWS OF 8″x8″x8″ CONC. BLOCK

TURNED

45°

FORESHORTENED

TILTED

30°   30°

35°16′

ISOMETRIC PROJECTION

FIGURE 4-6 Method of developing a true isometric projection, which is time consuming for the drafter.

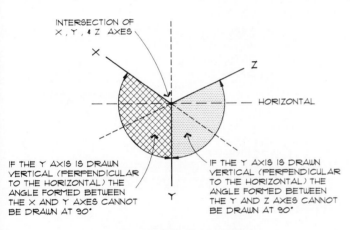

INTERSECTION OF X , Y , & Z AXES

X

Z

HORIZONTAL

IF THE Y AXIS IS DRAWN VERTICAL (PERPENDICULAR TO THE HORIZONTAL) THE ANGLE FORMED BETWEEN THE X AND Y AXES CANNOT BE DRAWN AT 90°

IF THE Y AXIS IS DRAWN VERTICAL (PERPENDICULAR TO THE HORIZONTAL) THE ANGLE FORMED BETWEEN THE Y AND Z AXES CANNOT BE DRAWN AT 90°

Y

AXONOMETRIC AXES

FIGURE 4-4 Axonometric drawing.

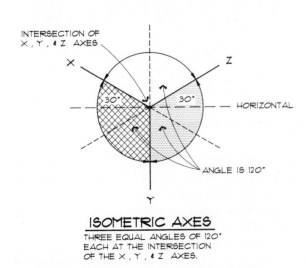

INTERSECTION OF X , Y , & Z AXES

X

Z

30°   30°

HORIZONTAL

ANGLE IS 120°

Y

ISOMETRIC AXES

THREE EQUAL ANGLES OF 120° EACH AT THE INTERSECTION OF THE X , Y , & Z AXES.

FIGURE 4-5 Isometric axes.

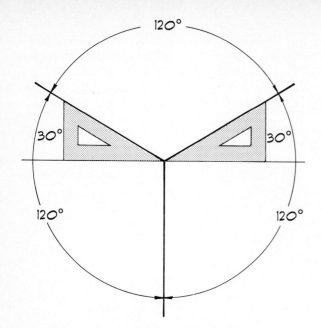

FIGURE 4-7 The three isometric axes.

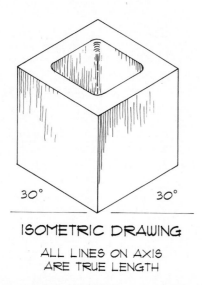

ISOMETRIC DRAWING

ALL LINES ON AXIS ARE TRUE LENGTH

FIGURE 4-8 The same block drawn with lines on the axis the same length as the orthographic views. An isometric drawing is about 22½ percent larger than an isometric projection, yet it has equal pictorial value and is simpler to draw.

necessary to show the underside of an object (so that it appears to be observed from below), the drafter employs a *reverse axis* (see Fig. 4-9). This axis position is more appropriate when drawing a high cornice view, or an overhead structural feature. The object appears to have been tilted backward instead of forward, as in the conventional position. Care must be taken to keep the major planes of the reverse axis clearly in mind.

Dimetric When two equally divided angles are created that are not 90° or 120° at the intersection of the *x, y*, and *z* axes, the principle of projection is known as *dimetric*

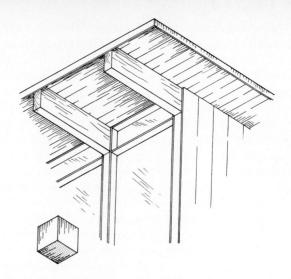

FIGURE 4-9 An isometric drawing exposing the underside.

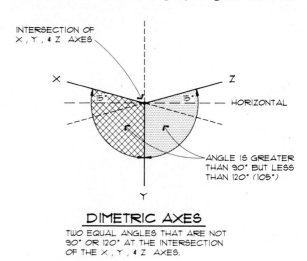

DIMETRIC AXES

TWO EQUAL ANGLES THAT ARE NOT 90° OR 120° AT THE INTERSECTION OF THE X, Y, & Z AXES.

FIGURE 4-10 Dimetric axes.

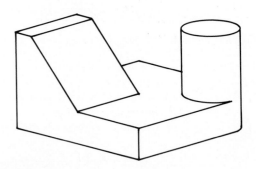

FIGURE 4-11 Dimetric drawing.

(the prefix *di*, in Greek, means twice or double). The most popular adoption of this principle results in the angle between the *x* and *y* axes and the angle between the *y* and *z* axes being equal and greater than 90° but less than 120° (Fig. 4-10). Important surfaces can be effectively illustrated by this principle. The drawing in (Fig. 4-11) demonstrates this rotation. The two surfaces in the foreground take prominence over the top surface.

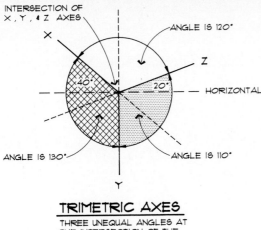

FIGURE **4-12** Trimetric axes.

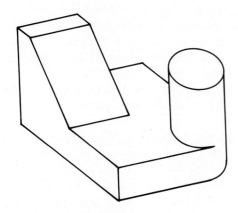

FIGURE **4-13** Trimetric drawing.

Trimetric When the intersecting *x*, *y*, and *z* axes form three unequal angles, the system of construction is known as a trimetric (the prefix *tri* comes from Greek meaning three). No two angles can be 90° angles, and the sum of all three angles must equal 360°. The wide choice of angle values gives the drafter flexibility and control of the pictorial view. Greater emphasis can be placed on a single plane in a trimetric view (Fig. 4-12). The right foreground plane of the object in (Fig. 4-13) takes precedence over the left side and the top.

4.2 Constructing a Pictorial Drawing

First, consider the most advantageous angle from which to view the object. Adopt the view that will show the important information on the three planes, even if it requires turning the object around. Avoid the need for hidden lines; they are usually omitted on paraline drawings. Then look for the major geometric forms. These forms are boxed in, first by drawing the correct axes lines, measuring the lines, and completing the boxed-in effect by drawing the surrounding parallel lines (see

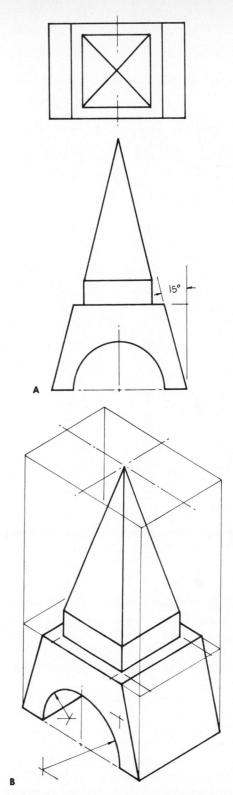

FIGURE **4-14** Constructing an isometric drawing within a box framework with axes distances taken from the ortho-graphic views.

Fig. 4-14B). This becomes a framework (very much like a cage) from which minor shapes or features can be taken away or added. The preliminary box construc-

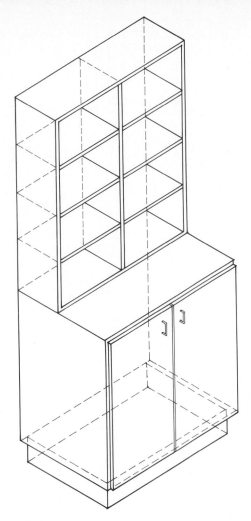

Figure 4-15 Some objects are better drawn by placing one block on the other.

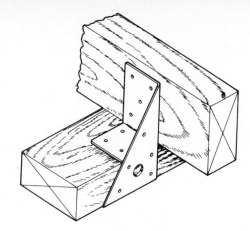

Figure 4-16 Isometric drawing of a metal framing anchor connection.

tion aids in placement of the drawing; if the view seems to be developing off to one side, the construction lines can be changed quickly and little time is lost. The basic enclosure also acts as reference surfaces, from which offset features can be measured during the development of the drawing.

If an object similar to Fig. 4-15 is to be drawn, a block-on-block method of construction may be simpler. Each basic shape is added to another, much as blocks are piled together, rather than by drawing a complete cage around the entire area of the object. After the base block is drawn, using this method, care should be taken to locate correctly the position of the succeeding block. Notice that the position of each new block is first laid out on the surface of the previous block. If the adjacency of the blocks falls on a hidden surface, often the features of the hidden surface must be constructed, even though they will not show and must be erased later. The block-on-block method usually requires less construction linework than the boxed-in method (see Fig. 4-16).

Angular Shapes   Angles specified in degrees do not appear in their shape on a three-dimensional drawing. The construction of an angular shape generally requires the use of coordinates from an orthographic view to determine the angular extremities (see Fig. 4-14A). The coordinate lengths are then transferred to the corresponding three-dimensional planes.

Irregular Curved Shapes   In three-dimensional drawings, irregular curved shapes are executed with the use of offsets (see Fig. 4-17). The drafter takes points from an orthographic view and transfers these to the framework of the three-dimensional projection. Profile sections can be used, or after the points are located on the drawing, they can be connected with curved lines to produce the pictorial feature. Coordinate distances must be obtained from orthographic views of the same scale, and they are projected on the three-dimensional planes.

Circles   Circles also appear distorted on three-dimensional drawings. A true circle becomes an ellipse. Other than construction with an elliptical template, satisfactory circles are generally constructed by the *four-center method* (see Fig. 4-18). The following procedure is used for drawing a three-dimensional circle:

1.   Construct center lines to locate it.
2.   Construct a square (rhombus) the size of the required diameter.
3.   From corners A and B, construct lines to the midpoint of the opposite sides of the square, which become perpendiculars of the sides.
4.   The intersections of these construction lines become the centers of the small arcs; draw the arcs using radius R_1.
5.   Points A and B become centers of the large arcs; draw both arcs of R radius, taking the size of R from the construction.

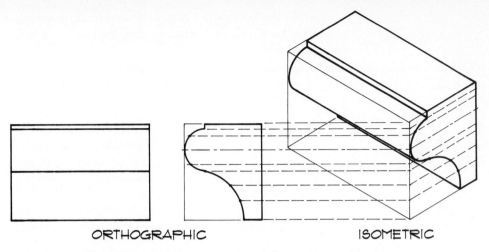

ORTHOGRAPHIC   ISOMETRIC

Figure 4-17 Constructing irregular curved shapes from orthographic views.

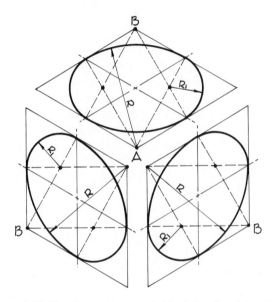

Figure 4-18 The four-center method of drawing isometric circles on the three axes.

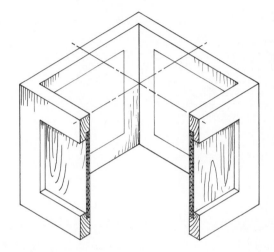

Figure 4-19 Isometric half-section.

All the construction is done with the use of the parallel bar, 30°–60° triangle, and compass. If an elliptical template is available, the center lines are first drawn; then the template is lined up accurately on the center lines. Circles and arcs on the three planes can be drawn by either method. If the circles fall on nonaxonometric planes, they can be plotted by the coordinate method from an orthographic view (see Fig. 4-17).

4.3 Pictorial Section Views

Because hidden lines are seldom used in pictorial drawings, sectioned surfaces showing interior assembly or construction often become necessary. The object is cut on either of the three-dimensional planes. If it is symmetrical, it is cut on center-line planes (Fig. 4-19), and

principles similar to orthographic sectioning are followed. On small, symmetrical objects, generally a *half-section* is used (see Fig. 4-19). First, the major shapes are drawn lightly; then the profiles of the sectioned surfaces are established, and the remaining lines are completed. The front quadrant of the object is removed to best reveal the interior. Usually, more of the exterior of a symmetrical object can be shown if a *broken-out* pictorial section is used (see Fig. 4-20). The axis cut is made on only one center-line plane, and only enough of the frontal material is removed to reveal the profile of the sectioned surface. The other broken edge of the opening is drawn with a freehand line. Crosshatch lines indicating the material are made less prominent, and their angle should not run parallel to the outline of the section. Diagonals are sufficient to indicate wood structural members (see Figs. 4-21 and 9-11 for building material symbols).

When strengthening the finish lines of pictorial drawings, start with the nearest features and continue

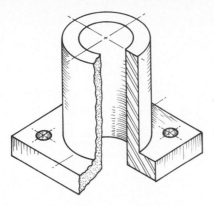

FIGURE 4-20 Isometric section, partially broken.

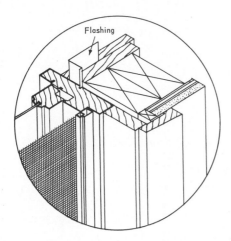

FIGURE 4-21 Isometric section of a window detail.

toward the back of the object. This procedure is time saving because it minimizes erasing; the result will be a neater piece of work.

4.4 Oblique Drawings

An oblique drawing shows an object with one set of planes in true orthographic projection on the frontal surface. The receding perpendicular sides are represented with parallel lines at various angles, which are projected from the frontal, true shape (see Fig. 4-22). It resembles an isometric drawing in that three sides are shown, and the three sides are represented with parallel lines upon which a drafter can make true measurements. The concrete block (C.M.U.) shown in the illustration has a true square, similar to an orthographic view, as its front surface. The receding top and right sides appear nearly axonometric.

Various Pictorial Effects One advantage of oblique drawings is their versatility in creating pictorial effects. By varying the angles of the receding axes, either one of the receding sides can be emphasized (see Fig. 4-22A, B, and C). Because drafting triangles conveniently provide angles of 30°, 45°, and 60°, these angles are most commonly used for the oblique axes. A 30° axis from the horizontal adds side-view emphasis, a 45° axis gives equal emphasis to both of the receding surfaces (commonly called a *Cavalier drawing*), and a 60° axis results in emphasis on the top view. If important information

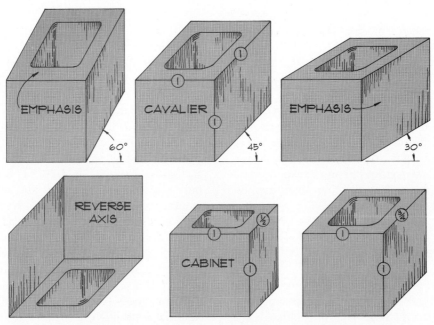

FIGURE 4-22 Pictorial appearance of various types of oblique drawings.

falls on one of the receding planes, the angle should be given careful consideration.

The axis can be projected to either right or left, depending on which side better describes the object. Also, the axis can be projected below the horizontal if the bottom surface yields more information than the top (see Fig. 4-22D).

On conventional oblique drawings, as we mentioned, the receding lines are measured true-length, producing a distorted effect. This applies especially to objects of considerable depth. The heavy appearance on receding surfaces often makes an oblique rendition objectionable. However, more pleasing proportions and a more realistic appearance can usually be achieved by reducing the depth by $1/4$, $1/3$, or $1/2$. The lines on the frontal planes remain full scale, giving the oblique lines proportional ratios of 1 to $3/4$, 1 to $2/3$, or 1 to $1/2$ (see Fig. 4-22E and F). The ratio of 1 to $1/2$ is referred to as a *Cabinet drawing* and generally has a too-thin appearance for most objects other than shallow cabinets.

One other expediency of oblique drawings is their convenience for showing circles or irregular shapes on the frontal planes. Circles can be drawn easily with a compass, and the other shapes do not have to be distorted (see Fig. 4-23). This is a definite advantage in giving technical information. Therefore, when selecting the layout of an oblique drawing, if possible, place the circular and irregular features on the frontal plane. Also, if a long object is drawn, place the long dimension on the frontal plane; the drawing will appear shallower in depth. Actually, objects of little depth are better

suited to oblique drawing because the distortion on their receding surfaces will hardly be noticeable (see Fig. 4-24).

If *circular shapes* fall on one of the oblique planes, they are made elliptical, similar to axonometric circles. Because of the construction involved, circles on oblique axes should be avoided; but if they become necessary, a rhombus similar to axonometric drawing is constructed around the intended circle, and the approximate, four-center method of ellipse construction is used. Different angular axes necessarily require differently shaped rhombus construction; the appropriate method can be taken from Fig. 4-18. Notice that the large arcs are drawn from the intersection of the two perpendicular bisectors of the two sides that form the larger rhombus angle; the smaller arcs are drawn from the intersection of the perpendicular bisectors of the two sides that form the smaller angle. The circle arcs must be tangent to the midpoints of the oblique-square sides. On the oblique axes, arcs representing rounded corners, and the like, are drawn by the same method, even though they may require only part of the construction.

4.5 Elevation Oblique

When the facade of a building or an important elevation of an object needs emphasis, the *elevation oblique* pictorial drawing is appropriate. It is drawn by turning a true-shape elevation parallel to the drawing surface. A side and top of the object will usually be drawn at a 30°, 45°, or 60° angle oblique to the elevation. This variation

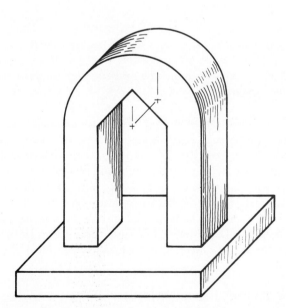

FIGURE 4-23 Circles and irregular shapes should be placed on the frontal plane of oblique drawings.

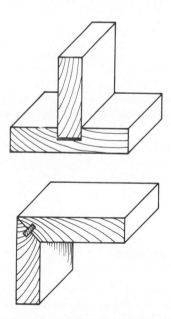

FIGURE 4-24 Sectioned orthographic details can be given a pictorial appearance by the addition of oblique receding surfaces.

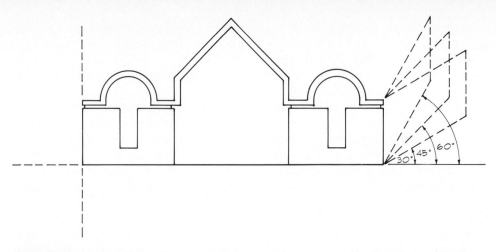

FIGURE 4-25 An elevation oblique is drawn by turning a true-shape elevation parallel to the drawing surface.

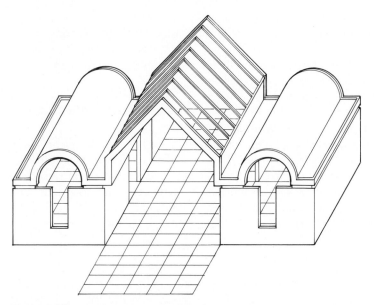

FIGURE 4-26 Elevation oblique drawing.

of the oblique pictorial is easy to construct and is appropriate when a slightly distorted depth is not objectionable (Fig. 4-25). A print of an orthographic projection is placed under the drafting paper with the elevation located parallel to the x and y axes. Triangles are used to draft the side and top views. Considerable emphasis is placed on the elevation or facade in this type drawing (Fig. 4-26).

4.6 Plan Oblique

A useful variation of the conventional oblique pictorial drawing is the *plan oblique* (referred to as an axonometric by many drafters). It is created by placing a true-shape plan beneath the tracing surface. Then the heights or vertical planes are projected from the plan and drawn to scale. The plan oblique has two subclasses: the *plan*

oblique with vertical projection and the *plan oblique with angular projection*.

Plan Oblique: Vertical Projection In executing this pictorial drawing, a true-shape plan is commonly rotated at a 45° or 30°–60° angle from the horizontal. Using a triangle, the vertical lines and planes are drawn perpendicular to the horizontal (Fig. 4-27). This projection method is popular because of the ease with which it can be drawn. The plan oblique with vertical projection can convey infinite detail about interior space and structural elements, as well as exterior mass and form (Fig. 4-28).

Plan Oblique: Angular Projection When a true-shape plan is placed parallel to the picture plane and the vertical planes are projected upward at an angle, usually 45° or 60°, and scaled, a plan oblique with angular

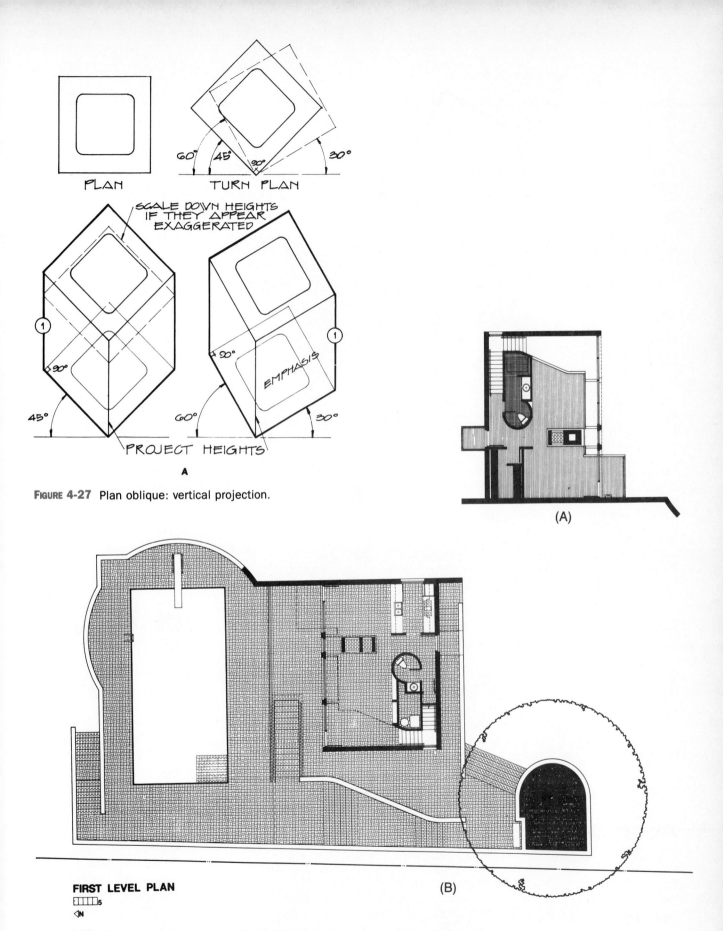

Figure 4-27 Plan oblique: vertical projection.

FIRST LEVEL PLAN

Figure 4-28 Turning a plan and projecting heights to draw a plan-oblique drawing. Floor plans (views A & B) and pictorial (views C & D) of a small house—Tony Ames, architect.

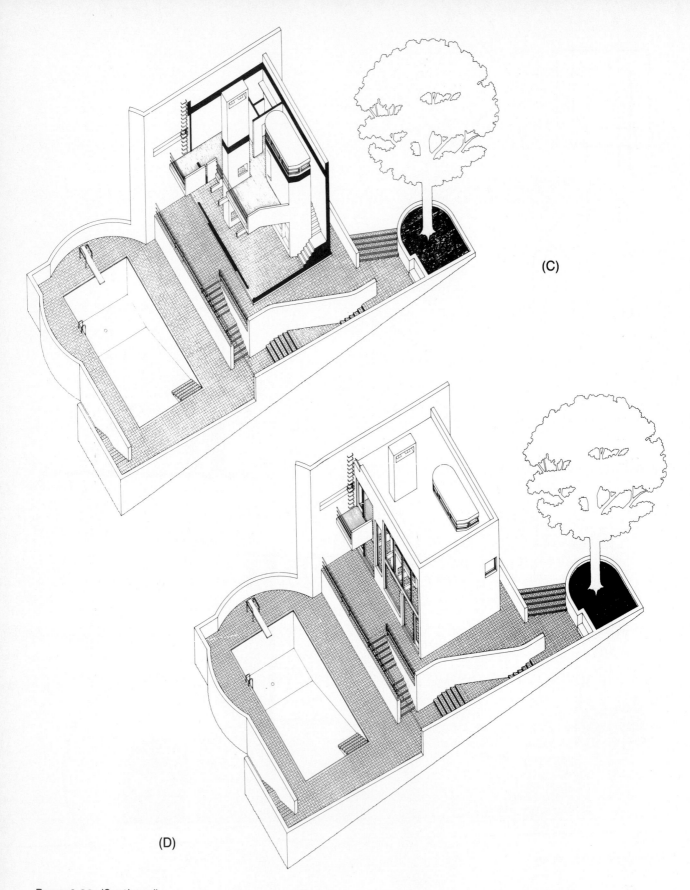

(C)

(D)

FIGURE 4-28 (Continued)

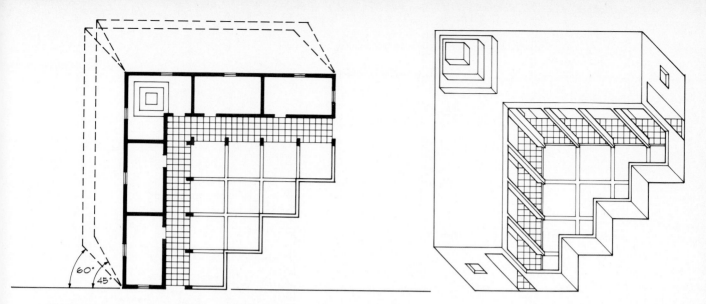

FIGURE 4-29 Plan oblique, angular projection.

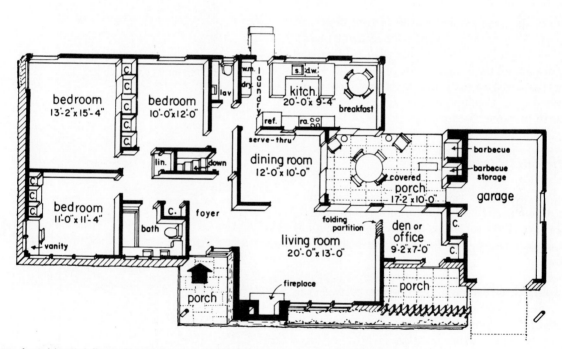

FIGURE 4-30 A residential floor plan given a pictorial nature with the addition of oblique lines. Cabinetwork and furniture may also be represented.

projection drawing is created. This form of projection places the viewer almost directly above the object and reveals a bird's-eye view (Fig. 4-29). Although not as widely used as the vertical projection method due to the appearance of greater distortion, the angular projection method is easily constructed (Fig. 4-30).

4.7 Planometric

Also referred to as an axonometric projection by some drafters, the *planometric* is probably the least used of all the pictorial drawings. A true-shape plan is positioned

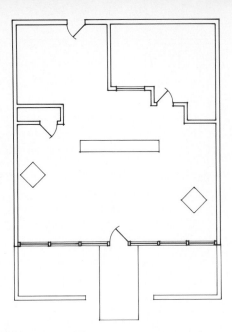

FIGURE 4-31 A true shape plan is positioned with one of its sides parallel to the picture plane.

with one of its sides parallel to the picture plane. A triangle is used to extrude vertically the receding planes that are perpendicular to the picture plane. The planometric negates all right-angled side planes (Fig. 4-31). Elements that are skew to the horizontal and vertical are best defined by this technique. Rectilinear distortion is common in planometric drawings (Fig. 4-32).

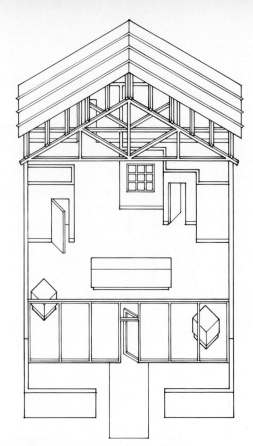

FIGURE 4-32 Planometric drawing.

4.8 Pictorial Dimensioning

Although many of the rules for dimensioning orthographic drawings are also valid for pictorial drawings, the rules have slight variations due to the pictorial nature of the drawings. The following rules should be observed:

1. Keep the dimension number midway between the arrowheads, and use a logical system to place the smallest dimension closest to the view and the successively larger farther out (Fig. 4-33).
2. If possible, dimension *visible* surfaces and features only.
3. Dimension lines must not connect extension lines that lie on different planes. Each plane has two axes—stay on these axes. Keep extension lines and dimension lines on the surface in question.
4. Occasionally, dimensions can be placed directly on the object, provided clarity is maintained and there is sufficient space. This method will usually eliminate unnecessary extension lines running through the object. Otherwise, place dimensions out beyond the extremities of the view so that they do not seem to crowd the exterior profile of the drawing.

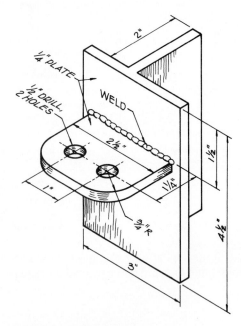

FIGURE 4-33 Dimensioning pictorial drawings.

5. Leaders should not be made parallel with the axes of the drawing. Leaders that dimension circular shapes should just touch the arc, and the arrowhead should point toward the center point. The other end of the leader should extend out to an

uncrowded space and have a $\frac{1}{4}''$ line attached, which should lie on the same axis as the circle center lines (see Fig. 4-33). Arc leaders dimensioning radii should originate at the center point of the arc, and the arrowhead should touch the *inner side* of the arc line.

6. Notes may be lettered on either of the pictorial planes or in a horizontal position. Whichever method is adopted should be maintained throughout the drawing.

7. On construction drawings, dimension lines should be made continuous and the dimension number placed just above the line (see Fig. 4-33). Letter the number so that it appears to lie on the same plane as the surface being dimensioned. This is accomplished by using vertical lettering, yet the vertical axis of the lettering is kept parallel with the extension lines of the dimension. To make the lettering appear pictorial, each figure is distorted very much like a square is distorted into a rhombus when it is placed on a pictorial plane.

EXERCISES

PICTORIAL DRAWING

The pictorial drawings in Figs. 4-34 through 4-37 should be made with instruments on small ($8\frac{1}{2}'' \times 11''$) sheets of drawing paper. All problems are shown in orthographic projection for the purpose of converting them into both isometric and oblique drawings. Double the size of each problem shown in Fig. 4-34; dimensions can be transferred with dividers. When drawing Figs. 4-36 and 4-37, merely let the grids equal any convenient size to fit your paper.

The pictorial drawings in Figs. 4-38 through 4-46 should be made with instruments on $11'' \times 17''$ sheets of drawing paper. These problems are shown in orthographic projection and should be doubled in size using proportional dividers when converting them to the required three-dimensional drawings. The drawings in Figs. 4-38 and 4-39 should be drawn in dimetric and trimetric views. The drawings in Figs. 4-40 and 4-41 should be drawn in elevation oblique views. The drawings in Figs. 4-42 and 4-43 should be drawn in plan oblique, vertical projection views. The drawings in Figs. 4-44 and 4-45 should be drawn in plan oblique, angular projection. The drawing in Fig. 4-46 should be drawn in a planometric view.

REVIEW QUESTIONS

1. What is the advantage of a mechanical pictorial drawing over an orthographic drawing?

2. What are the applications of axonometric and oblique drawings on working drawings?

3. Why does the oblique type of drawing have more versatility than the axonometric?

4. What angle from the horizontal gives emphasis to the top view in an oblique drawing?

5. Describe a *Cabinet drawing*.

6. Why is it advantageous to place the irregular shapes of an object on the frontal plane when making an oblique drawing?

7. How may a plan view of a building be quickly made into a pictorial drawing?

8. In dimensioning pictorial drawings, why are leaders drawn at angles other than those of the principal axes?

9. How are dimension numbers made to appear as though they lie on the planes of the drawing?

10. Are the longest dimensions placed closest to the view or farthest from the view, as compared to the shorter dimensions?

11. What is the difference between an axonometric drawing and a perspective drawing?

12. What is the proper title of a pictorial drawing that has x, y, and z axes and two of the angles between adjacent axes are equal?

13. What view of an object is revealed by a reverse axes drawing?

14. List the types of pictorial drawings that require a true-shape plan view that can be traced as a basis for the drawing.

15. Why are 30°, 45°, and 60° angles used in preparing most pictorial drawings?

16. What is the proper title of the pictorial drawing that has equal angles between the x, y, and z axes?

17. Define *paraline drawings*.

18. List the types of pictorial drawings that require true measurements for all lines making up the drawing.

19. What is the difference between a plan oblique with vertical projection and a plan oblique with angular projection?

20. What characteristic is lost in the planometric drawing that is evident in the plan-oblique drawing?

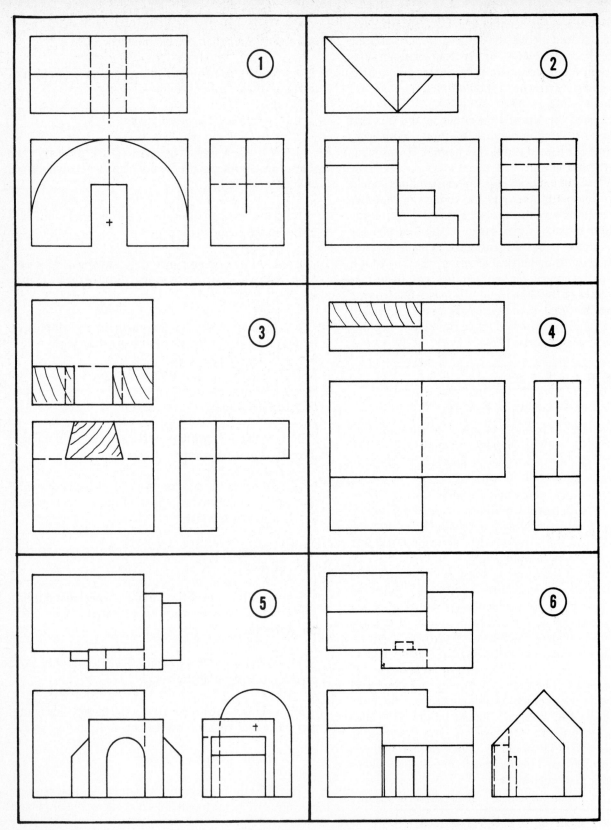

Figure 4-34 Exercises in axonometric and oblique drawing. The exercises should be enlarged to suitable scale.

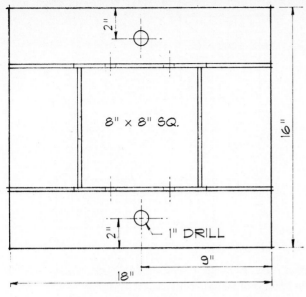

COLUMN SHOE
1/4" STEEL PLATE

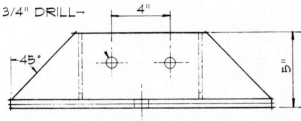

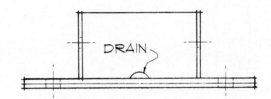

FIGURE 4-35 Exercise in axonometric or oblique drawing.

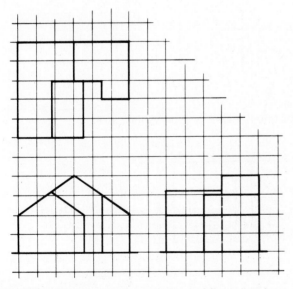

FIGURE 4-36 Exercise in axonometric or oblique drawing. Enlarge the grids to a convenient size.

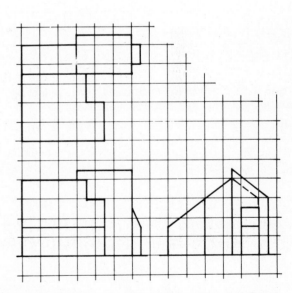

FIGURE 4-37 Exercise in axonometric or oblique drawing. Enlarge the grids to a convenient size.

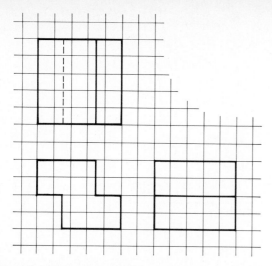

Figure 4-38 Exercise in dimetric and trimetric drawing. Enlarge the grids to a convenient scale.

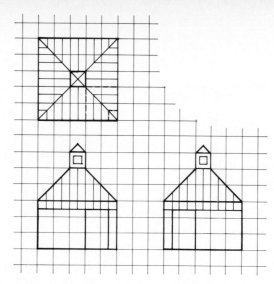

Figure 4-41 Exercise in elevation oblique drawing. Enlarge the grids to a convenient size.

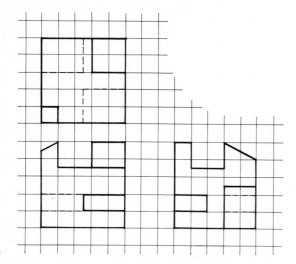

Figure 4-39 Exercise in dimetric and trimetric drawing. Enlarge the grids to a convenient scale.

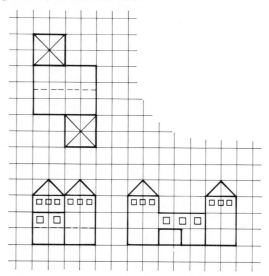

Figure 4-42 Exercise in plan oblique, vertical projection. Enlarge the grids to a convenient size.

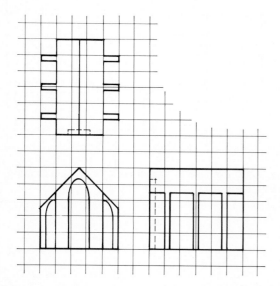

Figure 4-40 Exercise in elevation oblique drawing. Enlarge the grids to a convenient size.

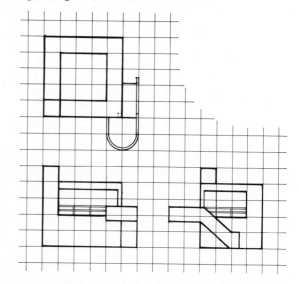

Figure 4-43 Exercise in plan oblique, vertical projection. Enlarge the grids to a convenient size.

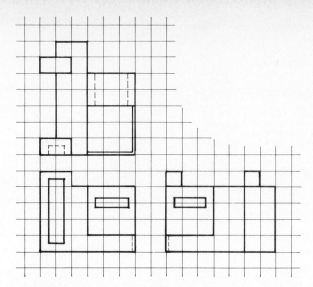

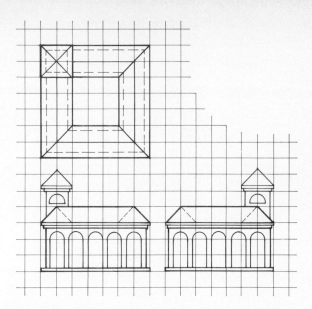

FIGURE 4-44 Exercise in plan oblique, angular projection. Enlarge the grids to a convenient size.

FIGURE 4-45 Exercise in plan oblique, angular projection. Enlarge the grids to a convenient size.

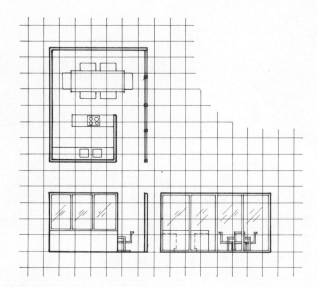

FIGURE 4-46 Exercise in planometric drawing. Enlarge the grids to a convenient size.

FREEHAND SKETCHING

FRANK BETZ

"Practice and thought might gradually forge many an art."
—VIRGIL

5

The often overlooked freehand sketch is a vital means of technical expression, not only for generating ideas, but also for making concepts workable realities. Drafters frequently find themselves in such a position. Without sketching ability, they are handicapped in many day to day drafting situations. Generally, every structure, no matter of what size, and each graphic problem that confronts the drafter or designer originates with a pencil sketch. Whether crudely or meticulously done, the sketch becomes an important exploratory instrument, as well as a means of conversing effectively between technically trained people. Whether one is concerned with the esthetic aspects of a building or with its structural properties, the ability to make spontaneous sketches is a considerable asset for architectural drafters and therefore should be an important part of their training.

To gain proficiency in this mode of expression, the student must invite situations entailing sketching at every opportunity. Graphic problems requiring solutions should be analyzed by preliminary sketches—not one, but as many as need be to develop the concept before it is put in final form on the drawing. Therein lies one of the many advantages of sketching—graphic ideas can be quickly developed on sketch paper before being drafted to scale on the board.

In addition, the sketch is necessary in planning and organizing intelligently the sheet layout of a complete set of drawings, which often includes many views and details. Numerous layout sketches are necessary to arrange drawings in proper sequence and to utilize the paper efficiently.

However, students are occasionally reluctant to resort to sketches when experimenting with their initial concepts. They seem to feel, evidently, that their early attempts will look unprofessional; but this is inconsequential at the outset. Rather, the desire to develop the concepts graphically should be their incentive for using sketches—appearance will improve with experience. Even the most proficient have had to start with crude beginnings.

The secret of learning to sketch, especially for those who are doubtful of their aptitude, is to begin by drawing simple things, such as lines and rectangular views, circles and circular shapes, and complete orthographic sketches. Then advance to axonometric and oblique pictorial sketches, and finally to realistic perspective drawings. This sequence, which leads the student to more difficult work progressively, also provides experience in all the necessary types of drawings encountered by the drafter.

So that the beginner will not be burdened with rules and restrictions, the following material is suggested as a series of guides for making freehand sketching as simple and easy as possible and as a means for eventually making it an enjoyable and rewarding accomplishment.

5.1 Sketching Materials

Few materials are needed: pencils, paper, pencil pointer, sandpaper pad, and an eraser. The majority of linework can be done with an H or B pencil, occasionally a 2B will be handy for darker accents, and a 2H pencil, if one is available, can be used for preliminary construction layout. Points on the pencils can be conical, or if both wide and thin lines are required (on floor plan sketches), a chisel-type point (see Fig. 5-1) can be dressed on a sandpaper pad to allow variation with the same point. Dressing the pencil point becomes very important in later shading exercises to represent various architectural textures, but for beginning work the medium-sharp point is satisfactory.

The pencil should be held in a natural way; avoid

FIGURE 5-1 Pencil points used in sketching.

FIGURE 5-2 Hold the pencil in a natural, comfortable position.

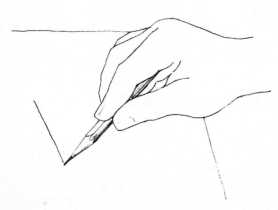

FIGURE 5-3 An alternate position for holding the sketching pencil during preliminary layouts.

clutching it too close to the point (see Fig. 5-2). Some drafters prefer to hold the pencil in a horizontal position, shown in Fig. 5-3, when laying in preliminary construction lines.

The most useful type of paper (for the student as well as the professional) is inexpensive tracing paper or sketch pad. As mentioned in Chapter 1, either a 12″ roll of tracing paper or an inexpensive pad (11″ × 17″) is convenient. The advantage of sketching on tracing paper is the ease with which sketches can be modified or redeveloped simply by placing the transparent paper over previously done sketches to minimize repetitious construction. Also, flaws that might possibly go unnoticed can be found by turning the paper over and observing the sketch in reverse. An eraser on the end of the pencil will be handy, but generally most erasing will be unnecessary when sketches can be redrawn quicker than mistakes can be erased.

Have a pointed felt-tip pen (Section 5.12) handy to practice basic exercises with after trial work with the pencil.

5.2 Beginning Line Exercises

Start your sketching practice with simple line exercises, drawn horizontally, vertically, and inclined in several directions (see Fig. 5-4). Make the short lines with finger and wrist movements and longer lines by attaching a series of shorter, more comfortable-length lines to each other (see Fig. 5-5). After each stroke, move the ball of the hand to a new position along the path of the long line. Usually, a very light trial line will help to establish the general direction of a long line. Or, before the long line is started, a termination point can be indicated; concentrate on the point as the line progresses and almost without exception the line will end at the point. Establish *parallel lines* by placing a few points along the original line, equidistant from it, and sketch the parallel line through the points, as in Fig. 5-6.

The right-handed person should sketch horizontal lines from left to right (the reverse if left-handed), and vertical lines should be drawn toward oneself. If a small sheet of paper is being used, the paper can be turned in

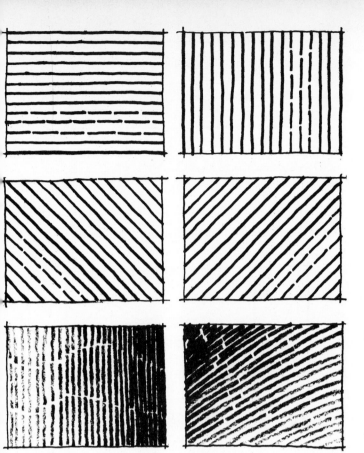

FIGURE 5-4 Beginning practice exercises.

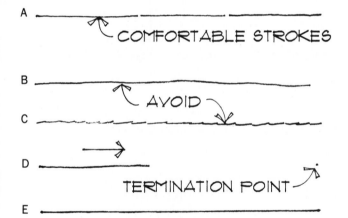

FIGURE 5-5 Sketching long lines freehand.

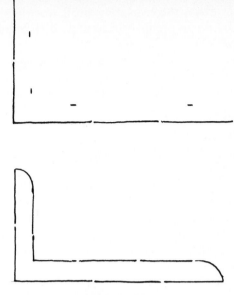

FIGURE 5-6 Laying out parallel lines.

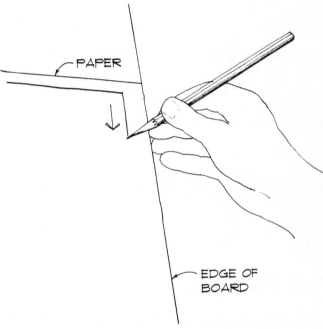

FIGURE 5-7 Drawing semi-freehand lines with a convenient edge.

a favorable position when sketching lines; usually it becomes easier to sketch a line in a horizontal direction. For practice, sketch straight lines in all directions without turning the paper; this improves coordination of the hand and eye.

If a board or pad is used when sketching, a semifreehand method of drawing long lines, shown in Fig. 5-7, can be employed. The edge of the board or pad is used as a guide, and the free hand holds the paper in a position parallel to the edge of the board. This method is especially helpful in establishing important center lines or major horizontal roof lines on an elevation, from

which other lines on the sketch can be made parallel. Borders are also easily made with this method.

5.3 Dividing Lines and Areas Equally

The ability to divide lines and areas into equal spaces is frequently necessary in arriving at many of the common geometric forms found in sketches. A line can be quickly divided if the pencil itself is used as a measuring stick. With the aid of the pencil, lay off approximate half-lengths of the line from each end; if the approximation is not exact, the remaining small space is easily bisected by eye to produce an accurate division of the entire line.

Another method of bisecting lines is by *visual comparison*. An entire line is observed and "weighed optically" in determining its fulcrum, or point of balance. Each half is compared visually before placing the bisecting point. This procedure can be repeated any number of times to divide a line into any number of equal divisions merely by dividing and redividing its line segments (see Fig. 5-8). It is especially effective in maintaining symmetry of sketches when lines as well as spaces must be kept uniform.

Centers of rectangular figures are also found by drawing their diagonals. If necessary, the halves can be divided with diagonals for smaller divisions (see Fig. 5-9).

5.4 Sketching Angles

The 90° angle is a predominant feature in the majority of construction sketches. Thus, it becomes important to be able to sketch right angles rather accurately, even if it entails checking them with the triangle occasionally. Frequently, the perpendicular edges of the drawing paper can serve as a guide for comparison. It is also helpful to turn the sketch upside down; nonperpendicular tendencies of horizontal and vertical lines will become evident. Correct shape of the right angles gives the sketch stability, without which effectiveness is lost.

A 45° angle is made by dividing a right angle equally by visual comparison and a 30° or 60° angle by dividing the right angle into three equal parts, which is slightly more difficult. Always start with the right angle for the most accurate estimation of angle shape (Figs. 5-10 and 5-11).

5.5 Sketching Circles and Arcs

Small circles are usually sketched without construction other than center lines, but larger circles require some preliminary construction to help maintain their symmetry and also to locate them properly on the sketch. Start larger circles (over ½″) with perpendicular center lines, around which you lay out a square and carefully check each quadrant of the square as it develops for unity of size and shape (see Figs. 5-12 and 5-13). If the square is not true, the finished circle will not come out round. Then, starting at the intersection of the top of the square and the center line, sketch each half of the circle with full, curved strokes that touch each center-line intersection within the square. Practice sketching circles of different sizes until they become balanced and well rounded. Be careful to maintain a "blown-up," full character on all circles, rather than a flattened or elliptical appearance.

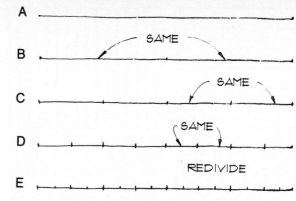

FIGURE 5-8 Bisecting lines by visual comparison.

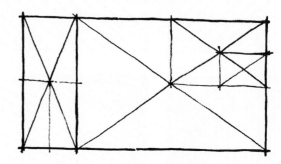

FIGURE 5-9 Finding centers by sketching diagonals.

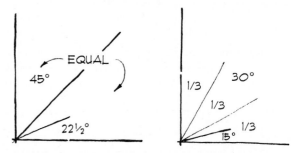

FIGURE 5-10 Sketching angles by convenient divisions.

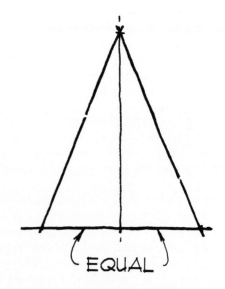

FIGURE 5-11 Using a center line for symmetry.

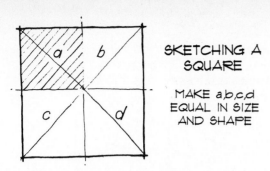

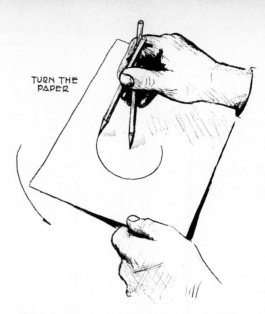

FIGURE 5-12 Sketch an accurate square by starting with center lines.

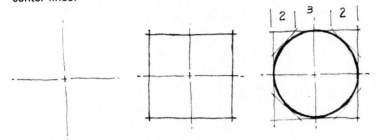

FIGURE 5-13 Sketching a circle.

FIGURE 5-14 Sketching a circle with the use of two pencils.

If several circles are required on a sketch, the *semi-mechanical* technique shown in Fig. 5-14 will produce them accurately and save considerable time. Try a few of different sizes for exercise. Hold two equally long pencils rigidly in the hand so that they act very much as a compass. One pencil becomes the pivot; the other scribes the circle when the paper is revolved under the pencils with the other hand.

Freehand arcs are drawn with similar construction as mentioned for circles (see Figs. 5-15 and 5-16). Often it is advisable to construct an entire square and circle in order to maintain the character of a regular curve on arcs. The construction linework can be quickly erased.

5.6 Developing Good Proportion

Proportion is an illusive characteristic of sketching—it is mastered only after training the eye to see correctly. Without a feeling of proper proportion, the sketch can be misleading and therefore of little value. Continually strive for correct proportion by astute observation and analysis of your sketching subject. Drawing in proportion is largely a matter of discerning how one thing relates to another—for instance, how length relates to width, height to length, the size of one feature to another, and one space to another. The trained drafter automatically sees these relationships and checks for accuracy at frequent intervals while sketching.

One of the simplest methods of arriving at correct proportion is seeing through incidental details of the subject and recognizing the *basic geometric forms* inherent in it (see Figs. 5-17 and 5-18), whether the subject is

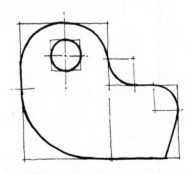

FIGURE 5-15 Sketching small circles.

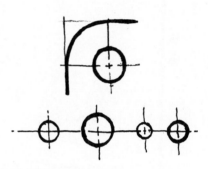

FIGURE 5-16 Sketching arcs with construction.

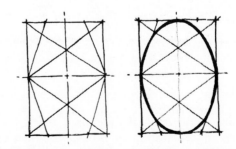

FIGURE 5-17 Construction for sketching an ellipse.

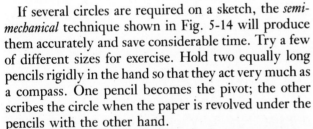

FIGURE 5-18 A page from the sketchbook of a thirteenth-century French architect, Villard D'Honnecourt, showing the use of geometric forms in sketching.

orthographic or pictorial. If these basic forms can be recognized, an important step in proportion has been accomplished (see Figs. 5-19 and 5-20). At this point we are mainly concerned with plane figures; pictorial sketches are discussed later.

When sketching from a dimensioned drawing, the

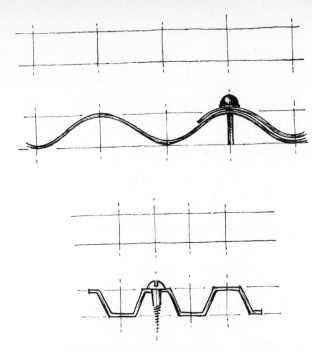

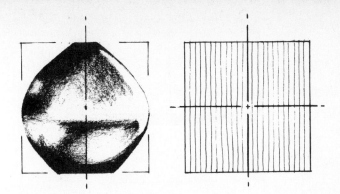

FIGURE 5-21 Using a simple square for arriving at proportion.

FIGURE 5-19 Sketching construction for simple shapes.

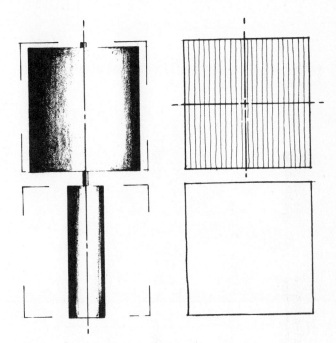

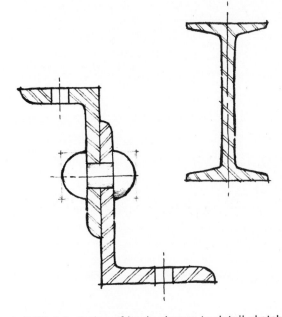

FIGURE 5-20 Adaptation of basic shapes to detail sketches.

FIGURE 5-22 Arriving at proportion in sketches.

dimensions themselves provide a definite basis for proportion—if they are carefully observed. To set the general size of a sketch, establish a major line or feature first; the remaining lines are then made proportional to that original line according to the given dimensions. For example, if a 20' × 40' floor plan is to be sketched, the 20' is represented with a line of any convenient length, depending on the size of the paper (preliminary sketches should be small); the line for the 40' should then be drawn twice this length. Similarly, if a partition within the plan is, say, 10' long, the line representing it should be only one-half as long as the 20' line. This

procedure introduces adequate proportion throughout the sketch.

But suppose we are sketching an object or view that has no given dimensions for measurement or tangible means for proportion. This presents more of a problem to the easily discouraged beginner, and some system must be developed to help create this necessary sense of relationship. The simple *square*, as a shape for comparing basic proportion, is the most effective and appropriate method. Although not particularly attractive in itself, the square is the ideal geometric form to look for when arriving at proportion of height and width. It has uniform sides, regardless of its size, and can be accurately sketched by comparing these sides. If you were analyzing the proportion of the vase in Fig. 5-21, you would observe that the body of the vase will fit neatly into a square. In sketching the lamp in Fig. 5-22, its shade has the general shape of a square, and its height is a little less than twice the height of the square. The

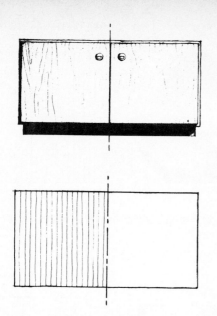

FIGURE 5-23 Many sketching subjects can be fitted into squares.

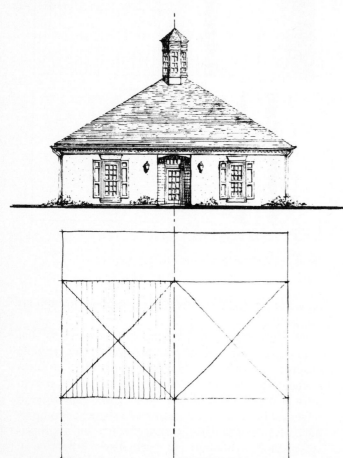

FIGURE 5-24 The use of the square in sketching elevations.

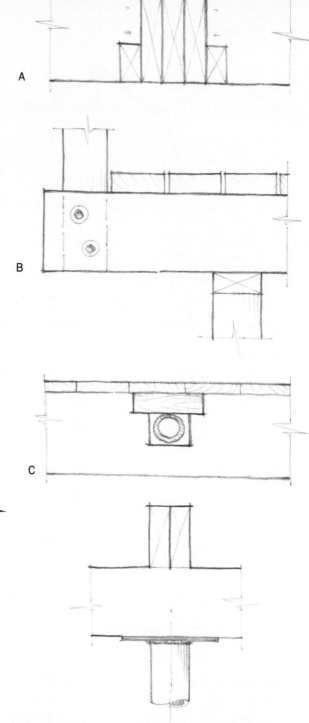

A

B

C

D

FIGURE 5-25 The use of parallel lines in detail sketches.

width of the base is one-third the width of the square. Two squares quickly give you the basic proportion of the piece of furniture in Fig. 5-23. If you were sketching the exterior elevation of the house in Fig. 5-24, a square would organize its general shape and smaller squares would give you the proportions of minor details.

The square, therefore, makes a suitable unit for sim-

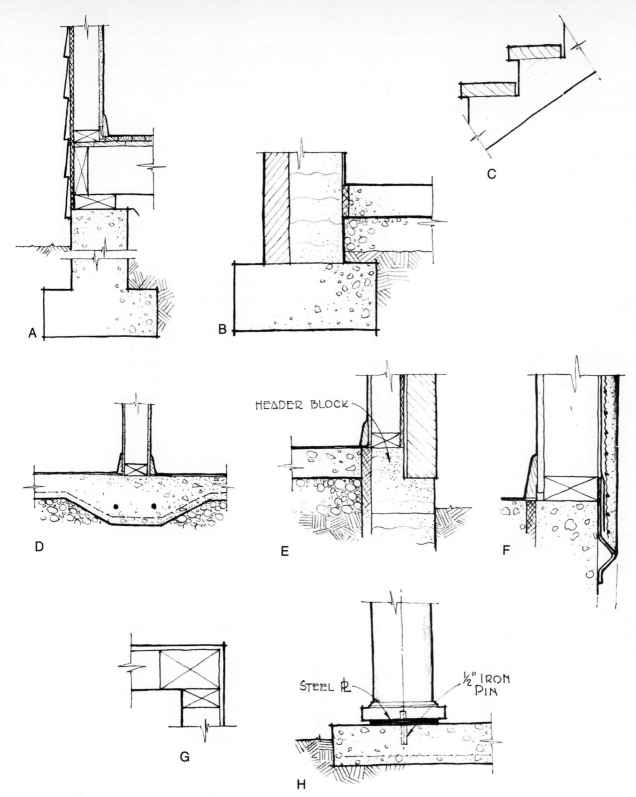

FIGURE 5-26 Quick construction sketches.

plifying a subject under observation and for quickly duplicating the units in the sketch. When you become "square conscious," you will automatically see squares of different sizes in your subjects; when these same squares are used as guides in your sketch, you will have arrived at a handy method of proportioning plans, ele-

vations, and section sketches of buildings as well as other subjects.

It is also important to be familiar with the general proportions of commonly used building materials, such as lumber, brick, concrete block, stock moldings, and stock doors (see Figs. 5-25 and 5-26). Once the proportions of these materials are committed to memory, other aspects of the sketch will assume relative proportions.

5.7 Acquiring Good Line Technique

At the start of a sketch, make the lines light and indefinite while the forms are still in a plastic state of development. These exploration and trial lines should be retained until satisfactory shapes emerge and the general nature of the sketch takes on a realistic proportion. Next, perfect and strengthen important lines so that the corrected shapes predominate the trial lines; work on minor details after major shapes seem right; in this way, the entire sketch will mature simultaneously. Light trial lines can be erased as the sketch progresses, although if they are left in, the light lines throughout the drawing seem to soften it and give it a "sketchy" quality.

The finished lines should have weight variations according to their importance. Object lines and key profile lines are made bold, whereas less important lines are made accordingly less prominent. Line variations provide the sparkle and depth so important in a successful sketch. Occasionally, a freehand line is broken at uneven intervals rather than made continuous, and the beginning and end of each stroke are made definite instead of appearing feathered out. One interesting quality of a freehand line is its slight waviness as compared to the sharp straightness of a mechanical line. This quality adds personality to the finished sketch, and there is no reason for trying to avoid it. On the other hand, a choppy, hesitating line technique, shown in Fig. 5-5C, is neither forthright nor pleasing in appearance. Progress in sketching is made only with *practice;* each successive exercise should be a deliberate effort to improve.

5.8 Sketching Plans and Elevations

The floor plan sketch is the logical start for depicting the architectural idea. After preliminary planning has produced a few general concepts of the structure, but definite limitations are not yet established, a *schematic sketch* showing possible room locations is drawn. Use only circular shapes for these trial layouts (see Fig. 5-27). Make similar sketches if necessary for second-floor plans as well. From these schematics, a more developed plan is made.

The best procedure for working out preliminary studies of tentative floor plans and elevations is the use of $1/8''$ coordinate paper. Either work directly on $8\frac{1}{2}'' \times 11''$ sheets, or tape your sketching tracing paper over a coordinate underlay pad, which has been fastened to the drawing board, as described in Chapter 1. The coordinate paper facilitates sketching horizontal and vertical lines and provides a preliminary sense of scale. Each coordinate space represents 1 square foot, and the sketch will have a convenient scale of $1/8'' = 1'\text{-}0''$. This

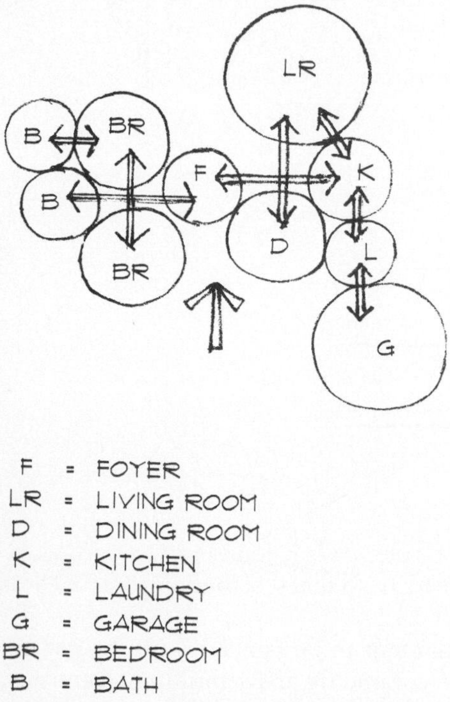

F   = FOYER
LR = LIVING ROOM
D   = DINING ROOM
K   = KITCHEN
L   = LAUNDRY
G   = GARAGE
BR = BEDROOM
B   = BATH

FIGURE 5-27 A schematic sketch for starting a floor plan.

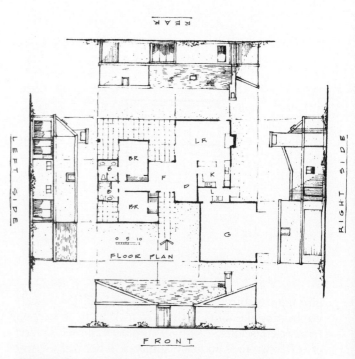

FIGURE 5-28 Plan development sketch and relating elevations.

scale is satisfactory for early studies. Frame walls on coordinate paper can be made a half-space wide (6″), large buildings can be put on a small sheet, and, more important, the small scale allows more command of the development. Even the scale of $\frac{1}{16}″ = 1′\text{-}0″$ will be found adaptable to beginning sketches on coordinate paper. Large sketches are clumsy to handle during the planning stage.

To sketch a plan, lightly draw the exterior walls with a single, continuous line; do not show windows and doors yet. Lay out all the partitions with a fine line; let the lines continue through doors and other openings. Establish all clothes closets with a minimum of 2′ in depth and fill in with close lines parallel to the 2′ dimension. Indicate the placement and width of all windows and doors on the wall lines. With the pencil dressed to a chisel point, widen the exterior walls and partitions with a broad line; stop at the window and door openings. Next, complete the window and door symbols (see Fig. 5-28) with a sharp point. On design sketches, door indications can merely be left as openings. Sketch the approximate locations of stairs; indicate risers with parallel lines (actual size about 11″ apart), and indicate the direction of travel with an arrow and the note UP or DOWN, as the case may be. Draw in fireplaces, entrance platforms, terraces, walks, and other minor features. Kitchen cabinets and bathroom fixtures are blocked-in freehand. Label the rooms and add as many dimensions as needed; usually only interior room sizes are indicated at this stage. Show the plan with the front side *down* on the paper.

If a second-floor plan is necessary for a 2-story house, develop the second-floor plan on tracing paper placed over the completed first-floor plan. Place bearing walls and major partitions above first-floor walls, if possible, for sounder construction. Stairwells and chimneys must coincide, and plumbing wet-walls are best aligned above each other. The vent stack of a first-floor bath must pass through a second-floor partition. Draw an end elevation of 1½-story houses before attempting the second-floor plan. Locations of half-walls and dormer windows become simpler on elevation views showing the roof profile.

Before the elevations can be sketched, a preliminary roof layout must be made on the plan view. The character of the roof plays an important role in the total design of a house, not only for the sake of appearance, but also from a standpoint of accommodating the outline of the plan. Consequently, several sketches may be necessary to find the most desirable type of roof. For economy, keep the roof simple; on the other hand, if an unassuming single gable or hip roof is used, its austere silhouette usually appears monotonous and contributes little architectural character to the structure. (Refer to Figure 7-82 for illustration of roof types.) Uniform roof overhangs are easier to frame than various extensions. But protection from the weather over entrances, walks, and terraces makes the roof more serviceable. Show the roof overhang with dashed lines, and indicate ridges, valleys, hips, and roof offsets. If the roof slopes are uniform, the intersections of gables and hips are always shown with 45° lines.

To sketch an elevation, place the floor plan sketch under a fresh sheet of tracing paper, take the longitudinal features from the plan, and merely transfer features from each exterior wall (see Fig. 5-28). The ridge and eave lines of sloping roofs can be established by first sketching the end elevations if necessary. Then they are transferred to the other elevations after satisfactory roof slopes have been developed. Stock door heights are shown about 6′-8″ above the estimated finished floor level, and the tops of windows are usually aligned with door tops in residential construction. Important details showing the character of the windows and doors should be added, as well as other significant features such as chimneys, columns, exterior steps, and symbols of exterior materials. Sketching some foliage near the ends of the elevation will project an impression of unity with the landscape (see Fig. 5-29).

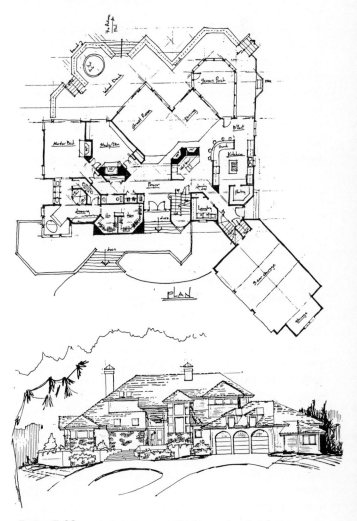

FIGURE 5-29 A professional preliminary sketch of a residence.

Sketching section details requires definite information about the construction of the tentative structure; nevertheless, exploratory section sketches must be made in conjunction with plan and elevation development.

Start details by blocking in important structural members, around which subordinate materials are added. If masonry is involved in the section, establish its shape before applying wood framing or other details. Add exterior and interior wall coverings, moldings, finish flooring, and the like, after major structural pieces are oriented correctly. Care must be taken to relate each member according to its structural position; proportion is important to reveal workability of the detail. Because section details are composed mainly of parallel and perpendicular lines, the right-angle nature of the lines deserves attention. Strengthen the outlines of important elements and make the symbols of the different sectioned materials lighter. In large areas of sectioned surface, except for the periphery of the surface, much of the symbol linework can be omitted (see Fig. 5-26).

Coordinate paper with 12 × 12 divisions within each 1″ square can be used to sketch accurate details in the following conventional scales: 1/4″ = 1′-0″, 1/2″ = 1′-0″, 1″ = 1′-0″, and 3″ = 1′-0″ (see Fig. 5-30). Especially when using the 1″ = 1′-0″ scale, you will find that section details can be quickly sketched over this paper, if scaled sketches are needed. In fact, many drafters find that details sketched over 12 × 12 per inch coordinate paper are perfectly satisfactory for developing working drawings. Using the different scales with the paper, each small square is equal to the following number of inches:

1/4″	= 1′-0″	4″
1/2″	= 1′-0″	2″
1″	= 1′-0″	1″
3″	= 1′-0″	(3 small squares = 1″)

5.9 Axonometric, Isometric, and Oblique Sketching

Not only are axonometric, isometric, and oblique sketches the next step in the logical development toward perspective sketching, but they also provide a quick method of examining tentative construction details pictorially if the need arises.

The principles of pictorial and orthographic sketching are similar, except that now we will deal with volumes rather than flat planes. Instead of the square being a convenient unit of proportion as in orthographic views, the *cube* becomes the ideal unit of pictorial proportion. In addition, all objects are simplified to their basic volumetric or platonic forms, and these forms are the first consideration in the pictorial sketch (see Fig.

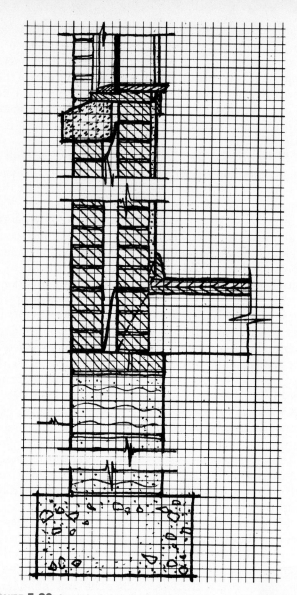

FIGURE 5-30 A scaled detail sketch on grid coordinate paper.

5-31). *Block out the basic forms of the object before attempting the minor details.* Since this simple procedure is effective for experienced technical illustrators, it should serve the student equally well. Study the forms shown in Fig. 5-32; careful analysis of any object being sketched reveals that these basic shapes are inherent forms, although sometimes only parts of these shapes or several of them in combination are perceived.

First, practice sketching the basic geometric shapes, using the construction principles indicated in Chapter 4. Then, look for these shapes in the object you are about to sketch and concentrate on the basic form representation. The object can be enclosed in a cube or box (Fig. 4-14), or it can be built up by a series of differently shaped blocks, one on top of the other (Fig. 4-15),

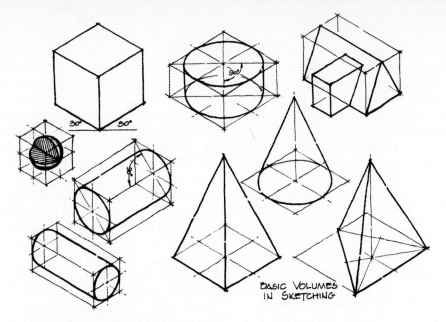

FIGURE 5-31 Volumetric platonic forms.

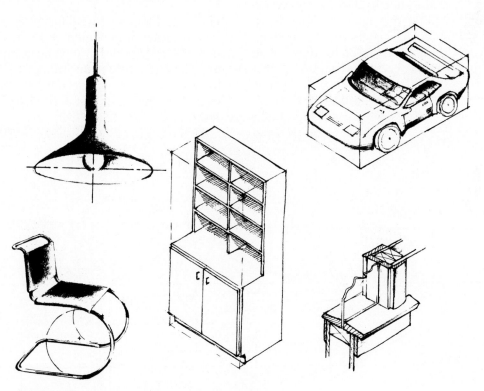

FIGURE 5-32 Sketches derived from basic forms.

depending on the nature of the object. Details are added or "carved" from these main blocks after shape and proportion are established.

If you are sketching from orthographic plans or elevations, the lines of each view can often be laid out on their respective pictorial planes for easier construction.

Occasionally, it becomes advisable to combine a pictorial sketch with an orthographic section sketch. Partial pictorial sections are also revealing sketches. Appropriate exercises should be devoted to sketching from actual models, drawing equipment, even books, or anything at hand.

5.10 Sketching a Quick Perspective

The realistic appearance of a perspective sketch is often helpful, not only in analyzing many of the esthetic aspects of the structure before the working drawings are completed, but in presenting preliminary ideas to a client. Exterior features that appear quite satisfactory on elevation views may not always be pleasing when observed from an oblique angle. Axonometric and oblique drawings usually are not entirely reliable for scrutinizing these design aspects, whereas perspective sketches are especially adaptable to critical examination of architectural ideas during their planning stages.

Briefly, a perspective drawing or sketch is based on the fact that all horizontal lines that recede from the observer appear to converge at a distant point (that is, if one side of the building is parallel to the picture plane). The receding lines will appear to vanish at two distant points if the building is observed from an angular position (see Fig. 5-33). Also, these points of convergence, called vanishing points, fall on a horizontal line or plane that is theoretically at the same level as the observer's eye and that appears on the drawing very similarly as the actual horizon appears on a landscape. Depending on the placement of the horizon line on the drawing, a structure will appear to have been viewed from either a raised or lowered position. Usually, the sketch is made with the natural height of observation in mind: about 6' high, the height of a person's eye above the ground.

In sketching a perspective, vanishing points and proportion are usually arrived at by eye; in fact, the points are commonly omitted except in early exercise sketches because the eye soon becomes trained to establish their correct position and horizon level mentally. Often the points do not fall within the confines of the paper.

Early exercises should consist of simple block studies as shown in Figs. 5-34 and 5-35. Basic building forms and shapes with a minimum of detail should be sketched in various positions until they look realistic; then more complex shapes can be attempted.

It will be beneficial at this point to turn to Chapter 13 and study the principles of perspective drawing. A background in the theory of perspective projection will definitely be helpful in learning to sketch freehand perspectives. Generally, the angular-type perspective, as shown in Fig. 5-36, is appropriate for small, planning-stage sketches.

For sketches of interiors, the 1-point parallel perspective, shown in Fig. 5-38, is adequate for most situations.

In general, follow these simple steps in sketching perspectives of architectural subjects:

STEP 1.   Draw a vertical line to represent the closest vertical corner of the building. On this line, assume a sense of vertical scale by stepping off equal divisions of, say, 5' to any height needed for the building. The divisions can be actually about 1/2", 1", or any similar length, depending on the desired size of the finished sketch.

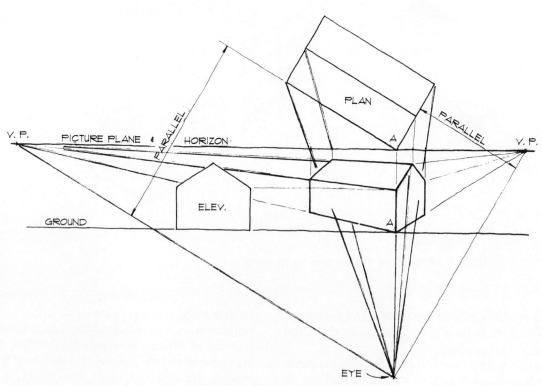

FIGURE 5-33 A perspective layout using a plan and elevation view.

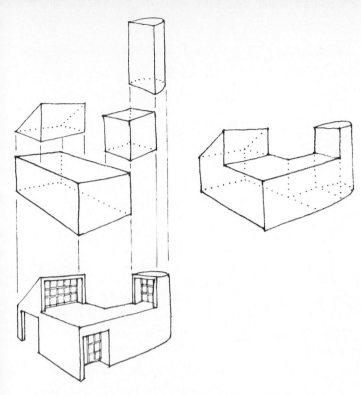

FIGURE 5-34 The basic geometric forms in a perspective sketch.

STEP 2. At a point near 6' high (height of the average person) on the vertical line, sketch a horizontal line across the paper to represent the horizon (see Fig. 5-36). Occasionally, the appearance of the building will be improved by raising the horizon line to more than 6'; however, avoid placing it at a level coinciding with major roof lines or other important horizontal features of the building.

STEP 3. Establish vanishing points on the horizon line by trial (see Fig. 5-37). Place the points on the horizon line well out beyond the area for the intended building so that the receding lines from the vertical forecorner will result in realistic forms.

STEP 4. From the vertical line, sketch a *trial block* of the general size and proportion of the building. The scale of the plan can be taken from the vertical line, but depth proportions become smaller as they recede from the viewer. If the basic block does not appear to have the desired shape, move the vanishing points to new locations on the horizon line. Even the horizon can be moved to create more desirable appearances. A few

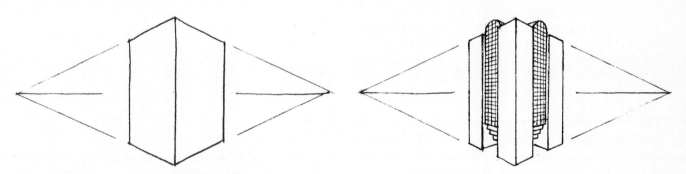

FIGURE 5-35 Blocking in forms to get proportion.

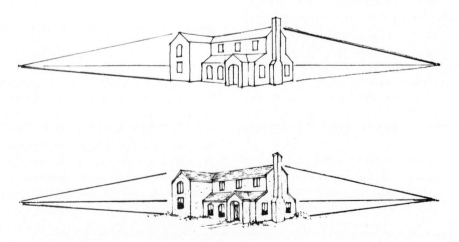

FIGURE 5-36 Blocking in residential forms.

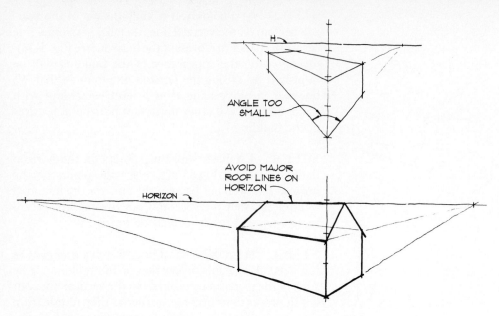

FIGURE 5-37 (A) Vanishing points too close together produce a distorted appearance. (B) Vanishing points placed further apart produce a natural appearance.

trials will produce the correct construction for the building. Wall lines of the block must converge at their respective vanishing points, and care should be taken to avoid a sharp angle formed by the receding walls at the bottom of the forecorner (see Fig. 5-37). If the building is a house with a gable or hip roof, block in the entire height of the roof at the ridge height; use the ground line as the bottom of the block.

STEP 5. Develop the irregularities and offsets of the building, using the basic block as a cage or framework. Symmetry can be maintained with the proper use of center lines. Remember that similar features will appear wider near the observer than they will farther away. Depth proportions are established by eye so that the entire sketch maintains a satisfactory appearance.

To simplify beginning perspective sketches, grid sheets are available that can be placed under tracing paper when sketching. These sheets or charts are laid out for various angles of view, and the grids eliminate the need for establishing vanishing points. A suitable scale is adopted to establish the basic block of the sketch; after this appears to be correct, the details are added, with grid lines serving as a guide for receding lines.

Interior sketches are started with an orthographic rectangular view of the facing wall (Fig. 5-38), inasmuch as we will be looking directly into the wall if we sketch a parallel perspective sketch. The height of the rectangle on the vertical plane can be considered to be the standard 8′ ceiling height, for convenience, and the length is made accordingly. For example, if the wall is 16′ long, it is drawn twice as long as whatever height we have

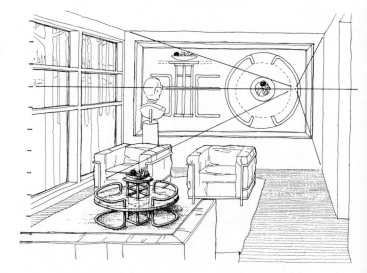

FIGURE 5-38 Interior sketch using 1-point perspective.

made the 8′ ceiling. Place a vanishing point about 6′ high near the center of the rectangle. Sidewall lines are drawn from the corners of the rectangle outward. Notice that the sidewall lines, if extended into the rectangle, converge at the vanishing point. All lines that are perpendicular to the picture plane converge at this point. Heights of relative features are horizontal on the facing wall and can be carried along the sidewalls as long as they vanish toward the vanishing point. This construction forms the basis for the sketch; all features such as doors, windows, beams, and furniture are added in proportion after completion of the basic room interior.

5.11 Shading Pictorial Sketches

A limited amount of shading on pictorial sketches adds to the effect of realism, although only lines may define the limits of a three-dimensional object. Shading also makes interpretation much simpler for the untrained person, and therefore its use is justified. A few major points seem appropriate here for the purpose of improving sketching technique, but it would be best to first refer to Chapter 13, under shades and shadows, for projection principles.

The observation of light as it affects the images of objects is especially helpful to students when learning to add shading to their sketches. Without light we would see nothing; light, therefore, must be considered if we are to represent a three-dimensional object realistically.

The *light source* is generally regarded as coming from an upper-left position, slightly in front of the object. We can think of the source as coming over our left shoulder as we work on the sketch. The top of our object, then, would be the lightest in value or tone, since it receives the most intense light; the front side would have a lesser value, and the right side would appear darkest (see Fig. 5-39). Also, reflected light plays on the sides of an object and must be shown. For that reason, surfaces are not usually shaded with a monotone over their entire area; generally, a graduating shade is more effective.

Highlights, which appear entirely white, are the result of direct reflection of the light source from a surface into our eyes. These white areas play an important part in representing the character of each surface and, therefore, should be handled carefully (see Fig. 5-39, which shows the nature of highlights on basic forms). Usually, it is advisable to omit the highlight in small areas until the shading is complete; then the exact shape of the highlight is rubbed out with an eraser. Overhangs and undercuts, as well as holes and recesses, require the use of shadows to reveal their relief and give them emphasis. Cylindrical surfaces must be made to appear round by applying a parallel highlight slightly to the side of the light source and darker tones near their receding edges.

Light patterns created by strong sunlight on outdoor subjects require more contrast at the shadows than interior subjects.

Contrast can be a useful tool for emphasizing important features on a sketch. When a white area and an extremely dark tone are placed adjacent to each other, the contrast provides a definite emphasis at their junction and gives the impression of bringing the white area forward. This quality is helpful in obtaining three-dimensional effects, especially when adjoining surfaces form abrupt intersections. Remember that shading indications merely supplement the outlines of the sketch and should not be overdone, nor should they produce

FIGURE 5-39 Shading of basic forms and masses.

FIGURE 5-40 A quick perspective sketch.

conflicting geometric shapes that interfere with the important features of the drawing.

An example of good shading technique, made with careful pencil strokes, is shown in Fig. 5-39. Darker tones of the shade are made with wide strokes spaced closely together and with considerable pressure on the pencil. Lighter tones are produced with fine lines spaced farther apart, and the lines are usually feathered out at their ends. Shade lines should reveal the basic form of the surface they represent—straight lines on flat planes and curved lines on curved surfaces (see Fig. 5-40). Other shading techniques, such as a series of dots or smudging can be employed to depict definite surface textures; smudge tones give the impression of a smooth, satiny surface, whereas dots appear to represent a rough texture. See Section 14.4 for further information on pencil rendering.

5.12 Sketching With the Felt-Tip Pen

Many architects use the felt-tip pen on tracing paper for quick sketches that can be reproduced if necessary. The pens are convenient and responsive, lending themselves to many architectural subjects. They are economical and easily available in most stationery and drafting supply stores. Many stores carry a full line of colors as well as black. Their only drawback for the student is that the lines are positive and cannot be erased like pencil lines. For that reason, use the felt tip only after you have gained confidence with the pencil, or lay out the principle lines of the sketch with pencil first before completing the drawing with the pen.

Several types of tips are available, but the most popular are the *cone* and *chisel* points (see Fig. 5-41). The cone point is best for outlines and finer detail requiring uniform-width lines, whereas the chisel is more versatile and allows different-width lines with the use of the corner, edge, or the broadside for flat sweeps when larger areas need to be covered. Various pressures also produce different widths with either point.

Experiment with the chisel point by holding it in different ways to see the many free-flowing lines that are possible.

Avoid using the felt-tip pen on porous paper since the ink will blot and spread throughout the paper. On some thin papers the ink may soak completely through and even stain paper below. A sized paper should be used; as previously mentioned, tracing paper is very satisfactory.

Keep the pens tightly capped when not in use or they will soon dry out. Rather than trying to revive a dried-out point, you will find that it is usually better to discard it. Points, however, can be redressed with a

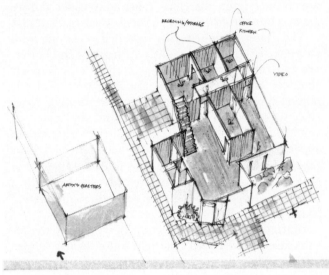

FIGURE 5-43 Interior sketch with the felt-tip pen.

FIGURE 5-41 Many types of felt-tip pens with chisel or pointed tips are available for sketching.

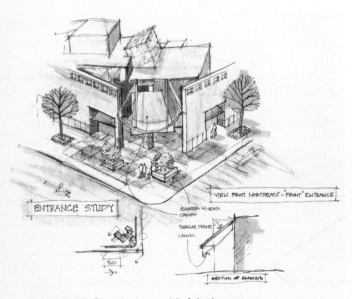

FIGURE 5-42 Sketch done with felt-tip pen.

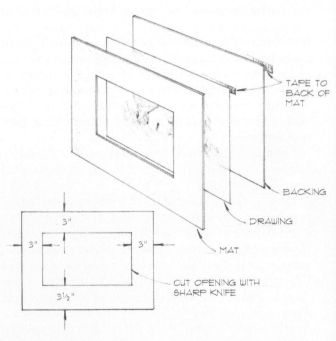

FIGURE 5-44 Making a mat and mounting a small drawing.

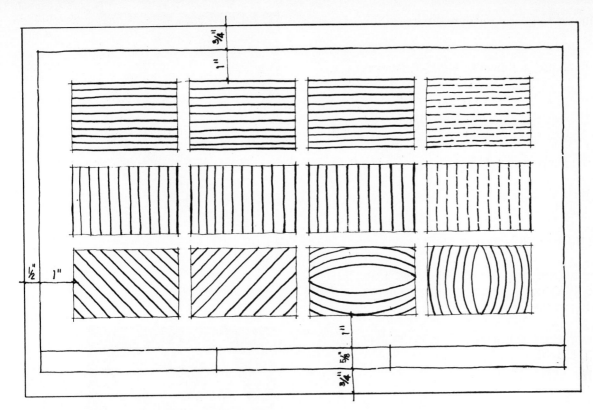

FIGURE 5-45 Layout of beginning sketching exercise.

razor blade should they become worn and blunt from repeated use.

After you have tried a few felt-tip sketches, it will be evident that they take on their own definite character, different from other mediums. Black linework combined with bold areas of soft gray or very light tan produces interesting architectural combinations. Bright colors should be avoided. Often masses of foliage can be stroked with bold sweeps and the edges of the masses given repeating, character lines with the fine point to quickly represent landscaping. The pen is also well adapted to masses of light and shadow on buildings (see Figs. 5-42 and 5-43).

Black line sketches on tracing paper can be easily mounted over colored board so that the tint shows through and then framed with a white mat to dramatize or display the sketch if necessary (see Fig. 5-44).

E X E R C I S E S

S K E T C H I N G

1. On $8\frac{1}{2}'' \times 11''$ drawing paper, lay out a border and divide the paper into 12 equal rectangles freehand, as shown in Fig. 5-45. With an HB pencil, carefully fill the rectangles with horizontal, vertical, and inclined lines as shown.

2. Sketch a 3″ square and bisect each side by eye.

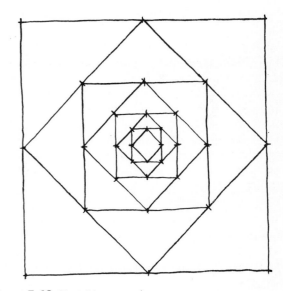

FIGURE 5-46 Sketching exercise.

Connect the points to form an inverted square within the original, as shown in Fig. 5-46; continue drawing squares within squares until the space is filled.

3. Sketch Fig. 5-20, showing the angle-iron assembly.

4. Sketch a section view of an I beam as shown in Fig. 5-20.

5. Sketch four 1¼″ squares and draw circles within each (Fig. 5-13).

6. Sketch an ellipse as shown in Fig. 5-17; major axis 3″, minor 2″.

7. Sketch the corrugated metal sections in Fig. 5-19.

8. Sketch the lamp in Fig. 5-22.

9. Sketch three orthographic views of the seven basic forms in Fig. 5-39.

10. Sketch the box sill section in Fig. 5-26A.

11. On coordinate paper, sketch the floor plan shown in Fig. 5-49A. Sketch your own grid coordinates over the drawing in the book.

12. On coordinate paper, sketch the front elevation shown in Fig. 5-49B. Sketch your own grid coordinates over the drawing in the book.

13. On 8½″ × 11″ drawing paper, sketch the basic isometric shapes in Fig. 5-31.

14. Sketch the building in an oblique view in Fig. 5-50.

15. Make an isometric sketch of the lamp in Fig. 5-22.

16. Sketch the sphere in Fig. 5-47.

17. Sketch the glass block in Fig. 5-48.

18. Make a perspective sketch of the piece of furniture in Fig. 5-23.

19. Make a perspective sketch of the small pool house in Fig. 5-49.

20. Make a perspective sketch of a small home from a magazine.

FIGURE 5-47 Sketching exercise.

FIGURE 5-48 Sketching exercise.

REVIEW QUESTIONS

1. Why does ability in sketching require a strong sense of observation?

2. Explain the *structural* or *skeleton* method of developing a sketch.

3. Why is a sketching subject reduced to its simplest geometric forms in organizing the sketch and the details drawn later?

4. What type of practice sketches should precede pictorial sketches?

5. Which simple geometric form aids in establishing proportion?

6. Why do architectural drafters prefer to do their sketching on inexpensive tracing paper?

7. For what reason is sketching a necessary part of drafting training?

8. What is meant by a *schematic* sketch of a floor plan?

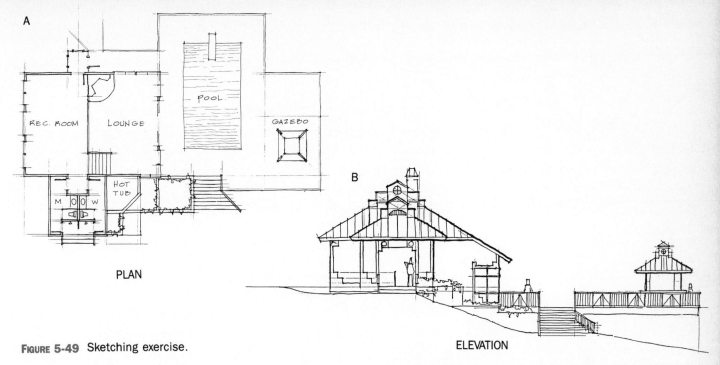

PLAN

ELEVATION

FIGURE 5-49 Sketching exercise.

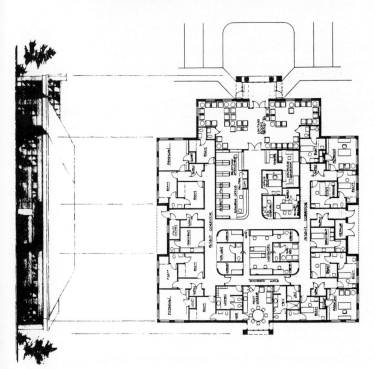

FIGURE 5-50 Sketching exercise.

9. Why is the use of coordinate paper underlays especially helpful in sketching floor plans?

10. In perspective sketching, why may it be necessary to try several basic-block forms before arriving at suitable vanishing points when drawing a building?

11. Why is it essential for the beginner to practice sketching basic geometric shapes?

12. Describe the method used for drawing a freehand circle using two pencils.

13. Why are shades and shadows essential elements of the sketch?

14. What type of perspective view is established when the ground line and horizon line are placed close to each other?

15. What advantage does the felt-tip pen sketch have over the pencil sketch when reproduction of the sketch is important?

16. How is good line technique acquired?

17. What method is recommended for sketching symmetrical objects?

18. Describe the step by step procedure used in setting up a freehand 2-point perspective.

19. Describe in detail the differences between a 1-point perspective and a 2-point perspective.

20. Why is it important for the drafter to have the ability to make freehand sketches?

BASIC RESIDENTIAL PLANNING

W. D. Farmer

"The beautiful is as useful as the useful. More so perhaps."

—Hugo

6

Because of the universal interest and the various aspects involved in home planning, the house is the most appropriate starting problem for students. It is appropriate not only because nearly everyone has been subjected to either the good or the bad qualities of residential planning at one time or another and has formed various opinions, but because the principles of good residential planning can be adapted to many of the other types of structures.

The successful design of buildings requires a deep insight about abstract design, the many construction methods, factors of cost, and even human psychology—all are important; and few individuals are generously gifted with such varied qualifications. However, drafters who can grasp the basic planning principles as they work on the drawing board have a definite advantage, whether they contribute creatively or not. Minor decisions must continually be made during the development of working drawings. Prudent decisions reflect drafters' backgrounds and will certainly contribute to their advancement. Planning also provides an insight into the real meaning of architecture and challenges the ultimate thinking ability of the student. Good planning should start with correctly sized and oriented living spaces.

6.1 Use a Planning Checklist

One inevitable aspect of residential planning is the unlimited variety of tastes and needs of different individuals. Almost every planning job brings together dissimilar combinations of these aspects. Realistic planning often becomes a matter of compromise—choosing between features that will genuinely contribute to the livability of the plan and those that the client feels he or she would like to have. Occasionally, choices are diffi-

cult to resolve. Within the limits of the budget, the custom-designed home should be a representation of the tastes and needs of the occupants, and it should please them. The role of the designer often becomes that of an arbitrator with a practical-minded attitude, yet one with a flair for individuality, if he or she is to be successful. The designer must be able to reconcile the special requests of individuals with their actual needs and come up with satisfying solutions. As a rule, this is not easy. The first step, then, must be a definite understanding of the tastes and needs of the client. To be certain that no important details have been overlooked or forgotten, a procedure must be followed that helps to organize these requirements before planning is started. One of the simplest methods for this purpose is a *checklist* similar to the following:

PLANNING CHECKLIST

_____ 1. Site:
     _____ Size of lot
     _____ Shape of lot
     _____ Type of contours (level, slope to rear, slope to front, slope to side)
     _____ Utilities available (water, electricity, gas, sewer)
     _____ Drainage (good, poor)
     _____ Types of trees, if any
     _____ Direction of most desirable view
     _____ North direction
     _____ Convenience to schools, shopping, churches, etc.
     _____ Satisfactory soil and topsoil
     _____ Wetlands
_____ 2. Occupants:
     _____ Number and age of adults

_____ Number and age of boys
_____ Number and age of girls
_____ Profession of owner
_____ Provision for guests
_____ Provision for servants, if any
_____ Others (in-laws, etc.)
_____ Pets

_____ 3. Individual requirements:
  _____ Formal entertaining
  _____ Separate formal dining area
  _____ Informal living areas
  _____ Outdoor living and eating areas
  _____ Supervised outdoor play area
  _____ Nursery
  _____ Recreation areas (billiards, swimming, tennis)
  _____ Hobby areas (music, sewing, woodworking, gardening, etc.)
  _____ Study or reading areas
  _____ Laundry area
  _____ Screened porch or deck
  _____ Entertainment center (TV, stereo, video)
  _____ Personal computer

_____ 4. General design:
  _____ One-story
  _____ Two-story (_____ elaborate stairway)
  _____ Split-level
  _____ Crawl space
  _____ Concrete slab
  _____ Basement (_____ exterior entrance)
  _____ Traditional exterior
  _____ Contemporary exterior
  _____ Type of roof
  _____ Exterior materials (brick, siding, stone, board-and-batten, plywood, stucco, E.I.F.S.
  _____ Finish floor materials
  _____ Garage (number of cars)
  _____ Carport (number of cars)
  _____ Provision for eventual expansion
  _____ Open planning

_____ 5. Budget restrictions:
  _____ Size of house in sq ft (1000 and under, 1500, 2000, 2500 and over)
  _____ How the house is to be financed
  _____ Number of bathrooms (tub or shower) (wall and floor material)
  _____ Fireplaces
  _____ Type of entrance
  _____ Quality of interior trim

_____ 6. Mechanical equipment required:
  _____ Central heating (warm air, hot water, radiant, heat pump, solar, etc.)
  _____ Air conditioning
  _____ Washer-dryer

_____ Dishwasher
_____ Range
_____ Oven
_____ Microwave
_____ Refrigerator
_____ Ironer
_____ Food freezer
_____ Garbage disposal
_____ Exhaust fans
_____ Water softener
_____ Size of hot water heater
_____ Solar panels
_____ Sauna
_____ Hot-tub

_____ 7. Storage areas required:
  _____ Entrance closet
  _____ Bedroom closets
  _____ Linen closets
  _____ Toy storage
  _____ Kitchen equipment storage
  _____ Cleaning equipment storage
  _____ Tool storage
  _____ China storage
  _____ Gardening equipment storage
  _____ Hobby equipment storage
  _____ Others

6.2 Building Codes

Building codes are minimum requirements which should be utilized in the construction of a residence or building. Its purpose is to protect the public's life, health and welfare in the built environment. Before beginning the design one should be familiar with requirements in the building codes. The building code will place limitations on the area and height of the structure permitted to be built based on the type of construction and occupancy. In some instances, in order to maximize the limitation of a certain type of construction or occupancy, the code will require for the installation of an automatic sprinkler system for fire protection. These and various other requirements will affect the design of a structure as well as impact economical considerations.

Presently in the United States there are three model building codes: the National Building Code (BOCA), the Standard Building Code (SBCCI) and the Uniform Building Code (ICBO). These model codes tend to be in use regionally and a particular edition is usually adopted by city, county or state governments by ordinance for enforcement. Model codes are not the only codes available for adoption, certain government bodies have chosen to write their own building codes. For example, Miami-Dade County in Florida, New York City and the State of North Carolina all have written their own codes. Always consult with the building department which has jurisdiction over the location where the proposed structure is to be constructed to determine what code and edition is under enforcement.

You will find after researching the building codes that some of the construction methods in this book are not only good practices but also are code requirements. For example, the use of natural light and ventilation in bedrooms, placing exhaust fans in bathrooms, using pressure treated wood plates on slab on grade construction, installing joint reinforcement and wall ties in masonry construction and ventilation of crawl spaces are all building code requirements. Information concerning the minimum width permitted for an exit door, the fire rating of walls and doors and the maximum safe loads that may be imposed on a floor or roof can all be found in the building codes.

6.3 Review the Restrictions and Legal Aspects of the Lot

First, make a thorough investigation of the property on which the house is to be built. If possible, check for any restrictions created by easements; acquaint yourself with the zoning regulations of the property. All legal restrictions must be carefully followed. *Easements* are the legal means by which a party other than the owner has been given access or certain rights to the property for various reasons. Utility companies have easements on property in many areas. For example, if electric power lines run across a piece of property, the power company no doubt has an easement on the property for the explicit purpose of running and maintaining the lines. The right is irrevocable and must be honored by the owner and future owners. Occasionally, easements are granted to individuals for trespass privileges on property and must be honored as well.

Zoning regulations or ordinances, usually binding to residential property, restrict the minimum size of a dwelling that can be put on a lot in a given area. These restrictions protect property owners from encroachment of undesirable structures, which might devaluate surrounding property values. From the standpoint of future resale of a house, it is wise to neither overbuild nor underbuild in a restricted area; it is advisable to maintain a consistent quality in keeping with neighboring homes. Overbuilding simply means the construction of a much larger or more expensive house than those in the immediate area, whereas underbuilding is the reverse—building a house much smaller or one in a lower price bracket than surrounding homes. Ordinances usually restrict the placement of a house on a lot (setback from the street as well as the side lot lines).

Of course, it is taken for granted that all conditions of lot selection, such as availability of utilities, conve-

nience to shopping centers, schools, churches, transportation, and suitable zoning regulations have been considered by the prospective home builder. The selection of the lot and an investigation of the clear-title legality of the deed (usually done by title guarantee companies) are the responsibility of the owner.

If possible, make a personal inspection of the lot. No written description is as valuable as first-hand observation of the property.

A *plat*, which is a graphic description of a subdivision or tract of land, is on file in county or city land registering offices. The plat and a written description constitute the legal documents of the property. Photocopies of registered plats may be obtained by the landowner for a small fee. The usual registered-plat drawing contains the following information: name of subdivision, district or section, county or city, state, north-point arrow, scale, name and width of all streets, bearing of street lines, lot lines, lot dimensions and numbers, description of any easements, setback lines, utility mains, protective covenants, references to adjoining property, and certification as to the correctness of the plat by a registered land surveyor (Fig. 6-1). A plat should not be confused with a *site plan*, which will be described later with working drawings. The site plan is drawn by the drafter to show the exact placement of the structure on the property, but it does not become part of the property's legal description.

Linear measurements describing the boundaries of land are usually given in feet and decimals of a foot carried to two places, such as 87.41' or 264.92'. Bearing angles are indicated in degrees and minutes from either north or south, whichever results in the smaller angle, such as N31° 17'E, S24° or 45'W. Land surface heights shown on plats or survey maps can be either distances in feet above sea level, or they can be distances above or below local permanent datum points, called *bench marks*. Either method is satisfactory for indicating various land surface heights.

Prior to construction planning, owners often have survey maps made of their property by a registered land surveyor. A survey map (Fig. 6-2) containing *contour lines* as well as other pertinent physical descriptions of the property will help the designer orient the structure properly. Contour lines indicate the elevation variations of the property. Each contour is plotted to represent similar elevations along the entire line. If you were to actually walk along a contour line, you would continually walk on the same level or elevation. The shoreline of a lake is a good example of a natural contour line. As the water's edge continues around the lake, it varies in shape and curvature depending on the nature of the terrain along the shore. If a small stream empties into the lake, the water's edge turns and follows the bed of the stream for a distance, then crosses the stream and returns toward the mouth and continues around the

FIGURE 6-1 A plat map of a residential subdivision.

edge of the lake. Each contour on the ground closes on itself, such as the complete shoreline of the lake, and eventually returns to itself. This fact is not always apparent on most contour maps as the closures usually fall off the map.

Adjacent contour lines normally have similar characteristics because of natural surface formations (see Fig. 6-3). Lines close together indicate a steep rise in elevation, whereas lines farther apart indicate a more level area. Lines will not cross each other except when indicating unusual conditions such as caves or overhanging cliffs, nor will they touch each other except when a vertical wall or cliff is represented. On riverbeds, the contour lines point upstream. Figure 6-4 shows typical contour indications.

The vertical distance between contour levels is known as the *contour interval*. These contour intervals are usually 1′, 2′, 5′, or 10′, depending on the scale of the map. Heights above sea level or heights above or below local datum points are usually shown along every fifth line, which is often drawn darker to facilitate identification. Because of the uneven nature of land surfaces, contour lines are generally drawn freehand on topographic maps; on plane surfaces they would appear more mechanical and therefore are occasionally drawn with instruments.

Slopes of land surfaces or roadbeds are generally expressed in percent of grade. A slope of 5 percent, for instance, rises vertically 5′ over a horizontal distance of 100′.

$$\frac{rise}{run} = slope \ (expressed \ in \ percent)$$

$$\frac{5}{100} = 0.05 = 5\%$$

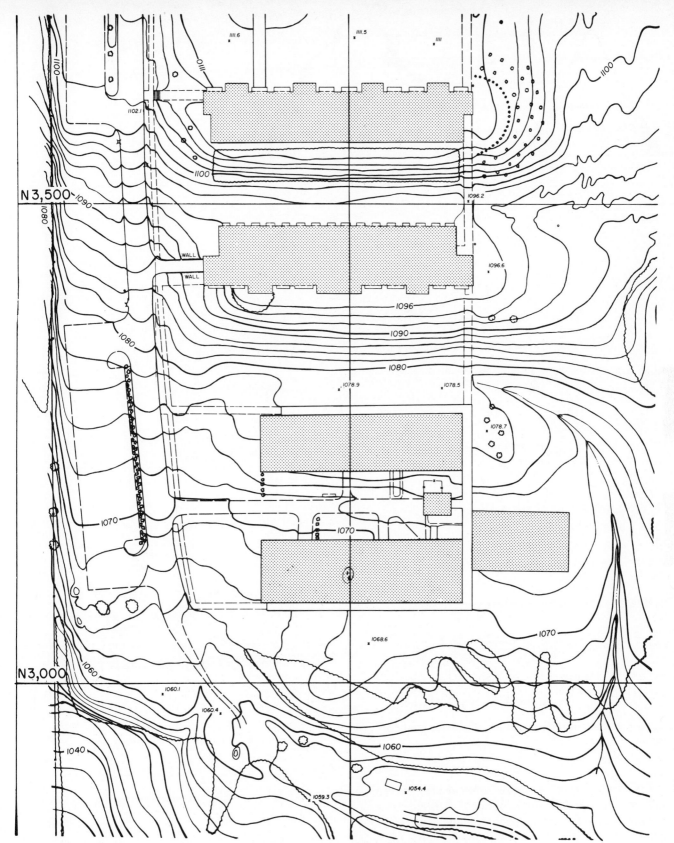

Figure 6-2 A survey map showing the use of contour lines to indicate surface variations.

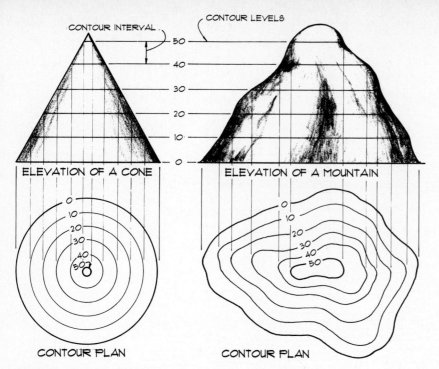

FIGURE 6-3 Contour lines showing the shape of a cone and a hill.

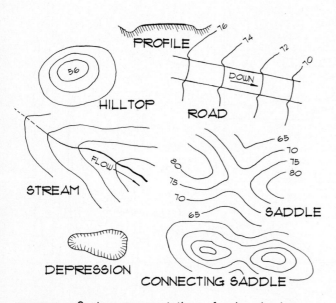

FIGURE 6-4 Contour representations of various land surfaces.

Figure 6-5 shows the contour lines of a typical building lot. The contour profile of line A-A is constructed by projecting the intersections of line A-A and the contour lines that pass through it to the contour levels laid out horizontally below. If the lot is to be leveled for a more desirable construction area, finish contours would appear similar to those shown in the lower drawing. The finish profile of line B-B could be found by projecting the new contour intersections as shown. Fills

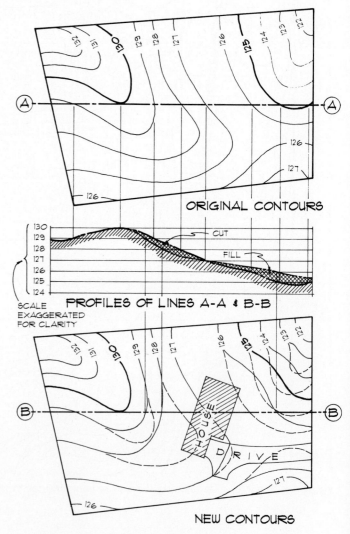

FIGURE 6-5 The method of plotting a contour profile and of indicating new contours on plot plans.

and cuts are accurately defined by superimposing original and finish contour profiles. Notice that on contour maps showing required surface changes the finish contour lines are usually made solid, and the original lines where the changes occur are shown as broken lines.

6.4 Prepare a Site Analysis

An important predesign step is to conduct a comprehensive *site analysis*. The analysis focuses on existing as well as future conditions that may affect the site and the proposed residence. Extensive research is required to address all the issues that may affect the site. Some information is easily obtained from the plat, land regis-

tering office, zoning office, land surveyor, utility companies, city or county engineers' office, and weather centers. Other information can only be assembled from site visits, observations, and surveys at and around the vicinity.

As a first step, organize the site considerations into broad-scope headings. Second, specific issues should be listed under broad-scope headings. Sketches can be prepared to graphically illustrate the analysis data.

Climate   Temperature highs and lows, average rainfall, average snowfall, relative humidity, prevailing winds, hurricanes, tornados, earthquakes, and the sun's orientation in summer and winter are all important climatic considerations (Fig. 6-6).

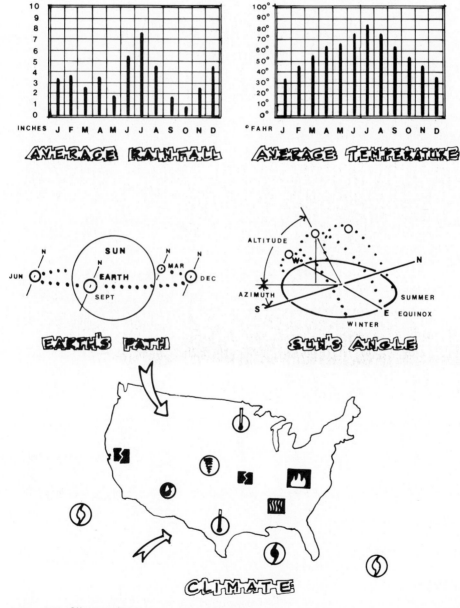

FIGURE 6-6 Climate data.

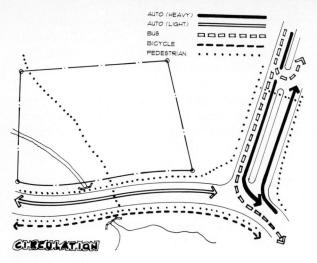

CIRCULATION

FIGURE 6-7 Circulation analysis.

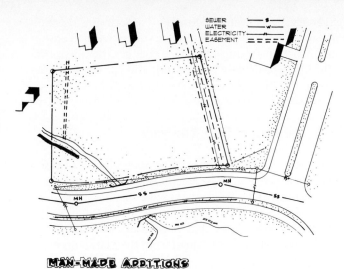

MAN-MADE ADDITIONS

FIGURE 6-10 Man-made additions.

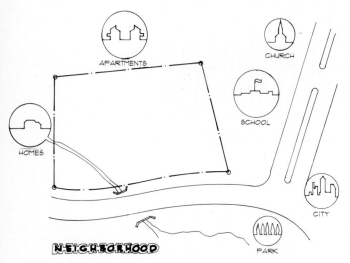

NEIGHBORHOOD

FIGURE 6-8 Neighborhood analysis.

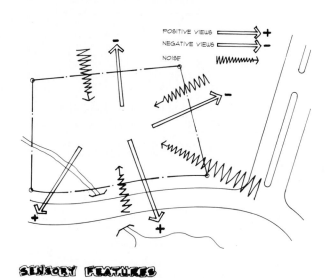

SENSORY FEATURES

FIGURE 6-11 Sensory features analysis.

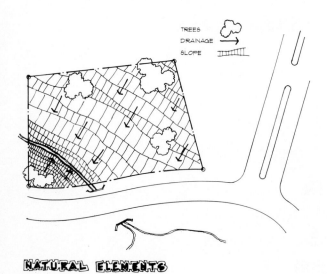

NATURAL ELEMENTS

FIGURE 6-9 Natural elements.

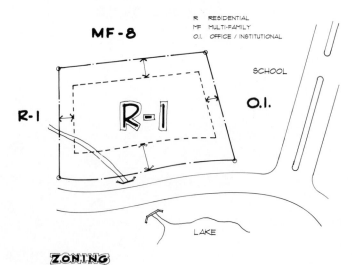

ZONING

FIGURE 6-12 Zoning analysis.

Circulation Vehicular and pedestrian traffic patterns and frequency of movement are of prime concern. Automobile, truck, train, taxi, streetcar, bicycle, bus, aircraft, subway, and overhead rail circulation patterns require study. Roads, sidewalks, and paths should be located on a site analysis drawing (Fig. 6-7).

Neighborhood The architectural, cultural, psychological, sociological, historical, ethnic, age, density, stability, recreational, safety, and economic factors of the neighborhood must be analyzed (Fig. 6-8).

Natural Elements Trees, vegetation, topography, soil, rocks, lakes, ponds, rivers, streams, slopes, ridges, valleys, and drainage are some of the natural features present on many sites. These features become important site advantages or disadvantages (Fig. 6-9).

Man-Made Additions People have changed the character of the land by adding fences, walls, pavements, streets, sidewalks, hard and soft landscaping, utilities, buildings, and outdoor furniture to the environment. Most such additions become major site considerations (Fig. 6-10).

Sensory Features Views, sounds, and odors repel or appease the senses. An effective site analysis should study views to and from the site and determine whether they are an asset or liability. The same holds true for noises and odors in the neighborhood (Fig. 6-11).

Zoning Land utilization plans show a designated zoning or land use for all parcels of property in a community. Lot size, building density, setbacks, and type and size of building are determined by zoning (Fig. 6-12).

Composite site analysis diagrams can be developed. These composite analyses combine a series of issues on a single graphic display (Fig. 6-13).

6.5 Plan the House to Fit the Site

After reviewing the legal restrictions and site analysis of the lot, analyze the natural advantages of the area so that the house will become an integral and compatible part of its environment. Study the following points for their individual adaptability:

Plan a 1-Story House if You Have Enough Space to Spread Out Houses on one level are easiest to build and maintain; there are no stairways that use up valuable floor space and constitute possible hazards for children and older people. Rambling 1-story houses are

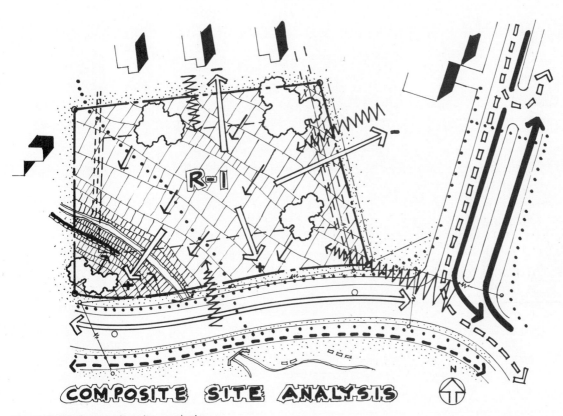

FIGURE 6-13 Composite site analysis.

FIGURE 6-14 One-story house, ranch type.

FIGURE 6-15 Split-level house.

FIGURE 6-16 Two-story house.

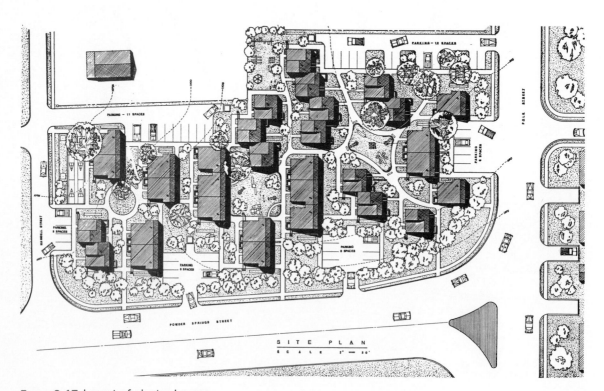

FIGURE 6-17 Layout of cluster houses.

often referred to as *ranch type* (Fig. 6-14). If the contours of the lot will accommodate offset floor levels, plan a *split-level* house (Fig. 6-15). If the space is limited, plan a *2-story house* (Fig. 6-16); build up instead of out. Less roof and less foundation will make the 2-story house more economical than a 1-story of comparative size. In areas where expensive land must be divided into very narrow lots, the best solution is *cluster houses* (Fig. 6-17). Their party walls afford more privacy than do facing windows 10′ or so apart on adjacent conventional houses. However, row houses can be considered only in tract or subdivision planning.

Make the House Part of the Land By utilizing the entire lot for livability (see Fig. 6-18), even a modest-size home can seem spacious if the inside is made to communicate with the exterior. Level areas adjacent to the house are the most inexpensive living space your planning can provide. If possible, open the back to private outdoor areas by the use of glass and a view— easily created with landscaping if necessary. On noisy streets, "turn your back" to the public by using few, if any, windows on the front.

Avoid Excessive Excavation Usually, selection of the proper house type will minimize expensive excavation work. You will find that the less you disturb the natural contours of the land, the kinder nature will be to the future inhabitants of the home (see Fig. 6-19).

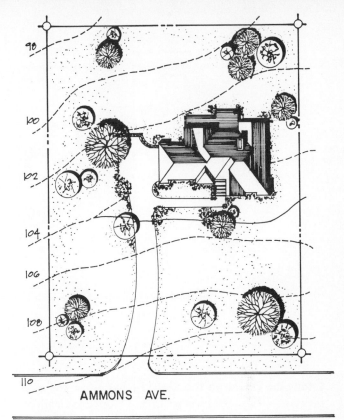

SITE PLAN

FIGURE 6-18 Landscaping sketch showing good site utilization.

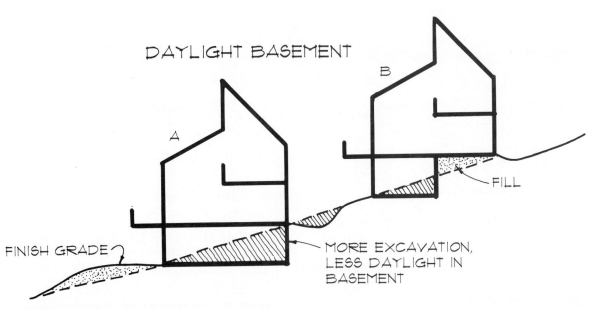

FIGURE 6-19 Planning for minimum excavation.

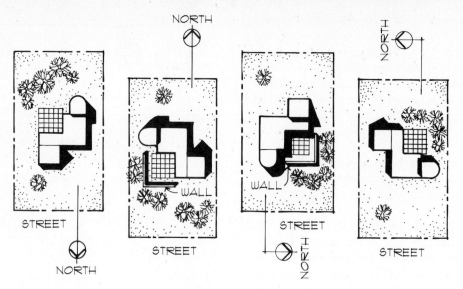

FIGURE 6-20 Orienting the house to the sun.

Orient the House to the Sun Living areas are more pleasant with southern exposures. However, not all lots can easily accommodate this favorable exposure and still provide the most desirable view. On lots with the street side facing south, a walled patio near the front of the house may be the only method of obtaining a southern exposure and privacy as well (Fig. 6-20). To gain southern exposure on other lots, it may be necessary to turn the plan or place living areas on various sides of the building. With correctly designed overhangs and sunshades, window walls can harness the sun in summer and provide warmth and comfort within the house during the winter (see Fig. 6-21). Sun charts, showing exact angles of the sun throughout various times of the day and year, should be consulted for accurate solar orientation of large glass walls, especially in warm cli-

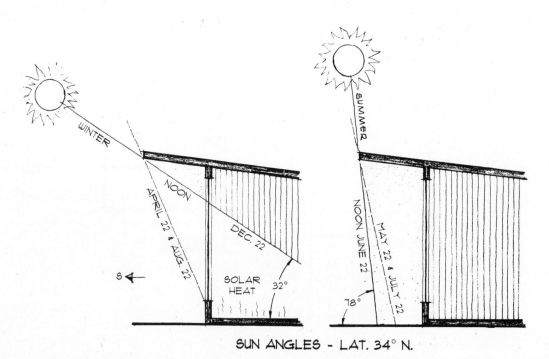

SUN ANGLES - LAT. 34° N.

FIGURE 6-21 Harnessing the sun with the overhangs for year-round comfort.

mates. Plan the roof overhangs accordingly. Sunlight in moderation can be pleasant, but in excess it can be severe and damaging.

Make Maximum Use of the Existing Trees as noise barriers and as shade producers during months of intense summer sun (see Fig. 6-22). Shade on a house reduces inside temperatures considerably (as much as 10°) during the summer and reduces the maintenance of painted surfaces. Deciduous trees are especially effective; by dropping their leaves in winter, they allow desirable winter sunshine to penetrate a house when it

is needed, and in summer they block the sun when it becomes destructive (see Fig. 6-23A). For maximum utility, trees should be on the south side of the house (see Fig. 6-23B). Evergreen trees, on the other hand, are more effective as windbreaks; they often make it possible to prolong the use of outdoor living areas well into the colder months of the year.

Consider Prevailing Winds By proper planning, breezes can be funneled through a house for additional comfort in warmer climates, and bitter winds can be diverted in colder climates (see Fig. 6-24).

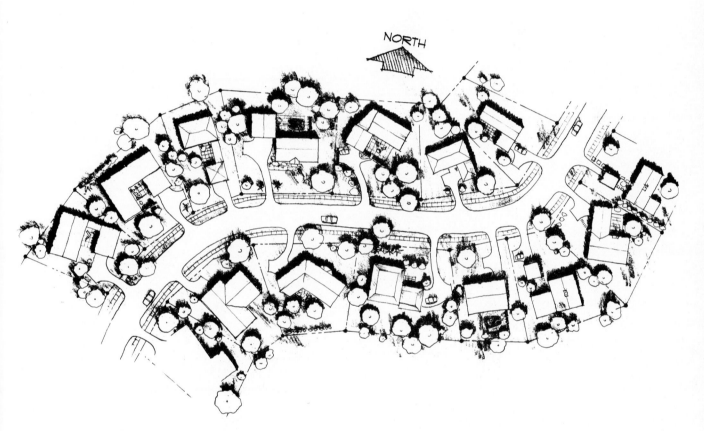

FIGURE 6-22 Plan the site for interest and privacy.

1. Avoid the lined-up look; vary the position and placement of the house on each lot.
2. Use curved streets; they prevent speeding.
3. Cut lots into a variety of shapes and sizes.
4. Curved driveways are more pleasing than straight drives.
5. Control the view from windows by planting or walls to gain privacy.
6. Place living areas on the south side if possible; avoid a western exposure.
7. Combine a variety of housing styles, some one-story, others two-story, to prevent the uniform-roofline look.
8. Use deciduous trees on the south side for summer shade; use conifers for windbreaks.
9. A rolling terrain improves interest and groundline variety.
10. Planting should be done in clusters to retain the natural look.
11. If possible, provide a turnaround drive so that cars will not have to back out into a busy street.
12. Split-level houses should be placed on a sloping lot, a flat-roof house on a flat site.
13. Preserve natural contours to prevent harsh drainage problems.
14. Avoid high planting near the intersection of the driveway and street, which will obstruct the view.
15. Provide greenery backgrounds for flowering shrubs.
16. Do not hide the front entrance; have the planting lead the eye to the door.

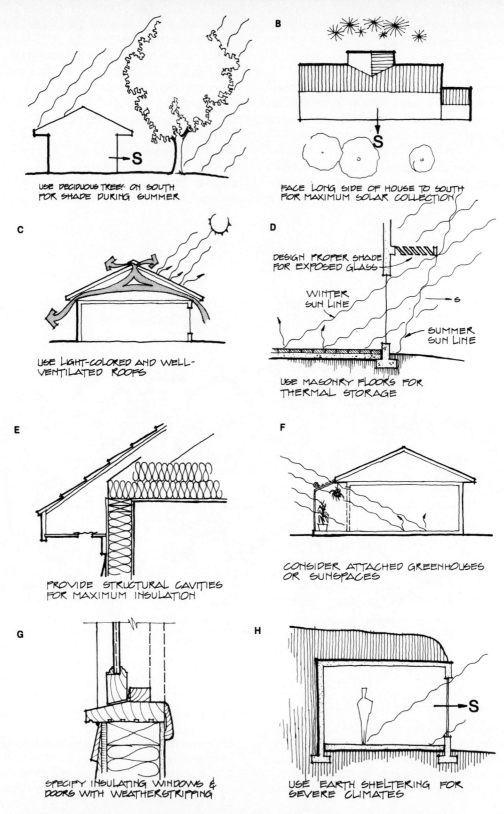

A

USE DECIDUOUS TREES ON SOUTH FOR SHADE DURING SUMMER

B

FACE LONG SIDE OF HOUSE TO SOUTH FOR MAXIMUM SOLAR COLLECTION

C

USE LIGHT-COLORED AND WELL-VENTILATED ROOFS

D

DESIGN PROPER SHADE FOR EXPOSED GLASS

WINTER SUN LINE

SUMMER SUN LINE

USE MASONRY FLOORS FOR THERMAL STORAGE

E

PROVIDE STRUCTURAL CAVITIES FOR MAXIMUM INSULATION

F

CONSIDER ATTACHED GREENHOUSES OR SUNSPACES

G

SPECIFY INSULATING WINDOWS & DOORS WITH WEATHERSTRIPPING

H

USE EARTH SHELTERING FOR SEVERE CLIMATES

FIGURE 6-23 Conserving energy in homes begins by planning passive solar features at the outset.

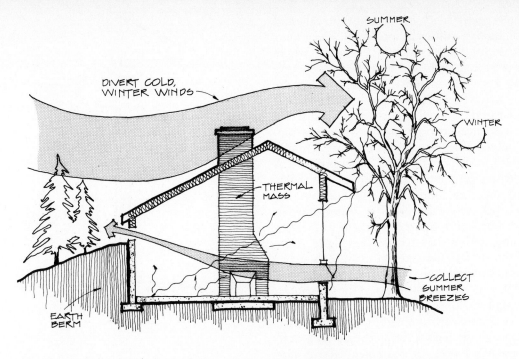

FIGURE 6-24 Using shape and orientation for natural ventilation in warmer climates.

Keep Bedrooms and Quiet Zones Isolated from noise-producing conditions. Cars, trains, play areas, and such, must be considered in house orientation.

Provide a Sense of Privacy from possible observers on public streets or from surrounding buildings or property. The house should be a sanctuary where the occupants can relax and feel protected.

6.6 Utilize Solar Planning to Reduce Energy Costs

During the middle 1970s, because of the oil shortage, the costs for heating and cooling homes in this country almost doubled. This fact placed a new emphasis on energy conservation and changed planning strategy in housing as well as commercial structures throughout the nation.

It has been found that by careful planning in home construction major savings in energy costs can be realized by capturing and controlling the heat from the sun. Many successful buildings have already been built that have verified the value of solar planning. Even the adobe houses (Fig. 6-87) built by the natives in the southwestern United States many years before the oil shortage, utilized heat from the sun to provide additional comfort within their dwellings. Because night-time temperatures in the area drop uncomfortably low, and daytime temperatures from the sun reach high levels, the massive adobe walls of their houses absorb the intense heat during the day and give it off within

during the night to maintain a more stable and comfortable temperature. Many of our contemporary homes are now keeping energy costs more manageable by using solar concepts during their construction.

Although various solar collectors and distribution equipment are now available to builders to incorporate active solar features in solar homes, the most cost-effective savings can be realized by planning *passive* solar features into the construction (see Fig. 6-23). Passive features have few moving parts and no operating or maintenance costs, and the advantage is gained largely by the original design and the materials selected by the builder.

Planning for passive solar homes involves site orientation, (see Fig. 6-28) careful interior layout, sufficient glass for solar energy collection, proper storage of the energy until it is needed, and a means of energy distribution throughout the home. The use of superinsulating material and a tight shell to minimize heat loss is important.

To benefit from solar energy, plan the shape of the house so that large window areas are placed with southern exposures; use deciduous trees on the south side, as previously mentioned so that their leaves will provide shade during summer and allow the sun to flood the glass during winter (see Fig. 6-24). Make use of evergreens for windbreaks from cold winter winds. Plan shade protection for the glass areas with accurately designed overhangs and shade louvers where necessary. Plan well-ventilated and light-colored roofs. Provide insulating glass in all windows; plan some operable windows to take advantage of cooler breezes and temperatures, and specify adequate space within walls and roof to accommodate sufficient insulation. Place thermal-mass masonry features within the home where they can absorb the sunlight and store the solar energy. For example, a massive masonry chimney within the house creates a flywheel effect by slowly taking on and giving off solar heat. Other features that can be used to store daytime solar energy are masonry floors of tile, brick, or concrete. If suitable, use a masonry Trombe wall (Fig. 6-25), which can be glazed and ventilated to bring inexpensive heat into habited spaces. Water is another convenient medium to store heat within. To supplement other storage features, use water tubes or tanks placed near south-exposed windows to soak up the energy and store it for later use (see Fig. 6-26).

Another economical heat storage feature is a bin filled with rocks placed underground below the house (see Fig. 6-27), if rocks are available near the site. Solar-heated air circulated through the bin will give off its heat to the rocks; then air from within the house when circulated through the bin will bring the stored heat to where it is needed. Forced-air equipment (active solar feature) must be installed with this arrangement.

An interesting feature that can be useful in contemporary solar planning is a sunspace or greenhouse (Fig. 6-23F) as part of the plan layout or attached to the house. These glassed-in areas provide ideal spaces for interior plants and greenery while collecting heat for human comfort. Although they are light and airy as part of the house, there are several problems that must be overcome in their use. Depending on the extent of planting within, high levels of water vapor and window condensation may result. Also, considerable heat loss through the glass at night and during winter months can be expected unless provision is made for it. Even excessive heat gain during the summer months must be controlled with ventilation and sunshades. The sunspace provides a satisfactory way to heat a thermal-mass wall if the air circulation to the house proper can be controlled.

Another type of construction that might be considered for energy efficiency is an *earth-sheltered* home. This alternative is not inexpensive, yet it is an easy home to heat and cool. If parts of the design are placed within the earth (see Fig. 6-23H), energy costs can be greatly reduced, the principle being that the earth itself maintains a more stable and moderate temperature than the air above. Therefore, less heat is needed in winter and less air conditioning in summer to maintain comfort temperatures for living. Site selection and orientation are extremely important. There are several subtypes of earth-insulated houses that might be considered. One is the atrium type built around courtyards that give light and ventilation to the interior. Typically, it is usually entirely underground. This type fits a south-sloping lot well in cold climates and a north-sloping lot in warm climates.

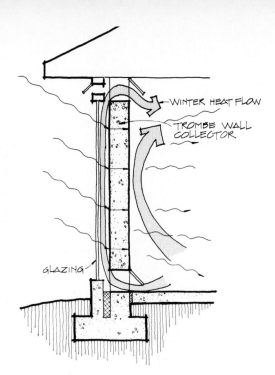

FIGURE 6-25 (On left) Use of a Trombe wall for solar energy collection.

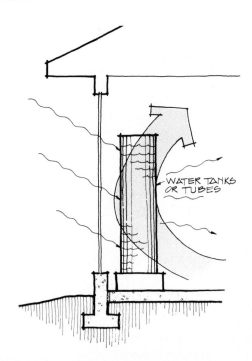

FIGURE 6-26 (At right) Water-filled tanks or tubes near south-exposed glass will store solar heat.

An earth-bermed type is one in which the windows and doors are placed in various locations in the walls with openings in the berms to allow for light and ventilation. Even the roof can be covered with earth in several of the types. This construction is dramatically effective in extremely cold climates where harsh winds prevail. Groundwater conditions and waterproof con-

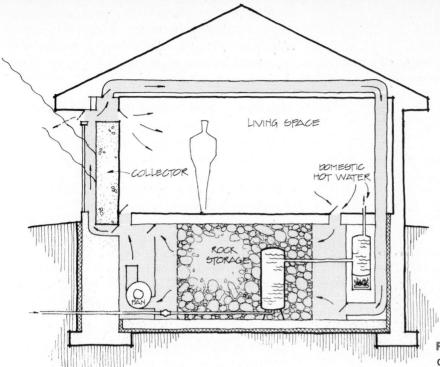

FIGURE 6-27 A rock bin underground can be used to store solar heat when air is circulated through it.

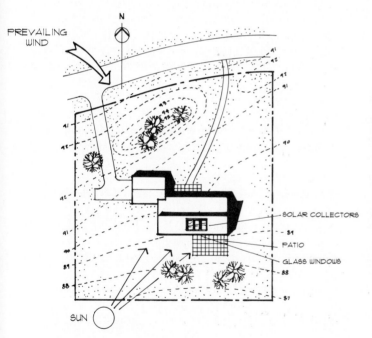

FIGURE 6-28 Solar planning involves correct house orientation.

struction below grade (usually concrete) are premier considerations. Insulation must be placed below floor slabs and to the exterior of walls and roof. Other problems, such as drainage of exterior below-grade areas to outfalls, must be solved, natural lighting to all interior living spaces is a layout problem, and the selection of durable building materials is another of the numerous considerations involved.

With the continuing rise of energy costs, it is only logical that more solar planning should be included in all future home construction. Many houses will utilize many of the manufactured components, such as efficient solar collectors, air-circulating equipment, and other energy-saving features that are now available to home builders. These include the active solar components. But wise planners will surely make the best use of the passive features mentioned here during the initial construction of future homes. Many of the solar features can also be applied to the remodeling of older homes.

6.7 Choose the Most Appropriate Basic Structure

There are many basic structures to consider and analyze before the most suitable is decided on. Each of the following has both advantages and disadvantages, but after considering the needs carefully, one type will prove to be the most appropriate.

One-Story with a Pitched Roof and Flat Ceilings (see Fig. 6-29)   This popular house type is built with conventional rafter and ceiling-joist framing methods, or the roof framing can be quickly erected with prefabricated roof trusses. It lends itself easily to prefabrication, which is gaining in acceptance throughout the United States. It also has the advantage of having its

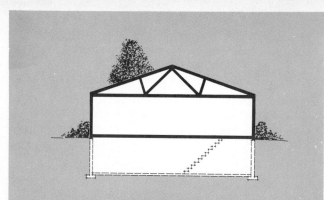

FIGURE 6-29 One-story house with pitched roof and flat ceilings.

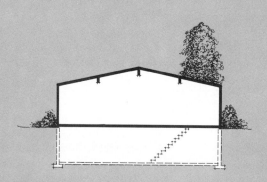

FIGURE 6-30 One-story house with pitched roof and sloping ceilings.

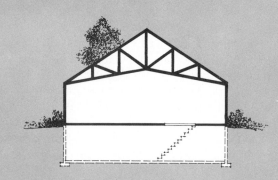

FIGURE 6-31 One-story house with pitched roof and ceilings, which allows the use of more insulation within the scissors-truss area.

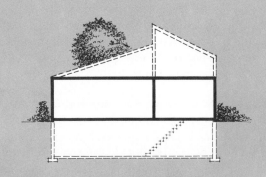

FIGURE 6-32 One-story house with a flat or shed-type roof and ceilings.

living areas on one level. This type of house can be built with or without a basement, with a crawl space, or on a concrete slab, or it can be used in conjunction with multilevel designs to produce many of our traditional home styles.

One-Story with a Pitched Roof and Sloping Ceilings (see Fig. 6-30) This type has evolved from the plank-and-beam type framing, and its popularity is due mainly to the massive exposed beams and sloping ceiling interiors, as well as the interesting architectural effects produced by the extensions of the beams on the cornice exteriors. The type looks well with large overhangs, which produce expansive, unbroken roof lines. Many exciting examples of this structural type can be found in contemporary designs. If a sloping ceiling with air space above for insulation is required, use the *sissors* truss as shown in Fig. 6-31. Gypsum board or other ceiling material can be fastened to the lower chords of the trusses.

One-Story with a Flat Roof and Ceilings (see Fig. 6-32) With built-up roofing materials comparing favorably with conventional roofing, this type has become definitely contemporary in nature and is a very economical type of construction (the same structural members are used for both the ceiling and the roof). It requires skillful design of its elevation views to overcome a boxy appearance, and its strong horizontal roof lines often appear monotonous unless broken with offsets or various roof levels. The flat roof can be combined effectively with the shed-type roof (see dashed lines in Fig. 6-32), or it can be used with gable roofs as carports, garages, or other attached wings for variety of roof lines.

One-and-One-Half-Story with Two Living Levels—less living space on the top level (see Fig. 6-33) This structural type is associated with the New England Cape Cod house. The basic simplicity of the true Cape Cod design should be retained, in proportion and in detail, if an approach to historical authenticity is desired. Even though the shape is traditional, many contemporary-type houses have resulted from the use of the steep roof and various adaptations of the story-and-one-half principle.

Two-Story with Two Living Levels—Pitched Roof and Flat Ceilings (see Fig. 6-34) Numerous 2-story houses are rich in traditional charm. Their heritage can be captured only by the correct proportion and detail usually associated with many of the New England houses. Either gable or hip roofs of various slopes can be used with the 2-story design; often lower roofed additions to the main box seem to enhance the overall silhouette. Upper-story projections (see Fig. 11-15) not only increase the second-story living space, but tend to reduce the strong vertical appearance.

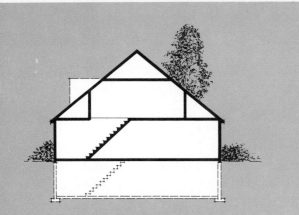

FIGURE 6-33 One-and-one-half-story house with the steep roof allowing partial living space on the second level.

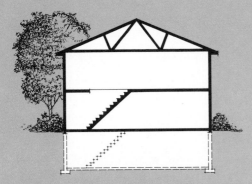

FIGURE 6-34 Two-story house with a pitched roof and flat ceilings.

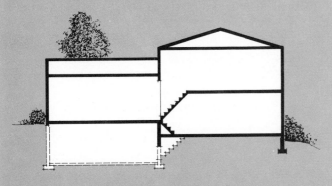

FIGURE 6-35 Split-level house with three living levels –pitched roof and flat ceilings.

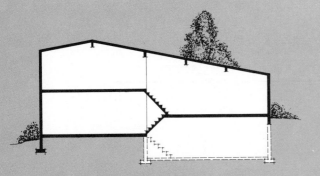

FIGURE 6-36 Split-level house with three living levels- pitched roof and various ceilings.

Split-Level with Three Living Levels—Pitched Roofs and Flat Ceilings (see Fig. 6-35) The majority of the comparatively new split-level type houses have three living levels and an optional basement level. All levels are connected with stair segments that combine in pairs to make one full-story height. Multilevels provide excellent zoning for different activities, and their exteriors can be given interesting variety. On sloping lots the split-level can be oriented to the site and still have full-story height exposure to outdoor living areas. Stair arrangements can become complicated, requiring considerable study to develop a successful design.

Split-Level with Three Living Levels—Continuous Sloping Roofs and Various Ceilings (see Fig. 6-36) This second type of split-level is identified by low-pitched roofs (usually 2:12 or 3:12 slopes) that continue over several levels to create sloping ceilings in various upper and middle rooms. The continuous ceilings produce several ceiling heights, thereby adding interest to the interior living spaces. Roof slopes and floor levels must be carefully controlled to result in satisfactory wall heights and proper proportions. Both types of split-levels are similar in livability and popularity.

6.8 Use a Matrix to Analyze Space Relationships

The *matrix* is a convenient aid in developing and understanding the relationships among the various spaces in a residence. First, you must prepare a list of all the rooms, spaces, or areas that are essential to the design program. The drafter must then lay out a two-dimensional grid to form the matrix. The grid may be drafted in a format where the room names are listed in both a horizontal column and a vertical column. This system results in a square grid where all lines drawn in the matrix are perpendicular to each other (Fig. 6-37). Another option is to develop the matrix by listing the room names in a vertical column and drafting the grid with

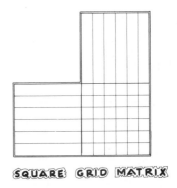

SQUARE GRID MATRIX

FIGURE 6-37 Square grid matrix.

45° degree lines (Fig. 6-38). The latter system eliminates the duplication of coding each space twice when completing the matrix.

A code must be established to differentiate between the relationships of adjacency of spaces listed on the matrix. A common scale used in defining the code for example could be in a range through *essential*, *desirable*, *neutral*, and *unimportant* to *detrimental*. A graphic symbol is assigned to each term in the code (Fig. 6-39).

To complete the matrix the user reads the names of the rooms and places a graphic symbol, which represents the relationship of adjacency between the two spaces, on the grid. For instance, in a residence, it would be essential for a foyer to be adjacent to a coat closet. The symbol of essential would be coded into the matrix where the grid lines for foyer and coat closet cross (Fig. 6-40A, B). When completed, the matrix reveals the relationship of adjacency between all spaces in the program. Patterns will surface that indicate a common bond among several spaces, which can be clustered in close proximity.

Use Zone Diagrams to Establish Major Elements of Design   The clusters that become obvious from the matrix can be transformed to a zone diagram (Fig. 6-40C). Several zone diagrams could be developed for most residences. Living space used for family activities and entertaining guests could be zone 1. Eating areas where meals are prepared and enjoyed by family members and guests could be zone 2. Sleeping areas used primarily by the family could be zone 3. To illustrate component spaces in zone 1, cluster the foyer, living room, and family room together. An example of zone 2

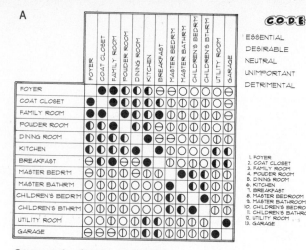

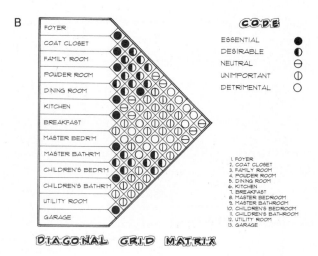

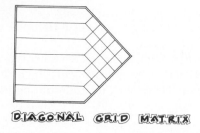

FIGURE 6-38 Diagonal grid matrix.

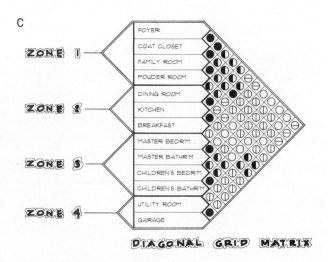

FIGURE 6-40 Matrix completed for a residence.

CODE

ESSENTIAL	●
DESIRABLE	◐
NEUTRAL	⊖
UNIMPORTANT	⦶
DETRIMENTAL	○

FIGURE 6-39 A common scale should be used to code the matrix.

126   Basic residential planning

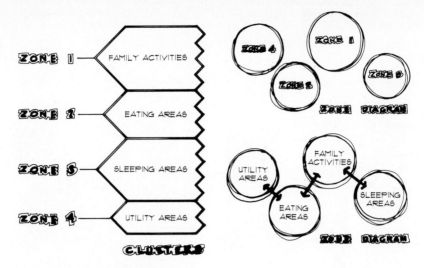

FIGURE 6-41 Zone diagrams.

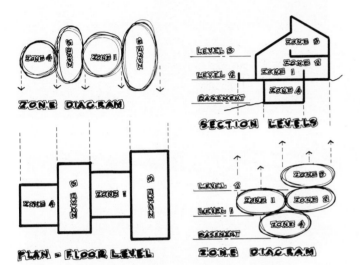

FIGURE 6-42 Using the zone diagram to develop the design.

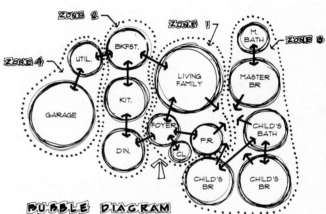

FIGURE 6-43 Bubble diagram sketches.

would be a grouping of the kitchen, dining room, and breakfast room. Zone 3, representing sleeping spaces, might include bedrooms, baths, and closets. Arrows are drawn to represent circulation between zones (Fig. 6-41).

Zone diagrams are useful tools in developing the mass and form of a residence. A cluster of space could easily represent a wing or floor level (Fig. 6-42).

Use Bubble Diagrams to Establish Adjacency Requirements   Although zone diagrams are useful, the main purpose of the matrix is to establish essential relationships between rooms. Once the degree of adjacency has been determined, the drafter can begin sketching *bubble diagrams*. Freehand circles or bubbles are drawn to represent each of the rooms listed in the matrix. The bubbles are placed in proximity according to their degree of adjacency indicated on the matrix. Arrows are used to depict circulation between spaces (Fig. 6-43).

Drafters frequently study several complete bubble diagrams before deciding which one best meets the criteria of the project. Once the appropriate diagram is determined, the drafter begins schematic site and floor plan studies. A good bubble diagram serves as the foundation for the development of a successful preliminary floor plan (Fig. 6-44).

6.9 Plan the Interior Spaces to Reflect the Life-Style of the Occupants

Understanding the life-style of the occupants of a home is important for effective interior space planning. Some occupants prefer casual living, while others desire a more formal life-style. Analyze the needs of the client before preparing preliminary sketches.

Regardless of the life-style, certain fundamentals are

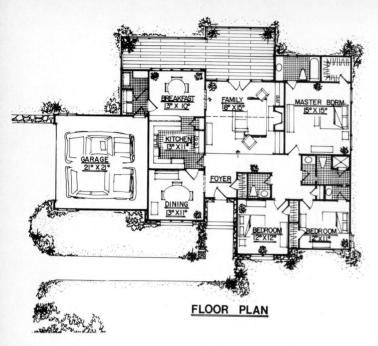

FLOOR PLAN

GARAGE
21° X 21°

BREAKFAST
13° X 10°

FAMILY
18° X 15°

MASTER BDRM.
15° X 15°

KITCHEN
13° X 11°

FOYER

DINING
13° X 11°

BEDROOM
12° X 12°

BEDROOM
12° X 11°

FIGURE 6-44 Floor plan developed from the bubble diagram in Figure 6-43.

Falling water

Falling water

FIGURE 6-45 Blending contemporary elements between interior and exterior design. (*Western Pennsylvania Conservancy.*)

essential to all residential planning. Successful interiors have a definite relationship to successful exteriors.

The character of a traditional-style home should be reflected both in its exterior and interior design. The same statement can be made for contemporary design. Frank Lloyd Wright was a modern architect who masterfully blended exterior and interior forms and materials (Fig. 6-45). Thomas Jefferson, the colonial designer, tastefully integrated classical elements of design on the interior and exterior (Fig. 6-46).

Allow the Correct Amount of Space for Each Major Activity   From a general standpoint, you can think of the basic activities in a home as being *eating, sleeping,* and *living.* Give each activity its proper allotment of space, according to the living habits of the inhabitants and the size of the plan. Use precious space generously where it counts most—in living and entertainment areas. And restrict floor space in individual-activity areas, such as kitchens and baths, where careful planning can make them adequately efficient. Living rooms set the interior atmosphere of the home and should not convey the impression of confinement. Isolate quiet zones—bedrooms, studies, and the like—from noisy family and recreation rooms. If possible, use closets for sound-barrier walls; a closet full of clothes makes the simplest method of preventing sound transmission between rooms (Fig. 6-47).

Make Areas Serve Dual, Nonconflicting Purposes   if you want maximum space utilization and a flexible plan. See if any of the following typical combinations might gain additional living space in the plan:

1. Living–dining
2. Living–family
3. Kitchen–laundry
4. Bath–laundry
5. Garage–laundry
6. Hall–laundry
7. Garage–workshop
8. Large bedroom with room divider
9. Carport adjacent to terrace

Monticello

Monticello

Figure 6-46 Blending classical elements between interior and exterior design. (*Monticello, Thomas Jefferson Memorial Foundation.*)

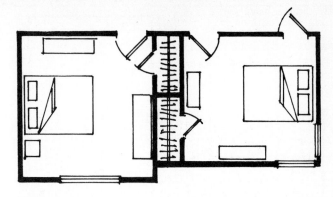

Figure 6-47 Using closets to prevent sound transmission between rooms.

TABLE 6-1		
Typical room sizes (inside dimensions)		
Living	14′	× 20′
Dining	12′	× 14′
Kitchen	8′	× 16′
Bath	5′	× 9′
Bedroom, master	12′	× 15′
Bedroom	11′	× 13′
Entrance hall	7′	× 8′
Powder room	4′	× 5′
Utility	8′	× 12′
Hall width	3′-6″ to	4′
Stairs width	3′	
Garage (single)	12′	× 20′
Garage (double)	20′	× 20′
Workshop	12′	× 14′

Plan the size of each room to fit the furniture to be used in it, especially the dining room and bedrooms. Minimize partitions, if possible, by eliminating offsets and by keeping partition walls in line with each other; unnecessary corners are expensive and they make furniture arrangement difficult.

Refer to Table 6-1 to help you size the various home areas.

Keep Major Traffic Routes Short Consider day to day activities so that the traffic patterns are minimized and hallways do not deprive the plan of important living space. Time, space, as well as maintenance of floors can be saved by efficient circulation. Traffic through rooms (especially through the center) is a characteristic of many older houses, which were designed around formal exteriors; little concern was given to the routes between different activity areas. If the main entrance of a plan is placed near the center (see Fig. 6-48), major

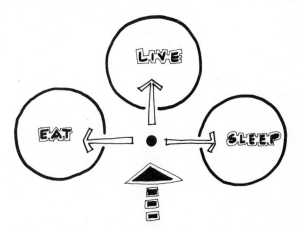

Figure 6-48 Defining major circulation patterns.

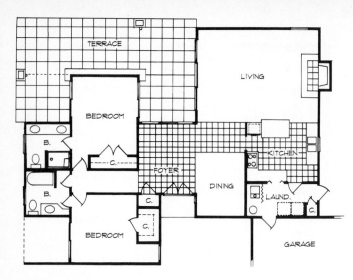

FIGURE 6-49 Floor plan with good traffic flow.

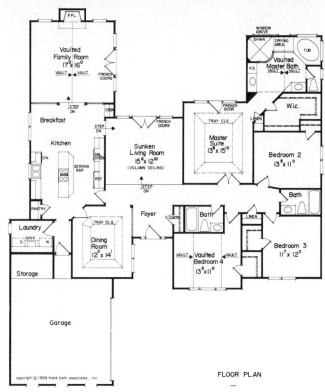

FIGURE 6-50 An efficient foyer.

traffic patterns can fan out in each direction and thus increase usable space within rooms and reduce hall lengths. The route from the carport or garage to the kitchen should definitely be short. If traffic must pass through a room, arrange the doors so that the traffic affects only a corner or an end. Often the correct placement of doors will reduce the length of routes. Avoid major traffic through an activity area, such as a kitchen work center. The activities of some families require many rooms, even if they are small; other families prefer fewer and larger rooms—commonly known as *open planning*. To sum up, provide convenient relationships between rooms, minimize traffic through rooms, and provide access to outdoor living areas if you want good traffic flow in your plan (Fig. 6-49).

Good design begins with an identifiable entry. The front door to a residence should be easily located and inviting to both occupants and guests. Make the foyer or entrance hall a transitional space from the exterior to the interior. With minimum use of floor space, make the foyer large enough to remove outer garments and yet provide a sense of orientation for visitors. Place the coat closet near the front entrance and adjacent to the foyer. The foyer should set the architectural character for the home and serve as a space from which other areas of the home are accessible (Fig. 6-50).

All homes need private and common spaces. Bedrooms and bathrooms, for example, are private spaces. Living rooms, dining rooms, and kitchens are common spaces. A good plan respects the needs of the occupants by recognizing the need for common space and private space. Clearly defined circulation between the areas of a home is most important.

Common Spaces Should Be Accessible from the foyer, since all the occupants of the home and many visitors will use them. It is desirable to move from the

foyer into a living room or family room (Fig. 6-51). Larger homes may have both a living and a family room. Living rooms are generally more formal in style and are frequently used for entertaining guests. The living room is usually located in the front of the house with windows facing the street. The size of the living room can be determined by the furnishings. A sofa, several lounge chairs, end tables for lamps, a coffee table, and bookcase are usual furnishings that must be accommodated into the layout. The shape of the room must be considered as well so that conversation groups can be arranged with as much flexibility as possible (Fig. 6-52).

A family room is a common space where members of a family gather for entertainment, reading, and conversing. Most family rooms are places for relaxation. The furnishings are usually casual, consisting of a sofa, lounge chairs, coffee table, end tables, lamps, bookcases, entertainment centers, and game tables (Fig. 6-53). Placing the family room at the rear of the house with pleasant views and circulation to the exterior is desirable. The kitchen and dining space should be accessible to the family room (Fig. 6-54).

Bedrooms are Private Spaces which are generally occupied by one or two people. North, east, or south exposures are mainly desirable for bedrooms. The occupant of a bedroom may have a preference for orienta-

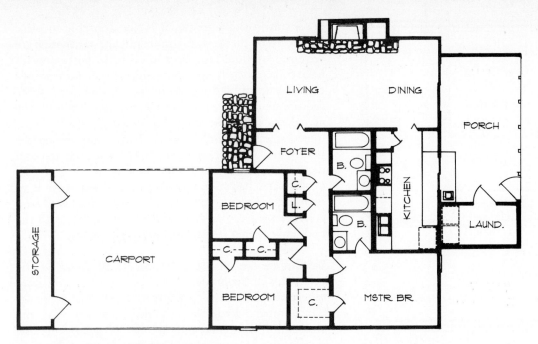

FIGURE 6-51 Living room/family room.

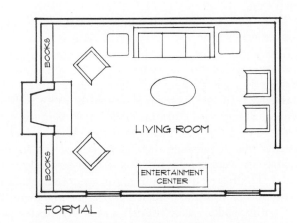

FORMAL

FIGURE 6-52 Placing furnishings in the living room.

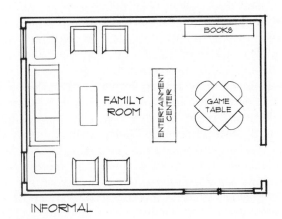

INFORMAL

FIGURE 6-53 An efficient family room.

FLOOR PLAN

FIGURE 6-54 Family room, kitchen, dining relationship.

tion. Bedrooms on the north are usually cooler. The morning sun will brighten a bedroom with windows toward the east. A south exposure will allow the sun to warm the room during winter months. Due to high temperatures and direct solar radiation from the after-

Sec. 6.9   Plan the interior spaces to reflect the life-style of the occupants   **131**

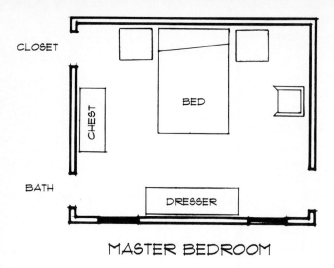

MASTER BEDROOM

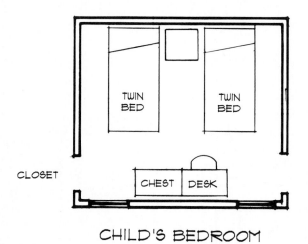

CHILD'S BEDROOM

FIGURE 6-55 Placing furniture in a bedroom.

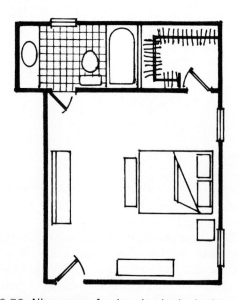

FIGURE 6-56 Allow space for dressing in the bedroom.

noon sun in the summer, it is not desirable to place bedrooms on the west. Natural light and ventilation are required by building codes in all bedrooms. Consult local codes to verify specific requirements. Furnishings can vary from bedroom to bedroom; therefore, space requirements vary. Be sure you are familiar with the actual sizes of twin beds, bunk beds, full-size beds, queen-size beds, and king-size beds before sizing the bedrooms. A chest, dresser, night tables, chairs, and desk are common bedroom furnishings (Fig. 6-55). Closets and bathrooms should be easily accessible to bedrooms. Provide suitable space near the closets for a convenient dressing area, and still have access to the bed and other major furnishings (Fig. 6-56).

Bathrooms are Essential for the Health Care of the occupants of the home. These spaces are private areas where the individual can practice personal hygiene. The number of bathrooms should be determined by the size of the residence and number of occupants. All homes should have one full-size bathroom with essential plumbing fixtures. Many residences have more than one bathroom and some have a half-bath or powder room. Two-story homes should have a bathroom on each floor.

Bathrooms in American homes are famous for their conveniences (Fig. 6-57). The half-bath usually has a lavatory and water closet. The full bath consisting of a lavatory, water closet, and tub can be economically arranged in a 8'-0" by 5'-0" space (Fig. 6-58). Put the standard 5' tub across the end so that the other fixtures will fit along one plumbing wall. A 4" vent stack is necessary in the wall near the water closet, which is usually placed between the other fixtures. To accommodate the vent stack, an 8" wet-wall is generally indicated. To shorten the plumbing runs, put baths back to back, and plan, if possible, a compact arrangement for the baths, sink, washer-dryer, and water heater (see Fig. 6-58). However, do not sacrifice a good plan for the extra cost of separating the baths or other plumbing.

Locate the doors in bathrooms to give maximum privacy and isolation. Often the bathroom door is left open, and direct views from living areas are undesirable. Minor rearrangements of bathroom positions in relation to halls usually eliminate this situation. Doors should swing into the bathroom (never into halls) without hitting bathroom fixtures. Use narrow doors; usually 2'-0" to 2'-6" widths are sufficient. By isolating the water closet or tub into compartments, the bathroom can be made useful to more than one person simultaneously. With children in a home, twin lavatories will reduce peak demands on the bathroom. Built-in lavatory cabinets (Fig. 6-59) will result in more storage space and allow countertop areas for grooming use. Large mirrors attached to the wall directly above the cabinets will further facilitate grooming and will also give the room a more spacious appearance. Do not

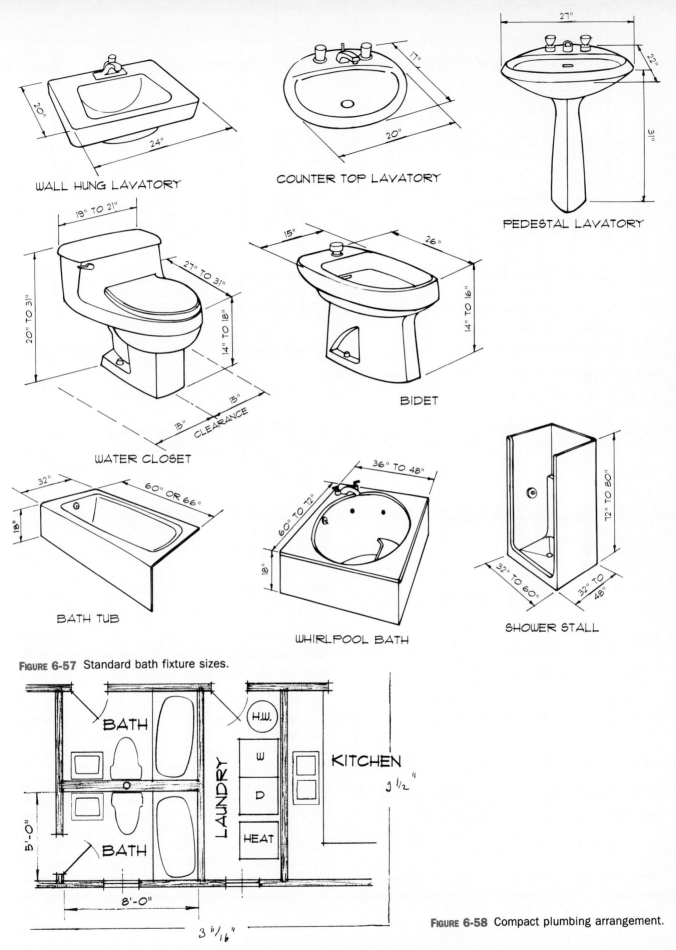

WALL HUNG LAVATORY

COUNTER TOP LAVATORY

PEDESTAL LAVATORY

WATER CLOSET

BIDET

BATH TUB

WHIRLPOOL BATH

SHOWER STALL

FIGURE 6-57 Standard bath fixture sizes.

BATH

H.W.

KITCHEN

LAUNDRY

W

D

HEAT

BATH

FIGURE 6-58 Compact plumbing arrangement.

Sec. 6.9   Plan the interior spaces to reflect the life-style of the occupants   **133**

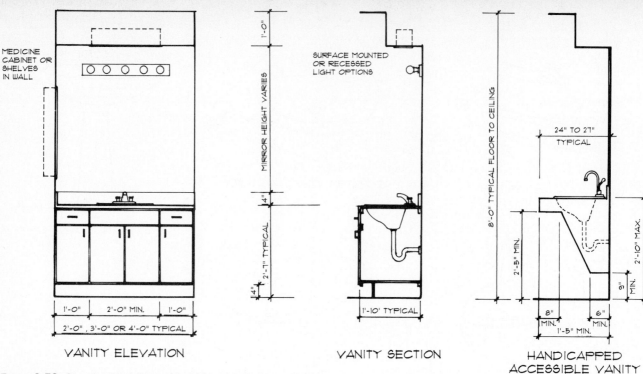

MEDICINE CABINET OR SHELVES IN WALL

1'-0"
MIRROR HEIGHT VARIES
4"
2'-7" TYPICAL
4"

1'-0" | 2'-0" MIN. | 1'-0"
2'-0", 3'-0" OR 4'-0" TYPICAL

VANITY ELEVATION

SURFACE MOUNTED OR RECESSED LIGHT OPTIONS

1'-10" TYPICAL

VANITY SECTION

8'-0" TYPICAL FLOOR TO CEILING

24" TO 27" TYPICAL

2'-5" MIN.
2'-10" MAX.
9" MIN.

8" MIN. | 6" MIN.
1'-5" MIN.

HANDICAPPED ACCESSIBLE VANITY

FIGURE 6-59 Standard heights and widths of bathroom vanities.

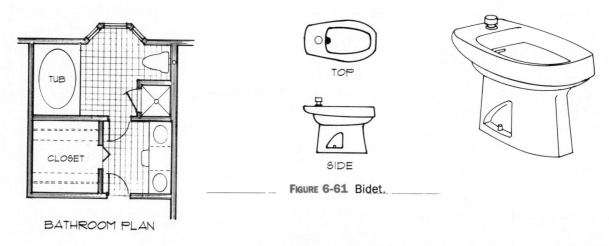

TUB

CLOSET

BATHROOM PLAN

TOP

SIDE

FIGURE 6-61 Bidet.

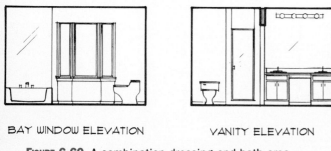

BAY WINDOW ELEVATION

VANITY ELEVATION

FIGURE 6-60 A combination dressing and bath area.

suites (see Fig. 6-60). Shower stalls are preferred by some people and require less floor space than tubs. A minimum shower should be 2'-6" × 2'-6". Tub and shower combinations are very popular. Versatility can be accommodated by the use of the tub or the shower in the same plumbing fixture. Luxury bathrooms may have both a tub and a separate shower stall. The whirlpool bath and exotic-shaped tub are common in many custom homes. The bidet, a plumbing fixture used in Europe for years, is now being manufactured in America and can be found in some modern bathrooms (Fig. 6-61). Ventilation is another important aspect of bathroom design. Forced-air exhaust fans are used in windowless bathrooms. Even bathrooms with windows should have an exhaust fan for more positive ventilation to the outside. Floors and wainscoting in bathrooms should be finished with durable, easily maintained materials that produce sanitary and pleasant interiors.

center medicine cabinets directly over the lavatory; use a mirror or a window above. Many master bedrooms have accessible private baths and adjacent dressing facilities (generous closets), resulting in complete master

Marble, tile, and vinyl are common flooring materials. Lighting should be soft and adequate, especially in front of mirrors.

Plan for Adequate Storage Space not only for clothes storage, but for the many items required in a modern home. Design the space to fit the items, provide it where it is needed, and make the storage easily accessible. Many types of modern closet-door units are available for built-in storage spaces. Sliding doors eliminate swinging space needed within a room, and full, 8' high closet doors provide maximum storage space above clothes rods. Walk-in closets are satisfactory if clothes rods can be installed along two long walls; otherwise, they are inefficient (see Fig. 6-62). Avoid a narrow closet with a door in the narrow end; the storage space has poor accessibility. Lining part of a carport or garage with 1/4" pegboard provides inexpensive storage for garden tools. Built-in cabinets installed above the hoods of stored cars make efficient use of otherwise wasted space. Diagonal areas below stairways can be devoted to storage. Often the attic can be utilized for dead storage by introducing a *scuttle* or disappearing stair unit in a convenient hall ceiling. If a basement is planned, a considerable amount of its space can be reserved for storage. However, according to experts, in most cases basement storage space is more expensive than aboveground storage space. The average home must provide storage for the following items (excluding kitchen equipment): clothes, linens, cleaning equipment, toys, hobby and sports equipment, sewing needs, guests' coats, tools, and lawn and garden equipment. Well-designed storage units make for a better organized home and thereby help to simplify housekeeping.

Plan a Functional Kitchen People who cook spend much time in the kitchen, planning meals, storing food, cooking and serving, and cleaning after meals. The kitchen should, first of all, be easy to work in, conveniently located, and pleasant in appearance to make these tasks no more difficult than necessary. Unlike furniture, kitchen cabinets and appliances are permanently installed and cannot be rearranged by merely pushing them about to rectify planning errors. Kitchens can be placed at the front of the house, to be close to the garage and front door; or they can be placed in the back, to be accessible to outdoor eating and play areas. Kitchens serve various purposes besides food preparation; many are designed to furnish room for snacking and informal meals. Others incorporate informal living and play areas for children. Some are even combined with entertainment centers. Many individuals, on the other hand, prefer a completely independent kitchen that can be closed off from other areas when cooking and eating are completed.

The layout of the actual work center of the kitchen deserves careful attention. The basic activity of this area is largely controlled by the placement of the sink, the cooking unit, and the refrigerator. If we were to connect these three major appliances with a triangle on the plan, it would represent the bulk of the travel within

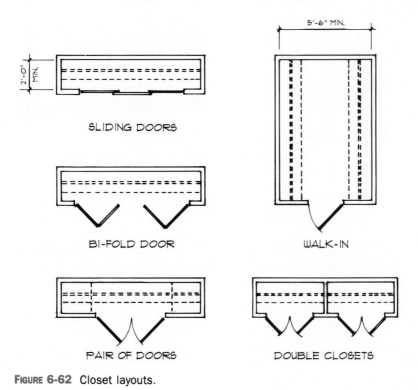

SLIDING DOORS

BI-FOLD DOOR

PAIR OF DOORS

5'-6" MIN.

WALK-IN

DOUBLE CLOSETS

FIGURE 6-62 Closet layouts.

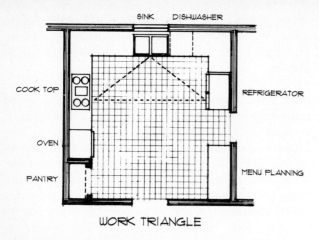

FIGURE 6-63 The efficiency of a kitchen depends on the size of the work triangle.

the kitchen and is known as the *work triangle* (see Fig. 6-63). Keep the perimeter of this triangle from 12′ to 20′ in length if you want an efficient kitchen; if it becomes longer, a rearrangement of the basic appliances should be made. Check manufacturers' literature for the actual size of the appliances to be included in your kitchen (to be sure they fit) before progressing too far with the planning of the cabinets and other features. According to the arrangement of the cabinets and appliances, kitchens can be made in these basic shapes: U shape, L shape, two-wall or corridor type, and the modest one-wall type (see Fig. 6-64). Tests have shown the U shape to be the most efficient. Occasionally, a peninsula or island cabinet is incorporated into the L shape or U shape to isolate the work center or to utilize excessive space within large kitchen areas. The ideal arrangement is to have the major appliances efficiently placed with continuous cabinets between and sufficient countertop space on each side of the appliances for satisfactory work surfaces (see Fig. 6-65). Whether or not the kitchen is used for eating, countertop surface must be provided for many activities: menu planning, actual food preparation (mixing, chopping, and so on), cooking, serving, and cleaning up. These countertops should be surfaced with heatproof, easy-to-clean material. Through traffic should bypass the kitchen work center to avoid interference with the preparation of meals. Provide maximum kitchen storage with both base cabinets and wall cabinets where possible (see Fig. 6-66). Run wall cabinets to the top of the standard 8′ high wall, and use the top 14″ for dead storage. Allow at least 40 square feet of shelf space for general kitchen storage, with an additional 6 square feet for each person living in the home. In U-shaped and two-wall types of kitchens, allow between 4′ and 6′ of floor space between faces of opposite cabinets. Various modifications of the basic arrangements can be made to create interest and to utilize the kitchen space effectively without destroying the function of the work center.

Water vapor, cooking odors, and heat should be con-

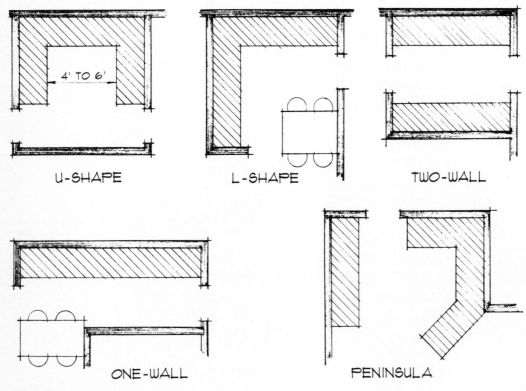

FIGURE 6-64 Basic kitchen layouts.

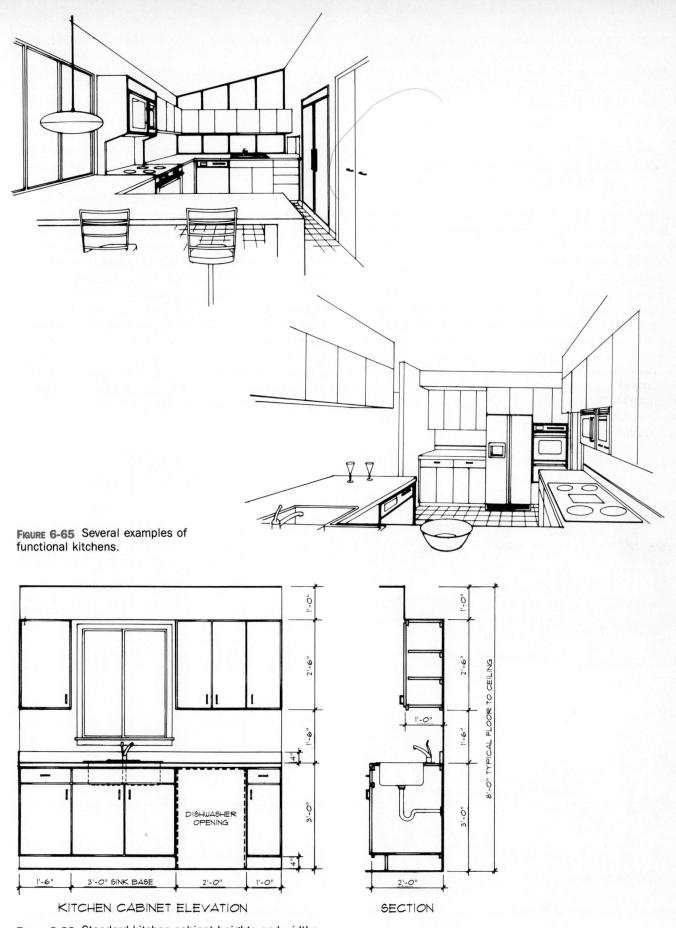

FIGURE 6-65 Several examples of functional kitchens.

1'-0"

2'-6"

1'-6"

4"

3'-0"

4"

1'-0"

1'-0"

2'-6"

1'-6"

8'-0" TYPICAL FLOOR TO CEILING

3'-0"

DISHWASHER OPENING

1'-6"   3'-0" SINK BASE   2'-0"   1'-0"

2'-0"

KITCHEN CABINET ELEVATION

SECTION

FIGURE 6-66 Standard kitchen cabinet heights and widths.

trolled in a modern kitchen with the use of an exhaust fan. Such fans are especially important in open-plan kitchens. Range hoods usually incorporate quiet-running fans for the rapid disposal of the undesirable side effects of food preparation.

6.10 Make the Elevations Express the Spirit of the Interior

The exterior of a house should evolve from the requirements of the inside; if a formal interior is planned, the exterior should reflect it; if the interior is informal, the exterior should create an impression of freedom and casual living. Traditional exteriors are usually based on the use of symmetry: identical features on both sides of a vertical center line, resulting in positive balance (see Fig. 6-67A). Informality is gained by combining areas and features of dissimilar size and placement, unrestricted by identical balance, to produce a different type of visual balance (see Fig. 6-67B). Either type should create a sense of tranquility. Both can be in good taste if they provide interest without too much busy "makeup" and if they reflect simplicity without being austere.

Unity, harmony, scale, balance, emphasis, and focal point are all essential elements of a pleasing design. Unity and harmony can be achieved by careful placement of repetitive elements such as windows. Scale relates one object to another relative to size and must be a major design consideration. All architecture should be sensitive to the human scale. Doors, steps, ceiling heights, furniture, and counters are elements that are designed around the scale of the human figure. Scale is also important in the proportions of the exterior and interior elements of the house. A column's diameter in relation to its height is an element of scale (Fig. 6-68). Awkward proportions should be avoided in design. Emphasis can be achieved by contrasting colors, shades, and tones and by contrasting geometric shapes. All pleasing houses should have a focal point on the exterior and interior. A portico, entrance door, or steps can serve as a focal point on the facade. A fireplace, entertainment center, stairs, or cabinets can create a focal point in interior space. It is important that the unity, harmony, scale, balance, emphasis, and focal point be considered in designing a home.

A

B

FIGURE 6-67 Formal and informal elevations.

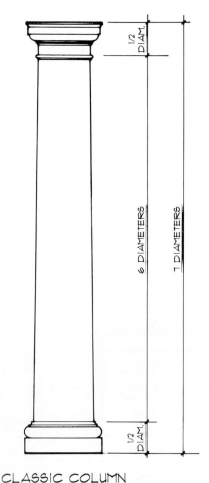

CLASSIC COLUMN

FIGURE 6-68 Elements of scale.

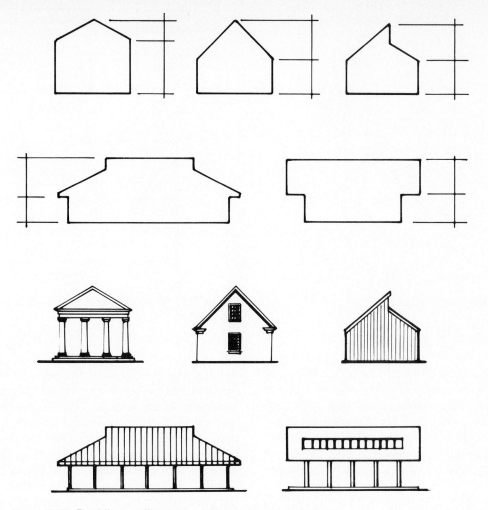

Figure 6-69 Providing a silhouette with pleasing proportions.

Consider the Basic Structural Masses Give them good proportions and pleasing visual shapes (Fig. 6-69). Unless its general form and silhouette are good, no amount of texture or ornament can improve a structure. Avoid extreme deviations from accepted building forms unless you are creative enough to start a new trend in architecture. Traditional shapes of the past have lived because their general proportions have been pleasing. Avoid awkward proportions.

Keep Important Roof Lines Simple Overly complex roofs not only look awkward, but they can also be expensive to build. A roof pitch must be proportional and related to the style and character of the building. Compare the height of exterior walls with the height of the roof. If the structure is L shape or T shape, make the wings the same width, if possible, so that the roof ridge line will be unified. If one wing must be narrower, be sure the narrow span roof is received against the larger span (Fig. 6-70). Consistency of roof pitch and type is important. When a roof pitch is selected, it is advisable to design all roof slopes on the building with the same

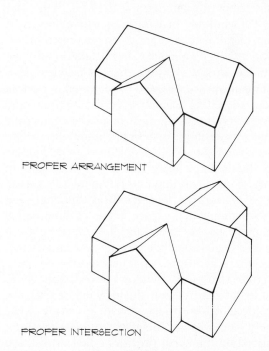

PROPER ARRANGEMENT

PROPER INTERSECTION

Figure 6-70 Arranging smaller gable roofs against larger ones.

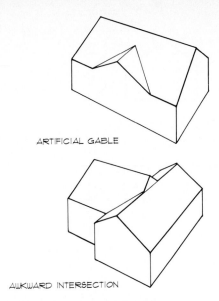

ARTIFICIAL GABLE

AWKWARD INTERSECTION

Figure 6-71 Avoiding artificial gables.

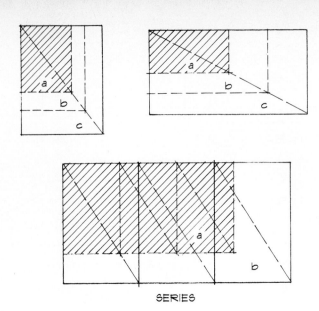

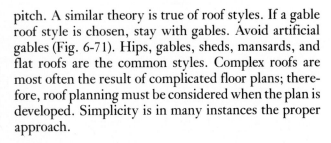

SERIES

Figure 6-72 Graphic method of arriving at similar window proportions.

pitch. A similar theory is true of roof styles. If a gable roof style is chosen, stay with gables. Avoid artificial gables (Fig. 6-71). Hips, gables, sheds, mansards, and flat roofs are the common styles. Complex roofs are most often the result of complicated floor plans; therefore, roof planning must be considered when the plan is developed. Simplicity is in many instances the proper approach.

Select Windows According to the Room Requirements
Room use, ventilation, and site orientation are the most important factors in determining the size, type, and placement of windows. In living areas where the view is important, windows can be large—to the floor if necessary. Incidentally, do not make the mistake of putting a large window in a wall where there is no view. Few pieces of furniture are designed to be placed in front of large floor to ceiling windows. In dining areas and bedrooms where furniture must be placed against the wall, it may be desirable to design windowsills 3'-0" to 4'-0" above the floor. Windows planned above kitchen cabinets should be at least 3'-8" above the floor. In baths, where privacy is important, windowsills should be at least 4'-0" from the floor. Windows admit light and induce ventilation into the space. Light for illumination of the interior space is important. Too much light can create excessive glare or admit too much solar radiation. In the northern hemisphere the best location for windows is on the south wall. Windows placed on the south allow sunlight to enter a room during winter months. A properly designed horizontal eave or overhang above the same window shades the glass from summer sun. Glass placed on the north provides excellent diffused light for reading but is an energy drain during the

winter. Minimize glass on the east and west or provide sun control devices such as blinds to regulate unwanted sunlight. Many windows can be opened to provide natural ventilation. In warm climates, large windows that allow plenty of air circulation are desirable. In cold climates, small windows may be sufficient to adequately ventilate a space. A study of the prevailing summer and winter breezes is desirable. Windows can be oriented to maximize the effect of natural ventilation.

Coordinate the Window Sizes and Types   Almost every house requires windows of different sizes, yet good fenestration (placement and sizing of window openings) will unify the exterior if you select window sizes of similar proportions. Use the graphic method of drawing a diagonal through one of the selected window shapes to find the correct proportions of the other windows (see Fig. 6-72). Today's wide range of window sizes and styles permits almost unlimited freedom in correct window coordination. Double-hung windows with small lights are typical of traditional exteriors; large window-walls are typical of contemporary exteriors. Line up the heads of windows and doors on the elevations. When making preliminary sketches, consider the appearance of the wall areas around window openings, as well as the windows themselves. If these shapes are not pleasing, or if the wall areas fail to produce the desired character, consider moving the windows one way or another without restricting their effectiveness from the interior. Avoid windows so close together or so near to exterior corners as to create extremely narrow interjacent wall areas (Fig. 6-73A and B). These areas appear unstable, especially if the wall is

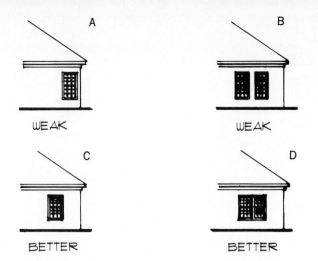

FIGURE 6-73 Placement of windows.

masonry. Bring the windows together by joining them with a narrow mullion, or place a unifying panel between the windows, or spread the windows farther apart (see Fig. 6-73C and D).

Select an Appropriate Front Door Style (as well as the other exterior doors), in keeping with the style of the house, and give this door the prominence it deserves. The treatment of the front entrance in traditional styles of the past has been highly ornamental. In present versions of these styles various adaptations of the *panel door*, with or without lights, are appropriate. Other-

wise, the *flush door*, painted or with natural wood finish, is the best selection for most contemporary entrances. If the front hall needs natural light, sash doors should be used, or side lights can be installed along the door frame (see Fig. 11-13). As a safety measure, it is advisable to place some type of small window in or near the front entrance so that the homeowner can identify callers before admitting them. Many types of *sliding glass doors*, framed in wood or metal, are available for easy access to outdoor living areas. To prevent serious accidents, sliding glass doors should be installed with tempered glass, or protection bars across the doors should be used. Refer to manufacturers' catalogues for details and availability of the various doors before you indicate the selection in your planning.

Keep Details in Scale Many of the details found on large traditional homes will not be successful on a small home. A suitable cornice detail is especially important (see Fig. 6-74).

Relate the Four Elevations by carrying out a repeating, interesting theme. Let some of the structural members be exposed, if appropriate, to contribute rhythmic enrichment. One exterior material should dominate, both in texture and color; use few additional materials. Especially avoid the pretentious use of too many contrasting materials on the front and only plain materials on the sides and rear. Design all four sides. Above all, select materials for the exterior that require minimum maintenance throughout the years.

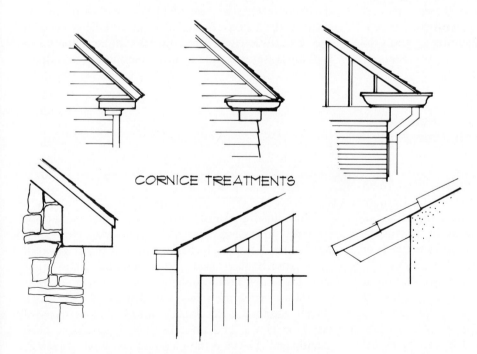

CORNICE TREATMENTS

FIGURE 6-74 Cornice treatments should be consistent with the character of the elevations.

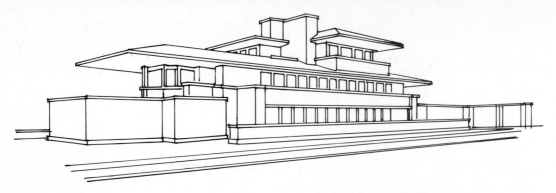

FIGURE 6-75 Accent horizontal lines if the house is to blend with the land.

Accent Horizontal Lines if you want the house to appear lower and longer. A lofty appearance is usually not pleasing. Wide overhangs of the roof and wall extensions from the house produce protected areas and help integrate the house to the land (see Fig. 6-75).

Make the Chimney Massive if you want this important design element to contribute character to the structure.

Remember that Much of the Value of a House is Created by the Design If the design is simple and in good taste, the house will continue to be desirable for many years.

Study the Prizewinning Residential Designs in leading architectural journals and home magazines. See if you can determine why prominent architects and home specialists have chosen these over other designs and what makes a house, whether large or small, exceptional and appealing. This understanding should provide you with one of the important requirements of successful planning—good taste.

6.11 Combine Exterior Design Elements that are in Keeping With Accepted Home Styles

Study the following home photographs (Figs. 6-76 through 6-90) for their identification with a definite style. Like our culture, home styles have their roots in many other countries. Each style, however, because of local climate, materials, topography, and the needs of individuals, is strictly American in development.

Colonial styles have survived because they are honest houses, usually unpretentious and simple, yet having pleasing architectural features. Many were passed on to descendants after having given each generation a lifetime of enjoyment. Houses erected in early colonial days in New England were built by carpenters and masons skilled in traditions of England, the Netherlands, and Germany. The styles in Louisiana were influenced by the French and in Florida, California, and Texas by the Spaniards, and some areas give evidence of oriental influences.

It can be said that many of the most admirable American homes were built 150 to 200 years ago; some are still in use. The value of these early houses lies in the degree to which they were copied as the population spread.

Today, very few houses exist that are pure examples of any one architectural style. All vary in proportion, window fenestration, or decorative treatment. These variations, however, give each house individuality and tend to show the stamp of a particular architect. But many retain enough features to allow us to make positive identification of their basic style. This is important—a well-designed home should give evidence of a definite styling, and you should be able to recognize those characteristics that identify it with a particular style. Today's home designer would be wise to keep an eye on tradition while focusing on the new materials and innovations available in contemporary building.

EXERCISES

The following planning exercises should first be done freehand on tracing paper or $1/8''$ coordinate paper. After you have gathered site data and various residential ideas from books, magazines, newspapers, and other sources, develop the problems as indicated in Chapter 5, under sketching plans and elevations. The plan sketch cannot be developed entirely before trials of elevation views, and possibly floor levels, have been established. Develop the plan and elevations together; do not be discouraged if numerous sketches are needed or if completely different approaches to the problem are necessary before a workable layout is finally attained.

FIGURE 6-76 Colonial saltbox styling. (*Hedrich-Blessing Photos.*)

FIGURE 6-77 New England colonial styling. (*Hedrich-Blessing Photos.*)

FIGURE 6-78 Cape Cod styling. (*Hedrich-Blessing Photos.*)

FIGURE 6-79 Regency styling. (*Hedrich-Blessing Photos.*)

FIGURE 6-80 Dutch colonial styling. (*Hedrich-Blessing Photos.*)

FIGURE 6-81 Southern colonial styling. (*Hedrich-Blessing Photos.*)

FIGURE 6-82 Ranch house styling. (*Hedrich-Blessing Photos.*)

FIGURE 6-83 French provincial styling.

FIGURE **6-84** Garrison styling. (*Hedrich-Blessing Photos.*)

FIGURE **6-85** English half-timber styling.

FIGURE **6-86** Contemporary styling. (*Frank Venning Photo.*)

FIGURE 6-87 Early adobe houses in the southwest.

FIGURE 6-88 Sketch of Spanish styling.

FIGURE 6-89 Williamsburg styling.

FIGURE 6-90 Contemporary styling.

1. Using the plat plan and topographic survey shown in Fig. 6-91, prepare a site analysis showing a separate drawing for each of the seven site considerations described in Section 6.4. Lay out the plat, double size, on 8½″ × 11″ paper using ink or felt-tip pens. Assume the property is in your hometown.

2. Using the plat plan and topographic survey shown in Fig. 6-92, prepare a comprehensive site analysis. Using 11″ × 17″ paper, draw the plan four times larger than the illustration with ink or felt-tip pens. Two drawings will be required to illustrate the comprehensive site analysis. One drawing should depict slope, drainage, climate, prevailing winds, and solar orientation. The other drawing should show vegetation, natural features, circulation, views, noise, zoning, and setbacks. Assume the property is located in the town where you are studying architectural drawing.

3. Prepare zone diagrams for a residence with the following space requirements:
    a. Living room
    b. Dining room
    c. Kitchen
    d. Family room
    e. Powder room
    f. Three bedrooms
    g. Two baths
    h. Two car garage

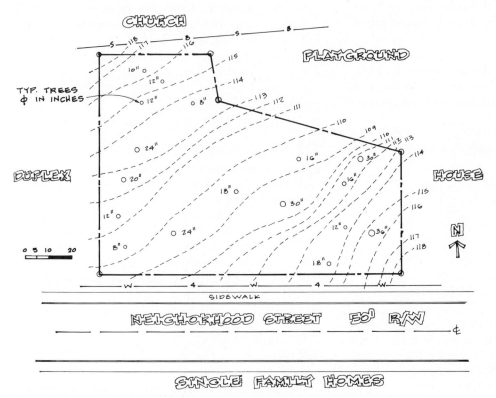

FIGURE 6-91 Plat plan and topographic survey for exercise 1.

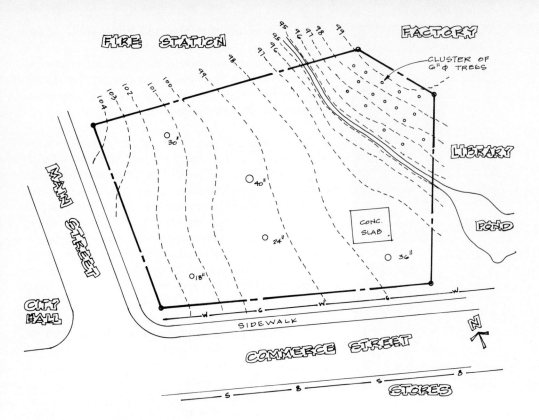

Figure 6-92 Plat plan and topographic survey for exercise 2.

4. Using the program and zone diagram from Exercise 3, prepare bubble diagrams for the same residence.

5. Prepare a freehand schematic plan of a residence using the spaces listed below for the site that you analyzed in Exercise 2. Use zone and bubble diagrams.
    a. Foyer
    b. Living room
    c. Dining room
    d. Breakfast room
    e. Kitchen
    f. Fitness room
    g. Powder room
    h. Two bedrooms
    i. Two bathrooms
    j. Library
    k. Workshop
    l. Two-car garage

6. Plan a *small beach house* for a young couple with a small daughter. The beach house should have minimum accommodations yet a festive spirit for vacation and weekend living. Provide for the following:
    a. Lot size: 65′ ocean front, 200′ deep
    b. 700-sq ft floor space, contemporary design
    c. Large living, dining, kitchen combination area with small kitchen utility unit behind folding doors
    d. Set house on preserved wooden piers to prevent damage from high water
    e. One easily accessible bath with shower
    f. Two sleeping rooms
    g. Fireplace, redwood exterior

7. Plan a bachelor's *retreat house*. The occupant to be is a young professor who requires space for books and study and space for occasional entertaining of large groups. Provide for the following:
    a. Lot size: 100′ × 185′, level and wooded
    b. 1500-sq ft floor space, plank-and-beam construction
    c. Master bedroom and guest bedroom
    d. Large living-dining room, modest kitchen
    e. One full bath
    f. Carport for one car, outdoor terrace area

8. Plan a *home for a young family* with one child. They are interested in a 1-story, colonial-type house with the following specifications:
    a. Lot size: 100′ × 200′, the lot slopes downward 10′ from the left to the right side

b. 1800-sq ft maximum floor space

c. Kitchen near family room with guest accommodations

d. Two bedrooms, 1½ baths

e. Full basement to be partially used as garage for one car

f. Provision for outdoor play area with supervision possible from kitchen

g. Brick-veneer construction with gable roof

9. Plan a *medium-priced home* for a family with two children, a boy and a girl. The clients indicate a preference for a ranch house on one level, with the following requirements:

a. Lot size: 150′ × 225′, with wooded view in rear

b. 2000-sq ft maximum floor space, exclusive of double carport

c. Two full baths, one to be private for master bedroom

d. Three bedrooms, separate dining room, family room, living room, kitchen, and utility area

e. Outdoor living area, rear entrance mud room

f. Adequate storage space

10. Plan a *traditional 2-story home* for a family of five (two boys and one girl), with the following specifications:

a. Lot size: 100′ × 175′

b. 2200-sq ft floor space plus double garage

c. Kitchen, dining room, entrance hall, powder room, and large living room on first floor (concrete slab-on-grade)

d. Three bedrooms and double bath on second floor

e. Outdoor terrace off living room with brick fireplace

f. Stone and/or wood exterior

g. Traditional-styled front entrance

11. Plan a *split-level* for a family of four (two teenage daughters). Provide the following:

a. Lot size: 125′ × 185′, rolling and wooded

b. 2000-sq ft floor space plus double carport

c. Separate dining and living room, three bedrooms, two full baths

d. Utility and laundry area

e. Large recreation room with fireplace and access to outdoor living area

f. Brick-veneer and board-and-batten exterior

12. Plan a modest *duplex for elderly people.* Two retired couples are interested in homes that will be easy to maintain and convenient to live in. They specify the following:

a. Lot size: 90′ × 200′, provision for gardening

b. 1000-sq ft in each unit

c. Frame construction, masonry party wall between units

d. Adequate storage, guest space, carport for one car for each unit

REVIEW QUESTIONS

1. Why is it important to use a planning checklist?

2. What is meant by an *easement?*

3. Do contour lines crossing a small stream point upstream or downstream?

4. Why is a southern exposure generally the most satisfactory direction in solar orienting a window-wall?

5. Which part of a home should have the most isolation and quiet?

6. What geometric shape is the most economical for a basic plan?

7. Evaluate the *traffic flow* in your own home from the standpoint of convenience.

8. What is the maximum length of a satisfactory kitchen *work triangle?*

9. Define the word *fenestration.*

10. Why are simple, uncomplicated exteriors usually the most pleasing?

LIGHT CONSTRUCTION PRINCIPLES

"Ah, to build, to build. That is the noblest art of all the arts."

—LONGFELLOW

This chapter introduces and explains many of the accepted principles and methods of light construction found in residences and small commercial buildings. The written material is supplemented with typical sections taken through walls, floors, roofs, and structural members. Pictorial drawings are also used when necessary to present this information as simply as possible. Some of the methods shown are adaptable to one area of the country; others are common construction practice in other areas, depending on building codes and local conditions. Some methods are conventional practice, having been in use for years; others are comparatively new. Together, they form details widely used and generally found satisfactory. More exhaustive treatments of construction details can be found in specialized texts to supplement this material. The actual drawing of details is treated later, but design drawing should not be attempted until a thorough study of construction methods has been made.

7.1 Developing a Background in Light Construction Methods

At this point in their training, students should acquire as much information and background relative to construction as they can find from various sources. Architecture, whether it is pursued by people who create and design the most elaborate structures or by others called on to draw the various working drawings of the simplest buildings, requires a searching interest and enthusiasm about the methods of building. To be successful in this field not only requires skill in knowing *how to draw*, but, equally important, requires the acquisition of background information in knowing *what to draw*. Unless drafters continually strive to increase their knowledge

of construction details, they can expect to become no more than junior drafters or merely tracers.

Technical courses in architectural print reading, building materials, and construction methods, which in technical schools often precede or are prerequisites to architectural drawing, provide this needed background. Monthly periodicals and trade magazines containing current and up to date information should be continually read by students and drafters. Literature from the many building construction trade organizations will be found valuable. Various governmental agencies concerned with housing and standardized construction practice, as well as the U.S. Government Printing Office, offer inexpensive manuals that should not be overlooked. Drafters must become familiar with *Sweet's Architectural Catalog File* (F. W. Dodge Corp., New York) for convenient reference on many construction materials. Many good books on construction are available in libraries.

Part-time employment with builders or contractors, as an adjunct to drafting training, is desirable for learning construction methods. In fact, actual on the job observation of a building in the process of construction is time well spent by drafters. Not only is it a thrilling experience, but it offers the opportunity of seeing many of the building materials in use and how they are put together within the building—mainly the structural members that are often concealed once the building is completed. Students who have familiarized themselves with the methods and techniques of construction will certainly be better equipped to draw more intelligently, progress more rapidly, and grow in stature as architectural drafters.

No attempt has been made to treat special situations requiring structural engineering design to solve the problems. Such information, which is beyond the scope of this book, is left to specialized texts.

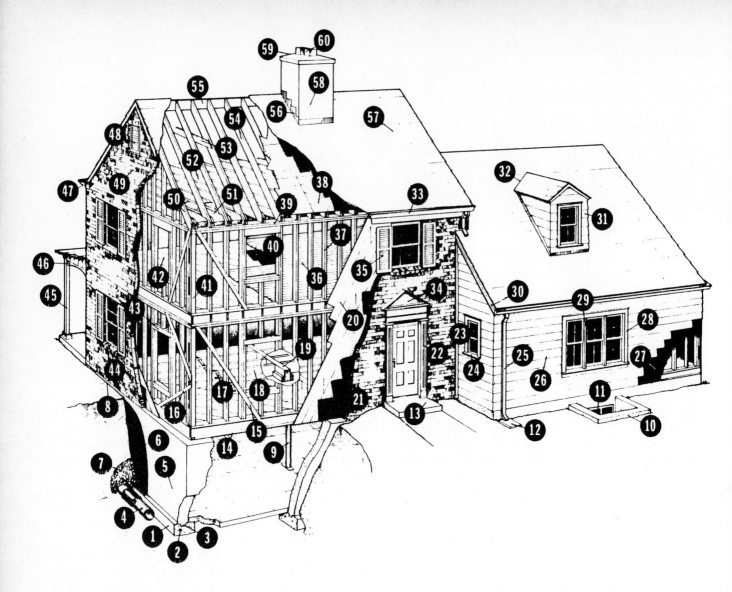

1. Footing	21. Building paper	41. Corner post
2. Reinforcing rod	22. Trim pilaster	42. Subfloor
3. Keyway	23. Double-hung window	43. Lintel; header
4. Drain tile	24. Window sill	44. Brick sill
5. Foundation wall	25. Downspout; leader	45. Porch post
6. Waterproofing	26. Bevel siding	46. Porch frieze board
7. Gravel fill	27. Fiberboard sheathing	47. Return cornice
8. Grade line	28. Window trim	48. Louver
9. Metal column	29. Mullion	49. Brick veneer; gable
10. Areaway wall	30. Rake mold	50. End rafter
11. Basement window	31. Dormer	51. Insulation
12. Splash block	32. Valley	52. Ceiling joist
13. Stoop	33. Gutter	53. Collar beam
14. Sill plate	34. Pediment door trim	54. Common rafter
15. Corner brace	35. Shutter	55. Ridge board
16. Knee brace	36. Finish flooring	56. Flashing
17. Bridging	37. Stud	57. Shingles
18. Floor joist	38. Roof decking	58. Chimney
19. Beam; girder	39. Double top plate	59. Cement wash; cap
20. Sheathing	40. Flooring paper	60. Chimney flues; pots

FIGURE 7-1 Typical residential terms.

7.2 Construction Terminology

Figure 7-1 is a guide to the terms found in light construction. Students should memorize these terms and know where they apply within a typical building. Definitions of other terms, which may be unfamiliar, can be found in the Glossary of Construction Terms in Appendix A. Students will occasionally encounter several designations for similar features in construction terminology because workers frequently use terms that are indigenous to their particular region; elsewhere the terms might have quite different applications. Despite widespread national distribution of building construction products, terminology has not been entirely standardized; but as students continue to improve their vocabulary and construction background, the ambiguities will become less confusing.

Some of the present terms used in residential construction, especially in wood framing, have been handed down from New England colonial history. For example, collar beam, soleplate, and ridge pole. Some terms have come from the ancient Greek civilization, especially terms relative to classic building exteriors, such as frieze, plinth, and dentils. Other parts derive their names from their physical shapes. For instance, the box sill, which has a boxed-in characteristic, the K brace, which has the shape of the letter K, and the T post, which resembles the letter T when shown in cross section, are just a few of the terms that are so labeled because of their shape. Most of the terms, however, have been derived from the logical use or placement of the part in relation to the building, for example, footing, foundation, baseboard, shoemold, and doorstop.

Girders, beams, and joists are terms given to horizontal structural members used in buildings. Often the heavy, structural support for the floor framing in light construction is referred to as either a girder or a beam.

In more complex construction, however, the heaviest members are referred to as girders. They support the beams, which are of intermediate weight, and which support the joists, the lightest members of the floor or roof structure.

7.3 Footings and Foundations

Every properly constructed building must be supported by an appropriate foundation, which will support the weight of the building and sustain the structure throughout all weather conditions to which it may be subjected. The *footing*, the enlarged base of the foundation wall, must be massive enough, depending on local soil conditions, to distribute the weight of the building to the ground below, and it must be deep enough to prevent frost action below. Poured concrete is usually the best and most widely used material. Footings can be formed and poured where soils are stable enough to hold their shape; trenches are dug the proper depth and concrete poured directly into the trenches to form adequate footings. See Fig. 7-2 for the method of laying out footings and foundation walls. Leveled batter boards are used to lay out the foundation of a building. Wooden stakes are driven into the soil several feet outside the corners of the proposed building. The top of the batter board is positioned at the finished floor elevation of the building. The batter board is then securely nailed to the wooden stakes. A taut string line that locates the exterior wall of the building and foundation is run between batter boards (see Fig. 7-2).

Frost action below the footing would raise and lower the building during freezing and thawing and soon fracture the foundation, as well as disrupt other parts of the building. Naturally, frost lines vary throughout the country; local building codes usually indicate the depth

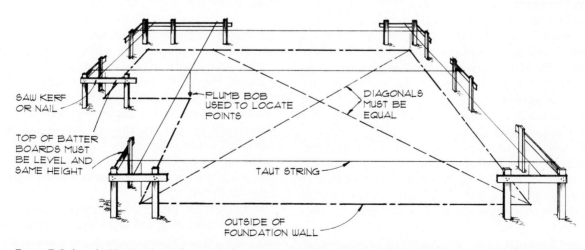

FIGURE 7-2 Leveled batter boards are used to lay out the foundation of a building.

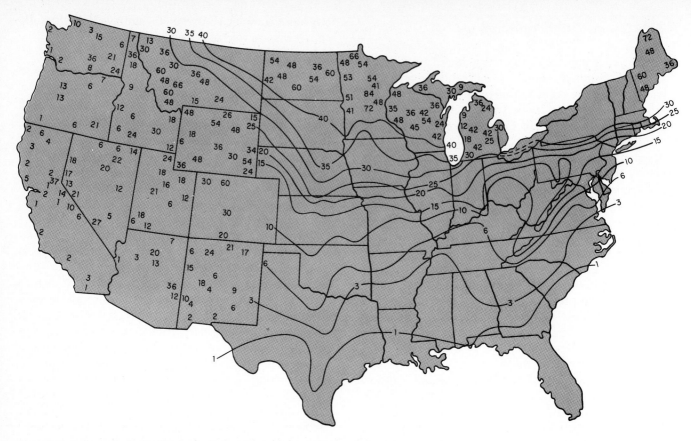

FIGURE 7-3 Average frost depths in inches throughout the United States.

to which footings must be placed below grade. Figure 7-3 shows average frost depths throughout the country compiled by the U.S. Weather Service. The *National Building Code* prescribes footings to be placed a minimum of 1'-0" below the frost line. Footings of buildings with basements are deep enough so that frost lines usually need not be considered. In northern areas, the cost of excavating for deep footings often makes the basement more economical than in southern areas, where footings are often merely trench footings several feet below grade.

Footings should also be placed on undisturbed soil; occasionally, if a building must be put over a fill, the soil should be well compacted and sufficient steel reinforcing should be in the footing to prevent cracking (see Fig. 7-6). Local codes in some areas require steel reinforcing in the footings to counteract specific conditions (Florida Hurricane Code, California Seismic Code). However, a good rule of thumb is that in firm soil, using light frame construction, the footing can be made twice as wide and the same depth or thickness as the width of the foundation wall (see Fig. 7-4A). Footings should project at least 4" beyond each side of a normal foundation wall and be centered below the wall for balance.

Stepped Footings are often required on sloping or steep lots where straight horizontal footings would be uneconomical (Fig. 7-5). The bottom of the footing is always placed on undisturbed soil and below the frost line, and horizontal runs should be level. The vertical rises of the footings are usually the same thickness as the horizontal portion and are poured at the same time. The vertical distance between steps should not exceed 2'; if concrete masonry units (C.M.U.) are used for the foundation wall, the vertical height of each step should be compatible with the unit height of the C.M.U. Horizontal lengths for the steps are usually not less than 3'.

Column or Post Footings are required to carry concentrated loads within the building. Usually, they are square with a pedestal on which the column or post will bear (see Fig. 7-4E). A steel pin is usually inserted into the pedestal if a wooden column is to be used. The footing will vary in size, depending on the load-bearing capacity of the soil and the load it will have to carry. Ordinary column footings for small residences might be 24" square by 12" deep, which would support 16,000 pounds if the soil-bearing capacity were 4000 lb/sq ft (see Table 7-1).

Footings for chimneys, fireplaces, and the like, should be poured at the same time as other footings, and they should be large enough to support the weights they will have to carry. Total weights of different types

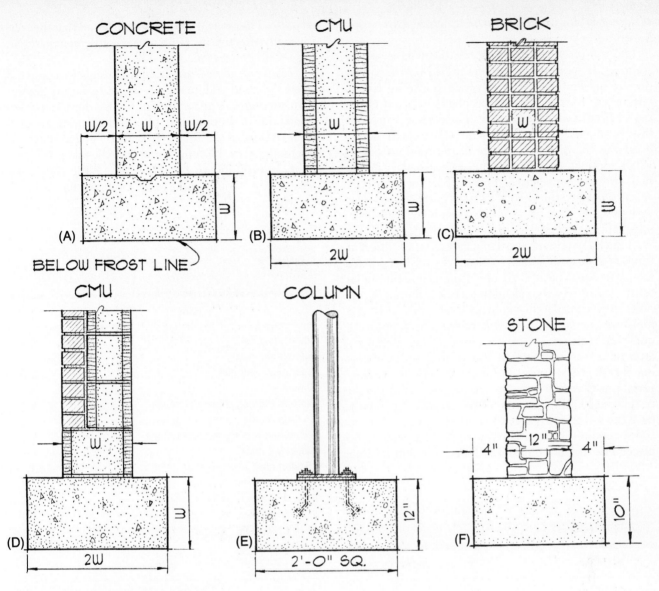

FIGURE 7-4 Footings for light construction.

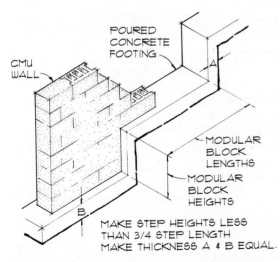

FIGURE 7-5 Stepped footings. Check local codes for various restrictions.

TABLE 7-1
Soil load-bearing qualities

	Safe load	
Type of soil	(tons/sq ft)	(lb/sq ft)
Soft clay, loam	1	2,000
Dry, firm sand, or clay	2	4,000
Compact, coarse sand	3	6,000
Coarse gravel	4	8,000
Hard pan or hard shale	10	20,000
Solid rock	No limit	

of masonry construction can be calculated by using Table 7-2.

The soil on which footings rest must be level and compact. In weak soils in which the load-bearing qualities are questionable, it is advisable to introduce steel reinforcing rods at intersecting points between chimney or fireplace footings and wall footings. In soft soils this is advisable also at corners, offsets, and where breaks in the direction or size of the footings occur. When footings are subjected to heavier loads, calculations should be made to determine their correct size in order to balance the various footings in relation to their various loads. The first consideration is the load-bearing qualities of the soil on which the footings rest. Table 7-1 indicates typical supporting capacities of different types of soil conditions in tons and pounds per square foot. The soil capacities are only general and cannot be relied on entirely for calculating critical footing sizes. Soils vary considerably even in local areas; also, the moisture content of some soils changes its supporting qualities. Only a soil expert or a local testing laboratory after numerous tests will be able to analyze load-bearing characteristics of a soil for critical footing design. Local practices that have been found successful should be relied on for this purpose. Careful builders generally have the soil tested before footings are poured. If local codes require steel reinforcing rods, they should be placed near the bottom in wall footings and in column or isolated footings. Engineers have found that the steel is usually effective in case of uneven settlement in resisting tensil stresses (see Fig. 7-6).

Because residences and frame buildings are comparatively light and seldom require accurate footing design, their footings are generally figured by the above-mentioned rule of thumb. In stable soil the footing for an 8″ foundation wall should be 16″ wide by 8″ deep or thick; the footing for a 12″ foundation wall should be 24″ wide by 12″ deep; and so on. However, if the soil is not trustworthy or the building gives indication of being

TABLE 7-2 Masonry weights	
Material	**Weight (lb/cu ft)**
Poured concrete	150
Concrete block (CMU)	75
Solid brick	120
Stone	160

TABLE 7-3 Typical weights of materials used in light construction	
Roof	**lb/sq ft**
Wood shingles	3
Asphalt shingles	3
Fiber-glass shingles	2.5
Copper	2
Built-up roofing, 3 ply and gravel	5.5
Built-up roofing, 5 ply and gravel	6.5
Membrane roofing, without ballast	1
Slate, 1/4″ thick	10
Mission tile	13
1″ Wood decking, with felt	2.5
2″ × 4″ Rafters, 16″ o.c.	2
2″ × 6″ Rafters, 16 ″ o.c.	2.5
2″ × 8″ Rafters, 16″ o.c.	3.5
1/2″ Plywood	1.5
Walls	
4″ Stud partition, plastered both sides	22
Window glass, DSB	2
2″ × 4″ Studs, 1″ sheathing, paper	4.5
Brick veneer, 4″	42
Stone veneer, 4″	50
Wood siding, 1″ thickness	3
1/2″ Gypsum wallboard	2.5
Floors, ceilings	
2″ × 10″ wood joists, 16″ o.c.	4.5
2″ × 12″ wood joists, 16″ o.c.	5
Oak flooring, 25/32″ thick	4
Clay tile on 1″ mortar base	23
4″ Concrete slab	48
Gypsum plaster, metal lath	10
Foundation walls	
8″ Poured concrete, at 150 lb/cu ft	100
8″ Concrete block	55
12″ Concrete block	80
8″ Brick, at 120 lb/cu ft	80

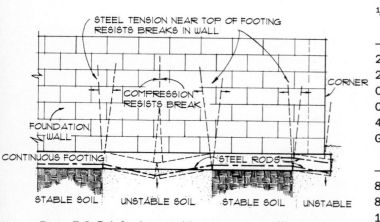

Figure 7-6 Reinforcing steel becomes most effective if placed in the lower part of a footing supporting C.M.U.

heavier than usual, the following method can be used to calculate the necessary size of the footings (see Tables 7-3, 7-4, and 7-5). Both dead load and live load must be considered in the calculations. *Dead load* refers to the weight of the structure as well as any stationary equipment fastened to it; *live load* refers to varying weights and forces to which parts of the building are subjected (people, furnishings, storage, wind, snow, and so on). Both weights are designated in pounds per square foot.

(see Fig. 7-7). Local codes generally require residential floors to be able to carry 40 lb/sq ft live load.

Foundation Walls for light construction are generally built of poured concrete or C.M.U. In areas where local stone has been found to be economical and dependable, it can be used for foundations. For residential structures, brick or stone masonry is used occasionally. Either material has sufficient load-bearing qualities; the

---

TABLE 7-4
Calculation for exterior wall footings (see Fig. 7-7)

Given: 1-story brick veneer frame, wood shingle roof, plaster interior walls, poured concrete foundation. Load-bearing value of soils 2000 lb/sq ft.

Roof

Dead load	1. Live load, snow, wind (varies locally)	30.0 lb/sq ft	
	2. Shingles, wood	3.0	
	3. Wood deck, 1″ thick and felt	2.5	
	4. Rafters, 2″ × 6″, 16″ o.c.	2.5	
	(Length of rafters measures 13′-0″)	38.0 lb/sq ft × 13′	= 494 lb

First-floor ceiling

Dead load	1. Live load (attic storage)	20.0	
	2. Wood floor, 1″ thick	2.5	
	3. Wood joists, 2″ × 8″, 16″ o.c.	3.5	
	4. Ceiling plaster, metal lath	10.0	
	(Half span of ceiling is 5′-0″)	36.0 lb/sq ft × 5′	= 180 lb

Exterior wall

Dead load	1. Brick veneer	42.0	
	2. Sheathing, wood 1″ thick and felt	2.5	
	3. Studs, 2″ × 4″, 16″ o.c.	2.0	
	4. Plaster, metal lath, interior	10.0	
	(Height of wall measures 9′-0″)	56.5 lb/sq ft × 9′	= 509 lb

Floor

Dead load	1. Live load (usual code requirements)	40.0	
	2. Finish oak floor	4.0	
	3. Subfloor, 1″ thick	2.5	
	4. 2″ × 10″ joists, 16″ o.c.	4.5	
	(Half span of floor to center beam is 5′-0″)	51.0 lb/sq ft × 5′	= 225 lb

Foundation

Dead load	1. Concrete wall, 8″ thick		
	(Height of foundation wall is 9′-0″)	100.0 lb/sq ft × 9′	= 900 lb
	2. Concrete footing, 16″ × 8″	100.0 lb/sq ft × 1.33′	= 133 lb
		Total load on soil per lin ft of wall	= **2471 lb**

$$\text{Required area of footing} = \frac{load}{soil\text{-}bearing\ capacity} = \frac{2471}{2000} = 1.23\ sq\ ft$$

Total area of footing required per linear foot of wall = 1.23 sq ft

For convenience use 1.25 : 12″ × 1.25 = 15″ *wide footing required*. To be on the safe side, it would be practical to make the footing 16″ wide, which would be the width if calculated by rule of thumb.

TABLE 7-5
Calculation for column footing (see Fig. 7-7)

1. Ceiling	180 lb/lin ft
2. Partitions	100
3. First floor	255
Total	535 lb/lin ft

The column supports 10 lin ft of beam

$$535 \times 10 = 5350$$

Dead load of beam	250
	5600 lb carried by column

Total load: $\dfrac{5600}{2000}$ = 2.8 sq ft footing required

Soil capacity:

$$X = \sqrt{2.8} = 1.7 = \mathbf{1'\text{-}8''}$$

Required column footing size = 1'-8" × 1'-8"
Make footing 2'-0" × 2'-0" × 12" deep

choice should be determined by availability, economy, and desired architectural effects.

Poured concrete is considered the most reliable, although it involves considerable labor in preparing forms and also requires time for the concrete to set and harden. The integral, one-solid-piece concrete foundation will resist fracturing from settling and differential soil pressures. It lends itself to steel reinforcement at critical points, and dimensions are not restricted by unit sizes, as would be the case when using C.M.U. brick, or other materials. Walls thinner than 6" or 8" would probably meet the load-bearing requirements for most small structures, yet they have a tendency to fail in shear or to buckle because of earth or water pressures. A good rule of thumb is to limit the height of unreinforced concrete foundation walls to *10 times their*

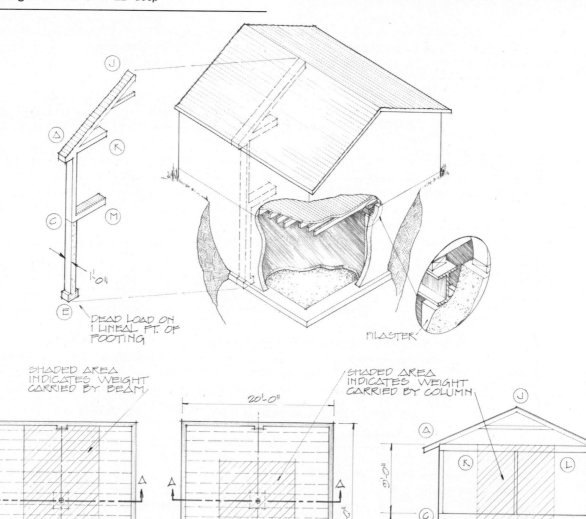

FIGURE 7-7 Footing loads.

thickness; otherwise, vertical reinforcing rods should be used.

Frequently, the thickness of the wall is determined by the thickness of the superstructure rather than the load it is to carry. If masonry is used above, the foundation should be as thick as the masonry. If brick or stone veneer frame construction is used, an 8″ thick foundation would be sufficient for 1-story heights. The height of a 2-story building with basement would require a 10″ thick foundation wall. Brick cavity walls, which are usually 10″ thick, can be supported on an 8″ foundation provided the 8″ thickness is corbeled with solid masonry to the thickness of the cavity wall. Long foundation walls, over 25′, should be increased in thickness or designed with integral pilasters at points in the wall where girders or beams rest. The pilasters should be extended one-half the thickness of the foundation wall (see Fig. 7-8).

Moisture conditions in the soil adjacent to the foundation walls may require the walls to be made thicker to ensure a dry basement. Also, exterior waterproofing and proper drainage along the base of the wall may be necessary. When concrete walls are poured separately from the footings, a key is used at their intersection to resist lateral ground pressures (see Fig. 7-9).

Concrete Masonry Unit (Concrete Block) foundations, because of their economy and speed of erection, are finding widespread use for foundations of residences as well as other types of buildings. Concrete masonry units have proved to be satisfactory if correct design has been used and good construction methods have been followed. The majority of foundation walls are made with the nominal 8″ × 8″ × 16″ and/or 8″ × 12″ × 16″ sizes. Their actual sizes are $7^5/_8$″ × $7^5/_8$″ × $15^5/_8$″ and $7^5/_8$″ × $11^5/_8$″ × $15^5/_8$″ (standard sizes vary slightly in different areas). The smaller height and length allow for vertical and horizontal mortar joints to attain modular dimensions. This feature can be a convenience to the designer or drafter. Common brick can be incorporated into C.M.U. walls if necessary—three brick courses are equivalent to the 8″ C.M.U. thickness, three brick wythes are the same as the 12″ C.M.U. thickness, and so on. Concrete masonry unit foundation walls should be capped with 4″ high solid cap units. This cap provides a smooth, continuous bearing surface for wood sills and makes the walls more resistive to termite infestation. Corner, joist, jamb, header, and other special units are also made in the standard sizes (see Fig. 7-10). Basement partitions can be built with 4″ or 6″ thick partition units. Very often, C.M.U. walls are veneered

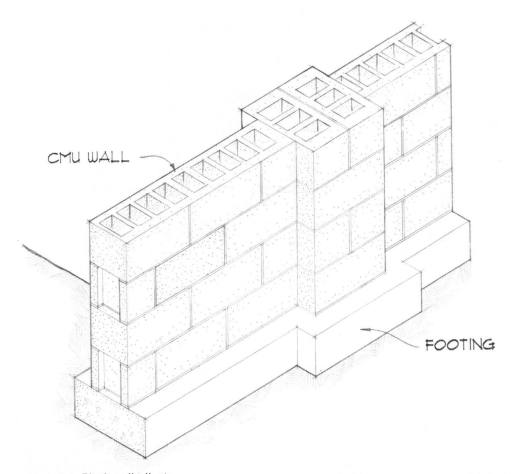

FIGURE 7-8 Block wall pilaster.

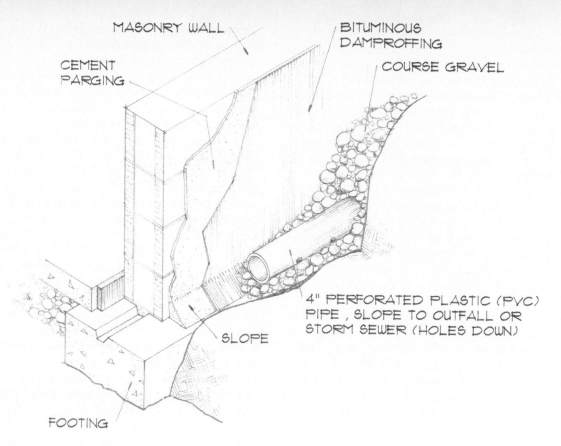

FIGURE 7-9 Dampproofing foundation walls.

Labels in figure: MASONRY WALL, BITUMINOUS DAMPROFFING, CEMENT PARGING, COURSE GRAVEL, 4" PERFORATED PLASTIC (PVC) PIPE, SLOPE TO OUTFALL OR STORM SEWER (HOLES DOWN), SLOPE, FOOTING

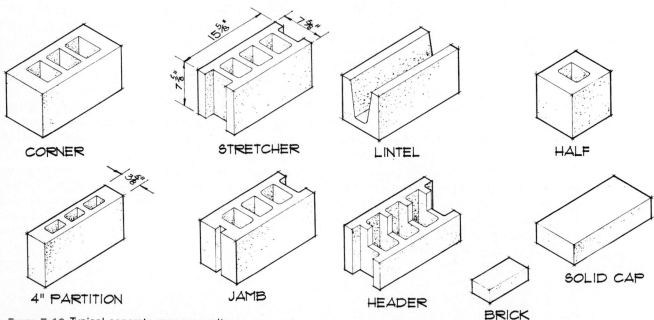

CORNER   STRETCHER   LINTEL   HALF

4" PARTITION   JAMB   HEADER   BRICK   SOLID CAP

FIGURE 7-10 Typical concrete masonry units.

with face brick to produce economical yet pleasing masonry walls of different thicknesses.

Points on foundation walls of C.M.U. on which beams or girders rest should have the cores filled with 1:2:4 concrete from the footing to the bearing surface. If heavy loads are anticipated, vertical steel rods should also be introduced to the cores. In long C.M.U. walls,

$8'' \times 16''$ vertical pilasters should be incorporated to the inside of the wall at a maximum of 10'-0" intervals (or as local building codes require) and filled with concrete for rigidity (see Fig. 7-8).

The load put on C.M.U. walls should be limited to 70 or 80 lb/sq in., which usually makes the 8" or 12" thick blocks adequate for foundations in the majority of

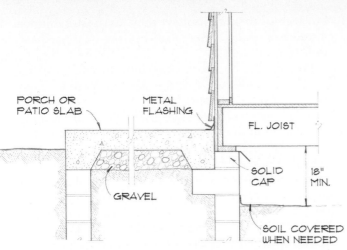

FIGURE 7-11 Anchoring exterior slabs to foundation walls.

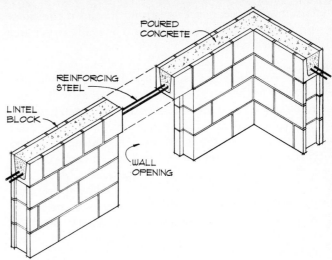

FIGURE 7-12 Lintel unit in masonry wall.

light construction buildings. In most situations, the mortar joints are the weakest part of the wall. Codes usually require units to be laid in full beds of portland cement mortar. Fully loaded walls would still have a safety factor of approximately 4 against failure. Walls supporting wood frame construction should extend at least 8″ above the grade line. Entrance platform slabs, porch slabs, and areaways should be supported or anchored to foundation walls (see Fig. 7-11). In straight walls, units should be laid in a lap bond (Fig. 7-8) so that vertical joints in every other course are directly above each other. Intersecting block walls should also be bonded for rigid construction by interlocking or lapping of alternate courses.

For economy and the sake of good construction, care should be taken to design C.M.U. walls so that units will not have to be cut by the mason. Wall lengths should be in modules of 8″ if the 16″ long unit is used. Openings for doors and windows should be placed, if possible, where vertical joints occur; both the width and the placement of the opening in the wall must be considered. Similarly, heights of C.M.U. walls should be determined by the heights of the units used. Care taken on the drawing board to provide wall lengths and openings compatible with the C.M.U. measurements used will result in sounder walls and neater construction.

Anchor bolts are required by most local codes in foundation walls. They are especially necessary to tie frame constructions such as open structures, carports, or garages to the foundations. Spaced 6′-0″ apart with at least two bolts in each sill member, anchors will resist winds if they are long enough to extend down into the second course of C.M.U. construction. The lower ends of the bolts are bent or secured by embedding a 4″ square steel washer into the mortar joints and filling the cavities with concrete.

If necessary, the heat loss through 8″ thick concrete

block can be reduced 50 percent by putting fill insulation into the cavities of the C.M.U.

In areas subject to earthquakes, C.M.U. walls are not practical for foundations. To resist earthquakes, they must be reinforced with vertical rods in cores and there must also be horizontal reinforcement in mortar beds.

Basement C.M.U. walls should be carefully laid with full, tight mortar joints. If the wall is to be waterproofed, the exterior surface below grade should be parged with a 1/2″ layer of cement mortar and coated with hot tar or asphalt. In case of extreme moisture conditions, roofing felt is applied over the hot asphalt and given another coat of hot asphalt. A foundation drain pipe set in gravel around the edge of the footings should also be used to carry off water that may build up around the wall (see Fig. 7-9).

Lintels over wall openings should be reinforced concrete rather than wood. Wood incorporated into C.M.U. walls for support often shrinks and causes cracks in the masonry work. Some codes require a reinforced bond beam capping the entire block wall. Precast concrete lintels are available that can be set in mortar above openings by the mason. Because of their weight in handling, split precast lintels are often used over wider openings. Lintel units can also be made into satisfactory lintels. The units are set on forms over the opening and filled with concrete and several reinforcing rods (see Fig. 7-12).

Piers are freestanding masonry posts. In basementless houses with wood floors, they are spaced 6′ to 8′ apart to support the girders. Usually, they need only be several feet high and 16″ square in section and capped with a 4″ solid cap unit. The units should be laid in a lapped bond for strength, and if the piers support heavy loads, they should be made larger and filled with concrete.

Stone Foundations using natural stone are not only pleasing to the eye, but are economical as well, especially where the stone can be found locally and has been pronounced suitable for construction work. Stone looks casual, yet gives the impression of solidity; its varied surface textures and uneven contours and sizes present a challenge to the artistry of the mason. Architects realize that stone eliminates the mechanical appearance so often present when C.M.U. materials are used. For this reason, stone is popular with architects and they use it frequently, especially in the building of better quality residences.

Stone masonry is generally referred to as either *field stone* or *ashlar*. Field stone is made up of individual stones more or less irregular in shape, size, and method of combining. In some masonry the irregularity may be less pronounced to give prominence to the horizontal coursing—hence the expression *coursed field stone*. To achieve the effect of horizontal dominance to the courses, the mason must dress the individual stones somewhat, forming horizontal setting beds and continuous uneven horizontal joints (see Fig. 7-13A). *Random field stone* is the term given to the more irregular and rustic-looking stonework, showing no evidence of coursing and very little dressing by the mason. The stones usually are massive in appearance and are combined to avoid the use of chips and fillers (see Fig. 7-13B). Bondstones are stones large enough to extend through the full thickness of the wall; good stonework will show evidence of bondstones at critical places as well as systematically throughout the entire wall. Fieldstones, gathered from river beds or open fields, produce a rubble-type stonework. They vary in color and size and usually are rounded by nature from water action, weathering, or movement on the earth's surface. Interesting textures on either exterior or interior walls above grade can be achieved with fieldstones, but due to their roundness they are unsuitable for foundation walls, where load-bearing qualities have to be considered.

Pilasters can be incorporated into stone foundations at critical points to serve the same purpose as mentioned for other masonry materials.

Ashlar stonework is the term given to masonry making use of custom-dressed and squared stones. The stones are usually processed at the quarry; each stone is cut to specifications to fit an exact place in the building. This type of stonework is costly; for this reason it is used mainly in large commercial or public buildings—seldom in residences. Ashlar stone can also be used as a veneer with other masonry materials as a backing. Ashlar-stone patterns impart the formal look, so prevalent on public buildings.

Any of the granites produce excellent foundation walls; their conchoidal fracture patterns reduce the amount of hammer dressing considerably. The use of granite results in typical random rubble masonry. Hard sandstones, blue shale, and conglomerates also produce suitable rubble walls. Coursed rubble can be conveniently made with sedimentary-type stones, hard sandstones, limestones, and others.

Sedimentary-type stone cut into 4″ thick veneering for wood frame construction is generally referred to as *ashlar-stone veneer*. The pieces have rock faces and squared setting surfaces and are combined to form similar horizontal courses.

Residential stone walls should be at least 16″ thick; thinner walls are more difficult for masons to lay. The unit of measurement of stone masonry is called a *perch*, usually 25 cubic feet of finished wall.

Precast concrete slip sills are usually used in stone-masonry under window and door openings.

Brick Foundations Brick foundation walls are satisfactory for light frame construction as far as strength and dependability are concerned. However, they require more skilled labor, and care must be used in selecting a hard-burned brick that will withstand below-grade

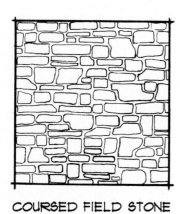

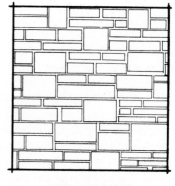

COURSED FIELD STONE   RANDOM FIELD STONE   CUT ASHLAR

FIGURE **7-13** Stonework textures.

conditions. Brick must be laid with high-grade portland cement mortar, and mortar joints must be completely filled to prevent water seepage. Poured concrete footings are recommended for brick foundation walls. (see Fig. 7-14)

Areaways Basements in residences require some method of ventilation and natural lighting. If the basement wall extends only 1' or 2' above grade, an areaway is needed so that basement windows that are on or below grade do not allow moisture to get into the basement (see Fig. 7-15). The areaway walls must be tied to the basement walls, and the same masonry materials are usually used for the areaway as for the foundation. Small areaways can be made of semicircular, corrugated galvanized steel. The bottom of the areaway can have a masonry floor with a drain leading to the storm sewer, or it can be filled with sufficient crushed gravel or stone with drainage tile below to carry the water away from the foundation wall. The areaway walls should extend several inches above grade and at least 4" below the bottom of the basement window. If the areaway is over 24" deep, it should be provided with a grill above to prevent children or animals from falling into it.

Freestanding Pier Foundations In warmer areas where floors need not be insulated, it is more economical to put 1-story houses on freestanding piers of masonry rather than on continuous foundations around the entire exterior wall (see Fig. 7-16). The piers must be of solid masonry: brick, poured concrete, or concrete masonry units. Customarily, piers 18" or 24" high above grade are used, never more than three times their least horizontal dimension unless reinforced. Usually, 8" × 16" or 12" × 16" piers spaced not more than 8' apart are sufficient. Piers should be spanned with either wood or metal beams large enough to carry the weight of the exterior walls. The beams act as sills, and the floor is built above the beams, which are well anchored to the piers.

Brick veneer can be used with freestanding piers by starting the brick veneer on a poured footing below grade. The footings must be poured integrally with the pier footings, and each must be the proper size. Despite masonry piers having been used, this brick-veneer curtain wall gives the exterior the appearance of a continuous foundation. When a brick-veneer curtain wall is used, sufficient ventilation and an access door must be provided as in continuous foundations (see Fig. 7-17).

Grade Beam Foundations One-story frame buildings can be adequately supported on foundations made of a

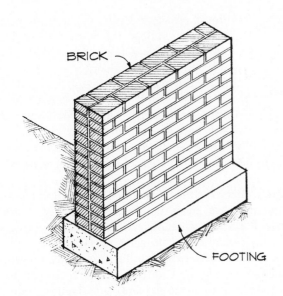

FIGURE 7-14 Poured concrete footings for brick foundations.

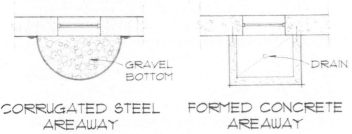

FIGURE 7-15 Areaways for basement windows.

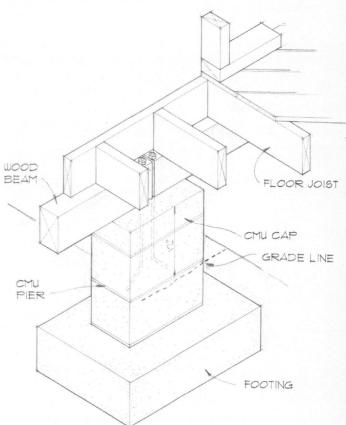

FIGURE 7-16 Freestanding masonry pier.

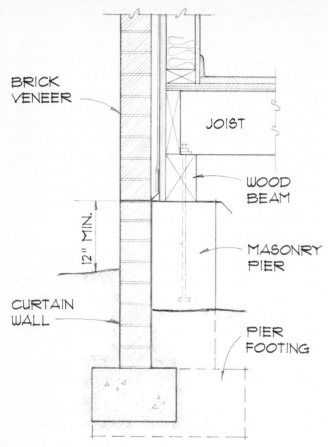

FIGURE 7-17 Economical pier construction with brick veneer and crawl space.

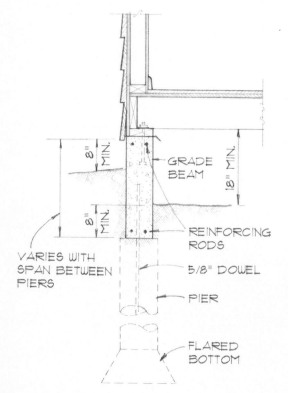

FIGURE 7-18 Detail showing the use of grade beam with frame construction.

system of poured concrete piers with suitable footings with the piers spanned by reinforced concrete beams that have been formed with trenches dug into the ground (see Fig. 7-18). The concrete beams must be designed in accordance with good engineering practice to carry the weight of the building above. Unless the soil below the beam has been removed and replaced with coarse rock or gravel not susceptible to frost action, the bottom of the grade beam must be below the frost line. If structural analysis has not been made, the following minimum conditions (F.H.A.) or (according to local building codes) should be met, based on a 1-story structure with average soil conditions:

1. Piers:
   a. Maximum pier spacing, 8'-0" o.c.
   b. Minimum size of piers, 10' diam; pier should be reinforced with a No. 5 bar for the full length of the pier and extending into the beam.
   c. Depth of pier should extend below the frost line and have a bearing area of at least 2 square feet for average soils.
2. Grade beam:
   a. Minimum width for frame buildings: 6"; an 8" beam can be flared if covered by base trim. Masonry or masonry veneer should be 8" wide.
   b. Minimum effective depth, 14"; if grade beam supports a wood floor, the beam must be deep enough to provide a minimum of 18" crawl space below the wood floor.
   c. Reinforce the beam with two top bars and two No. 4 bottom bars, if frame construction; if masonry or masonry veneer, reinforce with two top bars and two No. 5 bottom bars. If grade beam is flared at top, reinforce top with one No. 6 bar instead of two No. 4 bars.

Concrete Slab-on-Grade Construction In recent years, basements have been eliminated in many 1-story houses. Formerly, a basement was definitely necessary, for heating plants, fuel storage, and laundry or utility areas. With the advent of liquid and gas fuels, however, the need for bulky fuel and ash storage space has been eliminated. Both heating plants and laundry equipment have become more compact, thus requiring little space in the modern home. Basementless residences have become popular, especially in warmer climates where footings need not be placed so deep in the ground. With the elimination of the basement, one type of floor construction that has been found successful, if properly executed, is the concrete slab on ground (see Fig. 7-19).

Precaution should be used in placing a slab on certain lots. Sloping lots would not only require considerable excavation, they also present drainage problems; low lots where moisture often accumulates would also be

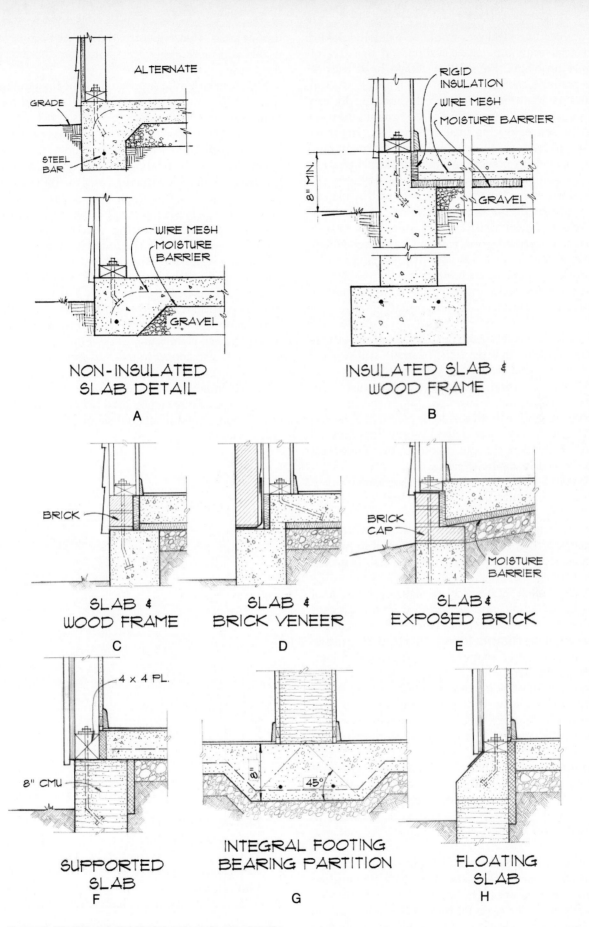

FIGURE 7-19 Sill details of slab-on grade construction.

unfavorable. The ideal area would be a nearly level lot requiring a minimum of excavation and one free of moisture problems. Finish floor should be at least 8″ above grade. Concrete floors have a tendency to feel cold and damp during winter and wet seasons; this can be eliminated by introducing either radiant heating coils or perimeter heating ducts into the slab. Care must be taken to have an absolutely watertight membrane below the slab to prevent moisture from penetrating from the ground, and, particularly in northern climates, the periphery of the slab must be well insulated. Concrete slabs can be finished with any of the many types of flooring materials: clay, ceramic, vinyl, or cork tile in mastic; carpeting over padding, or plywood block flooring in mastic; or hardwood strip flooring can be laid on sleepers over a concrete slab.

The following construction requirements should be met in using a concrete slab on ground:

1. Finish-floor level should be high enough above natural grade so that the finished grade will provide good drainage away from the building.
2. All debris, topsoil, and organic matter must be removed from below the slab. Loose soil must be compacted. Earth fill should be placed in 6″ layers.
3. All sewer, water, gas, and oil supply lines must be installed before the slab is poured. Gas lines must be placed in a pipe sleeve.
4. At least a 4″ layer of coarse gravel or crushed rock or course sand must be placed above the soil and well compacted.
5. A watertight vapor barrier must be placed over the crushed stone before the slab is poured to prevent moisture from seeping up into the slab from the soil.
6. A permanent, waterproof, nonabsorptive type of rigid insulation must be installed around the perimeter of the slab in accordance with the requirements of the climate. In very mild climates, insulation may not be required, but an expansion joint should be used.
7. The slab must be reinforced with wire mesh designated w 1.4 × w 1.4 fabricated in a 6″ × 6″ grid from No. 10 gauge steel wire. The slab must be at least 4″ thick and be troweled to a smooth, hard finish.
8. When ductwork is placed in the slab, it should be of noncorrodible, nonabsorbent material with not less than 2″ of concrete completely surrounding the ductwork. Heating coils and reinforcement, if used, must be covered with at least 1″ of concrete.

Slab-on-grade floors permit a lower silhouette in the overall appearance of the house. In areas where outdoor living spaces adjacent to the house are popular, the slab floor eliminates the need for four or five steps leading from interior floor levels to the surface of the outdoor terrace areas. Consequently, the terrace becomes more usable and more easily accessible from the interior of the house.

Slabs can either be supported by the foundation wall (Fig. 7-19F), or they can be independent of the foundation and supported entirely by the soil below the slab (Fig. 7-19H). Either method is satisfactory if the soil below is well compacted. If settlement should occur below the slab, the floating slab construction would be less likely to crack or fracture eventually. If considerable fill is necessary under a slab, it should be placed under the supervision of a soil engineer in accordance with acceptable engineering practice. Such a slab should be supported by the foundation wall, and have reinforcing steel bars placed in the slab and in thickened portions of the slab throughout the slab area (see Fig. 7-20). All load-bearing partitions and masonry nonbearing partitions should be supported on foundations bearing on natural ground independent of the slab, unless the slab is thickened and reinforced to distribute adequately the concentrated load (see Fig. 7-19G).

In northern areas, where insulation from heat loss is of prime importance, several inches of Zonolite® or insulating concrete can be used below the regular concrete. Proper rigid insulation should also surround the entire slab (see Fig. 7-19).

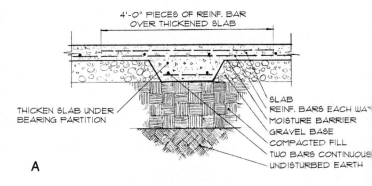

A

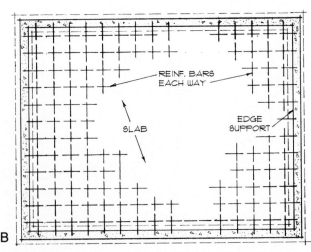

B

FIGURE 7-20 Use steel reinforcing in slabs placed on fill.

Structural Concrete Slabs are designed by a structural analysis of their intended load and contain steel reinforcing to make them strong enough to withstand the load they will bear independent of any central supports below. For example, garages with basements underneath may require structural slab floors.

Integral Slab and Footing Where frost lines are very shallow, slabs and their footings can be poured at one time, thus providing an integral foundation and floor, economical for 1-story buildings (see Fig. 7-19A). The footing is merely a flared thickening of the slab around its perimeter. For best results the bottom of the footing should be at least 1′ below the natural grade line and must be supported on solid, unfilled, and well-drained soil. Several No. 4 bars are placed near the bottom of the footing, and the wire mesh of the slab is rolled into the shape of the footing to tie the entire concrete mass together. Gravel fill and a waterproof membrane must be placed below the slab, similar to the other types of slabs. This type of slab is difficult to insulate, but construction time is gained by its use.

Termite Protection under Floor Slabs In areas where termite infestation is a problem, certain precautions should be taken for concrete slab-on-grade construction. Check with local authorities to verify acceptable methods for controlling termites. Where insulation or expansion-joint material has been specified around the perimeter of the slab, the material should be kept 1″ below the surface of the slab and the space filled with hot tar or asphalt. Insulation containing wood fiber should not be used in termite areas. Circular spaces around all plumbing pipes that pierce the slab should be dug out 1″ deep and also filled with hot asphalt. All framing lumber that comes in contact with the slab or is near it should be pressure treated. All plumbing walls should be provided with an access door for periodic inspection. Openings where anchor bolts are fastened to sill plates must be sealed. If slabs should happen to crack, a plastic waterproof membrane is more reliable than asphalt-saturated felt membranes in preventing moisture penetration.

Insulation for Floor Slabs In most areas of the United States, perimeter insulation must be installed around residential concrete slabs if the construction is to be satisfactory. Because of the density of concrete, it can be classified as a conductor of heat rather than an insulator (the reverse is true of wood and other cellular types of building materials). Heating engineers maintain that practically all the exterior heat loss from a slab on grade takes place along and near the edges of the slab. Very little heat is dissipated into the ground below the slab (see Fig. 7-21). Therefore, careful consideration must be given to the insulation of the slab edges, especially in colder areas. Insulation should be rigid, resistive to

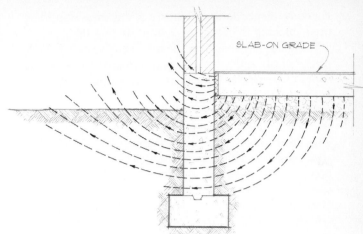

MAJORITY OF HEAT LOSS IS
AROUND PERIMETER OF SLAB

FIGURE 7-21 Heat loss of slab on ground.

dampness, immune to fungus and insect infestation, easy to cut and work, high in crushing strength, and of course resistive to transmission of heat.

Insulating qualities, referred to as R factors, are usually given for different insulation materials. The R factor for a material is the temperature difference in degrees Fahrenheit necessary to force 1 Btu/hr through 1 square foot of the material 1″ thick. Table 7-6 lists the resistance values, or R factors, that should be used in determining the minimum amount of insulation recommended for various design temperatures, with and without floor radiant heating. The table also indicates the minimum depth the insulation should extend below grade.

For example, if the table indicates an R factor of 2.62 is needed, and the insulation selected has an R factor of 1.50 per inch of thickness, then the total thickness needed would be calculated as follows:

$$\frac{2.62}{1.50} = 1.74'' \text{ of insulation}$$

TABLE 7-6

Resistance values for determining slab-on-ground perimeter insulations

Heating design temperature (°F)	Depth Insulation extends below grade	Resistance (R) Factor	
		No floor heating	Floor heating
−20	2′-0″	2.00	3.00
−10	1′-6″	1.75	2.62
0	1′-0″	1.50	2.25
+10	1′-0″	1.25	1.87
+20	1′-0″	1.00	1.50

For convenience and reliability, a 2″ thickness should be used, making the R factor 2 × 1.50 = 3.00.

Cellular-glass insulation board, asphalt-coated glass-fiber board, and synthetic-plastic foam are favorable types of perimeter insulation for concrete slabs.

Steel Reinforcement Poured concrete used in foundations for lintels or structural beams must be reinforced with steel rods to carry the weight imposed on it. For structural use, concrete in itself possesses good compression resistance qualities but has relatively poor tensile strength. Mild steel and concrete have nearly the same coefficients of expansion and contraction; they are, therefore, compatible in that they will expand and contract practically the same amount during temperature changes and so do not lose their bond when combined. When a force or weight is exerted downward on the top of a concrete beam, the tensile stresses would react outward on the lower part of the beam and cause it to break. For example, if a heavy weight were put on the center of a horizontal beam, supported on each end, the beam would crack open on its underside. To counteract this, steel, with its high tensile strength, should be placed in the lower part of the beam where the steel becomes the most effective. If the beam has a column or support below it at any point, the steel in the beam should continue over the column but be raised to the upper part of the beam directly over the column (see Fig. 7-22A). The tensile stresses directly above the column are in the upper part of the beam.

Steel wire mesh, used in concrete slabs on grade, should be placed in the upper part of the slab for most effectiveness; in a 4″ slab the mesh should be placed 1″ from the top of the slab. Steel mesh, also known as welded wire fabric, is available in 5′ wide rolls, and the 6″ × 6″ mesh opening size is usually used in slab reinforcement unless structural slabs are required. W 1.4 × w 1.4 wire size is sufficient.

In brickwork, steel angles are usually used above openings, unless brick arches or other types of masonry lintels are used. Steel angle sizes, 3½″ × 3½″ × 5/16″ and 6″ × 4″ × 3/8″, are often used because they lend themselves to the width of the brick and the mortar joint thickness; however, the thickness and size of the lintel depends on the load above and the span of the opening.

Steel reinforcement rods are available in sizes from No. 2 to No. 11, and they are labeled by their number or by their diameter (see Fig. 7-23). The number labeling is preferable because it indicates how many eighths of an inch the rod is in diameter. A No. 5 rod, for example, would be 5/8″ in diameter, a No. 7 rod 7/8″ in diameter, and so on. Deformed rods are rods that have ridges on their surfaces that provide a more mechanical bond between the steel and concrete. Steel reinforcement should be indicated and placed correctly when drawing section details.

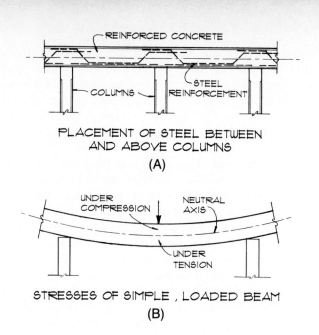

PLACEMENT OF STEEL BETWEEN AND ABOVE COLUMNS

(A)

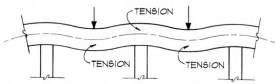

STRESSES OF SIMPLE, LOADED BEAM

(B)

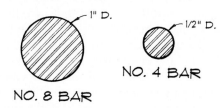

STRESSES BETWEEN AND ABOVE COLUMNS

(C)

FIGURE 7-22 Loading stresses of reinforced concrete beams. Similar stresses exist in wood beams.

FIGURE 7-23 Reinforcing steel is sized according to its diameter.

7.4 Conventional Wood-Frame Construction

Four out of five houses built in North America employ wood-frame construction. A frame structure will give many years of satisfactory service if careful planning has been done on the drawing board and is followed during construction. Correct details and good workmanship are two important factors in realizing durability from a frame building; however, the following methods will further ensure maximum service life from the use of wood:

1. Control the moisture content of the wood.
2. Provide effective termite and insect barriers throughout.

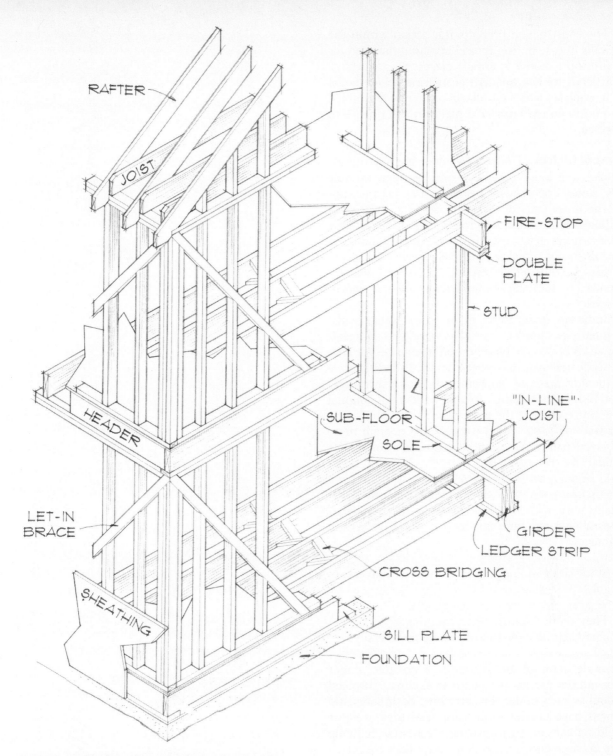

RAFTER

JOIST

FIRE-STOP

DOUBLE PLATE

STUD

"IN-LINE" JOIST

SUB-FLOOR

SOLE

HEADER

LET-IN BRACE

GIRDER

LEDGER STRIP

CROSS BRIDGING

SHEATHING

SILL PLATE

FOUNDATION

FIGURE 7-24 Platform (western) frame construction.

3. Use naturally durable or chemically treated wood in critical places in the structure.

7.4.1 Platform Frame Construction

Platform frame construction (also referred to as western frame) is identified by its story-level construction erected by the workers on each subfloor or platform (see Fig. 7-24). This method of construction has become popular throughout the country in recent years, mainly for the following reasons:

1. Long studding pieces required in balloon framing are not always available and are usually more costly.
2. The platform built at each level is convenient for carpenters to work on (the construction builds its own interior scaffolding).

3. The construction prevents flue action within the walls in case of fire, thus eliminating the need for firestop material in critical places.
4. It lends itself to modern prefabrication methods.
5. It is quicker to erect; wall sections can be assembled quickly on the horizontal platform and tilted into place.

Beams or Girders   Under wood floor framing, unless the joists are long enough to span between exterior walls, some type of heavy beam must be used to support the inner ends of the joists (see Fig. 7-25). If a building is wider than 15' or 16', which is generally the case, it is necessary to use additional support under the floor joists to avoid using excessively heavy floor joists. For this, wood or metal beams are used, and they are supported by the exterior foundation walls and piers or columns.

The beams under floors carry concentrated loads, and their sizes should be carefully considered. If steel is selected, S beams are usually used; their sizes for general residential use can be selected from Table 8-5. Steel has the advantage of not being subject to shrinkage. Wood beams can be either solid or built-up of nominal 2" lumber, usually of the same size lumber used for the floor framing joists. Solid wood beams contain more cross-sectional lumber than built-up beams of similar nominal size. For example, a 6" × 8" solid wood beam would have an actual size of 5½" × 7¼", whereas a built-up beam of 6" × 8" nominal dimension would be actually only 4½" × 7¼". However, from a practical standpoint the built-up wood beams have several advantages:

1. Stock-size framing lumber is more readily available.
2. Smaller pieces are easier to handle.
3. They reduce splitting and checking.
4. They can be nailed to the frame more easily.

It is desirable to locate beams, if possible, under major interior partitions in order to eliminate the need for double joists under the partitions. Bathrooms and kitchens have heavier dead loads, and their weights should be considered in placing the beams. If living space in basements is important, beam sizes are generally made larger to avoid numerous columns throughout the basement. Columns are usually spaced 8' to 10' on center in basements, depending on the beam sizes. Under basementless houses, piers are spaced no more than 7' to 8' on center. Wood beams should have at least a 4" bearing on masonry walls or pilasters, with a ½" air space around the ends of the beams for adequate ventilation if they are surrounded with masonry (see Fig. 7-26). If splices are necessary in wood built-up beams, they should be staggered and should be placed near the column for sound construction. The top edge of the

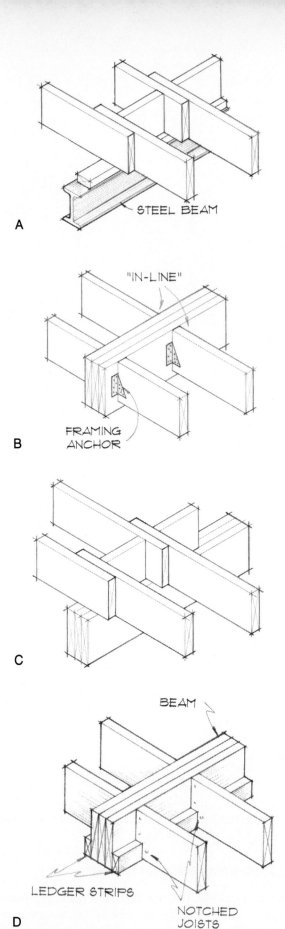

FIGURE 7-25 Joist and beam framing.

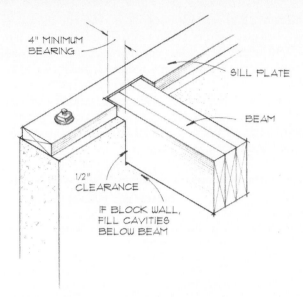

FIGURE 7-26 Beam pocket in foundation wall.

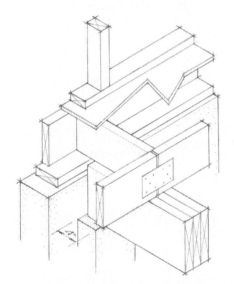

FIGURE 7-27 Box sill and girder support construction.

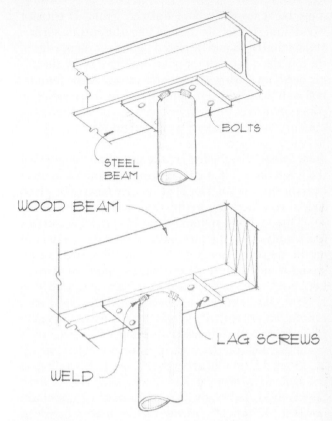

FIGURE 7-28 Steel columns supporting beams.

In 2-story houses, considerable weight is transferred from the upper story to the beams. For convenient selection of beam or girder sizes under wood floor construction, see Table 8-6, which designates maximum spans for the usual beam sizes used. The table is for those species of wood with a minimum of 1200-pound fiber stress, such as Douglas fir, southern pine, or eastern spruce. Beams supporting unusually heavy loads would have to be designed according to established engineering practice.

Columns In residential basements, either wood or metal columns can be used under the beams. The columns are usually 6 × 6 wooden posts or, preferably, round steel columns of 3″ or 4″ diameter with cap plates welded to both ends (see Fig. 7-28). Steel columns are available in stock lengths, or they can be fabricated in any lengths desired. Other types are adjustable. Select wood column sizes according to loads, unsupported heights, and lumber species (see Table 8-2).

Sills The box-type sill (Fig. 7-27) is generally used with platform frame construction. The sill plate, generally measuring 2 × 6 or 2 × 8, is placed over the foundation wall and anchored with ¹/₂″ diameter anchor bolts, spaced according to local codes (usually 6′ on center). Occasionally, builders use a 4 × 6 or 4 × 8 treated sill plate in box sill construction. The wood sill

beams must be the same height as the sill plates if joists are to rest on the beams (see Fig. 7-27). If the joists are to butt into the beams, a ledger strip is nailed to the beam, and either notched or narrower joists are toenailed over the ledger strip to the beams (see Fig. 7-24). Metal angle connectors or steel joist hangers can also be used for butt-fastening joists and beams. Joists butting into beams allow more headroom in basements and facilitate the installation of ductwork and plumbing under the floor, basement ceilings can without difficulty be finished with unbroken surfaces, and plywood subfloors can be more easily put over in-line joists. However, joists resting on the beams is the simpler method of floor framing.

Beams carry half the weight imposed on all the joists that rest on or are attached to the beams (see Fig. 7-7).

must be at least 8" above finished grade. If exterior wood siding is used on the building, the outside surface of the framing should be placed within the outer edge of the foundation so that the outside surface of the sheathing becomes flush with the outer surface of the foundation wall (see Fig. 7-24). This allows the finish siding to come down over the joint between the sill plate and the masonry wall to make a weathertight joint.

Floor Joists Floor joists are the structural members of the wood floor. Their size, spacing, and direction must be indicated on the floor plan, so they have to be given special consideration by the drafter. Joists rest on the sill plate, with a minimum of 1½" bearing surface (preferably 3" on the plate); this should be worked out on the sill detail (see Fig. 7-33). Joists are selected for strength and rigidity. The strength is required to carry both dead and live floor loads; the rigidity is needed to prevent vibration and movement when live load concentrations are shifted over the floor. Joists are usually of 2" (nominal) dimension thickness; 3" thick joists could be used, but they are often unavailable. The 6", 8", 10", or 12" (nominal) depths are used, depending on the load, span, spacing, and species and grade of lumber involved. Generally, joists are spaced 16" on center; however, 12" or 24" spacing can be used when load concentrations vary. Floor framing is simpler if the same depth joists are used throughout the floor, and for greatest rigidity they should run in the direction of the shorter span. Builders can gain additional strength and stiffness in joists by using lumber finished on only two sides [the narrow edges (S2E)], although rough lumber will ignite more quickly in case of fire, and some codes prohibit its use. If joists lap over beams or supports, the lap should be no more than 6" to 8" and no less than 4" for proper nailing together of joists (see Fig. 7-25A). If the lap is excessive, any sag or reflection at the center of the joists will cause the ends of the joists extending over the beams to raise the floor. If joists are supported by a steel beam, a 2" × 4" nailing strip should be bolted to the beam and the joists fastened to it.

For economy, the lengths of the joists should be limited to 2' increments. The header joists are end-nailed to each joist with 16-penny nails, and both the headers and the joists are toenailed to the sill plate or attached with metal joist anchors. If the bearing surface at the ends of the joists is critical, blocks between the joists can be used as a header; the blocks will function very much like block bridging (see Fig. 7-29B).

Local codes usually indicate the minimum joist sizes for various conditions. A rule of thumb for joist sizes using either Douglas fir, southern yellow pine, western larch, or hemlock (J & P Grade) would be to make their spans in feet one and one-half times their depth in inches, if the joists are spaced 16" on center. Thus, a 2" × 10" joist of the species indicated would span 15' if a 40-pound live load is required. Usually, lumber of a higher grade does not increase the allowable span, because rigidity is the controlling factor, which is not contingent on grades. For more accurate joist size selection according to spans required, refer to Chapter 8.

Note: As of September 1970, the various national lumber associations have adopted the American Softwood Lumber Standard, PS 20-70, which now unifies dressed lumber sizes as shown:

Nominal size	Dressed size (S4S) in inches	
	Surfaced dry	Surfaced green
2 × 4	1½ × 3½	1⁹⁄₁₆ × 3⁹⁄₁₆
2 × 6	1½ × 5½	1⁹⁄₁₆ × 5⁵⁄₈
2 × 8	1½ × 7¼	1⁹⁄₁₆ × 7½
2 × 10	1½ × 9¼	1⁹⁄₁₆ × 9½
2 × 12	1½ × 11¼	1⁹⁄₁₆ × 11½

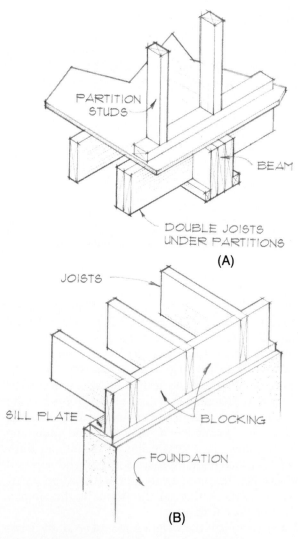

(A)

(B)

Figure 7-29 Double joist and header blocking.

Double joists should be used under all partitions running parallel with the joists, or some method of blocking must be employed so that partitions bear on framing rather than on the subfloor between the joists (see Fig. 7-29A).

Floor Trusses An alternative to framing floors with conventional floor joists is to use floor trusses or truss joists (Fig. 7-30). These systems of floor framing are appropriate when long spans are required and the use of load-bearing walls or columns to support floor loads is undesirable. Floor trusses or truss joists are used for first-floor framing in residences where open space in basements is essential.

Floor trusses are usually factory assembled units fabricated from 2 × 4 structural grade lumber. Engineered as flat trusses with top chords, bottom chords, and web members connected by stamped metal plates, these structural members are capable of spanning greater distances than wood floor joists. Most floor trusses are spaced at 24″ o.c., thus requiring a ³/₄″ thick or thicker subfloor. Diagonal bridging and continuous lateral bracing are required between floor trusses. Wiring and ductwork can easily be routed through openings between web members of floor trusses.

Truss joists are factory assembled wood floor framing members that resemble an I beam in cross section. These members consist of top and bottom chords and a solid web (Fig. 7-31). The top and bottom chords are cut from 2 × 4s or glue-laminated wood. The web is cut from plywood or structural-grade hardboard. Available in various depths and lengths, these members are similar to the floor trusses and are capable of spanning greater distances than conventional floor joists, thus requiring a ³/₄″ thick or greater subfloor. Diagonal bridging is essential between truss joists. Unlike with floor trusses, ductwork cannot be placed through the solid web; however, small openings can be cut through the webs to allow room for electrical wiring and plumbing pipes. Such openings should be placed at strategic locations designated by the manufacturer of the truss joists.

Trimmers and Headers Openings in floor framing for chimneys, stairways, and the like, must be surrounded by additional framing members for support. The joists that run parallel to the two sides of the opening are doubled and are called *trimmers*. The members that surround the other two sides of the opening are also doubled and are called *headers*; into these headers are framed the shortened joists called *header joists* or *tail joists* (see Fig. 7-32). Headers should not be over 10′-0″ long; if the spans are short and loads around the opening are not heavy, the assembly can be spiked together; otherwise, joist hangers or additional support must be used. Framing should not be fastened into chimneys; fire codes require a 2″ space around chimneys between the framed opening, which should be filled with incom-

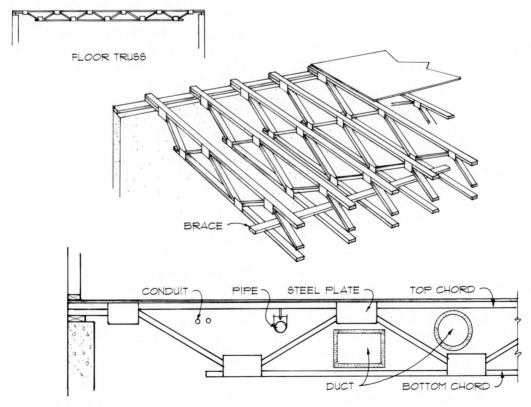

FIGURE 7-30 Wood floor trusses.

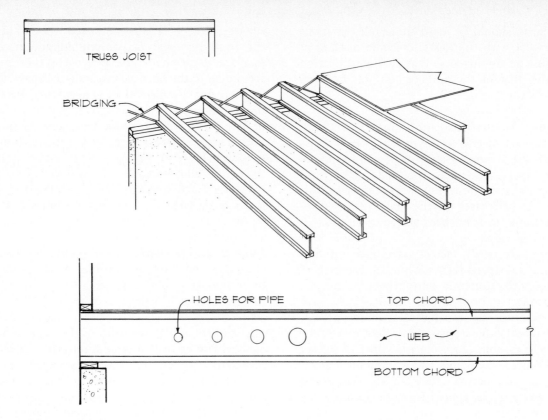

Figure 7-31 Truss joists.

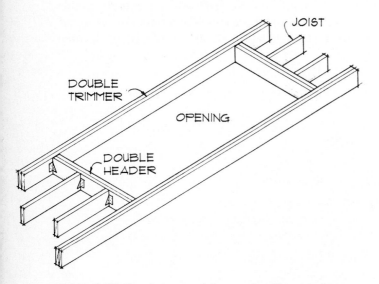

Figure 7-32 Framing around floor and ceiling openings.

bustible insulation. If the chimney flues are well surrounded with masonry, corbel masonry may be extended from the chimney on which framing may rest. Tail joists over 6'-0" long must be connected to headers in the same manner that joists are connected to beams or girders.

Cutting Openings in Joists The cutting or drilling through of joists that have been set in place should be

avoided if possible. However, plumbing or wiring must occasionally pass through floor joists. Small holes, if placed properly, are not too objectionable, but larger cuts often result in weakened or dangerous conditions (see Fig. 7-34). A horizontal structural member, such as a floor joist, with a load imposed on it can be considered to be under compression throughout the upper half of its depth; it is under tension throughout its lower half, with a neutral axis in the center of its depth. The farther away the wood fiber is from the center of the depth of the joist, the more important the fiber is to the strength of the member. Therefore, the closer to the center axis a hole is cut, the less destructive it will be. Joists may be notched at top or bottom if the notch does not exceed one-sixth of the depth of the joist, as long as the notch does not occur within the center one-third of the span. Holes with a maximum of 2" diameter can be bored within 2" of the edges of the joist without causing excessive damage.

Bridging consists of rows of short members between joists to produce a firm, rigid floor. Bridging not only prevents the deep, narrow shape of the floor joists from buckling sideways, but it distributes concentrated live loads to adjoining joists. Rows of bridging should be uninterrupted throughout the floor. Three types of bridging are seen in floor framing: 1 × 3 pieces of wood nailed diagonally between the joists, blocks the same depth as the joists nailed in staggered fashion perpendicular to the joists, or light metal bridging pieces

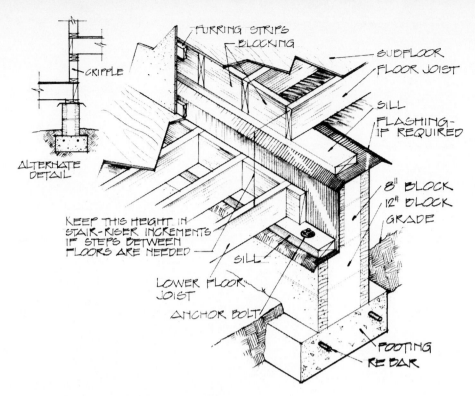

FIGURE 7-33 Framing for floor level offset.

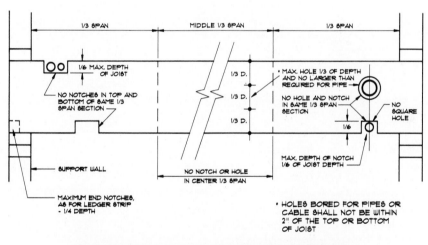

JOIST SIZE	MAX. HOLE	MAX. NOTCH DEPTH	MAX. END NOTCH
2 x 4	NONE	NONE	NONE
2 x 6	2"	1"	1 1/2"
2 x 8	2 1/2"	1 1/4"	2"
2 x 10	3"	1 1/2"	2 1/2"
2 x 12	4"	2"	3"

FIGURE 7-34 Cutting openings in wood floor joists.

nailed diagonally between the joists. Cross-bridging (see Fig. 7-35) allows wiring and piping to pass through without cutting. Joists with more than 8′ of span should have one row of bridging, but rows of bridging should be no more than 7′ or 8′ apart in longer spans.

Subfloor Nominal 1″ boards 4″, 6″, or 8″ wide, securely nailed to the joists, have traditionally been used for subfloors. The boards can be square edged, tongue and groove, or shiplap, and it is preferable to lay them diagonally (45° to the joists). Finish strip flooring can

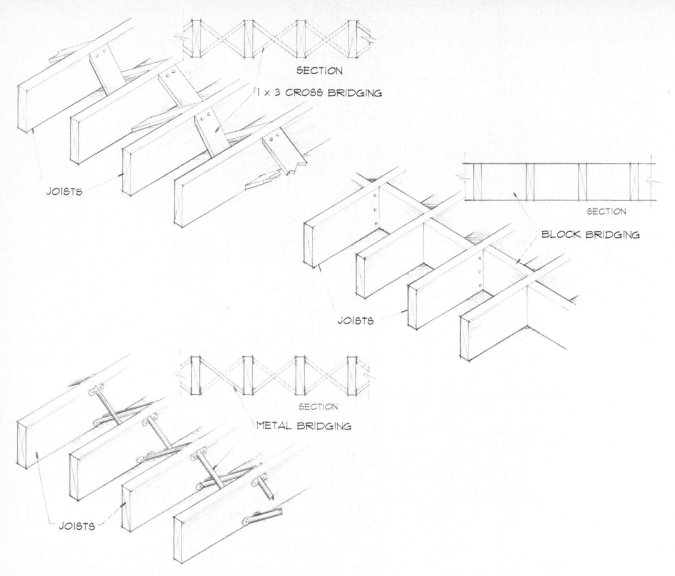

FIGURE 7-35 Types of bridging used in wood framing.

then be laid in either direction over the subfloor. Joints in the subflooring should fall in the center of the joists and they should be staggered. Square-edge boards laid up too tight often produce squeaky floors; rather, they should be nailed about ⅛″ apart. When subflooring is laid perpendicularly to the joists, the finish floor must be laid perpendicularly to the subfloor.

Because of the speed of erection, softwood plywood is the most popular material for subflooring today. Plywood produces a smooth surface for block flooring, tile, carpeting, and other nonstructural flooring materials. Sheets of plywood, usually ½″, ⅝″, or ¾″ thick for subfloors, should be laid with their face grain across the joists; the end joints of the sheets should be staggered and fall midway between adjoining sheets (see Fig. 7-36). If other than strip wood flooring is used, the joints around the plywood should have blocking below, or tongue-and-groove edge plywood can be used. Ply-

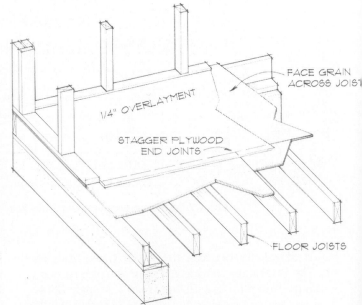

FIGURE 7-36 Use of plywood subflooring.

wood must be securely nailed around its edges as well as throughout central areas where backing occurs.

A hardboard or particle board overlayment $1/4''$, $3/8''$, $1/2''$, or $5/8''$ thick should be placed over plywood subfloors $1/2''$ or $5/8''$ thick. Tongue-and-groove plywood $3/4''$ thick or thicker does not require an overlayment when installed with screws and construction adhesive on floor joists spaced $16''$ o.c. or less. Structural-oriented strand board or wafer board $7/16''$ and $3/4''$ thick is used as subflooring in locations where it is acceptable by building codes.

Subfloor under Ceramic Tile In bathrooms and other areas requiring ceramic tile floors, some method must be used to lower the subfloor so that a concrete base for the tile can be provided for. If the joists are adequate for the load, they can be dropped several inches, or the top of the joists can be chamfered and the subfloor dropped $3''$ between the joists. If there is no objection to the finished tile floor being an inch or so above the other finished floor surface, the regular subfloor could be left as is. However, in economical construction, ceramic tile can be laid on mastic, on top of a substantial wood subfloor, which does not require a concrete subfloor, nor does it entail dropping of the wood floor.

Soleplates After the subfloor is in place, 2×4 plates, called *soles*, *shoe plates*, or *bottom plates*, are nailed directly over the subfloor to form the layout for all walls and partitions. Dimensions for this layout must be taken from the floor plan working drawing. It should be noted that unless floor plans show dimensions from the outer edge of the exterior wall framing to the center line of partitions, accurate layout of soleplates by workers becomes rather difficult. The plates are generally run through door openings and then cut out after the framing and rough openings have been established. Plumbing walls must be built of 2×6 or 2×8 studs to enclose soil stacks; partitions between closets can be built of 2×4 studs set sideways to increase usable space.

Studs usually 2×4 ($16''$ on center), are toenailed to the soleplate and are capped with a double 2×4 cap plate. Double studs, which support proper-size lintels or headers above the openings, should be used around all door and window openings. In 1-story buildings, studs can be spaced $24''$ on center, unless limited by the wall covering. If ceiling heights are to be $8'-0''$ high, the studs are generally cut between $7'-8''$ and $7'-9''$ in length. Blocking, halfway up the height of the studs, stiffens the wall and prevents the studs from warping. If vertical paneling is to be used as interior wall covering, horizontal blocking must be inserted between the studs in rows every $2'-0''$ of vertical height throughout the wall, or else 1×3 horizontal furring strips will have to be nailed to the studs to back up the vertical paneling.

With platform framing, it is convenient for workers

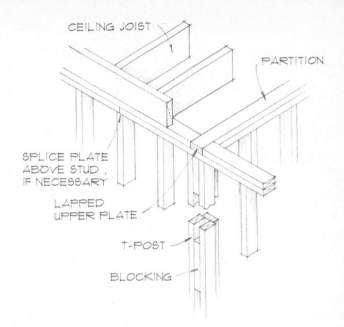

FIGURE 7-37 Framing at intersections of walls.

to lay out each wall horizontally on the platform, nail the pieces together without the second cap plate, and then lift the wall into place where it can be temporarily braced. All the walls and partitions are set in place and trued carefully. The top piece of the double cap plate is then attached so that all the walls and partitions are well lap jointed (see Fig. 7-37). Corner posts, T posts, and posts forming intersections of partitions are built up of 2×4s, well spiked together in a manner to provide for both inside and outside nailing surfaces at the corners (see Fig. 7-39).

Bracing Sufficient diagonal bracing must be used at the corners (see Fig. 7-38) as well as in major partitions to counteract wind pressures and to prevent lateral movement of the framing. Let-in, 1×4 braces placed as close to 45° as possible should be used, and they should be tied into both the top and bottom plates of the wall. If windows or openings are close to the corners, K braces can be used (see Fig. 7-1). Diagonal bracing can be eliminated if wood sheathing is used and nailed diagonally to the studs or if the frame is sheathed with plywood.

Lintels The horizontal supports above openings are usually built up of two pieces of nominal 2×4, 2×6, 2×8, 2×10, or 2×12 lumber with the wide dimension vertical. Extra strength and the exact $3 1/2''$ stud width can be gained by sandwiching a $3/8''$ plywood panel between the two vertical lintel pieces (see Fig. 7-40). Unless unusual loads bear over the opening, two 2×4s will support openings up to $3'-0''$ wide, two 2×6s up to $4'-0''$, and two 2×8s up to $5'-0''$; openings exceeding $6'-0''$ should be framed with diagonal truss-type framing or steel flitch plates introduced to the

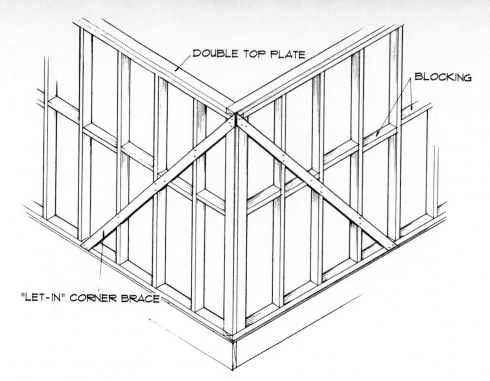

FIGURE 7-38 Diagonal bracing at corners.

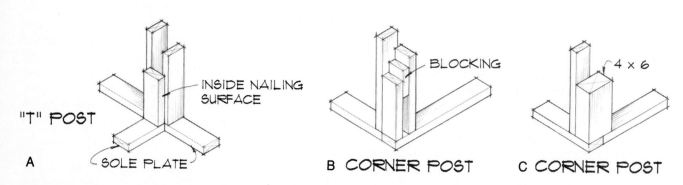

FIGURE 7-39 Stud framing at corners and intersections of walls.

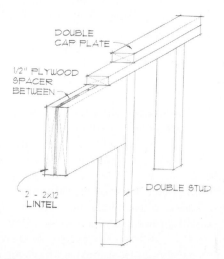

FIGURE 7-40 Lintels over typical wall openings.

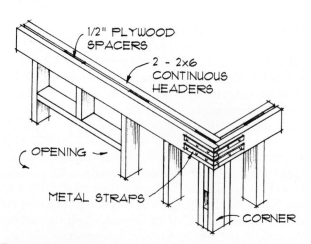

FIGURE 7-41 Wall framing with continuous headers instead of double cap plate.

lintels. Many builders use double 2 × 12 lintels above all wall openings; this eliminates the need for cripples or vertical blocking between the lintel and the top plate (see Fig. 7-40). For volume construction, some builders use a double 2 × 6 cap plate, set vertically, over all bearing walls, thus eliminating lintels. Such buildings generally have openings no wider than 4'-0" (see Fig. 7-41).

Second-floor Framing Each story in platform framing is a separate unit; if two stories are planned, the second-floor joists and headers are attached to the top plate of the first floor. The second-story walls are built on the platform or subfloor of the second floor. Second-story floor joists then become the first-floor ceiling joists. If possible, second-story partitions should fall directly above partitions below; otherwise, additional floor joists or blocking is required. Occasionally, second stories are cantilevered out beyond exterior walls below. Joists below cantilevered walls should be perpendicular to the walls and well anchored (see Fig. 7-42).

Ceiling Joists generally rest on the top wall plate if the roof is put directly above. If an attic floor is required (Fig. 7-43), headers and joists can be built up to the outside surface of the walls, with the attic floor nailed to the joists, and a 2" × 4" soleplate nailed over the floor around its perimeter on which the rafters bear. In ceiling framing, if a gable-type roof is used, it is more desirable to put the ceiling joists parallel to the roof rafters, making the ceiling joists actually bottom chords for the truss shape of the roof rafters. Ceiling joists are nailed to both the top plate and the roof rafters (see Fig. 7-44). A lateral brace or catwalk brace for ceiling framing is shown in Fig. 7-45.

When ceiling joists must be placed at right angles to the rafters, short joists are run perpendicularly to the long joists over the plate and nailed to both the plate and the rafters. The inner ends of the short joists are butted and anchored to a double long joist. Metal straps are used to tie the tops of the short joists across at least three of the long joists if no wood flooring is used (see Fig. 7-46).

Gable-roof Rafters Wind pressures against gable roofs (hip roofs as well) not only exert downward forces on the windward side, but also exert upward pressures on the leeward side, especially if the roof has a considerable overhang. Therefore, rafters must be well an-

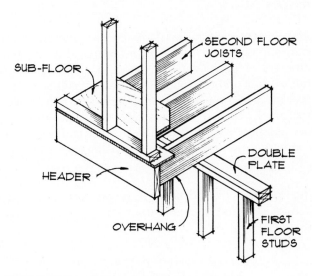

FIGURE 7-42 Framing a second-floor overhang.

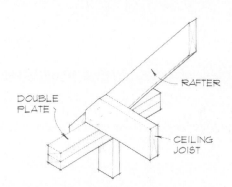

FIGURE 7-44 Fastening rafters and ceiling joists.

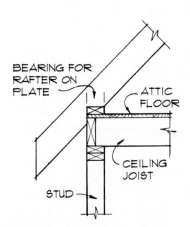

FIGURE 7-43 Fastening rafters to attic floor.

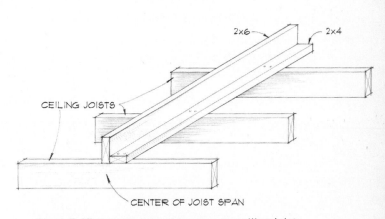

FIGURE 7-45 Catwalk lateral brace over ceiling joists.

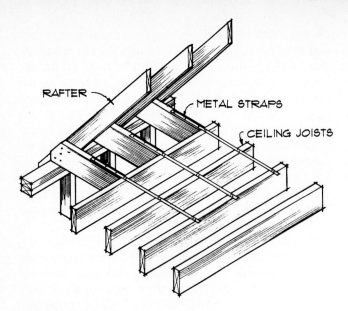

FIGURE 7-46 Framing with ceiling joists at right angles to rafters.

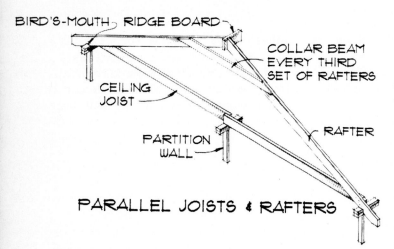

PARALLEL JOISTS & RAFTERS

FIGURE 7-47 Arrangement of opposite rafters and ceiling joists.

chored at their lower ends or bearing cuts. The triangular notch cut into the rafters for horizontal bearing is called a *bird's-mouth* (see Fig. 7-47 for roof-framing terminology). It should be deep enough so that the rafter bears on the full width of the 2 × 4 plate. The bird's-mouth is toenailed to the plate, and the rafter is also nailed to the ceiling joist; metal anchors are sometimes employed for more positive anchorage. Rafters are placed directly opposite each other at the ridge so that they brace against each other. Rafter lengths and cuts are carefully laid out on a pattern piece to ensure uniformity of all common rafters and to simplify their cutting. The ridgeboard can be either 1″ or 2″ nominal lumber, but it should be 2″ wider than the rafters so that the entire beveled ridge cut will make contact with the ridgeboard.

Valley Rafters   Valleys are formed by the intersection of two sloping roofs; the rafter directly below the valley is called the *valley rafter* (see Fig. 7-48). Valley rafters carry additional loads and should be doubled as well as widened to allow full contact with the diagonal cuts of the jack rafters.

Jack Rafters   are shorter than common rafters and run from hip or valley rafters to the plates. If roofs with different ridge heights intersect, the higher roof is framed first and the valley is formed by nailing a plate over the higher roof surface; the jack rafters of the lower roof are then nailed to the plate. Or the valley rafter can be incorporated into the larger roof framing if attic communication is needed between the gables or hips (see Fig. 7-48).

Hip Rafters,   like ridgeboards, do not carry any loads and are therefore the same size as the common rafters (Fig. 7-49).

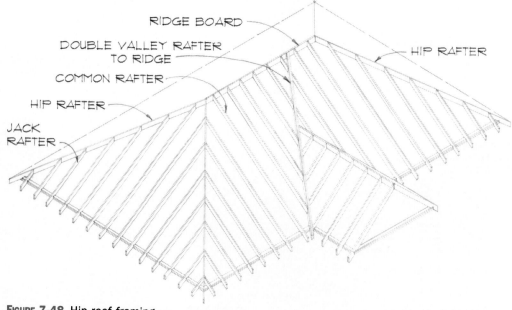

FIGURE 7-48 Hip-roof framing.

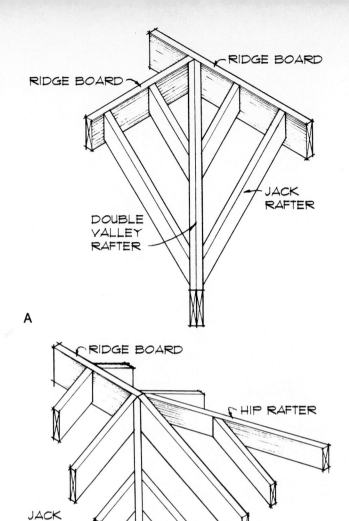

A

B

FIGURE 7-49 Roof framing: (A) valley rafter; (B) hip rafter.

Gambrel-roof Framing requires two sets of generally different length rafters. The first set of longer rafters receive a bird's-mouth cut and are nailed to the top plate of the exterior bearing walls. A knee wall or full stud wall is used to support these steeply pitched rafters at the opposite end of the span. The second set of rafters with less pitch is framed into the top end of the longer rafters and to a ridge beam at the center line of the structure. Collar beams or ceiling joists are placed at the junction between the two sets of rafters (see Fig. 7-50).

Dormer Framing is similar to gable roof framing. Double headers and double trimmers must be framed around the opening in the roof. Studs are nailed to the top of the double trimmers to form the vertical sides of the dormer. A ridge beam and rafters frame the gable roof structure of the dormers (see Fig. 7-52).

Flat-roof Framing consists of roof joists bearing on the top plate of stud walls. The roof joists may cantilever over the bearing wall to create an eave or overhang. When an overhang is desired around the perimeter of the structure, a double trimmer is placed to support cantilevered lookouts. These lookouts are perpendicular to the roof joists and form the overhang at the side of the structure (see Fig. 7-54).

Collar Beams (see Fig. 7-47). Collar beams are short lengths of 2 × 4's or 1 × 6's nailed across opposite gable rafters about one-third the distance down from the ridge. They stiffen the roof against wind pressures. If the attic is used for occupancy, the collar beams act as ceiling joists as well as rafter ties and must be placed at ceiling height. When the roof pitch is low and the rafter span is long, collar beams are nailed to each pair of rafters; otherwise, to every third pair.

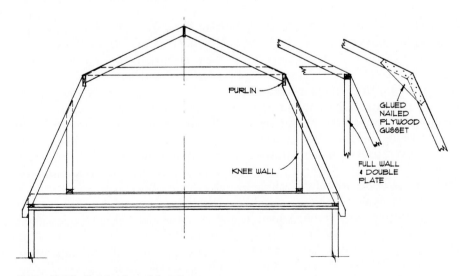

FIGURE 7-50 Gambrel-roof framing.

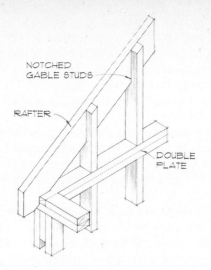

FIGURE 7-51 Gable studs.

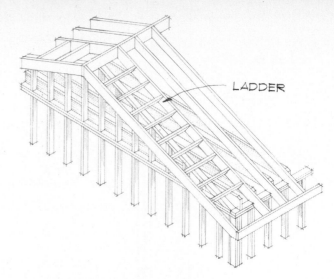

FIGURE 7-53 Gable-end roof framing.

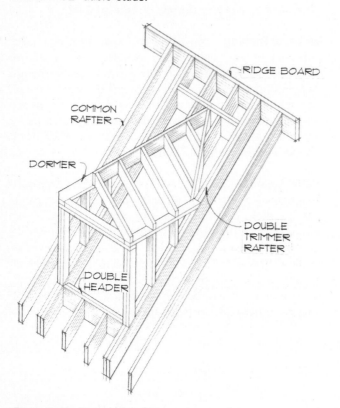

FIGURE 7-52 Dormer framing.

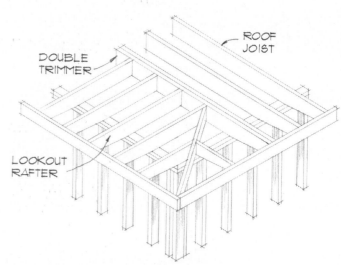

FIGURE 7-54 Flat-roof framing at corners.

Gable Studs must be framed with the same spacing as studs in the lower walls; they are diagonally cut and notched to fit the underside of the end rafters and butt to the double wall plate (see Fig. 7-51). It is customary to make provision for a louver, usually screened, near the ridge of the gable end wall. The net area of the opening should be at least $^1/_{300}$ of the area of the ceiling below. In most cases, prefabricated wood or metal louvers are used; they are inserted into the rough opening after the wall sheathing is applied. If a boxed overhang is required above the gable wall, a ladder-type framing can be cantilevered over the gable wall (see Fig. 7-53). If wood siding is used on the gable wall, and brick

veneer is used below, 2×8 gable studs can be used to bring the gable siding out flush with the brick veneer.

Roof Decking There are several methods of covering the roof framing, depending on the materials used and the type of roof covering. Nominal 1″ matched boards, usually 6″ wide and nailed perpendicularly to the rafters, can be used. They are started at the edge of the roof overhang and laid up tight to the ridge. Use of shiplap or tongue-and-groove lumber will result in a tighter deck and more solid surface for the roof covering. Splices should be well staggered and made over the center of the rafters. Long pieces of lumber are desirable for roof decking.

Softwood plywood makes a satisfactory roof deck; it goes on fast and makes a rigid roof when properly nailed down. Plywood joints should fall on the rafters, and vertical joints should be midway on succeeding rows. The face grain of the plywood should be laid perpendicularly to the rafters (see Fig. 7-55). Plywood that is

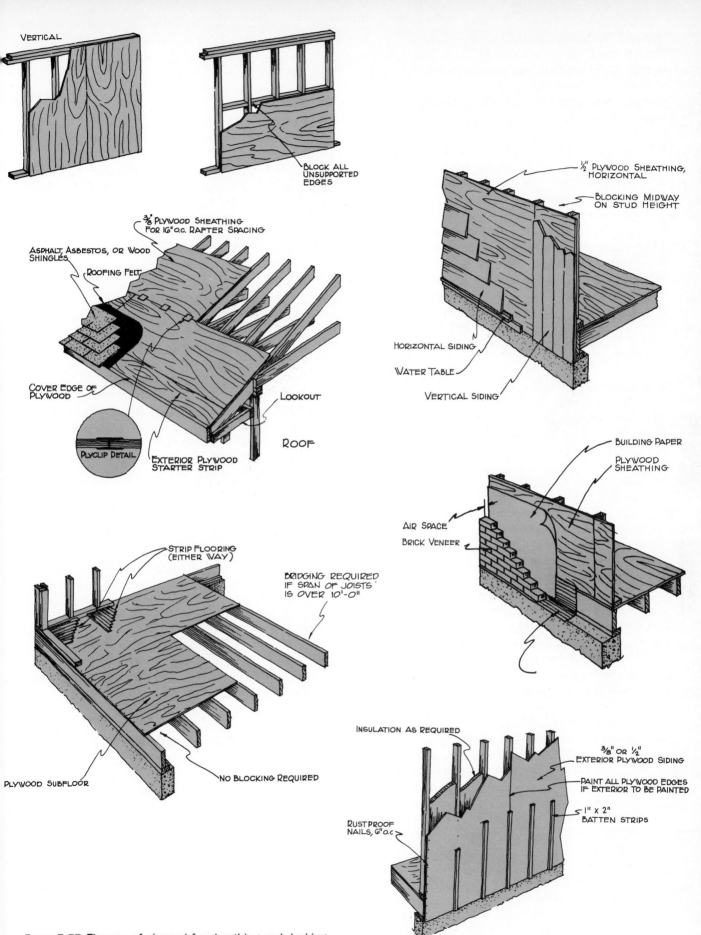

VERTICAL

BLOCK ALL
UNSUPPORTED
EDGES

⅜" PLYWOOD SHEATHING
FOR 16" o.c. RAFTER SPACING

ASPHALT, ASBESTOS, OR WOOD
SHINGLES

ROOFING FELT

COVER EDGE OF
PLYWOOD

PLYCLIP DETAIL

EXTERIOR PLYWOOD
STARTER STRIP

LOOKOUT

ROOF

½" PLYWOOD SHEATHING,
HORIZONTAL

BLOCKING MIDWAY
ON STUD HEIGHT

HORIZONTAL SIDING

WATER TABLE

VERTICAL SIDING

BUILDING PAPER

PLYWOOD
SHEATHING

AIR SPACE

BRICK VENEER

STRIP FLOORING
(EITHER WAY)

BRIDGING REQUIRED
IF SPAN OF JOISTS
IS OVER 10'-0"

PLYWOOD SUBFLOOR

NO BLOCKING REQUIRED

INSULATION AS REQUIRED

⅜" OR ½"
EXTERIOR PLYWOOD SIDING

PAINT ALL PLYWOOD EDGES
IF EXTERIOR TO BE PAINTED

1" x 2"
BATTEN STRIPS

RUSTPROOF
NAILS, 6" o.c.

FIGURE 7-55 The use of plywood for sheathing and decking.

$1/2''$ thick can be used as decking when light roof coverings are used; $5/8''$ or $3/4''$ thickness is necessary for the heavier roof coverings. All plywood edges should be well covered with molding or trim at the edges of the roof. As soon as the roof deck is completed it is covered with a good grade of roofing felt, preferably 30-pound felt. The felt is edge lapped and end lapped with at least a $2''$ lap and securely nailed every $6''$ with galvanized roofing nails. This covering is very important because it is rainproof and therefore protects the structure while the work is in progress.

If wood shingles are used as the roof covering, then 1×3 nailing strips can be used instead of solid decking. These strips are spaced the same distance apart as the part of the shingle that is exposed to the weather. The nailing strips provide an air space for ventilation and drying, thereby prolonging the life of the wood shingles. Wood shingle roofs can also have a tight, built-up deck covered with waterproof building felt; the 1×3 nailing strips are then attached over the felt, to which the wood shingles are nailed.

Wall Sheathing is the outer subwall, which is nailed directly to the studs and framework. Wall sheathing adds both strength and insulation to the building and forms a base for the exterior siding. The following types of materials are used for wall sheathing:

1. *Wood boards*, $1''$ nominal thickness, usually $6''$ or $8''$ wide; wider lumber will shrink more and leave wider gaps. Wood sheathing can be applied either horizontally or at a $45°$ angle. The horizontal method is more economical, but requires diagonal let-in bracing at the corners. Diagonal sheathing adds greatly to the rigidity of the wall and eliminates the need for corner bracing. It also provides an excellent tie between the framing and the sill plate. Wood sheathing can be either square edged, shiplap, or tongue and groove. End joints should be staggered and made over studs; two 8-penny nails are used at each stud bearing. Number 2 common lumber is usually specified.

2. *Fiberboard asphalt-coated sheathing* is available in $4'$ widths and $8'$, $9'$, $10'$, and $12'$ lengths. It can be applied either horizontally or vertically. The latter method usually requires a $9'$ long sheet to cover a wall that has $8'$-$0''$ ceilings. Fiberboard sheathing $1/2''$ thick is easy to handle by carpenters, and it goes on quickly compared to wood sheathing. Other types of fiberboard measure $2' \times 8'$ and have shiplap or tongue-and-groove edges; they are applied horizontally. Fiberboard must be carefully nailed with galvanized roofing nails.

3. *Plywood* used for sheathing usually comes in $4' \times 8'$ sheets and should be a minimum of $5/16''$ thick over studs spaced $16''$ on center (o.c.) and $3/8''$ thick over studs spaced $24''$ o.c. Six-penny nails

should be used and should be spaced not more than $6''$ apart for edge nailing and $12''$ apart for intermediate nailing. Plywood is usually applied vertically to permit perimeter nailing without additional blocking. When the $8'$ dimension is horizontal, blocking is desirable along the horizontal joints between the studs as a base for the finish-wall nailing. When the finish-wall material requires nailing between the studs (as with wood shingles), the plywood should be at least $3/8''$ thick. Wood shingles must be nailed to stripping if $5/16''$ plywood or other non-nail-holding sheathing is used. Plywood can be applied with power-driven staplers using galvanized wire staples. Asphalt building felt is placed over plywood sheathing in some locations.

4. *Gypsum sheathing*, composed of moisture-resistant gypsum filler faced on both sides with lightweight paper, can be used as a subwall. It is available in $2' \times 4'$ and $2' \times 8'$ sizes and $1/2''$ thick. Some gypsum sheathing has V-joint edges for easier application and better edge ties; this type is applied horizontally and nailed securely with galvanized roofing nails. Vertical joints are always staggered and made on the center of the studs. If finish siding is used that requires both nailing strips and a smooth base, the nailing strips are fastened directly to the studs, and the gypsum sheathing is nailed over the nailing strips.

5. *Styrofoam® and urethane sheathings*, usually $3/4''$ or $1''$ thick, some foil covered on one or both sides for added reflective insulation and resistance to moisture features, are light but fragile. They are obtainable in sheet sizes similar to plywood and must be carefully fastened to framing with large-headed nails or staples. Either has excellent insulating but poor structural qualities.

6. Wafer board available in $1/4''$ and $7/16''$ thicknesses and in $4'$ by $8'$ sheets is used for sheathing. This material can be applied vertically or horizontally over studs. Wafer board is fastened in the same manner as plywood.

7.4.2 Balloon Frame Construction

The distinguishing feature of balloon construction (Fig. 7-56) is that the studs run from the sill to the top plate. These vertical lengths of wall framing minimize the amount of wood shrinkage in the total height of the building. Even though the stud lengths are long, balloon framing is still an important type of construction in that there is less chance of the wood framing reducing in height when used with brick or stone veneer or stucco in 2-story buildings. Generally, in 1-story buildings the platform frame is employed; if a balloon frame is used, it can be identified by the studs

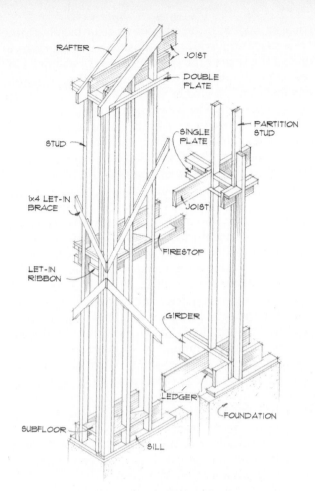

FIGURE 7-56 Balloon (eastern) frame construction.

placed directly on the sill plate, which is called a *solid sill*. Wood shrinks considerably more across grain than on end grain; therefore, the absence of horizontal members, with the exception of the sill and the plate, provides end-grain fiber almost throughout the entire height of the building. Even though balloon framing is not used as often as a platform frame, it has features that are noteworthy, and it is sometimes used in combination with platform construction.

Sill The sill plate, as in the platform frame, is well anchored to the foundation with ½" diameter anchor bolts. If the top of the foundation wall needs trueing, a bed of grout or mortar is placed below the sill. The sill is usually a 2 × 6 or 2 × 8; sometimes a double sill of well-spiked members is used. Both the studs and the first-floor joists rest on the sill plate, forming the solid sill. Usually, the sill plate is set the thickness of the sheathing inside the outer edge of the foundation wall (Fig. 7-29B).

Floor Joists The size and spacing of the floor joists, as in the platform frame, depend on their loads and span (refer to Chapter 8). Generally, the joists are spaced 16"

on center and are toenailed to the sill plate and the beam within the building. Joists can be butted to the beam and anchored, or they can be lapped over the beam. A row of bridging should be used if the joists span more than 10'-0". There are no headers at the ends of the joists.

Studs The studs are usually spaced 16" on center, as in other framing, and they run to the top plate. Each stud carries its own load from plate to sill without any lateral distribution by headers or beams. For this reason, studs have to be carefully selected, especially in balloon-frame, 2-story houses, where the studs must be considerably longer. The spacing of the studs must be compatible with the spacing of the floor joists and ceiling joists. This allows the joists in all floors to be nailed directly to the studs. Openings for doors and windows must be surrounded with double studs, and headers or lintels must be carefully selected; openings in first-story walls must have lintels or headers over them that are capable of carrying the entire weight of the studs above the openings.

One of the shortcomings of balloon framing is the ease with which a fire in the basement can burn through the sill and enter the cavities between the studs, causing flue action and rapid spread of the conflagration through the entire structure. To eliminate this hazard, codes require 2" blocking between the joists and studs above the sill plate and often prescribe that the cavity at the sill be filled with masonry or a noncombustible material.

Ribbon Another typical feature of the balloon frame is the method of supporting second-floor joists. Ceiling or second-floor joists rest on a 1 × 6 board, let into the studs, called a *ribbon*. The joists are also spiked to the studs. The ribbon is necessary only on those walls taking the ends of the joists. Fire stopping and blocking are also needed at the intersection of second-floor joists and the walls. In addition, horizontal blocking between the studs is required midway between room heights.

Posts Corner studs and posts at intersections of partitions and walls are built up, similar to the platform frame, so that nailing surfaces will be found on both inside and outside corners. Often balloon framing is used in partitions of 2-story, solid-masonry buildings to minimize vertical shrinkage.

Braces If horizontal board sheathing is used for the subwall, 1 × 4 let-in bracing must be used throughout the framing to resist raking stresses. The use of diagonal wood sheathing or plywood eliminates the need for the bracing. Diagonal 2 × 4 blocking at the corners does not have the strength the let-in braces have, especially if the blocking is not tightly fitted into the stud spacings.

Subfloor Boards, measuring 1 × 6 and laid diagonally, or plywood is generally used for the subfloor. The subfloor extends to the outer edge of the wall framing and is notched around the studs.

Top Plate and Roof Framing The top plate consists of a double 2 × 4 lapped at the corners and intersections of partitions and well-spiked together. If nailing surfaces are necessary for the application of gypsum board or other ceiling coverings, blocking must be inserted between the ceiling joists and spiked to the top plate. Rafters rest on the top plate and are nailed to both the plate and the ceiling joists, similar to platform framing. Metal framing anchors can be used to fasten rafters to the top plate if more rigidity is desired. The roof framing is done similarly to the method indicated in platform framing, and the treatment of the overhang varies with the type of architectural effect required. Some houses have very little overhang at the eaves; others may have as much as a 3′ overhang. Rafters can be left exposed at the eaves, or they can be boxed-in with a horizontal soffit. The treatment of the detail at the junction of the walls and roof plays an important part in the general character of the building (see Fig. 6-74).

7.4.3 Wood Roof Trusses

Lightweight, prefabricated wood trusses, often called trussed rafters, offer many advantages in roof framing of small- or average-size residences (see Figs. 7-57 and 7-58). Wood trusses can be used with either platform or balloon framing; when spaced 24″ on center, which is usually the case in small buildings, they become compatible with sheet sizes of plywood and other materials. Trusses can be lifted into place and quickly anchored on the job. Complete freedom can be exercised in the placement of partitions within the building; they can be made thinner, and when they are not load bearing, the foundation can be simplified, which constitutes a saving. The basic shape of the truss is a rigid structural triangle, and with the addition of strut members, the basic shape subdivides into smaller triangles, each reducing the span of the outer members or chords. This reduction of individual member spans allows narrower members, and less material is required to carry similar loads as compared to conventional framing.

The fasteners used to join the members of the truss can be nails, bolts, split rings, barb-pointed plates, or plywood gusset plates fastened with nails and glue. Many lumber dealers stock engineered trusses of standard lengths and roof pitches. Volume builders prefabricate their own trusses with simple jigs and production-line efficiency. Fabrication of trusses requires careful workmanship and attention to detail; the joints between members are critical, especially the heel joint, which is subjected to more lateral stresses. The heel joint should bear on the wall plate below (see Fig. 7-58). If an overhang is required, the top chords can be extended beyond the heel joint to support the overhang (see Fig. 7-57 and Fig. 7-59). Modified trusses are available for complete framing of hip-type roofs. Occasionally, conventional framing is combined with trussed-rafter framing; the trusses then replace the common rafters of the pitched roof, and conventional framing is used at the intersections of sloping roofs and around the hips of hip roofs.

One disadvantage of the trussed rafter is the relatively small amount of usable storage space remaining in the attic. However, if a W-type truss is used, the top of the lower chords between the center webs can be covered with a subfloor and used for storage if a 24″ disappearing stair is introduced between two trusses. The two trusses must be offset several inches from the 24″ spacing to take the stair unit. It is important to note that the bottom chords of trusses be designed to support live loads when attic storage is anticipated.

Also, by necessity, modular limitations with respect to building sizes, shapes, offsets, and the like, are encountered in the use of trusses.

Figure 7-57 shows an economical 32′-0″ truss designed by Byron Radcliff of Michigan State College. It

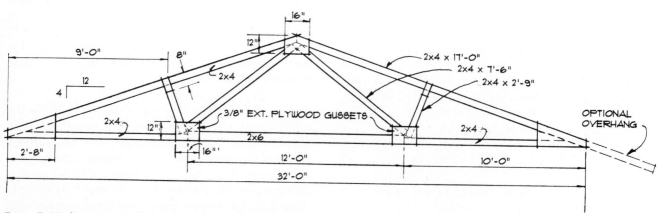

Figure 7-57 An economical wood truss for light construction.

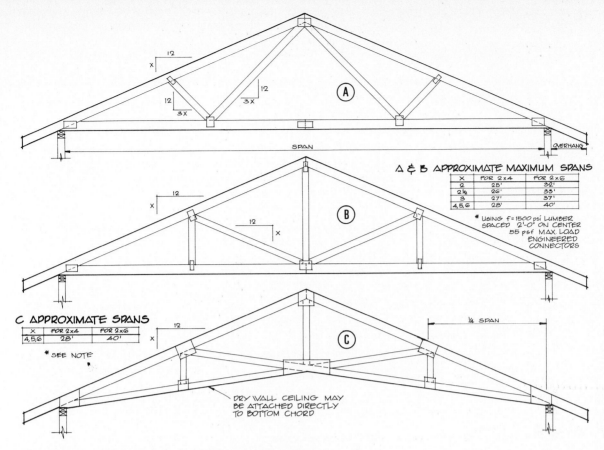

FIGURE 7-58 Prefabricated trusses for light construction.

A & B APPROXIMATE MAXIMUM SPANS

X	FOR 2×4	FOR 2×6
2	28'	32'
2½	26'	33'
3	27'	37'
4,5,6	28'	40'

* USING f=1500 psi LUMBER SPACED 2'-0" ON CENTER 55 psf MAX. LOAD ENGINEERED CONNECTORS

C APPROXIMATE SPANS

X	FOR 2×4	FOR 2×6
4,5,6	28'	40'

* SEE NOTE

DRY WALL CEILING MAY BE ATTACHED DIRECTLY TO BOTTOM CHORD

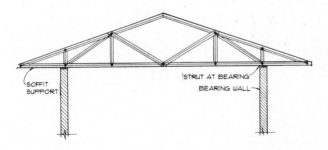

FIGURE 7-59 An alternate overhanging truss that provides for stable overhang.

is made entirely of 2 × 4s with the exception of the center of the bottom chord. The center 10′ section is designed for a 25-pound floor load to permit attic storage. In tests this truss took a 109-pound roof load before breaking, that is, twice the heaviest snow load for which trusses must be designed anywhere in this country. It requires only 73.1 board feet of lumber.

7.5 Plank and Beam Frame Construction

Plank and beam wood framing (see Figs. 7-60 and 7-61), now an established method of residential construction, has been adapted from the older type of mill construc-tion that utilized heavy framing members and thick wood floors and roofs. Plank and beam framing is similar to steel skeleton framing in concept; it develops structural stability by concentrating loads on a few large members, which in turn transfer their loads directly to the foundation by the use of posts or columns. In structures, these lines of load transfer from the beams should not be interrupted unless special provision has been made for their replacement. Posts needed to support beams in light construction must be at least 4″ × 4″. Where heavy, concentrated loads occur in places other than over main beams or columns, supplementary beams are necessary to carry the loads.

One structural advantage of plank and beam framing is the simplicity in framing around door and window openings. Because the loads are carried by posts uniformly spaced throughout the walls, large openings can be easily framed without lintels. Large window-walls, which are characteristic of contemporary construction, can be formed by merely inserting fixed glass between the posts. However, a window-wall should have several solid panels in appropriate places to stabilize it against lateral movement. All walls must be braced with diagonal bracing or suitable sheathing.

Plank and beam framing requires disciplined planning; savings will be realized by employing modular dimensions to the framing members and wall and roof

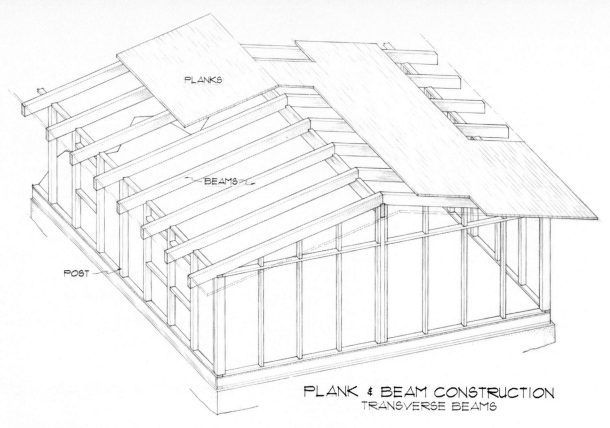

Figure 7-60 Plank and beam construction with transverse beams.

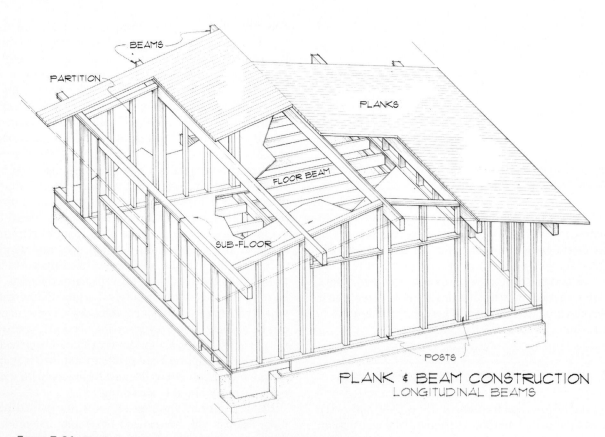

Figure 7-61 Plank and beam construction with longitudinal beams.

188 Light construction principles

coverings. (See Section 9.15 on modular dimensions.) It lends itself to the use of plywood. Stock plywood sizes can be used with a minimum of cutting and waste. Massive, exposed structural members within a house are instrumental in giving it a feeling of stability and rhythmic beauty, attributes that testify to the architect's competence.

With rising relative costs of labor in home building, plank and beam framing, which requires the handling of fewer pieces than does conventional framing, offers structural economies to home builders. In a study made by the National Lumber Manufacturers Association, the plank and beam method saved 26 percent on labor and 15 percent on materials over conventional joist framing. Bridging is eliminated between joists, nails are fewer and larger, and inside room heights are increased with no increase in stud or building heights. Masonry piers can be used instead of continuous foundation walls for economy. (The piers must be located under the structural posts.) Eave details and roof overhangs are simpler; usually, the 2″ roof decking is cantilevered over the wall and no material is needed for boxing in the cornice. Conventional framing can be successfully combined with plank and beam framing within the same building. Sometimes a plank and beam roof is used in only one room of the house, often the living or family area (Fig. 7-62). If so, sufficient column bearing must be provided within the stud walls for the beams of the one roof. If plank and beam wall framing supports conventional roof framing, a continuous header should be used at the top of the walls carrying the roof loads to transfer the load from the closely spaced rafters to the posts (see Fig. 7-41).

There are limitations to plank and beam framing, and attention to special details is necessary at these points of construction: partitions must be located over beams, or else supplemental framing must be installed; partitions perpendicular to the beams must rest on a 4 × 4 or 4 × 6 soleplate to distribute the load across the beam of the floor. Additional beams are needed under bathtubs and other concentrated loads. Because of the absence of concealed air spaces in floors and roofs, wiring and plumbing are more difficult to install. Often built-up cavity beams are used through which wiring or piping can pass. Flexible wiring cable can often be laid in the V joint on the top of 2″ roof decking. Surface-mounted electrical raceways may have to be used for electrical outlets. Plumbing, especially in 2-story houses, may have to be hidden within false beams or furred spaces. Moldings and raceways may have to be employed, and top surfaces of beams may have to be grooved to conceal wiring or piping.

Plank roofs with no dead air space below often require additional insulation and vapor barriers. Insulation is usually applied above the decking and must be rigid enough to support workers on the roof. The thickness of the insulation must conform to local climatic

FIGURE 7-62 Plank and beam interiors.

conditions. Vapor barriers should be installed between the decking and the insulation. Prefinished insulation board, 2″ to 4″ thick, is available in large sheets to replace decking and insulation combinations. It is light and can be installed rapidly by workers; no decorating of the underside ceiling is necessary. Prefinished insulation tile or panels can also be applied to the underside of regular wood decking. They can be attached directly to the decking, or furring strips can be used between the underside of the decking and the insulation. When rigid insulation is used above the decking, wood cant strips of the same thickness are fastened around the edges of the roof for application of flashing or gravel stops (see Fig. 7-63). Light-colored coverings for plank roofs also keep the house cooler in summer and warmer in winter.

Another consideration in plank and beam framing is the quality of the exposed structural lumber. Higher grades of framing lumber are required, because large knots, streaks, and resin blemishes are objectionable if painted and are even more unsightly if natural finishes are used. Workmanship in installing the structural pieces is especially important. Finishing nails must be used, metal anchors, if used, must be carefully fastened, and no hammer marks should be left on the

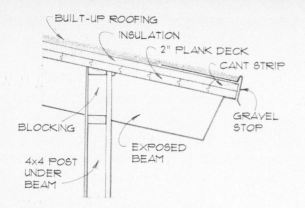

FIGURE 7-63 Typical plank and beam cornice detail.

each other and where beams join the posts. These connections must be strong and neatly done. Where gable roofs are used, provision must be made to absorb the horizontal thrust produced by the sloping roof beams (see Fig. 7-64). Partitions and supported ridge beams help relieve this thrust. Metal straps fastened over the ridge beam or metal ridge fasteners are effective in resisting the lateral stresses.

Plank and beam roofs can be supported with either transverse beams or longitudinal beams (see Figs. 7-60 and 7-61).

exposed structural surfaces. Planking should be accurately nailed to the beams, joints should occur above the beams, and the tongue and groove planking should be nailed up tightly so that shrinkage between planks will not be objectionable. Kiln-dried lumber should be specified, especially for visible ceilings. Blocking, or filler wall, between beams on exterior walls must be carefully fitted and detailed or leaky joints and air infiltration will result when the blocking dries and shrinks. Particular care must be given to connections where beams abut

Transverse Beams are usually supported at the ridge by a heavy ridge beam and by the long, exterior walls of the building. The planks then span the beams perpendicularly to the slope of the roof, if it is a gable type. Beams may be solid, glue laminated, or built up (see Fig. 7-65) of 2″ lumber, securely fastened together (fasteners are usually concealed). Strength and rigidity of the planks are improved if they are continuous over more than one span. Tests show that a plank that is continuous over two spans is nearly two and one-half times as stiff as a plank extending over only one span, under the same conditions. Planks, usually 6″ or 8″

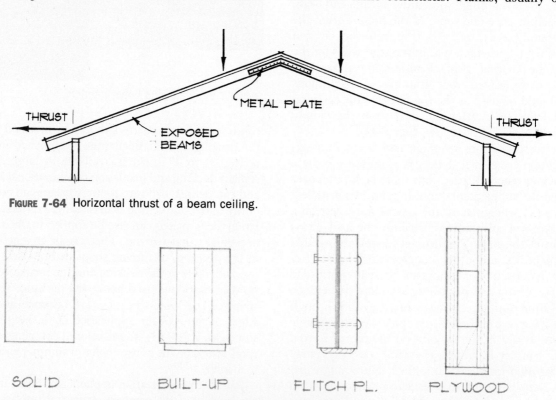

FIGURE 7-64 Horizontal thrust of a beam ceiling.

SOLID   BUILT-UP   FLITCH PL.   PLYWOOD

FIGURE 7-65 Types of beams used in plank and beam construction.

TONGUE & GROOVE - "V" JT.   SPLINE & "V" JT.

FIGURE 7-66 Wood decking used on plank and beam ceilings.

wide, can be tongue and grooved or splined (see Fig. 7-66) and are designed to support moderate loads. If beams are spaced more than 6' or 7' apart, noticeable deflection of common species of nominal 2" planking will result. 3" T&G planking will span up to 12'.

Longitudinal Beams, running the entire length of the building, can be used instead of transverse beams. In that case, the planking is applied parallel to the slope of the roof—down the slope. For either method, tables are used for the proper selection of beam size, span, and spacing, after the other architectural considerations have been resolved. Exterior beams at corners of gable ends are usually false or short beams, which are cantilevered out from the corner of the long, exterior walls (see Fig. 7-61). Beam sizes can be reduced when interior partitions become supports for the beams.

When either method of plank and beam framing is employed, interior partitions are often more difficult to frame than when conventional framing is used. If ceilings are sloping, the top of the partition must meet the underside of the slope and must be made diagonal. Other partitions, running perpendicularly to the slope of the ceiling, will have horizontal cap plates but must be built to different heights. Interior partitions, using 2 × 4 studs, can be framed by several methods. First, they can be framed with the studs cut the same length as the exterior walls and a double cap plate put over all the exterior and interior walls, tying them securely together as done in platform framing. Short studs are then attached above the plate to a single top plate that conforms to the slope of the ceiling and is attached to it.

Or the partitions can be erected after the roof is completed. The various-length studs are cut to fit the slope of the ceiling, and each partition with a single 2 × 4 cap is fitted into its proper place.

Finish strip flooring should be nailed at right angles to the plank subfloor, similar to conventional construction. Care must be taken to be sure flooring or roofing nails do not penetrate through the planks when the planks serve as a ceiling. The inside appearance should be considered when spacing beams; moving a beam several inches one way or another near a partition will often be an improvement. Partitions, on the other hand, should be placed in relation to beams so that the beams seem to form a uniform pattern throughout the room. The appearance of exposed beams on the exterior of the building is also of importance. Plank and beam framing lends itself to open planning, a characteristic of contemporary houses.

In most areas, the structural design of the plank and beam framing will be controlled by the local building code to the extent of specifying live load requirements. A live load of 40 lb/sq ft is usually specified for floors. For roofs, some codes specify 20 lb/sq ft, others 30 lb. Beam sizes, spacing, and species necessary for various spans of both roofs and floors can be taken from the plank and beam tables found in Chapter 8.

Glue-Laminated Structural Members offer many design possibilities in plank and beam construction that otherwise would be restricted by the structural limitations of sawed wood members (see Fig. 7-67). Many stock beam shapes are available (see Fig. 7-68), provid-

FIGURE 7-67 A California redwood home with an interesting roof of planks over laminated beams. (*Courtesy Dandelet.*)

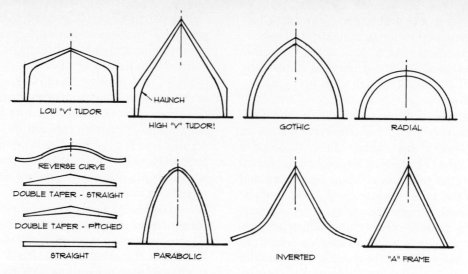

FIGURE 7-68 Glue-laminated structural shapes available in wood.

ing variations in conventional building silhouettes. Many church buildings successfully employ either laminated beams or arches for interesting ceilings and roof structures. Special waterproof glues are used for exterior exposures. Usually, comparative sectional sizes span one-third more than sawed timbers. Consult manufacturers' catalogues for specific shapes, loads, and spans.

In larger buildings, structural systems such as rigid frames, two-hinged barrel arches, and three-hinged arches, as well as bowstring arches and domes, make use of laminated members. Rigid frames are made of separate leg and arm members carefully joined at the haunch to maintain the desired roof slope. The two-hinged barrel arches must have provision for counteracting outward thrust at their bases with the use of either foundation piers, tie rods, or concrete foundation buttresses. Each support must be engineered to resist the horizontal thrust of the arch. Three-hinged arches such as Tudor and Gothic are popular in contemporary church architecture because of their beauty. Their spans vary typically from 30 to 100 feet. Their base construction is similar to the two-hinged arches. Because of the distance between arches, purlins are commonly placed perpendicularly between arches to carry the roof decking. Arch design data vary with the roof slope and span distance. Metal connectors at critical points ensure neat, engineered joining of the laminated members (see Fig. 7-69).

7.6 Brick and Stone Veneer Construction

In areas of the country where brick or building stone are economical, veneered frame dwellings are popular. Masonry veneer over wood framing is more economical than solid masonry; the combination wall (masonry over wood) utilizes the good qualities of both materials.

The exterior masonry is durable and requires no maintenance; the wood is economical, more flexible, and a good insulator. Any of the previously mentioned types of wood framing can be used with veneer; the wood frame supports the entire weight of the floors and roof—no loads are put on the masonry veneer. The single wythe of brick or stone is merely an exterior wall covering for the structure (see Fig. 7-71).

Bricks or 4″ or 6″ cut stone can be used for veneering. Hard-burned, moisture-resistant brick should be used. Sandstones and limestones are commonly used for stone veneers. Standard-size brick as well as oversized brick (jumbo, utility, or Norwegian) is available (Fig. 7-77). Bricks are manufactured in a wide range of colors and finishes. A better quality brick has the same clay throughout the brick, whereas a less expensive brick may have a color or sand finish applied only to the face of the brick. Wood-mold brick is available, which resembles the handmade brick of Colonial times. Adobe brick is popular in the Southwest.

It is common practice to start the veneer at the grade line. Provision must be made on the foundation for the width of the veneer and a 1″ air space between the veneer and the wall sheathing; at least 5″ bearing width on the foundation wall is allowed (see Fig. 7-72). Good construction usually starts the veneer lower than the wood sill on the foundation wall. Brick may be corbelled ³/₄″ beyond the edge of the foundation wall. Condensation often develops within the air space, and provision must be made to keep the moisture from penetrating the wood members. The exterior wood sheathing must be covered with a moisture barrier, such as roofing felt. If asphalt-coated sheathing board is used, the asphalt coating acts as a moisture barrier. Styrofoam and urethane sheathing are water-resistant materials and do not require a moisture barrier; however, both products are available with an aluminum foil face.

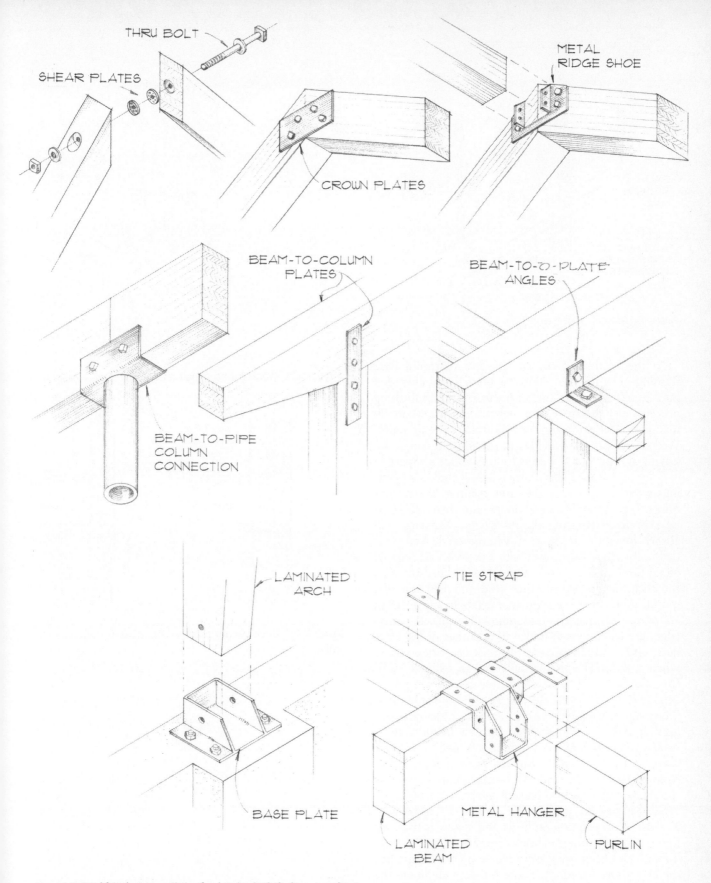

SHEAR PLATES

THRU BOLT

CROWN PLATES

METAL RIDGE SHOE

BEAM-TO-COLUMN PLATES

BEAM-TO-PIPE COLUMN CONNECTION

BEAM-TO-⊘-PLATE ANGLES

LAMINATED ARCH

BASE PLATE

TIE STRAP

METAL HANGER

LAMINATED BEAM

PURLIN

FIGURE 7-69 Metal connections for laminated timber members.

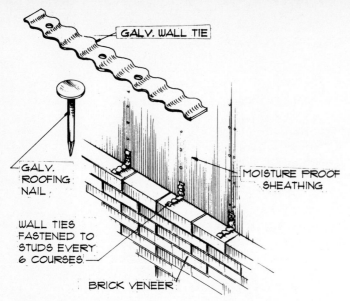

FIGURE 7-70 Brick wall ties.

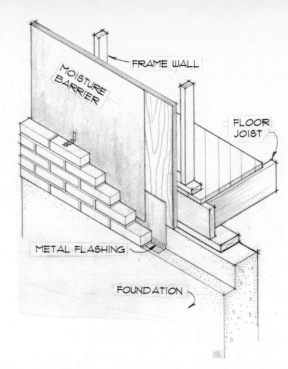

FIGURE 7-71 Wood frame construction with brick veneer.

At the bottom of the air space, a rustproof base flashing must be inserted under the felt and extended into the lower mortar joint of the veneer. This flashing prevents any moisture from penetrating the wood sill members after gathering at the bottom of the air space. Weep holes can be provided at the bottom course by leaving mortar out of vertical joints about 4′ apart.

Brick or masonry sills under window and door openings must be flashed in the same manner. Water running off from windows and doors onto their sills must be kept from entering the air cavity. Masonry will absorb moisture unless it is waterproofed. Veneer is tied to the wood frame wall with rustproof, corrugated metal ties (see Fig. 7-70). The ties are nailed through the sheathing to every other stud and laid into the mortar joints of every sixth course (about every 16″ to 20″ of vertical masonry). Sloping sills of brick, set on edge, are usually used under all openings of brick veneer, and a similar sloping sill must cap brick veneer when it extends only partially up an exterior wall. Combination brick and wood siding exteriors require a bead of caulking where the two materials join together. Stone veneer usually has a cut stone sill under all openings. It also extends out from the face of the veneer, similar to brick, and has a sloping top surface, called a *wash*, and a drip underneath to prevent water from running back to the wall. All mortar joints in veneers should be well tooled to prevent moisture penetration.

Steel angle iron, usually $3\frac{1}{2}″ \times 3\frac{1}{2}″ \times \frac{5}{16}″$ or $6″ \times 3\frac{1}{2}″ \times \frac{3}{8}″$ depending on loads and spans, is used for lintels above openings in brick veneer (see Fig. 7-73 and Table 7-7). Often brick *soldier courses* (Fig. 7-74) are put directly above openings. Some builders eliminate the use of steel lintels above veneer openings in 1-story houses by using a wide-trim frieze board and molding above all window and door openings. If a low, boxed-in

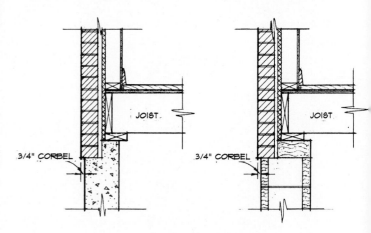

FIGURE 7-72 Brick veneer may be corbelled on foundation walls.

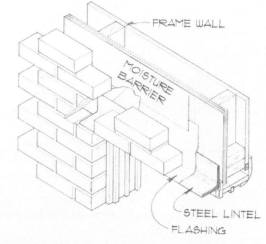

FIGURE 7-73 Steel lintel above brick veneer openings.

TABLE 7-7

Steel angle lintels for light-frame brick veneer construction

Span	Size
0'–5'	$3\frac{1}{2}'' \times 3\frac{1}{2}'' \times \frac{5}{16}''$
5'–7'	$4'' \times 3\frac{1}{2}'' \times \frac{5}{16}''$
7'–9'	$5'' \times 3\frac{1}{2}'' \times \frac{3}{8}''$
9'–10'	$6'' \times 3\frac{1}{2}'' \times \frac{3}{8}''$

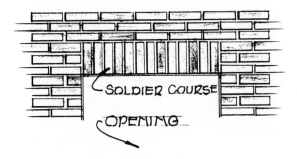

FIGURE 7-74 Brick soldier course above opening.

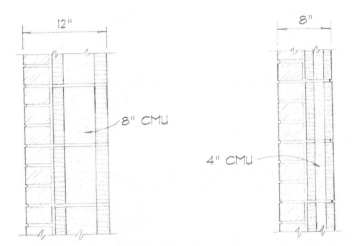

FIGURE 7-75 Concrete block and brick veneer wall details.

cornice is used, no masonry is necessary above the openings. The wide frieze board continues around the entire house below the cornice, and blocking is used to fur out to the face of the veneer above the windows and doors.

Brick or stone is often used to veneer concrete masonry units (see Fig. 7-75). In low walls, corrugated metal ties can be used to tie the two materials together; in larger walls, more positive bonds are attained with *header courses*—called "bonding" of brick set into the masonry backing.

7.7 Solid Masonry and Cavity Wall Construction

Solid masonry, especially brick and stone, has served people well for centuries as a desirable construction material. Many structures still standing and still beautiful are evidence of its pleasing as well as durable characteristics. Both brick and stone are available in many different colors, textures, and sizes to challenge the creativity and artistry of modern designers and builders. Even though many solid masonry buildings have been built of these materials in the past, the present-day trend is to use these materials as exterior veneers only, with either wood frame, metal studs, concrete block, or reinforced concrete as the structural, load-bearing material. Solid stone in residential work is limited mainly to foundations, as mentioned in the previous material on foundations, or small walls; in contemporary residences it is often used to create contrasting walls where the texture and color of the brick or stone are exposed both inside and outside. Many architects feel that the natural beauty of stone provides sufficient textural interest to make any further decoration of the walls unnecessary.

Local codes in some residential areas require solid masonry exterior walls in all structures. Usually 8″ thick brick walls are used in 1-story houses; local codes must be referred to if higher walls are involved. This type of construction, where solid masonry walls carry the weight of the floors and roof, is known as *bearing-wall construction*. The floors and roof are constructed of wood framing members, similar to conventional framing, except that the floor joists are set into the masonry walls and transfer their loads to them; the rafters rest on wood plates well anchored to the top of the walls. All the wood structural members of the floors, partitions, and roof are surrounded by the shell-like exterior masonry wall. This shell of incombustible material has the advantage of restricting the spread of fire to surrounding buildings. Floor joists setting in the masonry wall must have a diagonal cut, called a *fire cut*, on their ends to prevent the joists from rupturing the wall should a fire burn through the joists and cause them to drop to the bottom of the building (see Fig. 7-76). The fire cut allows full bearing at the bottom surface of the joist, yet is self-releasing in case of fire.

Because of the porous and noninsulating nature of solid brick or masonry, some method must be used to prevent moisture penetration and to insulate the exterior walls. The conventional method is to waterproof the inside surface of the masonry with hot asphalt or tar and then fasten 1×2 furring strips to the inside masonry surface, to which the interior wall covering is applied. Rigid insulation can also be inserted between the furring strips. Another method of furring the masonry wall, to get an air space between the exterior and

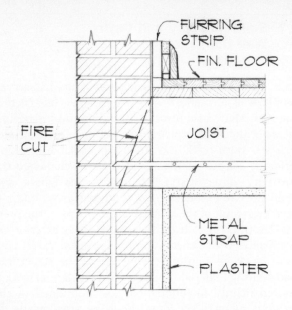

FIGURE 7-76 Wood joists in solid-brick wall detail.

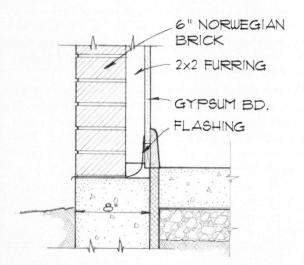

FIGURE 7-77 Norwegian brick wall detail for 1-story walls.

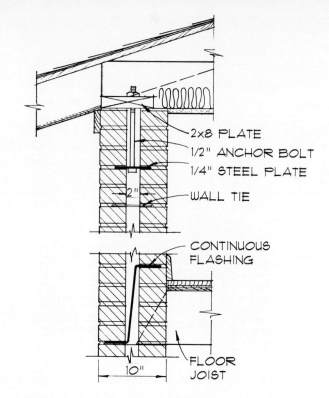

FIGURE 7-78 Brick cavity wall detail.

interior surfaces, is by using a self-furring metal lath over which ¾″ plaster is applied.

In economical 1-story buildings, a single-wythe brick called Norwegian brick can be used for the masonry load-bearing walls (see Fig. 7-77). Since the Norwegian brick is larger than common brick, a wall can be laid up much faster. It is 5½″ wide, 2³⁄₁₆″ high, and 11½″ long and can be furred with 2″ × 2″ furring strips, fastened to metal clips that are set into the mortar joints throughout the wall. Interior finish materials can be fastened to the furring strips.

Many other hollow brick units are available up to 8″ thick that are suitable for single-unit masonry walls. Interior plaster is often applied directly to the inside surface of these units. Many small commercial buildings are built with this method. For residential construction, however, small brick units are preferable be-

cause their texture imparts more interest than that of the larger units.

If a brick surface is required for both the outside and inside walls, a *brick cavity* wall can be used (Fig. 7-78). This method of construction was introduced from Europe in the late 1930s and has been widely accepted in this country. A 2″ air cavity is used between the wythes of common brick, making the wall usually 10″ thick. Rigid metal ties are placed in the mortar joints spaced 16″ on center horizontally and vertically to tie the two wythes together. No furring is necessary, since the air cavity prevents moisture penetration and insulates the wall. In colder climates, air stops are used at corners to minimize air circulation throughout the cavity. Added insulation can be given by applying rigid insulation to the inside wall of the air cavity; insulation should not touch the outside wythe of brick. Flashing must be used at floor levels, sills, heads of openings, and other critical places. Weep holes must be used in the outer base course to dissipate moisture accumulating in the lower part of the air cavity. This can be accomplished by omitting the mortar from header joints at intervals of 3′ to 4′. Another method is to insert cotton sash cord, cut 5″ to 6″ long, in the mortar joints every 4′ to produce a wick action and also seal the cavity from insects.

Wood floor joists can rest on the inside wythe of brick; additional metal ties must be used in the course below the joists, and the joists must not project into the cavity. Girders and beams must be supported by solid, 8″ wide pilasters that bond the inner and outer wythes together. Roof and ceiling construction must be supported by a 2″ thick wood plate that rests on both wythes and is anchored with ¹/₂″ anchor bolts 6′-0″ on center. The anchor bolts must extend down into the air cavity about 15″, and a 3″ × 6″ × ¹/₄″ plate is welded to the head of the bolt and anchored in the mortar joints of the brick (see Fig. 7-78). Mortar joints should be well tooled on both the outer and inner finish surfaces.

Concrete Masonry Units (Concrete Block) have become the most economical building material for small buildings, even for aboveground construction. It is estimated that a C.M.U. wall costs about 10 percent less than conventional stud wall with insulation construction. It is a widely available material that combines structure, insulation, and exterior and interior finish surfaces. Many various shapes and sizes of blocks are manufactured; as previously mentioned, the most used sizes are nominal 8″ × 8″ × 16″ and 8″ × 12″ × 16″. (Refer to Fig. 7-10 for other sizes and shapes.) The units are made either of dense concrete mixes, which give them good structural qualities, or of lightweight aggregate mixes, which result in blocks that are weaker structurally, but that provide better insulation. Lightweight blocks of foamed concrete are available in some areas; they have the same insulating qualities as stud walls with wood sheathing, siding, and 2″ of insulation.

Improperly cured units often result in cracks in C.M.U. walls. The blocks should be air cured for at least 28 days, or they should be cured under high-pressure steam, which is the better method for reducing ultimate shrinkage. Steam-cured units will shrink from ¹/₄″ to ³/₈″ in a 100′ wall; air-cured units will shrink about twice the amount. Cracking can often be eliminated by introducing wire mesh or lightweight C.M.U. steel reinforcement into every second or third horizontal mortar joint (see Fig. 7-79). Extra reinforcement is required above and below all wall openings. In long C.M.U. walls, control joints must be used to relieve contraction and other stresses; they are continuous vertical joints through the wall and are spaced at 20′-0″ intervals.

Concrete masonry unit walls are not successful in areas subjected to earthquakes, unless heavy reinforcement is used extensively at each floor and ceiling level. Refer to local seismic codes if blocks must be used.

In warm areas such as Florida, Arizona, and parts of Texas, concrete masonry units are a very popular aboveground construction material, even in fine houses. Units can be waterproofed on the exterior with waterproof, cement-base paints or directly covered with stucco. The inside is usually furred and plastered. Florida hurricane codes require continuous, reinforced concrete bond beams above each story-level of C.M.U. work, which must be tied to the foundation with vertical corner reinforcement (see Fig. 7-12).

Different architectural effects can be achieved by the

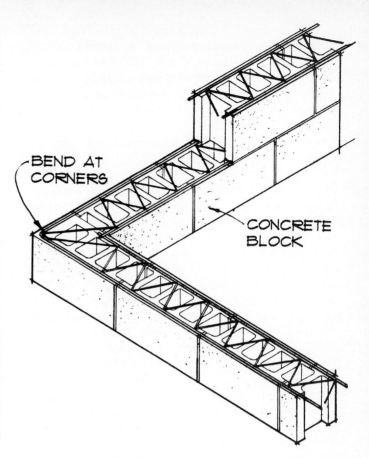

FIGURE 7-79 Horizontal reinforcement in C.M.U. courses.

use of different-sized units in various combinations; however, the *half-lapped bond* is used in structural walls. A *stacked bond* is occasionally used for novelty effects, but horizontal reinforcement must then be used in the horizontal joints. As mentioned in the material on foundations, use unit modules for lengths, heights, and opening sizes, as well as placement of the openings (see Fig. 7-5). Hollow units must be capped with solid cap blocks where framing joists or beams rest on them. Nonload-bearing partitions can be made with 4″ thick hollow units.

Ribbed or split-faced concrete masonry units in a wide variety of styles and colors are available from certain manufacturers. Although more expensive than standard units, the split-faced units eliminate the need for painting or furring the exterior or interior faces of the walls to apply other finishes.

Steel and Concrete Joists Steel joists are often used in small commercial buildings for the structural support of roofs and light-occupancy floors. Several different types of open-web steel joists are manufactured; details and allowable spans are obtained from manufacturers' catalogues.[1]

---

[1] Specifications and details can also be obtained from the Steel Joist Institute, 1346 Connecticut Avenue NW, Washington, DC 20036.

Total dead and live loads must be calculated, and preliminary considerations must be studied before open-web steel joists are adopted. After they have been found adaptable in the preliminary planning, a thorough engineering calculation is made of all aspects of their use before the steel joist construction is finally selected for the structure.

H series steel joists are available in standard depths of 8″, 10″, 12″, 14″, 16″, 18″, 20″, 22″, 24″, 26″, 28″, and 30″, each in different weights that can span up to 60′ for roofs. Maximum permissible spacing of the joists for floors is 24″ on center; for roofs it is 30″ on center. In flat roof construction with 2″ thick tongue and grooved decking, a 2″ × 4″ nailing strip is fastened to the top of the joists with metal clips or bolts to receive the decking. Some joists are made with wood nailing strips already attached to both the top and bottom chord. If a ceiling is required below the roof joists, 3/8″ ribbed metal lath can be clipped to the bottom chord and plaster applied over it (see Fig. 7-80). This construction will give the roof a 3/4-hour fire rating according to the National Bureau of Standards Report TRBM-44. Flat-type roof construction with steel joists also employs a 2″ concrete slab poured over paper-backed steel mesh or a 2″ gypsum slab as the deck. Usually, built-up roofing is applied directly over the slabs, unless rigid insulation is needed. Lightweight, insulating concrete makes a desirable roof. The steel joists rest on the load-bearing masonry walls, or, in wider buildings requiring a steel girder through the center, they would rest on the girder as well as on the walls. Metal bridging is attached to joists between spans. Suspended ceilings of acoustical tile can be supported with hangers and metal channels below the steel joists; the open-web character of the joists allows pipes, ducts, and wiring to be run through the dead air space above the ceiling.

In floor construction with steel joists, the joists are supported in the masonry wall similar to wood framing, as well as on steel girders through the center if the building is wider than the span of one joist. A 2″ or 2½″ poured concrete slab is placed over one of several types of permanent forming material—either paper-backed 6″ × 6″ No. 10 wire mesh, corrugated steel sheets, or 3/8″ expanded metal rib lath. The forming material is left in place. Floor slabs are reinforced with 1/4″ (No. 2) bars, 12″ on center both ways, or with the 6″ × 6″ welded wire mesh; no other reinforcing is generally used.

Precast, reinforced concrete slabs of similar thickness can also be used on floors. Asphalt tile or other floor finishes can be put over the concrete slabs.

Reinforced Concrete Joists are occasionally used in light construction (see Fig. 7-81). In case of a concrete floor with a basement below or a fireproof flat roof, the use of concrete joists is appropriate. They are manufactured in many areas, so a source can usually be found near any given building site. Depth and reinforcing size are custom designed according to the loads and spans required. Concrete joists are generally spaced 24″ on center and bear on concrete block walls. The slab can be poured over wood forming placed between the joists, or the permanent forming materials, mentioned above, can be used. Another method utilizes filler block laid tightly between the concrete joists and resting on the joists. A 2″ slab is poured over the filler block to form the floor or roof. Precast concrete joists are designed for each specific job and delivered to the site ready to be installed.

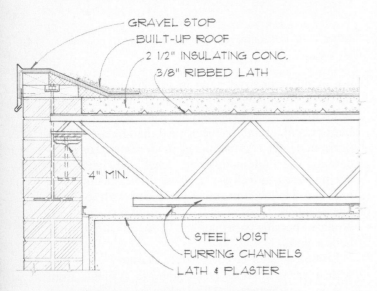

FIGURE 7-80 Bearing wall and steel joist detail.

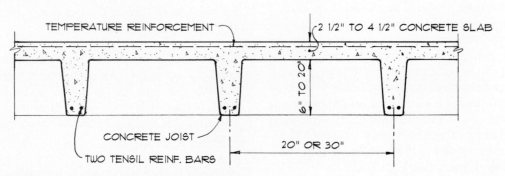

FIGURE 7-81 Reinforced concrete joist detail.

7.8 Roof Types and Roof Coverings

The roof is a very important part of any building, large or small, and it should therefore receive careful consideration. We might say a house is no better than the roof that covers it. Like an umbrella, it protects the structure from the elements; in some climates it is subjected to intense heat, most everywhere to rain and dampness, and in many areas to driving winds. Not only is the roof extremely functional, but its shape and nature play a vital role in the architectural appearance and styling of a house, which are often designated by its roof type. In commercial buildings, however, the roof is often flat and obscured by parapet walls, and therefore less important as far as the building's appearance is concerned.

In years past, the snow load of buildings in northern areas required steep roofs. However, with the improvement of roofing materials and more engineering design in buildings, the design of modern roofs has become less restrictive. Because architects and builders now have available a generous selection of roof coverings for any desired architectural treatment, we find successful roofs of all types and slopes in almost every area of the country regardless of climatic conditions.

7.8.1 Roof Types

The Flat Roof (see Fig. 7-82) is one of the simplest and most economical roofs as far as material is concerned. The roof joists become the framing members of both the roof and the interior ceiling. Sizes and spans of joists must be adequate to support both the live load of the roof and the dead loads of the roofing and the finished ceiling. The spacing of wood roof joists is generally 16″ on center. Comparatively little air space is provided in a flat roof; therefore, batt-type or blanket insulation, with the vapor barrier near the interior side, is recommended between roof joists. All the air cavities between the roof joists must be ventilated. Solid bridging should not be used in flat roofs; the blocking would prevent uniform air circulation.

Overhangs, for reason of weather protection or appearance, vary in width from 1′ to 4′; the usual overhang is 2′, so 4′-0″ wide plywood panels can be conveniently ripped and used for soffits. Overhangs of the flat roof are simply cantilevered over the exterior wall plates, and the joists are toenailed to the plates, or metal framing anchors can be used. If a boxed-in overhang is used, a header joist is recommended around the periphery of the roof (see Fig. 7-83A). The header joist becomes the backing for the finish fascia board, provides blocking for the soffit material, and tends to straighten the roof line. Overhangs from exterior walls that are parallel to the joists must be framed with *look-out joists* (sometimes called *tail joists*, see Fig. 7-54). Look-out joists are short and butt into a double, long joist. Generally, the distance from the double, long joist to the wall line is the same as the overhang. If wide joists are necessary, because of the span, the joist width is often tapered from the exterior wall to the outside end of the joist. This tapering of the joists prevents the fascia board from appearing too wide and heavy. Occasionally, to avoid wide fascias, narrow outlookers are lap nailed to the roof joists. Blocking is required on the top wall plate between each roof joist to provide nailing strips for the soffit and crown molding.

Flat roofs have the advantage of ease and flexibility of framing over odd building shapes and offset exterior walls. Other types of roofs often restrict the general shape of the building. Many architects resort to a flat roof when living spaces within the building do not conform to traditional shapes and relationships. Space planning can be almost unrestricted if a flat roof is used. However, the straight, horizontal roof line of a flat roof often appears hard and monotonous; variety and interest can be gained by combining other roof shapes with the flat roof, or by using several roof levels throughout the building. A watertight, built-up or single-ply membrane roof covering must be used on a flat roof, and metal gravel stops are put around the edges. The roof can have a slight pitch or it can be perfectly flat. Many flat roofs retain puddles after a rain, but this is not particularly objectionable.

The Shed-Type Roof (see Fig. 7-82) is framed very much like a flat roof yet it has a definite slope. As a rule the slopes are made low, unless the shed is used in combination with gable-type roofs. Ceilings can be applied directly to the rafters to provide interest and variety to interior living spaces. The span of a sloping rafter is the horizontal distance between its supports. Shed rafters should be well anchored to the plates of the exterior wall.

The Gable Roof used for centuries, is the traditional shape of most roofs. It consists of two inclined planes that meet at a ridge over the center of the house and slope down over the sidewalls. The inclined planes form a triangular shape at the ends of the house called a *gable* or *gable end* (see Fig. 7-53). Framing of the gable roof is discussed in the material under platform framing. Many different slopes or pitches can be used with the gable roof, depending on the architectural treatment and roofing materials.

Roof pitches must be indicated on drawings, and there are several methods of expressing the slope (refer to Section 10.3).

Details of the framing and architectural treatments of the intersection of the roof and the walls (see Fig. 7-84) are shown in *cornice details*, which will be discussed in Chapter 10 under Working Drawings. Steep gable roofs allow enough headroom for second-story living

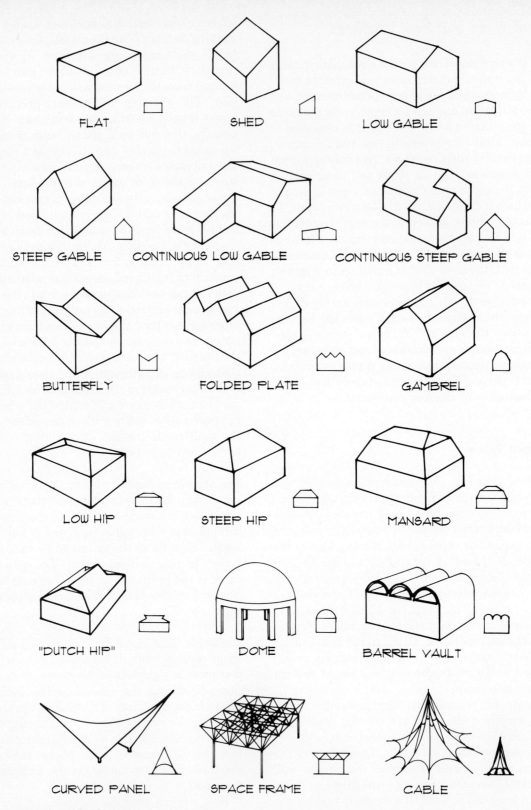

FIGURE 7-82 Roof types.

space, even though the floor area may not be as large as that of the first floor. Light and ventilation can be provided by dormers with windows, which are framed out from the main roof (see Fig. 7-52). In traditional, colonial-type houses, dormers must be symmetrically spaced on the roof; they should have good proportions so that they will appear light and neat. Massive dormers often ruin an otherwise attractively designed colonial-type house.

Low-slope gable roofs are characteristic of the newer,

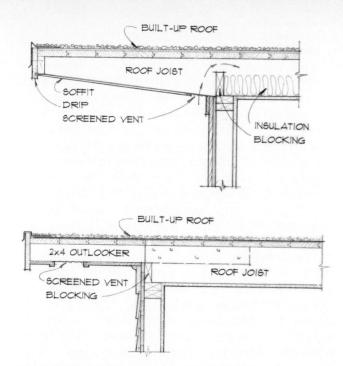

FIGURE 7-83 Flat roof with narrow fascia details.

rambling ranch-type house; they usually have wide overhangs. The space below the roof can be used, if at all, for minor storage.

The Hip Roof is another conventional-type roof that is popular in many areas of the country (see Fig. 7-82). The inclined roof planes slope to all outside walls, and the treatment of the cornice and roof overhang is identical around the entire house. It eliminates gable end walls but requires more roofing material than a gable roof of comparative size. Usually, the plan is rectangular, in which case common rafters are used to frame the center portion of the roof. Hip rafters, which carry very little of the load, are used at the exterior corners of the sloping intersections. Valley rafters, on the other hand, carry considerable loads, and are used at the interior intersections of the roof planes. Short jack rafters join either the hip rafter and the wall plate or the valley rafter and the ridge. More complex framing is required in hip roofs; hip, valley, and jack rafters require compound diagonal cuts at their intersections. For simple hip roofs, a roof layout is not necessary on the working drawings, but more complex roofs with

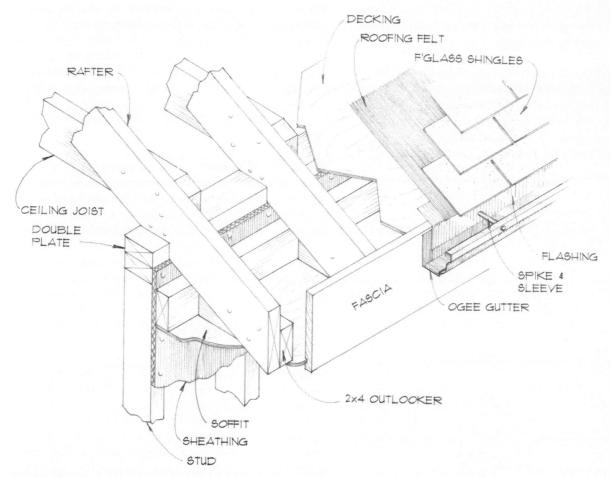

FIGURE 7-84 Roof construction at overhang with a boxed-in eave.

ridges of different heights and other offsets would definitely require a roof layout drawing.

Trussed rafters are available in some areas for framing standard span and pitch hip roofs. Regular trusses are used in the center section along the ridge, and modified trusses are made to conform to the end slope of the hip.

Like other roofs, hip roofs must be properly ventilated; because the roof covering is continuous over the higher areas of the roof, small metal vents or louvers are often employed on the rear side near the ridge to allow warm air to escape. Air inlets are provided by vents under the eaves.

Steep hip roofs often allow additional living space under the roof, similar to steep gable roofs. To be consistent, dormers on hip roofs usually have hip roofs as well.

The Dutch Hip Roof, a variation of the hip roof, is shown in Fig. 7-82. It is framed similarly to the gable roof throughout the center section to the ends of the ridge, where double rafters are used. The end hips are attached to the double rafters and are started below a louver and extend over the corners of the building. The louvers at each end of the ridge allow more positive ventilation under the roof.

Because a hip roof can become more complex to frame than other roofs, the following method is offered *to lay out a working drawing for a hip roof:*

Using Fig. 7-85 as an example, draw the outline of the building including all ells and offsets. Draw the main roof formed by the rectangle ABCD; the 45° hip lines are drawn from the main corners and corners of the ells. The intersections of the 45° hip lines will locate the ridgelines. Draw the 45° val-

ley lines connecting all roof intersections. A Dutch hip is indicated at point E; the ridge end can be indicated at any location along the diagonal hip lines, depending on the size of the louver used on the end elevation of the building. Uniform overhangs can be drawn around the exterior wall lines, and hip lines can be extended to the corners of the overhangs. This layout can be used regardless of the pitch that has been selected—low or steep slope. Hip roofs are more pleasing if the same pitch has been used on all planes of the roof. Rafters are drawn using either 16″ or 24″ o.c. spacing.

The Gambrel Roof is typical of Dutch colonial houses, and it is also found on many farm buildings. Each slope has a break or change of pitch; the lower part is always steeper than the upper (see Fig. 7-50). From a practical standpoint, this roof allows more headroom compared to a gable roof with the same ridge height. More labor is involved in framing a gambrel roof; as a result, it is seldom used in modern construction except on strictly colonial houses.

The Butterfly Roof is similar to an inverted gable roof (see Fig. 7-82). Caution should be exercised in the selection of a butterfly roof; roofers indicate that the intersection of the two inclined planes produces severe strain on the roof covering. Drainage of the valley is difficult, yet this can be accomplished with the use of tapered cant strips under the roofing, which act very much like a saddle that is used to spread water away from a chimney on a sloping roof. A bearing partition should be used below the valley for a stable support for the rafters.

The Barrel-Vault Roof employs precurved plywood panels or regular plywood attached to curved ribs (see Fig. 7-82). The panels are custom designed and made by authorized plywood manufacturers. With relatively thin cross sections, the curved, stressed-skin panels permit spanning long distances because of their arching action. Tie rods are usually required to counteract the thrust action when thinner panels are used. Insulation can be incorporated into the panels, and the underside of the panels can be used as the finished ceiling. Supported beams are uniformly spaced below the intersections of the vaults.

The Folded-Plate Roof (see Fig. 7-82) creates a roof line that is truly contemporary in profile. Its form is the result of engineered functional design. Reinforced concrete folded-plate roofs have been in use for years. Corrugated metal, on a small scale, obtains its stiffness similarly because of its folded characteristic. However, it has been largely through the efforts of the American Plywood Association that the shape has been adapted to

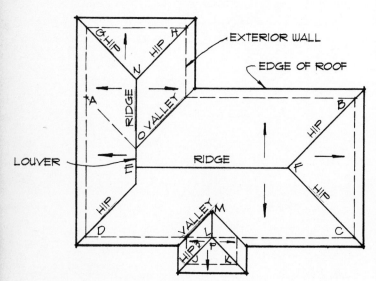

FIGURE 7-85 Layout of a hip roof.

wood construction, mainly because of the high shear strength and rigidity of plywood.

A plywood folded-plate roof differs from conventional pitched roof construction in that the roof sheathing and framing are designed to act together as a large inverted V-shaped beam to span from end to end of the building. A multiple-bay roof is made up of several such beams connected together side by side.

The inclined planes of the roof transfer their vertical loads to adjoining ridge and valley intersections, very much as cross-bridging in conventional floor construction transfers a concentrated load to surrounding floor joists. Loads on the inclined planes are carried in shear by the plywood diaphragm action to the ends of the building and by horizontal thrust action to the sides of the building.

Vertical supports are necessary at the ends of the building under the valleys and along the sides of the building. Either a beam or a bearing wall can be used along the sides. Horizontal thrust that is transferred to the sides of the building must be counteracted by horizontal ties of steel or wood.

The analysis of a multiple-bay folded plate differs slightly in that at the interior valleys additional support is gained by each plane supporting the other; for this reason, walls or vertical beams are not required, provided the valley chords are adequately connected. Omission of supports below valleys, of course, increases the shear that must be resisted by the interior sloping planes. Horizontal chord stresses are greater then as well.

The following lists point out the advantages and disadvantages of the folded-plate roof as compared to other methods of roof construction.

Advantages

1. Trusses or other members that span from valley to valley are eliminated, thereby resulting in clear, uncluttered interiors.
2. Inasmuch as the plywood sheathing constitutes part of the structural unit, long spans are possible with small framing units.
3. A plywood ceiling can be used as a finish as well as for additional resistance to shear.
4. Assembly can be with nails only; no gluing is required, although it will improve rigidity.
5. Either conventional site construction or prefabrication can be employed. Components of the folded plate can be stressed-skin panels, or one or more full-length plates can be prefabricated.
6. Interesting form can be achieved economically for buildings of all sizes, from residences to large industrial structures.

Disadvantages

1. Drainage requires special attention on multiple-bay structures.

2. A well-designed folded-plate roof necessitates more roofing material. At least a 5:12 slope is recommended, since shear in the roof diaphragm diminishes with increase in slope.
3. Folded plates do not readily lend themselves to incorporation of a flat ceiling.

7.8.2 Roof Coverings

Many roofing materials are available for small buildings, and each has its advantages and limitations. Consequently, selection of the proper roofing material is of paramount importance and, in so doing, the following points should be considered:

1. Slope of the roof, if any
2. Quality or permanence required of the roof
3. Inherent architectural features of the roofing in relation to the rest of the structure
4. Cost of the roofing material

Built-Up Roofing A flat roof or a roof of very little slope must, of necessity, be covered with a completely watertight material. The majority of flat roofs are now covered with built-up roofing (see Fig. 7-86), which, if properly installed, is durable. On a wood deck, the first heavy layer of felt is nailed to the decking with galvanized roofing nails. Each succeeding layer of felt is mopped with either hot asphalt or hot coal-tar pitch. The top layer is then well mopped and covered with a thin layer of pea gravel, fine slag, or marble chips. This mineral surface protects the roof to some degree from the elements, and the lighter colors reflect the sun's rays from the building. For every 100 square feet of roof, the use of 400 pounds of gravel or 300 pounds of slag is recommended.

A five-ply roof would normally be warrantied by roofing contractors for 20 years; economy three-ply roofs would be warrantied for 10 years. Over smooth concrete decks, fewer piles are required, and the first

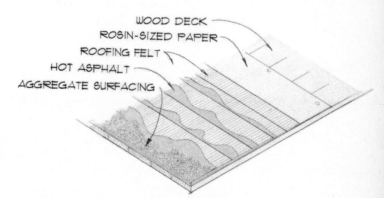

FIGURE 7-86 Built-up roof on wood deck (level to 2″-12″ pitch).

layer of felt is mopped directly to the slab. Asphalt pitch can be used on steeper slopes than can coal-tar pitch, but the limiting slope for a built-up roof is 2:12, if gravel is expected to stay on the roof. Even on a 2:12 slope, gravel will lose its grip during heavy rains. Metal gravel stops, preferably copper, are fastened to the

wood deck surrounding the entire roof. Proper use of base and cap flashing is shown in Figs. 7-87 and 7-88.

On flat roofs as well as pitched roofs, substantial and rigid roof decks play an important part in the success of the roof covering. Decks should be well nailed, clean, and dry before coverings are applied.

In roofing terminology, a *square* is an area of 100 square feet; thus a square of roofing material is the amount necessary to cover 100 square feet.

Membrane Roofing In recent years, major advances have been made in the membrane roofing industry. High-strength, reinforced synthetic sheets suitable for single-ply roofing systems have been developed. Although many membrane systems are installed over concrete roof decks or rigid insulation on metal decks, they can also be applied over wood decks. Most systems use mechanical fasteners to anchor the sheets to the roof deck. Special flashings are installed at roof penetration. Seams are usually heat welded. Some systems require a stone ballast to stabilize the membrane during high winds. The majority of such systems are easily repaired, if damaged, and have a warranty.

Shingle Roofing When a building has a sloping roof, more consideration must be given to the appearance of the roofing material. Shingles or multiple-unit type roofing materials are designed for sloping roofs; the incline allows water to drain off quickly without readily

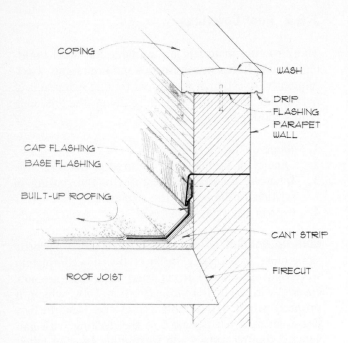

FIGURE 7-87 Roof flashing at a parapet wall.

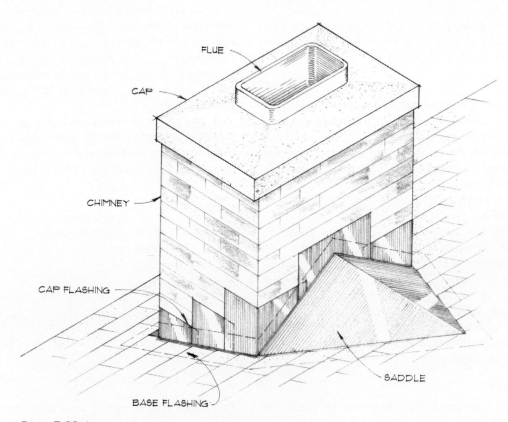

FIGURE 7-88 Chimney flashing on a sloping roof.

challenging the watertightness of the roof. The small, individual units of such roofing are also not subjected to stresses or shock from severe temperature changes; each piece can expand and contract individually without producing a noticeable effect, as in a built-up roof. The degree of resistance to water penetration of shingle materials varies directly with the slope of the roof and indirectly with the amount of exposure of each unit to the weather. Usually, the steeper slopes will allow more exposure of the units than the flatter slopes because the water drains off quicker. Strong winds tend to drive moisture under roof units unless some provision is made for sealing the edges or holding them down. This tendency is especially noticeable on lower slopes. Exposure to the weather is specified in inches; some roofing materials are exposed 4″ between laps; other materials, for example, can be allowed 10″ exposure. However, manufacturers' recommendations should be followed in applying all roofing materials.

Sloping roofs in light construction are generally covered with one of the following roofing materials:

1. Asphalt shingles
2. Fiberglass shingles
3. Wood shingles
4. Slate shingles
5. Clay tile units
6. Cement tile units
7. Metal shingles or panels

Asphalt Shingles Asphalt-saturated felt, coated with various colored mineral granules, is manufactured into strip shingles of different shapes and sizes. The most popular shape is the square-butt strip shingle, 12″ wide and 36″ long, with slotted butts to represent individual shingles at the exposure. Strips with hexagonal exposures are also made. The amount of 4″ or 5″ is the usual exposure to the weather, and weights per square vary according to the quality of the shingles. Quality shingles should weigh at least 235 lb square. The shingles are attached to the wood deck with 1¼″ galvanized roofing nails; four nails are needed for each strip. Each nail is driven about ½″ above each slot on the square-butt shingles. Two layers of shingles are then fastened with each nail, and the nailhead is just covered with the succeeding course. A double course is fastened at the eave. Occasionally, a starter strip of 55-pound roll roofing or one course of wood shingles is used under the double layer of strip shingles at the eave. Along the gable edge of the roof, a strip of wood bevel siding is often nailed to the deck with the thin edge in, to guide water from the edge as it drains along the incline. Metal edge flashing can also be used at gable edges. Roof decks should be first covered with 15-pound asphalt felt, lapped 6″ at ends and sides, before asphalt shingles are applied.

Asphalt strip shingles can be used on low-slope roofs if self-sealing shingles are used. This type has asphalt adhesive under the exposed edges, which seals the edges against driving rains and capillary action. Often, starter strips near the eaves are full mopped with adhesive, rather than nailed, to prevent this moisture penetration.

To cover ridges and hips, strip shingles are cut into

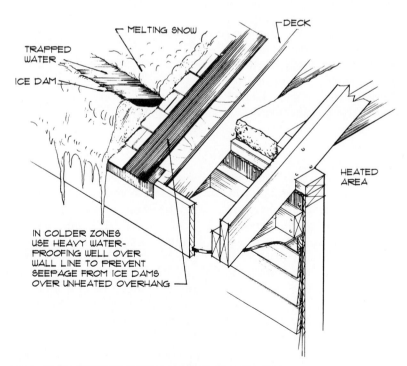

FIGURE 7-89 Preventing water seepage from ice dams.

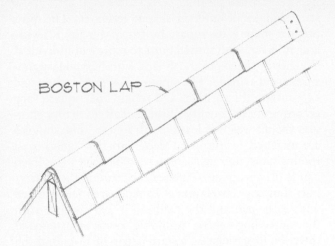

FIGURE 7-90 Covering ridge, fiberglass shingles.

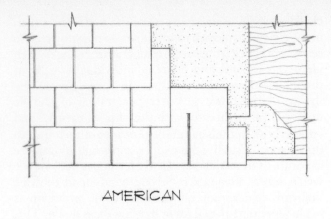

AMERICAN

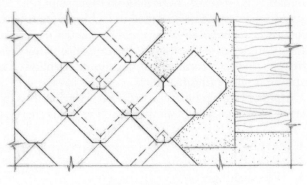

HEXAGONAL

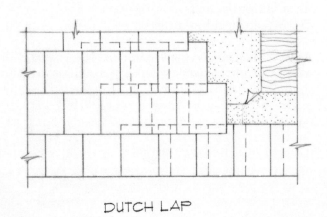

DUTCH LAP

FIGURE 7-91 Shingles are available in a variety of patterns.

smaller pieces and nailed over the ridges in a lapped fashion called a *Boston lap* (see Fig. 7-90). Intersections of roofs and walls must be flashed with durable metal flashing, preferably copper, and valleys are flashed with similar metal flashing, usually 18″ wide. Shingles are available in a variety of patterns (see Fig. 7-91).

Although they burn readily when ignited, asphalt shingles are more resistant to combustion than wood shingles, and many local codes that prohibit wood shingle roofs will allow the use of asphalt shingle materials.

Fiberglass Shingles A recent variation of the asphalt shingle is known as the *fiberglass roof shingle*. It has better fire and weathering resistance qualities than the conventional asphalt shingle because of the inorganic fiberglass-mat base. With these additional properties, it is rapidly replacing the organic-based asphalt shingle in the marketplace. Those with self-sealing adhesive strips below each shingle allow them to be used on low-slope (2:12 minimum) roofs if additional underlayment is provided. The self-sealing adhesive is activated by the heat of the sun to seal down the shingle tabs and help to prevent wind damage. In colder zones use heavy water proofing well over the wall line to prevent seepage from ice dams (see Fig. 7-89)

Wood Shingles have been used for many years in residential construction. Standard wood shingles or shakes, because of their inherent combustibility, are prohibited by many local fire codes. Recently, a chemical treatment process has been developed that makes it possible to obtain a wood shingle or shake with a class B or class C fire rating. In other than restricted areas, the standard wood shingle and shake is being used; they make handsome, durable roofs when properly installed. Wood weathers to a soft, mellow color after exposure to the elements and, if properly installed, can be expected to last 25 years.

Two types of wood shingles are available: machine-

sawed and handsplit. Both kinds are made chiefly of western red cedar, redwood, or cypress, all highly decay resistant woods. The machine-sawed shingles are made in 16″, 18″, and 24″ lengths and in random widths. They are taper sawed in shingle mills and graded No. 1, 2, or 3 according to the absence of knots and defects. To prevent cupping after exposure, the better grades are cut from the logs so that the annular rings of the log are perpendicular to the flat surfaces of the shingles. Butt ends vary in thickness from 1/2″ to 3/4″.

Handsplit shingles, often called *shakes*, are split from the log to reveal a natural, irregular wood-grain surface.

Their butts are thicker, ranging from 5/8" to 1 1/4", which produces strong horizontal course lines that give the roof a rustic quality. Thick, natural butt shingles are popular on ranch-type houses. Lengths of handsplit shingles are generally 24", 32", and 36", and widths vary from 5" to 18". In dry areas, wood shingles are usually put directly on plywood or tight wood decks. In damp areas, installation of nailing strips, spaced the same distance apart as the shingle exposure, provides ventilation directly below the shingles (see Fig. 7-92). Air space below the shingles prolongs the life of the roof.

The starting course for wood shingles is doubled at the eave, or better tripled, and projects beyond the edge of the roof board at least 2" to form a drip. A strip of 30-pound roll roofing felt is first nailed over the overhang, to make the roof watertight over the exterior wall. This precaution will prevent water from penetrating the shingles if ice dams occur on the lower part of the roof in colder areas. A cant strip of bevel siding along the gable edges is also recommended, as mentioned under asphalt shingles.

The standard exposure for wood shingles is 5 1/2". Longer shingles, however, can be laid with exposures up to 12", depending on the slope of the roof and method of application. More course-line texture can be obtained by doubling each course, usually with No. 2 grade shingles below. Careful nailing technique must be used to see that joints in preceding and successive courses are staggered or are offset at least 1 1/2" to allow good drainage and eliminate water penetration into the roof along the edges of the shingles. Shingles are loosely spaced to allow for swelling and shrinking, and zinc-coated or copper threepenny nails should be used; thicker shingles require larger nails. At least two nails must be used for each shingle and three for wider shingles, and care must be taken not to split the shingle when it is nailed. Open valleys are flashed with durable metal flashing; wide shingles are neatly cut to form the valleys. Hips and ridges can be covered by several methods, but the alternating Boston lap is the most popular as it retains the shingle texture to the edge of the ridge.

Many variations can be used in laying shingles. Sometimes every fifth or sixth course is doubled to vary the shadow line throughout the roof, sometimes the shingles are laid at random with no set course, sometimes they are staggered so that alternate shingles project beyond adjoining ones, and sometimes the course lines are made wavy to simulate thatch roofs with even the rakes and eaves turned over slightly to emphasize the effect of the thatch. Stained shingles are occasionally used to give definite color to the roof; staining also prolongs the life of the shingles. Regardless of the treatment and variations that are possible with wood shingles, the basic water-shedding principles of application must be followed.

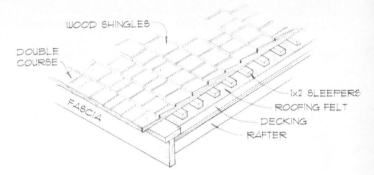

FIGURE 7-92 Installing wood shakes.

Slate Roofing Natural slate taken from quarry beds and split into thin sheets has provided builders with one of our more aristocratic roofing materials. The marked cleavage of the slate rock imparts a natural, irregular, and pleasing surface to a roof, and the natural color variations of slate from different quarries produce subtle shades ranging from blacks and grays to blues and greens, and even to browns and reds. Some slate changes in color after weathering. A well-laid slate roof is very durable and will outlast the life of the building. Slate is used only on the finest homes and more formal commercial buildings, yet its use has diminished in recent years.

Slate is split, cut into sheets, and punched for nails at the quarry. Common commercial sizes of the sheets are 12" × 16" and 14" × 20" and 3/16" or 1/4" thick. Random sheets vary in size and thickness. Each sheet is attached with at least two copper nails; pieces near ridges and hips are often secured with copper wire and roofing cement. Slate roofs are heavy, and therefore the roof-framing members must be more substantial than those for wood or asphalt shingles or other light roofing materials. Because of the weight of the slate, the sheets hug the roof well against driving wind. Damaged slate sheets are difficult to replace after the roof has been completed; experienced slate roofers are required to properly install a slate roof.

Under most conditions, at least a 6:12 pitch is necessary for slate. Roof boards are nailed up tight, over which a heavy roofing felt is applied and secured with roofing nails. A cant strip is used at the eaves to give the starter course the same slant as successive courses. Usually, the starter course is laid along the eave with the long dimension parallel to it, and the doubled course is started flush with the edge. Depending on the slope of the roof, slate should be laid with a 3" or 4" head lap. The head lap is the amount a lower edge of a course laps or covers the top edge of the second course underneath it. The amount of slate exposure is found by deducting the lap from the total length of the sheet and dividing the difference by 2. For example, the exposure of a 16" long sheet with a 4" head lap is 1/2 (16 − 4) = 6. Slate can be laid with different exposures on the same roof, however. As with wood shingles, all joints must be staggered to shed water effectively. After random sizes are sorted, it is preferable for the slater to attach the large, thick slates near the eaves, the medium slates near the center, and leave the smaller, thin pieces for the ridge area. This method produces rather interesting slate textures on a roof.

Hips and ridges are generally finished with the Boston-lap method. Both flashing and roofing cement are used to make the ridges and hips water resistant. Closed valleys, made with trapezoidal pieces of copper flashing placed under each course and lapped at least 3″, are the most popular on slate roofs.

Simulated slate shingles manufactured of fiber-reinforced cement resemble natural slate shingles in appearance. The simulated slate is lighter in weight and stronger than natural slate. The installation procedure for these shingles is similar to natural slate. Simulated slate carries a class A fire rating and can be warranted up to 30 years.

Clay Tile Roofing

Many variations of clay roofing tile are manufactured. They are generally very durable, made from different types of clay, and burnt in kilns, as are many other types of terracotta building products. Roofs of clay tile are characteristic of Mediterranean and Spanish architecture. The early Jesuits of Mexico first brought tile roof construction to this country when they built the old Spanish missions of California and the Southwest.

Traditionally, clay tiles were available in natural, burnt-orange colors. Today a wide selection of natural colors, ranging from light tan to dark brown, is available. Some manufacturers produce a glazed ceramic roofing tile that comes in a spectrum of colors from white to dark blue (Fig. 7-91).

Even though there are various patterns or shapes, all clay tile can be divided into two general categories: flat and roll type. The flat tiles vary from simple pieces to pieces with interlocking edges and headers. Roll tiles are available in semicircular shapes, reverse S shapes, and pan and cover types. Each type requires a tightly sheathed roof covered with heavy roofing felt. On low-pitched roofs and on all ridges and hips, the paper should be doubled; cant strips are needed at the eaves, as in slate roofs. Although some flat tile is fastened by hanging it on wooden cleat strips across the roof, the majority is secured with copper nails through prepunched holes. The semicircular roll tile require wooden strips running from the eaves to the ridges between the pans. Tile application requires careful planning inasmuch as tile pieces must fit together and very little latitude is allowed in their placing. Allowance must be made for expansion and contraction of the roofing at intersections of walls and projections. Because clay tile is one of the heavier roofing materials, roof framing must be adequate to support it.

Open valleys are usually used with tile, and copper flashing is placed below. Manufacturers furnish special shapes and pieces for covering hips and ridges, as well as pieces for rake edges and starter strips at the eaves. Often, starter pieces at the eaves as well as ridge and eave pieces are set in mastic or cement, both of which are available in colors to match the tile. Ridge rolls often require wood strips along the ridge for fastening the tile. Some tile shapes tend to look bulky on residential roofs; however, if carefully chosen to complement the style of the house, tile will help in creating a picturesque effect.

Cement Tile Roofs

This type of roof has become popular in Florida for residential construction. Precast concrete tiles with wide exposures are attached to the roof and neatly grouted with mortar. Heavy roofing felt is used below, and white waterproofing cement-base paint is applied as a finish over gray cement tiles. Cement tile can be used on low pitches, and the roof becomes resistant to sun and heat. Cement tiles are now available in a number of colors. Colored cement is used in the manufacture of the tiles. This eliminates the need for painting the tiles after installation (Fig. 7-91).

Metal Roofing

Occasionally, metal roofing is the most appropriate material to cover residences or light construction buildings. The principal metals used in roofing are copper, terneplate, aluminum, painted steel, and galvanized iron. Because of the cost of material and labor, metal is generally restricted in use to finer residences and more expensive structures. On moderately priced residences, we often see metal employed for small dormers, projections over front entrances, and minor roofs, in combination with other roofing material on the major roof. Metal must be applied by experienced roofers, who are aware of the individual properties of the different metals.

Copper is the most durable as well as one of the more expensive metals for roofing. It is malleable, tenacious, easy to work, and does not require maintenance after installation. It weathers to a gray-green color and looks well in combination with other building materials.

Terneplate is made of sheet iron or steel coated with an alloy of 25 percent tin and 75 percent lead. Metal roofers purchase the metal in small sheets that have been shopcoated with an oil-base paint. After application, the top surface must be painted with two coats of paint long in oil. If properly maintained, terneplate will last from 30 to 50 years. One advantage of terneplate is its light weight; also, it expands less than copper.

Both copper and terneplate are applied on tight board roof decks covered with rosin-sized paper. On roof pitches from 3″ to 12″, either the standing-seam or batten-seam method is used (see Fig. 7-93). After joining the small sheets into long strips, the standing seam is formed by turning up one edge 1½″ and the adjoining

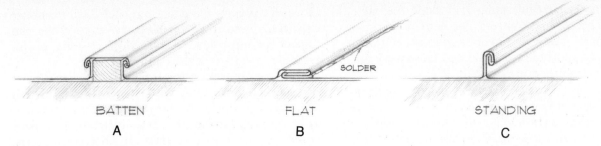

FIGURE 7-93 Metal roof seams.

edge 1¼″. The edges are bent and locked together without soldering. Cleats are nailed to the roof deck and incorporated into the seam to hold the metal to the deck, but no nails are driven through the sheets.

Batten seams are formed by nailing wood strips, ranging in size from 2″ × 2″ to 4″ × 4″ to the deck, which run from the eaves to the ridge and which are parallel to each other. Metal lengths are put between the battens and bent up along the edges of the battens to form pans down the slope of the roof. Cleats of the same metal are nailed to the edges of the battens and are incorporated into lock joints, which are formed by the edges of metal caps that rest on the battens, as well as the edges of the metal pans. Batten strips are used on the ridges and hips where necessary. The ends of wood batten strips at the edges of the roof must be covered with metal.

Several types of aluminum and steel roofing are used on residences and small buildings. Both aluminum and steel sheets, flat or corrugated, with baked enamel and other patented finishes are popular metal roofing materials (Fig. 7-93). Some are laid beginning at the ridge and continuing down to the eave; others are laid beginning at the eave and proceeding up to the ridge, similar to the method of applying copper sheets. Snap-on battens usually seam the joints between sheets, which are commonly 12″, 16″, or 24″ wide. Special caps are designed to cover ridges and hips. Pressed aluminum or steel shingles and tiles are available that resemble wood shakes and roll tiles. Like metal sheets, these roofing materials have baked enamel or special finishes. Available in strips, the roofing is nailed in place; concealed locking devices connect one strip to the other at each end. Metal sheets, shingles, and tiles can be installed on wood furring strips nailed perpendicular to the roof framing members. These roofing materials can be installed over roofing felt on a plywood deck.

Corrugated aluminum sheets are employed mainly for temporary buildings. They are fastened directly to the deck with aluminum nails and neoprene washers; the fastening is done through the high portion of the lapped corrugations.

On economy roofs, corrugated galvanized iron sheets can be used. However, galvanized iron has a limited service life as well as an unpleasing appearance. This material should be reserved for temporary or less important structures.

7.9 Exterior Finish Materials

The exterior finish material plays a very important part in the esthetics of a building, and if maintenance is a factor, the selection of the finish is especially important. Many finish materials are available; some of the more common materials for wood construction are wood siding, wood shingles, plywood, hardboard, aluminum, stucco, exterior insulation and finish systems (E.I.F.S.) and masonry veneer (see Section 7.6 on masonry veneer). Wood siding has been used successfully for years and is typical of American-built houses. Much of it requires periodic repainting; some of the durable wood species, such as redwood, western red cedar, and cypress, can be left natural with merely an application of several coats of water repellent. Kiln-dried lumber is preferred, and select grades with a minimum of knots and defects should be used. Figures 7-94 through 7-96 illustrate some of the more common types of wood siding available.

Bevel Siding is widely used in present-day construction. It is cut into widths varying from 4″ to 12″ and butt thicknesses range from ⁷⁄₁₆″ to ³⁄₄″. The usual amount of lap is from 1″ to 2″. For example, a bevel siding 6″ wide is usually applied with 4½″ to the weather, and a siding 10″ wide is usually applied with 8″ to the weather. Wider sizes have a tendency to cup and warp.

Much of the warping in siding can be prevented by the application of a prime coat of paint to all sides of the siding, including ends, before installation. Rustproof nails should be used: rust stains bleed through the paint film (Fig. 7-95 indicates the correct nailing technique). Notice in the figure that the nails do not pass through the underpiece of the lap; this allows for expansion in the lap without taking the risk of splitting the thin portion of the underpiece, should the nails be put through both pieces of the lap. Strong, horizontal shadow lines are characteristic of bevel siding. Various corner treatments are shown in Fig. 7-96. A starter strip must be nailed to the bottom of the sheathing so that the first course of siding will slope the same amount as succeeding courses. The bottom course is started about 1″ below the top of the foundation wall to weatherproof and hide the wood and masonry joint. Bevel siding exposures are worked out exactly by carpenters so that horizontal butt lines coincide with sill and head edges of windows and doors, and courses are similar throughout the wall height. Minor variations of exposure on a wall are permissible inasmuch as they are not readily noticeable. Water tables should be used

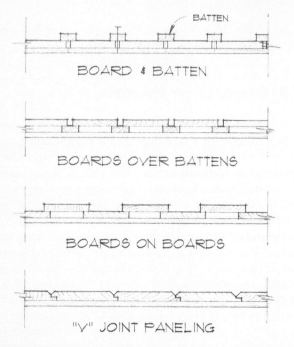

FIGURE 7-94 Various vertical wood siding as shown through horizontal sections.

above all windows and doors; a rabbeted trim member is generally used at the top of the wall to cover the thin edge of the top course. Rabbeted bevel siding is also available in various widths and thicknesses.

On economy walls, drop siding, also known as novelty siding, is acceptable without sheathing. Building felt is tacked directly to the studs and the drop siding is nailed over the felt. Figure 7-95 shows one of the typical profiles of drop siding. Corners can be treated as mentioned under bevel siding, or square-edged corner boards can be nailed directly over the siding.

Board and Batten Siding can be used to obtain a rustic texture on exterior frame walls (see Fig. 7-94). Either surfaced or unsurfaced square-edged boards can be used. The wide boards are nailed vertically with at least 1/8″ space between them for expansion. Battens of the same type of lumber, usually only 2″ wide, are nailed over the vertical joints of the wide boards. The 2″ batten strips are also used for trim around doors and windows, as well as along the top of the wall. Joints between the wide boards are often caulked before the batten strips are applied. Horizontal blocking must be installed in the stud wall if insulation board sheathing has been used so that the boards and battens can be nailed at a minimum of four levels of vertical height throughout a 1-story wall. If nominal 1″ wood or plywood sheathing has been used, the boards and battens can be secured by nailing into the sheathing. Care should be exercised in nailing the batten strips; the nails should pass between the wide boards in the joint, or the nails

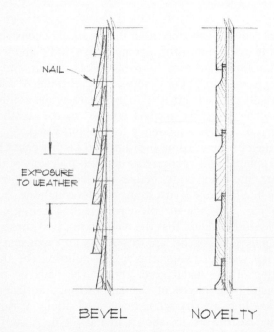

FIGURE 7-95 Vertical details of bevel and novelty siding.

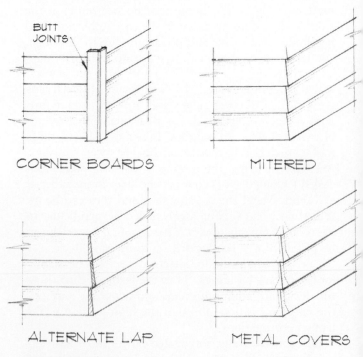

FIGURE 7-96 Treatments of outside corners on horizontal wood siding.

can pass through the batten and one of the wide boards *only* (see Fig. 7-95). This allows expansion of the joint without splitting either the boards or the batten. Only rustproof nails should be specified.

Another interesting effect can be gained by applying the wide boards over the narrow batten strips. This application becomes a reverse board and batten method, which produces narrow grooves and a slightly different overall effect. Redwood lumber is frequently applied in this manner.

V-Joint, Tongue and Groove Paneling can also be used for vertical siding. Adequate wood sheathing or horizontal blocking must also be installed to provide proper nail anchoring; blind nailing is generally used along the tongue to hide the nails within the joint. Kiln-dried lumber with minimum-shrinkage characteristics should be selected, and joints should be nailed up tight so that moisture will not penetrate between the boards. Either random-width or uniform-width paneling can be used. Bottom cuts at the base of the wall should be beveled to provide a drip. Because of cupping, paneling over 8″ wide should be avoided.

In recent years, rough-sawn cedar paneling has been widely used in contemporary-style homes and small commercial buildings, in many applications with diagonal coursing. The paneling can be stained to gain various color treatments or left to weather with natural wood appearance. Both cedar and redwood are soft and require careful nailing with rustproof nails.

Wood Shingles produce warm and charming exterior finishes that are popular in many areas of the country. The shingles are versatile in that many effects can be obtained by various applications. They can be painted, stained, or left to weather naturally. Unfinished shingles weather unevenly because of projections, overhangs, and the like. Handsplit shakes can be used for rustic effects, double courses of regular shingles can be used for strong horizontal shadow lines, or regular shingles can be applied in staggered course lines for unusual effects (see Fig. 7-97). More exposure widths can be allowed on wood shingle walls than is necessary when applying similar shingles to a roof. Table 7-8 can be used to determine the amounts of weather exposure of shingles according to their lengths.

Western red cedar is the most popular wood used for commercial shingles, and the application to walls is similar to the methods mentioned under roof coverings (Section 7.8.2). For siding, No. 1 grade is usually specified; No. 2 or 3 grade can be used for underlays of double courses. Wood shingles must have substantial wood backing for nailing; if insulation board sheathing is used on the wall, horizontal nailing strips, usually 1 × 3 are nailed over the insulation board. The strips are spaced the same distance apart as the exposure width of the shingles.

RANDOM COURSING

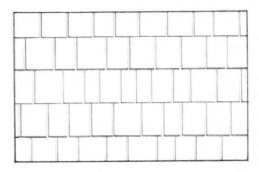

REGULAR COURSING

Figure 7-97 Wood shingle textures.

Table 7-8

Maximum weather exposure for wood shingle siding

Length of shingle	Single course	Double course
16″	7½″	12″
18″	8½″	14″
24″	10″	16″

Exterior Plywood is now used extensively for siding. Plywood can be applied vertically with 1 × 2 batten strips placed vertically either 16″ or 24″ on center to hide the joints of the plywood (see Fig. 7-98). Plywood must be well painted or stained. Also, texture one-eleven plywood, ⅝″ thick, with rabbeted joining edges, can be nailed vertically on stud walls to resemble vertical paneling. Plywood is also available in strips to be applied horizontally similar to shingles.

Sheet Hardboard is a popular exterior siding material; that if properly applied and painted, will give years of satisfactory service. Hardboard is made from natural wood fibers that are subjected to heat and pressure to form sheets or strips of various sizes and thicknesses; it comes in various surface textures: smooth, grooved, and ribbed. Hardboard must have solid backing sup-

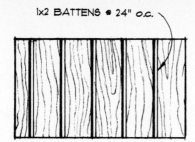
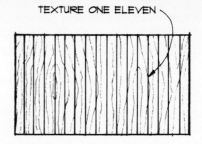

FIGURE 7-98 Plywood siding. Battens can be spaced either 24″ or 16″ o.c.

port and is durable if kept painted. Strips can be applied horizontally to resemble bevel siding, or larger panels can be applied vertically to resemble board and batten siding.

The horizontally applied panels are usually 8″ to 1′ wide by 16′ long by ³/₈″ to ⁷/₁₆″ thick, applied generally with 7″ or 11″ exposures. Starter strips at the base of the wall and corner treatments are handled similarly to wood bevel siding. Vertical joints should be made over studs, and nailing is done through the lap at each stud location.

For vertical application, 4′ wide panels are used. Lengths are obtainable up to 16′, and recommended thicknesses are ¹/₄″ and ⁵/₁₆″. Vertical wood battens spaced 16″ on center can be used to hide vertical joints on smooth hardboard edges; a ¹/₈″ space must be left between panels, and joints are caulked before batten strips are applied. Grooved and ribbed panels have shiplap edges for concealing the joints. Manufacturers' directions should be followed in applying either type of hardboard exterior panels.

Aluminum Siding is a low maintenance material, used for both residential and commercial construction and is also popular for remodeling exterior walls. Two types of aluminum panels are most popular: those applied horizontally to resemble either narrow- or wide-bevel siding, and those applied vertically to resemble board and batten siding. Both styles are available with baked-on enamel finishes of various colors, and can be painted if necessary, similar to wood siding. Aluminum siding is light in weight, easy to apply, and resistant to weathering.

The horizontal panels are started at the base of the sheathing with a wood cant strip nailed below the bottom edge of the first course, and each course is nailed to the sheathing along its top edge. Courses are held to the adjacent course with a lock joint. Matching corner pieces, backer strips for end joints, and trim pieces are furnished by the manufacturers for each type of panel. Horizontal panels are made 12¹/₂′ long, with either a bevel exposure 8″ wide or two 4″ bevel exposures. Some panels have foam insulation backing.

Vertical aluminum panels are applied by first nailing

a starter corner strip vertically along one corner and then locking the first panel into the strip and nailing the panel along the edge opposite the lock joint. This procedure is continued across the wall. Aluminum can be cut with a hacksaw or tinsnips when fitting around openings and such; appropriate pieces are furnished by manufacturers to form water tables and trim members. Vertical panels are made in lengths to cover 1-story heights so that joints are eliminated.

Vinyl Siding is available in a wide range of colors and does not require painting. Manufactured from polyvinyl chloride sheets, the siding comes in 10′ and 12′ long panels. The panels are preformed to resemble either horizontal or vertical wood siding. The surface of the siding may be smooth or embossed to replicate wood graining. Both the vertical and horizontal panels have perforated edge strips for nailing. Galvanized nails should be used to attach the siding to wood studs, wood strips or to a solid nailable sheathing. A variety of vinyl trim pieces are available to compliment the siding. These pieces are especially convenient for finishing corners, cornices, soffits, fascias and around doors and windows (see Fig. 7-99).

Stucco has been used for years as a satisfactory exterior siding material, but present-day use is limited largely to direct application over concrete block and other masonry materials. Some application for stucco over wood frame walls in residential construction is still found, however.

On masonry walls of concrete block, tile, or brick, two coats of portland cement stucco are applied like plaster to form a coat ⁵/₈″ thick. This particular stucco should be made of 1 part portland cement, 3 parts sand, and 10 percent by volume of hydrated lime. Or a prepared portland cement stucco may be used and applied according to the manufacturers' directions. The masonry wall is first cleaned with a wire brush and a scratch coat is applied. After the scratch coat is thoroughly dry, the finish coat is applied and given whatever surface texture is desired. A finish may be smooth with a metal trowel finish, sand-finished with a wood float, or stippled by applying various tooling or stroking

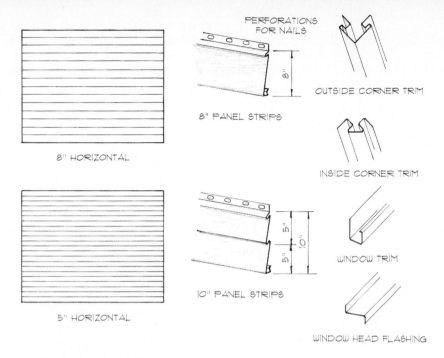

8" HORIZONTAL

5" HORIZONTAL

PERFORATIONS
FOR NAILS

8" PANEL STRIPS

10" PANEL STRIPS

OUTSIDE CORNER TRIM

INSIDE CORNER TRIM

WINDOW TRIM

WINDOW HEAD FLASHING

FIGURE 7-99 Vinyl siding.

effects. To render the finish waterproof, cement-base paints are usually applied after the finish coat is completely dry. Colored stucco can be obtained by mixing mineral pigments into the finish coat, or colored cement-base paints may be applied to the final stucco surface.

On wood frame walls, stucco is applied over ribbed metal lath that is backed up with heavy asphalt-treated paper (see Fig. 7-100). Wood or metal furring strips 15" on center can also be used under galvanized wire fabric, or galvanized furring nails can be used to keep the fabric at least 1/4" away from the paper and sheathing. Foundations must be adequate to prevent settling and subsequent cracking of the stucco. Stucco-covered 2-story buildings should be constructed with balloon framing to minimize vertical shrinkage. Usually, a rustproof metal ground strip is placed at the base of the wood wall to close the opening between the stucco and the sheathing. Flashing must be used above all doors and windows, and the tops of stucco walls must be protected by overhangs and trims members. When applied over wood frame walls, a three-coat stucco job is standard (consisting of scratch coat, brown coat, and finish coat) to make the stucco 3/4" thick.

Stucco is used to produce imitation, half-timber-type exterior walls used mainly in Normandy-style houses. Treated boards representing the timbers are fastened directly to the sheathing, and stucco is applied to the furring lath in the areas between the timbers. In this construction, attention must be given to the prevention of moisture penetration between the timbers and the stucco. Flashing must be used liberally over horizontal timber pieces as well as joints in the timber pieces, which are especially susceptible to the accumulation of moisture.

All the aforementioned exterior siding materials must be applied over a suitable moisture-resistant building paper that has been fastened to the wall sheathing. This paper is important in preventing moisture penetration under and between siding pieces, and in preventing air infiltration through the exterior walls from wind pressures.

Exterior Insulation and Finish Systems (E.I.F.S.) Exterior wall treatment systems have gained significant acceptance on residences and commercial buildings that at one time could have only been surfaced with stucco (Fig. 7-100). E.I.F.S. can be applied to smooth masonry walls or to stud walls that have exterior-grade gypsum sheathing. The application is generally a four-step process. First, an adhesive is applied to one side of an insulating panel such as Styrofoam®, which then is attached to the masonry wall or gypsum sheathing. Next, an adhesive with an admixture of portland cement is troweled over the insulating panel. Third, a fiberglass mesh reinforcement is embedded into the wet adhesive, which is allowed to cure. Last, an acrylic polymer finish coat is troweled over the exterior wall surface. Color tints can be added to the finish coat. The tints are usually blended into the acrylic polymer at the factory. The E.I.F.S. treatment adds insulating value to the wall system, will not crack like stucco, and is a low-maintenance material. Sharp objects or strong im-

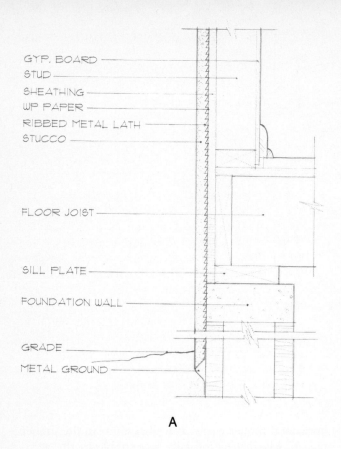

GYP. BOARD
STUD
SHEATHING
WP PAPER
RIBBED METAL LATH
STUCCO

FLOOR JOIST

SILL PLATE

FOUNDATION WALL

GRADE
METAL GROUND

A

pacts can damage the soft surface; however, a heavy-duty reinforcing mesh with substantial impact resistance can be used. Creative designs and trims are easily achieved by varying the thickness or cutting sculptural shapes into the Styrofoam.

Further technical information on E.I.F.S. design and detailing is available from:

Drynit Systems, Inc.
One Energy Way
P.O. Box 1014
West Warlock, R.I. 02893

7.10 Interior finishes and trim

Gypsum Wallboard, commonly called gypsum drywall construction, is now used as the interior finish in the majority of American homes under construction. The paper-covered gypsum sheets are made in $4' \times 8'$, $4' \times 10'$, and $4' \times 12'$ sizes. Standard thicknesses are $3/8''$, $1/2''$, and $5/8''$. Gypsum is light to handle and has good thermal and fire-resistance qualities. The sheets can be easily cut and nailed to framing, joints and nailheads can be smoothly finished with joint compound and perforated tape, and very little moisture is introduced into the structure from the material, which is the case when plaster is used (see Figs. 7-101 and 7-102).

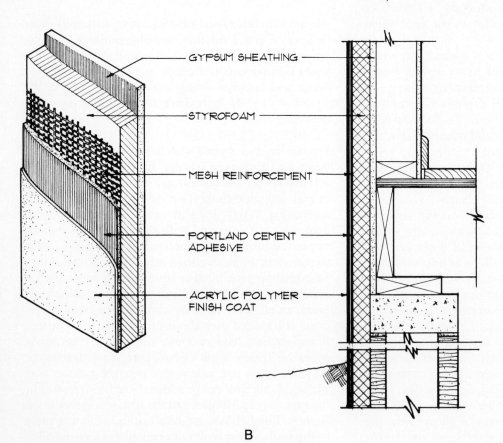

GYPSUM SHEATHING

STYROFOAM

MESH REINFORCEMENT

PORTLAND CEMENT
ADHESIVE

ACRYLIC POLYMER
FINISH COAT

B

FIGURE 7-100 Stucco and exterior insulation finish system.

214 Light construction principles

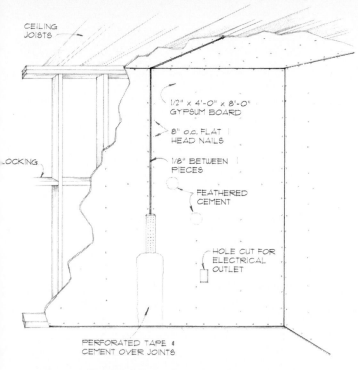

FIGURE 7-101 Application of gypsum board applied vertically for interior walls.

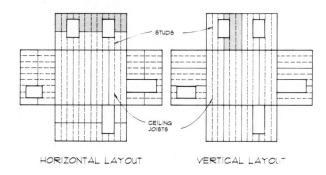

HORIZONTAL LAYOUT   VERTICAL LAYOUT

FIGURE 7-102 Two methods of gypsum board layout.

Plaster is still preferred by many architects for first-class construction. A two-coat job, consisting of ³/₈″ rocklath, a brown coat, and a finish coat, results in a ⁷/₈″ total thickness. Metal lath strips are fastened in corners and at critical points around openings where cracking tends to occur. If metal lath is used for the entire base instead of the rocklath, a three-coat job (scratch, brown, and finish coats) is required. A water-resistant plaster, called Keene's Cement, is usually specified in kitchens and baths.

Prefinished Plywood Sheets in various natural wood finishes are becoming popular in many room interiors. They are blind nailed directly to studs and never require painting or finishing. Other manufactured sheet

materials as well as solid wood paneling are also available for various wall coverings. To straighten nailing surfaces when using sheet materials or ceiling acoustical tile, furring strips can be applied perpendicularly to studs or ceiling joists.

Trim is the general term given to molding, base, casing, and various other finish members that must be carefully fitted by finish carpenters to complete the appearance of the structure (see Fig. 7-103). Many stock pieces and patterns are available at lumber dealers. In higher-class construction, custom-made moldings and trim pieces are often shown in detail on the working drawings and therefore must be specially milled. Care must be taken to select consistent patterns to be used throughout a building so that harmony in the trim results. Colonial interiors traditionally require ogee profiles, whereas contemporary styles usually appear best with simpler tapered or teardrop profiles. Casing and finishing nails are used to apply trim members; the nails are driven below the surface of the wood with a nail set so that the holes can be filled, and care must be exercised to prevent hammer marks from injuring the surface of the wood.

7.11 Insulation, Vapor Barriers, and Ventilation of Frame Structures

Present-day builders are fully aware that indoor comfort is of primary importance to the individual. Consequently, proper insulation becomes a major consideration in warm climates as well as cold. Many types of insulation are available; the most suitable usually depends on the details of the construction; the amount depends on the extent of comfort desired. When care in selection and installation is taken, optimum benefit will be realized. Experience has shown that it is more economical to employ modern insulation materials than to rely on structural materials for insulating requirements.

Heat-loss calculations and the design of heating and cooling systems are not discussed in this material; however, the general aspects of insulation, such problems as water vapor within buildings, and the ventilation of unheated air spaces are of concern to the drafter if details of construction are to be correctly conceived and drawn.

Basically, all construction materials can be classified more or less as either insulators or conductors, depending on their porosity or density. Still air is an excellent insulator if confined into small spaces such as the matrix of insulating materials or small cavities within walls. On the other hand, dense materials, such as glass or masonry, are relatively poor insulators. All materials, however, resist the flow of heat to a certain extent, the resistance of the given material being directly proportional to its thickness. (see Fig. 7-104)

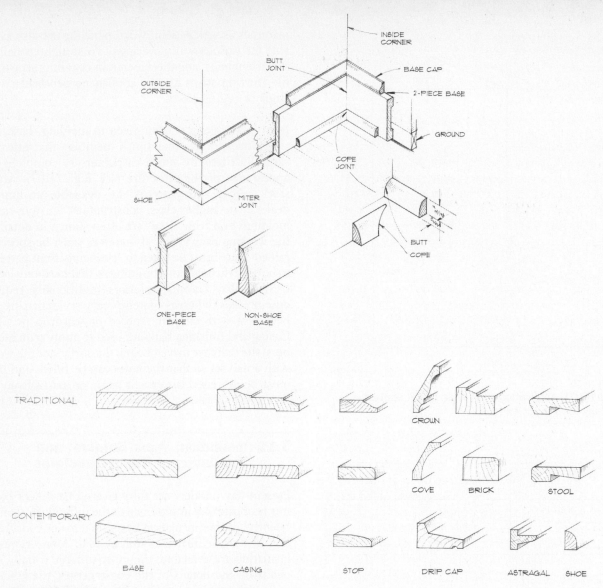

FIGURE 7-103 Stock trim and base applications.

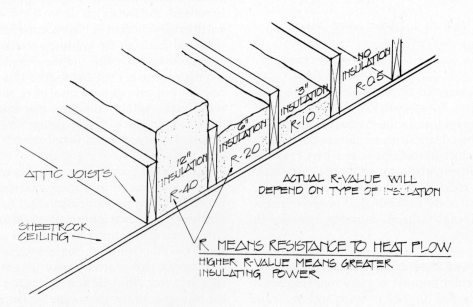

FIGURE 7-104 Insulation R values.

Heat may be transmitted by three different methods: conduction, convection, and radiation. *Conduction* is the transfer of heat by direct molecular contact; metals, for instance, conduct heat more readily than wood, yet all materials conduct heat if a temperature difference exists between their surfaces. It must be remembered that *heat flows from the warm to the cold surfaces. Convection* is the transfer of heat by air or other agent in motion. Even though air is a good insulator, when it circulates it loses part of its value as an insulator. Air spaces about ³/₄" wide within walls or ceilings are the most restrictive to circulation. In larger spaces, air acts like a conveyor belt, taking heat from warm surfaces and depositing it on cold surfaces. *Radiation* is the transfer of heat through space from a warm surface to a cold surface, very much as light travels through space. Effective resistance to radiation can be provided by shiny surfaces, such as aluminum foil; the more actual surfaces a heat ray has to penetrate, the more effective the reflective insulation becomes. Actual heat transfer through walls and ceilings usually employs all three of the above-mentioned methods of transfer, to various degrees. Of course, some heat is also dissipated from buildings through openings around doors and windows.

To compare the suitability or insulating qualities of different building materials and insulations, a standard of reference must be used. By accurate experimentation, the thermal qualities of individual building materials have been determined; when these materials are incorporated into typical combinations found in walls, floors, roofs, and so on, including occasional air spaces, the rate of heat flow or coefficient of transmission, known as the *U factor*, can be calculated. This factor can be defined as the number of Btu's (British thermal units—heat units) that will flow through 1 square foot of the structure from one air region to another due to a temperature difference of 1°F in 1 hour.

Easy reference can be made from tables giving the *U* factors with and without insulation, put out by the American Society of Heating, Refrigeration, and Air Conditioning Engineers (A.S.H.R.A.E.). Tables for *U* factors of typical constructions and various insulation combinations can also be found in the Forest Products Laboratory Report R1740. Comparisons of these *U* factors make it possible to evaluate different combinations of materials and insulations on a basis of overall heat loss, potential fuel savings, influence on comfort, and cost of installation.

Other than the reflective insulators, commercial insulations are usually made of glass fibers, glass foam, mineral fibers, organic fibers, polystyrene and polyurethane. The best materials should be fireproof and vermin-proof, as well as resistant to heat flow. The cellular materials utilize tiny isolated air cells to reduce conduction and convection; the fibrous materials utilize tiny films of air surrounding each fiber. These efficient insulating materials are manufactured into blankets, batts, and sheets in sizes and shapes to fit conveniently into conventional structural spaces. Some have tabs or edges for stapling to wood frame members; others are sized so that they can be tightly wedged into conventional structural cavities. Proper selection depends on initial cost, effectiveness, and the adaptation of the insulation to the construction features. Blankets and batts should be installed between framing members to form isolated air spaces between their faces and the interior wall surfaces. Sheet insulation should be used where rigidity is important, such as on roof decks and perimeters of floor slabs. Fill insulation (loose mineral wool or mineral pellets) is used mainly in ceilings where it can be poured between ceiling joists, or it can be used to fill the cavities of concrete block. Reflective foil insulations are best put into cavities where the reflective surfaces can be adjacent to air spaces. All insulation should be installed according to manufacturers' directions, and care must be taken to cut the material carefully around outlet boxes and other obstructions within the walls. Figure 7-105 illustrates the proper placement of insulation within typical frame buildings.

If the restriction of heat flow were the only consideration in the application of insulation within buildings, it would be a simple matter to provide enough insulation around heated spaces to theoretically reduce fuel bills sufficiently and thereby offset the initial cost of the insulation. However, air usually contains water vapor, and because water vapor acts like a gas to penetrate porous materials and always flows from areas of high temperature to areas of lower temperatures, many types of insulation soon lose their effectiveness if they become saturated with water vapor.

Air is saturated or has a relative humidity of 100 percent when it contains as much moisture as it will hold. Warm air has the ability to retain more moisture than cold air. If saturated air is lowered in temperature, some of its moisture will be given off as condensation. This point in temperature change at which a specimen of air gives off moisture in the form of condensation is known as its *dew point*. When high temperature differences exist between insulated wall surfaces (between inside and outside air), the dew point often occurs in the insulation itself, where the resistance to heat flow is greater than in the structural members. The condensation that can gather in the insulation from the cooling of the vapor as it passes through a wall may not only reduce the value of the insulation, but may eventually cause permanent damage to the structural members. This problem generally arises in winter, during the heating season, especially when the humidity within the building is high.

The simplest solution to the problem is to prevent water vapor from getting into the wall structures. This is partially done by providing a vapor barrier near the *inside surface* of the wall. To be effective, the vapor

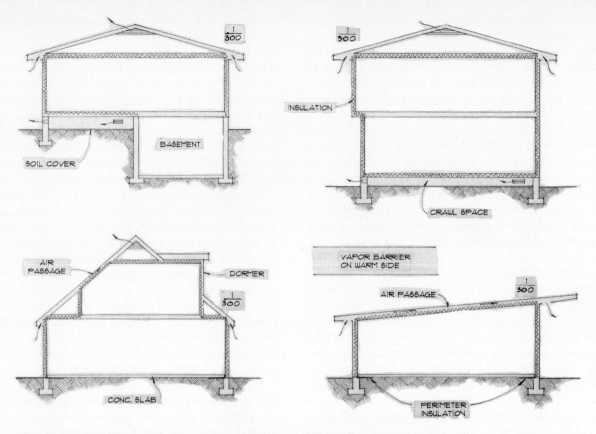

Figure 7-105 Placement of insulation in wood-frame buildings. Ventilation of attic and crawl spaces is necessary. The fraction indicates the ratio of minimum net vent opening to the ceiling area for proper ventilation of enclosed spaces.

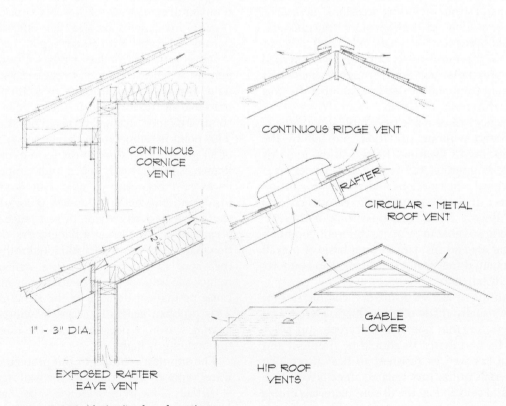

Figure 7-106 Methods of roof venting.

barrier must be as airtight as possible. One of the most common vapor barriers is aluminum foil, which also acts as a reflective insulator. Asphalt and aluminum paints are other effective vapor barriers. The glue layers in plywood act as vapor barriers. Polyethylene film and glossy, asphalt-treated heavy paper are satisfactory barriers; however, ordinary building-paper does not offer much resistance to the passage of vapor. Many types of commercial insulation have one face covered with a vapor barrier; this is the side that should always be placed toward the inside of the building.

Even good vapor barriers do not prevent some moisture from penetrating through minor breaks in the barrier around pipes, electric outlets, joints, and the like; some will even permeate the barrier itself, not necessarily through minor breaks. Water vapor that has possibly found its way into walls can be released to the outside by *cold side venting*. This condition requires sheathing paper to be weather-resistant but not vapor-proof. Lightweight roofing felt is satisfactory—it can breathe. Siding materials must not be airtight, yet they must have the ability to shed water and resist driving rains. Many of the newer, water-base exterior paints possess this feature of allowing water vapor from the inside to escape through the paint film.

Another suggestion that will help minimize the vapor problem in homes is the installation of forced-air fans in rooms of excess humidity, such as bathrooms, kitchens, and utility areas. The use of exhaust fans directly to the outside relieves the home of much of the otherwise destructive concentrations of humidity.

Some engineers maintain that no moisture barrier need be used in ceilings below an attic that is adequately vented with louvers. The water vapor can permeate through insulation in the ceiling and be carried out of the building by the air movement in the attic space. For this reason, louvers in vent spaces should never be closed during the winter. If air spaces exist below roofs and the air spaces are not heated, adequate ventilation must be provided below the roof (Fig. 7-106). Since most roofing materials are resistant to vapor flow, trapped moisture within the spaces would soon cause damage.

In gable roofs, the vents should be a minimum of $1/300$ of the ceiling area, depending on local codes. If vents can be provided along the eaves of a gable roof, a more positive circulation will result, and the vents near the ridge on the gable can be made smaller. Hip roofs are more difficult to vent; openings are necessary around the roof in the soffit of the eaves. Small metal outlet vents can also be incorporated into the roofing, near the ridge of the hip, to allow air to circulate and escape. Numerous types of small metal vents are available for hip roof venting. The area size of vents under hip roof eaves should be a minimum of $1/300$ of the ceiling area; the outlet vents near the ridge of hip roofs should be at least $1/600$ of the ceiling area, check local codes.

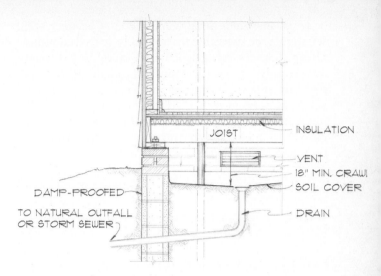

Figure 7-107 Crawl-space construction.

Flat roofs should be vented with a continuous vent along the soffit of the overhang (see Fig. 7-83). Spaces between all framing members should have access to outside air if the ceiling material is supported by the roof members. A minimum vent area of $1/300$ of the ceiling area should be provided, check local codes. All wood-framed roofs with unheated spaces directly below should be adequately vented by either of the above-mentioned methods.

Crawl spaces in basementless houses also require adequate ventilation. At least four foundation wall vents should be provided, preferably located near the corners. The aggregate net ventilating area should be calculated as follows: a = 2L/100 + A/300 a = total net vent area (sq.ft) L = crawl space perimeter A = crawl space area (sq.ft). Fewer vents can be used if the ground below the floor is completely covered with a vapor barrier, check local codes.

In colder localities, floors in basementless houses should have insulation applied between the floor joists (see Fig. 7-107). Crawl spaces will be troublefree if:

1. Insulation is applied below the floors.
2. Sufficient vents are installed in the foundation walls.
3. A vapor barrier is provided over the entire ground area within the foundation walls.

EXERCISES

The following exercises should be done on $8\frac{1}{2}'' \times 11''$ drawing paper with a $\frac{1}{2}''$ border. Some of the drawings require the use of instruments; others may be done freehand.

1. Using guide lines $1/4''$ high and $5/16''$ between each set, divide the sheet into three equally spaced columns. Using architectural style lettering, number 1 through 39 vertically (each vertical row will contain thirteen $1/4''$ high guidelines and thirteen numbers). Using Fig. 7-1, cover the written terms with opaque paper, read the numbers on the drawing of the house, and letter on the numbered lines the proper term for the items identified by numbers 1 through 39.

2. Using the scale $1/4'' = 1'-0''$, draw dashed lines to represent the outside wall of a $24'-0''$ long by $12'-0''$ wide building. Illustrate in plan view the placement of batter boards, string lines, and diagonal measurements that are required to locate the foundation wall and footings for this small structure.

3. Lay out a floor framing plan at a scale of $1/4'' = 1'-0''$ with 2 × 8 floor joists at $16''$ o.c. for the $24'-0''$ by $12'-0''$ building. Show headers and two rows of bridging. Label materials and sizes on the drawing.

4. Using the scale $1/4'' = 1'-0''$, lay out a hip roof framing plan with 2 × 6 rafters at $16''$ o.c. for the $24'-0''$ by $12'-0''$ building using a $2'-0''$ projection beyond the exterior wall to form an overhanging eave. Label materials and sizes on the drawing.

5. Draw the elevation view of a standard W pattern truss with an 8:12 pitch and a clear span of $28'-0''$ at a scale of $1/4'' = 1'-0''$. Top and bottom chords are 2 × 6s, web members are 2 × 4s, and gussets are $1/2''$ plywood. Eaves extend $1'-6''$ beyond the face of the exterior wall. Label materials and sizes on the drawing.

6. Draw freehand sketches of the front elevation and one side elevation of small buildings with these roof types: gable, hip, shed, mansard, folded plate, and gambrel. Scale the sketches to fit neatly on the sheet.

7. Draw a freehand section sketch through a 1-story wood frame structure with crawl space below the floor framing and a pitched gable roof with an attic. Using arrows, graphically show where the crawl space and attic should be ventilated. Label vents and show the ratio of vent area to surface areas.

8. Draw nine $2''$ wide by $1 1/2''$ high rectangles equally spaced on the sheet; sketch within each rectangle an elevation view of the following types of exterior siding: horizontal bevel, board and batten, novelty, boards on boards, V joint, boards over boards, wood shingles with random coursing, wood shingles with regular-coursing, and stucco.

9. Sketch a front elevation view of a 1-story gable roof residence with a brick chimney penetrating the roof surface. Draw one side elevation of the same house and show a saddle on the roof at the chimney.

10. Sketch four elevations of the end portion of a building with a hip roof. Show a different roofing material on each of the four sketches. Include the following roofing materials: fiberglass shingles, standing seam copper, Spanish clay tile, and wood shakes.

REVIEW QUESTIONS

1. Why must local frost depths be considered when drawing footings?

2. What is a good rule of thumb for sizing footings in light construction?

3. Describe a stepped footing and indicate its application.

4. What condition may require accurate calculation of footing sizes?

5. List three materials that are commonly used for foundation walls.

6. What is a pier?

7. Indicate the logical application of grade beam foundation construction.

8. What are the advantages of a slab on ground floor construction in comparison to crawl space construction?

9. What are the identifying characteristics of platform (western) frame construction?

10. Why are trussed rafters widely used in small home construction?

11. In plank and beam framing, how is the load on roof beams transmitted to the foundation?

12. Why should the location of beams in plank and beam framing be shown on the working drawings?

13. What part of the construction limits the spacing of beams in plank and beam framing?

14. What is a transverse beam?

15. List the good points of brick veneer construction.

16. Explain modular sizing of concrete block walls.

17. What are the important factors in the selection of a roofing material?

18. What is the purpose of a vapor barrier in a wood wall, and why should it be placed facing the interior side?

19. What are metal framing anchors and where are they used in construction?

20. What is flashing and identify two places where flashing is used?

STRUCTURAL MEMBER SELECTION

"There is always a best way of doing everything, if it be to boil an egg."

—RALPH W. EMERSON

8

It is common practice to indicate the sizes of structural members on working drawings. This chapter is concerned with this information and the span and loading tables that must be used to obtain the sizes. The tables are readily available to drafters and designers. On residential drawings this information is placed on the details, floor plans, or other views that seem the most appropriate. In a set of commercial-building working drawings, structural information is found on separate structural drawings included with the architectural set—usually completed by a structural engineer or other specialist in the area involved.

The tables are compiled and published by the various lumber manufacture associations (for example, the National Forest Products Association) as well as federal government departments involved with housing and construction. Some are included as part of local code manuals, which often include a nationally recognized building code as a part, and which are available at local building inspection offices. These local code restrictions should be available to drafters before making any decisions on structural members. Notice that each species of framing lumber has its own loading table; a number of the tables are included in this material. The tables give minimum sizes, and sometimes good judgment may require that sizes taken from the tables should be modified for structural soundness. Only experience in wood framing can provide this valuable background. Occasionally, it becomes feasible to use steel members in critical situations in wood framing; several steel tables are included here for that purpose. Many steel shapes and sizes are available to builders; consult the latest *Manual of Steel Construction* by the American Institute of Steel Construction for detailed information on steel shapes. Often a structural problem can be solved by the introduction of a steel member

where wood may not be entirely adequate. For unusual framing problems, it is safest to employ the services of a competent structural engineer experienced in wood structures.

But the drafter or designer should be familiar with the span tables and other structural information that are available for specifying and selecting the correct sizes of structural members needed in residential working drawings—mainly so that the builder will not be confronted with a hit or miss situation and the building will serve its purpose satisfactorily.

8.1 Stresses in Members

Let us begin by discussing lumber and its ability to support loads. Wood, being a natural material as opposed to human-made, quality-controlled materials such as steel or aluminum, has structural variations and limits. These variations are caused by species characteristics, natural defects, manufacture, moisture content, and so on. Some species, for example, oak and maple, have excellent resistance to wear qualities as needed on finish floors; other species resist weathering, insect and fungi attack, and decay, such as redwood, cedar, and cypress, yet they possess less desirable structural qualities. The widely cut Douglas fir and southern pine are especially suited for structural use. The majority of structural lumber manufactured today is made from these two species, even though considerable amounts of lumber are made from several other minor species. Notice from the tables that even those species that have less favorable load-bearing qualities are readily used if need be, yet their sizes must be increased or spans reduced to carry comparable loads. Normal safety factors are reflected in some tables. Final selection of lumber, however, is usually based on economy and availability of the lumber locally. Higher grades of similar species of lumber can be expected to carry greater loads, as indicated by the tables. Although the innate character of the wood does not change with lower grades, the fewer defects in the better grades will no doubt result in more reliability, (see Table 8-1) and, as a result, longer spans are given on the tables.

For economy reasons, residential framing lumber is usually visually graded rather than machine graded as is needed for select structural lumber where critical strength and loading properties are needed.

The several structural species of lumber mentioned previously are usually stiffer than other types, especially under loads. The tendency for a member to bend when loaded is known as *deflection* (see Fig. 8-1). In some situations within the structure, excessive deflection can cause serious damage, as for example in a plastered ceiling supported by undersized ceiling joists. The deflection under load could cause plaster cracking. Therefore, many tables show several spans, each limited by a different deflection factor. The standard for maximum allowable deflection where very little deflection can be tolerated is $L/_{360}$ of the span; for less critical situations, $L/_{240}$ of the span is used. Deflection on long beams can be significant. As an example, a horizontal beam or joist limited to, say, a $L/_{240}$ deflection and selected to span 20'-0" would possibly deflect 1" near its center and still support its designed load. The less restrictive deflection factor is usually specified for rafters or other members where the actual deflection is not as visible as in floor or ceiling framing. Deflection varies inversely with the depth of the beam; so, if suitable, select sizes with maximum depth. Members loaded with continuous heavy loads are affected by long-term deflection, often referred to as live-load

TABLE 8-1
Basic grade classifications for yard lumber

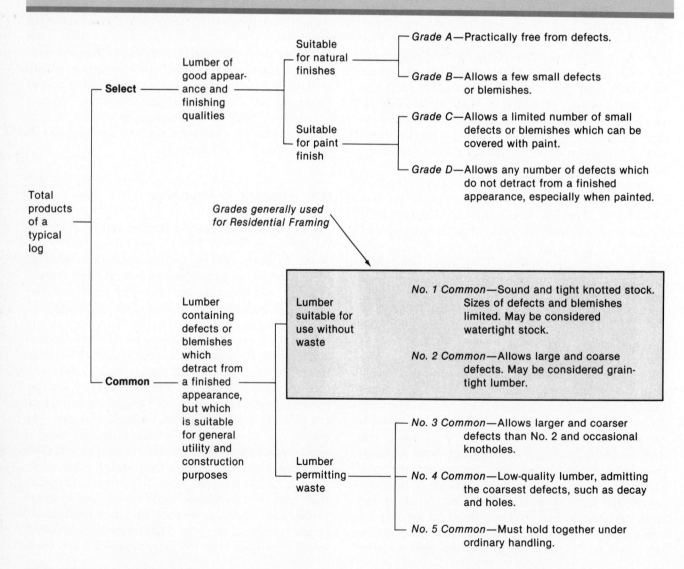

creep. Over a period of years the deformation may be substantial. We see evidence of this in older buildings where floors are under continual heavy load; the loaded wood beams often sag considerably. To overcome creep, stiffer and larger members, or steel, can be used.

Elasticity is another important characteristic in selecting framing lumber; the greater the modulus of elasticity (E), the stiffer the lumber. Notice in the tables that both southern pine and Douglas fir rate high in this quality.

The stress to be considered in column selection is *buckling* (see Fig. 8-1). The fiber in wood columns is under *compression* (parallel to grain) when loaded; some species can resist this squeezing-type stress better than others. *Tension* is a pulling-type stress, not of major concern in most light-frame members, except those in triangular-shaped trusses. While columns resist mainly compressive forces parallel to the grain, flexural members, such as beams and joists, are subject to a combination of stresses as shown by Fig. 8-1. This bending (flexure) produces longitudinal stresses. For simply supported members, this results in compression at the top fiber and tension at the bottom fiber. Vertical, applied loads are also resisted by internal shear stresses, which produce a sliding or cutting action. Where joists or beams are supported, compression stresses perpendicular to the grain are developed; if the bearing length is too short, the bearing area is reduced, thus increasing the unit stresses to the extent that the wood fiber collapses.

8.2 Moisture Content

Moisture content also affects the strength of lumber. It is the weight of the water in the wood, expressed as a percentage of the completely dry weight of the wood. Green lumber is not as strong as dried lumber, and we must remember that wood, especially dry wood, is a very good insulator from heat transfer. Lumber, however, tends to take on or give off moisture according to its environment. When it gives off moisture, it shrinks; when it takes it on, it swells. Lumber will shrink more in the dry, southwestern United States than it will in, for example, the coastal and southeastern states. The swelling and shrinking in various amounts is inevitable in wood structures, and the designer should be aware of it. Wood fiber, however, tends to shrink and swell less on end grain than across grain. Critical supports therefore would be best placed with stresses against end grain (such as with studs and posts) wherever possible. Temperature changes, on the other hand, affect the structural properties of wood very little.

For economy and availability, residential framing lumber is universally specified at 19 percent moisture content; structural lumber used for more critical design loads is often specified at 15 percent moisture content. Check these criteria on tables as values on identical members will vary. Finish lumber is usually specified at 12 percent; above 19 percent, moisture content lumber is considered unseasoned.

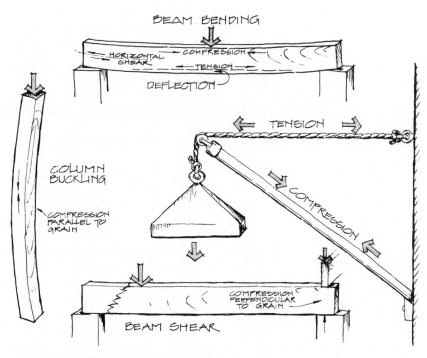

FIGURE 8-1 Stresses in structural members.

8.3 Local Codes

Since every building must conform to building codes and restrictions, drafters must be familiar with these documents when doing residential drawings. Their purpose is to provide for safety and protect the health and welfare of the occupants. Live loads on floors and roofs are especially important in wood framing (see Fig. 8-2). Local conditions throughout the United States vary considerably, and therefore local restrictions must be used to reflect these conditions; yet most local codes also include one of the national codes—*Uniform Building Code*, *Standard Building Code*, and others—as part of the document. Some areas use the F.H.A. Minimum Property Standards as a supplement to their codes. Remember that codes indicate minimum values, and any departures should be on the restrictive side.

8.4 First Determine the Loads

Before using the tables in this chapter to size framing members, calculate the total load that will be imposed on each supporting member. The weights of materials can be found in Table 7-3. More complete building material weights can be obtained from Architectural Graphic Standards. Include all materials that will form the tributary load (see Fig. 7-7). Roof loads are usually transmitted directly to exterior walls, especially roofs that are supported with prefabricated trusses, and therefore need not be considered in column and girder loading. The total applied load supported by a structural member includes both the *dead load* and the *live load*. Refer to the following table for typical minimum live loads in residential framing.

Minimum residential live loads	
Location	**Live load (psf)**
Dwelling rooms (other than sleeping)	40
Dwelling rooms (sleeping only)	30
Attics (served by any type of stairs)	30
Attics (limited storage)	20
Attics (no storage)	15
Stairs	60
Public stairs, corridors (2-family duplex)	60
Garage or carport (passenger cars)	100
Walks	100

8.4.1 Columns

Indicate the size and type of basement columns on the *basement plan*. Because steel columns are readily available and their smaller-size allows more usable floor space, they have become more popular than wood columns, especially in 1-story heights (see Fig. 8-3). Welded $^1/_4''$ steel plates are attached to each end for securing (Fig. 7-28). The hollow center may be filled with concrete to increase their strength. However, if wood columns are more suited, their sizes and loading capacities can be taken from Table 8-2.

Try to locate columns at load points if possible. The spacing of columns and the sizing of girders are best done by trial and error at the drawing board. When the floor area to be framed is established, make several sketches on overlay paper above the plan to determine the best framing and support method possible. Establish where concentrations of weight will be so that direct support can be placed below whenever possible, rather than having unnecessary loads over the center of joist spans. Closer-spaced columns will reduce beam size but will also diminish space utilization at the lower level. Usually, a compromise is the best solution.

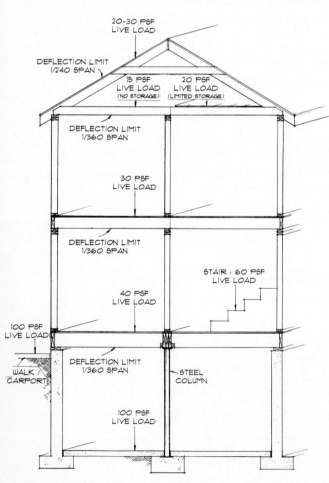

FIGURE 8-2 Live loads in residential construction.

Nominal size	Actual size	Area (sq in.)	Wood columns: lumber species	Maximum loads in kips (1000 lb) Heights (unsupported)			
	Solid or glued			7'-0"	8'-0"	9'-0"	10'-0"
4" × 4"	3½" × 3½"	12.25	Sou. pine; Douglas fir	11.22	8.59	6.79	5.50
			Redwood	8.42	6.44	5.09	4.12
			Hemlock, eastern	7.72	5.91	4.67	3.78
4" × 6"	3½" × 5½"	19.25	Sou. pine; Douglas fir	17.64	13.51	10.67	8.64
			Redwood	13.23	10.13	8.00	6.48
			Hemlock, eastern	12.13	9.28	7.33	5.94
6" × 6"	5½" × 5½"	30.25	Sou. pine; Douglas fir	68.47	52.42	41.42	33.55
			Redwood	51.35	39.31	31.06	25.16
			Hemlock, eastern	47.07	36.04	28.47	23.06
6" × 8"	5½" × 7¼"	39.88	Sou. pine; Douglas fir	90.26	69.10	54.60	44.22
			Redwood	67.69	51.82	40.95	33.17
			Hemlock, eastern	62.05	47.51	37.53	30.40
8" × 8 "	7¼" × 7¼"	52.56	Sou. pine; Douglas fir	206.74	158.28	125.05	101.30
			Redwood	155.05	118.71	93.79	75.97
			Hemlock, eastern	142.13	108.82	85.98	69.64
8" × 10"	7¼" × 9¼"	67.06	Sou. pine; Douglas fir	263.77	201.95	159.56	129.24
			Redwood	197.83	151.46	119.67	96.93
			Hemlock, eastern	181.34	138.84	109.70	88.85
10" × 10"	9¼" × 9¼"	85.56	Sou. pine; Douglas fir	547.82	419.42	331.40	268.43
			Redwood	410.86	314.57	248.55	201.32
			Hemlock, eastern	376.63	288.35	227.83	184.54

8.4.2 Beams

Indicate size and type of beams that support first-floor joists on the basement or foundation plan. Usually, a heavy broken line is a sufficient symbol. Here again, if living space is important in the basement area, it may be advantageous to use a steel beam rather than wood to allow columns to be spaced farther apart. In crawl spaces this is not critical; C.M.U. piers are universally used at ground level since they can be located at critical points under the framing and be somewhat closer together to minimize beam sizes.

Wood beams can be either solid or built up from 2" framing lumber well spiked together. Notice that built-up beams span slightly shorter spans than similar-size solid members. This is reflected in the tables because more sides have been planed during finishing, which results in a smaller cross section. In small homes it is usually more practical to build up the wood beam using the same-size framing material as that used for joists, shown in Fig. 7-25D. If headroom or an uninterrupted ceiling is important below, or if a beam must be introduced into the joist framing and be at the same level, ledger strips or hangers can be used (Fig. 7-25D) to

TABLE 8-3

Standard steel pipe columns maximum loads in kips (1000 lb) ($F_y = 35$ ksi)

Column diameter (nominal)	Column diameter (outside)	Unbraced length				
		6'-0"	7'-0"	8'-0"	9'-0"	10'-0"
3"	3.5"	38	36	34	31	28
3½"	4.0"	48	46	44	41	38
4"	4.5"	59	57	54	52	49
5"	5.56"	83	81	78	76	73

support the joists against the beam rather than rest on the beam.

A flitch beam, having a steel plate sandwiched between two wood members, such as is often used above openings in carports or above garage doors, may be the solution for the beam in floor framing as well. (See Table 8-4 for loading values.)

Two types of manufactured wood beams are also available, both feature high load-carrying capacity and dimensional stability.

TABLE 8-4
Flitch beams

Maximum Load in Kips   No. 2 Grade Sou. Y. Pine   Steel A–36

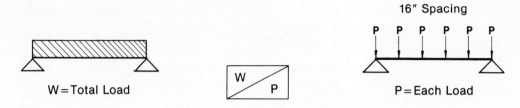

W = Total Load | W / P | P = Each Load — 16" Spacing

Size	Wt./Ft.	10'-0"	12'-0"	14'-0"	16'-0"	18'-0"	20'-0"	22'-0"
2–2×8 ³⁄₈″ × 7½″ PLT.	14.6	6.72 / .84	5.12 / .58	4.0 / .34	3.7 / .24	3.4 / .23	2.8 / .19	2.3 / .13
2–2×8 ⁷⁄₁₆″ × 7½″ PLT.	16.1	7.5 / .94	5.71 / .64	5.2 / .38	4.2 / .27	3.8 / .24	3.1 / .21	2.5 / .14
2–2×8 ½″ × 7½″ PLT.	17.6	8.3 / 1.03	6.3 / .70	5.3 / .42	4.6 / .30	4.2 / .29	3.4 / .22	2.8 / .16
2–2×10 ³⁄₈″ × 9¼″ PLT.	18.5	11.0 / 1.37	9.09 / 1.02	7.7 / .71	6.0 / .50	4.8 / .34	3.8 / .26	3.2 / .18
2–2×10 ⁷⁄₁₆″ × 9¼″ PLT.	20.5	12.3 / 1.5	10.1 / 1.1	8.6 / .79	6.7 / .56	5.3 / .38	4.3 / .29	3.5 / .20
2–2×10 ½″ × 9¼″ PLT.	22.4	13.5 / 1.7	11.2 / 1.3	9.5 / .90	7.4 / .62	5.8 / .42	4.7 / .32	3.9 / .22
2–2×12 ³⁄₈″ × 11¼″ PLT.	22.6	16.3 / 2.0	13.5 / 1.5	11.5 / 1.0	10.0 / .83	8.5 / .61	6.9 / .46	5.7 / .32
2–2×12 ⁷⁄₁₆″ × 11¼″ PLT.	24.9	18.2 / 2.3	15.1 / 1.7	12.8 / 1.2	11.1 / .93	9.5 / .68	7.7 / .51	6.4 / .35
2–2×12 ½″ × 11¼″ PLT.	27.3	20.1 / 2.5	16.6 / 1.9	14.2 / 1.3	12.3 / 1.0	10.5 / .75	8.5 / .57	7.0 / .39

*Loads after darker line are governed by span divided by 240

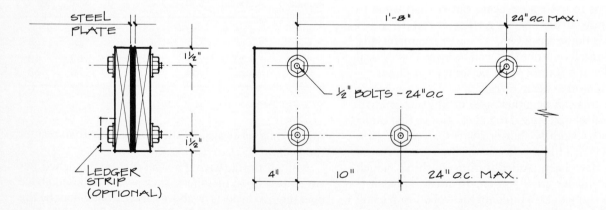

The Glu-Lam® beam (Fig. 8-3) is built up of ³⁄₄″, 1³⁄₈″, or 1½″ sawn lumber, horizontally laminated with an adhesive. Widths vary from 3⅛″ to 10¾″ and depths from 3″ to 75″. Load tables and details for these beams are published by the American Institute of Timber Construction, Englewood, Colorado.

The Micro-Lam® beam is a vertically laminated member built up of thin roll peeled veneers, bonded

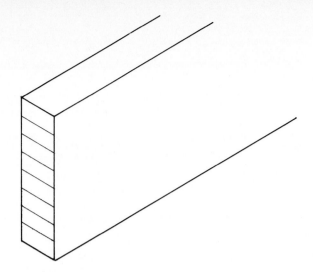

FIGURE 8-3 Glu-Lam® beam.

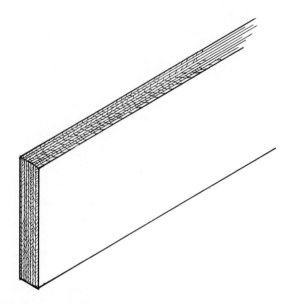

FIGURE 8-4 Micro-Lam® beam.

TABLE 8-5

Steel beam loads, F_y = 36 ksi (A36 steel): allowable uniform load in kips

	Span						
	8'	10'	12'	14'	16'	18'	20'
W6 × 9	11	8.8	7.3	6.3			
W8 × 10	15	12	10	8.8	7.7	6.9	6.2
W10 × 12	22	17	14	12	11	10	8.6
W12 × 14	30	24	20	17	15	13	12
W14 × 22	57	46	38	33	29	26	23
W14 × 30	83	67	55	48	42	37	33

together by a waterproof adhesive. Beams are made in 1³/₄″ wide and in depths from 5¹/₂″ to 18″ (Fig. 8-4). Load tables and details are published by the Trus Joist MacMillian, A Limited Partnership, Boise, Idaho.

Steel beams are usually W sections; typical sizes for light framing and their spans are shown in Table 8-5. Allow for a wood plate to be fastened above the beam for securing the wood joists. The wood joists can also be framed to the side of the steel beam as shown by Fig. 7-25E. Steel column cap plates are welded or fastened to the beam with bolts (Fig. 7-27). As mentioned previously, steel beams usually allow more headroom below.

Steel angle lintels, usually needed over brick veneer openings, can be found in Table 7-7.

8.4.3 Floor Joists

Floor framing requires careful consideration in residential construction. Often the type of subfloor (plywood or 1″ lumber), the span required, and the species of lumber available play a part in selecting a satisfactory solution. Codes require 40 lb/sq ft in living areas, but it is common practice to maintain the same live load throughout the building. Indicate joist size, spacing, and direction with a note and short line with arrows at each end. Plan the joist layout so they span the shorter dimension, which should be reflected in the overlay sketch.

Normally, joists are spaced 16″ apart, yet situations may arise where 12″ or 24″ spacing may be more suitable. Plan the joist layout also so that a minimum of cutting is necessary; that is, plan joist lengths in 2′ increments if possible. Select the joist size from Table 8-6 after the span and type of load are determined. Notice in this table that no dead-load calculations are necessary.

A living room floor, as an example of using Table 8-6, with a 40-pound live load and a span of 14′-0″ requires 2 × 10 joists spaced 16″ o.c. if No. 2 southern pine is used. Notice that the joists are capable of spanning 15′-8″ if necessary. Should a span of 17′-0″ be needed in another area of the house, for instance, it may be best to space this set of joists 12″ o.c. rather than go to larger 2 × 12 joists spaced at the same 16″ o.c. spacing. This solution results in neater and less complex framing unless a higher grade of lumber is used. Other situations occur where some latitude in joist selection must be available to arrive at the most economical yet sound arrangement. It is usually most practical to stay with one grade and cross-sectional size throughout the entire floor framing. Ceiling joists that support another floor above must be considered as floor joists as well.

In addition to sawn lumber floor joists, manufactured type members are available. One is a wood I-shaped member, as shown by Fig. 8-5. It is made in depths of 9¹/₂″ to 24″ and in lengths to 40′. The flanges

TABLE 8-6

Joist and rafter spans (19% maximum moisture content)

Spans based on American Softwood Lumber Standard (PS 20-70) sizes.

SELECTED SPECIES AND GRADES		SOUTHERN YELLOW PINE No. 1 Kiln Dried $F_b = 1900$ $E = 1,900,000$	SOUTHERN YELLOW PINE No. 2 $F_b = 1200$ $E = 1,400,000$	DOUGLAS FIR-LARCH No. 2 $F_b = 1450$ $E = 1,700,000$	EASTERN SPRUCE Structural $F_b = 1300$ $E = 1,300,000$	SOUTHERN YELLOW PINE No. 1 Kiln Dried $F_b = 1900$ $E = 1,900,000$	SOUTHERN YELLOW PINE No. 2 $F_b = 1200$ $E = 1,400,000$	DOUGLAS FIR-LARCH No. 2 $F_b = 1450$ $E = 1,700,000$	EASTERN SPRUCE Structural $F_b = 1300$ $E = 1,300,000$
Nominal Size	Spc'g. " o.c.	**FLOOR JOISTS**							
		30# Live Load				40# Live Load			
2″ x 6″	12	12–6	11–3	12–0	11–0	11–4	10–3	10–11	10–1
	16	11–4	10–10	10–11	10–0	10–4	9–4	9–11	9–2
	24	9–11	8–8	9–7	8–9	9–0	7–9	8–8	7–11
2″ x 8″	12	16–6	14–11	15–10	14–6	15–0	13–6	14–5	13–2
	16	15–0	13–6	14–5	13–2	13–7	12–3	13–1	12–0
	24	13–1	11–6	12–7	11–6	11–11	10–3	11–3	10–6
2″ x 10″	12	21–0	19–0	20–3	18–6	19–1	17–3	18–5	16–10
	16	19–1	17–3	18–5	16–10	17–4	15–8	16–9	15–3
	24	16–8	14–7	16–1	14–8	15–2	13–1	14–6	13–4
2″ x 12″	12	25–7	23–1	24–8	22–6	23–3	21–0	22–5	20–6
	16	23–3	21–0	22–5	20–6	21–1	19–1	20–4	18–7
	24	20–3	17–9	19–7	17–11	18–5	15–11	17–6	16–3
		CEILING JOISTS							
		No Attic Storage—Drywall Ceiling				Limited Attic Storage—Plaster Ceiling			
2″ x 4″	12	13–2	11–10	12–8	11–7	9–1	8–3	8–9	8–0
	16	11–11	10–9	11–6	10–6	8–3	7–6	8–0	7–3
	24	10–5	9–5	9–11	9–2	7–3	6–6	7–0	6–4
2″ x 6″	12	20–8	18–8	19–11	18–2	14–4	12–11	13–9	12–7
	16	18–9	16–11	18–1	16–6	13–0	11–9	12–6	11–5
	24	16–4	14–2	15–7	14–5	11–4	10–0	10–11	10–0
2″ x 8″	12	27–2	24–7	26–2	24–0	18–10	17–0	18–2	16–7
	16	24–8	22–4	23–10	21–9	17–2	15–6	16–6	15–1
	24	21–7	18–8	20–6	19–0	15–0	13–2	14–5	13–2
2″ x 10″	12	34–8	31–4	32–9	30–7	24–1	21–9	23–2	21–2
	16	31–6	28–6	29–9	27–9	21–10	19–9	21–1	19–3
	24	27–6	23–1	26–0	24–3	19–1	16–10	18–5	16–10
		LOW SLOPE ROOF RAFTERS (3″ in 12″ or less)							
		20# Live Load—No Finished Ceiling				40# Live Load—No Finished Ceiling			
2″ x 6″	12	16–5	14–2	15–4	14–4	13–0	11–0	11–11	11–5
	16	14–8	12–4	13–3	12–10	11–9	9–6	10–3	9–11
	24	12–8	10–0	10–10	10–5	9–9	7–9	8–5	8–1
2″ x 8″	12	21–7	18–9	20–3	19–4	17–2	14–6	15–8	15–1
	16	19–6	16–3	17–6	16–10	15–6	12–7	13–7	13–1
	24	16–8	13–3	14–4	13–9	12–11	10–3	11–1	10–8
2″ x 10″	12	27–6	23–11	25–10	24–6	21–10	18–6	20–0	19–3
	16	24–8	20–8	22–4	21–6	20–0	16–0	17–4	16–8
	24	21–3	16–11	18–3	17–7	16–6	13–1	14–2	13–7
2″ x 12″	12	33–5	29–1	31–4	30–0	26–6	22–6	24–4	23–5
	16	30–0	25–2	27–2	26–2	24–4	19–6	21–1	20–3
	24	25–10	20–6	22–2	21–5	20–0	15–11	17–2	16–7
		HIGH SLOPE ROOF RAFTERS (over 3″ in 12″)							
		20# Live Load—Light Roofing				40# Live Load—Heavy Roofing			
2″ x 4″	12	11–6	10–3	11–0	9–11	8–5	7–4	7–8	6–11
	16	10–5	9–1	9–6	8–7	7–3	6–4	6–8	6–0
	24	8–6	7–4	7–9	7–0	5–11	5–2	5–5	4–11
2″ x 6″	12	18–1	15–0	16–2	15–7	13–2	10–6	11–4	10–11
	16	16–4	13–0	14–0	13–6	11–5	9–1	9–10	9–5
	24	13–4	10–7	11–5	11–0	9–4	7–5	8–0	7–9
2″ x 8″	12	23–8	19–9	21–4	20–6	17–5	13–10	14–11	14–5
	16	21–6	17–1	18–5	17–9	15–1	12–0	12–11	12–6
	24	17–7	13–11	15–1	14–6	12–4	9–9	10–7	10–2
2″ x 10″	12	30–3	25–2	27–2	26–2	22–2	17–8	19–1	18–4
	16	27–5	21–10	23–7	22–8	19–3	15–3	16–6	15–11
	24	22–5	17–10	19–3	18–6	15–8	12–6	13–6	13–0

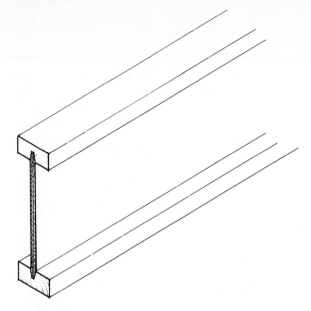

FIGURE 8-5 Truss joist.

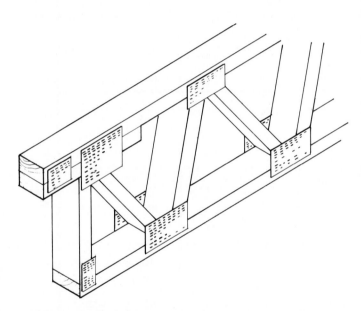

FIGURE 8-6 Factory fabricated wood trusses.

are made of microlaminated wood or solid wood and the webs of plywood or oriented strand board. These members are lightweight, easy to handle, and dimensionally stable and have the capacity to support large loads. Such members as the residential TJI® joists are fabricated by Trus Joist MacMillian.

Another member is the fabricated wood flat truss. It is built up of 2 × 4 material and assembled with metal truss-plate connectors. It is usually available from roof trussed rafter suppliers. Large load capacity on longer spans means that load-bearing partitions and interior beams, posts, and footings can frequently be eliminated (see Fig. 8-6).

8.4.4 Ceiling Joists

Indicate the ceiling joist size and direction with a symbol and note on the floor plan that requires the ceiling above; always indicate framing information that is overhead or over the plane of the floor plan. Notice that ceiling joists may be subjected to various types of loads. Ceilings where storage above is necessary must be adequately framed to prevent objectional deflection. If ceiling joists are to tie with the rafters to counteract lateral thrust, consideration must be given to their direction; otherwise, joists are placed to result in the shortest span for economy. Select ceiling joists sizes from Table 8-6 in the group directly below floor joists.

8.4.5 Rafters

As we mentioned previously, roof loads are usually transmitted directly to exterior walls; occasionally, partial loads are transmitted to interior partitions. Notice in Table 8-6 that rafter size is affected by roof slope; lower slopes require larger rafters. The span of a rafter is the horizontal distance from the wall plate to the ridgeboard (see Fig. 10-8 and Table 8-20). Collar beams, usually 1 × 4 or 1 × 6 ties, fastened midway between the ridge and plate to opposing rafters, are meant to stiffen the roof. They are conventionally applied to every second or third set of rafters. Design loads are figured from span to collar beam only, but in actual practice the full horizontal span of the rafter is used. The weight of roofing material is also important. Fiberglass or wood shingles are considered light roofing, whereas slate or mission tile, for example, are considered heavy roofing. Select rafter size from Table 8-6 after roofing materials have been determined.

If wood trusses are used for roof framing, refer to Section 7.4.3.

8.5 Plank and Beam Framing[1]

The following tables provided by the National Forest Products Association are included for sizing beams (6'-0", 7'-0", and 8'-0" spacings) and planking, often used in contemporary construction. Refer to the material in Section 7.5 for more information on this type of framing.

8.5.1 Design Data for Planks

Design data for plank floors and roofs are included in Table 8-7. Computations for bending are based on the

---

[1] From *Plank-and-Beam Framing for Residential Buildings* (Manual No. 4). By and with permission from the National Forest Products Association.

TABLE 8-7
Nominal two-inch plank

Required values for fiber stress in bending (f) and modulus of elasticity (E) to support safely a live load of 20, 30, or 40 pounds per square foot within a deflection limitation of l/240, l/300, or l/360.

PLANK SPAN IN FEET	LIVE LOAD psf	DEFLECTION LIMITATION	TYPE A f psi	TYPE A E psi	TYPE B f psi	TYPE B E psi	TYPE C f psi	TYPE C E psi	TYPE D f psi	TYPE D E psi
6′	20	$\frac{l}{240}$	360	576000	360	239000	288	305000	360	408000
		$\frac{l}{300}$	360	720000	360	299000	288	381000	360	509000
		$\frac{l}{360}$	360	864000	360	359000	288	457000	360	611000
	30	$\frac{l}{240}$	480	864000	480	359000	384	457000	480	611000
		$\frac{l}{300}$	480	1080000	480	448000	384	571000	480	764000
		$\frac{l}{360}$	480	1296000	480	538000	384	685000	480	917000
	40	$\frac{l}{240}$	600	1152000	600	478000	480	609000	600	815000
		$\frac{l}{300}$	600	1440000	600	598000	480	762000	600	1019000
		$\frac{l}{360}$	600	1728000	600	717000	480	914000	600	1223000
7′	20	$\frac{l}{240}$	490	915000	490	380000	392	484000	490	647000
		$\frac{l}{300}$	490	1143000	490	475000	392	605000	490	809000
		$\frac{l}{360}$	490	1372000	490	570000	392	726000	490	971000
	30	$\frac{l}{240}$	653	1372000	653	570000	522	726000	653	971000
		$\frac{l}{300}$	653	1715000	653	712000	522	907000	653	1213000
		$\frac{l}{360}$	653	2058000	653	854000	522	1088000	653	1456000
	40	$\frac{l}{240}$	817	1829000	817	759000	653	968000	817	1294000
		$\frac{l}{300}$	817	2287000	817	949000	653	1209000	817	1618000
		$\frac{l}{360}$	817	2744000	817	1139000	653	1451000	817	1941000
8′	20	$\frac{l}{240}$	640	1365000	640	567000	512	722000	640	966000
		$\frac{l}{300}$	640	1707000	640	708000	512	903000	640	1208000
		$\frac{l}{360}$	640	2048000	640	850000	512	1083000	640	1449000
	30	$\frac{l}{240}$	853	2048000	853	850000	682	1083000	853	1449000
		$\frac{l}{300}$	853	2560000	853	1063000	682	1354000	853	1811000
		$\frac{l}{360}$	853	3072000	853	1275000	682	1625000	853	2174000
	40	$\frac{l}{240}$	1067	2731000	1067	1134000	853	1444000	1067	1932000
		$\frac{l}{300}$	1067	3413000	1067	1417000	853	1805000	1067	2415000
		$\frac{l}{360}$	1067	4096000	1067	1700000	853	2166000	1067	2898000

live load indicated, plus 10 pounds per square foot of dead load. Computations for deflection are based on the live load only. The table shows four general arrangements of planks as follows:

Type A—Extending over a single span
Type B—Continuous over two equal spans
Type C—Continuous over three equal spans
Type D—A combination of types A and B

On the basis of a section of planking 12″ wide, the following formulas were used in making the computations:

For type A: $M = \dfrac{wL^2}{8}$ and $D = \dfrac{5wL^4 (12)^3}{384EI}$

For type B: $M = \dfrac{wL^2}{8}$ and $D = \dfrac{wL^4 (12)^3}{185EI}$

For type C: $M = \dfrac{wL^2}{10}$ and $D = \dfrac{4wL^4 (12)^3}{581EI}$

For type D:

$M = \dfrac{wL^2}{8}$ and $D = \dfrac{1}{2}\left(\dfrac{5wL^4 (12)^3}{384El} + \dfrac{wL^4 (12)^3}{185EI} \right)$

Notations   In the preceding formulas and in the tables, the symbols have the following meanings:

w = load in pounds per linear foot
L = span in feet
M = induced bending moment in pound-feet
f = fiber stress in bending in pounds per square inch
E = modulus of elasticity in pounds per square inch
I = moment of inertia in inches to the fourth power
D = deflection in inches

To use Table 8-7, first determine the plank arrangement (types A, B, C or D), the span, the live load to be supported, and the deflection limitation. Then select from the table the corresponding required values for fiber stress in bending (f) and modulus of elasticity (E). The plank to be used should be of a grade and species that meets these minimum values. The maximum span for a specific grade and species of plank may be determined by reversing these steps.

For those who prefer to use random-length planks (instead of arrangements type A, B, C, or D), similar technical information is included in *Random Length Wood Decking*, a publication of the National Forest Products Association.

In addition to the nominal 2″ plank described above, decking is available in nominal 3″ thickness and in various laminated deck systems, as shown by Fig. 8-7.

8.5.2 Design Data for Beams

Design data for beams are included in Tables 8-8 through 8-18. Computations for bending are based on the live load indicated plus 10 lb/sq ft of dead load. Computations for deflection are based on the live load only. All beams in the table were designed to extend over a single span and the following formulas were used:

For type A:

$$M = \dfrac{wL^2}{8} \quad and \quad D = \dfrac{5wL^4 (12)^3}{384EI}$$

To use the tables, first determine the span, the live load to be supported, and the deflection limitation. Then select from the tables the proper size of beam with the corresponding required values for fiber stress in bending (f) and modulus of elasticity (E). The beam used should be of a grade and species that meets these minimum values. The maximum span for a beam of specific size, grade, and species can be determined by reversing these steps.

Lumber Sizes   Tabular data provided herein are based on net dimensions (S4S) as listed in American Softwood Lumber Standard, VPS 20-70, Table 8-19.

TABLE 8-8
Floor and roof beams

Required values for fiber stress in bending (f) and modulus of elasticity (E) for the sizes shown to support safely a live load of 20 pounds per square foot within a deflection limitation of l/240.

SPAN OF BEAM	NOMINAL SIZE OF BEAM	6'-0" f	6'-0" E	7'-0" f	7'-0" E	8'-0" f	8'-0" E
10'	2-3x6	1070	780000	1250	910000	1430	1040000
	1-3x8	1235	680000	1440	794000	1645	906000
	2-2x8	1030	570000	1200	665000	1370	760000
	1-4x8	880	485000	1030	566000	1175	646000
	3-2x8	685	380000	800	443000	915	506000
	2-3x8	615	340000	720	397000	820	453000
	2-2x10	630	273000	735	219000	840	364000
11'	2-3x6	1295	1037000	1510	1210000	1730	1382000
	1-3x8	1490	905000	1740	1056000	1990	1206000
	2-2x8	1245	754000	1450	880000	1660	1005000
	1-4x8	1065	647000	1245	755000	1420	862000
	3-2x8	830	503000	970	587000	1105	670000
	2-3x8	745	453000	870	529000	995	604000
	2-2x10	765	363000	890	424000	1020	484000
12'	2-3x6	1545	1346000	1800	1571000	2060	1794000
	1-3x8	1775	1175000	2070	1371000	2370	1566000
	2-2x8	1480	980000	1725	1144000	1970	1306000
	1-4x8	1270	840000	1480	980000	1690	1120000
	3-2x8	985	653000	1150	762000	1315	870000
	2-3x8	890	588000	1035	686000	1185	784000
	1-6x8	755	483000	880	564000	1005	644000
	2-2x10	910	472000	1060	551000	1210	629000
	1-3x10	1090	566000	1275	660000	1455	754000
13'	2-3x6	1815	1711000	2110	1997000	2415	2281000
	1-3x8	2085	1494000	2430	1743000	2780	1991000
	2-2x8	1740	1245000	2025	1453000	2315	1660000
	1-4x8	1490	1067000	1735	1245000	1985	1422000
	3-2x8	1160	830000	1350	969000	1545	1106000
	2-3x8	1045	747000	1215	872000	1390	996000
	1-6x8	885	614000	1040	716000	1185	818000
	2-2x10	1070	600000	1245	700000	1420	800000
	1-3x10	1280	719000	1495	839000	1710	958000
14'	2-2x8	2015	1555000	2350	1815000	2685	2073000
	3-2x8	1340	1037000	1570	1210000	1790	1382000
	2-3x8	1210	933000	1410	1089000	1610	1244000
	1-6x8	1025	766000	1200	894000	1370	1021000
	1-3x10	1485	899000	1730	1049000	1980	1198000
	2-2x10	1235	749000	1445	874000	1650	998000
	1-4x10	1060	642000	1240	749000	1415	856000
	3-2x10	825	499000	965	582000	1100	665000
	2-3x10	740	449000	865	524000	990	598000
15'	3-2x8	1540	1275000	1800	1488000	2055	1699000
	2-3x8	1390	1148000	1620	1340000	1850	1530000
	1-6x8	1180	943000	1375	1100000	1570	1257000
	1-3x10	1705	1105000	1990	1289000	2270	1473000
	2-2x10	1420	921000	1660	1075000	1895	1228000
	1-4x10	1220	789000	1420	921000	1625	1052000
	3-2x10	950	614000	1105	717000	1265	818000
	2-3x10	850	553000	995	645000	1135	737000
	1-6x10	735	464000	855	541000	980	618000
	4-2x10	710	461000	830	538000	945	614000
	2-2x12	960	512000	1120	597000	1280	682000
16'	3-2x8	1755	1548000	2045	1806000	2340	2063000
	2-3x8	1580	1393000	1840	1626000	2105	1857000
	2-2x10	1615	1118000	1890	1305000	2155	1490000
	1-4x10	1385	958000	1615	1118000	1845	1277000
	3-2x10	1075	745000	1260	869000	1435	993000
	2-3x10	970	671000	1130	783000	1290	894000
	1-6x10	835	563000	975	657000	1130	750000
	4-2x10	810	559000	945	652000	1080	745000
	1-8x10	615	413000	715	482000	815	550000
	1-3x12	1310	746000	1530	871000	1750	994000
	2-2x12	1090	621000	1275	725000	1455	828000
17'	2-2x10	1825	1341000	2125	1565000	2430	1787000
	1-4x10	1565	1149000	1825	1341000	2085	1532000
	3-2x10	1215	894000	1420	1043000	1620	1192000

SPAN OF BEAM	NOMINAL SIZE OF BEAM	6'-0" f	6'-0" E	7'-0" f	7'-0" E	8'-0" f	8'-0" E
17'	2-3x10	1095	804000	1280	938000	1460	1072000
	1-6x10	945	675000	1100	788000	1260	900000
	4-2x10	910	670000	1065	782000	1215	894000
	1-8x10	690	495000	805	578000	910	660000
	1-3x12	1480	894000	1725	1043000	1975	1192000
	2-2x12	1235	745000	1440	869000	1645	993000
	1-4x12	1060	639000	1230	746000	1410	852000
	3-2x12	820	497000	960	580000	1095	663000
18'	2-2x10	2045	1592000	2385	1858000	2725	2123000
	1-4x10	1755	1364000	2045	1592000	2340	1819000
	3-2x10	1365	1061000	1590	1238000	1815	1415000
	2-3x10	1270	955000	1480	1114000	1695	1273000
	1-6x10	1060	801000	1235	935000	1415	1068000
	4-2x10	1020	796000	1195	929000	1365	1062000
	1-8x10	780	588000	910	686000	1040	784000
	1-3x12	1660	1062000	1935	1239000	2210	1416000
	2-2x12	1380	885000	1615	1033000	1845	1180000
	1-4x12	1185	758000	1385	885000	1580	1011000
	3-2x12	920	590000	1075	688000	1230	786000
	2-3x12	830	531000	970	620000	1105	708000
19'	3-2x10	1520	1248000	1775	1456000	2025	1664000
	2-3x10	1365	1123000	1595	1310000	1825	1497000
	1-6x10	1170	943000	1365	1100000	1560	1257000
	4-2x10	1140	936000	1330	1092000	1520	1248000
	2-4x10	975	802000	1140	936000	1300	1070000
	1-8x10	860	691000	1005	806000	1145	921000
	1-3x12	1850	1249000	2155	1457000	2465	1665000
	2-2x12	1540	1041000	1800	1215000	2055	1388000
	1-4x12	1320	892000	1540	1041000	1760	1190000
	3-2x12	1025	694000	1200	810000	1370	926000
	2-3x12	925	624000	1080	728000	1230	832000
	1-6x12	805	531000	940	620000	1070	708000
20'	3-2x10	1685	1456000	1965	1699000	2245	1942000
	2-3x10	1515	1310000	1770	1529000	2020	1747000
	1-6x10	1300	1099000	1515	1282000	1735	1465000
	4-2x10	1260	1092000	1475	1274000	1685	1456000
	2-4x10	1080	936000	1265	1092000	1445	1248000
	1-8x10	960	806000	1120	941000	1280	1075000
	2-2x12	1705	1214000	1990	1417000	2275	1619000
	1-4x12	1465	1040000	1710	1214000	1950	1387000
	3-2x12	1140	809000	1330	944000	1520	1079000
	2-3x12	1025	728000	1195	850000	1365	971000
	1-6x12	970	620000	1130	723000	1295	826000
	2-4x12	730	520000	855	607000	975	694000
21'	3-2x10	1855	1685000	2165	1966000	2475	2247000
	2-3x10	1670	1516000	1950	1827000	2225	2088000
	1-6x10	1430	1273000	1670	1485000	1905	1697000
	4-2x10	1390	1264000	1625	1475000	1855	1686000
	2-4x10	1195	1083000	1390	1264000	1590	1444000
	1-8x10	1050	933000	1225	1089000	1400	1244000
	2-2x12	1880	1405000	2195	1640000	2510	1874000
	1-4x12	1615	1204000	1880	1405000	2150	1606000
	3-2x12	1255	937000	1465	1093000	1670	1249000
	2-3x12	1130	843000	1320	984000	1505	1124000
	1-6x12	970	717000	1130	837000	1295	956000
	2-4x12	805	602000	940	702000	1075	802000
22'	1-6x10	1580	1463000	1845	1707000	2105	1951000
	4-2x10	1525	1453000	1780	1696000	2035	1938000
	2-4x10	1310	1245000	1530	1453000	1745	1660000
	1-8x10	1160	1073000	1355	1252000	1545	1431000
	1-4x12	1770	1384000	2065	1615000	2360	1846000
	3-2x12	1375	1077000	1605	1257000	1835	1436000
	2-3x12	1240	969000	1445	1130000	1655	1291000
	1-6x12	1080	825000	1260	963000	1440	1100000
	2-4x12	885	692000	1035	807000	1180	922000
	4-2x12	1035	808000	1205	943000	1375	1078000
	5-2x12	825	646000	965	754000	1105	862000
	3-3x12	825	639000	965	746000	1105	852000

TABLE 8-9
Floor and roof beams

Required values for fiber stress in bending (f) and modulus of elasticity (E) for the sizes shown to support safely a live load of 20 pounds per square foot within a deflection limitation of l/300.

SPAN OF BEAM	NOMINAL SIZE OF BEAM	6'-0" f	6'-0" E	7'-0" f	7'-0" E	8'-0" f	8'-0" E
10'	2-3x6	1070	975000	1250	1138000	1430	1300000
	1-3x8	1235	850000	1440	992000	1645	1133000
	2-2x8	1030	712000	1200	831000	1370	949000
	1-4x8	880	606000	1030	707000	1175	808000
	3-2x8	685	475000	800	554000	915	633000
	2-3x8	615	425000	720	496000	820	566000
	2-2x10	630	341000	735	398000	840	455000
11'	2-3x6	1295	1296000	1510	1512000	1730	1727000
	1-3x8	1490	1131000	1740	1320000	1990	1508000
	2-2x8	1245	942000	1450	1099000	1660	1256000
	1-4x8	1065	809000	1245	944000	1420	1078000
	3-2x8	830	629000	970	734000	1105	838000
	2-3x8	745	566000	870	660000	995	754000
	2-2x10	765	454000	890	530000	1020	605000
12'	2-3x6	1545	1682000	1800	1963000	2060	2242000
	1-3x8	1775	1469000	2070	1714000	2370	1958000
	2-2x8	1480	1225000	1725	1429000	1970	1633000
	1-4x8	1270	1050000	1480	1225000	1690	1400000
	3-2x8	985	816000	1150	952000	1315	1088000
	2-3x8	890	735000	1035	858000	1185	980000
	1-6x8	755	604000	880	705000	1005	805000
	2-2x10	910	590000	1060	688000	1210	786000
13'	1-3x8	2085	1867000	2430	2179000	2780	2439000
	2-2x8	1740	1556000	2025	1816000	2315	2074000
	1-4x8	1490	1334000	1735	1557000	1985	1778000
	3-2x8	1160	1037000	1350	1210000	1545	1382000
	2-3x8	1045	934000	1215	1090000	1390	1245000
	1-6x8	885	767000	1040	895000	1185	1022000
	2-2x10	1070	750000	1245	875000	1420	1000000
	1-3x10	1280	899000	1495	1049000	1710	1198000
	1-4x10	915	642000	1070	749000	1220	856000
14'	3-2x8	1340	1296000	1570	1512000	1790	1727000
	2-3x8	1210	1166000	1410	1361000	1610	1554000
	1-6x8	1025	957000	1200	1117000	1370	1276000
	1-3x10	1485	1124000	1730	1312000	1980	1498000
	2-2x10	1235	936000	1445	1092000	1650	1248000
	1-4x10	1060	802000	1240	936000	1415	1069000
	3-2x10	825	624000	965	728000	1100	832000
	2-3x10	740	561000	865	655000	990	748000
	1-6x10	640	471000	745	550000	850	628000
	4-2x10	620	468000	720	546000	825	624000
	2-2x12	835	520000	975	607000	1115	693000
15'	3-2x8	1540	1594000	1800	1860000	2055	2125000
	2-3x8	1390	1435000	1620	1675000	1850	1913000
	1-6x8	1180	1179000	1375	1376000	1570	1572000
	1-3x10	1705	1381000	1990	1612000	2270	1841000
	2-2x10	1420	1151000	1660	1343000	1895	1534000
	1-4x10	1220	986000	1420	1151000	1625	1314000
	3-2x10	950	767000	1105	895000	1265	1022000
	2-3x10	850	691000	995	806000	1135	921000
	1-6x10	735	580000	855	677000	980	773000
	4-2x10	710	576000	830	672000	945	768000
	2-2x12	960	640000	1120	747000	1280	853000
	1-4x12	825	549000	960	641000	1100	732000
16'	2-3x8	1580	1741000	1840	2032000	2105	2321000
	2-2x10	1615	1397000	1890	1630000	2155	1862000
	1-4x10	1385	1197000	1615	1397000	1845	1596000
	3-2x10	1075	931000	1260	1086000	1435	1241000
	2-3x10	970	839000	1130	979000	1290	1118000
	1-6x10	835	704000	975	821000	1130	938000
	4-2x10	810	699000	945	816000	1080	932000
	1-8x10	615	516000	715	602000	815	688000
	1-3x12	1310	932000	1530	1087000	1750	1242000
	2-2x12	1090	776000	1275	905000	1455	1034000
	1-4x12	935	666000	1090	777000	1250	888000
	3-2x12	730	518000	850	604000	970	690000
17'	2-2x10	1825	1676000	2130	1956000	2435	2234000
	1-4x10	1565	1437000	1825	1677000	2085	1915000
	3-2x10	1215	1117000	1420	1303000	1625	1489000
	2-3x10	1095	1005000	1280	1173000	1460	1340000
	1-6x10	945	844000	1100	985000	1260	1125000
	4-2x10	910	837000	1065	977000	1215	1116000
	1-8x10	690	619000	805	722000	910	825000
	1-3x12	1480	1117000	1725	1303000	1975	1489000
	2-2x12	1235	931000	1440	1086000	1645	1241000
	1-4x12	1060	799000	1230	932000	1410	1065000
	3-2x12	820	621000	960	725000	1095	828000
	2-3x12	740	559000	865	652000	990	745000
18'	1-4x10	1755	1705000	2045	1990000	2340	2273000
	3-2x10	1365	1326000	1590	1547000	1815	1767000
	2-3x10	1270	1194000	1480	1393000	1695	1592000
	1-6x10	1060	1001000	1235	1168000	1415	1334000
	4-2x10	1020	995000	1195	1161000	1365	1326000
	1-8x10	780	735000	910	858000	1040	980000
	1-3x12	1660	1327000	1935	1549000	2210	1769000
	2-2x12	1380	1106000	1615	1291000	1845	1474000
	1-4x12	1185	947000	1385	1105000	1580	1262000
	3-2x12	920	737000	1075	860000	1230	982000
	2-3x12	830	664000	970	775000	1105	885000
	1-6x12	720	565000	840	659000	960	753000
19'	3-2x10	1520	1560000	1775	1820000	2025	2079000
	2-3x10	1365	1404000	1595	1638000	1825	1871000
	1-6x10	1170	1179000	1365	1376000	1560	1572000
	4-2x10	1140	1170000	1330	1365000	1520	1560000
	2-4x10	975	1002000	1140	1169000	1300	1336000
	1-8x10	860	864000	1005	1008000	1145	1152000
	1-3x12	1850	1561000	2155	1822000	2465	2081000
	2-2x12	1540	1301000	1800	1518000	2055	1734000
	1-4x12	1320	1115000	1540	1301000	1760	1486000
	3-2x12	1025	867000	1200	1012000	1370	1156000
	2-3x12	925	780000	1080	910000	1230	1040000
	1-6x12	805	664000	940	775000	1070	885000
20'	3-2x10	1685	1820000	1965	2124000	2245	2426000
	2-3x10	1515	1637000	1770	1910000	2020	2182000
	1-6x10	1300	1374000	1515	1603000	1735	1831000
	4-2x10	1260	1365000	1475	1593000	1685	1819000
	2-4x10	1080	1170000	1265	1365000	1445	1560000
	1-8x10	960	1007000	1120	1175000	1280	1342000
	2-2x12	1705	1517000	1990	1770000	2275	2022000
	1-4x12	1465	1300000	1710	1517000	1950	1733000
	3-2x12	1140	1011000	1330	1180000	1520	1348000
	2-3x12	1025	910000	1195	1062000	1365	1213000
	1-6x12	970	775000	1130	904000	1295	1003000
	4-2x12	855	759000	995	886000	1135	1012000
21'	2-3x10	1670	1895000	1950	2211000	2225	2526000
	1-6x10	1430	1591000	1670	1857000	1905	2121000
	4-2x10	1390	1580000	1625	1844000	1855	2106000
	2-4x10	1195	1354000	1390	1580000	1590	1805000
	1-8x10	1050	1166000	1225	1361000	1400	1554000
	2-2x12	1880	1756000	2195	2049000	2510	2341000
	1-4x12	1615	1505000	1880	1756000	2150	2006000
	3-2x12	1255	1171000	1465	1366000	1670	1561000
	2-3x12	1130	1054000	1320	1230000	1505	1405000
	1-6x12	970	896000	1130	1046000	1295	1194000
	4-2x12	940	878000	1100	1025000	1255	1170000
	2-4x12	805	752000	940	877000	1075	1002000
22'	4-2x10	1525	1816000	1780	2119000	2035	2421000
	2-4x10	1310	1556000	1530	1816000	1745	2074000
	1-8x10	1160	1341000	1355	1565000	1545	1787000
	1-4x12	1770	1730000	2065	2019000	2360	2306000
	3-2x12	1375	1346000	1605	1571000	1835	1794000
	2-3x12	1240	1211000	1445	1413000	1655	1614000
	1-6x12	1080	1031000	1260	1203000	1440	1374000
	4-2x12	1030	1010000	1205	1179000	1375	1346000
	2-4x12	885	865000	1035	1009000	1180	1153000
	5-2x12	825	807000	965	942000	1105	1076000
	3-3x12	825	799000	965	932000	1105	1065000

TABLE 8-10
Floor and roof beams

Required values for fiber stress in bending (f) and modulus of elasticity (E) for the sizes shown to support safely a live load of 20 pounds per square foot within a deflection limitation of l/360.

SPAN OF BEAM	NOMINAL SIZE OF BEAM	6' - 0" f	6' - 0" E	7' - 0" f	7' - 0" E	8' - 0" f	8' - 0" E
10'	2-3x6	1070	1170000	1250	1365000	1430	1560000
	1-3x8	1235	1020000	1440	1192000	1645	1359000
	2-2x8	1030	855000	1200	997000	1370	1140000
	1-4x8	880	727000	1030	847000	1175	969000
	3-2x8	685	570000	800	667000	915	759000
	2-3x8	615	510000	720	600000	820	679000
	1-6x8	525	419000	615	489000	700	558000
11'	2-3x6	1295	1555000	1510	1815000	1730	2073000
	1-3x8	1490	1357000	1740	1584000	1990	1809000
	2-2x8	1245	1131000	1450	1320000	1660	1507000
	1-4x8	1065	970000	1245	1132000	1420	1293000
	3-2x8	830	754000	970	880000	1105	1005000
	2-3x8	745	679000	870	793000	995	906000
	1-6x8	635	558000	740	651000	845	744000
12'	1-3x8	1775	1762000	2070	2056000	2370	2349000
	2-2x8	1480	1470000	1725	1716000	1970	1959000
	1-4x8	1270	1260000	1480	1470000	1690	1680000
	3-2x8	985	979000	1150	1143000	1315	1305000
	2-3x8	890	882000	1035	1029000	1185	1176000
	1-6x8	775	724000	880	846000	1005	966000
	2-2x10	910	708000	1060	826000	1210	943000
	1-3x10	1090	849000	1275	991000	1455	1132000
13'	2-2x8	1740	1867000	2025	2179000	2315	2490000
	1-4x8	1490	1600000	1735	1867000	1985	2133000
	3-2x8	1160	1245000	1350	1453000	1545	1659000
	2-3x8	1045	1120000	1215	1308000	1390	1494000
	1-6x8	885	921000	1040	1074000	1185	1227000
	2-2x10	1070	900000	1245	1050000	1420	1200000
	1-3x10	1280	1078000	1495	1258000	1710	1437000
	1-4x10	915	771000	1070	900000	1220	1028000
14'	3-2x8	1340	1555000	1570	1815000	1790	2073000
	2-3x8	1210	1399000	1410	1633000	1610	1866000
	1-6x8	1025	1149000	1200	1341000	1370	1531000
	1-3x10	1485	1348000	1730	1573000	1980	1797000
	2-2x10	1235	1123000	1445	1311000	1650	1497000
	1-4x10	1060	963000	1240	1123000	1415	1284000
	3-2x10	825	748000	965	873000	1100	997000
	2-3x10	740	673000	865	786000	990	897000
	1-6x10	640	565000	745	660000	850	753000
	4-2x10	620	561000	720	655000	825	749000
	2-2x12	835	624000	975	728000	1115	832000
15'	3-2x8	1540	1912000	1800	2232000	2055	2548000
	2-3x8	1390	1722000	1620	2010000	1850	2295000
	1-6x8	1180	1414000	1375	1650000	1570	1885000
	1-3x10	1705	1657000	1990	1933000	2270	2209000
	2-2x10	1420	1381000	1660	1612000	1895	1842000
	1-4x10	1220	1183000	1420	1381000	1625	1578000
	3-2x10	950	921000	1105	1075000	1265	1227000
	2-3x10	850	829000	995	967000	1135	1105000
	1-6x10	735	696000	855	811000	980	927000
	4-2x10	710	691000	830	807000	945	921000
	2-2x12	960	768000	1120	895000	1280	1023000
	1-4x12	825	659000	960	769000	1100	878000
16'	2-2x10	1615	1677000	1890	1957000	2155	2235000
	1-4x10	1385	1437000	1615	1677000	1845	1915000
	3-2x10	1075	1117000	1260	1303000	1435	1489000
	2-3x10	970	1006000	1130	1174000	1290	1341000
	1-6x10	835	844000	975	985000	1130	1125000
	4-2x10	810	838000	945	978000	1080	1117000
	1-8x10	615	619000	715	723000	815	825000
	1-3x12	1310	1119000	1530	1306000	1750	1491000
	2-2x12	1090	931000	1275	1087000	1455	1242000
	1-4x12	935	799000	1090	932000	1250	1066000
	3-2x12	730	622000	850	725000	970	828000
	2-3x12	655	559000	765	652000	875	745000

SPAN OF BEAM	NOMINAL SIZE OF BEAM	6' - 0" f	6' - 0" E	7' - 0" f	7' - 0" E	8' - 0" f	8' - 0" E
17'	2-2x10	1825	2011000	2125	2347000	2430	2680000
	1-4x10	1565	1723000	1825	2011000	2085	2298000
	3-2x10	1215	1341000	1420	1564000	1620	1788000
	2-3x10	1095	1206000	1280	1407000	1460	1608000
	1-6x10	945	1012000	1100	1182000	1260	1350000
	4-2x10	910	1005000	1065	1173000	1215	1341000
	1-8x10	690	742000	805	867000	910	990000
	1-3x12	1480	1341000	1725	1564000	1975	1788000
	2-2x12	1235	1117000	1440	1303000	1645	1489000
	1-4x12	1060	958000	1230	1119000	1410	1278000
	3-2x12	820	745000	960	870000	1095	994000
	2-3x12	740	671000	865	782000	990	894000
18'	3-2x10	1365	1591000	1590	1857000	1815	2122000
	2-3x10	1270	1492000	1480	1671000	1695	1909000
	1-6x10	1060	1201000	1235	1402000	1415	1602000
	4-2x10	1020	1194000	1195	1393000	1365	1593000
	1-8x10	780	882000	910	1029000	1040	1176000
	1-3x12	1660	1593000	1935	1858000	2210	2124000
	2-2x12	1380	1327000	1615	1549000	1845	1770000
	1-4x12	1185	1137000	1385	1327000	1580	1516000
	3-2x12	920	885000	1075	1032000	1230	1179000
	2-3x12	830	796000	970	930000	1105	1062000
	1-6x12	720	678000	840	790000	960	904000
	4-2x12	690	663000	805	774000	920	884000
19'	3-2x10	1520	1872000	1775	2184000	2025	2496000
	2-3x10	1365	1684000	1595	1965000	1825	2245000
	1-6x10	1170	1414000	1365	1650000	1560	1885000
	4-2x10	1140	1404000	1330	1638000	1520	1872000
	2-4x10	975	1203000	1140	1404000	1300	1605000
	1-8x10	860	1036000	1005	1209000	1145	1381000
	2-2x12	1540	1561000	1800	1822000	2055	2082000
	1-4x12	1320	1338000	1540	1561000	1760	1785000
	3-2x12	1025	1041000	1200	1215000	1370	2055000
	2-3x12	925	936000	1080	1092000	1230	1248000
	1-6x12	805	796000	940	930000	1070	1062000
	4-2x12	770	780000	900	910000	1025	1040000
20'	2-3x10	1515	1965000	1770	2293000	2020	2620000
	1-6x10	1300	1648000	1515	1923000	1735	2197000
	4-2x10	1260	1638000	1475	1911000	1685	2184000
	2-4x10	1080	1404000	1265	1638000	1445	1872000
	1-8x10	960	1209000	1120	1411000	1280	1612000
	2-2x12	1705	1821000	1990	2125000	2275	2428000
	1-4x12	1465	1560000	1710	1821000	1950	2080000
	3-2x12	1140	1213000	1330	1416000	1520	1618000
	2-3x12	1025	1092000	1195	1275000	1365	1456000
	1-6x12	970	930000	1130	1085000	1295	1239000
	4-2x12	855	911000	995	1063000	1135	1214000
	2-4x12	730	780000	850	910000	975	1040000
21'	4-2x10	1390	1896000	1625	2212000	1855	2529000
	2-4x10	1195	1624000	1390	1896000	1590	2166000
	1-8x10	1050	1399000	1225	1633000	1400	1866000
	1-4x12	1615	1806000	1880	2107000	2150	2409000
	3-2x12	1255	1405000	1465	1639000	1670	1873000
	2-3x12	1130	1264000	1320	1476000	1505	1686000
	1-6x12	970	1075000	1130	1255000	1295	1434000
	4-2x12	940	1054000	1100	1230000	1255	1404000
	2-4x12	805	903000	940	1053000	1075	1203000
	3-3x12	750	834000	875	973000	1000	1112000
	1-8x12	720	789000	840	921000	960	1052000
	1-10x12	570	623000	665	727000	760	830000
22'	2-4x10	1310	1867000	1530	2179000	1745	2490000
	1-8x10	1160	1609000	1355	1878000	1545	2146000
	3-2x12	1375	1615000	1605	1885000	1835	2154000
	2-3x12	1240	1453000	1445	1695000	1655	1936000
	1-6x12	1080	1237000	1260	1444000	1440	1650000
	4-2x12	1035	1212000	1205	1414000	1375	1617000
	2-4x12	885	1038000	1035	1210000	1180	1383000
	5-2x12	825	969000	965	1131000	1105	1293000
	3-3x12	825	958000	965	1119000	1105	1278000
	1-8x12	790	907000	920	1058000	1055	1209000
	1-10x12	625	716000	730	835000	835	954000

TABLE 8-11
Floor and roof beams

Required values for fiber stress in bending (*f*) and modulus of elasticity (*E*) for the sizes shown to support safely a live load of 30 pounds per square foot within a deflection limitation of *l*/240.

SPAN OF BEAM	NOMINAL SIZE OF BEAM	6'-0" f	6'-0" E	7'-0" f	7'-0" E	8'-0" f	8'-0" E
10'	2-3x6	1430	1170000	1670	1365000	1905	1560000
	1-3x8	1645	1020000	1920	1190000	2195	1360000
	1-4x8	1175	727000	1370	848000	1565	969000
	3-2x8	915	570000	1070	665000	1220	760000
	2-3x8	820	510000	955	595000	1095	680000
	2-4x8	590	364000	690	425000	785	485000
	2-2x10	840	409000	980	477000	1120	545000
11'	2-3x6	1725	1555000	2015	1815000	2300	2073000
	1-3x8	1990	1357000	2320	1584000	2655	1809000
	1-4x8	1420	970000	1660	1132000	1895	1293000
	3-2x8	1105	754000	1290	880000	1475	1005000
	2-3x8	995	679000	1160	792000	1325	905000
	2-4x8	710	485000	830	566000	945	646000
	2-2x10	1020	544000	1190	635000	1360	725000
12'	1-4x8	1690	1260000	1970	1470000	2255	1679000
	3-2x8	1315	979000	1535	1142000	1755	1305000
	2-3x8	1185	882000	1385	1029000	1580	1176000
	2-4x8	845	630000	985	735000	1125	840000
	1-6x8	1005	724000	1175	845000	1340	965000
	2-2x10	1210	708000	1410	826000	1615	944000
	3-2x10	810	472000	945	551000	1080	629000
	2-3x10	725	424000	845	495000	965	565000
13'	1-4x8	1985	1600000	2315	1867000	2645	2133000
	3-2x8	1545	1245000	1805	1453000	2060	1659000
	2-3x8	1390	1120000	1620	1307000	1855	1493000
	2-4x8	990	801000	1155	935000	1320	1068000
	1-6x8	1180	921000	1375	1075000	1575	1228000
	2-x10	1425	900000	1665	1050000	1900	1200000
	3-2x10	950	600000	1110	700000	1265	800000
	2-3x10	855	540000	1000	630000	1140	720000
	1-4x10	1220	923000	1425	1079000	1625	1230000
14'	3-2x8	1790	1555000	2090	1815000	2385	2073000
	2-3x8	1610	1400000	1880	1634000	2145	1866000
	2-4x8	1150	1000000	1340	1167000	1535	1333000
	1-6x8	1370	1149000	1600	1341000	1825	1532000
	2-2x10	1650	1123000	1925	1310000	2200	1497000
	3-2x10	1100	748000	1285	873000	1465	997000
	2-3x10	990	673000	1155	785000	1320	897000
	1-4x10	1415	963000	1650	1124000	1885	1283000
	1-6x10	915	943000	1070	1100000	1220	1257000
	2-4x10	705	481000	825	561000	940	641000
15'	2-4x8	1320	1230000	1540	1435000	1760	1640000
	1-6x8	1570	1414000	1830	1650000	2095	1885000
	2-2x10	1895	1381000	2210	1612000	2525	1841000
	3-2x10	1260	921000	1470	1075000	1680	1228000
	2-3x10	1135	829000	1325	967000	1515	1105000
	1-4x10	1620	1183000	1890	1380000	2160	1577000
	1-6x10	980	696000	1145	812000	1305	928000
	2-4x10	810	592000	945	691000	1080	789000
	4-2x10	945	691000	1105	806000	1260	921000
	1-8x10	720	510000	840	595000	960	680000
	2-2x12	1280	768000	1495	896000	1705	1024000
	1-4x12	1095	658000	1280	768000	1460	877000
16'	2-2x10	2155	1677000	2515	1957000	2875	2235000
	3-2x10	1435	1117000	1675	1303000	1915	1489000
	2-3x10	1290	1006000	1505	1174000	1720	1341000
	1-4x10	1845	1437000	2155	1677000	2460	1915000
	1-6x10	1115	844000	1300	985000	1485	1125000
	2-4x10	925	719000	1080	839000	1235	958000
	4-2x10	1075	838000	1255	978000	1435	1117000
	1-8x10	815	619000	950	722000	1085	825000
	2-2x12	1455	931000	1700	1086000	1940	1241000
	1-4x12	1250	799000	1460	932000	1665	1065000
	3-2x12	970	621000	1130	725000	1295	828000
	2-3x12	875	559000	1020	652000	1165	745000

SPAN OF BEAM	NOMINAL SIZE OF BEAM	6'-0" f	6'-0" E	7'-0" f	7'-0" E	8'-0" f	8'-0" E
17'	3-2x10	1620	1341000	1890	1565000	2160	1787000
	2-3x10	1460	1206000	1705	1407000	1945	1607000
	1-4x10	2085	1723000	2435	2011000	2780	2297000
	1-6x10	1255	1012000	1465	1181000	1675	1349000
	2-4x10	1040	862000	1215	1006000	1385	1149000
	4-2x10	1215	1005000	1420	1173000	1620	1340000
	1-8x10	920	742000	1075	866000	1225	989000
	2-2x12	1645	1117000	1920	1303000	2195	1489000
	1-4x12	1410	958000	1645	1118000	1880	1277000
	3-2x12	1095	745000	1280	869000	1460	993000
	2-3x12	985	671000	1150	783000	1313	894000
	4-2x12	820	559000	955	652000	1095	869000
18'	2-3x10	1695	1432000	1980	1671000	2260	1909000
	1-6x10	1415	1201000	1650	1401000	1885	1601000
	2-4x10	1170	1023000	1365	1194000	1560	1364000
	4-2x10	1360	1194000	1590	1393000	1815	1592000
	1-8x10	1040	882000	1215	1029000	1385	1176000
	2-2x12	1840	1327000	2150	1549000	2455	1769000
	1-4x12	1580	1137000	1845	1327000	2105	1516000
	3-2x12	1230	885000	1435	1033000	1640	1180000
	2-3x12	1105	796000	1290	929000	1475	1061000
	4-2x12	920	663000	1075	774000	1225	884000
	2-4x12	790	569000	920	664000	1055	758000
	5-2x12	735	531000	860	620000	980	708000
19'	2-4x10	1300	1203000	1515	1404000	1735	1604000
	4-2x10	1520	1404000	1775	1638000	2025	1871000
	1-8x10	1145	1036000	1335	1209000	1525	1381000
	1-4x12	1760	1338000	2055	1561000	2345	1783000
	3-2x12	1370	1041000	1600	1215000	1825	1388000
	2-3x12	1230	936000	1435	1092000	1640	1248000
	4-2x12	1025	780000	1195	910000	1365	1040000
	2-4x12	880	669000	1025	781000	1175	892000
	5-2x12	820	624000	955	728000	1095	832000
	1-6x12	1070	796000	1250	929000	1425	1061000
	3-3x12	820	617000	955	720000	1095	822000
	1-8x12	785	584000	915	681000	1045	778000
20'	4-2x12	1680	1638000	1960	1911000	2240	2183000
	1-8x10	1280	1209000	1495	1411000	1705	1611000
	3-2x12	1520	1213000	1775	1415000	2025	1617000
	2-3x12	1365	1092000	1595	1274000	1820	1456000
	4-2x12	1025	910000	1195	1062000	1365	1213000
	2-4x12	975	780000	1140	910000	1300	1040000
	5-2x12	910	728000	1060	849000	1215	970000
	1-6x12	1295	930000	1510	1084000	1725	1239000
	3-3x12	910	720000	1060	840000	1215	960000
	1-8x12	870	682000	1015	795000	1160	909000
	1-10x12	690	538000	805	628000	920	717000
	4-3x12	680	546000	795	637000	905	728000
21'	1-8x10	1400	1399000	1635	1633000	1865	1865000
	3-2x12	1670	1405000	1950	1640000	2225	1873000
	2-3x12	1505	1264000	1755	1475000	2005	1685000
	4-2x12	1255	1054000	1465	1230000	1675	1405000
	2-4x12	1075	903000	1255	1054000	1435	1204000
	5-2x12	1005	843000	1175	984000	1340	1124000
	1-6x12	1295	1075000	1510	1255000	1725	1434000
	3-3x12	1005	833000	1175	972000	1340	1110000
	1-8x12	960	789000	1120	921000	1280	1052000
	1-10x12	760	623000	885	727000	1015	830000
	4-3x12	750	632000	875	737000	1000	842000
	2-3x14	1085	774000	1265	903000	1445	1032000
22'	2-3x12	1655	1453000	1930	1696000	2205	1940000
	4-2x12	1375	1212000	1605	1414000	1835	1615000
	2-4x12	1180	1038000	1380	1211000	1575	1384000
	5-2x12	1100	969000	1285	1131000	1465	1292000
	1-6x12	1440	1237000	1680	1443000	1920	1649000
	3-3x12	1100	958000	1285	1118000	1465	1277000
	1-8x12	1055	907000	1230	1058000	1405	1209000
	1-10x12	830	716000	970	835000	1105	954000
	4-3x12	825	727000	965	848000	1100	969000
	2-3x14	1190	890000	1390	1039000	1585	1186000
	1-6x14	1045	765000	1220	893000	1395	1020000
	3-3x14	795	589000	930	687000	1060	785000
	2-4x14	820	601000	955	701000	1095	801000

TABLE 8-12
Floor and roof beams

Required values for fiber stress in bending (f) and modulus of elasticity (E) for the sizes shown to support safely a live load of 30 pounds per square foot within a deflection limitation of I/300.

SPAN OF BEAM	NOMINAL SIZE OF BEAM	6'-0" f	6'-0" E	7'-0" f	7'-0" E	8'-0" f	8'-0" E
10'	2-3x6	1430	1462000	1670	1706000	1905	1948000
	1-3x8	1645	1275000	1920	1488000	2195	1699000
	1-4x8	1175	909000	1370	1061000	1565	1212000
	3-2x8	915	712000	1070	831000	1220	949000
	2-3x8	820	637000	955	743000	1095	849000
	2-4x8	590	455000	690	531000	785	606000
	2-2x10	840	511000	980	596000	1120	681000
11'	1-3x8	1990	1696000	2320	1979000	2655	2261000
	1-4x8	1420	1212000	1660	1414000	1895	1615000
	3-2x8	1105	942000	1290	1099000	1475	1255000
	2-3x8	995	849000	1160	991000	1325	1132000
	2-4x8	710	606000	830	707000	945	808000
	2-2x10	1020	680000	1190	793000	1360	906000
	1-3x10	1220	817000	1425	953000	1625	1089000
12'	1-4x8	1690	1575000	1970	1838000	2255	2099000
	3-2x8	1315	1224000	1535	1428000	1755	1631000
	2-3x8	1185	1102000	1385	1286000	1580	1469000
	2-4x8	845	787000	985	918000	1125	1049000
	1-6x8	1005	905000	1175	1056000	1340	1206000
	2-2x10	1210	885000	1410	1033000	1615	1180000
	3-2x10	810	590000	945	688000	1080	786000
	2-3x10	725	530000	845	618000	965	706000
13'	1-4x8	1985	2000000	2315	2334000	2645	2666000
	3-2x8	1545	1556000	1805	1816000	2060	2074000
	2-3x8	1390	1400000	1620	1634000	1855	1866000
	2-4x8	990	1001000	1155	1168000	1320	1334000
	1-6x8	1180	1151000	1375	1343000	1575	1534000
	2-2x10	1425	1125000	1665	1313000	1900	1500000
	3-2x10	950	750000	1110	875000	1265	1000000
	2-3x10	855	675000	1000	788000	1140	900000
	1-4x10	1220	1154000	1425	1347000	1625	1538000
14'	3-2x8	1790	1944000	2090	2268000	2385	2591000
	2-3x8	1610	1750000	1880	2042000	2145	2333000
	2-4x8	1150	1250000	1340	1459000	1535	1666000
	1-6x8	1370	1436000	1600	1676000	1825	1914000
	2-2x10	1650	1404000	1925	1638000	2200	1871000
	3-2x10	1100	935000	1285	1091000	1465	1246000
	2-3x10	990	841000	1155	981000	1320	1121000
	1-4x10	1415	1204000	1650	1405000	1885	1605000
	1-6x10	915	1179000	1070	1376000	1220	1572000
	2-4x10	705	601000	825	701000	940	801000
15'	2-4x8	1320	1537000	1540	1794000	1760	2049000
	1-6x8	1570	1767000	1830	2062000	2095	2355000
	2-2x10	1895	1726000	2210	2014000	2525	2301000
	3-2x10	1260	1151000	1470	1343000	1680	1534000
	2-3x10	1135	1036000	1325	1209000	1515	1381000
	1-4x10	1620	1479000	1890	1726000	2160	1971000
	1-6x10	980	870000	1145	1015000	1305	1160000
	2-4x10	810	740000	945	863000	1080	986000
	4-2x10	945	864000	1105	1008000	1260	1152000
	1-8x10	720	637000	840	743000	960	849000
	2-2x12	1280	960000	1495	1120000	1705	1280000
	1-4x12	1095	822000	1280	959000	1460	1096000
16'	2-2x10	2155	2096000	2515	2446000	2875	2794000
	3-2x10	1435	1396000	1675	1629000	1915	1861000
	2-3x10	1290	1257000	1505	1467000	1720	1675000
	1-4x10	1845	1796000	2155	2096000	2460	2394000
	1-6x10	1115	1055000	1300	1231000	1485	1406000
	2-4x10	925	899000	1080	1049000	1235	1198000
	4-2x10	1075	1047000	1255	1222000	1435	1395000
	1-8x10	815	774000	950	903000	1085	1032000
	2-2x12	1455	1164000	1700	1358000	1940	1552000
	1-4x12	1250	999000	1460	1166000	1665	1332000
	3-2x12	970	776000	1130	905000	1295	1034000
	2-3x12	875	699000	1020	816000	1165	932000

SPAN OF BEAM	NOMINAL SIZE OF BEAM	6'-0" f	6'-0" E	7'-0" f	7'-0" E	8'-0" f	8'-0" E
17'	3-2x10	1620	1676000	1890	1956000	2160	2234000
	2-3x10	1460	1507000	1705	1759000	1945	2009000
	1-6x10	1255	1265000	1465	1476000	1675	1686000
	2-4x10	1040	1077000	1215	1257000	1385	1435000
	4-2x10	1215	1256000	1420	1466000	1620	1674000
	1-8x10	920	927000	1075	1082000	1225	1236000
	2-2x12	1645	1396000	1920	1629000	2195	1861000
	1-4x12	1410	1197000	1645	1397000	1880	1596000
	3-2x12	1095	931000	1280	1086000	1460	1241000
	2-3x12	985	839000	1150	979000	1315	1118000
	4-2x12	820	699000	955	816000	1095	932000
	2-4x12	705	599000	820	699000	940	799000
18'	2-3x10	1695	1790000	1980	2089000	2260	2386000
	1-6x10	1415	1501000	1650	1752000	1885	2000000
	2-4x10	1170	1279000	1365	1492000	1560	1705000
	4-2x10	1360	1492000	1590	1741000	1815	1989000
	1-8x10	1040	1102000	1215	1286000	1385	1469000
	2-2x12	1840	1659000	2150	1936000	2455	2211000
	1-4x12	1580	1421000	1845	1658000	2105	1894000
	3-2x12	1230	1106000	1435	1291000	1640	1474000
	2-3x12	1105	995000	1290	1161000	1475	1326000
	4-2x12	920	829000	1075	967000	1225	1105000
	2-4x12	790	711000	920	830000	1055	948000
	5-2x12	735	664000	860	775000	980	885000
19'	1-6x10	1570	1767000	1830	2062000	2095	2355000
	2-4x10	1300	1504000	1515	1755000	1735	2005000
	4-2x10	1520	1755000	1775	2048000	2025	2339000
	1-8x10	1145	1295000	1335	1511000	1525	1726000
	1-4x12	1760	1672000	2055	1951000	2345	2229000
	3-2x12	1370	1301000	1600	1518000	1825	1734000
	2-3x12	1230	1170000	1435	1365000	1640	1560000
	4-2x12	1025	975000	1195	1138000	1365	1300000
	2-4x12	880	836000	1025	976000	1175	1114000
	5-2x12	820	780000	955	910000	1095	1040000
	1-6x12	1070	995000	1250	1161000	1425	1326000
	3-3x12	820	771000	955	900000	1095	1028000
20'	1-8x10	1280	1511000	1495	1763000	1705	2014000
	3-2x12	1520	1516000	1775	1769000	2025	2021000
	2-3x12	1365	1365000	1595	1593000	1820	1819000
	4-2x12	1025	1137000	1195	1327000	1365	1516000
	2-4x12	975	975000	1140	1138000	1300	1300000
	5-2x12	910	910000	1060	1062000	1215	1213000
	1-6x12	1295	1162000	1510	1356000	1725	1549000
	3-3x12	910	900000	1060	1050000	1215	1200000
	1-8x12	870	852000	1015	994000	1160	1136000
	1-10x12	690	672000	805	784000	920	896000
	4-3x12	680	682000	795	796000	905	909000
	2-3x14	985	836000	1150	976000	1315	1114000
21'	3-2x12	1670	1756000	1950	2049000	2225	2341000
	2-3x12	1505	1580000	1755	1844000	2005	2106000
	4-2x12	1255	1317000	1465	1537000	1675	1755000
	2-4x12	1075	1129000	1255	1317000	1435	1505000
	5-2x12	1005	1054000	1175	1230000	1340	1405000
	1-6x12	1295	1344000	1510	1568000	1725	1791000
	3-3x12	1005	1041000	1175	1215000	1340	1388000
	1-8x12	960	986000	1120	1151000	1280	1314000
	1-10x12	760	779000	885	909000	1015	1038000
	4-3x12	750	790000	875	922000	1000	1053000
	2-3x14	1085	967000	1265	1128000	1445	1289000
	1-6x14	950	832000	1110	971000	1265	1109000
22'	4-2x12	1375	1515000	1605	1768000	1835	2019000
	2-4x12	1180	1297000	1380	1513000	1575	1729000
	5-2x12	1100	1211000	1285	1413000	1465	1614000
	1-6x12	1440	1546000	1680	1804000	1920	2061000
	3-3x12	1100	1197000	1285	1397000	1465	1596000
	1-8x12	1055	1134000	1230	1323000	1405	1511000
	1-10x12	830	895000	970	1044000	1105	1193000
	4-3x12	825	909000	965	1061000	1100	1212000
	2-3x14	1190	1112000	1390	1298000	1585	1482000
	1-6x14	1045	956000	1220	1116000	1395	1274000
	3-3x14	795	736000	930	859000	1060	981000
	2-4x14	820	751000	955	1114000	1095	1001000

TABLE 8-13
Floor and roof beams

Required values for fiber stress in bending (*f*) and modulus of elasticity (*E*) for the sizes shown to support safely a live load of 30 pounds per square foot within a deflection limitation of *I*/360.

SPAN OF BEAM	NOMINAL SIZE OF BEAM	6'-0" f	6'-0" E	7'-0" f	7'-0" E	8'-0" f	8'-0" E
10'	2-3x6	1430	1754000	1670	2047000	1905	2338000
	1-3x8	1645	1530000	1920	1785000	2195	2039000
	1-4x8	1175	1091000	1370	1273000	1565	1454000
	3-2x8	915	854000	1070	997000	1220	1138000
	2-3x8	820	764000	955	891000	1095	1018000
	2-4x8	590	546000	690	637000	785	728000
	2-2x10	840	613000	980	715000	1120	817000
11'	1-3x8	1990	2035000	2320	2375000	2655	2713000
	1-4x8	1420	1454000	1660	1697000	1895	1938000
	3-2x8	1105	1130000	1290	1319000	1475	1506000
	2-3x8	995	1019000	1160	1189000	1325	1358000
	2-4x8	710	727000	830	848000	945	969000
	2-2x10	1020	816000	1190	952000	1360	1088000
	1-3x10	1220	980000	1425	1144000	1625	1306000
12'	1-4x8	1690	1890000	1970	2206000	2255	2519000
	3-2x8	1315	1469000	1535	1714000	1755	1958000
	2-3x8	1185	1322000	1385	1543000	1580	1762000
	2-4x8	845	944000	985	1102000	1125	1258000
	1-6x8	1005	1086000	1175	1267000	1340	1448000
	2-2x10	1210	1062000	1410	1239000	1615	1416000
	3-2x10	810	708000	945	826000	1080	944000
	2-3x10	725	636000	845	742000	965	848000
	1-4x10	1040	909000	1215	1061000	1385	1212000
13'	3-2x8	1545	1867000	1805	2179000	2060	2489000
	2-3x8	1390	1680000	1620	1960000	1855	2239000
	2-4x8	990	1201000	1155	1401000	1320	1600000
	1-6x8	1180	1381000	1375	1612000	1575	1841000
	2-2x10	1425	1350000	1665	1575000	1900	1799000
	3-2x10	950	900000	1110	1050000	1265	1200000
	2-3x10	855	810000	1000	945000	1140	1080000
	1-4x10	1220	1385000	1425	1616000	1625	1846000
	1-6x10	735	679000	855	792000	980	905000
14'	2-4x8	1150	1500000	1340	1750000	1535	1999000
	1-6x8	1370	1723000	1600	2011000	1825	2297000
	2-2x10	1650	1684000	1925	1965000	2200	2245000
	3-2x10	1100	1122000	1285	1309000	1465	1496000
	2-3x10	990	1009000	1155	1177000	1320	1345000
	1-4x10	1415	1445000	1650	1686000	1885	1926000
	1-6x10	915	1415000	1070	1651000	1220	1886000
	2-4x10	705	721000	825	841000	940	961000
	4-2x10	825	842000	960	983000	1100	1122000
	1-8x10	625	622000	730	726000	835	829000
15'	2-2x10	1895	2071000	2210	2417000	2525	2760000
	3-2x10	1260	1381000	1470	1612000	1680	1841000
	2-3x10	1135	1243000	1325	1450000	1515	1657000
	1-4x10	1620	1775000	1890	2071000	2160	2366000
	1-6x10	980	1044000	1145	1218000	1305	1392000
	2-4x10	810	888000	945	1036000	1080	1184000
	4-2x10	945	1037000	1105	1210000	1260	1382000
	1-8x10	720	764000	840	891000	960	1018000
	2-2x12	1280	1152000	1495	1344000	1705	1536000
	1-4x12	1095	986000	1280	1151000	1460	1314000
	3-2x12	855	768000	1000	896000	1140	1024000
	2-3x12	770	691000	900	806000	1025	921000
16'	3-2x10	1435	1675000	1675	1955000	1915	2233000
	2-3x10	1290	1508000	1505	1760000	1720	2010000
	1-6x10	11.5	1266000	1300	1477000	1485	1687000
	2-4x10	925	1079000	1080	1259000	1235	1438000
	4-2x10	1075	1256000	1255	1466000	1435	1674000
	1-8x10	815	929000	950	1084000	1085	1238000
	2-2x12	1455	1397000	1700	1630000	1940	1862000
	1-4x12	1250	1199000	1460	1399000	1665	1598000
	3-2x12	970	931000	1130	1086000	1295	1241000
	2-3x12	875	839000	1020	979000	1165	1118000
	4-2x12	730	699000	850	816000	975	932000
	2-4x12	625	599000	730	699000	835	798000

SPAN OF BEAM	NOMINAL SIZE OF BEAM	6'-0" f	6'-0" E	7'-0" f	7'-0" E	8'-0" f	8'-0" E
17'	2-3x10	1460	1808000	1705	2110000	1945	2410000
	1-6x10	1255	1518000	1465	1771000	1675	2023000
	2-4x10	1040	1292000	1215	1508000	1385	1722000
	4-2x10	1215	1507000	1420	1758000	1620	2009000
	1-8x10	920	1112000	1075	1298000	1225	1482000
	2-2x12	1645	1675000	1920	1955000	2195	2233000
	1-4x12	1410	1436000	1645	1676000	1880	1914000
	3-2x12	1095	1117000	1280	1303000	1460	1498000
	2-3x12	985	1007000	1150	1175000	1315	1342000
	4-2x12	820	839000	955	979000	1095	1118000
	2-4x12	705	719000	820	839000	940	958000
	5-2x12	655	671000	765	783000	875	894000
18'	2-4x10	1170	1535000	1365	1791000	1560	2046000
	4-2x10	1360	1790000	1590	2089000	1815	2386000
	1-8x10	1040	1322000	1215	1543000	1385	1762000
	2-2x12	1840	1991000	2150	2323000	2455	2654000
	1-4x12	1580	1705000	1845	1990000	2105	2273000
	3-2x12	1230	1327000	1435	1549000	1640	1769000
	2-3x12	1105	1194000	1290	1393000	1475	1591000
	4-2x12	920	995000	1075	1161000	1225	1326000
	2-4x12	790	853000	920	995000	1055	1137000
	5-2x12	735	797000	860	930000	980	1062000
	1-6x12	960	1016000	1120	1186000	1280	1354000
	3-3x12	740	787000	865	918000	985	1049000
19'	2-4x10	1300	1805000	1515	2106000	1735	2406000
	1-8x10	1145	1554000	1335	1813000	1525	2071000
	3-2x12	1370	1561000	1600	1822000	1825	2081000
	2-3x12	1230	1404000	1435	1638000	1640	1871000
	4-2x12	1025	1170000	1195	1365000	1365	1560000
	2-4x12	880	1003000	1025	1170000	1175	1337000
	5-2x12	820	936000	955	1092000	1095	1248000
	1-6x12	1070	1194000	1250	1393000	1425	1592000
	3-3x12	820	925000	955	1079000	1095	1233000
	1-8x12	785	877000	915	1023000	1045	1169000
	1-10x12	620	692000	725	807000	825	922000
	4-3x12	615	702000	715	819000	820	936000
20'	3-2x12	1520	1819000	1775	2123000	2025	2425000
	2-3x12	1365	1638000	1595	1911000	1820	2183000
	4-2x12	1025	1364000	1195	1592000	1365	1818000
	2-4x12	975	1170000	1140	1365000	1300	1560000
	5-2x12	910	1092000	1060	1274000	1215	1456000
	1-6x12	1295	1394000	1510	1627000	1725	1858000
	3-3x12	910	1080000	1060	1260000	1215	1440000
	1-8x12	870	1022000	1015	1193000	1160	1362000
	1-10x12	690	806000	805	941000	920	1074000
	4-3x12	680	818000	795	955000	905	1090000
	2-3x14	985	1003000	1150	1170000	1315	1337000
	1-6x14	860	862000	1005	1006000	1145	1149000
21'	2-3x12	1505	1896000	1755	2213000	2005	2527000
	4-2x12	1255	1580000	1465	1844000	1675	2106000
	2-4x12	1075	1355000	1255	1581000	1435	1806000
	5-2x12	1005	1265000	1175	1476000	1340	1686000
	1-6x12	1295	1613000	1510	1882000	1725	2150000
	3-3x12	1005	1249000	1175	1457000	1340	1665000
	1-8x12	960	1183000	1120	1380000	1280	1577000
	1-10x12	760	935000	885	1091000	1015	1246000
	4-3x12	750	948000	875	1106000	1000	1264000
	2-3x14	1085	1160000	1265	1354000	1445	1546000
	1-6x14	950	998000	1110	1165000	1265	1330000
	3-3x14	725	769000	845	897000	965	1025000
22'	4-2x12	1375	1818000	1605	2122000	1835	2423000
	2-4x12	1180	1556000	1380	1816000	1575	2074000
	5-2x12	1100	1453000	1285	1696000	1465	1937000
	3-3x12	1100	1436000	1285	1676000	1465	1914000
	1-8x12	1055	1361000	1230	1588000	1405	1814000
	1-10x12	830	1074000	970	1253000	1105	1432000
	4-3x12	825	1091000	965	1273000	1100	1454000
	2-3x14	1190	1334000	1390	1557000	1585	1778000
	1-6x14	1045	1147000	1220	1338000	1395	1529000
	3-3x14	795	883000	930	1030000	1060	1177000
	2-4x14	820	901000	955	1051000	1095	1201000
	4-3x14	595	667000	695	778000	795	889000

TABLE 8-14
Floor and roof beams

Required values for fiber stress in bending (f) and modulus of elasticity (E) for the sizes shown to support safely a live load of 40 pounds per square foot within a deflection limitation of I/240.

SPAN OF BEAM	NOMINAL SIZE OF BEAM	6'-0" f	6'-0" E	7'-0" f	7'-0" E	8'-0" f	8'-0" E
10'	2-3x6	1785	1560000	2085	1820000	2380	2079000
	1-3x8	2055	1360000	2400	1587000	2740	1813000
	2-2x8	1710	1134000	1995	1323000	2280	1512000
	1-4x8	1470	969000	1715	1131000	1960	1291000
	1-6x8	875	558000	1020	651000	1165	744000
	2-2x10	1050	545000	1225	636000	1400	726000
	1-3x10	1260	655000	1470	764000	1680	873000
11'	2-2x8	2070	1509000	2415	1761000	2760	2011000
	1-4x8	1775	1293000	2070	1509000	2365	1723000
	1-6x8	1055	743000	1230	867000	1405	990000
	2-2x10	1275	725000	1490	846000	1700	966000
	1-3x10	1525	872000	1780	1017000	2030	1162000
	1-4x10	1090	623000	1270	727000	1455	830000
	3-2x10	850	484000	990	565000	1135	645000
12'	1-4x8	2110	1680000	2460	1960000	2810	2239000
	1-6x8	1255	965000	1465	1126000	1670	1286000
	3-2x8	1645	1305000	1920	1523000	2190	1739000
	2-2x10	1510	944000	1760	1101000	2010	1258000
	1-3x10	1820	1132000	2125	1321000	2425	1509000
	1-4x10	1300	808000	1515	943000	1735	1077000
	3-2x10	1010	629000	1180	734000	1345	838000
	2-3x10	905	565000	1055	659000	1205	753000
13'	1-6x8	1475	1228000	1720	1433000	1965	1637000
	2-3x8	1735	1493000	2025	1742000	2315	1990000
	2-4x8	1235	1068000	1440	1246000	1645	1423000
	2-2x10	1780	1200000	2075	1400000	2370	1600000
	3-2x10	1185	800000	1380	934000	1580	1066000
	1-3x10	2130	1439000	2485	1679000	2840	1918000
	2-3x10	1070	720000	1250	840000	1425	960000
	1-4x10	1525	1230000	1780	1435000	2035	1640000
	2-4x10	760	514000	890	600000	1015	685000
14'	2-4x8	1435	1333000	1675	1555000	1915	1777000
	3-2x10	1375	997000	1605	1163000	1830	1329000
	2-3x10	1235	897000	1440	1047000	1645	1196000
	1-4x10	1770	1284000	2065	1498000	2360	1711000
	2-4x10	830	641000	1025	748000	1175	854000
	3-3x10	825	599000	960	699000	1100	798000
	1-6x10	1145	1257000	1335	1467000	1525	1675000
	1-8x10	780	553000	910	645000	1040	737000
	4-2x10	1030	749000	1200	874000	1375	998000
	2-2x12	1395	832000	1630	971000	1860	1109000
15'	3-2x10	1575	1228000	1840	1433000	2100	1637000
	2-3x10	1420	1105000	1655	1289000	1890	1473000
	2-4x10	1010	789000	1175	921000	1345	1052000
	3-3x10	945	737000	1100	860000	1260	982000
	1-6x10	1225	928000	1430	1083000	1635	1237000
	1-8x10	900	680000	1050	793000	1200	906000
	4-2x10	1180	921000	1375	1075000	1575	1228000
	2-2x12	1600	1024000	1865	1195000	2130	1365000
	3-2x12	1065	683000	1240	797000	1420	910000
	1-3x12	1920	1229000	2240	1434000	2560	1638000
	4-2x12	800	512000	935	597000	1065	682000
	2-3x12	960	614000	1120	716000	1280	818000
16'	3-2x10	1795	1489000	2095	1738000	2395	1985000
	2-3x10	1610	1341000	1880	1565000	2145	1787000
	2-4x10	1155	959000	1350	1119000	1540	1278000
	3-3x10	1075	894000	1255	1043000	1435	1192000
	1-6x10	1395	1125000	1625	1313000	1860	1500000
	1-8x10	1020	825000	1190	962000	1360	1100000
	4-2x10	1345	1117000	1570	1303000	1790	1489000
	2-2x12	1820	1241000	2120	1448000	2425	1654000
	3-2x12	1210	828000	1410	966000	1610	1104000
	4-2x12	910	621000	1060	724000	1215	828000
	5-2x12	730	497000	850	580000	975	662000
	2-3x12	1095	745000	1280	869000	1460	993000

SPAN OF BEAM	NOMINAL SIZE OF BEAM	6'-0" f	6'-0" E	7'-0" f	7'-0" E	8'-0" f	8'-0" E
17'	2-3x10	1825	1608000	2130	1876000	2430	2143000
	2-4x10	1300	1149000	1520	1341000	1735	1532000
	3-3x10	1215	1073000	1420	1252000	1620	1430000
	1-8x10	1150	989000	1340	1154000	1535	1318000
	3-2x12	1370	993000	1600	1159000	1825	1323000
	4-2x12	1025	745000	1195	869000	1365	993000
	5-2x12	820	596000	955	695000	1095	794000
	2-3x12	1230	895000	1435	1044000	1640	1193000
	3-3x12	820	590000	955	688000	1095	786000
	2-4x12	880	639000	1025	746000	1175	852000
	1-6x12	1070	761000	1250	888000	1425	1014000
	1-8x12	785	558000	915	651000	1045	744000
18'	2-3x10	2120	1909000	2475	2228000	2825	2545000
	2-4x10	1460	1364000	1705	1592000	1945	1818000
	3-3x10	1365	1273000	1595	1485000	1820	1697000
	1-8x10	1300	1176000	1515	1372000	1730	1568000
	3-2x12	1540	1180000	1800	1377000	2050	1573000
	4-2x12	1150	884000	1340	1032000	1530	1178000
	5-2x12	920	708000	1075	826000	1225	944000
	2-3x12	1380	1061000	1610	1238000	1840	1414000
	3-3x12	920	700000	1075	817000	1225	933000
	2-4x12	990	759000	1155	886000	1320	1012000
	1-6x12	1200	903000	1400	1054000	1600	1204000
	1-8x12	880	663000	1025	774000	1175	884000
19'	1-8x10	1430	1381000	1670	1612000	1905	1841000
	3-2x12	1710	1388000	1995	1620000	2280	1850000
	4-2x12	1280	1040000	1495	1214000	1705	1386000
	5-2x12	1025	832000	1195	971000	1365	1109000
	2-3x12	1540	1248000	1795	1456000	2050	1663000
	3-3x12	1025	823000	1195	960000	1365	1097000
	2-4x12	1100	892000	1280	1041000	1465	1189000
	1-6x12	1335	1061000	1560	1238000	1780	1414000
	1-8x12	980	779000	1145	909000	1305	1038000
	3-4x12	735	595000	860	694000	980	793000
	4-3x12	770	624000	900	728000	1025	832000
	2-6x12	670	1063000	780	1240000	895	1417000
20'	3-2x12	1900	1617000	2220	1887000	2530	2155000
	4-2x12	1280	1213000	1495	1415000	1705	1617000
	5-2x12	1135	971000	1325	1133000	1515	1294000
	3-3x12	1135	960000	1325	1120000	1515	1279000
	2-4x12	1220	1040000	1425	1214000	1625	1386000
	1-6x12	1620	1240000	1890	1447000	2160	1653000
	1-8x12	1085	909000	1265	1061000	1445	1212000
	3-4x12	810	693000	945	809000	1080	924000
	4-3x12	850	728000	990	849000	1135	970000
	2-6x12	740	620000	865	723000	985	826000
	1-10x12	860	717000	1005	837000	1145	956000
	2-3x14	1230	891000	1435	1040000	1640	1188000
21'	3-2x12	2090	1873000	2440	2186000	2785	2497000
	4-2x12	1570	1405000	1830	1640000	2095	1873000
	5-2x12	1255	1124000	1465	1312000	1675	1498000
	3-3x12	1255	1111000	1465	1296000	1675	1481000
	2-4x12	1345	1204000	1570	1405000	1795	1605000
	1-8x12	1200	1052000	1400	1228000	1600	1402000
	3-4x12	895	803000	1045	937000	1195	1070000
	4-3x12	935	843000	1090	984000	1245	1124000
	2-6x12	820	717000	955	837000	1095	956000
	1-10x12	950	831000	1110	970000	1265	1108000
	2-3x14	1355	1032000	1580	1204000	1805	1375000
	1-6x14	1190	887000	1390	1035000	1585	1182000
22'	4-2x12	1720	1616000	2005	1886000	2295	2154000
	5-2x12	1375	1292000	1605	1508000	1830	1722000
	3-3x12	1375	1277000	1605	1490000	1830	1702000
	3-4x12	985	923000	1150	1077000	1315	1230000
	4-3x12	1030	969000	1200	1131000	1375	1292000
	2-6x12	900	825000	1050	963000	1200	1100000
	1-10x12	1035	955000	1205	1114000	1380	1273000
	2-3x14	1485	1187000	1730	1385000	1980	1582000
	1-6x14	1305	1020000	1525	1190000	1740	1360000
	2-4x14	1025	801000	1195	935000	1365	1068000
	3-3x14	995	785000	1160	916000	1325	1046000
	3-4x14	680	534000	795	623000	905	712000

TABLE 8-15
Floor and roof beams

Required values for fiber stress in bending (f) and modulus of elasticity (E) for the sizes shown to support safely a live load of 40 pounds per square foot within a deflection limitation of l/300.

SPAN OF BEAM	NOMINAL SIZE OF BEAM	6'-0" f	6'-0" E	7'-0" f	7'-0" E	8'-0" f	8'-0" E
10'	1-3x8	2055	1700000	2400	1984000	2740	2266000
	2-2x8	1710	1417000	1995	1654000	2280	1889000
	1-4x8	1470	1211000	1715	1413000	1960	1614000
	1-6x8	875	697000	1020	813000	1165	929000
	2-2x10	1050	681000	1225	795000	1400	908000
	1-3x10	1260	819000	1470	956000	1680	1092000
	1-4x10	900	585000	1050	683000	1200	780000
11'	2-2x8	2070	1886000	2415	2201000	2760	2514000
	1-4x8	1775	1616000	2070	1886000	2365	2154000
	1-6x8	1055	929000	1230	1084000	1405	1238000
	2-2x10	1275	906000	1490	1057000	1700	1208000
	1-3x10	1525	1090000	1780	1272000	2030	1453000
	1-4x10	1090	779000	1270	909000	1455	1038000
	3-2x10	850	605000	990	706000	1135	806000
12'	1-6x8	1255	1206000	1465	1407000	1670	1607000
	3-2x8	1645	1631000	1920	1903000	2190	2174000
	2-2x10	1510	1180000	1760	1377000	2010	1573000
	1-3x10	1820	1415000	2125	1651000	2425	1886000
	1-4x10	1300	1010000	1515	1179000	1735	1346000
	3-2x10	1010	786000	1180	917000	1345	1048000
	2-3x10	905	706000	1055	824000	1205	941000
	1-6x10	785	594000	915	693000	1045	792000
	2-4x10	650	505000	760	589000	865	673000
13'	1-6x8	1475	1535000	1720	1791000	1965	2046000
	2-3x8	1735	1866000	2025	2178000	2315	2487000
	2-4x8	1235	1335000	1440	1558000	1645	1779000
	3-2x10	1185	1000000	1380	1167000	1580	1333000
	2-2x10	1780	1500000	2075	1750000	2370	2000000
	1-3x10	2130	1799000	2485	2099000	2840	2398000
	2-3x10	1070	900000	1250	1050000	1425	1200000
	1-4x10	1525	1537000	1780	1794000	2035	2049000
	2-4x10	760	642000	890	749000	1015	856000
14'	2-4x8	1435	1666000	1675	1944000	1915	2221000
	3-2x10	1375	1246000	1605	1454000	1830	1661000
	2-3x10	1235	1121000	1440	1308000	1645	1494000
	1-4x10	1770	1605000	2065	1873000	2360	2139000
	2-4x10	880	801000	1025	935000	1175	1068000
	3-3x10	825	749000	960	874000	1100	998000
	1-6x10	1145	1571000	1335	1833000	1525	2094000
	1-8x10	780	691000	910	806000	1040	921000
	4-2x10	1030	936000	1200	1092000	1375	1248000
	2-2x12	1395	1040000	1630	1214000	1860	1386000
15'	3-2x10	1575	1535000	1840	1791000	2100	2046000
	2-3x10	1420	1381000	1655	1612000	1890	1841000
	2-4x10	1010	986000	1175	1151000	1345	1314000
	3-3x10	945	921000	1100	1075000	1260	1228000
	1-6x10	1225	1160000	1430	1354000	1635	1546000
	1-8x10	900	850000	1050	992000	1200	1133000
	4-2x10	1180	1151000	1375	1343000	1575	1534000
	2-2x12	1600	1280000	1865	1494000	2130	1706000
	3-2x12	1065	854000	1240	997000	1420	1138000
	1-3x12	1920	1536000	2240	1792000	2560	2047000
	4-2x12	800	640000	935	747000	1065	853000
	2-3x12	960	767000	1120	895000	1280	1022000
16'	3-2x10	1795	1861000	2095	2172000	2395	2481000
	2-3x10	1610	1676000	1880	1956000	2145	2234000
	2-4x10	1155	1199000	1350	1399000	1540	1598000
	3-3x10	1075	1117000	1255	1303000	1435	1489000
	1-6x10	1395	1406000	1625	1641000	1860	1874000
	1-8x10	1020	1031000	1190	1203000	1360	1374000
	4-2x10	1345	1396000	1570	1629000	1790	1861000
	2-2x12	1820	1551000	2120	1810000	2425	2067000
	3-2x12	1210	1035000	1410	1208000	1610	1380000
	4-2x12	910	776000	1060	905000	1215	1034000
	5-2x12	730	621000	850	725000	975	828000
	2-3x12	1095	931000	1280	1086000	1460	1241000

SPAN OF BEAM	NOMINAL SIZE OF BEAM	6'-0" f	6'-0" E	7'-0" f	7'-0" E	8'-0" f	8'-0" E
17'	2-3x10	1825	2010000	2130	2345000	2430	2679000
	2-4x10	1300	1436000	1520	1676000	1735	1914000
	3-3x10	1215	1341000	1420	1565000	1620	1787000
	1-8x10	1150	1236000	1340	1442000	1535	1647000
	3-2x12	1370	1241000	1600	1448000	1825	1654000
	4-2x12	1025	931000	1195	1086000	1365	1241000
	5-2x12	820	745000	955	869000	1095	993000
	2-3x12	1230	1119000	1435	1306000	1640	1492000
	3-3x12	820	737000	955	860000	1095	982000
	2-4x12	880	799000	1025	932000	1175	1065000
	1-6x12	1070	951000	1250	1110000	1425	1268000
	1-8x12	785	697000	915	813000	1045	929000
18'	2-4x10	1460	1705000	1705	1990000	1945	2273000
	3-3x10	1365	1591000	1595	1857000	1820	2121000
	1-8x10	1300	1470000	1515	1715000	1730	1959000
	3-2x12	1540	1475000	1800	1721000	2050	1966000
	4-2x12	1150	1105000	1340	1289000	1530	1473000
	5-2x12	920	885000	1075	1033000	1225	1180000
	2-3x12	1380	1326000	1610	1547000	1840	1767000
	3-3x12	920	875000	1075	1021000	1225	1166000
	2-4x12	990	949000	1155	1107000	1320	1265000
	1-6x12	1200	1129000	1400	1317000	1600	1505000
	1-8x12	880	829000	1025	967000	1175	1105000
	3-4x12	660	632000	770	737000	880	842000
19'	3-3x10	1520	1872000	1775	2184000	2025	2495000
	3-2x12	1710	1735000	1995	2025000	2280	2313000
	4-2x12	1280	1300000	1495	1517000	1705	1733000
	5-2x12	1025	1040000	1195	1214000	1365	1386000
	2-3x12	1540	1560000	1795	1820000	2050	2079000
	3-3x12	1025	1029000	1195	1201000	1365	1372000
	2-4x12	1100	1115000	1280	1301000	1465	1486000
	1-6x12	1335	1326000	1560	1547000	1780	1767000
	1-8x12	980	973000	1145	1135000	1305	1297000
	3-4x12	735	744000	860	868000	980	992000
	4-3x12	770	780000	900	910000	1025	1040000
	2-6x12	670	1329000	780	1551000	895	1771000
20'	3-2x12	1900	2021000	2220	2358000	2530	2694000
	4-2x12	1280	1516000	1495	1769000	1705	2021000
	5-2x12	1135	1214000	1325	1417000	1515	1618000
	3-3x12	1135	1200000	1325	1400000	1515	1600000
	2-4x12	1220	1300000	1425	1517000	1625	1733000
	1-6x12	1620	1550000	1890	1809000	2160	2066000
	1-8x12	1085	1136000	1265	1326000	1445	1514000
	3-4x12	810	866000	945	1011000	1080	1154000
	4-3x12	850	910000	990	1062000	1135	1213000
	2-6x12	740	775000	865	904000	985	1033000
	1-10x12	860	896000	1005	1046000	1145	1194000
	2-3x14	1230	1114000	1435	1300000	1640	1485000
21'	4-2x12	1570	1756000	1830	2049000	2095	2341000
	5-2x12	1255	1405000	1465	1640000	1675	1873000
	3-3x12	1255	1389000	1465	1621000	1675	1851000
	2-4x12	1345	1505000	1570	1756000	1795	2006000
	1-8x12	1200	1315000	1400	1535000	1600	1753000
	3-4x12	895	1004000	1045	1172000	1195	1338000
	4-3x12	935	1054000	1090	1230000	1245	1405000
	2-6x12	820	896000	955	1046000	1095	1194000
	1-10x12	950	1039000	1110	1212000	1265	1385000
	2-3x14	1355	1290000	1580	1505000	1805	1719000
	1-6x14	1190	1109000	1390	1294000	1585	1478000
	2-4x14	930	871000	1085	1016000	1240	1161000
22'	4-2x12	1720	2020000	2005	2357000	2295	2693000
	5-2x12	1375	1615000	1605	1885000	1830	2153000
	3-3x12	1375	1596000	1605	1862000	1830	2127000
	3-4x12	985	1154000	1150	1347000	1315	1538000
	4-3x12	1030	1211000	1200	1413000	1375	1614000
	2-6x12	900	1031000	1050	1203000	1200	1374000
	1-10x12	1035	1194000	1205	1393000	1380	1592000
	2-3x14	1485	1484000	1730	1732000	1980	1978000
	1-6x14	1305	1275000	1525	1488000	1740	1700000
	2-4x14	1025	1001000	1195	1168000	1365	1334000
	3-3x14	995	981000	1160	1145000	1325	1308000
	3-4x14	680	667000	795	778000	905	889000

TABLE 8-16
Floor and roof beams

Required values for fiber stress in bending (f) and modulus of elasticity (E) for the sizes shown to support safely a live load of 40 pounds per square foot within a deflection limitation of l/360.

SPAN OF BEAM	NOMINAL SIZE OF BEAM	6'-0" f	6'-0" E	7'-0" f	7'-0" E	8'-0" f	8'-0" E
10'	1-3x8	2055	2040000	2400	2381000	2740	2719000
	2-2x8	1710	1701000	1995	1985000	2280	2267000
	1-4x8	1470	1453000	1715	1696000	1960	1937000
	1-6x8	875	837000	1020	977000	1165	1116000
	2-2x10	1050	817000	1225	953000	1400	1089000
	1-3x10	1260	982000	1470	1146000	1680	1309000
	1-4x10	900	702000	1050	819000	1200	936000
11'	1-4x8	1775	1939000	2070	2263000	2365	2585000
	1-6x8	1055	1114000	1230	1300000	1405	1485000
	2-2x10	1275	1087000	1490	1268000	1700	1449000
	1-3x10	1525	1308000	1780	1526000	2030	1743000
	1-4x10	1090	934000	1270	1090000	1455	1245000
	3-2x10	850	726000	990	847000	1135	968000
	2-3x10	765	654000	890	763000	1020	872000
12'	1-6x8	1255	1447000	1465	1689000	1670	1929000
	3-2x8	1645	1957000	1920	2284000	2190	2609000
	2-2x10	1510	1416000	1760	1652000	2010	1887000
	1-3x10	1820	1698000	2125	1981000	2425	2263000
	1-4x10	1300	1212000	1515	1414000	1735	1615000
	2-3x10	905	847000	1055	988000	1205	1129000
	3-2x10	1010	943000	1180	1100000	1345	1257000
	1-6x10	785	713000	915	832000	1045	950000
	2-4x10	650	606000	760	707000	865	808000
13'	2-4x8	1235	1602000	1440	1869000	1645	2135000
	2-2x10	1780	1800000	2075	2100000	2370	2400000
	3-2x10	1185	1200000	1380	1400000	1580	1600000
	2-3x10	1070	1080000	1250	1260000	1425	1440000
	1-4x10	1525	1845000	1780	2153000	2035	2459000
	2-4x10	760	771000	890	900000	1015	1028000
	3-3x10	710	719000	830	839000	945	958000
	1-6x10	920	906000	1075	1057000	1225	1208000
	4-2x10	890	899000	1040	1049000	1185	1198000
14'	2-4x8	1435	1999000	1675	2333000	1915	2665000
	3-2x10	1375	1495000	1605	1745000	1830	1993000
	2-3x10	1235	1345000	1440	1570000	1645	1793000
	2-4x10	880	961000	1025	1121000	1175	1281000
	3-3x10	825	898000	960	1048000	1100	1197000
	1-6x10	1145	1885000	1335	2200000	1525	2513000
	1-8x10	780	829000	910	967000	1040	1105000
	4-2x10	1030	1123000	1200	1310000	1375	1497000
	2-2x12	1395	1248000	1630	1456000	1860	1663000
	3-2x12	930	832000	1085	971000	1240	1109000
15'	3-2x10	1575	1842000	1840	2150000	2100	2455000
	2-3x10	1420	1657000	1655	1934000	1890	2209000
	2-4x10	1010	1183000	1175	1380000	1345	1577000
	3-3x10	945	1105000	1100	1289000	1260	1473000
	1-6x10	1225	1392000	1430	1624000	1635	1855000
	1-8x10	900	1020000	1050	1190000	1200	1360000
	4-2x10	1180	1381000	1375	1612000	1575	1841000
	2-2x12	1600	1536000	1865	1792000	2130	2047000
	3-2x12	1065	1024000	1240	1195000	1420	1365000
	1-3x12	1920	1843000	2240	2151000	2560	2457000
	4-2x12	800	768000	935	896000	1065	1024000
	2-3x12	960	921000	1120	1075000	1280	1228000
16'	2-3x10	1610	2011000	1880	2347000	2145	2681000
	2-4x10	1155	1438000	1350	1678000	1540	1917000
	3-3x10	1075	1341000	1255	1565000	1435	1787000
	1-6x10	1395	1687000	1625	1969000	1860	2249000
	1-8x10	1020	1237000	1190	1443000	1360	1649000
	4-2x10	1345	1675000	1570	1955000	1790	2233000
	2-2x12	1820	1861000	2120	2172000	2425	2481000
	3-2x12	1210	1242000	1410	1449000	1610	1655000
	4-2x12	910	931000	1060	1086000	1215	1241000
	5-2x12	730	745000	850	869000	975	993000
	2-3x12	1095	1117000	1280	1303000	1460	1489000
	3-3x12	730	737000	850	860000	975	982000

SPAN OF BEAM	NOMINAL SIZE OF BEAM	6'-0" f	6'-0" E	7'-0" f	7'-0" E	8'-0" f	8'-0" E
17'	2-4x10	1300	1723000	1520	2011000	1735	2297000
	3-3x10	1215	1609000	1420	1878000	1620	2145000
	1-8x10	1150	1483000	1340	1731000	1535	1977000
	3-2x12	1370	1489000	1600	1738000	1825	1985000
	4-2x12	1025	1117000	1195	1303000	1365	1489000
	5-2x12	820	894000	955	1043000	1095	1192000
	2-3x12	1230	1342000	1435	1566000	1640	1789000
	3-3x12	820	885000	955	1033000	1095	1180000
	2-4x12	880	958000	1025	1118000	1175	1277000
	1-6x12	1070	1141000	1250	1331000	1425	1521000
	1-8x12	785	837000	915	977000	1045	1116000
	3-4x12	585	639000	680	746000	780	852000
18'	3-3x10	1365	1909000	1595	2228000	1820	2545000
	1-8x10	1300	1764000	1515	2058000	1730	2351000
	3-2x12	1540	1770000	1800	2065000	2050	2359000
	4-2x12	1150	1326000	1340	1547000	1530	1767000
	5-2x12	920	1062000	1075	1239000	1225	1416000
	2-3x12	1380	1591000	1610	1857000	1840	2121000
	3-3x12	920	1050000	1075	1225000	1225	1400000
	2-4x12	990	1138000	1155	1328000	1320	1517000
	1-6x12	1200	1354000	1400	1580000	1600	1805000
	1-8x12	880	994000	1025	1160000	1175	1325000
	3-4x12	660	758000	770	884000	880	1010000
	4-3x12	690	796000	805	929000	920	1061000
19'	4-2x12	1280	1560000	1495	1820000	1705	2079000
	5-2x12	1025	1248000	1195	1456000	1365	1663000
	2-3x12	1540	1872000	1795	2185000	2050	2495000
	3-3x12	1025	1234000	1195	1440000	1365	1645000
	2-4x12	1100	1338000	1280	1561000	1465	1783000
	1-6x12	1335	1591000	1560	1857000	1780	2121000
	1-8x12	980	1168000	1145	1363000	1305	1557000
	3-4x12	735	892000	860	1041000	980	1189000
	4-3x12	770	936000	900	1092000	1025	1248000
	2-6x12	670	1594000	780	186000	895	2125000
	1-10x12	775	923000	905	1077000	1035	1230000
	2-3x14	1110	1146000	1295	1337000	1480	1528000
20'	4-2x12	1280	1819000	1495	2123000	1705	2425000
	5-2x12	1135	1456000	1325	1699000	1515	1941000
	3-3x12	1135	1440000	1325	1680000	1515	1919000
	2-4x12	1220	1560000	1425	1820000	1625	2079000
	1-8x12	1085	1363000	1265	1591000	1445	1817000
	3-4x12	810	1039000	945	1212000	1080	1385000
	4-3x12	850	1092000	990	1274000	1135	1456000
	2-6x12	740	930000	865	1085000	985	1240000
	1-10x12	860	1075000	1005	1254000	1145	1433000
	2-3x14	1230	1336000	1435	1559000	1640	1781000
	1-6x14	1075	1149000	1255	1341000	1430	1532000
	2-4x14	845	903000	985	1054000	1125	1204000
21'	5-2x12	1255	1686000	1465	1967000	1675	2247000
	3-3x12	1255	1666000	1465	1944000	1675	2221000
	2-4x12	1345	1806000	1570	2107000	1795	2407000
	1-8x12	1200	1578000	1400	1841000	1600	2103000
	3-4x12	895	1204000	1045	1405000	1195	1605000
	4-3x12	935	1264000	1090	1475000	1245	1685000
	2-6x12	820	1075000	955	1254000	1095	1433000
	1-10x12	950	1246000	1110	1454000	1265	1661000
	2-3x14	1355	1548000	1580	1806000	1805	2063000
	1-6x14	1190	1330000	1390	1552000	1585	1773000
	2-4x14	930	1045000	1085	1219000	1240	1393000
	3-3x14	905	1032000	1055	1204000	1205	1375000
22'	5-2x12	1375	1938000	1605	2262000	1830	2583000
	3-3x12	1375	1915000	1605	2235000	1830	2553000
	3-4x12	985	1384000	1150	1615000	1315	1845000
	4-3x12	1030	1453000	1200	1695000	1375	1937000
	2-6x12	900	1237000	1050	1443000	1200	1649000
	1-10x12	1035	1432000	1205	1671000	1380	1909000
	2-3x14	1485	1780000	1730	2077000	1980	2373000
	1-6x14	1305	1530000	1525	1785000	1740	2039000
	2-4x14	1025	1201000	1195	1401000	1365	1600000
	3-3x14	995	1177000	1160	1373000	1325	1569000
	3-4x14	680	801000	795	935000	905	1068000
	1-8x14	955	1122000	1115	1309000	1275	1495000

TABLE 8-17

Design values for visually graded structural lumber

Species and commercial grade	Size classification	Extreme fiber in bending "F_b" Single-member uses	Extreme fiber in bending "F_b" Repetitive-member uses	Tension parallel to grain "F_t"	Horizontal shear "F_v"	Compression perpendicular to grain "F_{C⊥}"	Compression parallel to grain "F_C"	Modulus of elasticity "E"	Grading rules agency
SOUTHERN PINE (Surfaced dry. Used at 19% max. m.c.)									
Select Structural		2000	2300	1150	100	565	1550	1,700,000	
Dense Select Structural		2350	2700	1350	100	660	1800	1,800,000	
No. 1		1700	1950	1000	100	565	1250	1,700,000	
No. 1 Dense	2" to 4" thick	2000	2300	1150	100	660	1450	1,800,000	
No. 2	2" to 4"	1400	1650	825	90	565	975	1,600,000	
No. 2 Dense	wide	1650	1900	975	90	660	1150	1,600,000	
No. 3		775	900	450	90	565	575	1,400,000	
No. 3 Dense		925	1050	525	90	660	675	1,500,000	
Stud		775	900	450	90	565	575	1,400,000	
Construction	2" to 4"	1000	1150	600	100	565	1100	1,400,000	
Standard	thick	575	675	350	90	565	900	1,400,000	
Utility	4" wide	275	300	150	90	565	575	1,400,000	
Select Structural		1750	2000	1150	90	565	1350	1,700,000	
Dense Select Structural		2050	2350	1300	90	660	1600	1,800,000	
No. 1		1450	1700	975	90	565	1250	1,700,000	SPIB
No. 1 Dense	2" to 4" thick	1700	2000	1150	90	660	1450	1,800,000	
No. 2	5" and	1200	1400	625	90	565	1000	1,600,000	
No. 2 Dense	wider	1400	1650	725	90	660	1200	1,600,000	
No. 3		700	800	350	90	565	625	1,400,000	
No. 3 Dense		825	925	425	90	660	725	1,500,000	
Stud		725	850	350	90	565	625	1,400,000	
Dense Standard Decking	2" to 4"	2000	2300	—	—	660	—	1,800,000	
Select Decking	thick	1400	1650	—	—	565	—	1,600,000	
Dense Select Decking	2" and	1650	1900	—	—	660	—	1,600,000	
Commercial Decking	wider	1400	1650	—	—	565	—	1,600,000	
Dense Commercial Decking	Decking	1650	1900	—	—	660	—	1,600,000	
Dense Structural 86	2" to 4"	2600	3000	1750	155	660	2000	1,800,000	
Dense Structural 72	thick	2200	2550	1450	130	660	1650	1,800,000	
Dense Structural 65		2000	2300	1300	115	660	1500	1,800,000	
DOUGLAS FIR-LARCH (Surfaced dry or surfaced green. Used at 19% max. m.c.)									
Dense Select Structural		2450	2800	1400	95	730	1850	1,900,000	
Select Structural		2100	2400	1200	95	625	1600	1,800,000	
Dense No. 1		2050	2400	1200	95	730	1450	1,900,000	
No. 1	2" to 4"	1750	2050	1050	95	625	1250	1,800,000	
Dense No. 2	thick	1700	1950	1000	95	730	1150	1,700,000	
No. 2	2" to 4"	1450	1650	850	95	625	1000	1,700,000	
No. 3	wide	800	925	475	95	625	600	1,500,000	
Appearance		1750	2050	1050	95	625	1500	1,800,000	WCLIB
Stud		800	925	475	95	625	600	1,500,000	WWPA
Construction	2" to 4"	1050	1200	625	95	625	1150	1,500,000	
Standard	thick	600	675	350	95	625	925	1,500,000	
Utility	4" wide	275	325	175	95	625	600	1,500,000	
Dense Select Structural		2100	2400	1400	95	730	1650	1,900,000	
Select Structural		1800	2050	1200	95	625	1400	1,800,000	
Dense No. 1	2" to 4"	1800	2050	1200	95	730	1450	1,900,000	
No. 1	thick	1500	1750	1000	95	625	1250	1,800,000	
Dense No. 2	5" and	1450	1700	775	95	730	1250	1,700,000	
No. 2	wider	1250	1450	650	95	625	1050	1,700,000	
No. 3		725	850	375	95	625	675	1,500,000	
Appearance		1500	1750	1000	95	625	1500	1,800,000	
Stud		725	850	375	95	625	675	1,500,000	
Dense Select Structural		1900	—	1100	85	730	1300	1,700,000	
Select Structural	Beams and	1600	—	950	85	625	1100	1,600,000	
Dense No. 1	Stringers	1550	—	775	85	730	1100	1,700,000	
No. 1		1300	—	675	85	625	925	1,600,000	WCLIB
Dense Select Structural		1750	—	1150	85	730	1350	1,700,000	
Select Structural	Posts and	1500	—	1000	85	625	1150	1,600,000	
Dense No. 1	Timbers	1400	—	950	85	730	1200	1,700,000	
No. 1		1200	—	825	85	625	1000	1,600,000	
Select Dex	Decking	1750	2000	—	—	625	—	1,800,000	
Commercial Dex		1450	1650	—	—	625	—	1,700,000	
Dense Select Structural		1900	—	1250	85	730	1300	1,700,000	
Select Structural	Beams and	1600	—	1050	85	625	1100	1,600,000	
Dense No. 1	Stringers	1550	—	1050	85	730	1100	1,700,000	
No. 1		1350	—	900	85	625	925	1,600,000	WWPA
Dense Select Structural		1750	—	1150	85	730	1350	1,700,000	
Select Structural	Posts and	1500	—	1000	85	625	1150	1,600,000	
Dense No. 1	Timbers	1400	—	950	85	730	1200	1,700,000	
No. 1		1200	—	825	85	625	1000	1,600,000	
Selected Decking	Decking	—	2000	—	—	—	—	1,800,000	
Commercial Decking		—	1650	—	—	—	—	1,700,000	
Selected Decking	Decking	—	2150	(Surfaced at 15% max. m.c. and				—	1,900,000	
Commercial Decking		—	1800	used at 15% max. m.c.)				—	1,700,000	
EASTERN WOODS (Surfaced dry or surfaced green. Used at 19% max. m.c.)									
Select Structural		1300	1500	775	60	270	850	1,100,000	
No. 1	2" to 4"	1100	1300	650	60	270	675	1,100,000	
No. 2	thick	925	1050	525	60	270	550	1,000,000	
No. 3	2" to 4"	500	575	300	60	270	325	900,000	NELMA
Appearance	wide	1100	1300	650	60	270	825	1,100,000	NHPMA
Stud		500	575	300	60	270	325	900,000	
Construction	2" to 4"	650	750	400	60	270	625	900,000	
Standard	thick	375	425	225	60	270	500	900,000	
Utility	4" wide	175	200	100	60	270	325	900,000	
Select Structural		1150	1300	750	60	270	750	1,100,000	
No. 1	2" to 4"	950	1100	650	60	270	675	1,100,000	NHPMA
No. 2	thick	775	900	425	60	270	575	1,000,000	
No. 3	5" and	450	525	250	60	270	375	900,000	
Appearance	wider	950	1100	650	60	270	825	1,100,000	
Stud		450	525	250	60	270	375	900,000	

TABLE 8-18

Design values for visually graded structural lumber

Species and commercial grade	Size classification	Extreme fiber in bending "F_b" Single-member uses	Extreme fiber in bending "F_b" Repetitive-member uses	Tension parallel to grain "F_t"	Horizontal shear "F_V"	Compression perpendicular to grain "$F_{C\perp}$"	Compression parallel to grain "F_C"	Modulus of elasticity "E"	Grading rules agency
WESTERN CEDARS (Surfaced dry or surfaced green. Used at 19% max. m.c.)									
Select Structural	2" to 4"	1500	1750	875	75	425	1200	1,100,000	
No. 1	thick	1300	1500	750	75	425	950	1,100,000	
No. 2	2" to 4"	1050	1200	625	75	425	750	1,000,000	
No. 3	wide	600	675	350	75	425	450	900,000	
Appearance		1300	1500	750	75	425	1100	1,100,000	
Stud		600	675	350	75	425	450	900,000	
Construction	2" to 4"	775	875	450	75	425	850	900,000	WCLIB
Standard	thick	425	500	250	75	425	700	900,000	WWPA
Utility	4" wide	200	225	125	75	425	450	900,000	
Select Structural	2" to 4"	1300	1500	875	75	425	1050	1,100,000	
No. 1	thick	1100	1300	750	75	425	950	1,100,000	
No. 2	5" and	925	1050	475	75	425	800	1,000,000	
No. 3	wider	525	625	275	75	425	500	900,000	
Appearance		1100	1300	750	75	425	1100	1,100,000	
Stud		525	625	275	75	425	500	900,000	
Select Structural	Beams and	1150	—	675	70	425	875	1,000,000	
No. 1	Stringers	975	—	475	70	425	725	1,000,000	
Select Structural	Posts and	1100	—	725	70	425	925	1,000,000	WCLIB
No. 1	Timbers	875	—	600	70	425	800	1,000,000	
Select Dex	Decking	1250	1450	—	—	425	—	1,100,000	
Commercial Dex		1050	1200	—	—	425	—	1,000,000	
Select Structural	Beams and	1150	—	775	70	425	875	1,000,000	
No. 1	Stringers	975	—	650	70	425	725	1,000,000	
Select Structural	Posts and	1100	—	725	70	425	925	1,000,000	WWPA
No. 1	Timbers	875	—	600	70	425	800	1,000,000	
Selected Decking	Decking	—	1450	—	—	—	—	1,100,000	
Commercial Decking		—	1200	—	—	—	—	1,000,000	
Selected Decking	Decking	—	1550	(Surfaced at 15% max. m.c. and			—	1,100,000	
Commercial Decking		—	1300	used at 15% max. m.c.)			—	1,000,000	
WHITE WOODS (WESTERN WOODS) (Surfaced dry or surfaced green. Used at 19% max. m.c.)									
Select Structural	2" to 4"	1350	1550	775	70	315	950	1,100,000	
No. 1	thick	1150	1300	650	70	315	750	1,100,000	
No. 2	2" to 4"	925	1050	550	70	315	600	1,000,000	
No. 3	wide	525	600	300	70	315	375	900,000	
Appearance		1150	1300	650	70	315	900	1,100,000	
Stud		525	600	300	70	315	375	900,000	
Construction	2" to 4"	675	775	400	70	315	675	900,000	
Standard	thick	375	425	225	70	315	550	900,000	
Utility	4" wide	175	200	100	70	315	375	900,000	
Select Structural	2" to 4"	1150	1300	775	70	315	850	1,100,000	WWPA
No. 1	thick	975	1100	650	70	315	750	1,100,000	
No. 2	5" and	800	925	425	70	315	625	1,000,000	
No. 3	wider	475	550	250	70	315	400	900,000	
Appearance		975	1100	650	70	315	900	1,100,000	
Stud		475	550	150	70	315	400	900,000	
Select Structural	Beams and	1000	—	700	65	315	675	1,000,000	
No. 1	Stringers	850	—	575	65	315	550	1,000,000	
Select Structural	Posts and	950	—	650	65	315	700	1,000,000	
No. 1	Timbers	775	—	525	65	315	625	1,000,000	
Selected Decking	Decking	—	1300	—	—	—	—	1,100,000	
Commercial Decking		—	1050	—	—	—	—	1,000,000	
Selected Decking	Decking	—	1400	(Surfaced at 15% max. m.c. and			—	1,100,000	
Commercial Decking		—	1150	used at 15% max. m.c.)			—	1,000,000	
EASTERN SPRUCE (Surfaced dry or surfaced green. Used at 19% max. m.c.)									
Select Structural	2" to 4"	1400	1600	800	70	390	1050	1,500,000	
No. 1	thick	1200	1350	700	70	390	825	1,500,000	
No. 2	2" to 4"	975	1100	575	70	390	650	1,400,000	
No. 3	wide	550	625	325	70	390	400	1,200,000	
Appearance		1200	1350	700	70	390	1000	1,500,000	
Stud		550	625	325	70	390	400	1,200,000	NELMA
Construction	2" to 4"	700	800	400	70	390	750	1,200,000	NHPMA
Standard	thick	400	450	225	70	390	625	1,200,000	
Utility	4" wide	175	225	100	70	390	400	1,200,000	
Select Structural	2" to 4"	1200	1350	800	70	390	925	1,500,000	
No. 1	thick	1000	1150	675	70	390	825	1,500,000	
No. 2	5" and	825	950	425	70	390	700	1,400,000	
No. 3	wider	475	550	250	70	390	450	1,200,000	
Appearance		1000	1150	675	70	390	1000	1,500,000	
Stud		475	550	250	70	390	450	1,200,000	
Select Structural	Beams and	1050	—	725	65	390	750	1,400,000	
No. 1	Stringers	900	—	600	65	390	625	1,400,000	
Select Structural	Posts and	1000	—	675	65	390	775	1,400,000	
No. 1	Timbers	800	—	550	65	390	675	1,400,000	
Select	Decking	—	1300	—	—	—	—	1,500,000	NELMA
Commercial		—	1100	—	—	—	—	1,400,000	

From National Forest Products Association.

TABLE 8-19
Properties of sections (S4S)

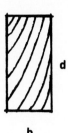

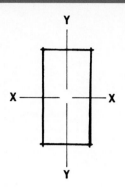

Nominal Size Inches b d	Actual Size Inches b d	Area In.²	AXIS XX S In.³	AXIS XX I In.⁴	AXIS YY S In.³	AXIS YY I In.⁴	Board Measure per Lineal Foot	Weight per Lineal Foot Lbs.
2 x 2	1-1/2 x 1-1/2	2.25	.56	.42	.56	.42	.33	.63
3	2-1/2	3.75	1.56	1.95	.94	.70	.50	1.05
4	3-1/2	5.25	3.06	5.36	1.31	.99	.67	1.46
6	5-1/2	8.25	7.56	20.80	2.06	1.55	1.00	2.29
8	7-1/4	10.88	13.14	47.63	2.72	2.06	1.33	2.98
10	9-1/4	13.88	21.39	98.93	3.57	2.62	1.67	3.87
12	11-1/4	16.88	31.64	177.98	4.23	3.18	2.00	4.68
14	13-1/4	19.88	43.89	290.77	4.97	3.75	2.33	5.50
3 x 3	2-1/2 x 2-1/2	6.25	2.61	3.25	2.6	3.24	.75	1.73
4	3-1/2	8.75	5.10	8.93	3.64	4.56	1.00	2.43
6	5-1/2	13.75	12.60	34.66	5.73	7.16	1.50	3.82
8	7-1/4	18.13	21.90	79.39	7.56	9.53	2.00	5.03
10	9-1/4	23.13	35.65	164.88	9.63	12.16	2.50	6.44
12	11-1/4	28.13	52.73	296.63	11.75	14.79	3.00	7.83
14	13-1/4	33.13	73.15	484.63	14.91	17.34	3.50	9.18
4 x 4	3-1/2 x 3-1/2	12.25	7.15	12.50	7.14	12.52	1.33	3.39
6	5-1/2	19.25	17.65	48.53	11.23	19.64	2.00	5.34
8	7-1/4	25.38	30.66	111.15	14.82	26.15	2.67	7.05
10	9-1/4	32.38	49.91	230.84	18.97	33.23	3.33	8.98
12	11-1/4	39.38	73.82	415.28	23.03	40.30	4.00	10.91
14	13-1/2	46.38	106.31	717.61	27.07	47.59	4.67	12.90
6 x 6*	5-1/2 x 5-1/2	30.25	27.73	76.25	27.73	76.25	3	8.40
8	7-1/2	41.25	51.56	193.35	37.81	103.98	4	11.46
10	9-1/2	52.25	82.73	392.96	47.89	131.71	5	14.51
12	11-1/2	63.25	121.23	697.07	57.98	159.44	6	17.57
14	13-1/2	74.25	167.06	1127.67	68.06	187.17	7	20.62
8 x 8*	7-1/2 x 7-1/2	56.25	70.31	263.67	70.31	263.67	5.33	15.62
10	9-1/2	71.25	112.81	535.86	89.06	333.98	6.67	19.79
12	11-1/2	86.25	165.31	950.55	107.81	404.30	8	23.96
14	13-1/2	101.25	227.81	1537.73	126.56	474.61	9.33	28.12
10 x 10*	9-1/2 x 9-1/2	90.25	142.89	678.75	142.89	678.75	8.33	25.07
12	11-1/2	109.25	209.39	1204.03	172.98	821.65	10	30.35
14	13-1/2	128.25	288.56	1947.80	203.06	964.25	11.67	35.62
12 x 12*	11-1/2 x 11-1/2	132.25	253.48	1457.51	253.48	1457.51	12	36.74
14	13-1/2	155.25	349.31	2357.86	297.56	1710.98	14	43.12
14 x 14*	13-1/2 x 13-1/2	182.25	410.06	2767.92	410.06	2767.92	16.33	50.62

Note: Properties are based on minimum dressed green size which is ½ inch off nominal in both b and d dimensions.

TABLE 8-20
Conversion diagram for rafters

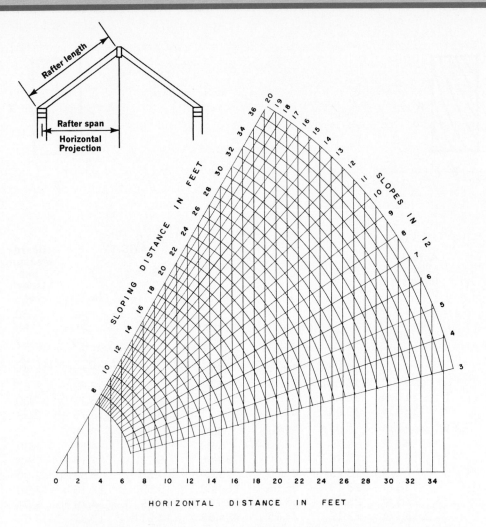

To use the diagram select the known horizontal distance and follow the vertical line to its intersection with the radial line of the specified slope, then proceed along the arc to read the sloping distance. In some cases it may be desirable to interpolate between the one foot separations. The diagram also may be used to find the horizontal distance corresponding to a given sloping distance or to find the slope when the horizontal and sloping distances are known.

Example: With a roof slope of 8 in 12 and a horizontal distance of 20 feet the sloping distance may be read as 24 feet.

EXERCISES

The following exercises should be done on $8\frac{1}{2}'' \times 11''$ drawing paper with a $\frac{1}{2}''$ border, using drawing instruments; drawings do not have to be drawn to a particular scale.

1. Draw an elevation view and a section of a wood beam; graphically illustrate which fibers are in tension and which fibers are in compression; show where the neutral axis is located to illustrate that the stress changes from tension to compression.

2. Draw the elevation view of a beam that is supported by two columns and cantilevers beyond the end of one of the columns; graphically illustrate which fibers are in tension and which fibers are in compression.

3. Draw the elevation view of a W-pattern truss. Identify the members of the truss that are in tension

and the ones that are in compression; use arrows to indicate tension and compression.

4. Draw a section of each of the following structural members; poché and label the materials: a wide-flange beam (W section), a glue-laminated beam, a flitch beam, and an I-shaped floor joist.

5. Draw an elevation view of a flat floor truss with metal truss plate connectors; show a bearing wall at one end of the trusses and a steel beam at the other end.

REVIEW QUESTIONS

1. What lumber grades are generally used for the major amount of residential framing throughout the country?

2. What physical characteristics must structural lumber possess?

3. List the two major species of wood that are now used for framing houses.

4. What is the main use in home construction for oak lumber?

5. Explain the word *deflection* as used in structural terminology.

6. Wood columns used to support a girder in a structure would be subjected to what type of stresses?

7. What is the maximum amount of moisture allowed in seasoned framing lumber?

8. Local building codes require what minimum live load on living room floors?

9. Why must both the live load and the dead load be considered when determining the size of a structural framing member?

10. If using No. 2 Douglas fir for framing a kitchen floor, what size joists would be necessary if they are spaced 16″ o.c. and span 11′-6″?

11. Specify the ceiling joist size for the following situation: no attic storage, No. 2 southern yellow pine, 16″ o.c. spacing, and 13′-0″ span.

12. Define the term *safety factor*.

13. Differentiate between light roofing and heavy roofing when sizing rafters.

14. Why is it important in conventional roof framing to have ceiling joists parallel to the rafters?

15. In planning a plank and beam roof with wide spacing of the beams, why is the stiffness of the planking an important consideration?

16. Is the rafter length or the rafter span used in selecting a proper size for a rafter from Table 8-6?

17. What is the maximum allowable span for 2 × 10 Douglas fir floor joists spaced at 16″ o.c. if the live load is 30 lb/sq ft?

18. What will be the length of a rafter if the roof slope is 9:12 and the horizontal span is 16′-0″?

19. What advantage is gained by the use of a flitch beam?

20. What size of standard steel pipe column is required to support 50 kips if the unsupported length is 10′-0″?

DRAFTING EXPRESSION

"All things require skill but an appetite."

—GEORGE HERBERT

9

Expression in drafting concerns itself mainly with the manner and technique employed by the drafter in conveying correct information on working drawings simply and clearly. The preparation of working drawings becomes an important part of architectural service, entailing ideas and skillful graphic communication. Tradespeople, estimators, contractors—all concerned with the construction of a building—must rely on the drawings for much of the technical information needed to execute their work. The drawings, therefore, must be expressive and somewhat tailored to locally accepted conventions, as well as accurately scaled. It helps if drafters as they work put themselves in the shoes of the carpenter or contractor, usually pressed for time, who must search the drawings for each bit of information. The following points on expressive drafting will be helpful in communicating your ideas on paper with a minimum of misinterpretation.

9.1 Vary Line Weights According to Their Importance

All lines on a drawing should have significance or they have no reason for being there. This significance, naturally, varies, and it should be reflected by the weight or width of each line. If a line has little importance, it should appear light; on the other hand, if a line contributes an important aspect to the drawing, it should appear heavy and prominent. Other lines will have intermediate importance. However, if all the lines on a drawing appear prominent or if all are made light, the drawing loses much of its expressiveness. We might say, then, that line variations (contrast) contribute definite meaning to drawings (see Fig. 9-1). Students should study various examples of good linework to know where to place the correct emphasis and where to restrain it. For added clarity, heavy lines are effective in more situations than beginners usually realize. For example, a plan or elevation can be improved by a heavy outline, and the silhouette of a section can be made more readable (see Fig. 9-2). Also, grade lines and roof overhang lines on elevation views look more realistic if they are heavy. Features nearer to the observer can add depth to the drawing by being outlined with heavy lines. In contrast, center lines, extension lines, and dimension lines require only minor emphasis and should be made fine. Consistent variations in linework are one of the important fundamentals of professional graphic expression. Pencils must be kept sharp, and various pressures must be used; it may even be necessary to go over important lines. To gain extreme emphasis, some drafters use the technical drafting pen on a few important lines on a drawing (see Fig. 9-3). The ink can go directly over pencil construction lines with very satisfactory results.

Develop the habit of putting a slight pressure on the beginnings and endings of pencil lines to make them sharp and distinct, rather than fizzled-out and ragged at their ends. Architectural linework should end exactly at the corners (Fig. 9-4).

See the full-size drawing in Fig. 9-5 for actual line weights and lettering sizes.

9.2 Learn to Make Crisp Looking Broken Lines

Many types of broken lines are found to be necessary on drawings, and a little care in their execution will pay off in added expression. Broken lines can be phantom lines

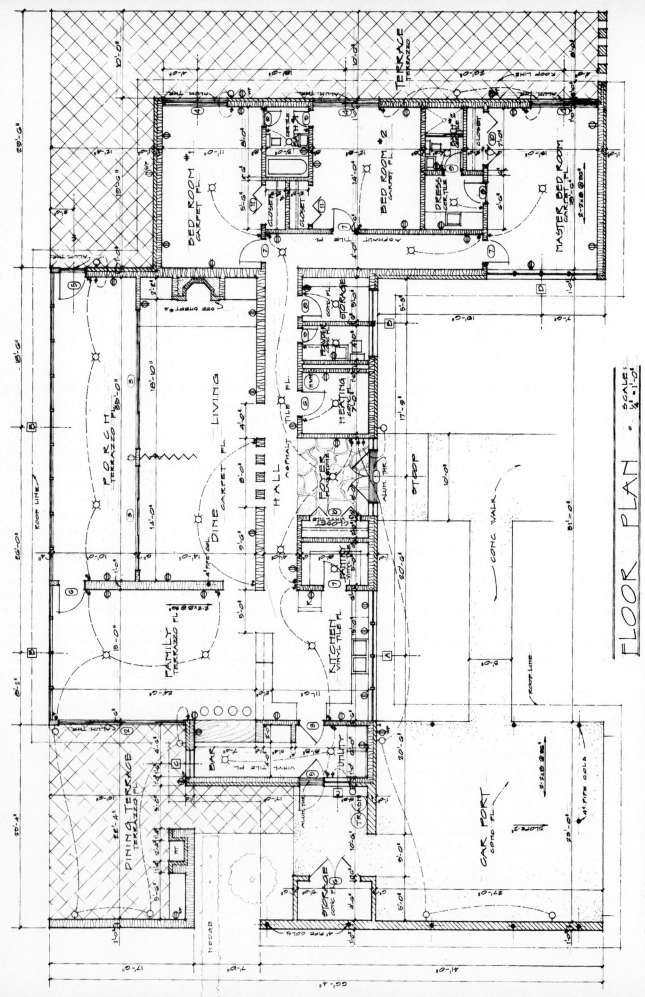

Figure 9-1 Expressive linework on a working drawing.

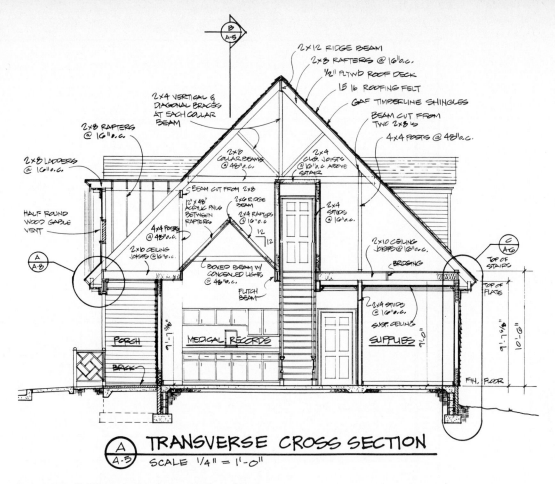

FIGURE 9-2 Outline emphasis on section views.

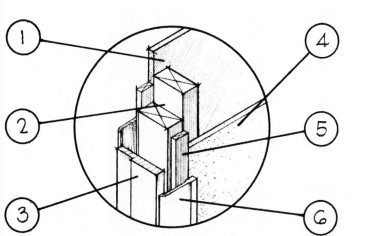

FIGURE 9-3 For more emphasis, some lines may be inked.

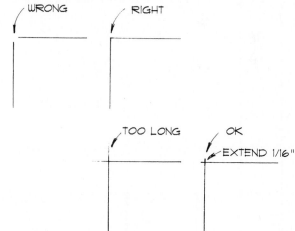

FIGURE 9-4 Intersection of lines on architectural drawings.

representing hidden surfaces, or they can represent alternate positions of movable features, or they can represent structural pieces, or they can be employed to provide information in other situations. After observing various working drawings, you will notice many uses for dissimilar broken lines (see Fig. 9-6). Like other linework, the dashes in broken lines should be given emphasis at their ends with slight pencil pressure, and the dashes should not be spaced too far apart; that is, they should have more line than openings. Make the dashes uniform in length and spacing. If several features are represented with broken lines, use a different dash length for each representation. Each will then have an obvious meaning. For example, on floor plans, bro-

Sec. 9.2　Learn to make crisp looking broken lines　**251**

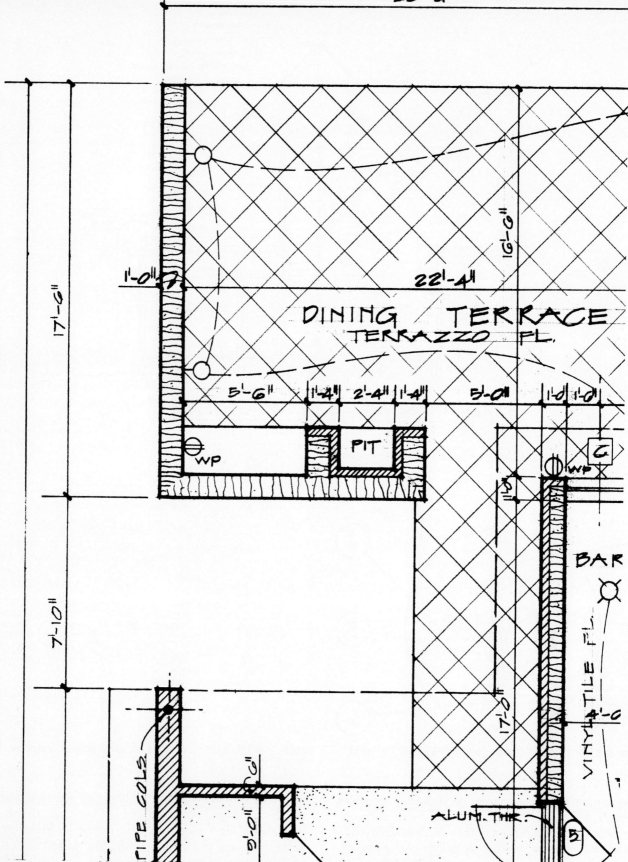

FIGURE 9-5 The actual size (partially shown) of the original drawing in Fig. 9-1. Notice the typical size of lettering, symbols, and the like, used by the drafter.

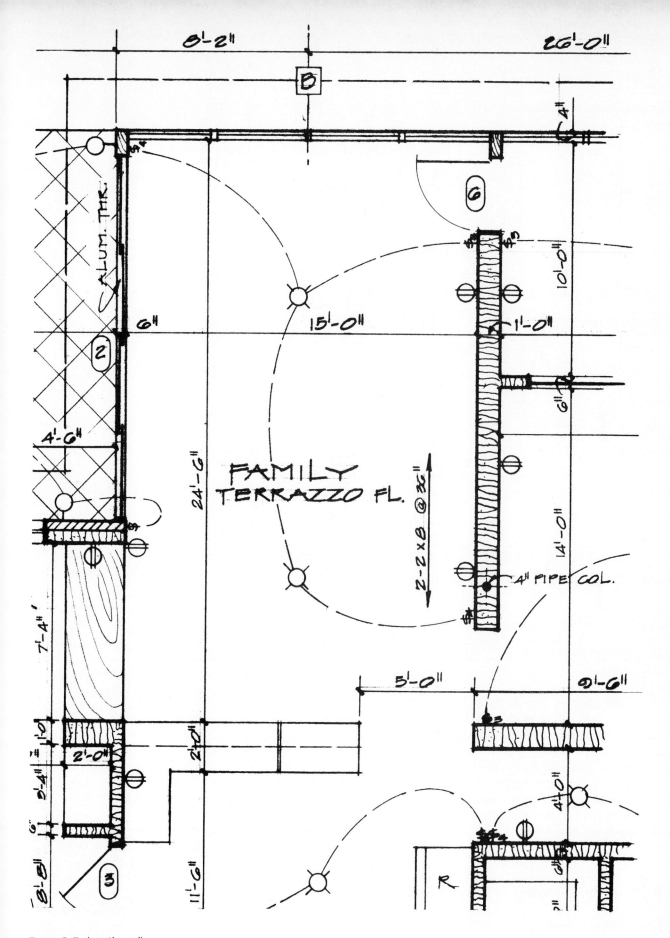

FAMILY
TERRAZZO FL.

FIGURE 9-5 (continued)

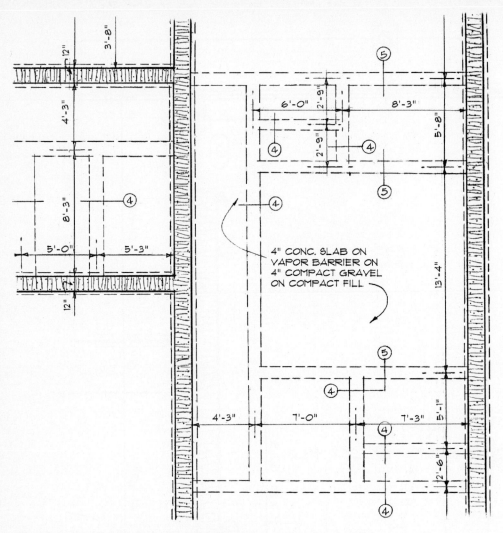

Figure 9-6 A partial foundation plan showing the use of broken lines.

ken lines are used to represent roof outlines, electric wiring to an outlet and switch connections, and so on. When selecting a dash technique for each, the roof outline could have 1/4" dashes, the electric wiring to an outlet and switch connections could have 1/2" dashes, and so on. Should they cross each other or appear near one another, there will be an obvious difference and no mistake will be made in their identification (Fig. 9-7A). If possible, complete each type of broken line on the drawing before starting other types so that individual techniques will be maintained. When a broken line changes in direction at a corner, make dashes intersect at the actual corner, rather than at an opening with no corner point (see Fig. 9-7B).

9.3 Make the Dimensions Easy to Read

The usefulness of a working drawing depends to a large extent on the correctness and manner of placement of its dimensions. If the dimensions are orderly and have been determined with the builder's needs in mind, information is readily obtained from the drawing. Numerous expensive mistakes are often the result of faulty dimensions.

Regardless of the scale of a drawing, numerical dimensions always indicate the actual size of the structure or feature. For example, if the side of a carport is represented by a line 5" long on a plan drawn to the scale 1/4" = 1'-0", the numerical dimension shown on the drawing should be 20'-0", which is the dimension workers must use to build the wall.

Extension Lines are light lines drawn from the extremities of a feature requiring a dimension (see Fig. 9-7C). Extension lines should not touch the feature, but rather they should begin 1/32" from the object line and extend about 1/8" beyond the arrowhead of the dimension line. If features within a drawing are best dimensioned outside the view, extension lines pass through the object lines and are unbroken.

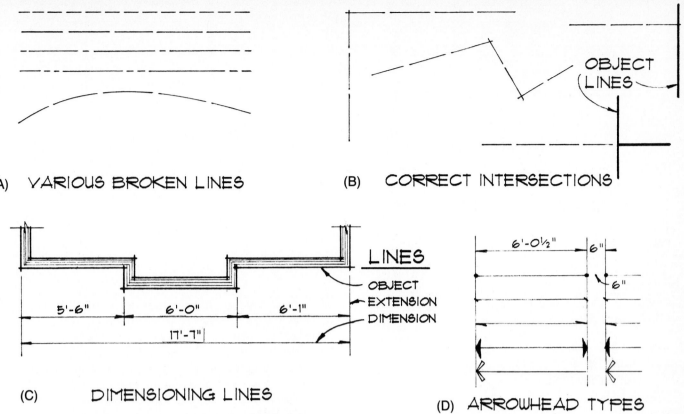

(A) VARIOUS BROKEN LINES

(B) CORRECT INTERSECTIONS

OBJECT LINES

(C) DIMENSIONING LINES

5'-6" 6'-0" 6'-1"

17'-7"

LINES
— OBJECT
— EXTENSION
— DIMENSION

6'-0½" 6"

6"

(D) ARROWHEAD TYPES

FIGURE 9-7 Broken lines, arrowheads, and dimensions.

Dimension Lines are also light lines and have arrowheads on each end, indicating the exact extremities of the dimension (see Fig. 9-7C). On architectural and structural drawings, dimension lines are made continuous, and the numerical dimension is placed just above the line, about midway between the arrowheads (see Fig. 9-7C). When placing a numerical dimension above adjacent parallel dimension lines, be careful to place it closer to the line it identifies. On shop or engineering drawings, the dimension line is broken near its center, and the numerical dimension is centered in the opening.

Arrowheads are drawn at the ends of dimension lines. Various types of arrowheads are seen on drawings (Fig. 9-7D), but the student should learn to make conventional arrowheads well before trying other types. Make them neat and uniform, with their points just touching the extension lines. A sharp, narrow arrowhead about ⅛" long is the most appropriate. Avoid clumsy arrowheads made with dull pencils, giving the drawing a spotty appearance.

Dimensions should be neatly lettered, and they should be made to read from the bottom and right side of the drawing—never from the top or left side. Dimensions under 12" are given in inches, such as 6", 3⅝", or 11½". Over 12" long they are usually given in feet and inches, such as 3'-4", 25'-7½", or 12'-0". However, on detail drawings, some features that are well over 12" in

size are commonly expressed in inches only. For example, joist spacing is usually indicated as 16" on center, kitchen base cabinets as 36" high, and minimum crawl space as 18". When lettering dimensions, never place the numbers directly on linework nor allow the numbers to touch lines on the drawing; it often mutilates the figure, and after a print is made of the drawing, the dimension is usually misread.

9.4 Place Dimensions for Obvious Association With Their Features

Dimension lines should be placed outside the view or drawing, if possible. On large plans, however, features such as partitions that are well inside the exterior walls must be dimensioned inside the view for obvious association. Dimensions that are too remote from their features are difficult to find, and the excessively long extension lines that are then necessary make the drawing confusing. The placement of dimensions within a drawing should be studied carefully to be sure that they do not interfere with other lines on the view. Avoid a dimension line that coincides with an object line at the arrowhead; offset the dimension slightly. Judgment must also be used in placing dimensions around the periphery of a plan or detail. If they are too close, they interfere with the outline of the view, and the numerical dimensions often become crowded; if they are too far

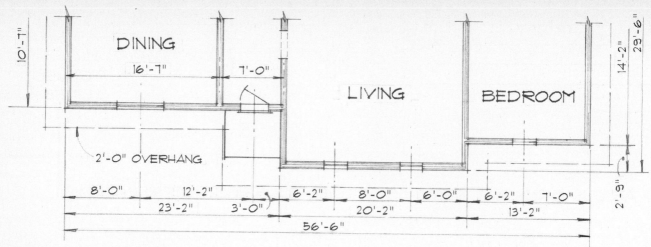

Figure 9-8 In-line dimensions on a plan view.

away, they give the impression of pertaining to features other than their own.

9.5 Line Up Dimensions in Series for Simplicity

If possible, a series of dimensions should be lined up so that they can be quickly drawn with one setting of the ruling edge, even if the view has offset edges (see Fig. 9-8). With arrowheads at each extension line intersection, the continuous dimension line effect simplifies the appearance of the drawing. The smallest dimensions are placed nearest, and the larger ones are placed farther away from the view. On a floor plan, for example, which often has many features requiring complex dimensions, similar features should be brought to each series for unity. The location of window and door center lines can be dimensioned along one series, closest to the plan; the offsets in the exterior wall and abutting partitions can be dimensioned along another series about 1/2″ farther out; and the overall length of the building can be shown as a single dimension about the same distance out again. Almost each dimensioning situation requires a different solution. Be sure to check the total of a series, arithmetically, to verify the overall dimension. Occasionally, it becomes necessary to cross extension lines, but avoid crossing dimensional lines.

9.6 Do Not Duplicate Dimensions

Basically, dimensions are either *size* dimensions or *location* dimensions. Only those that contribute to the construction of the building or feature should be shown—needless repetition only clutters. Often the method of construction dictates their correct choice. For example, in frame wall construction, the window and door openings are located to their center lines on the plan, whereas in solid masonry construction, they are dimensioned to their edges or rough openings (see Fig. 9-9). In frame partitions, the locations, of doors are often superfluous, inasmuch as their symbol indicates an obvious placement. Correct dimensioning eliminates the need for workers to make unnecessary addition or subtraction calculations on the job.

9.7 Use Leaders to Avoid Overcrowding

Leaders are straight or curved lines leading from a numerical dimension or note to the applying feature (see Fig. 9-10A). Usually, an arrowhead or dot is drawn on the feature end of the leader. Various leader techniques have been devised by drafters, but the most effective leaders are those that identify themselves as leaders and do not become confused with object lines or other lines on the drawing. Leaders should appear as connectors only and should not be misinterpreted. This is the purpose for using angular or offset-curve leaders. It is usual practice to add leaders to the drawing after dimension lines have been completed; then satisfactory, uncrowded spaces can be found for the leader dimension or note, without placing this information too far from the feature. If a series of leaders must identify a number of materials or features, on section views for example, be sure the notes are arranged in a logical sequence so that the leaders do not cross (Fig. 9-10A). For readability, bring the leader to the beginning of a note. Leaders with circles or balloons attached are effective for identifying parts of an assembly or similar drawing requiring a sequence of letters or numbers (see Fig. 9-3).

Use angular leaders also to label circular shapes and holes. Place the leader indicating a diameter dimension on the exterior of the circle, with the arrowhead touch-

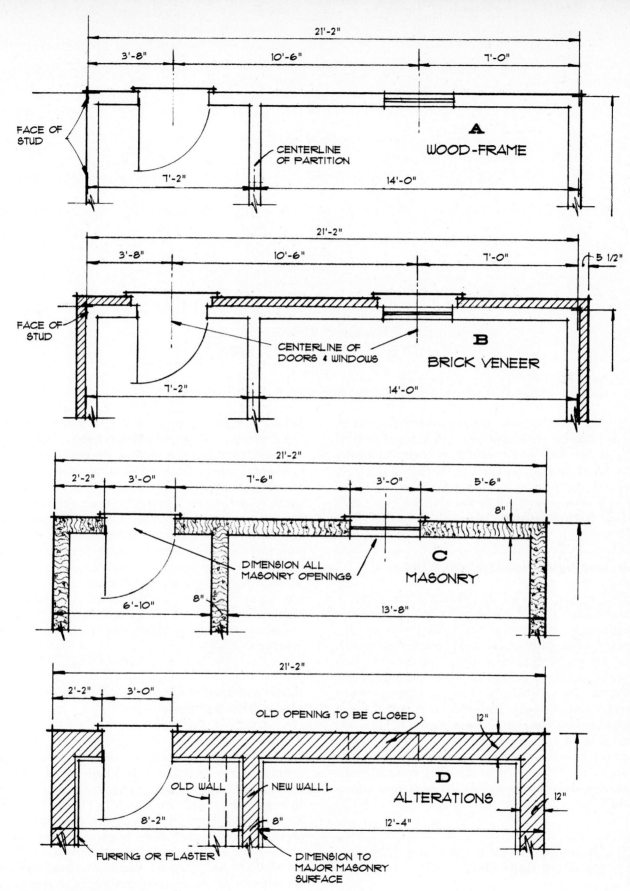

FIGURE 9-9 Dimensioning conventions.

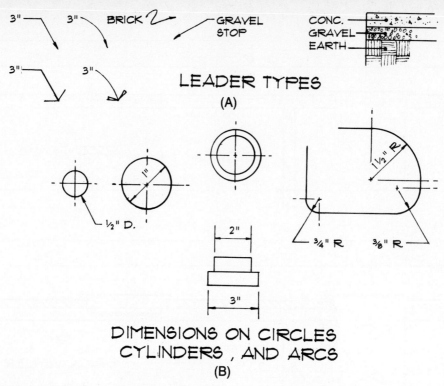

LEADER TYPES
(A)

DIMENSIONS ON CIRCLES
CYLINDERS , AND ARCS
(B)

FIGURE 9-10 Various types of leaders; dimensions for circles and arcs.

ing the circumference and pointing toward its center. A regular, angular dimension line can be used to label large circles; dimension cylinders on their rectangular view. Draw the leaders indicating the radii of arcs from their radiating points to the arcs, with the arrowhead of the leader on the inner side of the curvature (Fig. 9-10B) and the letter R following the numerical radius.

9.8 Use Notes Sparingly on a Drawing

Unless a note clarifies the graphic representation, chances are it can be better included in the written specifications and thereby save the drafter's time. If a note is needed, however, use small lettering and make it clear and concise. If a note, such as, "See detail A–A" is used, be sure there is a detail A–A to which the reader can refer. Check spelling carefully; even drafters need a dictionary occasionally. Extensive notes should be organized in neat blocks away from linework. These lettered areas of unusually long notes (if they definitely must be put on the drawing) should be considered in the sheet layout planning. Allow breathing space around a note, regardless of size, so that the reader can understand it.

9.9 Abbreviations Save Time, but They are Often Confusing

Even though the American Standards Association has established abbreviation standards for the construction

industry, many variations still exist throughout the country. Some architectural offices insist on abbreviating every word possible on their drawings, mainly to economize; other offices, knowing the inconsistencies and chances of misinterpretation, will not tolerate the use of abbreviations. The drafter must use discretion, however, and abbreviate only those words that have commonly identified abbreviations and use them in such a way that they cannot possibly be misconstrued. Capital lettering is usually employed, and, as a rule, the period at the end is omitted. If it becomes necessary to use unusual abbreviations throughout a set of drawings, indicate their meanings on a legend. A list of common construction abbreviations is included in Appendix B.

9.10 Indicate Materials and Features With Symbols

Because most buildings are a complexity of different materials and components, a simplified method of representation is necessary on a drawing—the smaller the scale, the simpler the symbol. Many of the conventional architectural symbols are shown in Fig. 9-11. Study these symbols carefully and commit to memory the important, most used ones: brick, concrete, stone, earth, wood, concrete masonry unit, insulation, glass, gravel, doors, and windows. Notice that most symbols are different on elevations from those in section or on plans. Learn all representations. Like other aspects of architectural drawing, symbols also vary slightly in

MATERIAL SYMBOLS - SECTION

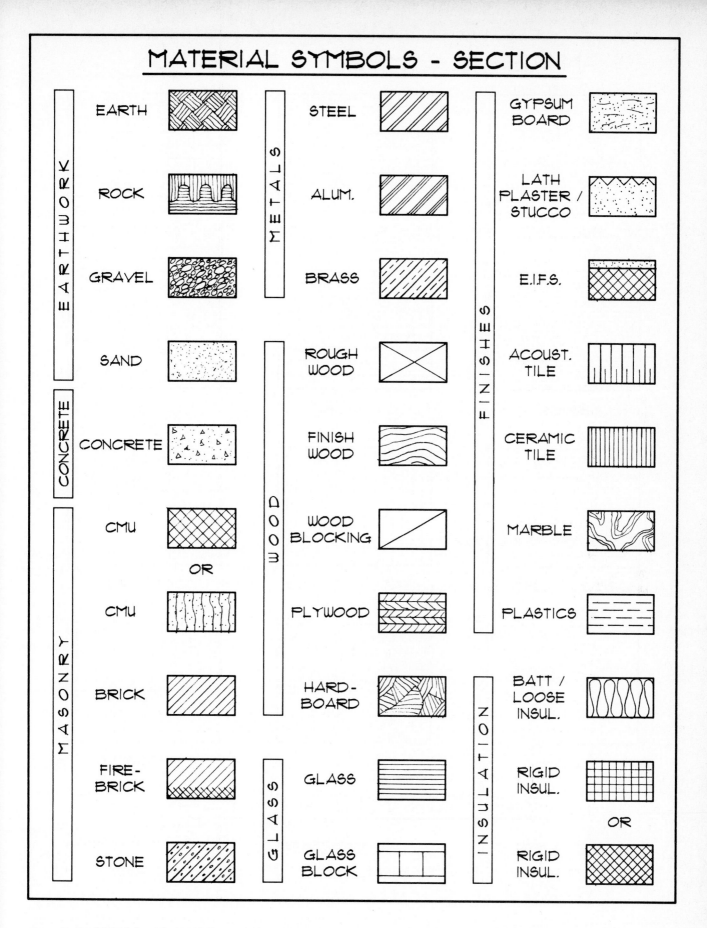

EARTHWORK
- EARTH
- ROCK
- GRAVEL
- SAND

CONCRETE
- CONCRETE

MASONRY
- CMU
- OR
- CMU
- BRICK
- FIRE-BRICK
- STONE

METALS
- STEEL
- ALUM.
- BRASS

WOOD
- ROUGH WOOD
- FINISH WOOD
- WOOD BLOCKING
- PLYWOOD
- HARD-BOARD

GLASS
- GLASS
- GLASS BLOCK

FINISHES
- GYPSUM BOARD
- LATH PLASTER / STUCCO
- E.I.F.S.
- ACOUST. TILE
- CERAMIC TILE
- MARBLE
- PLASTICS

INSULATION
- BATT / LOOSE INSUL.
- RIGID INSUL.
- OR
- RIGID INSUL.

FIGURE 9-11 Material symbols used on working drawings.

MATERIAL SYMBOLS - ELEVATION

CONC./STUCCO/PLASTER

CMU - RUNNING BOND

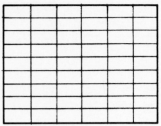

CMU - STACKED BOND

BRICK

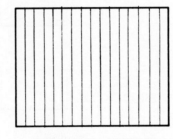

CUT STONE

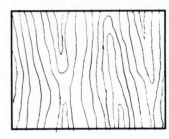

FIELD STONE

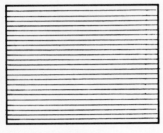

HORIZONTAL SIDING

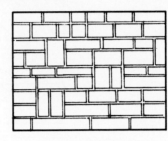

VERTICAL SIDING

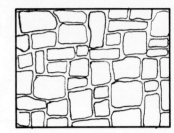

WOOD PANEL

GLASS

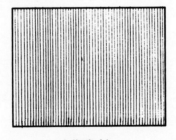

METAL

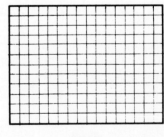

TILE

PARTITION SYMBOLS - PLAN

WOOD FRAME

METAL FRAME

GLASS

FIGURE 9-11 (continued)

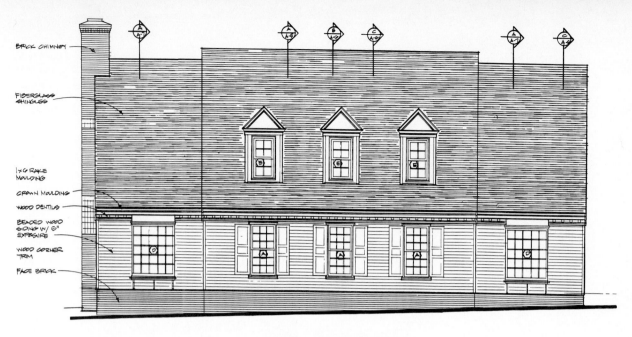

EAST ELEVATION
SCALE 1/4" = 1'-0"

FIGURE 9-12 An elevation showing application of material symbols.

different areas and in different offices. If nonstandard symbols are used on drawings, a symbol legend can be drawn on one of the sheets. Although simply drawn, all symbols should be indicative of the material they represent; if a symbol is misleading or gives the impression of the wrong material, clarify it with a simple note. Material symbols or hatching need not be made with heavy line weights. In fact, their representation in rather large areas will appear more pleasing if the linework fades out near the center, thus resembling a highlight on the surface, and it is given more emphasis near the edges (see Fig. 9-12). Make the highlights nongeometric in shape to eliminate any possibility of their appearing as construction features on the surface. The edges of hatched areas should be distinct. Contrast of adjacent materials is especially important on section views. To aid expression, hatch adjacent pieces on section views in different directions. Otherwise, use the same tone and technique for a material or member reappearing in different places throughout the section. If an overall gray pencil tone is used to indicate a predominant material, usually it is more tidy to apply the shading on the reverse side of the tracing. Wood structural members in section are merely indicated with diagonals (Fig. 9-11); finish lumber is indicated with an end-grain symbol done freehand.

If notes or dimensions must go into hatched areas, leave out enough of the linework so that the number or note can be inserted and can be read without difficulty (see Fig. 9-12).

In drawing wood frame construction, the exterior walls of the floor plan of a home can be represented with parallel lines, scaled 6″ apart, which is usually close to the actual thickness of the combined studs, inside material, and outside wall coverings. Parallel lines are often the only symbol needed to represent the wood walls. But by the addition of either straight or wavy lines (resembling wood grain) within the parallel lines, a more prominent outline of the plan is attained (see Fig. 9-13). The tone of the symbol makes the plan more readable. This principle of giving prominence to important features by shading, either freehand or mechanical, is adaptable to many situations in drafting. The symbols for windows and doors on plans drawn at small scales are shown in Fig. 9-9. Several methods are shown for indicating doors. On elevation views, draw windows and doors accurately to reveal their characteristics.

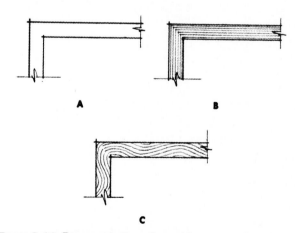

FIGURE 9-13 Representation of wood frame on plan views.

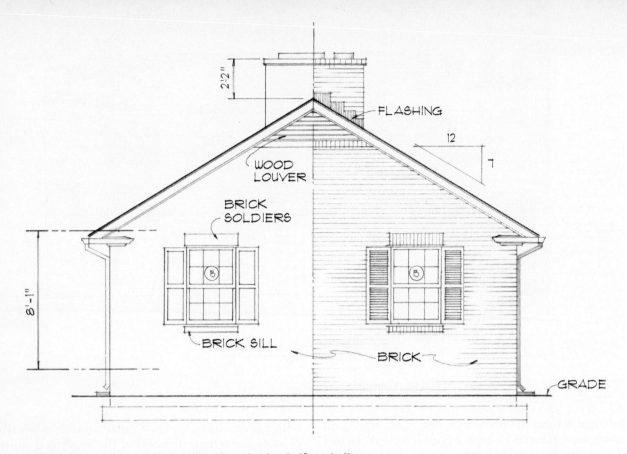

FIGURE 9-14 A symmetrical elevation view showing half-symboling.

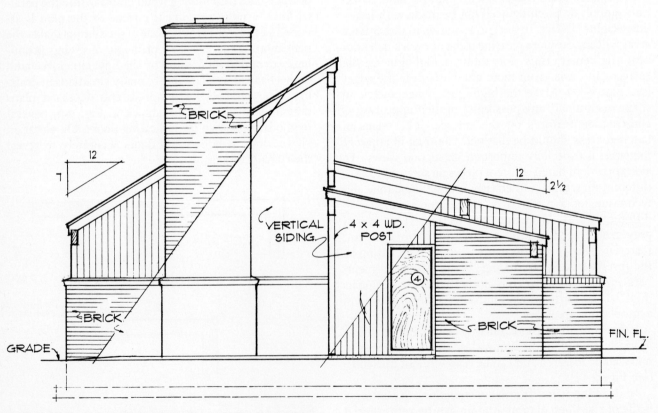

FIGURE 9-15 Partial symboling with the use of a diagonal line.

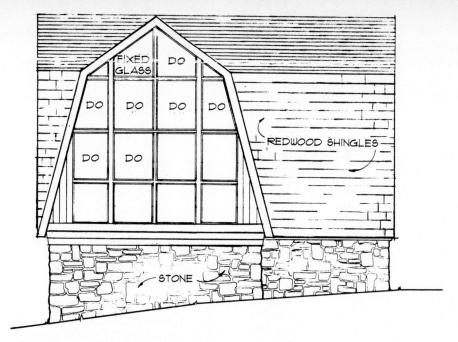

FIGURE 9-16 Method of indicating obvious similar features.

9.11 Avoid Unnecessary Repetition of Symbol Hatching

When drawing elevation views of a symmetrical nature, the material symbol on one side of the center line can often be omitted if there is no special reason for hatching the entire elevation (see Fig. 9-14). In design drawings, however, completion of the various material tones may be necessary in analyzing the esthetic aspects of the building. Another method of suggesting materials on an elevation without taking the time to hatch the entire drawing is shown in Fig. 9-15. A light diagonal line that does not conflict with other important lines is drawn on the elevation to limit the hatching to a typical area. Sometimes merely a note is sufficient to indicate the material if it does not require careful delineation. When a series of identical features is shown, it is permissible to provide a symbol for only one feature completely and add a ditto (DO) note to the remaining ones (see Fig. 9-16). Time is saved if laborious hatching is omitted where repetition is not informative.

9.12 Use a Drafting Template for Difficult Symbols

Many symbols such as bathroom fixtures, electrical symbols, kitchen equipment, circles, and irregular shapes can be quickly drawn with appropriate architectural templates (see Fig. 1-1). Refer to Section 1.16 for the correct use of drafting templates. Drafters may develop their own templates or symbols for items such as north arrows (see Figs. 9-17 and 9-18).

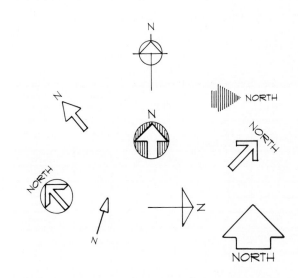

FIGURE 9-17 Suggestions for north-point arrows.

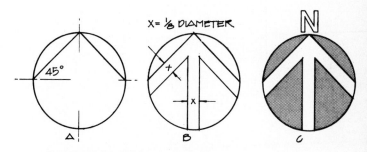

FIGURE 9-18 Steps in drawing a standardized north arrow.

9.13 Use Schedules to Organize Extensive Information

A schedule is an organized arrangement of notes or information usually lettered within a ruled enclosure and conveniently placed on the drawing (see Fig. 9-19). Extensive information placed in a schedule, rather than lettered in various places on the drawing, makes the information easily accessible to estimators and builders who appreciate the organized arrangement. Schedules commonly list information pertaining to doors, windows, interior trim, painting, structural detail elements, and so on. Door and window schedules are usually placed on the floor plan sheet, where they can be studied in relation to the plan drawing. When drawing a schedule enclosure, make the horizontal ruled lines 1/4" or 3/8" apart so that there will be sufficient space between the lines for the lettering (which need be only 1/8" high) to avoid touching the ruled linework. The title should be slightly larger, and a top-horizontal and a left-vertical column for identifications and headings should be isolated from the remaining spaces with heavy lines. Draw a heavy border line around the entire schedule.

Identify windows with letters (A, B, C, D) both in the schedule and near the windows on the plan; identify doors with numbers (1, 2, 3, 4) or vice versa, so that each can be easily distinguished. Rough-opening sizes for windows installed in frame walls are important information and should be included in the schedule along with window size, type, and material. Often the name of the manufacturer and the item's exact catalogue number are also provided. Instead of a lettered schedule, door information can also be shown by drawing small elevation views of each door type. Sometimes the small elevations are included as part of a lettered schedule. If the doors are similar stock heights, they become simplest to draw if arranged in a horizontal row (see Fig. 9-20). Dimensions and material information should both be included in this type of graphic schedule. On noncomplex floor plans using only stock doors, door sizes can be lettered along the door symbol on the plan with a note such as 1 3/8" × 2'-6" × 6'-8" FLUSH, and no schedule is required.

MARK	NO. NEEDED	ROUGH OPNG.	TYPE	MFG. NO.	MULLION	REMARKS
A	2	2'-11" × 4'-6"	DH	BW 2749	NONE	BY BILT-WELL
B	6	3'-10" × 4'-6"	DH	BW 2749	1 - 3 1/8"	SEE DETAIL
C	4	8'-9" × 4'-6"	DH	BW 2749	2 - 3 1/8"	DO
D	2	1'-11" × 3'-2"	DH	BW 2749	NONE	DO
E	3	1'-5" × 2'-3 7/8"	CAS.	A461	NONE	BY TRUSCON

WINDOW SCHEDULE

FIGURE 9-19 A typical window schedule.

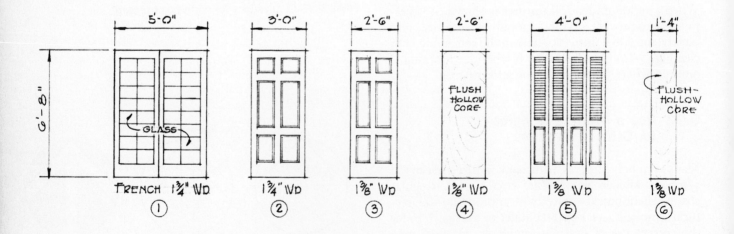

FIGURE 9-20 A method of describing doors on working drawings.

9.14 Avoid Smudged Pencil Linework

Slight smudging of pencil linework with triangles and instruments cannot be entirely avoided, but care should be taken to refrain from unnecessary rubbing or touching the finished pencil lines. Beginning students, especially, are confronted with the problem of smudged drawings. Listed below are a number of suggestions for keeping a pencil drawing clean while on the drawing board:

1. Use a systematic and organized procedure in the sequence of drawing lines so that instruments will not have to be placed over existing lines any more than necessary; for example, start from the top of the layout and draw as many major, horizontal lines as possible, proceeding to the bottom of the layout. For vertical lines, start from the left of the layout and draw as many vertical lines as convenient, proceeding toward the right of the drawing (if left-handed, proceed toward the left). In other words, draw lines so that the triangle can be moved away from the lines already completed. This will

become a time-saving habit if conscientiously applied during early training.
2. Protect completed parts of a drawing by covering them with extra sheets of paper. Do this also at the end of the day or work period.
3. Small triangles will reduce smudging if extensive work must be done on small details.
4. Form the habit of raising the T-square, parallel bar and triangle blade slightly when moving it up or down on the drawing board. This can be done by merely bearing down on the head as it is moved.
5. Keep the instruments clean by wiping with a damp cloth regularly. Avoid soap and water on wooden parts. The fine graphite from pencil leads has the habit of lodging in the surface pores of almost any material. Always wipe the pencil point after sharpening. Do not store the pencil pointer in direct contact with other drafting equipment, either on the drawing board or in portable kits. Keep it in an isolated container.
6. Use the dry cleaning pad sparingly to prevent smudged linework (see Fig. 9-21). Sweep the drawing occasionally with the drafting brush to reduce the amount of loose graphite on the surface. Avoid rubbing the drawing with the hand or any hard objects, as well as with sleeves or cuffs (see Fig. 9-22).
7. Be sure your hands are clean and dry. If necessary, use a little talcum powder on them to reduce perspiration.

FIGURE 9-21 Using a dry cleaning pad to prevent smudged linework.

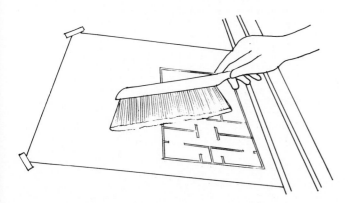

FIGURE 9-22 Sweeping loose graphite from drawings.

9.15 Learn the Principles of Modular Drafting

To meet the rising cost of construction, the building industry has developed a method for simplifying the details of structures so that building components, materials, and equipment can be assembled easily with a minimum of alterations, such as cutting, fitting, and other minor modifications. It is felt that by reducing hand labor for such job-site alterations, the application of this principle effects the only definite economies yet to be realized in present-day construction, and that this fuller utilization of our technical advances in the building industry can be made without sacrificing any of the architectural qualities of the design. The industry's recommendation is *modular coordination*, which involves these four aspects:

1. Thinking modular during all stages of the design process
2. Drawing the working drawings so that modular concepts are represented simply, yet with some flexibility
3. Sizing building products so that they will conform to modular assembly

4. Devising construction techniques that will economically utilize coordinated materials with a minimum of modification and waste

Modular drafting concerns itself with these concepts. Some architectural offices use modular coordination and dimensioning on their working drawing; others, because of the occasional difficulty in obtaining a full range of modular products and local difficulty in obtaining construction personnel who fully understand the system, are reluctant to convert to the modular method. But there is merit in coordination; and, like any advance in an industry involving large numbers of people in various areas and trades, time is required before the method is universally understood and accepted.

Beginning students should first learn the conventional methods for representing and dimensioning working drawings. Then, after an intimate acquaintance with construction methods and building products, the benefits of modular methods will become apparent. Well thought out conventional drawings often result in modular characteristics, whether it is realized or not. The first step is "thinking modular," both in conceiving the building structurally and esthetically, and continuing this thinking throughout the working drawings. Modular drawings are not necessarily restricted to the use of modular materials only.

The following points are given briefly to serve as an introduction to the fundamentals of modular drafting.

9.15.1 Use a Modular Grid in Laying Out Preliminary Design Sketches

From the very outset, design trial sketches must be developed over a modular grid, which has only one restriction—that it be sized in 4″ multiples: 16″, 24″, 4′-0″, 10′-8″, 24′-0″, and so on. The selection of the basic grid may be almost any convenient multiple size (see Fig. 9-23). If plywood or other sheet materials are to be a dominant material in the construction, a 4′-0″ × 4′-0″ grid size might be a logical selection. If the spans of structural members seem to satisfy a 12′-0″ spacing, a grid size of 12′ may be appropriate. If concrete masonry units are to be a major material, a 16″ grid size could be used (it may be a bit small for design sketches, however). The size of the building or repeating spaces within the building should be considered in selecting a design grid size, just so the selected size of the grid can be divided by 4.

The basic 4″ module was adopted by the American Standards Association, after careful study, as being the most convenient unit from which major materials could be sized and construction features could be dimen-

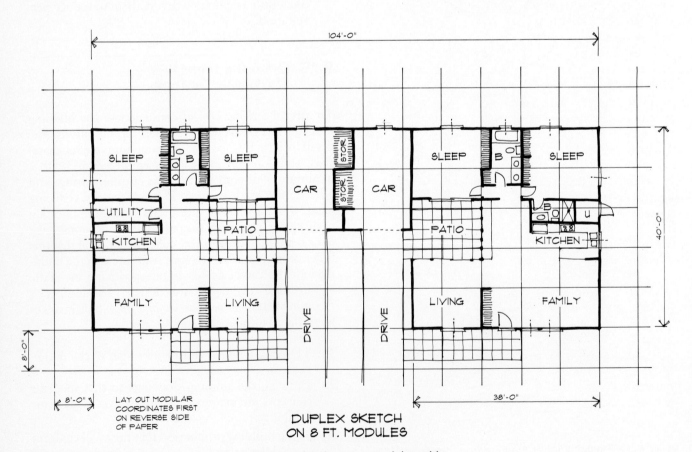

FIGURE 9-23 Modular drawings start with preliminary sketches over modular grids.

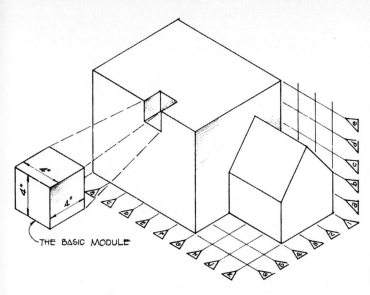

FIGURE 9-24 The basic module of an architectural volume.

sioned. The module is three-dimensional, resembling a 4″ cube (Fig. 9-24), yet it appears in all three principal building planes as a 4″ grid. Some drawings do not show the grids; but because the building was created over a grid, important points will fit, even if the grid lines are imaginary. The basic module is also compatible with sizing of products from countries using the metric system; 4″ is nearly identical with 10 cm.

When the preliminary sketches are converted to large-scale drawings, multiples of the 4″ module become easy to dimension, and all parts of the building can be conveniently related. The design grid can be laid out directly on the sketch paper, or it can be inserted below tracing paper as an underlay. If the structural system and the planning layout can be combined into unified modules, both the working drawings and the construction will be simplified. Grid-disciplined design sketches are the foundation, so to speak, for modular coordination, making possible the benefits of modular drawings.

9.15.2 Develop the Details of the Building on Grid Lines

In developing the details of a building, the 4″ grid lines must be drawn first and become a part of the drawing. The grids can be drawn on the reverse side of the tracing paper, or they can be done in ink so that they cannot be erased if changes must be made. Draw the grids only where each detail will appear; but they must be made to show clearly on the reproduction prints. Because of their small size, 4″ grid lines are not put on a small-scale drawing. Any scale smaller than 3/4″ = 1′-0″ is considered a small-scale drawing. On complex plans and elevations it may be necessary to use

reference grid lines to relate the details to their correct placement in the building. Some of the grids in the details may coincide with the reference grids shown on the plans and elevations and others may not; regardless, the continuity of the 4″ module is related with modular dimensions at key points throughout the building.

The accompanying details show where units and surfaces usually best fit within or on grid lines. Each unit of a detail does not necessarily have to fall on grid lines, nor does the modular system restrict the use of only modular materials. However, key points have been worked out in conventional construction to best utilize standard materials in the system. Notice that generally the nominal sizes and surfaces fit the grid lines (see Figs. 9-25 and 9-26). The actual size is usually a fraction of an inch smaller than the nominal size (an exception is the height of a wide-flange beam). For example, the nominal cross-section size of a 2 × 4 wooden lumber actually measures only 1½″ × 3½″ when the lumber is dressed and dry (19 percent moisture content or less); the actual size of the 8″ × 8″ × 16″ concrete block measures 7⅝″ × 7⅝″ × 15⅝″. To eliminate the need for excessive fractions, the grid line conveniently falls within the joint in masonry and just outside the edge of a 2″ × 4″ member, allowing some flexibility. Because 3/8″ is usually the width of a mortar joint between masonry units, 3/16″ is, therefore, a constant dimensional relationship of unit surfaces to the controlling grid. It becomes convenient for grid lines to fall on the center lines of columns, window openings, partitions, and the like. When grid lines indicate nominal sizes, it is important that the drafter as well as the construction contractor be fully aware of this fact. Working drawings can also be based on actual sizes, but a consistent

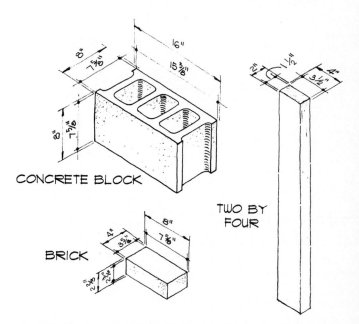

FIGURE 9-25 Actual and nominal sizes of common building materials.

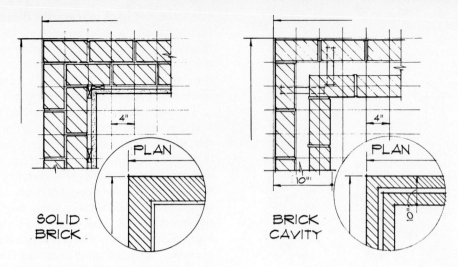

FIGURE 9-26 Typical walls and their treatment.

method must be used throughout the drawings. Comparatively few fractions are required in modular drafting, which should make the system of particular interest to drafters.

9.15.3 Use an Arrowhead to Indicate a Grid Dimension; a Dot to Indicate a Nongrid Dimension

The dots and arrowheads at the ends of dimension lines have a definite significance on modular drawings. To distinguish between grid and off the grid dimensions, an arrowhead is always used to indicate a dimension on a grid line and a dot to indicate a dimension off the grid

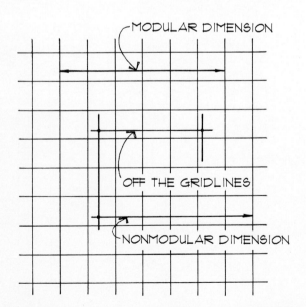

FIGURE 9-27 The use of arrowheads and dots on modular drawings.

lines (see Fig. 9-27). Dimensions that have an arrowhead at each end of the dimension line will be in 4″ multiples. Dimensions that have dots on each end may or may not be modular, but their extremities do not fall on grid lines. If a dimension has an arrowhead on one end and a dot on the other, it cannot be a 4″ multiple and therefore is not a modular dimension. Even though the grid lines do not actually appear on a modular drawing, the designer or drafter imagines them to be there, and their presence is always implied by the 4″ multiple dimensions. As we mentioned, reference grids with heavy triangles at their ends, enclosing a consecutive numbering system (see Fig. 9-24), can be used to give additional coordination between details and the plans and elevations. Any point within the total volume of the building can be located with the reference grids.

9.15.4 Coordinate Vertical Dimensions with Modular Floor Heights

Usually the nominal finished floor is placed on a grid line; the actual finished floor surface is located ⅛″ below a grid line (Fig. 9-28). In wood frame construction, however, the top of the subfloor or the surface of a slab on grade foundation is placed on a grid line (Fig. 9-29). Three brick heights as well as one 8″ concrete masonry unit height coincide with two grid heights. A difficult point of modular coordination concerns the use of stock doors. If the finished floor coincides with a grid line, then the 6′-8″ or 7′-0″ stock door heights will not allow enough space for the head jamb to make the rough opening modular. If special doors and frames are not available to fit the modular heights, consideration must be given to this point in the details. Other important vertical heights are windowsills, ceiling heights, and table heights.

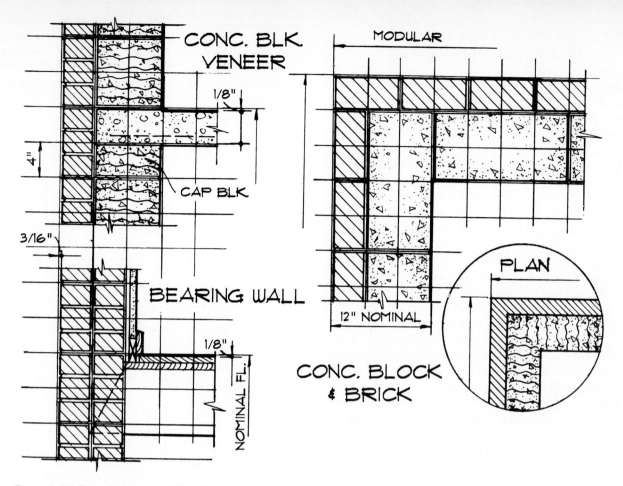

FIGURE 9-28 The placement of floor levels within modular grids.

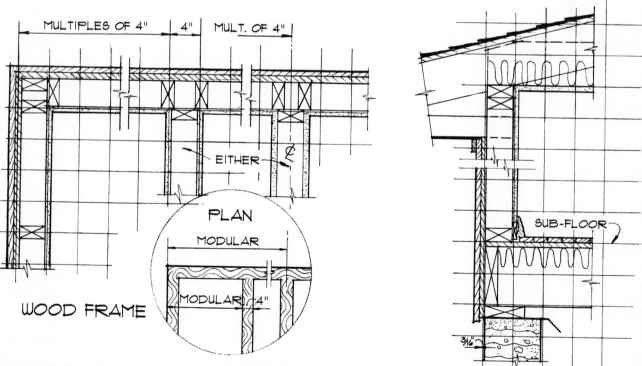

FIGURE 9-29 The placement of frame details within modular grids.

9.15.5 Use a Note to Indicate That the Drawings Are Modular

Because a set of drawings drawn and dimensioned to modular measure appears very much like a set of conventional drawings, a note stating that the drawings are modular should be used as a guideline for contractors, bidders, estimators, and workers. The note, usually placed on the first sheet of the drawings, should be simple and clear; if it is accompanied by several simple drawings illustrating the method of dimensioning employed, as well as by any special representations found on the drawings, all the advantages of modular measure will be readily understood. To standardize the modular note, an easily applied translucent appliqué[2] has been devised by the A.I.A. modular coordinator and is recommended by the Modular Measure Committee of the American Standards Association (see Fig. 9-30). It can be affixed by a pressure-sensitive adhesive to the tracing itself and will clearly show on all prints. Some architectural offices design their own modular note and merely letter it, along with any illustrative drawings, directly on the first sheet of their drawings.

Figures 9-31 and 9-32 show a residential floor plan and various details drawn and dimensioned modular.

A type of modular construction for small buildings is shown in Fig. 9-33 (MOD 24, devised jointly by the major U.S. wood products associations). The framing is placed on 24″ centers so that standard 4′ × 8′ plywood and sheeting materials can be used with a minimum of waste and cutting. Many factory manufactured small homes are now produced using a 4″ module for sizing.

9.16 Metric System of Measurement

It is expected that U.S. industry will eventually convert to the metric system of measurement. In construction, many standards will have to be established before complete conversion will be possible. Lumber, materials, and building components will have to be manufactured in metric measurement before the industry can be expected to adopt the system.

A module of 10 centimeters, almost identical to our present 4″, would be a logical new module for construction materials (see Fig. 9-34). Otherwise, the *meter* would be a convenient unit for sizing buildings and dimensioning drawings. A suggested method of dimensioning drawings is shown in Fig. 9-35. Until a complete conversion is made, the metric dimension could be placed above the dimension line and the English equivalent placed below.

[2]Available from Standpat Co., 150-42 12th Road, Whitestone, NY 11357.

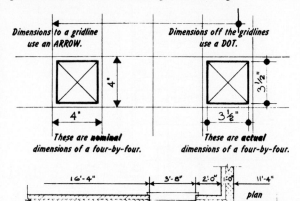

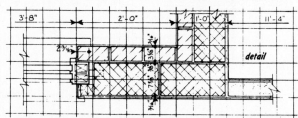

NOTE — All drawings are dimensioned by Modular Measure in conformance with the American Standard Basis for Coordination of Dimensions of Building Materials and Equipment (A62.1-1956).

This system of dimensioning is used for greater efficiency in construction: less cutting, fitting and waste of material, less chance for dimensional errors. The Modular Method uses a horizontal and vertical grid of reference lines. The gridlines are spaced 4 inches apart in length, width and height.

Dimensions to a gridline use an ARROW.

Dimensions off the gridlines use a DOT.

These are *nominal* dimensions of a four-by-four.

These are *actual* dimensions of a four-by-four.

SMALL-SCALE plans, elevations and sections ordinarily give only nominal and grid dimensions (from gridline to gridline in multiples of four inches, using arrows at both ends). Dimension-arrows thus indicate *nominal* faces of walls, jambs, etc., finish floor, etc., coinciding with invisible gridlines, which are not drawn in at such small scales.

LARGE-SCALE detail drawings actually show these same gridlines drawn in, every 4 inches. On these details, reference dimensions give the locations of *actual* faces of materials in relation to the grid.

FIGURE 9-30 A preprinted applique available for attachment to working drawings to indicate that they are modular.

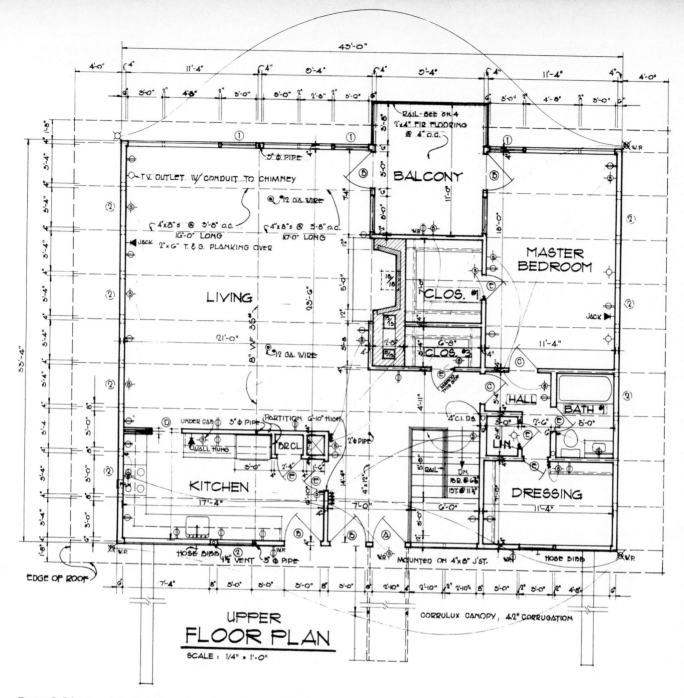

FIGURE 9-31 A residential floor plan drawn and dimensioned modular.

2. Draw sixteen ¹/₂″ high by 1″ wide rectangles equally spaced on the paper; ¹/₄″ below each rectangle draw guidelines ³/₁₆″ high; letter the titles of the following material symbols and poché the proper symbol in the rectangle above: compact fill, gravel, rock, concrete, C.M.U., brick, fire brick, field stone, steel, finish wood, rough wood, plywood, hardboard, batt insulation, rigid insulation, and glass.

3. Draw four floor plans of a small storage facility

8′-0″ wide by 12′-0″ long (outside dimensions) at scale of ¹/₄″ = 1′-0″. Center a six-panel 3′-0″ by 6′-8″ door on the 12′-0″ wall and a 4′-6″ by 5′-2″ double casement window on the 8′-0″ wall. Four different materials will be used for wall construction; draw one plan with 4″ wood stud walls, draw the second plan with 6″ C.M.U. walls, draw the third plan with 8″ concrete walls, and draw the fourth plan with 6″ wood stud walls and 4″ brick veneer. Place exterior and interior dimensions on each plan.

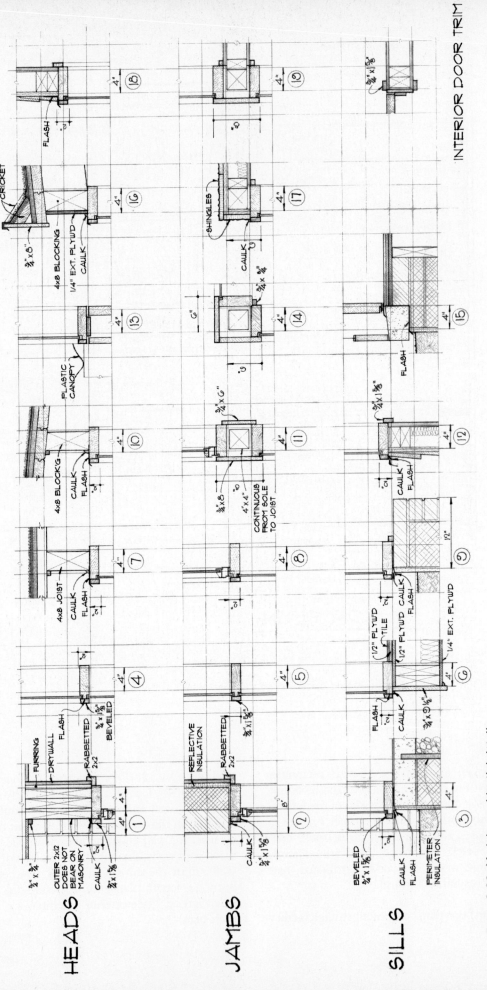

Figure 9-32 Modular residential details.

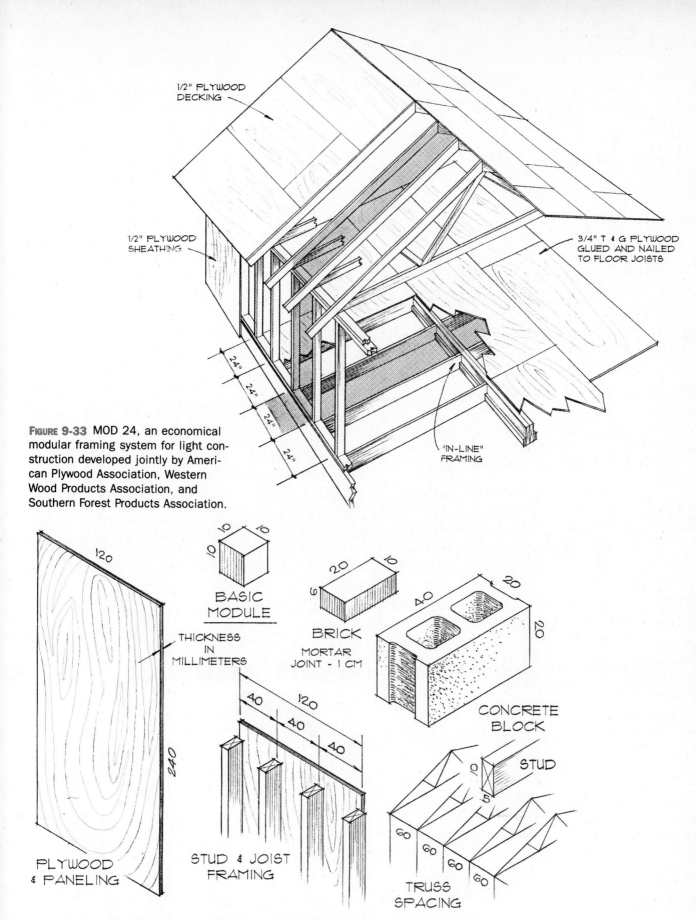

1/2" PLYWOOD
DECKING

1/2" PLYWOOD
SHEATHING

3/4" T & G PLYWOOD
GLUED AND NAILED
TO FLOOR JOISTS

24"
24"
24"
24"
24"

'IN-LINE'
FRAMING

FIGURE 9-33 MOD 24, an economical modular framing system for light construction developed jointly by American Plywood Association, Western Wood Products Association, and Southern Forest Products Association.

120

10
10
10
BASIC
MODULE

THICKNESS
IN
MILLIMETERS

20
10
6
BRICK
MORTAR
JOINT - 1 CM

40
20
20
CONCRETE
BLOCK

240

40
120
40
40
STUD & JOIST
FRAMING

10
5
STUD

60
60
60
60
TRUSS
SPACING

PLYWOOD
& PANELING

FIGURE 9-34 Suggested modular materials in metric measure.

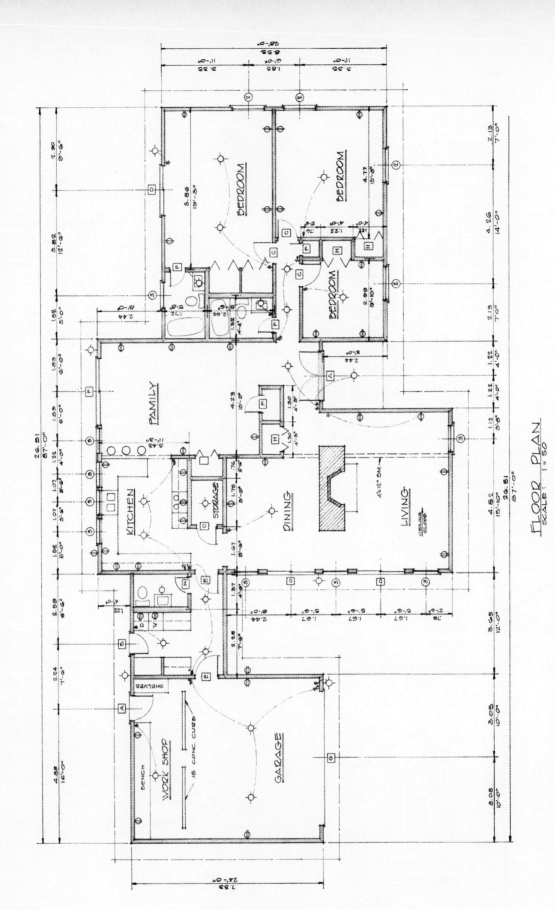

Figure 9-35 Metric dimensions. Although no standards for metric dimensioning have yet been adopted, one method for converting may be used as shown. The metric dimension is placed above the line and the English units below.

4. Draw elevation views and plan views of the following doors at a scale of $3/8'' = 1'-0''$: six-panel wood doors, $3'-0''$ by $6'-8''$; flush wood door, $2'-8''$ by $6'-8''$; full louvered wood door, $2'-4''$ by $6'-8''$; two-panel bi-fold doors, $6'-0''$ by $6'-8''$; and two-panel nine-light $3'-0''$ by $6'-8''$ door; all doors are $1^3/4''$ thick. Dimension and label each door.

5. Using two of the floor plans developed in Exercise 3 at a scale of $1/4'' = 1'-0''$, draw the side and end elevation views of the door and window walls. Use the $6''$ C.M.U. plan with $12''$ board and batten siding at the triangular gable ends of the roof. Use the brick veneer plan with a hip roof. Floor to ceiling heights are $8'-0''$, roof pitches are 7:12 with fiberglass shingles, overhangs are $1'-4''$ with a 1×6 fascia, and buildings are slab on grade. Poché and label all materials.

REVIEW QUESTIONS

1. What do we mean by *contrast* in linework?

2. How may broken lines or dashed lines be varied to represent various features on a drawing?

3. What is a typical architectural characteristic of line intersections at corners?

4. From what directions on a drawing are dimensions made to read?

5. Why is a series of dimensions best placed along a continuous line on a floor plan?

6 What is the conventional method of expressing architectural measurement with numbers?

7. Why are the basic structural features of a plan the first dimensions to be given consideration?

8. Why is it preferable to use only those abbreviations that have been standardized and commonly accepted?

9. What is the advantage of using a schedule when considerable information is involved?

10. Describe *modular coordination*.

11. How can pencil smudging be removed from tracings?

12. Describe three techniques used by drafters to keep drawings neat while drafting.

13. Draw the proper symbol for expressing a 5:12 roof pitch on a working drawing.

14. What is another term used for symbol hatching?

15. On floor plans of commercial buildings, dimensions are shown from wall to wall. How are the corresponding dimensions shown on residential floor plans?

16. What is the primary unit of measurement for modular dimensioning?

17. Why is it necessary to draw a north arrow on floor plans?

18. An arrowhead is used at the ends of dimension lines, what other symbol may be used at the ends of dimension lines?

19. What is the metric equivalent measurement to a $4''$ modular measurement.

20. Identify two types of schedules used on working drawings and describe how they are organized.

TYPICAL ARCHITECTURAL DETAILS

"Genius is the ability to reduce the complicated to the simple."

—C. W. CERAN

The word *details* covers the broad category of isolated and enlarged drawings that, together with the plans and elevations, form the complete set of working drawings. Each detail furnishes specific information at key points throughout the construction. Almost every set of drawings requires a different set of details, the choice of which is determined by the architect or drafter. Only a few standard details may be necessary, however, on drawings of modest structures incorporating conventional construction. In fact, some sets of drawings contain very few details, allowing the builders considerable latitude in the choice of construction, whereas other sets contain details for almost every construction arrangement in the building.

This chapter will be limited to the basic general details found in average residential and light-construction sets of drawings. Other minor details will be discussed in Chapter 11.

10.1 Selecting the Correct Scale for Details

Before starting a detail drawing, take a minute or two to decide on the most appropriate scale. Suitable scale depends on the size of members in the detail, the amount of detail that must be shown, as well as the space available in the layout of the sheet; all these factors must be considered. Plan the sheets so that details are placed for their most logical association with other drawings and that all sheets of a set are utilized for economy as well as appearance. Scales for details range from $\frac{1}{2}'' = 1'\text{-}0''$ to full size. Small pieces, such as moldings, are usually drawn full size to show clearly profiles and small detail. Larger members or assemblies can be drawn at smaller scales. It is worth noting that

the preferable larger scales can be used in minimum spaces if *break symbols* are employed to remove unimportant areas of long members. This method of condensing details to show only the significant points is common practice in architectural drawings since many members are necessarily large, and reducing the scale would only make smaller pieces difficult to show. However, if space permits, the true heights and lengths of important members of a detail are definitely more informative to workers. Break symbols should be resorted to only when limited space prevents drawing the entire detail.

The choice of scale may also be affected by the units in the detail. For example, if concrete block coursing is used, by selecting the $\frac{3}{4}'' = 1'\text{-}0''$ scale, the 8'' coursing can be easily layed out with the $\frac{1}{2}'' = 1'\text{-}0''$ architects' scale.

10.2 Drawing Typical Wall Details

If the construction of a house is identical throughout all the exterior walls, only one wall section may be necessary; if the construction varies, several sections should be drawn. A typical wall section conveniently incorporates the *footing detail*, *sill detail*, and *cornice detail*—all properly in line for relative reference (see Figs. 10-1, 10-2, and 10-3).

To draw a wall section, start with the poured footing (usually twice as wide and the same height as the thickness of the foundation wall) and center the foundation wall directly above. If footing depths vary below grade and if a basement is required, the foundation wall can be drawn with a break symbol, and only a convenient amount of the wall need be shown.

The construction at the top of the foundation, known as the sill detail, is important, and various arrange-

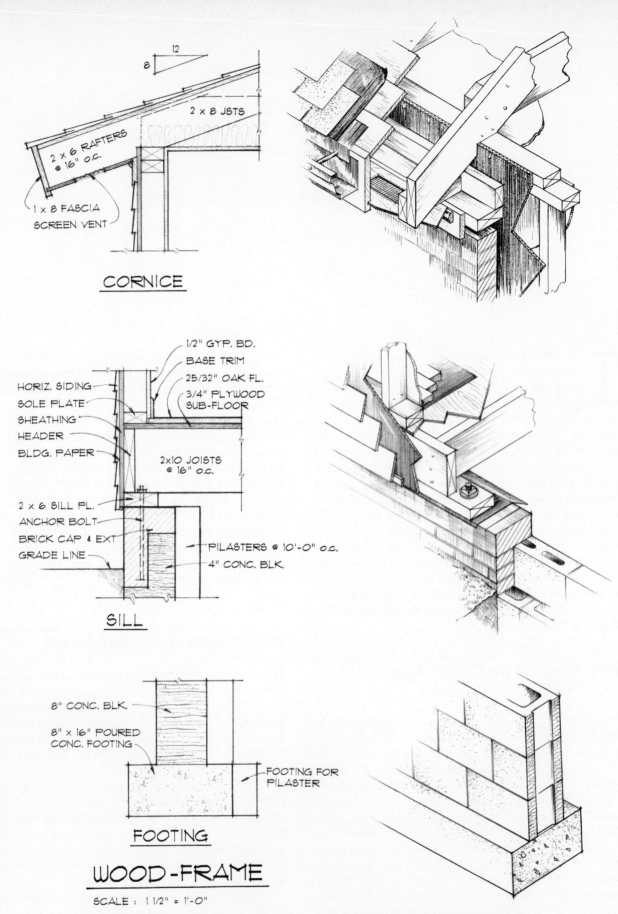

CORNICE

1/2" GYP. BD.
BASE TRIM
25/32" OAK FL.
3/4" PLYWOOD
SUB-FLOOR

HORIZ. SIDING
SOLE PLATE
SHEATHING
HEADER
BLDG. PAPER

2x10 JOISTS
@ 16" o.c.

2 x 6 SILL PL.
ANCHOR BOLT
BRICK CAP & EXT
GRADE LINE

PILASTERS @ 10'-0" o.c.
4" CONC. BLK.

SILL

2 x 6 RAFTERS
@ 16" o.c.

2 x 8 JSTS

1 x 8 FASCIA
SCREEN VENT

8
12

8" CONC. BLK

8" x 16" POURED
CONC. FOOTING

FOOTING FOR
PILASTER

FOOTING

WOOD-FRAME

SCALE : 1 1/2" = 1'-0"

FIGURE 10-1 Typical wall details (the isometric views help to visualize the construction).

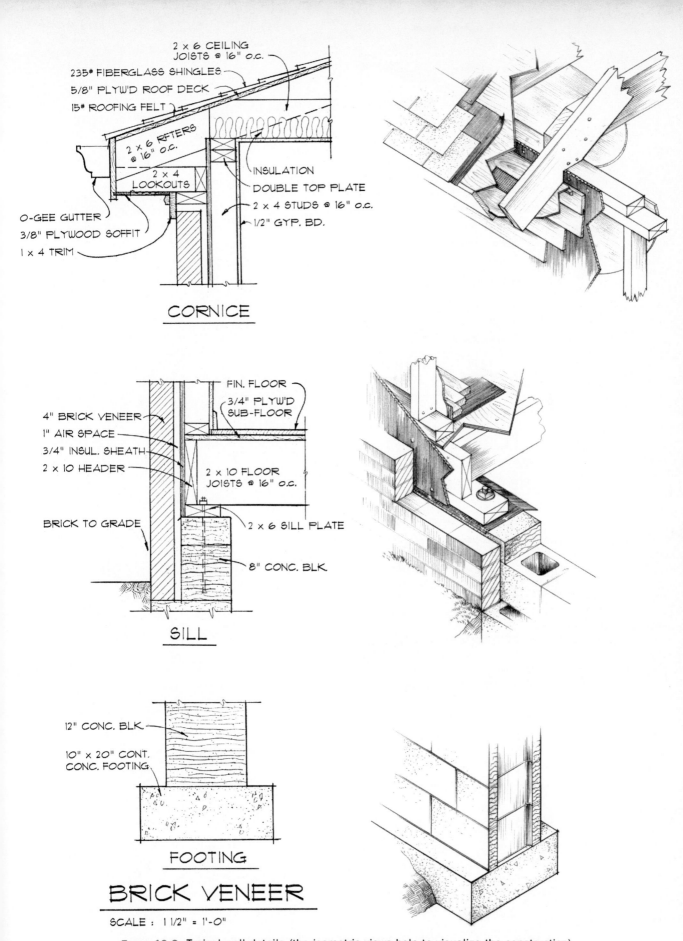

2 x 6 CEILING
JOISTS @ 16" o.c.

235# FIBERGLASS SHINGLES
5/8" PLYW'D ROOF DECK
15# ROOFING FELT

2 x 6 RFTERS
@ 16" O.C.

2 x 4
LOOKOUTS

INSULATION
DOUBLE TOP PLATE
2 x 4 STUDS @ 16" o.c.
1/2" GYP. BD.

O-GEE GUTTER
3/8" PLYWOOD SOFFIT
1 x 4 TRIM

CORNICE

FIN. FLOOR
3/4" PLYW'D
SUB-FLOOR

4" BRICK VENEER
1" AIR SPACE
3/4" INSUL. SHEATH.
2 x 10 HEADER

2 x 10 FLOOR
JOISTS @ 16" o.c.

BRICK TO GRADE

2 x 6 SILL PLATE

8" CONC. BLK.

SILL

12" CONC. BLK.

10" x 20" CONT.
CONC. FOOTING

FOOTING

BRICK VENEER

SCALE : 1 1/2" = 1'-0"

FIGURE 10-2 Typical wall details (the isometric views help to visualize the construction).

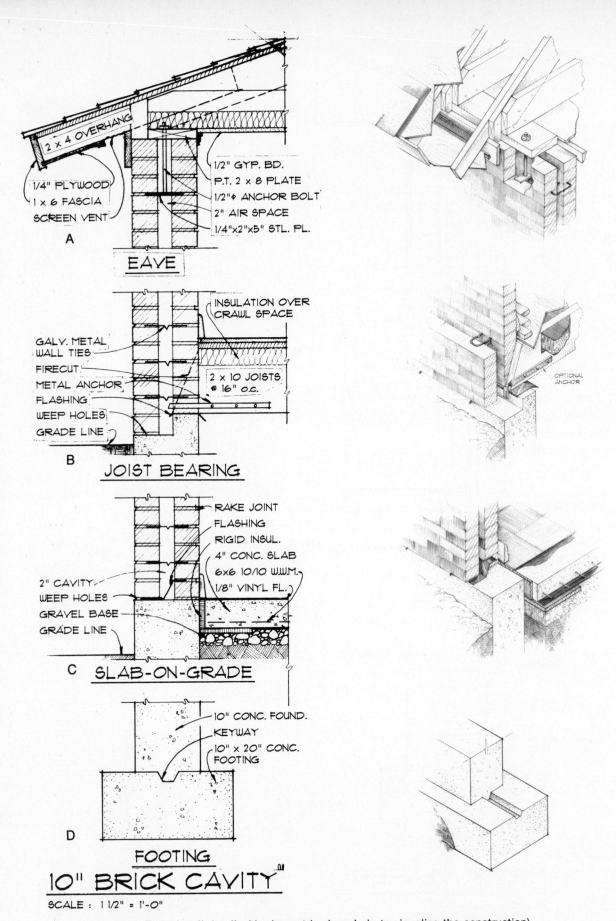

A

2 × 4 OVERHANG

1/4" PLYWOOD
1 × 6 FASCIA
SCREEN VENT

1/2" GYP. BD.
P.T. 2 × 8 PLATE
1/2"⌀ ANCHOR BOLT
2" AIR SPACE
1/4"×2"×5" STL. PL.

EAVE

B

GALV. METAL
WALL TIES
FIRECUT
METAL ANCHOR
FLASHING
WEEP HOLES
GRADE LINE

INSULATION OVER
CRAWL SPACE

2 × 10 JOISTS
@ 16" O.C.

JOIST BEARING

C

2" CAVITY
WEEP HOLES
GRAVEL BASE
GRADE LINE

RAKE JOINT
FLASHING
RIGID INSUL.
4" CONC. SLAB
6×6 10/10 W.W.M.
1/8" VINYL FL.

SLAB-ON-GRADE

D

10" CONC. FOUND.
KEYWAY
10" × 20" CONC.
FOOTING

FOOTING

10" BRICK CAVITY

SCALE : 1 1/2" = 1'-0"

OPTIONAL
ANCHOR

FIGURE 10-3 Typical wall details (the isometric views help to visualize the construction).

ments of the framing members at this point determine the height of the finished floor from grade. If the foundation is concrete masonry units, show the courses and insert an anchor bolt through the sill plate into the C.M.U. Wood members should be kept at least 8″ from grade. If a wood floor over a crawl space has been decided on, allow at least 18″ clearance between floor joists and the grade line. This condition usually places the finished floor at least 28″ or 30″ above grade (unless excavation is done within the foundation). Exterior steps to the floor surface will then be necessary. If a basement is planned, such as in the house of Fig. 11-3, the foundation must extend far enough above grade to meet local codes and to allow installation of basement windows. If slab on ground construction is required, the finish floor level will usually fall about 8″ above the grade level, requiring one step height for entry. Other variations of the sill detail may result in still other floor heights; usually, it is advantageous to keep the house as low as possible. Draw the grade line after the sill is completed. Be sure the wood joists have at least 3″ bearing surface on the sill plate. In western frame construction, the box sill requires the soleplate and studs to be placed over the subfloor.

In brick veneer construction, a better sill detail results if the brick starts at, or just below, grade and the wood plate is raised above the bottom of the veneer and frame air space (see Fig. 10-2B). This prevents moisture, which usually forms at the bottom of the air space during cold weather, from penetrating the wood framing. Otherwise, the wood members are identical to frame construction. Brick rowlock sills (Figs. 10-4F and 10-5) must have flashing below.

In solid masonry construction, several methods can be used to support wood floor joists. A diagonal fire cut can be used at the ends of the floor joists resting within the solid masonry walls (see Fig. 10-4D). Or the masonry wall can be widened to provide bearing for the floor joists.

The cornice detail shows all the construction at the intersection of the walls and the roof, including the roof overhang. In conventional frame construction, both the notched bird's-mouth of the rafters and the ceiling joists bear on the double wall plate, and the joists usually are shown parallel to the rafters. A bird's-mouth cut provides a horizontal bearing surface for the rafters, and because it supports the main weight of the roof, the surface should be a minimum of 3″ wide. **Remember that members in details should be drawn actual size rather than nominal size.**

Extend the rafters to form the overhang (often as much as 2′ on some homes). The overhang can be given various treatments, depending on the decisions made on the design sketches. If a wide, boxed-in cornice seems advisable, draw 2 × 4 horizontal outlookers from the studs to the rafter ends (Fig. 10-2A). Attach soffit material to the underside of the outlookers, and show a screened vent under the eave when applicable. At the ends of the rafters, draw either a vertical or inclined fascia board, making it wide enough to allow about a ¾″ drip below the surface of the soffit material. If a sloping soffit is desirable, the soffit material is attached directly to the underside of the rafter overhang; on other treatments, the rafters can be left exposed on the exterior. Cornice details showing exposed rafters, either in conventional or post and beam construction, must have blocking and exterior wall covering shown between the rafters. This detail must be carefully conceived to produce an airtight joint between the wall and the underside of the roof decking; exterior trim at this point also requires consideration.

Complete the decking, roofing material, gravel stops, gutter, and the like, and include all hatching, notes, and applicable dimensions. Avoid scattering descriptive notes on section views in a disorderly fashion. Plan the notes in a logical sequence, with noncrossing leaders touching the identifying part. Line up the notes on a vertical guide line insofar as possible, and make the spacing between notes uniform when they occur in groups. Keep the notes as close to their counterparts as practical for minimum misinterpretation. Outline the section with *bold lines*. See Fig. 10-6 for cutting plane indications. Roof slopes, as discussed below, should be indicated with a roof slope diagram.

10.3 Indicating Roof Pitches on Drawings

The slope of a roof largely determines the kind of roofing; this in turn influences preliminary planning when pleasing roof lines have been established. Although any slope can be made workable, it is advisable to modify the roof lines of the sketch slightly if necessary so that the working drawings will have roof slopes that are not too difficult to measure. This affects the appearance very little and makes the construction of the roof somewhat simpler (see Fig. 10-7 for typical roof slopes).

Roof slopes or pitches can be shown by any of three methods on drawings:

1. Slope-ratio diagram
2. Fractional pitch indication
3. Angular dimension

The slope-ratio triangle is drawn with its hypotenuse parallel to the roof profile; and its opposite sides, representing the rise and run slope ratio, are drawn vertically and horizontally. The horizontal leg of the triangle is usually measured 1″ long for convenience and given a numerical value of 12. The rise value shown on the vertical leg of the triangle can then be easily measured off on the 1″ = 1′-0″ scale. This ratio of the rise of the roof to its run is stated, for example, as 3:12, 7:12, or 1½:12, making it consistent with conventional refer-

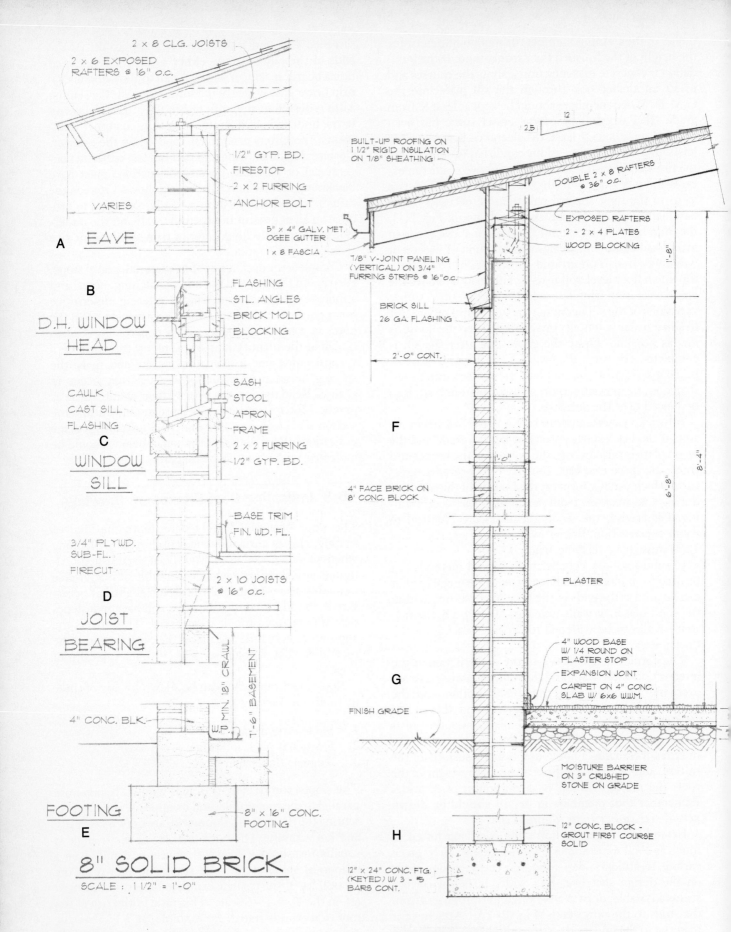

2 x 8 CLG. JOISTS

2 x 6 EXPOSED
RAFTERS @ 16" O.C.

1/2" GYP. BD.

FIRESTOP

2 x 2 FURRING

ANCHOR BOLT

VARIES

A EAVE

5" x 4" GALV. MET.
OGEE GUTTER

1 x 8 FASCIA

B

FLASHING

STL. ANGLES

BRICK MOLD

BLOCKING

D.H. WINDOW
HEAD

CAULK

CAST SILL

FLASHING

SASH

STOOL

APRON

FRAME

2 x 2 FURRING

1/2" GYP. BD.

C

WINDOW
SILL

BASE TRIM

FIN. WD. FL.

3/4" PLYWD.
SUB-FL.

FIRECUT

2 x 10 JOISTS
@ 16" O.C.

D

JOIST
BEARING

4" CONC. BLK.

U.P. MIN. 18" CRAWL

7'-6" BASEMENT

FOOTING

E

8" x 16" CONC.
FOOTING

8" SOLID BRICK

SCALE : 1 1/2" = 1'-0"

BUILT-UP ROOFING ON
1 1/2" RIGID INSULATION
ON 7/8" SHEATHING

2.5 12

DOUBLE 2 x 8 RAFTERS
@ 36" O.C.

EXPOSED RAFTERS

2 - 2 x 4 PLATES

WOOD BLOCKING

1'-8"

7/8" V-JOINT PANELING
(VERTICAL) ON 3/4"
FURRING STRIPS @ 16" O.C.

BRICK SILL
26 GA. FLASHING

2'-0" CONT.

F

4" FACE BRICK ON
8' CONC. BLOCK

1'-0"

8'-4"

6'-8"

PLASTER

4" WOOD BASE
W/ 1/4 ROUND ON
PLASTER STOP

EXPANSION JOINT

CARPET ON 4" CONC.
SLAB W/ 6x6 W.W.M.

G

FINISH GRADE

MOISTURE BARRIER
ON 3" CRUSHED
STONE ON GRADE

H

12" CONC. BLOCK -
GROUT FIRST COURSE
SOLID

12" x 24" CONC. FTG.
(KEYED) W/ 3 - #5
BARS CONT.

BLOCK & BRICK VENEER

SCALE : 1" = 1'-0"

FIGURE 10-4 Typical wall details.

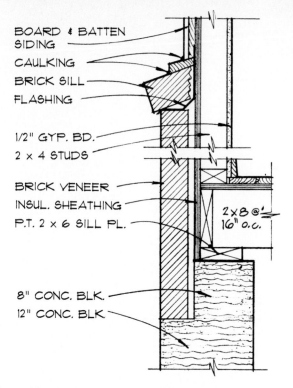

BOARD & BATTEN SIDING
CAULKING
BRICK SILL
FLASHING

1/2" GYP. BD.
2 x 4 STUDS

BRICK VENEER
INSUL. SHEATHING
P.T. 2 x 6 SILL PL.

2 x 8 @ 16" O.C.

8" CONC. BLK.
12" CONC. BLK.

FIGURE 10-5 Wood and brick half-wall detail.

ences associated with roofing materials and other construction applications. In Fig. 10-8 the 4:12 right-triangle symbol means, briefly, that for every 12" of horizontal run the roof rises 4". Most architects use this method for slope indications.

The fractional pitch of a roof is derived from a standard formula:

$$\text{pitch} = \frac{\text{rise}}{\text{span}}$$

The span is the total distance between top-plate supports (twice the run). The pitch of the roof in Fig. 9-8 would be $^4/_{24}$ or $^1/_6$. Fractional pitches are infrequently found on working drawings; yet carpenters have traditionally used fractional pitches for many of their rafter layouts.

Angular slopes are shown with an arc dimension line, revealing the angular dimension in degrees from the horizontal (Fig. 10-7). Its use is limited mainly to minor construction features.

10.4 Windows and Their Representation

Windows provide, first of all, the light and ventilation necessary in dwellings; they are the eyes through which the surrounding landscape can be enjoyed, bringing in the outdoors to make the interior more spacious and less confined. Windows, then, must be carefully selected as to size, type, and placement if they are to provide the desired architectural character to the structure; both practical and esthetic considerations are important in their selection. As a rule, the total window area should be at least 10 percent of the floor space.

Glassed areas can be either preassembled window units or *fixed glass*, which is directly affixed to the framing. The fixed glass allows large window areas to be installed with a minimum of expense, inasmuch as no operating sash, hardware, or screens are necessary. If ventilation is needed, occasional opening sash or panels can be incorporated into window-walls. Today's market offers a wide assortment of preassembled window units; most of them are made of wood, aluminum, or steel. Some wood windows are available with a metal or vinyl cladding, that eliminates the need for painting. Each material has its merits; their choice should be contingent on the specific requirements of the design. Units should be selected for appropriateness, durability, and ease of maintenance. Many units are man-

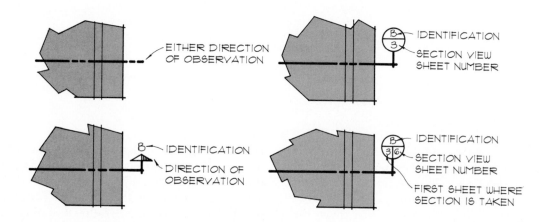

EITHER DIRECTION OF OBSERVATION

IDENTIFICATION
SECTION VIEW
SHEET NUMBER

IDENTIFICATION
DIRECTION OF OBSERVATION

IDENTIFICATION
SECTION VIEW
SHEET NUMBER
FIRST SHEET WHERE SECTION IS TAKEN

FIGURE 10-6 Methods of indicating cutting planes for sections.

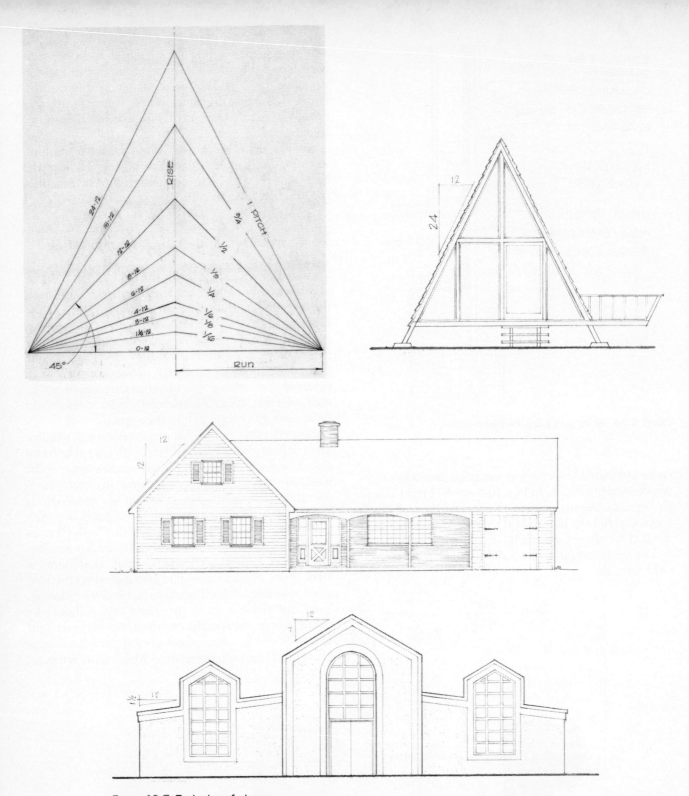

Figure 10-7 Typical roof slopes.

ufactured with insulating (double) glass. This type has the advantage of reducing heat loss (up to 60 percent over single-glass units); in addition, no damaging condensation can form on the inside pane. Tinted glass is also obtainable. Figure 10-9 shows the major types of window units currently used in residential construction.

Double-Hung or vertical-slide windows are the most familiar, having two sashes that operate vertically. A double-hung window allows a maximum of 50 percent ventilation and is typically American. The unit, including the two sash, frame, weather stripping, and hardware, is set into the rough opening, plumbed, and nailed to the double studs and header. Inside trim is

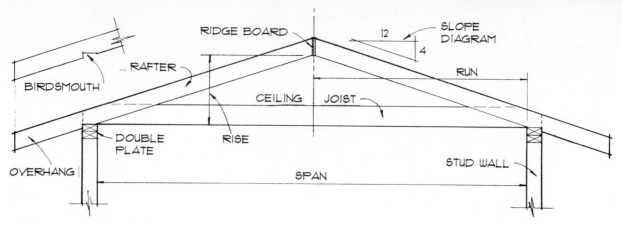

FIGURE 10-8 Roof slope and framing terms.

FIGURE 10-9 Major residential window types: (1) double hung; (2) casement;
(3) horizontal sliding; (4) awning; (5) jalousie; (6) basement; (7) bow or bay;
(8) hopper and fixed; (9) skylight; (10) single hung; (11) arch top; (12) Palladian.

applied after the interior walls are complete. If units are combined into groups, a structural mullion is shown between the units. The sloping sill member rests on the lower member of the rough opening (see Fig. 10-10).

Casement windows have their sash hinged on the side. Most of them open out, but some are available that open in. Casement sash have the advantage of directing breezes into the room when open, and 100 percent

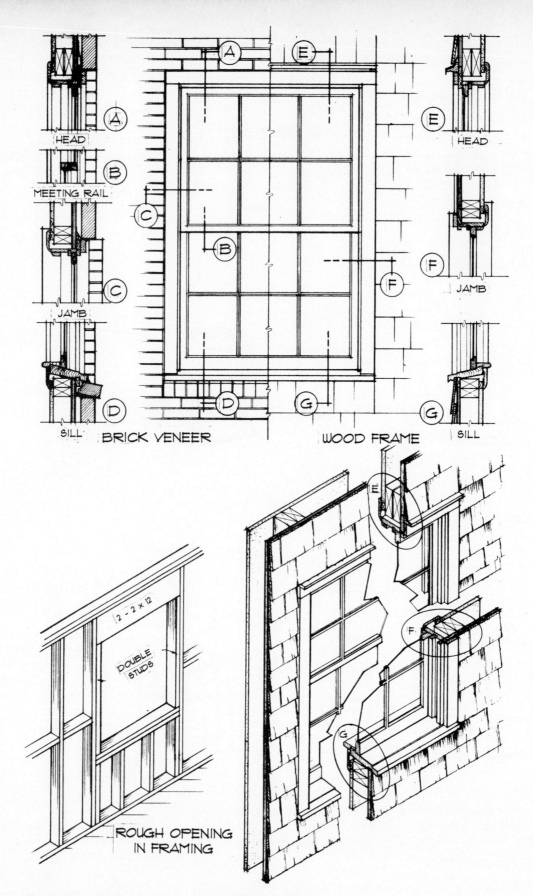

FIGURE 10-10 Typical sections of a double-hung window.

Labels within the figure:

BRICK VENEER
- A HEAD
- B MEETING RAIL
- C JAMB
- D SILL

WOOD FRAME
- E HEAD
- F JAMB
- G SILL

2 - 2 x 12

DOUBLE STUDS

ROUGH OPENING IN FRAMING

ventilation is possible. Operating cranks open and close the sash.

Horizontal Sliding windows operate horizontally like sliding doors. Horizontal slide windows, like double-hung windows, allow only 50 percent ventilation when open. Units are often combined with fixed picture-window sash.

Awning windows open out horizontally, with the hinges of each sash at the top and the cranking hardware operating all the sash in each unit simultaneously. Their major advantage is that they can be left open during rain without adverse effects. Dust collects on the opened windows readily, however.

Jalousie window units have small, horizontal glass panels that operate horizontally, much like awning sash. The individual glass panels do not have frames. The advantages are similar to those of awning windows, except that jalousie windows are seldom as weathertight when closed. Therefore, they should be reserved mainly for glass-enclosed porches or for residences in warmer climates.

Hopper windows have small sash, opening either in or out, which are combined with larger fixed windows. The complete unit is set into the rough opening like other window units.

Palladian windows are a comparitively recent adaptation from the 16th-century Italian architect, Andrea Pallidio. They are tall, semi-circular center windows combined with straight-headed side windows, which have become popular in many American homes within the last twenty years (See Fig . . . .). Often classical pilasters and heads are trimmed out in the interior to form very elegant windows, especially in rooms with high ceilings.

The Palladian window should be carefully proportioned to compliment the other windows and features, they must be properly placed without crowding other elements and spaces, and should be used sparingly to avoid dominating the main architectural features. Usually small lights within the combined units are most pleasing.

The windows are generally used to provide added light to large rooms with high ceilings, as we mentioned, and often to illuminate stairways where a focal point might contribute style to the exterior. Manufacturers frequently refer to the arched windows as "cathedral windows". Stock windows properly sized can be combined using a larger central unit and semi-circular head and two smaller side windows to form very satisfactory combinations.

Skylights are actually roof windows that can be placed over openings in roofs of little or no slope and sealed into the roofing material. Residential skylights are usually bubble-shaped plastic units with flanges or sealing rims around the base (see Fig. 10-9). Small skylights are convenient for giving natural light to interior hallways or windowless bathrooms. However, in warm climates the direct glare of the sun through a skylight can be troublesome unless some manner of light control is provided. Caution should be exercised in the use of skylights on roofs.

Clerestory windows are so named because of their placement—usually high in a wall above a lower roof level. They are often a series of small windows; their height affords privacy and permits them to cast dramatic light effects within the room.

Picture Windows so called because usually no muntins interfere with the framed view, are fixed-glass units (as a rule rather large), which often become the center unit of several regular windows.

Study the many manufacturers' catalogues for more detailed information of various windows and observe the recommended method of attaching each in different wall openings (see Fig. 10-11). Notice that window sizes and the *rough-opening* sizes are given in the literature. This information is important to the builders. Rough opening means the width and height of the framed opening that receives the window unit. In Fig. 10-10, note the method of framing window openings in wood frame construction. As mentioned previously, the units are supported by the wood framing, and the section views reveal the relationship of the unit to the framing, how they are attached, and what trim is necessary for completion. These details should be shown on working drawings for proper installation of the windows.

To better understand the details of a double-hung window, observe the cutting planes shown on the elevation view of Fig. 10-10. The head, jamb, and sill sections to the left of the elevation clearly explain these important points in the construction. A meeting rail section is also shown merely to familiarize you with the relationship of the two sashes. Note that, for more information, the right side of the elevation appears to be in a brick veneer wall, and the same sections to the right show typical construction around the double-hung window in brick veneer construction. The isometric view in Fig. 10-10 describes the pictorial representations of the same head, jamb, and sill sections in wood frame. Study these details carefully. Similar sections of a metal window are shown in Fig. 10-12. Details of windows vary with different manufacturers; therefore, after window selections have been made, details of the windows must be taken from the manufacturers' catalogues.

To draw a window detail, first establish the wood

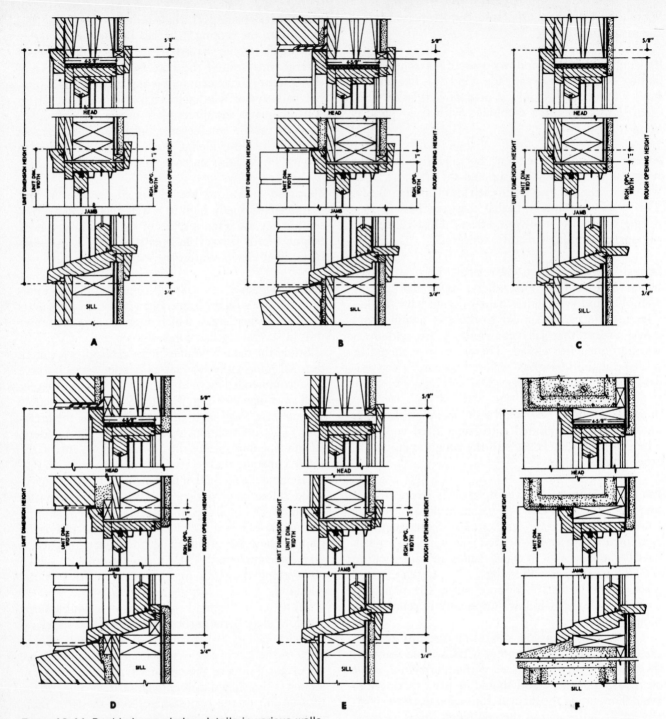

FIGURE 10-11 Double-hung window details in various walls.

frame members, or the rough openings of masonry if the window is to go into solid masonry. Use large scales such as $3'' = 1'\text{-}0''$ or $1\frac{1}{2}'' = 1'\text{-}0''$ if small members are present in the section. Then draw the sheathing and inside wall covering. Next locate the window frame in relation to the rough-opening surface, and complete the sash, trim, and exterior wall covering. Use the conventional break symbol so that only the necessary amount of detail need be drawn. Be sure that the structural members line up vertically and that the head section is drawn at the top, the jamb in the center, and the sill section at the bottom.

10.5 Doors and Their Representation

Because of their economy and the wide assortment of available sizes, stock doors are universally used in resi-

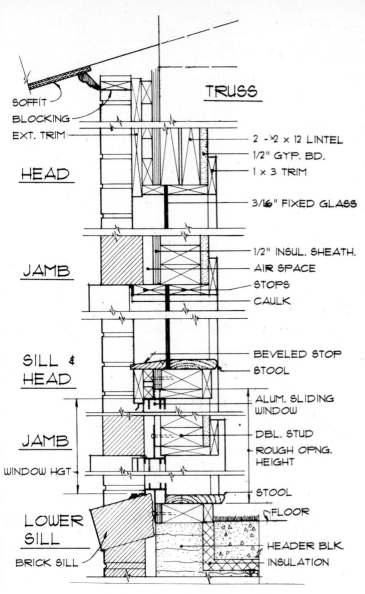

SOFFIT
BLOCKING
EXT. TRIM

TRUSS

HEAD

2 - 2 × 12 LINTEL
1/2" GYP. BD.
1 × 3 TRIM
3/16" FIXED GLASS

JAMB

1/2" INSUL. SHEATH.
AIR SPACE
STOPS
CAULK

SILL &
HEAD

BEVELED STOP
STOOL

ALUM. SLIDING
WINDOW

JAMB

DBL. STUD
ROUGH OPNG.
HEIGHT

WINDOW HGT

STOOL
FLOOR

LOWER
SILL

BRICK SILL

HEADER BLK.
INSULATION

FIGURE 10-12 Fixed-glass and metal window detail.

dential and light construction. Two major types are manufactured: flush and panel (see Fig. 10-13).

Flush Doors are built of solid-wood stiles and rails with various wood veneering glued to both sides, producing smooth, easy to paint surfaces. This type is popular in contemporary architecture because of its clean-cut appearance and easy to maintain features. Various shaped lights can be introduced to flush doors for lighting dark entrances, and decorative moldings can be applied directly to the veneered surfaces for style treatments. Flush doors can be subdivided into two types: *hollow core* and *solid core*. The hollow core have grillage-filled cavities, making them lighter and ideal for interior use. The solid core have their cavities filled with wood blocking or other dense materials, making them heavier and more appropriate for exterior en-

trances. The heavier construction reduces warping during extreme temperature differences between inside and outside. Many decorative wood grain veneers are available on flush doors to match natural wood interior wall coverings. See Fig. 10-14 for typical sizes.

Panel Doors, manufactured in a wide variety of styles, are generally made of ponderosa pine or Douglas fir. Various arrangements of the panels and lights are surrounded with stiles and rails, usually of solid wood, to produce handsome and sturdy doors. Panel doors have been used for many years in American homes. Some panel doors are manufactured with glue and veneer stiles and rails. They are sometimes preferred for exterior installation. For colonial and traditional homes, panel doors are the most authentic in character. Elaborate panel door and frame units are available for classic entrances (Fig. 10-15). Variations of the panel door include the following styles.

French Doors have glazed lights separated with muntins throughout, rather than panels. When additional light is needed, or a view is desired between rooms, these doors find application, especially in traditional homes. Often they are used in pairs with an astragal molding between.

Dutch Doors, also typical of some colonial styles, are cut in half horizontally, and each half operates on its own set of hinges. The bottom half can act as a gate while the top remains open.

Louver Doors, which have horizontal strips placed on the diagonal for vents instead of panels, are attractive in both traditional and contemporary settings. They are excellent for closet doors, because of their venting characteristics, but are time consuming to paint.

Jalousie Doors, usually suitable for enclosed porches or exterior doors in warmer climates, have operating glass panel units inserted within the stiles and rails.

10.5.1 Wood Stock Door Sizes

Both flush and panel doors are available in $1\frac{3}{8}''$, $1\frac{3}{4}''$, and $2\frac{1}{4}''$ stock thicknesses. Stock heights are 6'-8" and 7'-0"; narrow doors can be obtained in 6'-6" heights. Widths are available in 2" increments, from 1'-6" to 3'-0"; a few styles are made in 4'-0" widths. See Fig. 10-14 for the conventional door widths applicable to residential construction.

10.5.2 Folding- or Sliding-Door Units

With the increase in private outdoor living areas, large sliding glass doors have found widespread acceptance.

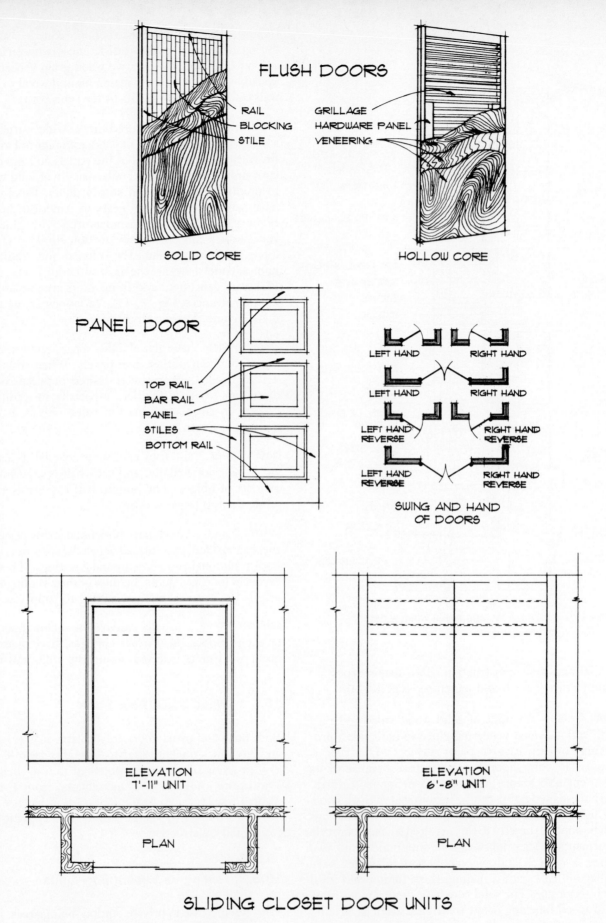

FLUSH DOORS

RAIL
BLOCKING
STILE

GRILLAGE
HARDWARE PANEL
VENEERING

SOLID CORE

HOLLOW CORE

PANEL DOOR

TOP RAIL
BAR RAIL
PANEL
STILES
BOTTOM RAIL

LEFT HAND
RIGHT HAND
LEFT HAND
RIGHT HAND
LEFT HAND REVERSE
RIGHT HAND REVERSE
LEFT HAND REVERSE
RIGHT HAND REVERSE

SWING AND HAND
OF DOORS

ELEVATION
7'-11" UNIT

ELEVATION
6'-8" UNIT

PLAN

PLAN

SLIDING CLOSET DOOR UNITS

FIGURE 10-13 Doors and their representation.

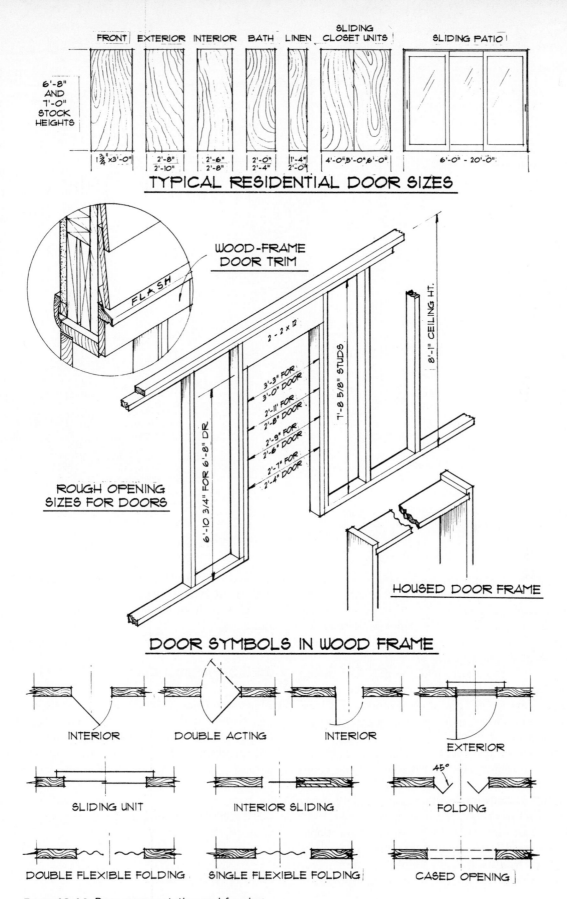

TYPICAL RESIDENTIAL DOOR SIZES

WOOD-FRAME DOOR TRIM

ROUGH OPENING SIZES FOR DOORS

HOUSED DOOR FRAME

DOOR SYMBOLS IN WOOD FRAME

INTERIOR   DOUBLE ACTING   INTERIOR   EXTERIOR

SLIDING UNIT   INTERIOR SLIDING   FOLDING

DOUBLE FLEXIBLE FOLDING   SINGLE FLEXIBLE FOLDING   CASED OPENING

FIGURE 10-14 Door representation and framing.

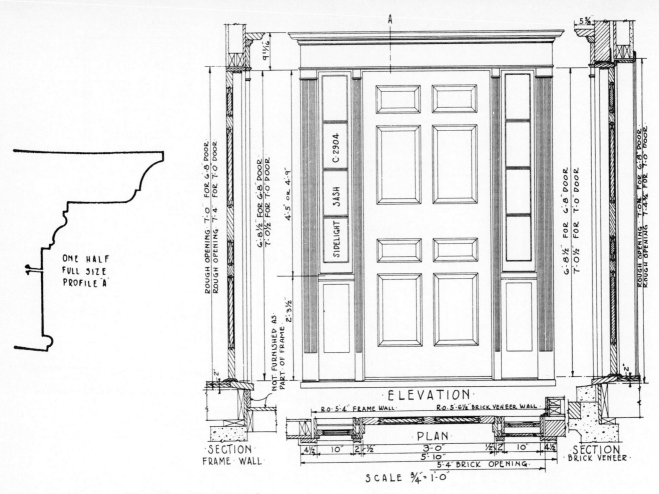

ONE HALF
FULL SIZE
PROFILE A

FIGURE 10-15 Details of a traditional entrance door.

Sliding units are manufactured of aluminum, steel, or wood (see Fig. 10-16). Stock heights are usually 6'-10", and unit widths, ranging from 6'-0" to 20'-0", utilize various sliding and fixed-glass panel arrangements. Like other component sizing indications, door unit widths are given first, such as 8'-0" × 6'-10" or 12'-0" × 6'-10". Exact sizes and specifications should be taken from manufacturers' literature. Because of serious accidents involving large glass doors, many local codes require either tempered glass or protection bars across the doors.

For interior use, many types of folding- and sliding-door units are appropriate for closet doors and room dividers. Stock sizes conform to the 6'-8", 7'-0", and 8'-0" heights, and custom-built units are available from some manufacturers for special situations. The 8'-0" high closet door units (Fig. 10-13) allow an additional amount of accessible storage space in a closet in comparison to lower heights and are highly recommended. Their use reduces the amount of framing around the door as well.

Accordion doors, available in 6'-8" and 8'-0" stock heights and in widths ranging from 2'-4" to 8'-2", are made of flexible plastic material and require little space at the jambs when open. Distinctive wood folding doors are also made of various wood panels. Sliding closet units come in 3', 4', 5', and 6' widths.

10.5.3 Fireproof Doors

Flush wood doors filled with heat-resisting materials and treated with fire-resisting chemicals (1-hour fire rating) are available for light construction. Some codes require fireproof doors between the house and attached garages. Many types of metal doors having hollow, grillage-filled, or wood cores are manufactured mainly for commercial and industrial application and are labeled according to the amount of time of fire resistance: C = $3/4$, B = $1\frac{1}{2}$, A = 2 hours.

10.5.4 Doorframes

Exterior wood doorframes usually are made and assembled at the mill and delivered to the site, ready for

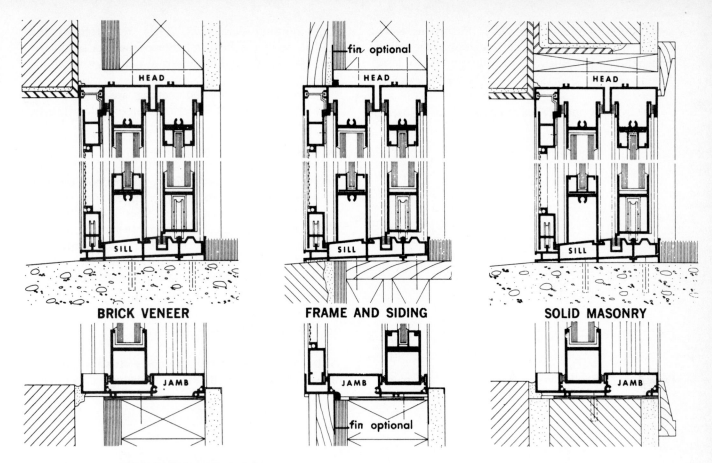

BRICK VENEER FRAME AND SIDING SOLID MASONRY

Stock Sizes and Types

Door Types Viewed from exterior		Door Sizes Width	Height	Stock Numbers	Glass Sizes Width only All heights 76¾″	Rough Openings All heights 6′–10½″
▶ XO		5′–11″	6′–10″	G2- 6	33″	5′–11½″
		7′–11″	6′–10″	G2- 8	45″	7′–11½″
		9′–11″	6′–10″	G2-10	57″	9′–11½″
◀ OX		5′–11″	6′–10″	G2- 6	33″	5′–11½″
		7′–11″	6′–10″	G2- 8	45″	7′–11½″
		9′–11″	6′–10″	G2-10	57″	9′–11½″
▶ OXO		8′–10¼″	6′–10″	G3- 9	33″	8′–10¾″
		11′–10¼″	6′–10″	G3-12	45″	11′–10¾″
		14′–10¼″	6′–10″	G3-15	57″	14′–10¾″
◀ ▶ OXXO		11′- 8⅞″	6′–10″	G4-12	33″	11′- 9⅜″
		15′- 8⅞″	6′–10″	G4-16	45″	15′- 9⅜″
		19′- 8⅞″	6′–10″	G4-20	57″	19′- 9⅜″

FIGURE 10-16 Aluminum sliding glass door details.

installation into the rough openings. In wood frame floor construction, the header joist and subflooring below an entrance must be cut out slightly to receive the sloping sill member of a doorframe (Fig. 10-15). Frames must be heavy enough to carry the weight of the doors and to take the strain of door closures. Generally, exterior frames are 1¹/₁₆″ thick, and the sill member is made of hardwood to resist wear. Heavy doors may require thicker jamb members. A planted threshold of either hardwood or metal is necessary to hide the joint between the sill and the finished floor below entrance doors.

Interior doorframes are purchased in sets and usually assembled on the job. Usually 1″ or 1⅛″ thick lumber is satisfactory for interior use. Other dimensions depend on the size of the door and the thickness of the walls in which they are installed. To provide simple door installation, planted doorstops are preferred on interior frames.

Metal doorframes, called *door bucks*, are being used by some housing developers. They are prefitted and drilled, ready for the installation of the door hardware. Both wood and metal frames are available with prehung doors.

Representations of cased openings are shown in Fig. 10-17. See Fig. 10-18 for various entrance doorframes.

10.5.5 Overhead Garage Doors

Because of their size and weight, garage doors must be operated with counterbalances or springs on overhead tracks. Stock sizes range from $8'-0'' \times 7'-0''$ to $9'-0'' \times 7'-0''$ for single garage widths; double garage openings require a $16'-0'' \times 7'-0''$ door size. Their symbol on plans is merely a line through the opening, accompanied by a dimensional note and the manufacturer's number.

10.5.6 Drawing Door Details

Although accurate details of door sections are seldom shown on working drawings involving conventional

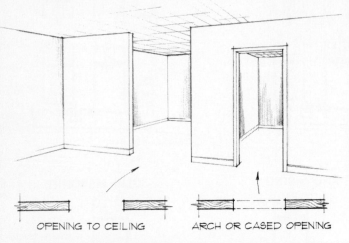

OPENING TO CEILING   ARCH OR CASED OPENING

FIGURE 10-17 Variation in wall-opening symbols on plans.

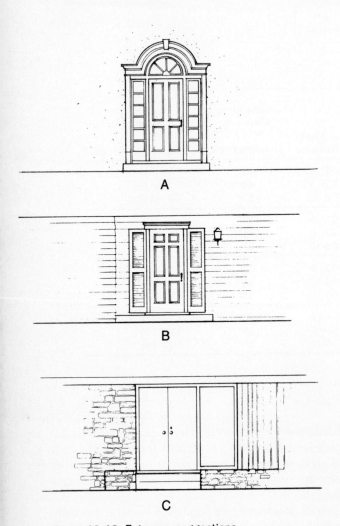

A

B

C

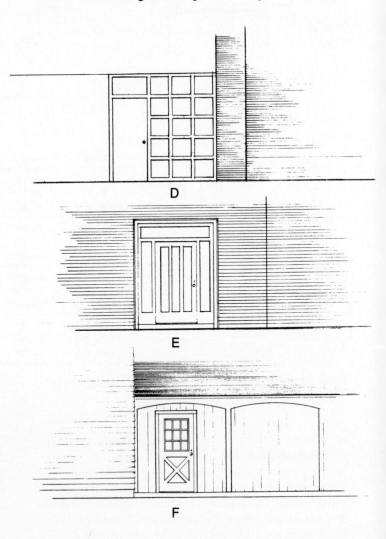

D

E

F

FIGURE 10-18 Entrance suggestions.

construction, the drafter must choose the size, type, and style to best fit the situation. If doors are incorporated into special framing or if they are placed in walls of different construction, section views of the jambs and the surrounding construction, as well as the trim, must be drawn. To show the proper installation methods in various types of walls, several door details are included in this material (also refer to Fig. 9-32).

In Fig. 10-15 note that the cutting planes on the door elevation indicate sections similar to window details, described previously. Section A reveals the construction through the head jamb and sill, and the plan section reveals the construction through the side jambs. The sections are placed in a position for convenient projection, as well as for analyzing the relationships of the members. In drawing the sections, start by laying out the frame walls, then the wall coverings, and finally the doorjambs and surrounding trim. In solid masonry construction, the masonry outlines are drawn first; then the jambs and trim are added. Steel angles or reinforced concrete lintels must be used to support the weight of the masonry above the door opening and must be shown on the head section.

10.6 Fireplace Design and Details

For centuries, fireplaces were the only method of heating homes; and even with our modern fuels and central heating systems, the fireplace is still as popular as ever because we have not found a substitute for the sheer fascination of an open fire, which provides warmth and a peaceful gathering place in the home.

Because the old-time fireplace mason, who knew by experience the necessary dimensional requirements of successful fireplaces, is slowly disappearing, complete working drawings of fireplaces must be included in plans to ensure their correct construction. If an honest house is to be built, the fireplace must be honest as well and must be designed to be workable.

Residential fireplaces of various forms and styles are being constructed. Some are merely openings in massive interior masonry walls, with no mantel or other decor other than the texture of the masonry. Some have provision for log storage near the opening; others may have outdoor barbecue grills incorporated into the chimneys. Many are masonry walls with metal hoods above to concentrate the draft and carry off hot gases and smoke. For general purposes, fireplaces can be divided into the following groups:

1. Single-face fireplaces (conventional)
   a. Wall
   b. Corner
   c. Back to back
2. Multiple-face fireplaces (contemporary)
   a. Two adjacent faces (corner)
   b. Two opposite faces (through opening)
   c. Three faces, 2 long, 1 short
   d. Three faces, 1 long, 2 short
   e. Hooded
   f. Freestanding

The successful operation of a fireplace depends on its construction. Even special fireplaces, which incorporate various shapes and materials, can be made workable if the basic principles of fireplace design are followed, instead of resorting to chance or mere luck. Here are the critical points in single-face fireplace design and construction.

10.6.1 Size of Fireplace Opening

Not only should the fireplace be given a prominent position in a room, away from major travel routes, but the fireplace opening should be in keeping with the room size. Small rooms should have small fireplace openings; large rooms, large ones. The opening should have pleasing proportions; a rectangle is more desirable than a square; the width should exceed the height. A fireplace width of, for instance, 28″ to 36″ would be adequate for a room of 250 square foot floor space. In Fig. 10-19, notice some of the more common opening sizes. A raised hearth, usually 16″ above the floor, brings the opening nearer to eye level and often makes the fireplace appear larger. Keep wood trim at least 8″ from the opening and use a steel angle-iron lintel to support the masonry above the opening.

Figure 10-19 shows that fireplace openings have relative proportions of height, width, and depth; however, minor variations may be made to meet the various masonry courses and other restrictions of layout. The size of the opening becomes the starting feature in the design of a fireplace.

10.6.2 Flue Size and Chimney Height

Each fireplace in a building should have an independent flue, unconnected to other vents or flues, and it must start on the center line of the fireplace opening. A chimney can take care of a number of fireplaces, and each flue must continue to the top with as little offset as necessary. Each flue must be large enough in cross-sectional area to create the proper draft through the fireplace opening. Unless the sectional flue area is at least one-tenth of the fireplace opening area (rule of thumb), a troublesome condition may result (see the table that accompanies Fig. 10-20 for exact sizes). Chimney heights under 14′ may even require larger flue sizes, as the height of the chimney, surrounding buildings, and prevailing winds affect flue velocities. The higher the chimney, the more draft velocity. For

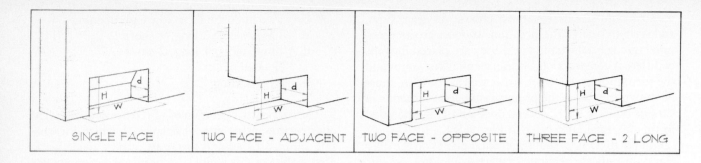

| SINGLE FACE | TWO FACE - ADJACENT | TWO FACE - OPPOSITE | THREE FACE - 2 LONG |

FIREPLACE DIMENSIONS

Fireplace Type	Opening Height h, in.	Hearth Size w by d, in.	Modular Flue Size, in.
Single Face	29	30 × 16	12 × 12
	29	36 × 16	12 × 12
	29	40 × 16	12 × 16
	32	48 × 18	16 × 16
Two Face— adjacent	26	32 × 16	12 × 16
	29	40 × 16	16 × 16
	29	48 × 20	16 × 16
Two Face— opposite	29	32 × 28	16 × 16
	29	36 × 28	16 × 20
	29	40 × 28	16 × 20
Three Face— 2 long, 1 short	27	36 × 32	20 × 20
	27	36 × 36	20 × 20
	27	44 × 40	20 × 20

FIGURE 10-19 Typical fireplace openings and workable dimensions.

fire protection of the roofing materials, the height of the chimney should be at least 2' above the highest point of the roof. Flue sizes are important and therefore should be clearly indicated on the drawings; a flue too large is better than one too small. Vitrified clay flue linings are used to resist high chimney temperatures and to provide smooth flue interiors. Without the lining, cracks tend to develop in the chimney walls. Round linings operate more efficiently, but rectangular types can be more easily fitted into chimney spaces.

10.6.3 Shape of Combustion Chamber

The combustion chamber (Fig. 10-20) is lined with 4" thick firebrick set in fireclay. It is shaped not only to reflect heat into the room, but to lead hot gases into the throat with increased velocity. If the fireplace is too deep, less heat will be radiated into the room. The sections in Fig. 10-20 indicate the conventional shape of combustion chamber walls. The back and end walls should be at least 8" thick. Slight variations are permissible in the layout of the chamber, but long experience has shown that the conventional shapes and proportions are the most satisfactory, as far as operation is concerned.

10.6.4 Design of the Throat

The throat offsets the draft above the chamber, and if a metal damper is used, the door of the damper acts as a valve for checking downdrafts while the fireplace is in operation. The inclusion of a damper is a convenient method of preventing heat loss and outside drafts when the fireplace is not in use. Notice that the door of the damper hinges so that it opens toward the back of the fireplace. The opening of either the damper or the throat should be larger than the area of the flue lining. Also, the damper should be the same length as the width of the fireplace and be placed at least 6" (preferably 8") above the top of the fireplace opening. Both steel and cast iron dampers are available; check manufacturers' catalogues for types and sizes.

10.6.5 Shape of the Smoke Shelf and Smoke Dome

The location of the damper establishes the height of the smoke shelf, which is directly under the flue and which stops downdrafts with its horizontal surface. The smoke dome is the area just above the shelf. Notice that the back wall is built vertically; the only offset on the back is a corbeled brick course that supports the flue lining, where a corbeled brick course is also shown for flue support. Usually, the sloping walls are represented with lines drawn 60° from the horizontal.

10.6.6 Support for the Hearth

The hearth is best supported with a reinforced concrete slab resting on the walls of the fireplace foundation and extending in front at least 18". (Previously, a brick trimmer arch was used to support the forward hearth against the chimney foundation in conventional construction.) Number 3 reinforcing rods are placed near the upper part of the slab, and brick, stone, or other masonry material is applied directly on the slab for a textured hearth covering. If an ash dump is feasible and accessible to a basement ash pit or outdoor cleanout door, the reinforced slab may simply be formed with ribbed metal lath having a hole cut for the ash dump and

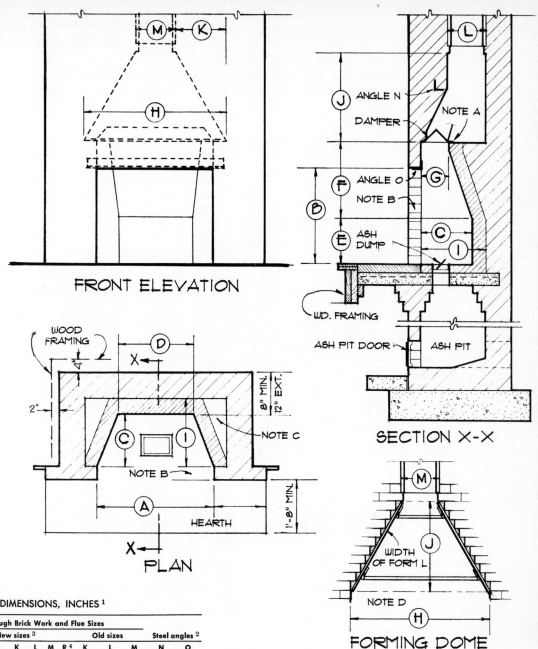

FRONT ELEVATION

PLAN

SECTION X-X

FORMING DOME

FIREPLACE DIMENSIONS, INCHES [1]

							Rough Brick Work and Flue Sizes												
Finished Fireplace Opening							**New sizes** [3]							**Old sizes**			**Steel angles** [2]	
A	B	C	D	E	F	G	H	I	J	K	L	M	R [4]	K	L	M		N	O
24	24	16	11	14	18	8¾	32	20	19	10	8×12	8		11¾	8½×	8½		A-36	A-36
26	24	16	13	14	18	8¾	34	20	21	11	8×12	8		12¾	8½×	8½		A-36	A-36
28	24	16	15	14	18	8¾	36	20	21	12	8×12	10		11½	8½×	13		A-36	A-36
30	29	16	17	14	23	8¾	38	20	24	13	12×12	10		12½	8½×	13		A-42	A-36
32	29	16	19	14	23	8¾	40	20	24	14	12×12	10		13½	8½×	13		A-42	A-42
36	29	16	23	14	23	8¾	44	20	27	16	12×12	12		15½	13	×13		A-48	A-42
40	29	16	27	14	23	8¾	48	20	29	16	12×16	12		17½	13	×13		A-48	A-48
42	32	16	29	14	26	8¾	50	20	32	17	16×16	12		18½	13	×13		B-54	A-48
48	32	18	33	14	26	8¾	56	22	37	20	16×16	15		21½	13	×13		B-60	B-54
54	37	20	37	16	29	13	68	24	45	26	16×16	15		25	13	×18		B-72	B-60
60	37	22	42	16	29	13	72	27	45	26	16×20	15		27	13	×18		B-72	B-66
60	40	22	42	16	31	13	72	27	45	26	16×20	18		27	18	×18		B-72	B-66
72	40	22	54	16	31	13	84	27	56	32	20×20	18		33	18	×18		C-84	C-84
84	40	24	64	20	28	13	96	29	61	36	20×24	20		36	20	×20		C-96	C-96
96	40	24	76	20	28	13	108	29	75	42	20×24	22		42	24	×24		C-108	C-108

[1] See Fig. 10-20.
[2] Angle sizes: A. 3″ x 3″ x 3/16″; B. 3½″ x 3″ x ¼″; C. 5″ x 3½″ x 5/16″.
[3] New flue sizes: Conform to modular dimensional system. Sizes shown are nominal. Actual size is ½″ less each dimension.
[4] Round flues.

Note A. The back flange of the damper must be protected from intense heat by being fully supported by the masonry. At the same time, the damper should not be built in solidly at the ends, but given freedom to expand with heat.

Note B. The thickness of the fireplace front will vary with the material used: brick, marble, stone, tile, etc.

Note C. The hollow, triangular spaces behind the splayed sides of the inner brickwork should be filled to afford solid backing. If desired to locate a flue in either space, the outside dimensions of the rough brickwork should be increased.

Note D. A good way to build a smoke chamber is to erect a wooden form consisting of two sloping boards at the sides, held apart by spreaders at the top and bottom. Spreaders are nailed upward into cleats. The form boards should have the same width as the flue lining.

FIGURE 10-20 Successful fireplace construction. (*Courtesy Donley Bros. Co.*)

any upcoming flues; the concrete is poured over the lath.

In homes with slab floors the fireplace and the hearth are built up from an isolated footing to the floor level. For easy cleaning, the fireplace floor can be made 1″ higher than the outer hearth.

10.6.7 Wood Framing Precautions Around the Fireplace and Chimney

Precautions must be taken when fireplaces or their chimneys pass through wood frame floors, roofs, and the like. Fire codes prohibit direct contact between

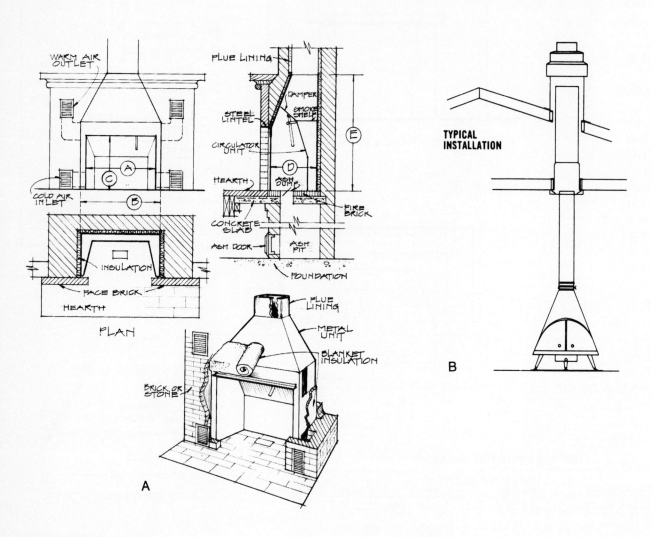

Steel Fireplace Units

| Vestal Model No. | Unit Dimensions in Inches | | | | | Chimney Flue Sizes | | | | | |
| | | | | | | Under 20' High from Hearth | | | Over 20' High from Hearth | | |
	A	B	C	D	E	Std. Flue	Modular Flue	Round Flue	Std. Flue	Modular Flue	Round Flue
30	30	34	25	18½	46¼	8½″ × 13″	12″ × 12″	10″ D.	8½″ × 13″	12″ × 12″	10″ D.
34	34	38	27	19¾	49¾	8½″ × 13″	12″ × 12″	10″ D.	13″ × 13″	12″ × 16″	12″ D.
38	38	42	29¼	21¼	53¾	13″ × 13″	12″ × 16″	12″ D.	13″ × 13″	12″ × 16″	12″ D.
42	42	47	32	23¼	58¼	13″ × 13″	12″ × 16″	12″ D.	13″ × 18″	16″ × 16″	15″ D.
50	50	56	34	25¼	62¾	13″ × 18″	16″ × 16″	15″ D.	13″ × 18″	16″ × 20″	15″ D.

From Vestal Manufacturing Co.

FIGURE 10-21 (A) Prefabricated metal circulating fireplaces. (B) Freestanding metal fireplace unit and flue.

framing members and chimney surfaces (see Fig. 10-20). Usually a 2″ air space is provided between the masonry and wood; this space is filled with incombustible insulating material. Trimmers and headers around wood openings are doubled to give support to the cut joists or rafters, and the subflooring or decking is applied closer to the masonry. The hearth slab, which is independent of the wood framing, usually has its outer edge resting on a ledger strip fastened to the headers or floor joists.

10.6.8 Steel Fireplace Boxes

Prefabricated, one-piece, steel fireboxes are available (see Fig. 10-21 and *Sweet's Architectural Catalog File*) that combine the combustion chamber, smoke dome, and even a steel lintel for the masonry opening. The firebox is merely set on a masonry hearth, and the brick or stone enclosure is built up around it, thus eliminating any necessity for fireplace design other than the correct flue size. Because they are hollow, the fireboxes can utilize warm and cold air ducts and vents to improve heating efficiency. After the desired openings have been determined, correct catalogue numbers can be established.

10.6.9 Special Fireplaces

Special fireplaces include variations of the multifaced and hooded types, often referred to as "contemporary." Because of their unusually large openings and their complexity of shapes, special fireplaces occasionally cause smoking in the room and have poor draw through their throats. Generally, if these fireplaces operate poorly, the flue is too small, the damper throat is too narrow, the chimney height is too low, or possibly nearby buildings or trees prevent proper draft through the flues. Also, fireplaces with the sides of the combustion chamber exposed so as to allow room drafts to pass directly through, such as freestanding or open-back fireplaces, will tend to allow smoke into the room unless room drafts are prevented or glass sides are installed. Special metal smoke dome and damper boxes are available to improve multiface fireplace operation (see *Sweet's File*). Hooded fireplaces require heat-resisting insulation below the metal hoods.

Freestanding, complete fireplace units are sold that require no masonry enclosures nor a masonry chimney. The units, complete with chimney and hearth, can be installed in existing structures.

In drawing special fireplace details, design data can be taken from the fireplace dimensions table and the accompanying drawings (Fig. 10-20); further information can be found in Ramsey and Sleeper's *Architectural Graphic Standards*. But the best source for information about special fireplaces, as well as the equipment needed for regular fireplaces, is from manufacturers' catalogues and literature. See Fig. 10-22 for chimney heights.

10.7 Stair Design and Layout

Let us now consider the problems encountered in stair construction. A flight of stairs is part of the system of

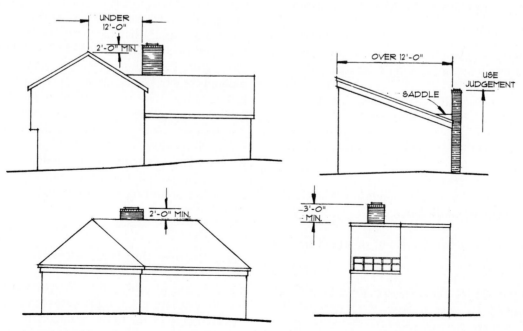

Figure 10-22 Chimney heights.

hallways communicating between the occupied floor levels of a building. In multistory buildings, the stairs, both interior and exterior, must be given careful consideration in the total design. Main stairways in homes, as well as in public buildings, have long been objects of special ornament by architects. Many beautiful staircases are evident in scores of buildings throughout the country. The present trend, however, is toward simplicity and comfort in residential stairs, although dramatic stairways are occasionally found in contemporary public buildings.

STAIR TERMINOLOGY

Stairs have their own terminology in construction work; the following terms are commonly encountered:

BALUSTERS the thin vertical supports for the handrail of open stairs.

BULLNOSE the first step on an open stair, which has been extended out forming a semicircle and often receiving the newel post.

CARRIAGE the rough structural support (usually 2″ × 12″) for treads and for risers of wood stairs, sometimes called string or stringer.

CLOSED STRINGER the visible member of a stairs that abuts the risers and treads and that is not cut to show the profile of the stairs.

HANDRAIL the round or decorative member of a railing which is grasped with the hand during ascent or descent.

HEADROOM the narrowest distance between the surface of a tread and any ceiling or header above.

HOUSED STRINGER the stringer that has been grooved to receive the risers and treads.

LANDING the floor at either the top or bottom of a flight of stairs.

NEWEL the main post of the railing at the bottom of a stair or at changes in direction of the railing.

NOSING the round projection of the tread beyond the face of the riser.

OPEN STRINGER the stringer that has been cut to fit the profile of the stairs; the riser cut is mitered, the tread cut is square.

PLATFORM the intermediate landing between various parts of the stair flight.

RAILING the handrail and baluster forming the protection on open stairs.

RISE the total floor to floor vertical height of a stairs.

RISER the vertical face of the step.

RUN the total horizontal length of a stairs, including platform.

STAIRWELL the enclosed chamber into which the stairs are built.

STEP the combination of one riser and one tread.

STRINGER the inclined member supporting the risers and treads, sometimes a visible trim member next to the profile of the stairs.

TREAD the horizontal surface member of each step, usually hardwood.

WINDER the radiating or wedge-shaped treads at turns of stairs.

10.7.1 Types of Construction

Previously, stair building was a highly specialized craft, especially in home construction; many stairs required considerable hand labor. Today, stairways are often ordered directly from a mill or shops, fabricated according to details furnished by the designer. Usually, first-quality construction accepts only shop-made stair units (Fig. 10-23) having expert crafting, which are delivered to the site and quickly installed by carpenters. Figure 10-24 shows a more economical stair that is built on the job. Usually, 2 × 12 carriages are cut to the profile of the stairs and the treads are attached. Three carriages are preferred construction if the stair width is 3′-0″ or over. Double trimmers and headers must surround the stairwell framing, and the carriages must have sufficient bearing at both ends.

Other structural methods of stair support have been devised by architects to produce both novel and sturdy stair flights.

10.7.2 Riser and Tread Proportions

Because considerable effort is expended in ascending and descending stairs, regardless of type, comfort and safety should be the first consideration in their design.

In designing a comfortable stair, there must be a definite relationship between the height of the risers and the width of the treads; all stairs should be designed to conform to established proportions. If the combination of riser and tread is too great, the steps become tiring, and a strain develops on the leg muscles and the heart; if the combination is too short, the foot has a tendency to kick the riser at each step in an attempt to shorten the stride, also producing fatigue. Experience has shown that risers 7″ high with an 11″ tread result in the most satisfactory combination for principal residential stairs.

10.7.3 Stair Formulas

The following three formulas have been devised for checking riser and tread proportions, exclusive of molding; each will be satisfactory:

Two risers + 1 tread = between 24″ and 25″
Riser × tread = between 72″ and 77″
Riser + tread = between 17″ and 18″

As an example of formula application, suppose that a 11″ tread were found suitable on a preliminary stair layout; then, after examining each of the stair formulas, it will be seen that a riser height of 7″ satisfies any formula. If a 12″ tread were selected, the riser would have to be 6″, and so on. Minor variations would still make the stairs workable, but treads are seldom made less than 11″ or more than 12″ wide.

10.7.4 Angle of Stairs

Stair flights should be neither too steep nor too flat in incline. An angle of from 30° to 33° from the horizontal is the most comfortable. Long flights are also tiring; usually a platform about midway in a long flight helps relieve fatigue. There will always be one less tread than there are risers in all stairs.

10.7.5 Plan Layout Variations

Various plan layouts are shown in Fig. 10-25. If space on the plan prohibits the use of a straight run, other layouts are shown for the purpose of flexibility in fitting stairs in restricted spaces and for lending stairs various character treatments. In limited space, a winder stair (Fig. 10-25) can be used if necessary; yet it is more hazardous than a platform arrangement. The winder-stair profile should be considered at a line 1′-4″ from the winder corner. Remember that a landing counts as a tread and should conform to the width of the rest of the stairs.

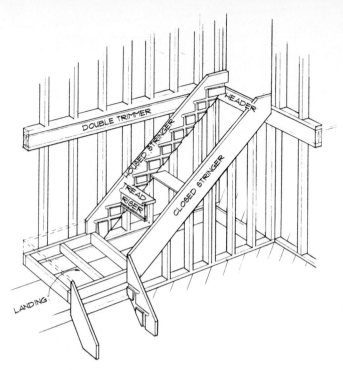

FIGURE 10-23 Mill-made stair construction.

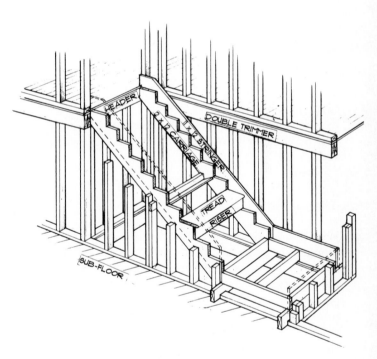

FIGURE 10-24 On-the-job stair construction.

10.7.6 Headroom

Headroom should be between 6′-8″ and 7′-4″ over major stairs; 6′-6″ is usually sufficient over minor flights to the basement or attic. Individual conditions may neces-

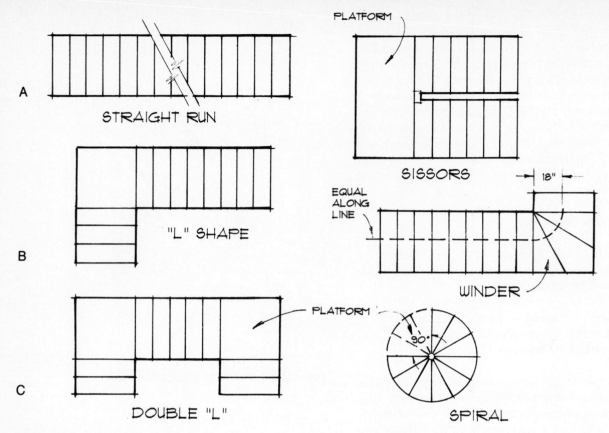

FIGURE 10-25 Various stair layouts.

sitate slight variations of headroom. Disappearing stairs to attic storage spaces are usually prefabricated units, which can be shown on the plan with a dashed rectangle and a note.

10.7.7 Railings

Whether a stair is open or enclosed between walls, a railing must be installed to be within easy reach in case of stumbling or loss of balance. It is general practice to use a continuous handrail from floor to floor. It can be plain or ornamental—in keeping with the design features of the building—but it should be smooth and sturdy. The most comfortable handrail height is 32″ above the tread surface measured from the edge of the tread to the top of the handrail. Landings in residences should have 36″ high railings and in commercial building they should be 42″ high.

10.7.8 Exterior Stairs

Exterior stairs are usually designed with smaller riser heights and therefore with wider treads than interior stairs. A popular proportion is a 6″ riser and a 12″ tread for maximum safety on long flights. Landings should

be provided every 16 risers on continuous stairs. If slopes are gradual, ramps (up to 12°) are often preferable to steps for outside use. Usually, masonry with reinforcing and well-anchored footings is the most practical exterior material.

Requirements of all classes of stairs are given in the NFPA 101, Life Safety Code, published by the National Fire Protection Association. The design of all stairs should meet their specifications.

10.7.9 Drawing Stair Details (Figs. 10-26 and 10-27)

STEP 1. *To draw a stair detail*, first, the finished floor to finished floor height must be known, even though carriages rest on rough framing. The number of risers necessary to ascend the height can be found arithmetically by dividing the heights by 7″ (typical risers). If the floor to floor dimension is conveniently divisible by either typical riser height, calculation is simplified. But seldom will it come out even, unless ceiling heights have been purposely figured. In Fig. 10-27, the total height or rise needed for the stairs is 108″ (8′-1⅛″ stud and plate height, plus 9¼″ joist height, plus 1⅝″ flooring thickness). When we divide 108 by 7, the quotient is 15.42. Since all risers must be the same height, 16 risers

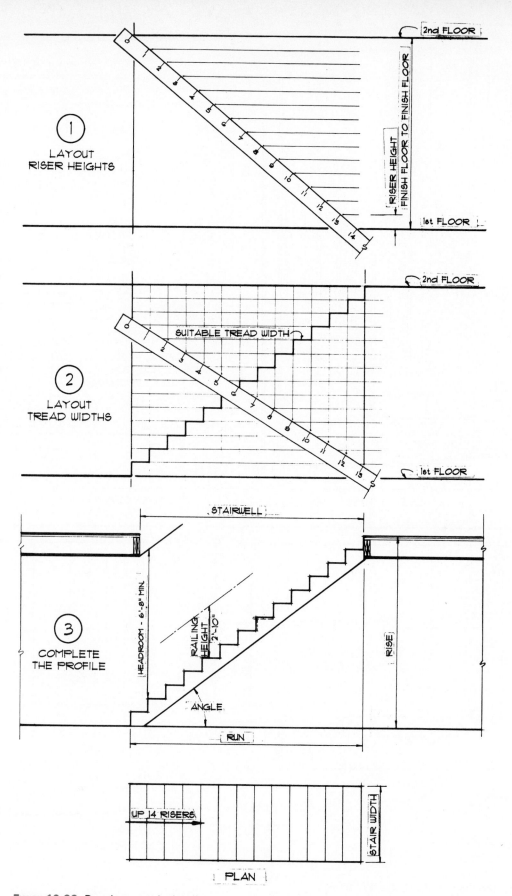

FIGURE 10-26 Drawing a stair detail.

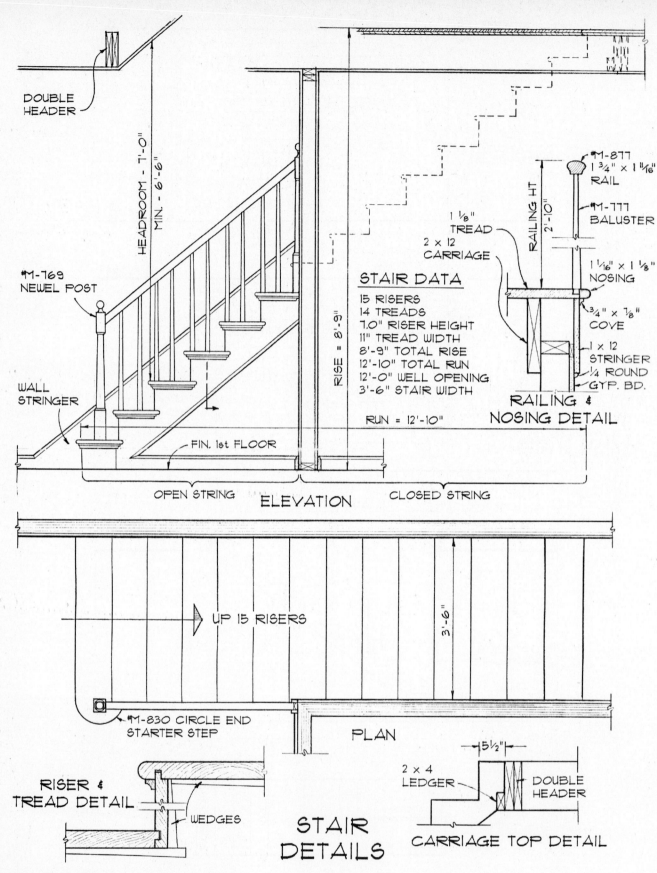

DOUBLE HEADER

HEADROOM - 7'-0"
MIN. - 6'-6"

#M-769 NEWEL POST

WALL STRINGER

RISE = 8'-9"

FIN. 1st FLOOR

OPEN STRING

ELEVATION

CLOSED STRING

STAIR DATA

15 RISERS
14 TREADS
7.0" RISER HEIGHT
11" TREAD WIDTH
8'-9" TOTAL RISE
12'-10" TOTAL RUN
12'-0" WELL OPENING
3'-6" STAIR WIDTH

RUN = 12'-10"

1 ⅛" TREAD

2 x 12 CARRIAGE

RAILING HT

#M-877
1 ¾" x 1 ¹¹⁄₁₆"
RAIL

#M-777 BALUSTER

2'-10"

1 ¹⁄₁₆" x 1 ⅛" NOSING

¾" x ⅞" COVE

1 x 12 STRINGER
¼ ROUND
GYP. BD.

RAILING & NOSING DETAIL

UP 15 RISERS

3'-6"

#M-830 CIRCLE END STARTER STEP

PLAN

RISER & TREAD DETAIL

WEDGES

STAIR DETAILS

2 x 4 LEDGER

5½"

DOUBLE HEADER

CARRIAGE TOP DETAIL

FIGURE 10-27 Details of a traditional stairs.

can be adopted. Using 16 risers with 11¼" tread width seems to satisfy the stair formulas:

$$\frac{108''}{16} = 6.75'' \text{ riser}$$

Formula 1: $2(6.75) + 11.25 = 24.75$
Formula 2: $6.75 \times 11.25 = 75.93$
Formula 3: $6.75 + 11.25 = 18$

Therefore, the stair data for Fig. 10-28 would be:

Total number of risers	16
Total number of treads	15
Riser height	6.75″
Tread width	11.25″
Total rise	108″
Total run	168.75″

STEP 2. Because odd fractions are difficult to measure on a drawing, the graphic method of stair profile layout is recommended. Scale the floor to floor height and draw the floor lines between which the stair is to be drawn. Divide the between-floor space into 16 divisions graphically. Divisions on the scale can be used by adopting 16 convenient divisions and adjusting them diagonally across the space and marking to form the tread surfaces (see left side of Fig. 10-26). Draw the 15 vertical riser surfaces similarly, or measure them if feasible. The top riser meets the second-floor surface. This results in the correct stair profile from floor to floor. Strengthen the profile and erase the construction lines.

STEP 3. Next, locate the ceiling or soffit surface above the stairs, keeping in mind that the headroom for important stairs should be 6'-8" to 7'-4" high, if possible; slightly less is permissible if the stairwell above must be made smaller. This headroom line locates the header framing and the sloping ceiling above. In basement stairs, less headroom is satisfactory. To conserve stairwell space, usually two or more flights of stairs are superimposed directly above one another in multistory buildings. Openings for the stairwell can now be dimensioned for the framing, and final adjustments on second-floor walls near the stairs can be made.

STEP 4. If the carriage outline is to be drawn, the thickness of the treads (usually 1¹¹⁄₁₆″) is shown below the profile surface, and the thickness of the risers (usually ¾″) shown within the vertical lines. The original profile will remain the surface of the risers and treads. Usually, the carriage is cut from 2 × 10 or 2 × 12 lumber, and at least 3″ of solid material must remain below the depth of the cuts for stability. Nosings commonly extend 1⅛″ beyond the surface of the risers. Basement stairs seldom require covered risers.

STEP 5. For safety, railings are a necessary part of the stairs and should be drawn next. If necessary, details of railings, ornamental newel posts, balusters, and trim can be taken from manufacturers' catalogues. Draw the railing 2'-6" above surface of the treads. Major stairs should be made from 3'-0" to 3'-6" wide in residences and 3'-8" wide or wider in commercial buildings.

Complete the stair plan layout by projecting the risers from the elevation detail. Show the riser surfaces and indicate the number of risers; include either an UP or DOWN note and arrow (see Fig. 10-27). About half of the complete stair symbol is shown on each floor plan, and a conventional diagonal break line is drawn near the symbol center. A concrete stair detail is shown in Fig. 10-28.

EXERCISES

1. Draw a typical wall detail of a brick-veneer, 1-story residence, using the scale: 1″ = 1'-0″. Use a crawl space with concrete-block foundation wall. Floor joists: 2″ × 10″; ceiling joists: 2″ × 8″; roof slope 4:12.

2. Draw a typical wall detail of a concrete-block wall with a slab-on-ground floor, using the scale: ¾″ = 1'-0″. Show a flat roof with 2″ × 8″ roof joists and box-in the 2' overhang (see roof overhang details in Chapter 7).

3. Draw a typical wall detail of a frame wall for a house with a basement of 8″ poured concrete walls, using the scale: ¾″ = 1'-0″. Use a plank-and-beam roof with 3″ × 8″ beams. Roof slope: 3:12, board-and-batten siding.

4. Draw a section detail of an aluminum awning window, using the scale: 1″ = 1'-0″. Select an actual window from *Sweet's File*.

5. Draw a section and an elevation of a wood hopper window, using the scale: 1½″ = 1'-0″. Use information from a manufacturer's catalogue.

6. Draw the head, jamb, and sill section of a door detail in a solid-brick (8″) wall, using the scale: ¾″ = 1'-0″. Use 1¼″ wood jambs, suitable trim, and 1¾″ flush door.

7. Draw the elevation, plan, and vertical section details for a contemporary fireplace, using the scale ¾″ = 1'-0″. Use stone masonry with a flagstone hearth. Size of fireplace opening: 42″ × 28″.

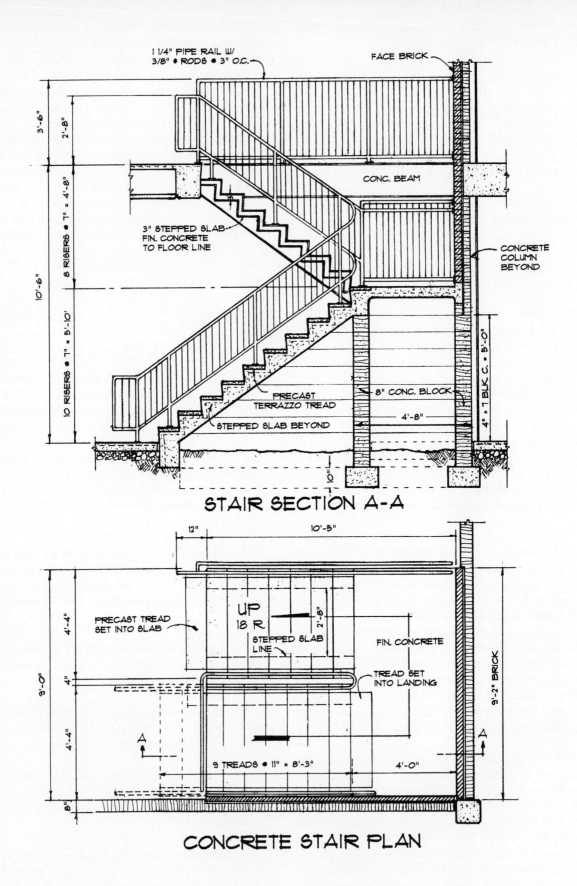

STAIR SECTION A-A

1 1/4" PIPE RAIL W/ 3/8" ⌀ RODS @ 3" O.C.

FACE BRICK

3'-6"

2'-8"

CONC. BEAM

3" STEPPED SLAB FIN. CONCRETE TO FLOOR LINE

8 RISERS @ 7" = 4'-8"

10'-6"

CONCRETE COLUMN BEYOND

10 RISERS @ 7" = 5'-10'

PRECAST TERRAZZO TREAD

8" CONC. BLOCK

STEPPED SLAB BEYOND

4'-8"

4" + 7 BLK C. = 5'-0"

10"

CONCRETE STAIR PLAN

12"

10'-5"

4'-4"

PRECAST TREAD SET INTO SLAB

UP 18 R

2'-8"

STEPPED SLAB LINE

FIN. CONCRETE

9'-0"

4"

TREAD SET INTO LANDING

9'-2" BRICK

4'-4"

A

A

9 TREADS @ 11" = 8'-3"

4'-0"

8"

FIGURE 10-28 Details of a commercial stairs.

8. Design and draw the details for a colonial stairs. Single-flight using the scale $\frac{3}{4}'' = 1'-0''$. Finish-floor to finish-floor height: $9'-8''$. Select a suitable scale, trim, and railing.

9. Draw a wall detail of a 2-story contemporary wood frame house with slab on ground, aluminum and glass siding doors, 2×10 second floor joists, $4'-6''$ high aluminum casement windows on second floor, $18''$ deep flat roof trusses, membrane roofing with stone ballast, $2'-0''$ high parapet, exterior walls and parapet to have $1\frac{1}{2}''$ thick E.I.F.S.; scale at $\frac{3}{4}'' = 1'-0''$.

10. Draw a section through a covered patio, slab on ground with $2''$ stone flooring, $8''$ square by $10'$ high wood posts, 6×12 wood beam between posts, 4×8 wood rafters, $3''$ laminated T&G decking, Spanish tile roof with 5:12 slope, $36''$ high railing with 2×4 top and bottom rails and 2×2 vertical balusters between posts using a scale of $1'' = 1'-0''$.

REVIEW QUESTIONS

1. What factors are used to determine the choice of scale when drawing details?

2. What information does a typical wall detail usually show?

3. Why are structural members in detail drawings drawn actual size rather than nominal size?

4. In gable-roof terminology, what is the difference between "span" and "run"?

5. Why must manufacturers' catalogues be consulted when determining rough-opening sizes for windows?

6. Differentiate between a window sash and a window frame.

7. Why are doorjambs usually the only sections needed when drawing door details?

8. What dimensions are first selected in fireplace design, and what should be the basis for their selection?

9. For a workable fireplace, what should be the proportion of the cross-sectional flue area to the fireplace opening area?

10. What two dimensions are the most critical in satisfactory stair design?

11. Describe how an architect's scale can be used to lay out the riser height and tread width of stairs in elevation or section without measuring each riser and tread from floor to floor.

12. Write the three formulas for checking riser and tread proportions.

13. What is a fire door and what do the labels A, B, and C designate?

14. What are anchor bolts and where are they used in wood frame construction?

15. What is used to support brick masonry above a door or window opening?

16. What type of cut is usually placed on a rafter where it rests on a bearing wall?

17. Residential doors are usually $6'-8''$ high. What is the common height of commercial doors?

18. What is the minimum headroom above stairs?

19. Where is a brick rowlock used in window detailing?

20. What is a clerestory window?

WORKING DRAWINGS OF SMALL HOMES

11

This chapter is concerned, mainly, with typical working drawings of small, custom-designed homes and the steps necessary for the satisfactory completion of these drawings by the student. To show traditional methods of depicting technical instructions for building houses, several sets of house plans have been included in this chapter. Each set is typical of current architectural practice and should be studied carefully for its manner of showing construction information. Occasionally, modifications will be necessary to satisfy local conditions and code requirements.

The *2-story solar home* (Fig. 11-1) is a conservative small home with three bedrooms for the average family that should be economical to heat and cool even with the rising home energy costs. Eighty percent of the total heating needs will be provided by the passive features. The home was designed by the Solar and Design section of the Tennessee Valley Authority (TVA) for use throughout the Tennessee valley area. If used in other climates of the United States, some modifications must be made to conform to local solar conditions. Larger blueprints and specifications are available from TVA, Knoxville, TN 37900 for a nominal fee.

Notice that the house is to be oriented on a south-facing sloping lot with the entry on the north. The two-level plan has 1008 square feet on each level. The double

FIGURE 11-1 Perspective rendering of solar home.

garage and storage feature are optional. Conventional building materials and construction skills that are universally available are used throughout. To maintain more heat in the living areas, the major bedroom area is in the lower level. Various passive solar features are used: a sun porch to collect solar energy, a 12″ concrete-filled block Trombe wall to help store solar energy, water-filled drums also for energy storage, shaded overhangs to prevent solar penetration of glass areas during the summer, earth-berming of the lower back wall to temper year-round temperatures, maximum use of insulation throughout ceiling and walls, and the use of insulating glass in all windows. Everything about the design is ideal for contemporary living.

The *2-story home* (Figs. 11-9 through 11-14) is traditional in nature, resembling many homes built in New England during colonial times and still popular in many areas (Fig. 11-15). Built over a crawl space with a cantilevered second story, the house has about 3000 square feet of floor space including the double carport, which makes it suitable for a larger family than the 1-story home shown in Appendix F. The sleeping area is organized on the second floor for isolation from the downstairs living and eating areas. Because of the overhang, brick veneer is used on the garage–first-floor level and bevel siding for the walls above.

Instructor assignments—limiting the size of a home, giving the tastes of a tentative client, and indicating the major type of construction and materials—are very much like the actual situations in an architectural office. Usually, the architect first consults with the client about his or her wishes, design sketches are prepared, and further consultation may be necessary to resolve information about the project. In fact, more sketches may have to be done before all ideas are clearly in mind and working drawings can be started. Student problems should be developed in the same manner—first by sketches, preferably on ⅛″ coordinate paper, and then on tracing paper with instruments. In the architectural office, the sketches of a project, together with any written information, are given to an experienced drafter, or project chief for their development. Some consultation may be necessary, yet one person usually assumes the responsibility for the completion of a small project. Student drafting assignments provide similar learning situations.

The following plates (Figs. 11-2 through 11-8, showing conventional drafting practice, should serve merely as guides for developing original ideas into complete working drawings. If only manipulative drafting exercise is advisable, the plates can be duplicated directly (they are shown approximately half size). While working on the drawings, the student is urged to continually refer to *Sweet's catalogs*, Ramsey and Sleeper's *Architectural Graphic Standards*, and other reference sources for additional help.

11.1 Start With the Floor Plan

In general, follow these steps in developing the first-floor plan.

STEP 1. *Lay out the major exterior walls with light lines.* Use the ¼″ = 1′-0″ scale and take the dimensions from the sketch. A 3H or 4H pencil works best for preliminary construction lines. Extend the lines beyond their termination points during construction until definite measurements are established. The following wall thicknesses are satisfactory on small plans, unless special conditions exist:

Wood frame exterior walls	6″
Wood frame partitions	5″
Brick veneer	10″ (4″ brick, 6″ wood)
Concrete block (C.M.U.)	4″, 8″, 12″ (nominal)
Solid brick	8″, 12″ (plus furring)
Brick cavity	10″ (2″ air space)

Draw the light lines completely through window and door openings at this preliminary stage. Then lay out all partitions, including, if necessary, an 8″ wide wet-wall for the bathroom 4″ vent stack enclosure. Block in the areas for stairs, fireplaces, door stoops, and so on. Give clothes closets a minimum of 2′ interior width.

STEP 2. *Locate all windows and doors with center lines.* Refer to the elevation sketches, if necessary, for window placements, and check manufacturers' catalogues for available sizes (see Figs. 11-4 and 11-11 for various window symbols). Select window types for their practicality and for their harmony with the spirit of the exterior. If elevations are not definite and window changes seem inevitable, draw the window symbols with only light lines and come back later for strengthening after the elevation fenestration is completed. After considering the proper door widths that become necessary in the different rooms (Fig. 10-14), lay out the door symbols. Scale the symbol the same width as the door. Study the traffic flow through doors before indicating their swing. Since interior doors are frequently left open, be sure to provide sufficient clear space for doors when in an open position. Exterior residential doors swing in; interior doors should not swing into hallways. For convenient accessibility, provide either sliding- or folding-door units in closets; louver doors are especially appropriate, since they allow ventilation for the clothes. Symbols are shown for doors (see Fig. 10-14). Erase the construction lines within the door symbols before completing the symbols. Indicate doorsills or waterproof thresholds below exterior doors. Cased openings or archways, which drop below ceiling heights, must be shown with broken lines (see Fig. 10-17).

A SOLAR HOME

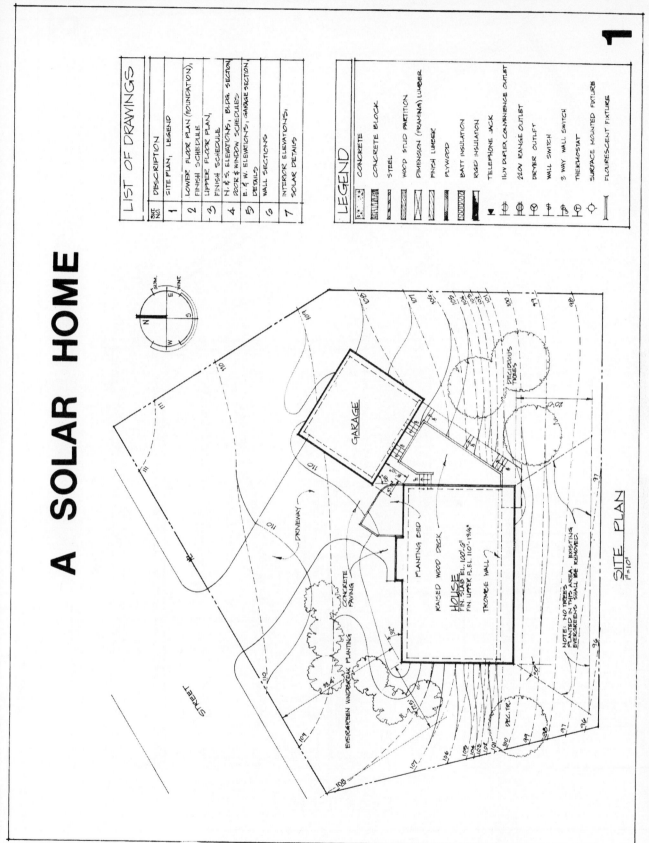

LEGEND

	CONCRETE
	CONCRETE BLOCK
	STEEL
	WOOD STUD PARTITION
	DIMENSION (FRAMING) LUMBER
	FINISH LUMBER
	PLYWOOD
	BATT INSULATION
	RIGID INSULATION
	TELEPHONE JACK
	110V DUPLEX CONVENIENCE OUTLET
	220V RANGE OUTLET
	DRYER OUTLET
	WALL SWITCH
	3 WAY WALL SWITCH
	THERMOSTAT
	SURFACE MOUNTED FIXTURE
	FLOURESCENT FIXTURE

SITE PLAN
1"=10'

GARAGE

DRIVEWAY

STREET

EVERGREEN WINDBREAK PLANTING

CONCRETE PAVING

PLANTING BED

RAISED WOOD DECK

HOUSE
FIN. SLAB EL. 100'-0"
FIN. UPPER FL. EL. 110'-13/4"

TROMBE WALL

NOTE: NO TREES PLANTED IN THIS AREA. EXISTING EVERGREENS SHALL BE REMOVED.

DECIDUOUS TREES

FIGURE 11-2 Site plan of solar home.

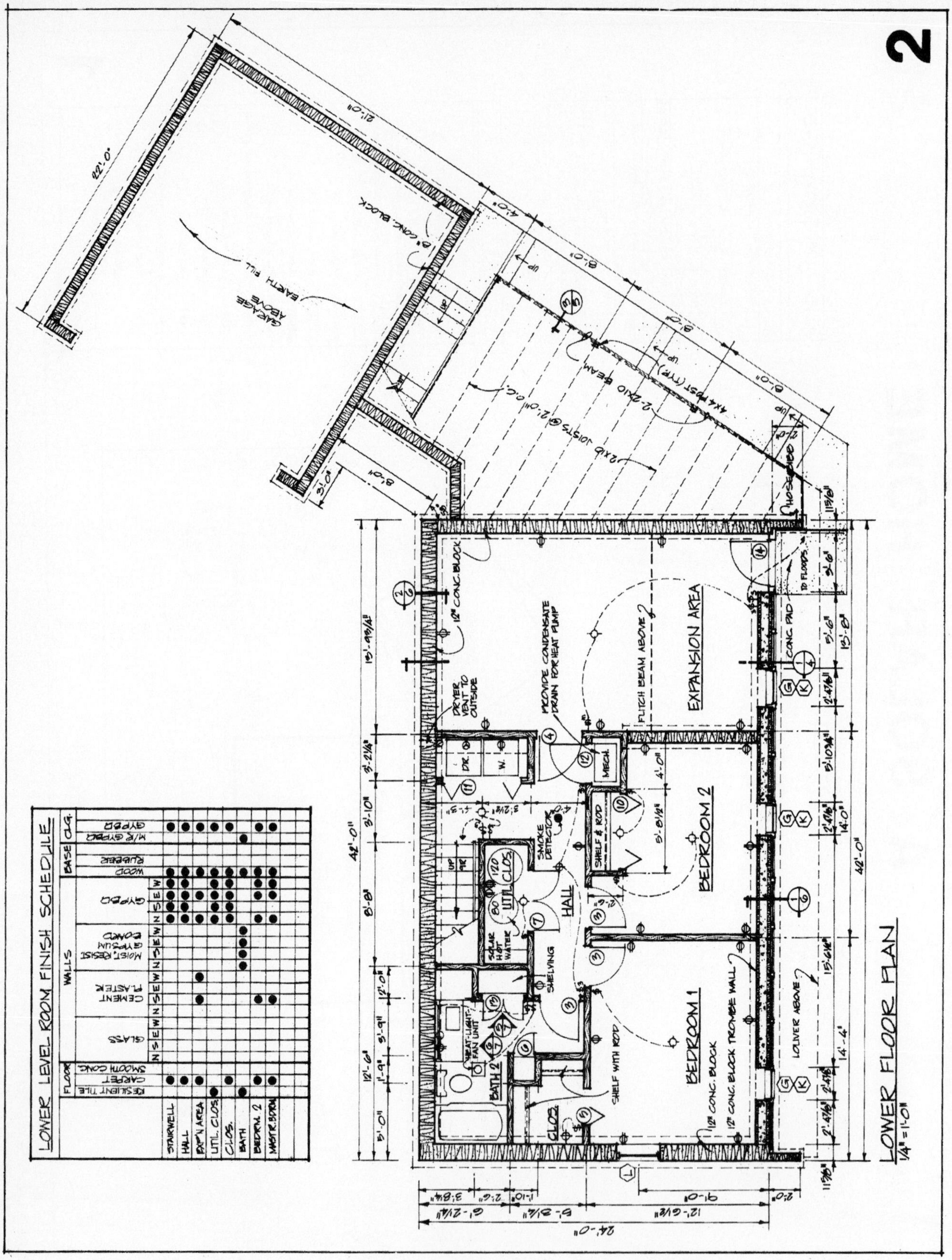

FIGURE 11-3 Lower floor plan of solar home.

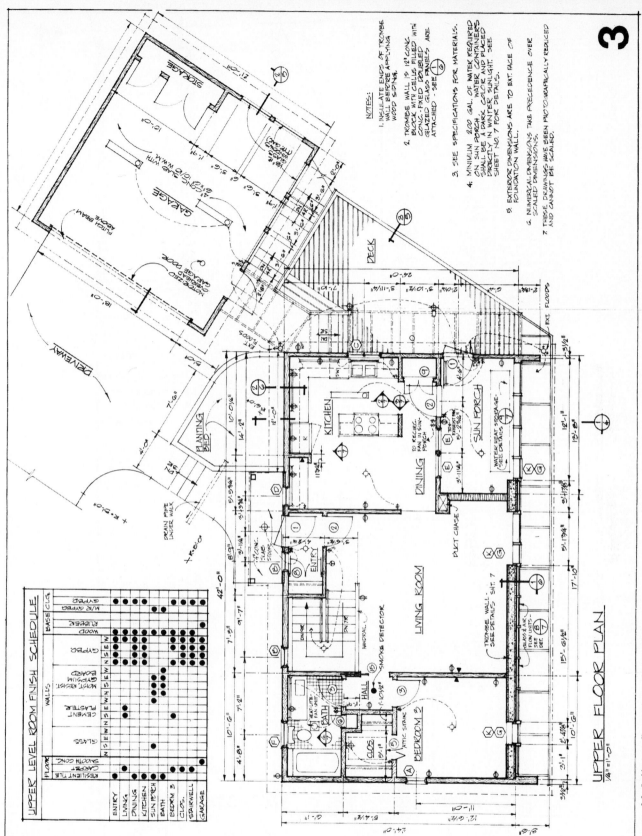

FIGURE 11-4 Upper floor plan of solar home.

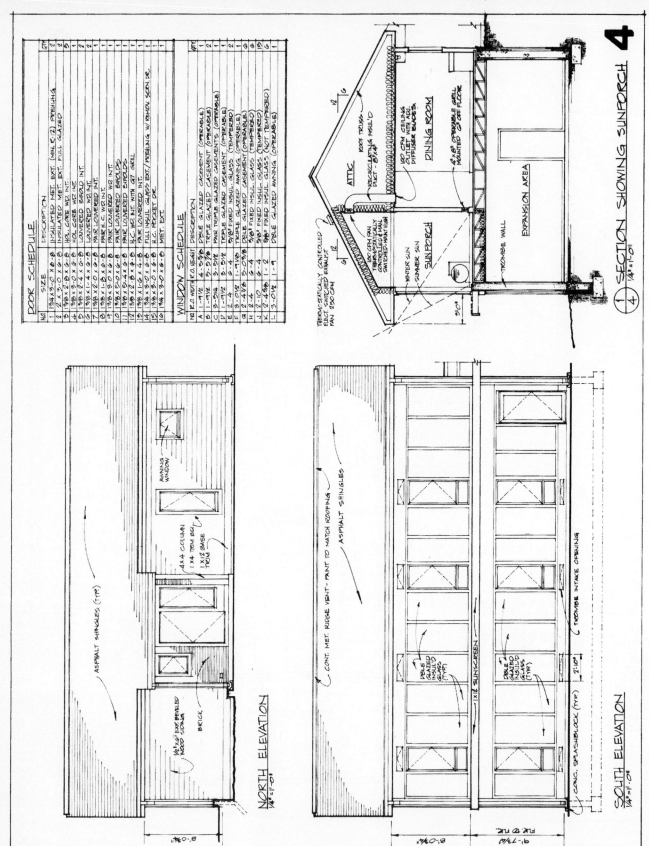

FIGURE 11-5 Elevations, section, and schedules of solar home.

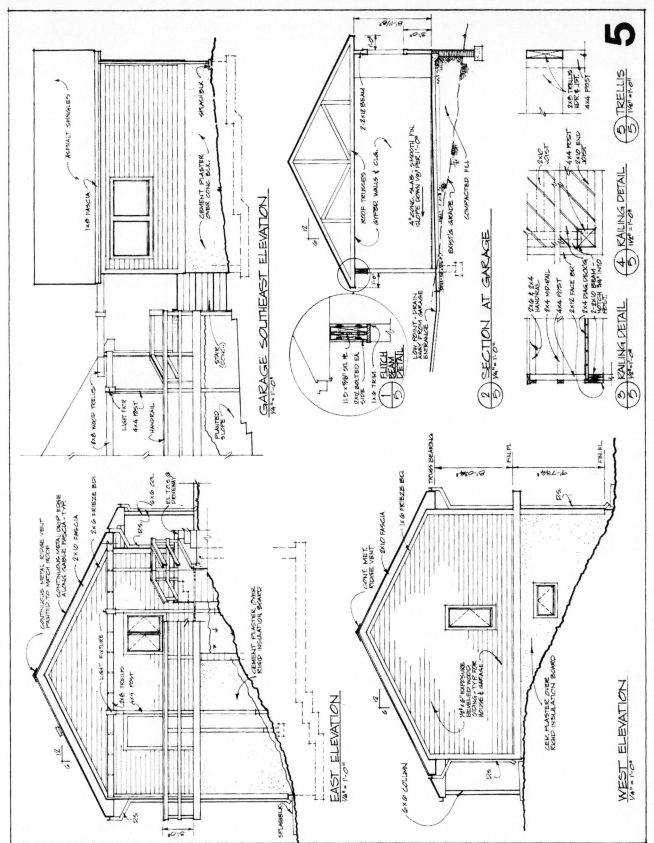

5

GARAGE SOUTHEAST ELEVATION
1/4" = 1'-0"

ASPHALT SHINGLES

1×8 FASCIA

CEMENT PLASTER OVER CONC. BLK.

SPLASH BLK.

STAIR (CONC.)

HANDRAIL

4×4 POST

LIGHT FIXR.

1×8 WOOD TRELLIS

PLANTED SLOPE

2-2×12 BEAM

ROOF TRUSSES

GYPSD. WALLS & CLG.

4" CONC. SLAB - SMOOTH FIN.
SLOPE DOWN 1/8" PER 1'-0"

EXIST'G GRADE

COMPACTED FILL

LOW POINT - DRAIN
AWAY FROM GARAGE
ENTRANCE

FLITCH BEAM DETAIL
1 / 5

11.5 × 5/8" STL. PL.
2×10 BOLTED EA. SIDE
1×8 TRIM

SECTION AT GARAGE
2 / 5   1/4" = 1'-0"

2×8 TRELLIS
HDR. & 1ST.
4×4 POST

TRELLIS
5 / 5   1/4" = 1'-0"

2×10 JOIST

4×4 POST
2×10 END JOIST

RAILING DETAIL
4 / 5   1/2" = 1'-0"

2×6 & 2×4 HANDRAIL
2×4 MID-RAIL
4×4 POST
2×12 FACE BD.
2×4 DIAG DECK'G
2-2×10 BEAM -
NOTCH 3/4 INTO POST

RAILING DETAIL
3 / 5   1/2" = 1'-0"

CONTINUOUS METAL RIDGE VENT
PAINTED TO MATCH ROOF

CONTINUOUS METAL DRIP EDGE
ALONG GABLE FASCIA - TYP.

2×6 FRIEZE BD.

6×6 COL.

EL. T.O.S. @ DRIVEWAY

2×10 FASCIA

LIGHT FIXTURE

2×8 TRELLIS

4×4 POST

CEMENT PLASTER OVER
RIGID INSULATION BOARD

SPLASHBLK.

EAST ELEVATION
1/4" = 1'-0"

TRUSS BEARING

FIN. FL.

FIN. FL.

CONT. MET. RIDGE VENT

2×10 FASCIA

1×8 FRIEZE BD.

1/4 × 6" EXPOSURE
BEVELED WOOD
SIDING - TYP FOR
HOUSE & GARAGE

CEM. PLASTER OVER
RIGID INSULATION BOARD

6×6 COLUMN

WEST ELEVATION
1/4" = 1'-0"

Figure 11-6 Elevations and details of solar home.

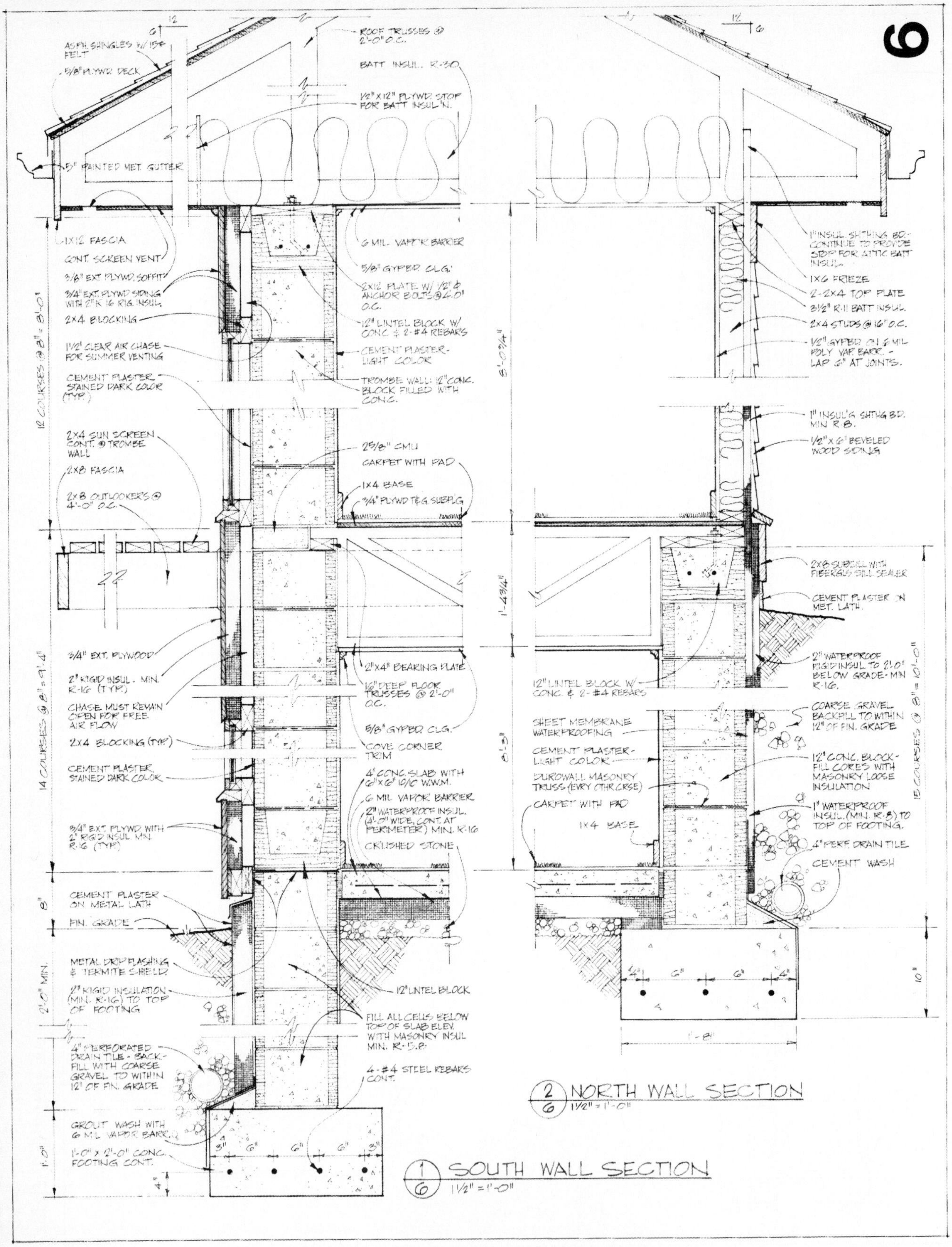
6
ASPH. SHINGLES W/ 15# FELT
5/8" PLYWD. DECK
ROOF TRUSSES @ 2'-0" O.C.
BATT INSUL. R-30
1/2" x 12" PLYWD. STOP FOR BATT INSUL'N.
5" PAINTED MET. GUTTER
1X12 FASCIA
CONT. SCREEN VENT
3/8" EXT. PLYWD. SOFFIT
3/4" EXT. PLYWD. SIDING WITH 2" K 16 RIG. INSUL.
2X4 BLOCKING
1 1/2" CLEAR AIR CHASE FOR SUMMER VENTING
CEMENT PLASTER STAINED DARK COLOR (TYP.)
2X4 SUN SCREEN CONT. @ TROMBE WALL
2X8 FASCIA
2X8 OUTLOOKERS @ 4'-0" O.C.
12 COURSES @ 8" = 8'-0"
6 MIL. VAPOR BARRIER
5/8" GYPBD. CLG.
2X12 PLATE W/ 1/2" ϕ ANCHOR BOLTS @ 4'-0" O.C.
12" LINTEL BLOCK W/ CONC. & 2-#4 REBARS
CEMENT PLASTER - LIGHT COLOR
TROMBE WALL: 12" CONC. BLOCK FILLED WITH CONC.
2 5/8" CMU
CARPET WITH PAD
1X4 BASE
3/4" PLYWD T&G SUBFLG
5'-0 3/4"
1'-4 3/4"
8'-3"
1" INSUL. SHTHING BD. - CONTINUE TO PROVIDE STOP FOR ATTIC BATT INSUL.
1X6 FRIEZE
2-2X4 TOP PLATE
3 1/2" R-11 BATT INSUL.
2X4 STUDS @ 16" O.C.
1/2" GYPBD. ON 6 MIL POLY VAP. BARR. - LAP 6" AT JOINTS.
1" INSUL'G SHTHG BD. MIN R-8.
1/2" x 6" BEVELED WOOD SIDING
2X8 SUBSILL WITH FIBERGLS SILL SEALER
CEMENT PLASTER ON MET. LATH
2" WATERPROOF RIGID INSUL. TO 2'-0" BELOW GRADE - MIN R-16.
COARSE GRAVEL BACKFILL TO WITHIN 12" OF FIN. GRADE
12" CONC. BLOCK - FILL CORES WITH MASONRY LOOSE INSULATION
1" WATERPROOF INSUL. (MIN. R-8) TO TOP OF FOOTING.
4" PERF. DRAIN TILE
CEMENT WASH
15 COURSES @ 8" = 10'-0"
3/4" EXT. PLYWOOD
2" RIGID INSUL. MIN. R-16 (TYP.)
CHASE MUST REMAIN OPEN FOR FREE AIR FLOW
2X4 BLOCKING (TYP.)
CEMENT PLASTER STAINED DARK COLOR
3/4" EXT. PLYWD. WITH 2" RIGID INSUL. MIN. R-16 (TYP.)
14 COURSES @ 8" = 9'-4"
2"X4" BEARING PLATE
16" DEEP FLOOR TRUSSES @ 2'-0" O.C.
5/8" GYPBD. CLG.
COVE CORNER TRIM
4" CONC. SLAB WITH 6"X6" 10/10 W.W.M.
6 MIL. VAPOR BARRIER
2" WATERPROOF INSUL. (4'-0" WIDE, CONT. AT PERIMETER) MIN. R-16
CRUSHED STONE
12" LINTEL BLOCK W/ CONC. & 2-#4 REBARS
SHEET MEMBRANE WATERPROOFING
CEMENT PLASTER - LIGHT COLOR
DUROWALL MASONRY TRUSS (EVRY OTHR CRSE)
CARPET WITH PAD
1X4 BASE
CEMENT PLASTER ON METAL LATH
FIN. GRADE
METAL DRIP FLASHING & TERMITE SHIELD
2" RIGID INSULATION (MIN. R-16) TO TOP OF FOOTING
4" PERFORATED DRAIN TILE - BACKFILL WITH COARSE GRAVEL TO WITHIN 12" OF FIN. GRADE
GROUT WASH WITH 6 MIL VAPOR BARR.
1'-0" x 2'-0" CONC. FOOTING CONT.
8"
2'-0" MIN.
1'-0"
4"
12" LINTEL BLOCK
FILL ALL CELLS BELOW TOP OF SLAB ELEV. WITH MASONRY INSUL. MIN. R-5.8
4-#4 STEEL REBARS CONT.
3"
6"
6"
6"
3"
4"
6"
6"
4"
1'-8"
10"
2/6 NORTH WALL SECTION
1 1/2" = 1'-0"
1/6 SOUTH WALL SECTION
1 1/2" = 1'-0"

FIGURE 11-7 Wall sections of solar home.

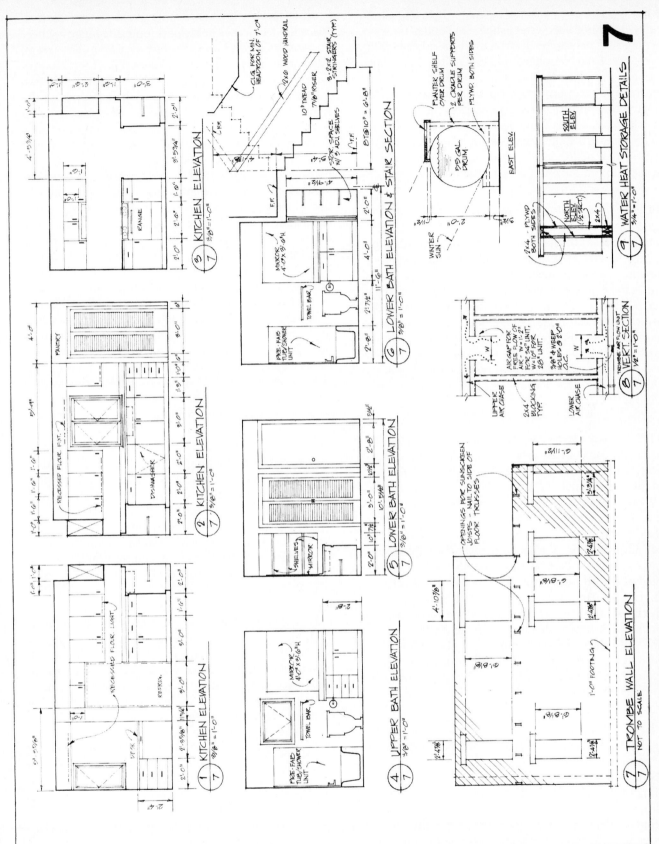

FIGURE **11-8** Kitchen, bath, and Trombe wall elevations.

STEP 3. *Draw the layout of the stairs.* If exact ceiling heights have not been established, stair indications on the plan may have to be delayed until stair details (Fig. 10-27) have been completed. However, after stair information is complete, the risers are indicated with lines. An arrow indicating either up or down and a note showing the number of risers completes the stair symbol. A diagonal break line near the center of the stair run terminates the amount of stair symbol necessary on each floor. Usually an 11″ tread, requiring about a 7″ riser, results in a comfortable residential stair.

STEP 4. *If a fireplace is required, draw the outline of the fireplace lightly.* The cutting plane of a fireplace representation passes through the lower part of the opening (see Fig. 10-20). Here again, details may require development on another sheet before the indication on the plan can be accurately drawn. Usually, a masonry hearth, 18″ or 20″ wide, is necessary in front of the opening. Size the fireplace opening and the masonry around it according to the proportions of the room in which it will serve. If a metal fireplace lining is used, the size and number should be indicated with a note. Refer to Section 10.6 for fireplace designs, details, and methods of representation.

STEP 5. *Lay out the kitchen cabinets and bath fixtures.* Locate the sink, dishwasher, range, microwave, and refrigerator; show the kitchen base cabinets 24″ wide and the wall cabinets 12″ wide. Use broken lines for the wall cabinets inasmuch as they are above the cutting plane of the plan. Carefully locate and draw the symbols for the bathroom fixtures. Sizes and clearances can be taken from Fig. 6-57 or from manufacturers' catalogues. Sizes of bath fixtures should be accurately scaled to indicate correct placement and workability of the arrangement. Bathroom templates save considerable time in this step. Indicate a medicine cabinet if no storage space is provided in built-in lavatory cabinets. Show all other built-in cabinetwork throughout the house in its correct place. All built-in features, which become a permanent part of the construction, must be shown on the plan.

STEP 6. *Draw all electrical outlets and switch symbols* (see Fig. 12-41). On ¼″ = 1′-0″ floor plans, use a circle ³/₁₆″ in diameter for the majority of the electrical symbols; a circle template will be handy for this. Locate ceiling outlets in the centers of room areas for general lighting. Long, rectangular rooms may require several ceiling outlets in order to distribute light evenly throughout the room. Living areas are best illuminated with table and floor lamps that can be operated from duplex outlets and convenient wall switches. Show a ceiling outlet above the tentative placement of a dining room table. Local lighting should be provided for work centers such as kitchen counters and sewing centers. Place light switches near doors (opposite hinges) where entrance is made into the room. If a room has several entrances, use two 3-way switches (Fig. 12-41) to provide convenient light operation. If necessary, use two 3-way switches and one 4-way switch to operate the lights from three different locations. Place the switches so that the lighting can be turned on before entering a room. Show 3-way switches at the top and bottom of stairways. In addition, outside outlets are needed for entrances, yard floodlights, and terrace requirements. When connecting switch symbols with their outlets, use an irregular curve as a ruling edge and maintain a consistent broken-line technique. Place duplex wall outlets about 8′-0″ apart in living areas; then lamps can be positioned at will throughout the room. Halls should have outlets for vacuum cleaners. It is important to provide a sufficient number of outlets for the many electric appliances now being used in a modern home: refrigerator, food freezer, range, heating units, washer, dryer, motors, and diverse equipment for food preparation, grooming, and so on. Some appliances may even require 220 volts, which is easily indicated with a special-purpose symbol. Waterproof outlets are specified for outdoor use. (Refer to Chapter 12 for further information on electrical drawings.)

STEP 7. *Complete and verify all dimensions.* Several methods of dimensioning the framing can be used on wood frame construction. For example, in one method, applied for the traditional house, the dimensions are taken from the outside surface of the exterior stud wall to the center lines of the partitions. This method is conventional, and it provides workers with the necessary dimensions for laying out the soleplates over the subfloors in western frame construction. Even on brick veneer construction, only the wood framing is dimensioned (refer to Chapter 9 for more details). On the 1-story home shown in Appendix F, as another method, the outside dimensions start at the surface of the sheathing, which coincides with the surface of the foundation wall on the detail. Continuous dimensions are carried through the house from partition surfaces, and the thickness of each partition is dimensioned. This method gives a better indication of inside room dimensions and is preferred by some architects. In either method, dimensions are shown to the center lines of windows and doors. Generally, the obvious placement of interior doors in narrow areas, such as hallways, seldom needs dimensions for location. Notice that dimensions are placed on each drawing where they are legible, uncrowded, and related to their features. Make guide lines for all dimension figures no larger than ⅛″ high. Check cumulative dimensions to be sure they equal the overall dimensions. Dimension solid masonry from wall surfaces, and indicate the thickness of each wall or partition so that masons will have definite surfaces to work from. They need to know the dimensions of door and window masonry openings as well. Avoid duplication of dimensions.

Students should remember that workers cannot construct frame buildings with the same precision found in, for instance, the machine trades. Finished buildings often show slight variations from dimensions indicated on working drawings. This condition, however, does not give license to careless and inaccurate dimensions on working drawings, but it is a situation that drafters should be aware of when dimensioning the drawings.

STEP 8. *Letter the room titles, notes, and scale of the plan.* Place the room titles near the center of the room, unless dimensions or ceiling electrical symbols interfere and would result in a crowded appearance. Unless a finish schedule is to be used, the finish flooring should be indicated with a small note below the room title. All notes that clarify features on the drawing should be completed; however, avoid excessive notes that can better be included in the specifications. Door sizes must be given either in door schedules or on the door symbols. Scale indications are lettered very small.

Use a note to show the size, direction, and spacing of ceiling or floor joists above (see Fig. 11-10). In conventional framing, ceiling joists must rest on bearing walls. To determine the size and spacing of the joists, based on their longest span, refer to the table on maximum spans for wood joists and rafters (Table 8-6). Ceiling joists on 1-story houses should preferably run parallel with the rafters to act as lateral ties. On 2-story houses, the ceiling joists become the floor joists of the second floor, and their sizes must be computed as joists capable of supporting 40-lb sq ft live load. Number 2 common, southern yellow pine or standard and utility-grade Douglas fir is widely used in house framing.

STEP 9. *Complete all hatching of materials according to the symbols shown in Fig. 9-11.* If lettering or dimensions fall in the hatching areas, leave enough of the symbol out to make the lettering readable. Prepare a border and title block similar to Figs. 11-9 through 11-14 or to those shown in Chapter 2.

STEP 10. *Check the plan carefully for discrepancies or omissions.* For this, the following list will prove helpful.

FIRST-FLOOR PLAN INFORMATION CHECKLIST

_____ 1. All necessary dimensions.
    _____ a. Outside walls
    _____ b. Interior partitions
    _____ c. Window and door center lines
    _____ d. Edges and thicknesses of solid masonry

    _____ e. Sizes of terraces, walks, and driveways
    _____ f. Special construction
    _____ g. Arrowheads on all dimension lines

_____ 2. Window symbols, door symbols with swing.
_____ 3. Window and door identification.
_____ 4. Center lines in windows.
_____ 5. Type of passageways through partitions.
_____ 6. Stair symbol and note: UP or DOWN and number of risers.
_____ 7. Steps necessary at exterior doors, different floor levels.
_____ 8. Vent stack in 8″ wet-wall.
_____ 9. Window and door schedules.
_____ 10. Thresholds under exterior doors or between rooms of different flooring materials.
_____ 11. Symbols for all stationary kitchen, bath, and laundry fixtures.
_____ 12. Built-in millwork.
_____ 13. Shelves and rods in clothes closets.
_____ 14. Fireplace symbol including hearth.
_____ 15. Broken line indicating roof outline, on 1-story plans or on second floor plans.
_____ 16. All lighting symbols.
    _____ a. Ceiling outlets
    _____ b. Wall fixture outlets
    _____ c. Switches with broken lines to outlets
    _____ d. Outside outlets and floodlights
    _____ e. Mechanical equipment outlets
    _____ f. Sufficient wall outlets
    _____ g. Special lighting
_____ 17. Medicine cabinets or closets in bathroom.
_____ 18. Ventilating fan in interior baths.
_____ 19. Note indicating size, spacing, and direction of ceiling framing.
_____ 20. Dashed lines showing scuttle to attic, if any.
_____ 21. Any special beams or structural members in overhead construction.
_____ 22. Any metal or wood columns.
_____ 23. Symbol for hot-water heater, central heating unit, or fixed mechanical equipment.
_____ 24. Hose bibbs.
_____ 25. Note indicating the drainage slope of concrete slabs (usually ⅛″ per ft).
_____ 26. Cutting-plane lines showing section detail locations.
_____ 27. Titles for all rooms, hallways, and areas.
_____ 28. Note indicating floor finish in each room (if no finish schedule is used).
_____ 29. Correct symbol hatching for materials.
_____ 30. Floor plan title and scale.

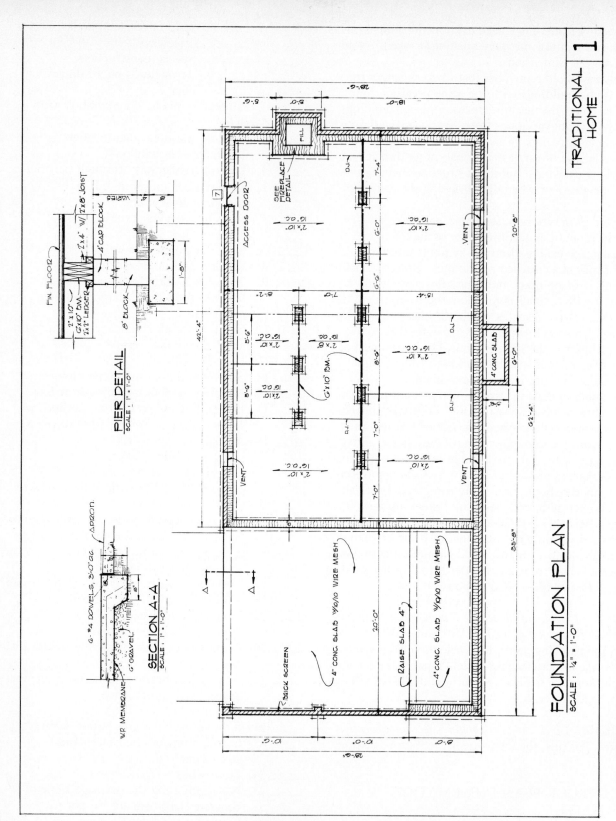

FIGURE 11-9 Foundation plan of a traditional home.

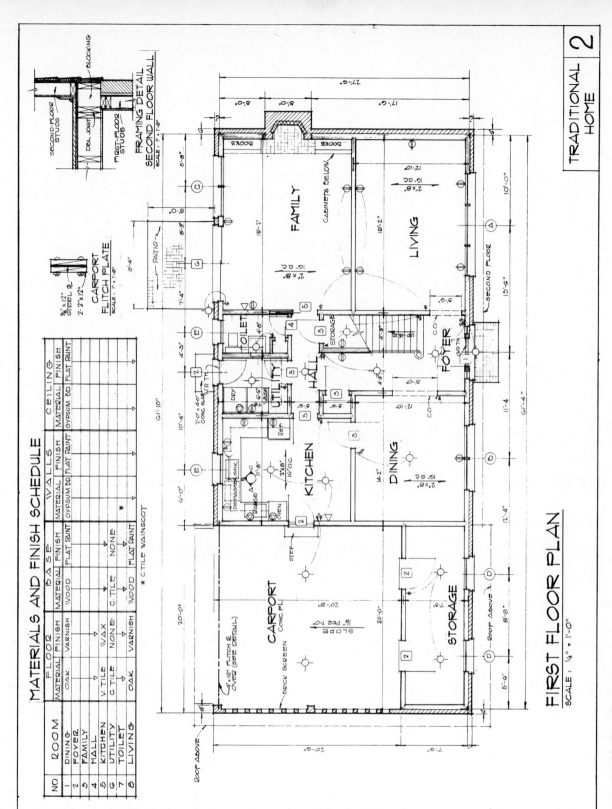

FIGURE 11-10 First-floor plan.

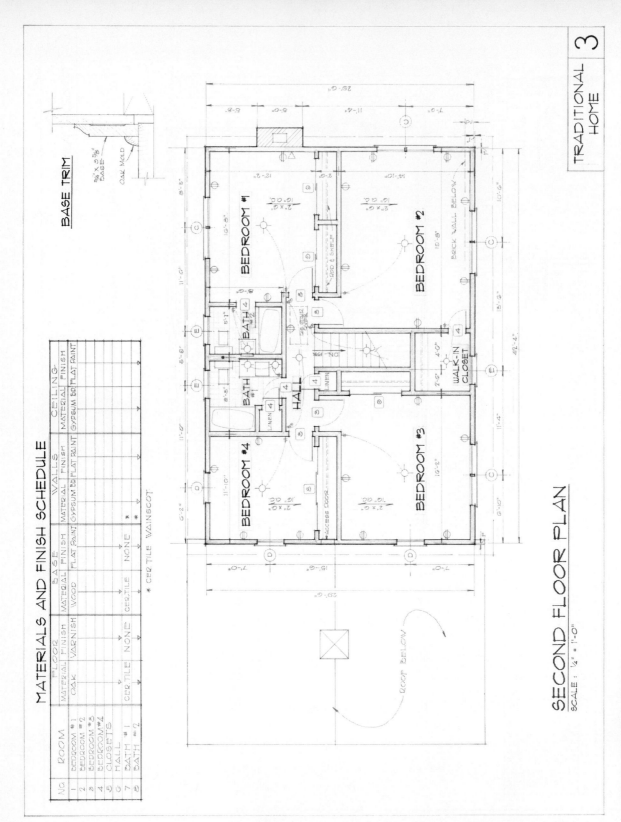

FIGURE **11-11** Second-floor plan.

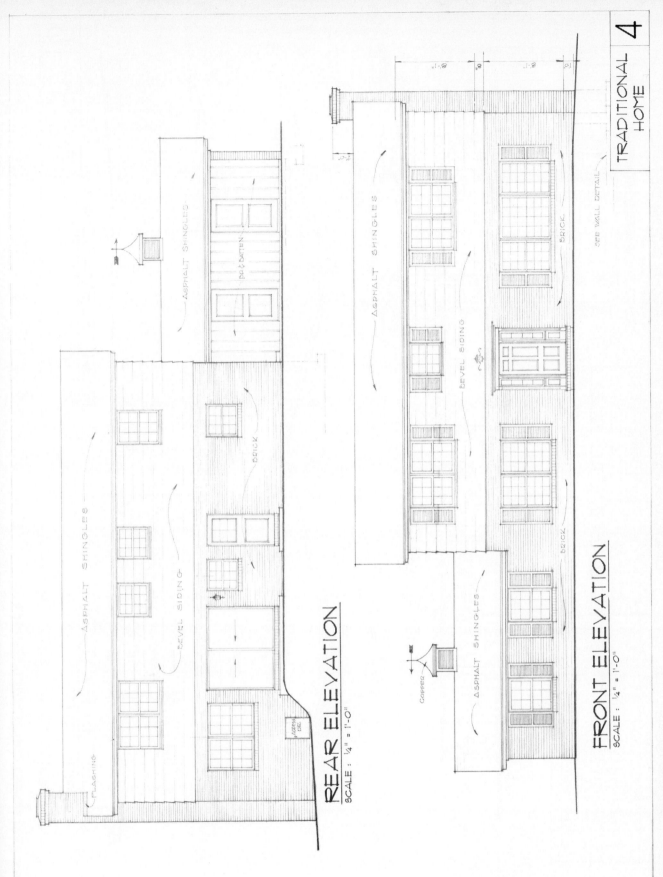

REAR ELEVATION

SCALE: 1/4" = 1'-0"

FRONT ELEVATION

SCALE: 1/4" = 1'-0"

TRADITIONAL HOME

4

FIGURE 11-12 Elevation views.

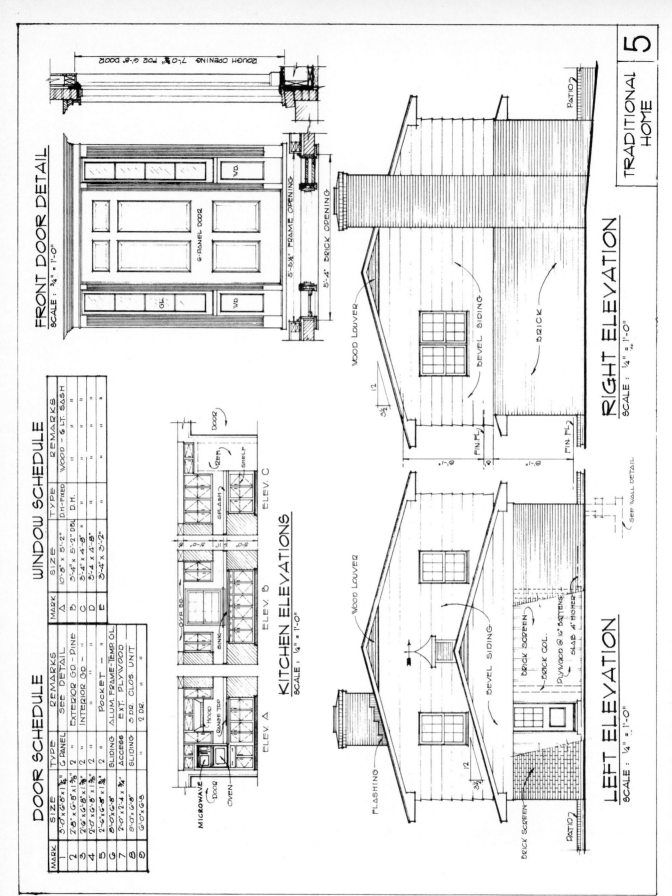

FIGURE 11-13 Elevation views, schedules, and details.

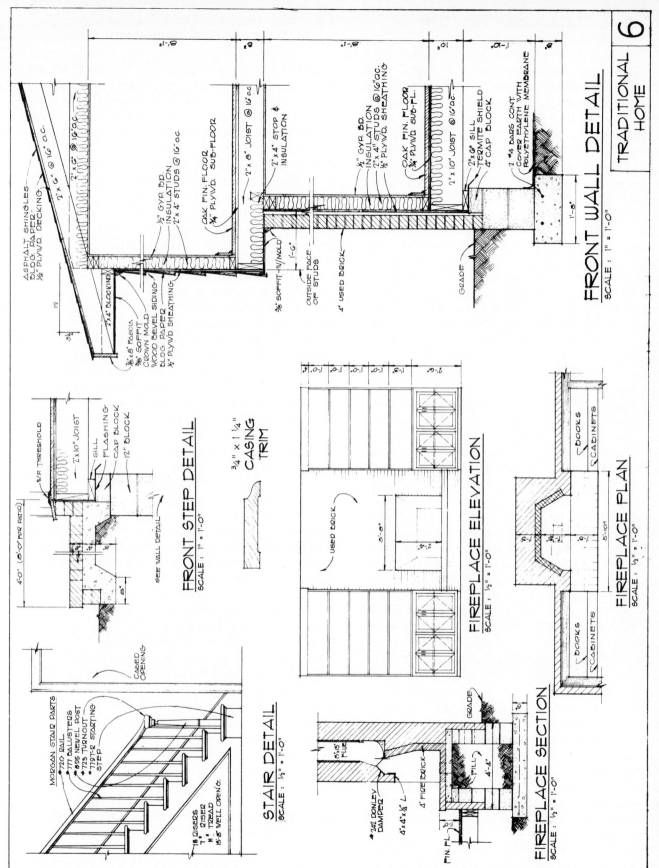

FIGURE 11-14 Wall section and details.

11.2 Develop the Second Floor Over the First-Floor Plan

If a 2-story house, similar to those in this chapter, is to be drawn, the second-floor plan is developed directly over the first-floor drawing. Sometimes architects make a print of the first floor and use it instead of the tracing. Start the second floor by first drawing the outside walls the same size as the walls below, unless a second-floor cantilever arrangement (Fig. 11-14) or a 1½-story house is being drawn. The knee walls under sloping roofs of typical 1½-story houses must be located on end elevations to determine the proper headroom in the living spaces. Knee walls should be a minimum of 4'-6" in height. Since light and ventilation are necessary in rooms with sloping walls, dormers must be planned so that the dormer windows will be on vertical planes. The position of the knee wall can be used to locate the position of the vertical dormer face, or smaller dormers can be placed higher on the roof. Additional sketches may be necessary in developing neat appearing dormers.

Partition layouts in second floors are somewhat restricted by the bearing walls below. Whenever possible, locate second-floor partitions directly over first-floor walls to avoid the need for additional support. Keep in mind that chimneys, stairs, and plumbing must be relative to the first floor when locating the walls, and that the vent stacks from first-floor plumbing must come up through second-floor partitions. Stairways should begin and end in hallways. Draw the top half of the stair representation from the first-floor half and include the proper note. Locate the center lines of second-floor windows; usually they are located directly above first-floor windows or centered over first-floor wall spaces. Complete the window symbols and identification. Generally, window and door identifications are incorporated with first-floor schedules. All rooms must communicate with halls. Locate and draw the door symbols with the correct swing. Usually, doors 2'-6" or 2'-8" wide are used in bedrooms, and bathroom doors can be 2'-0" to 2'-6" wide. Wider doors are required for wheelchairs. Partial, 1-story roofs, which are lower than the second-story roofs, should be shown to clearly describe their relationships. Also show scuttles or ceiling exhaust fans with broken lines. Locate and draw all bathroom fixtures and built-in cabinetwork to scale. Show the lighting symbols and dimension partitions, walls, and windows, similar to the first-floor plan. Draw in the hatching symbols for materials, where necessary, and complete all appropriate construction notes.

Because of the similarity between first- and second-floor plan requirements, use the first-floor plan checklist to verify all the necessary second-floor plan information upon completion.

11.3 Use the First-Floor Plan to Develop the Foundation (Basement) Plan

In modern residential construction, basements are not as popular as they once were. Living space aboveground is usually more comfortable, and may be more economical. However, a basement is included in the 1-story house located in Appendix F to show its correct representation. Foundation plans of houses with crawl spaces would appear similar except that usually masonry piers are employed instead of metal columns for the floor framing supports Fig. 11-9.

Develop the foundation plan, like the second-floor plan, on tracing paper taped down directly over the first-floor plan. As with other steps in the completion of working drawings, the foundation plan requires information about the total concept of the structure before it can be drawn. Reference must be made to a *typical sill detail* or wall section in order to relate the framing of the first floor and its position on the foundation wall Fig. 11-14. This information must be carefully observed if a satisfactory foundation is to be developed for the building. From the typical wall section of the 1-story house, notice that the exterior sheathing surface is flush with the outside surface of the foundation walls, and that the dimensions on the floor plan are given for the sheathing surface in Appendix F. In this case, the outside foundation lines are simply drawn exactly over the floor plan exterior lines. Relationships with other types of sill detail may not be as simple. For example, brick veneer construction must have a foundation surface about 5" to 6" wide beyond the wood framing upon which the brick must bear. Other sill details may require still different relationships between the wood framing and the foundation walls. For this reason, the typical wall construction detail must be worked out (at least on preliminary sketches) before the foundation plan can be started. Study various sill details and observe the relative positions of the wood framing and the foundation wall. Western frame sills are commonly called *box sills*.

The general shape of the foundation is drawn first, and since economical 8" C.M.U. has been selected for the foundation in this home, the thickness of the wall is scaled 8" wide. Because the front entrance requires a concrete walk, which is exposed to the weather, this area could not be excavated; yet a C.M.U. wall, for continuity, surrounds the area. A note is added to indicate the area is not excavated. Represent footing widths with broken lines. A satisfactory footing for 8" block walls is usually 16" wide. Even though the footings for the carport and terrace slab are poured integrally, the bearing surface of slabs is also shown with a broken line.

One important problem involved in foundation plan development is the method of supporting the first floor if wood framing is employed. It becomes obvious that

FIGURE 11-15 Pen-and-ink elevation rendering of a traditional home.

floor joists cannot span the entire width of the plan, even if they are placed parallel to the short dimension. To best utilize the lengths of available joists and to provide direct support under important points of load-bearing walls above, a 4 × 10 wood beam or girder is indicated along the stairwell through the entire length of the basement. This beam is supported by the foundation and equally spaced metal columns. Each column has an independent footing, also shown by broken lines. Columns are also necessary on the opposite side of the stairwell to prevent overloading the header joists at the ends of the stairwell.

As mentioned previously, concrete block piers would be used instead of the metal columns if a similar wood frame floor were constructed above a crawl space with no basement. Ordinarily, the piers would be 8″ × 16″, hatched like the walls, and shown with independent footings and locating dimensions.

Another important consideration is the support for load-bearing walls above, other than those above the main girder. Outside walls are directly supported by the foundation walls, but interior walls must depend on floor joists for support. If a partition is perpendicular to the floor joists, no extra support is necessary, since its weight is distributed over a number of joists. But if the partition is parallel to the joists, often no joist falls directly below and, therefore, extra joists must be introduced to carry the load. Notice that double joists are indicated below parallel partitions. The layout of the first-floor plan, then, is a definite aid in placing these additional members in the first-floor framing. Extra joists are also necessary below concentrations of bathroom fixtures and other special dead loads.

Place all notes and information pertaining to the first-floor framing on the foundation plan. Notes indicating details of the second-floor framing are included on the first-floor plan. In other words, the framing notes on any plan should pertain to the framing construction *directly overhead*. Use the conventional note for showing the size, spacing, and direction of first-floor joists (see Table 8-6 for joist sizes).

Windows should be installed in basements to allow light and ventilation. Screened vents and an access door are necessary in crawl spaces. Here, again, it may be necessary to refer to elevation sketches or typical sections for more information about the placement of basement windows. Until the elevations are completed, it is usually difficult to determine the level of the grade line and whether areaways around certain basement windows are necessary. If they are needed, include a section detail on the foundation plan sheet.

Dimension all masonry (to faces), partitions, columns or piers (to centers), slabs, and special framing; and complete all notes indicating the floor material, windows, doors, and framing sizes. Title the plan and show its scale.

FOUNDATION (BASEMENT) PLAN INFORMATION CHECKLIST

_____ 1. All necessary dimensions.
      _____ a. Masonry walls, surfaces, and thicknesses
      _____ b. Partitions
      _____ c. Columns or pilasters
      _____ d. Girders or beams
      _____ e. Double joists
      _____ f. Outside slabs
      _____ g. Arrowheads on all dimension lines

_____ 2. Window symbols, door symbols with swing.

_____ 3. Stair symbol and riser notes.

_____ 4. Footing indications under walls, columns, exterior stoops, piers.

_____ 5. Special floor framing.

_____ 6. Areaways, if necessary.

_____ 7. Lighting symbols.
      _____ a. Ceiling outlets
      _____ b. Switches with broken lines to outlets
      _____ c. Sufficient wall outlets
      _____ d. Mechanical equipment outlets

_____ 8. Symbol hatching of materials.

_____ 9. Note indicating unexcavated areas.

_____ 10. Note indicating floor surfaces.

_____ 11. Exterior slabs.

_____ 12. Plumbing fixtures, heating units.

_____ 13. Foundation wall vents and access door.

_____ 14. Fireplace foundation.

_____ 15. Basement door.

_____ 16. Foundation plan title and scale.

11.4 Project Elevations from the Floor Plan

Elevations (Fig. 11-16) are the drawings of a house, revealing not only the height dimensions and exterior materials, but also providing carpenters and workers a total view of the building. This total representation is more important than generally realized. Specific information about various parts of a building is shown in details, drawn large enough to reveal small members; but unless these details can be related to the total concept of the building, they cannot be understood. The elevations help tie together these bits of information. Also, if minor construction details and dimensions are not shown on working drawings, workers must continually refer to elevation views for the specified finished appearance. Builders have slightly different methods of arranging members and trim during construction without violating given details. A graphic representation of the correct finished appearance, then, places considerable importance on the elevation views. Drawing these views is not difficult if the proper procedure is followed.

Although we have not discussed wall sections (Figs. 10-1 through 10-4), which are necessary in determining definite elevation view heights, the student should at this point develop a typical wall section, if the drafter has not already done so for the foundation plan (see Section 10.2). Consideration should also be given to the general roof layout and the amount of roof overhang, especially if offset exterior walls are encountered, which may require a roof plan drawn on another sheet of paper.

Draw the elevations by taking their widths from the plan view and their heights from the developed wall sections. If the house has a gable roof, start with an end elevation so that the profile of the roof can be established and transferred directly to the other elevations. Tape the plan to the board directly above the intended space for the elevation so that projection can be made with instruments. Or a tick strip (a narrow strip of paper with the necessary markings) can be used to transfer all outside walls, window and door openings, center lines, and even roof overhangs to the elevation view. Use the same scale as the plan ($\frac{1}{4}'' = 1'\text{-}0''$), allowing direct transfer. Elevations of larger buildings are usually drawn to the $\frac{1}{8}'' = 1'\text{-}0''$ scale; however, if possible draw the elevations at the same scale as the floor plan.

Inasmuch as an elevation must have a horizontal line from which to spring, the tentative _grade line_ is the logical beginning. Draw a light horizontal line (even if the finished grade must be made to slope later) and allow enough space on the paper for the foundation below and the height of the building above. From the sill detail or wall section, lay out the _finish floor line_ lightly—it will become an important reference line later. Various types of construction establish definite dimensions from the grade to the finished floor surface. Ceiling heights are indicated by distances to the top of the double wall plate, which usually are $8'\text{-}1''$ above the floor line. Draw two plate heights if two stories are required. Remember that both the ceiling framing and roof rafters bear on a double plate on top of the wall.

Take roof pitches and cornice construction from details or sketches and lay out the profile of the roof after the center line of the ridge is established. On sloping roofs, be sure the roof line allows for the width of the rafters at the bird's-mouth on the top-plate bearing surface (see Figs. 10-1A and 10-2A). If trussed rafters are used, the lower chord of the trusses rests directly on the wall plates. Extend the roof lines beyond the walls to show the proper amount of overhang, draw the fascia board, and complete the exterior treatment of the cornice area. After critical examination, slight changes may be necessary in the roof profile to obtain the desired pleasing appearance.

To establish the heights of windows and doors on the

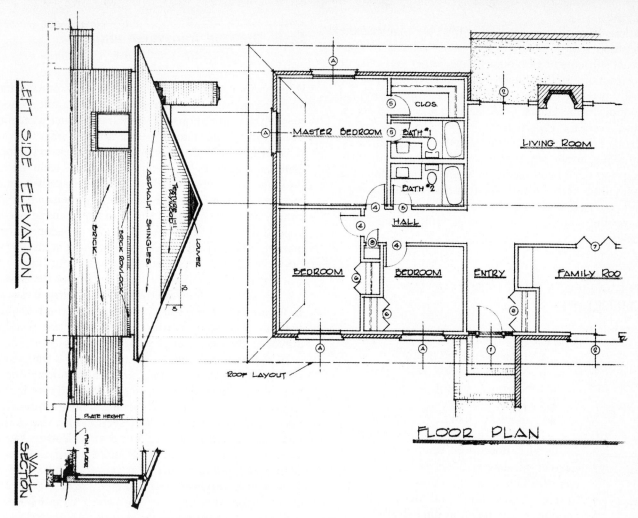

FIGURE 11-16 Project elevation views from the plan so that correct measurements can be quickly made.

elevation, measure the height of exterior doors (usually 6'-8" or 7'-0" stock doors) from the *finish floor surface*, and extend this height as the head for all windows and doors on the first-floor level. Correct window sizes, taken from manufacturers' literature, are then established from the head height. Features of windows and doors, including trim and brick sills if necessary, are carefully drawn on elevation views. If a number of similar windows are needed, it usually becomes simpler to draw the window accurately on a small piece of paper first and then slip this drawing under each window position and trace it. Second-floor windows are located according to inside requirements and outside appearance; generally, upper windows line up with lower windows, and higher windows are reduced in size. Place window identifications (letters or numbers within small circles) directly on the window symbol.

Project chimneys from the plan also, and extend their heights at least 2' above the ridge line (see Fig. 10-22). Slight changes in position are possible through attic spaces if chimneys must appear symmetrical after piercing the roof.

Draw the footing and foundation lines below the grade lines with broken lines. Basement heights are usually 7' to 8' and footings should extend down below local frost depths. The grade line can be changed, if necessary, to the desired finished level or slope. Strengthen all important elevation lines, especially the outline of the view and the eave line, and show the symbol for the various exterior materials. Portions of the hatching should be left out near the centers of large areas to prevent a mechanical appearance.

Dimensions on elevations need be only those that cannot be shown on details and plans. Dimension the finish floor and ceiling heights, chimney heights, extended wall heights, window heights (other than standard door heights), and other features requiring a vertical dimension. To make the elevations informative without appearing too cluttered, simple notes should indicate exterior materials such as flashings, gutters, downspouts, and steps. Indicate the roof pitch with a graphic diagram (see Section 10.3).

Usually, four elevations must be drawn for a complete description of the building; project the other elevations from the correct wall of the floor plan and the elevation just completed. It is advantageous to construct subsequent elevations in line, either vertically or horizontally, so that the layout of major features can be easily projected, even though features appear reversed in opposite elevations. Occasionally, it becomes necessary, even for experienced drafters, to make minor changes in the elevations and plans as work progresses. Students surely can expect changes to occur in early exercises until more facility is attained in handling the many interrelated conditions that exist in developing a complete set of working drawings. But perseverance is rewarding—subsequent drawings will become much easier.

ELEVATION VIEWS INFORMATION CHECKLIST

_____ 1. All necessary dimensions.
     _____ a. Floor-to-ceiling heights
     _____ b. Window heights
     _____ c. Chimney heights
     _____ d. Footing depths
     _____ e. Roof overhang
     _____ f. Special feature heights or depths
_____ 2. Grade line, floor lines, ceiling lines.
_____ 3. Correct window symbols and identification.
_____ 4. Correct door symbols and identification.
_____ 5. Footing and foundation lines (broken).
_____ 6. Roof slope indications.
_____ 7. Exterior materials symbols.
_____ 8. Exterior materials notes.
_____ 9. Louvers; attic, crawl space, roof.
_____ 10. Notes indicating special features.
_____ 11. Section cutting plane lines and identifications.
_____ 12. Exterior steps, stoops, roofed open areas, railings.
_____ 13. Columns, shutters.
_____ 14. Dormers.
_____ 15. Flashing, gutters, downspouts.
_____ 16. Elevation title and scale.

11.5 Select Scales Suitable to the Details

To utilize remaining spaces on working drawings, details must be drawn to accommodate the layout. Usually, a detail is easier to read if it is drawn to a large scale. When there are many details, one or more additional sheets may be required. Follow the procedure indicated in Section 10.2 when drawing the _wall sections_ as well as other major details. For clarity, the typical wall section in the 2-story house has been drawn in its entirety. (see Fig. 11-14).

11.6 Drawing Transverse and Longitudinal Sections

When buildings have various floor levels or unusual interior construction, such as split levels, a full section through the entire house is often drawn. Such a section shows features in their relative positions, rather than as isolated details on the drawing, and becomes very informative to workers on the job. A full section taken through the narrow width of a house is known as a _transverse_ section; through the long dimension, it is known as a _longitudinal_ section. Either can be used, depending on which plane reveals the necessary information. The cutting plane can be straight across, or it can be offset to conveniently gather in features on several planes, thereby increasing the value of the drawing. Broken lines are also effective in showing, if necessary, important structural members beyond visible surfaces. For convenience, full sections are usually drawn to the same scale as the elevations.

In the drawings for the 1-story house, a transverse section has been included to show, among other things, the construction of the sloping ceiling and roof in the living–dining area and the shape and position of cabinets in the kitchen area. The section also shows the basement and unexcavated foundation clearly, as well as information about the walls and the roof overhang. It reveals the shape of the total living–dining volume.

To draw a transverse or longitudinal section, tape the tracing paper directly over the proper elevation view and trace the outline of the house, the floor levels, heights of windows and doors, the foundation, grade line, and so on. Considerable time is saved by working directly over the elevation. Interior partitions, stairs, and the like, are taken from the plans. Keep in mind the direction and spacing of ceiling and floor framing members, the placement of girders, headers, columns, and so on. Limit the notes on the section to important features within the building. Place the cutting plane indication on the floor plan where offsets, if any, can be seen. Floor and ceiling heights, other vertical dimensions, footing depths, and roof pitch are easily dimensioned on the full section.

11.7 Drawing the Kitchen Details (Interior Elevations)

Kitchens generally require built-in cabinets for work counters, fixture enclosures, and storage. Builders usually subcontract this millwork and have it installed prebuilt instead of building it on the job.

Kitchen details, showing the size, shape, and general cabinet design, are helpful to the subcontractors, who must not only estimate the cost, but must fabricate and install the units as well. The heights and widths of kitchen cabinets have been standardized according to body measurements Fig. 6-66; however, special arrangements and conditions often exist in custom-designed kitchens, requiring accurately drawn details on the working drawings.

To draw the kitchen details, select a scale that will make the finished elevations neither too large nor too small; usually, $1/2'' = 1'-0''$ is the best scale on residential drawings. Lay out each wall elevation upon which the cabinets are to be installed (keep them in a horizontal row if space allows) and lightly draw the horizontal heights of the cabinet features: 4" toe space, 36" base cabinet height, thickness of the countertop, heights of the wall cabinets, and so on. Notice that wall cabinets often only go to a point 14" below the standard 8' ceiling because of difficulty in reaching any higher. This area above wall cabinets can be furred out flush with the face of the cabinets, or cabinets can be extended to the ceiling to be used for additional storage. Sometimes a shelf is left above wall cabinets, but it becomes a dust collector. These features must be shown on the details. When the kitchen is U or L shaped, the cabinets must return toward the viewer at one or both corners. At this point a *profile* section of the cabinetwork is drawn, and either the cut profile is hatched entirely, or it can be shown as a section with the top, doors, shelf construction, and the like, carefully described. After the returning sections are drawn, the remaining cabinet elevation surfaces are carefully laid out to show the doors and drawer faces (they look best if symmetrical and larger drawers are shown at the bottom of the cabinet) with hardware indications simply drawn. Use broken lines to indicate the door swing and the shelves within the cabinets. Show any windows or doors with their trim, which can be seen on the kitchen elevations. If necessary, draw an enlarged plan of the kitchen; otherwise, the arrangement of the cabinets shown on the floor plans is satisfactory. Include a symbol on the plan indicating the proper view of each kitchen detail, such as A, B, and C. Indicate all installed kitchen equipment, sink, range, range hood, oven units, dishwasher, and so on, with a note, strengthen important lines, and add appropriate dimensions. Do not forget a splash above the countertops, and indicate the countertop covering material.

11.8 Drawing the Bathroom Details (Interior Elevations)

Here, again, details must be drawn of bathroom interiors if wall tile or other specially applied surfacing is to be used for the wall covering so that subcontractors can estimate and satisfactorily complete the work. Many bathrooms have built-in cabinetwork also Fig. 6-59.

To draw the bathroom details, use a scale similar to the kitchen details (usually $1/2'' = 1'-0''$), and lay out in a horizontal row if possible the heights and widths of the walls that are to receive special covering or cabinetwork. Show the height of the wall wainscoting (6' high around shower areas, and 4' high or higher on other walls), all mirrors, cabinets, bathroom fixtures, tile fixtures, wall offsets, windows, and doors, all at their proper scale and heights. Relate each bathroom elevation to the floor plan layout with a direction indication. Use light horizontal and vertical lines to represent the elevation symbol for wall tile; the most common ceramic tile size is scaled 4" square. Complete the necessary notes and dimensions, title each view, and show the scale.

11.9 Drawing Fixed-Glass Details

With the increased use of glass in many homes, fixed glass has become a popular method of providing generous window openings without the use of prefabricated window units. Some prefabricated units, however, incorporating both fixed glass and opening sash, can be installed into rough openings that have been sized according to the units. Fixed glass installed in framing on the job is not restricted by manufacturers' sizes and can be made satisfactory if well-conceived details are followed. Appearance may require finish lumber for the structural framing around the glass, or finish lumber must surround rough framing when the fixed glass is trimmed out (Fig. 10-12).

In drawing fixed-glass details, sections must be drawn through the sill, jamb, head, and adjoining mullions showing the following conditions: first, the rough opening must be made substantial enough to eliminate any structural changes in the framing caused by shrinkage or bending of members from overhead wall loads. Proper lintels must be provided above fixed glass to prevent stresses, unless plank and beam framing relieves the window opening of this necessity.

Second, the surrounds within the rough window opening, which receive the glass, must have rabbets at least $1/2''$ deep to allow a loosely sized piece of glass to be set in a bed of putty and be held firmly, yet allowing slight flexibility. Window stops (usually attached on the interior) must be sized as thick as the rabbets so that their surface coincides with the exterior trim surface in contact with the glass. The trim member forming the exterior sill should be inclined slightly to allow water to drain properly from the sill surface. This principle of water drainage is true of all exposed materials forming ledges on walls. Drips should also be provided on head and sill exteriors to prevent water from running back under the members into the construction. Outside and inside wall edges must be kept in line so that inside casing trim will cover the joint between the surrounds and the interior wall surfacing and the exterior will work out with exterior surfacing materials. In brick veneer construction, the glass is placed within the stud wall, yet the trim must be wide enough to cover the air space between the stud wall and the brick. A masonry sill must be shown in masonry wall openings with fixed glass. Inside stools below the fixed glass must extend beyond the inside wall surface and have proper apron trim. Each detail should be labeled, and dimensions should be applied to the different trim members. If prefabricated, operating sash for ventilation may be incorporated with fixed windows, the glass surface of both should line up on the same vertical plane.

11.10 The Site Plan Orients the House to the Lot

The site plan, showing important natural features, orients the building accurately on the property. Information about lot size, shape, elevation, contours, roads, setback requirements, and the like, must be taken from a survey map or legal description of the property and drawn to a convenient scale. Use the engineering scale to lay out and dimension all land measurements in feet and decimal parts of a foot. The dimensions on construction features, however, should be shown in feet and inches. Usually, a scale of $1'' = 20'$ or $1'' = 10'$ is satisfactory, depending on the size of the lot; sometimes the scale $1/16'' = 1' - 0''$ is used, but the drawing should be large enough to show features and dimensions clearly.

After the outline of the lot is blocked in, determine the most favorable position of the house, and draw the outline of the foundation and all the exterior slabs, terraces, walks, drives, and the like. (Occasionally, a roof plan is drawn instead of the foundation.) If contour lines are available from the survey map, show the original lines broken and the finish contour lines as solid lines. On the site plan of the solar home (Fig. 11-2), the contour lines are shown with $1'$ intervals, and upon

investigation it will be noticed that the lot slopes toward the left-rear corner. Excavation from the basement has been used to build up the terrace slab to its necessary level, and the finish contour lines indicate this surface change. Hatch the house area to give it prominence, and, if necessary, use other hatching variations to show relative contrast on other important indications. Often trees or other natural features are shown on the site plan to denote their removal or retention during excavation and grading. See Fig. 11-17 for drive layouts.

Use the following checklist, from FHA site plan information requirements, as a guide for dimensioning and completing the plot plan.

SITE PLAN INFORMATION CHECKLIST

_____ 1. Scale of the drawing and title.

_____ 2. Dimensions of the site and north point.

_____ 3. Lot and block number of the site.

_____ 4. Dimensions of front, rear, and side yards (setbacks from property line to the house).

_____ 5. Location and dimensions of garage, carport, or other accessory buildings.

_____ 6. Location of walks, driveways, and approaches, with dimensions and materials.

_____ 7. Location of steps, terraces, porches, fences, and retaining walls.

_____ 8. Location and dimensions of easements and established setback requirements, if any.

_____ 9. Elevation level of first floor, floor of garage, carport, or other buildings.

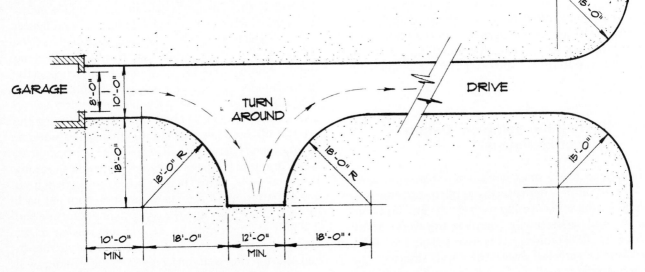

FIGURE 11-17 Layout of private drives and turning radii.

_____ 10. Finish-grade level at each principal corner of the structure.

_____ 11. Finish grade at both sides of abrupt changes of grade such as walls and slopes.

_____ 12. Other elevation levels that may be necessary to show grading and drainage.

_____ 13. Location of a reference bench mark and its elevation, from which contractor can relate all grades.

_____ 14. Existing trees, if any, to be removed or retained and their identification.

_____ 15. Location and identification of utility lines or pipes that will service the structure.

_____ 16. Septic tank and leaching field, if required.

_____ 17. Obstructions such as utility poles, catch basins, and hydrants.

EXERCISES

WORKING DRAWINGS OF SMALL HOMES

The following exercises should be done on 22″ × 34″ drawing paper with graphite lead or Mylar with plastic lead. Lay out a ½″ border at the top, bottom, and right side and a 1½″ border on the left side. Select a title block of your choice. All drawings are to be drawn to scale using instruments.

1. Draw the first floor plan of the residence in Fig. 11-10; use the scale of ¼″ = 1′-0″.

2. Draw the foundation plan of the residence in Fig. 11-9; use the scale of ¼″ = 1′-0″.

3. Draw the front elevation from Fig. 11-12 and the left side elevation from Fig. 11-13; use the scale of ¼″ = 1′-0″. Draw the finish schedule (make room title spaces ⅜″ high) and kitchen elevation at a scale of ¼″ = 1′-0″.

4. Draw the front wall detail from Fig. 11-14 using a scale of 1″ = 1′-0″, and the fireplace plan, section, and elevation at a scale of ½″ = 1′-0″.

5. Using the small beach house from Residential Planning Exercise 1, prepare working drawings of the following at a scale of ¼″ = 1′-0″: floor plan, foundation plan, exterior elevations, cross section, and bath elevation; at a scale of 1″ = 1′-0″, draw a typical wall section. Show a room finish schedule. Combine views on a drawing to create good composition.

REVIEW QUESTIONS

1. When starting a floor plan, why is it necessary to begin with general shapes and light lines?

2. What is meant by a _wet-wall?_

3. On wood frame construction drawings, why is it convenient for workers to have dimensions shown from the outside of exterior wall studs to the center lines of partitions?

4. Why are lengthy notes about construction commonly put in the specifications rather than on the working drawings?

5. Why is a floor plan more readable when symbol hatching has been used throughout the walls?

6. Does a joist note, giving size, spacing, and direction and shown on a floor plan, pertain to the framing above or below?

7. Why are piers within a crawl space generally masonry? How is this indicated?

8. What does the term _unexcavated_ mean when shown on part of a foundation plan?

9. Of what value is the finish floor line indication on an elevation view?

10. What dimensions must necessarily be put on elevation views?

11. What is the minimum width for a residential driveway for one-way traffic?

12. At what scale are bathroom elevations usually drawn?

13. How can columns and load-bearing walls be eliminated from a basement and at the same time maintain the structural integrity of the floor above?

14. What is the standard height from the floor to the top of doors and windows in residences?

15. Why is the floor plan developed before the foundation plan in working drawings?

16. Place the following drawings in the order they would appear in a set of residential working drawings: exterior elevations, foundation plan, bathroom and kitchen details, site plan, typical wall sections, and floor plan.

17. Why are doors numbered on a working drawing floor plan?

18. How are section cuts referenced on floor plans?

19. What working drawing contains the most information about the construction of the residence from the foundation to the roof?

20. How far should wood siding be placed above the exterior grade at the perimeter of the building?

RESIDENTIAL MECHANICAL AND ELECTRICAL SYSTEMS

"A comfortable house is a great source of happiness. It ranks immediately after health and good conscience."
—SYDNEY SMITH

12

Much of the comfort and livability of our present-day structures is provided by the wide variety of mechanical and electrical equipment now available to us. The various methods of conditioning the air within a building, the host of electrical appliances and lighting devices, the accommodations for plumbing facilities, arrangements for use of public utilities—all must be given careful attention by the designer of both homes and commercial buildings. No structure is considered complete without adequate provision for this equipment and the human comfort it affords (see Fig. 12-1).

For large jobs, architects commonly employ the services of registered engineers to design layouts and furnish drawings dealing with mechanical and electrical systems. Engineering firms, who employ engineers specializing in this type of work, are equipped to handle the complexity of problems involved. Separate drawings such as a "Heating, Ventilation, and Air-Conditioning Plan," "Electrical Plan," and "Plumbing Plan," are prepared and combined with the architectural set of working drawings. However, much of the technical information needed on larger installations is not usually required for the majority of residential work; subcontractors can design and install conventional residential equipment with a minimum of information on working drawings. Commonly, this information can be included on the regular floor plan. Of course, when regular floor plans become overcrowded with notes, symbols, and information, it frequently is advisable to draw separate plans for each of these areas of information, especially for the heating system.

Even though subcontractors usually lay out and design conventional residential heating–cooling, plumb-

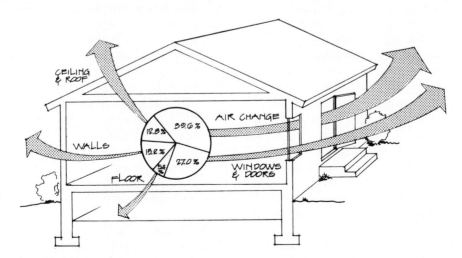

FIGURE 12-1 Heat loss in the typical home. Calculations based on one air change per hour and double pane windows and doors.

ing, and electrical systems, the student of architectural drawing, in order to plan for accommodating this equipment, should understand the general characteristics of the currently used systems and the problems involved in making them successful. Their provision in the structure contributes to the workability of the total concept and thereby justifies their careful study.

12.1 Planning the Heating and Cooling Systems

In homes, the selection of the most appropriate heating system is closely related to other aspects of the building, such as necessity for a utility room, feasibility of a basement, and selection of floor construction materials, and probably requires more consideration during early planning than other equipment installations. The type and cost of fuel available in the area are important factors; the client's preference as to the method of heating the house requires attention. Local climate, degree of comfort desired, initial cost of equipment, efficiency, and amount of insulation should also be given serious thought. In many areas, year-round space conditioning is now almost a requirement, and equipment capable of providing interior comfort in all seasons is a sound investment.

Local and national codes relating to heating and cooling installation must be carefully observed.

12.2 Architectural Considerations for Heating and Cooling

Comfort and efficiency of heating and cooling equipment begin with incorporating the following construction features into the building during the design stage:

1. Protect the west walls of the house from direct afternoon sun. This can be done by placing the carport or garage on the west side or by using trees, plantings, or fences for protection.
2. Use large glass areas on the south side, with sufficient overhangs or sunshades to protect the glass from direct sun during the summer months.
3. Protect the house, if possible, from cold winter winds. This is a matter of orientation and the intelligent use of windbreaks.
4. Use a light-colored roof to reduce heat absorption during summer for more cooling efficiency.
5. Specify sufficient insulation in both the walls and the ceilings. Use 3″ minimum in exterior walls, 6″ minimum in ceilings for continual year-round comfort.
6. Provide for sufficient ventilation in attics, kitchens, baths, and laundries to eliminate excessive interior moisture.

7. In colder areas, specify insulating (double) glass in all fixed-glass windows and window units. Double panes will not only reduce important heat losses, but will prevent destructive condensation from forming on glass and surrounding wood trim.
8. Locate the heating unit near the chimney or provide as short and direct a vent pipe as possible.
9. For the most heating efficiency, plan a compact shape of the house perimeter.
10. In 2-story houses, provide coinciding first- and second-floor partitions for heat risers to the second story; chases may even be necessary.
11. Specify weather stripping on all doors and windows.
12. Follow state energy codes regarding architectural choices for insulation, glass and fresh air.

12.3 Current Residential Heating Systems

Employing various fuels and methods of installation, the following basic systems are now generally used for residential central heating:

1. *Forced warm air*, which heats the air in a furnace, forces it through ducts with the use of a fan to all the heated areas of the house, returns the cooled air, and filters it.
2. *Hot-water systems*, either one- or two-pipe, which heat water in a central boiler and circulate it through piping to the different rooms where various types of convectors, radiators, baseboard, or radiant panels supply the heat to the air.
3. *Electric resistance systems*, using electricity as an energy source, provide a comfortable radiant-type heat with the use of resistance wiring embedded in either floors or ceilings or mounted in metal baseboards.
4. *Heat pumps*, which use no primary fuel other than electricity to run the reverse cycle compressor, operate as a combination heating and cooling system. However, supplementary electric resistance heating elements are necessary during extreme temperature drops. The application for heating and cooling purposes is recent; heat pumps have been found adequate primarily in mild climates. A heat-pump unit is basically a refrigeration system using electrical energy to pump the natural heat from either air or water outside the house to produce a useful temperature level within the house. The procedure is reversed during summer cooling.

Although steam heat is occasionally used, its popularity as a method of residential heating is steadily declining.

In warm climates, small wall or floor units are sometimes more satisfactory than central systems. Also, unit heaters can be combined with central systems when isolated areas are difficult to heat with a main system.

12.3.1 Forced Warm Air Systems

These systems utilize a motor-driven fan to circulate filtered and hot water, gas, or oil flame heated air from the central heating unit, called an exchanger, through a system of ducts to each part of the house. Often provision is made for the introduction of a small amount of fresh outside air to the system. Warm air has become the most popular heating method in the majority of new homes throughout the country, mainly because of its economical initial cost and its compatibility and ease in combining with summer cooling systems. Heat distribution throughout the house is instantaneous, almost as soon as the furnace is turned on. Filters, introduced into the return ductwork, provide clean air throughout the operation. This heating system has an additional advantage: location of the furnaces is not restricted to basements or utility rooms. Furnaces of various types and sizes can conveniently be installed in crawl spaces, attics, small closets, or adjoining garages. In addition, the design features of many modern furnaces make them acceptable for installation in living spaces, such as recreation and play rooms. The furnace can be either the conventional *up-flow* or reverse *counterflow* or *hori-*

zontal-flow unit (see Fig. 12-2), depending on its placement and necessary duct system. Counterflow furnaces must be used when ducts are embedded in concrete slab floors or when above the floor furnaces must supply the warm air through ducts located in crawl spaces.

Various types of ductwork can be used with warm air furnaces. Circular sheet-metal or circular fiberglass ducts are usually the most economical. Fiberglass ducts are often used in attic installations and PVC coated steel ducts in concrete slab construction. Many systems utilize a perimeter arrangement, both in slabs and crawl spaces, as well as in some basement installations, whereby a continuous duct is placed near the periphery of the building, and a number of feeder ducts radiating out from the central plenum supply the perimeter duct with warm air (Figs. 12-3, 12-4, and 12-5). Room registers receive the warm air from the perimeter duct only. Another method utilizes a main trunk duct through the central part of the building, and smaller branch ducts carry the warm air to the different rooms. Rectangular sheet-metal ducts are usually used for this system, and a more compact and neater arrangement for basement installation results. Another system has a large central duct, called an *extended plenum*, with small circular ducts to each register (see Fig. 12-6).

Return ducts, usually shorter and larger in cross section, bring the cooled air back to the furnace.

The trend in residential installations is to give more consideration to return air duct sizing. Many systems

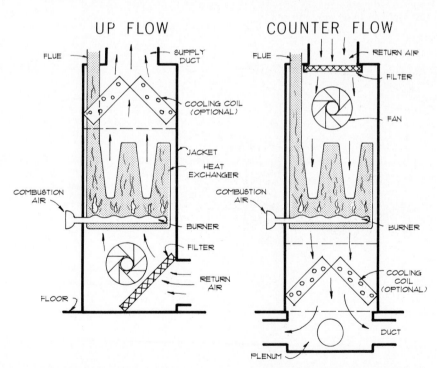

FIGURE 12-2 Section diagrams of typical gas-fired furnaces for warm air heating systems. Similar furnaces are made for other fuels and various furnace shapes are available. Cooling coils are shown for the combination cooling–heating operation. The counterflow furnace is usually used in slab or crawl space construction.

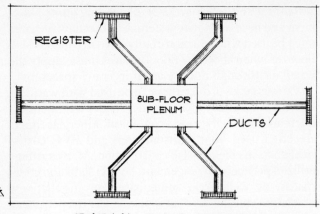

RADIAL-DUCT SYSTEM

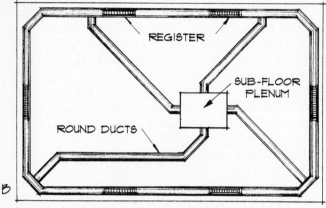

PERIMETER-LOOP SYSTEM

FIGURE 12-3 Warm air duct systems used in slabs and crawl spaces.

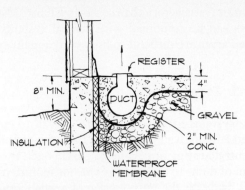

FIGURE 12-4 Sketch detail of slab construction and perimeter heat duct.

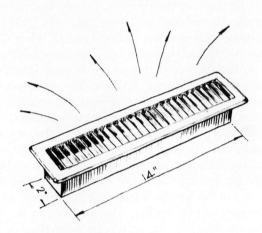

FIGURE 12-5 Typical floor register.

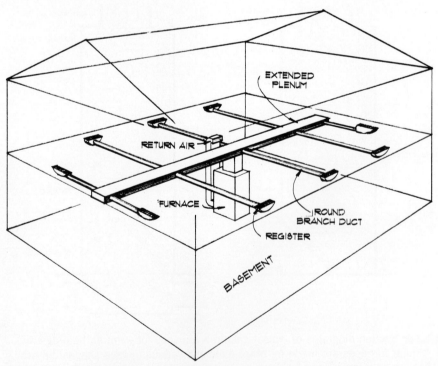

FIGURE 12-6 Warm air distribution system with an extended plenum and round ducts to the room registers. The furnace is located in the basement.

now provide for the introduction of fresh air through adjustable outside registers capable of compensating for air not returned from kitchens, baths, and vent fans. This maintains a continual supply of fresh air in the home and, because of infiltration, equalizes return air pressures.

We see, then, that various systems of warm air distribution are available to the home designer and that each system has slightly different characteristics and applications (Figs. 12-6 through 12-10).

The modern warm air system, comprising the furnace, ductwork, fan, and registers, usually has automatic controls to make it almost self-sufficient in opera-

tion. The controls necessary to operate a typical warm air system are:

1. Room thermostat
2. Fan thermostat
3. High-limit control

Occasionally, warm air furnaces are equipped with humidifiers that add water vapor to dry air in spaces in which case a *humidistat*, or humidity detector, is used to control the correct humidity level. Residential humidifiers are used in approximately 10 percent of residential heating systems.

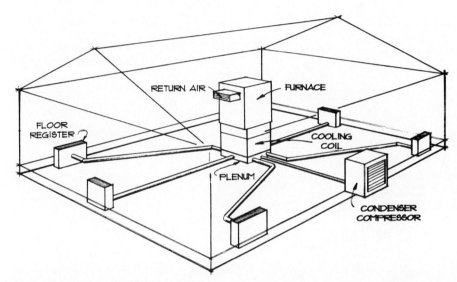

FIGURE 12-7 A radial distribution system using round ducts for a slab or crawl space. If used for heating only, the cooling coils and compressor–condenser unit are omitted. The counterflow furnace is necessary in this installation.

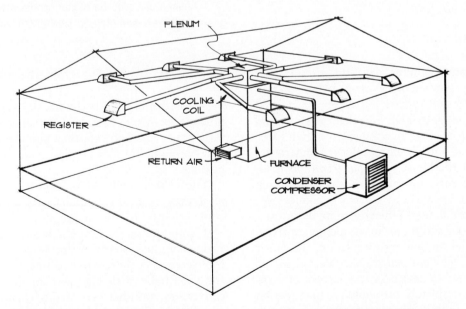

FIGURE 12-8 Attic distribution system using round ducts is practical when ceiling registers are used.

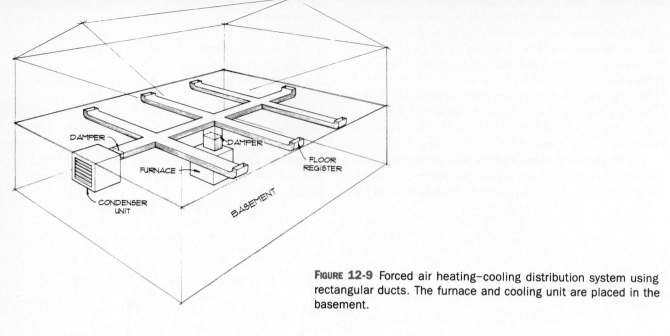

Figure 12-9 Forced air heating–cooling distribution system using rectangular ducts. The furnace and cooling unit are placed in the basement.

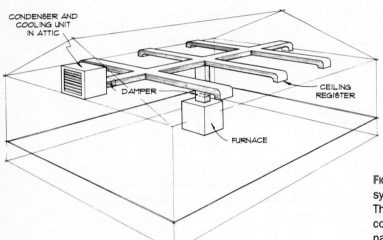

Figure 12-10 Forced air heating–cooling distribution system using rectangular ducts to ceiling registers. The furnace is placed on the first floor, and the cooling unit is placed in the attic. Warm air furnaces can also be placed in the attic, and cooling units are available for placement outside.

The *room thermostat* automatically turns the burner on when inside temperatures drop below a pre-established setting and turns it off when the desired temperature has been attained. The thermostat should be located 5′ from the floor on an inside wall with free air circulation that will provide uniform temperature levels throughout the house. The *fan thermostat* is located within the furnace unit and turns the fan on when the heated air in the plenum reaches a comfortable temperature for circulation. When the room thermostat turns the burner off, and the air in the plenum drops to a temperature level too low for circulation, the fan is turned off. The *high-limit control*, also located in the furnace unit, is a safety device for the purpose of turning the furnace completely off should a malfunction occur, causing the temperature within the plenum to become dangerously high.

12.3.2 Hot-water Systems (Hydronic Systems)

Heat distribution with the use of water has been in practice for many years and is still considered a very satisfactory method; approximately one-fourth of all new homes built today employ some form of hot-water heating.

The central boiler (Fig. 12-11), utilizing gas, oil, electricity, or coal as a fuel, heats water from a cold-water supply to the required temperature (usually 180°F) and pumps it throughout the rooms by means of various piping systems. A simple *one-pipe system*, having room converters or radiators connected in series, allows the water to be carried in the main pipe, diverted to the convectors, and then returned to the boiler for reheating. Special fittings allow restricted amounts of water into each convector so that the temperature of the water

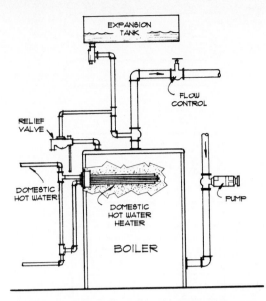

FIGURE 12-11 Diagram of a boiler used with hot-water heating systems.

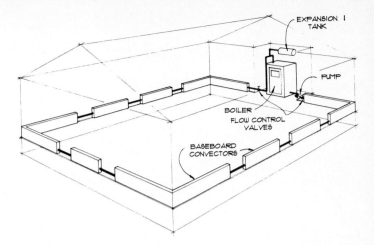

FIGURE 12-12 One-pipe hot-water heating system with baseboard convectors in the rooms.

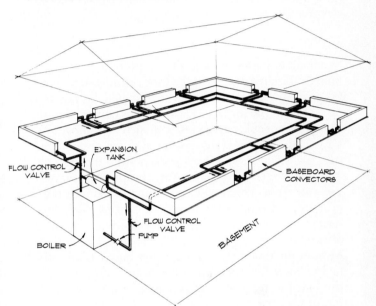

FIGURE 12-13 Two-pipe, reverse-return hot-water heating system with baseboard convectors. The boiler is installed in the basement.

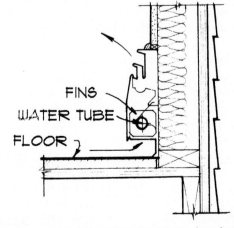

FIGURE 12-14 Sectional detail of a hot-water baseboard convector. Fins conduct the heat from the water tube to the air, creating air circulation through the baseboard.

in the later ones varies only slightly from the convectors closest to the boiler (see Fig. 12-12). A *two-pipe system* works more efficiently; of course, the initial installation cost is higher. One pipe supplies the rooms with hot water; the other, called the *return*, carries the cooled water back to the boiler (see Fig. 12-13). The return can be either direct or reverse, meaning the order in which the cooled water returns in relation to the order in which the warm water enters each convector. The reverse-return method is usually preferred.

Another system, referred to as a *radiant system*, distributes the hot water through pipes embedded either in concrete floor slabs or plastered ceilings (which, when warm, act as large radiators).

Various types of units can be used to dissipate the heat from the water to the air within each room. The conventional radiator has been used for years, but is a dust collector and uses floor space unless recessed into walls. More popular convectors are enclosed heaters with extended surface coils or finned tubes that give off the heat readily when air circulates through the units. Various sizes are available for wall-hung, recessed, or completely concealed installation.

A popular adaptation of the convector is the baseboard unit. The finned piping is arranged along the base of the outside walls and covered with a metal enclosure to resemble a baseboard. Heat is given off near the floor where it is needed, and various lengths of convectors can be combined with suitable trim to produce unobstructive heaters with pleasing appearances (see Fig. 12-14). Forced-air convectors must be used with residential heating–cooling hydronic systems, and they are adaptable to many commercial applications.

Hot-water boilers or heaters must be located in the

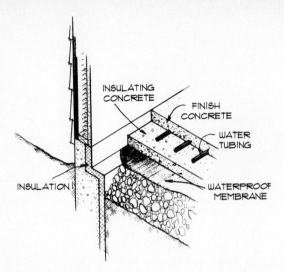

FIGURE 12-15 Floor panel hot-water heating embedded in concrete slab construction.

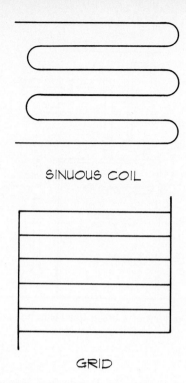

SINUOUS COIL

GRID

FIGURE 12-16 Two methods of installing hot-water pipe in radiant panel systems.

basement or in first-floor utility rooms of basementless homes. If coal or oil is used as a fuel, consideration must be given to storage space, which should be not too distant from the furnace. Each boiler is equipped with an expansion tank, either closed or open, to compensate for variations of the water volume at different temperature levels and to relieve air pockets from the system.

Another variation of a hot-water heating system is to use water from a high-efficiency water heater to supply heat to air handlers for forced-air heating. In many residences, hot water is used for bathing, washing dishes, and clothing only a couple of hours each day. Most of the time the domestic water heater is idle. By taking hot water from the water heater and passing it through a water to air heat exchanger, warm air can be forced into the home through a duct system.

Radiant panel hot-water systems employ either iron pipe, copper tubing embedded in floor slabs (Fig. 12-15), or copper tubing in ceiling plaster. Although copper is more expensive than steel, its installation is simpler and cheaper because it can be easily formed to fit panel areas and requires fewer fittings. Usually, a serpentine coil system is employed (see Fig. 12-16). Copper, being smaller in diameter and lighter, is practical for ceiling installation; the coils are fastened directly to metal or gypsum lath before the plaster is applied. Heat in floor slabs eliminates the usual coldness of concrete, yet because of its mass, concrete does not respond as quickly to heating as do ceiling panels. Higher surface temperatures (100° to 120°F) are allowable on radiant ceilings than on slab surfaces (80° to 85°F). Radiant surfaces heated to a temperature of 85° or 86°F will keep the occupants comfortable even with air temperatures slightly less than 60°. Balancing valves, usually located in closets or in other inconspicuous areas, allow complete control of heat within each room. The piping is usually taken off main supply lines to each room and fed back to the boiler by return mains, similar to typical two-pipe hot-water systems. Standard thermostatic controls cause the pump and boiler burner to maintain comfortable room temperatures. Because of the heat lag of slab radiant systems, it becomes necessary in many areas to include an exterior temperature change anticipator (outdoor thermostat), which controls the heat of the water in the piping in the system, balancing it with the actual need within the house.

The advantages of radiant panel heating are that:

1. The heat is clean, creating little dust and reducing the need for frequent repainting.
2. There are no visible registers or heating units within the rooms.
3. There are no drafts or noise from blower equipment.

12.3.3 Electric Heating Systems

Basically, electric heating systems convert electrical energy into heat with the use of resistance wiring installed in various ways throughout the structure. Both radiant- and convection-type heat are produced. In areas where electrical energy is economical, this type of fuel produces a very desirable method of heating residences. The heat is clean and easy to distribute and control, and installation of the system is economical. From a standpoint of safety, little damage can be done by fire since elements are designed to operate below 150°F. The heat can be placed exactly where it is needed as, for example, bathroom heaters or other auxiliary heaters.

Electrical resistance elements in baseboards, similar in appearance to hot-water baseboard units, can be installed along exterior walls to provide instantaneous and comfortable heat.

Radiant plaster ceilings are produced by attaching resistance wiring to gypsum lath. The wiring is manufactured in specific lengths to provide exact wattage ratings for a room according to its heat loss. Wattage sizes are based on the conversion ratio of *1 watt = 3.41 Btus*. The wiring is insulated with a protective covering and should not be cut or spliced. After the circuit has been carefully tested, a ½″ brown and finish plaster coat is applied. Connector wiring is regular nonheating type. Control thermostats are installed in each room. Care must be taken to keep the embedded wiring at least 6″ from walls and at least 8″ from any ceiling outlet boxes. It is recommended that 6″ of mineral insulation be applied over all radiant ceilings. Resistance wiring can also be installed between two layers of gypsum wall board in dry-wall construction (see Fig. 12-17). Spacing of the wiring on the first layer must allow for the nailing of the second layer, however, and a 3″ wide space below each ceiling joist is left void of the resistance wiring for this purpose. Otherwise, the installation is identical to plastered ceilings.

Resistance wiring can also be embedded in concrete slabs. Usually, 3″ of insulating concrete (vermiculite aggregate) is used as a base, the wiring is carefully stapled in place, and 1½″ or 2″ of surfacing concrete is applied over the wiring (see Fig. 12-18). The perimeter of the slab should be well insulated, and it is advisable to place more wiring near the periphery to compensate for heat loss to the exterior. This method of central heating is not recommended except in mild climates where floor surface temperatures will not have to be made uncomfortably warm. Resistance wiring in slabs is often satisfactory for auxiliary heating and for preventing snow from accumulating on driveways and walks.

One architectural advantage of any of the electrical resistance-type heating systems is the fact that no floor space need be reserved for a central heating unit, including chimney or flues. Another point, which is often overlooked, is that electrical heating installations are subject to minimum wear and therefore require less maintenance.

12.3.4 Heat Pumps

As mentioned earlier, the heat pump uses no combustion of fuel, such as gas, oil, or coal, as a primary heat source; rather, it operates on the principle that freely available outside air (or an economical water supply)

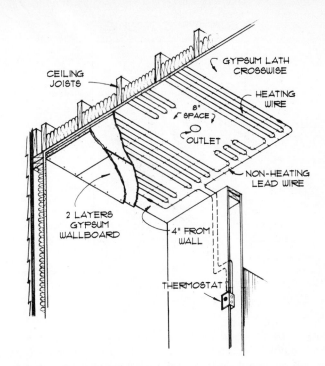

FIGURE 12-17 Installation of radiant heating electrical wire in dry-wall ceilings.

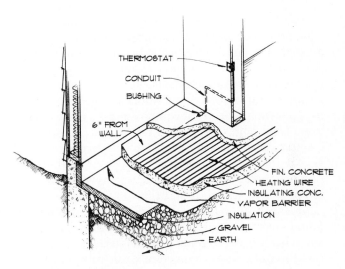

FIGURE 12-18 Installation of radiant heating electrical wire in concrete floor slabs.

contains useful heat even during colder weather, and that this heat can be controlled and pumped into the house to maintain desirable temperature levels. Like electrical heat, it is clean and free of soot particles. In summer the system operates in reverse, taking the heat from within the house and pumping it to the outside, working on a principle similar to that of the household refrigerator (see Fig. 12-19). Actually, the system is more efficient for cooling than for heating, but since it performs a dual function, the heat pump is commercially feasible for year-round inside comfort in some climates.

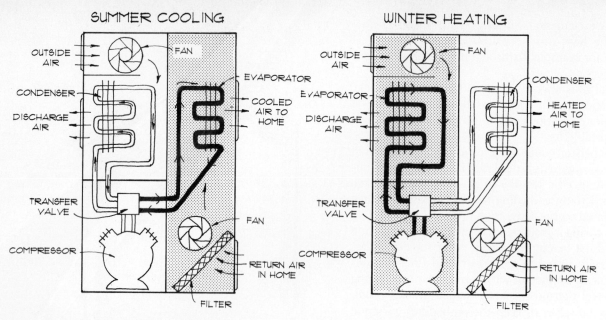

FIGURE 12-19 Diagram of heat-pump operation in summer and winter. The unit acts as a two-directional refrigeration system, taking the heat from the inside air and discharging it outside in summer, and taking the heat from outside air in winter and discharging it inside the house.

As a heating method, the system's efficiency drops considerably as the outside air drops in temperature. At a point just above freezing it becomes necessary to supplement the heat supply, usually with resistance-type electric heating elements, in order to maintain a required heat supply. The additional expense for such supplementary electrical equipment may make operation of the pump impractical in many sections of the country unless electrical rates are low. Experience has shown that the most practical adoption of the heat pump for home heating has been in areas where outside temperatures seldom drop below 30°F.

Several heat source and delivery media have been found successful: water to water, water to air, and air to air. When a water to water system is used, an economical source of uniform temperature water must be available for the heat exchanger. Distribution of the conditioned water within the house is handled with conventional piping systems. To date, the air to air system has been most highly commercialized for residential use. With this system, the air distribution within the house resembles the forced warm air heating methods, and consideration must be given to duct sizing and register placement for cooling as well.

In appearance, the heat pump is either a single metal-covered unit, placed outside the house, or it is contained in two cabinets, called a remote unit, with one installed inside, usually in the basement, utility room, or attic near an outside wall, and the other outside. Some manufacturers make a unit that can be hung on an outside wall, but because of noise the condensing unit is more satisfactory if it is not attached to the building in any way.

In operation, the pump draws in outside air (or water), and the refrigerant in the evaporator absorbs the air's natural heat; a compressor pumps the refrigerant to a higher temperature and pressure level, and the condenser gives off the heat to the inside air, creating the heating cycle. The heat pump is considered efficient in operation up to the point where supplemental resistance heat must be introduced. This supplementary heat must be sufficient to supply at least 75 percent of the total calculated heat loss requirements (100 percent is recommended in case of compressor failure). Cooling is done with the fixed-refrigerant circuit by interchanging the air over the evaporator and the condenser. Automatic reversing refrigerant valves makes the changeover possible.

Because frost on the evaporator coils reduces efficiency, automatic hot-gas defrosting cycles or electric defrosters are necessary in air source systems. Another required control is the inside air temperature regulating thermostat, similar to other heating and cooling systems, which controls inside temperature, fans, and the heating and cooling changeover. Also, an outdoor temperature change anticipator is advisable in order to maintain uniform inside comfort during sudden weather changes. An emergency switch should be installed, however, so that outdoor thermostats can be bypassed and the auxiliary heat can be controlled with the indoor thermostat only.

In planning a heat-pump installation, a 220-volt service outlet must be provided. No provision, of course, is necessary for a chimney or smoke vent, but it would be wise to plan for some other type of emergency heat in case of power failure.

12.4 Air-conditioning Methods

Cooling, dehumidifying, and filtering of air to provide a desired level of comfort for occupants of the space is commonly called *air conditioning*.

Summer cooling can be done most simply in residences with the use of individual room units placed in appropriate window openings. Or, in new construction, openings the size of window units can be provided in outside walls with electric outlets (usually 220 volts) nearby. This method of air conditioning may be the most economical in regions where summer temperatures are moderate and only one or two rooms in the home may require air conditioning. Basic planning for this type of cooling is not important and is not usually considered on working drawing, other than possibly a note on the floor plan where a unit is to be installed in an opening.

In areas where the cooling season is comparatively long, a central air-conditioning system, usually combined with the heating system equipment, is considered the most satisfactory for year-round inside climate control. As previously pointed out, these central systems, like heating systems, require consideration during initial planning of the structure; usually, the type of heating system selected will have a bearing on the most appropriate cooling system. If warm air heating is selected, cooling equipment utilizing the same circulating fan, ductwork, and registers will minimize the installation cost of the combination arrangement.

A mechanical refrigeration system, as mentioned under heat pumps, requires two basic units connected by closed-circuit refrigerant piping. The one unit, called the *evaporator*, allows the refrigerant to vaporize under low pressure and absorb heat from the surrounding air or water. This unit must be placed within the house and is commonly combined within the central furnace jacket of combination systems. The other unit, called the *condenser*, dissipates the heat absorbed by the evaporator as well as the heat of compression. Higher pressures in the condenser change the vaporized refrigerant into a liquid, requiring the heat taken up in the evaporator to be given off as it circulates through the condenser. The condenser, then, must be placed outside the building where it can give off its heat; or if installed inside, it must be adjacent to an outside wall opening.

Single-package cooling units are manufactured to fit conveniently on flat roofs, near louvers in attics, in crawl spaces, or in basement openings. Yet dual units are usually incorporated with heating systems requiring the condenser to be located on the exterior of the building. Many types of cooling units are available for combining with warm air heating systems.

In dry regions, such as the southwestern part of the United States, where outside air contains comparatively little moisture, air-conditioning units utilizing *evaporative cooling* rather than mechanical systems are being used successfully for summer cooling. Dry air can be economically cooled by forcing it through a spray of recirculated water. This system is based on the fact that evaporation is a cooling process. Both individual room units and central systems working on this principle are manufactured.

If the home is to be heated with hot water, an entirely separate cooling unit and ductwork system (split system) may be economically installed in an attic or crawl space to cool the house with air and yet allow the hot-water system to heat the house independently with water. Also, an indirect cooling unit, called a *water chiller*, may be combined with a hot-water system to circulate chilled water through the same piping system. During the winter, heated water is piped through the system, and during the summer, chilled water for cooling. If a water-cooled type of condenser is used with the chiller, space must also be planned for a cooling tower near the rear of the building or on a level roof.

Usually the two-pipe, reverse-return piping system is the most popular with water heating–cooling combinations. One thermostatic control may be used to regulate both the boiler and the water chiller. Circulating chilled water through radiant floor slabs or ceiling panels is not considered practical for cooling, mainly because of condensation problems on cold surfaces.

12.5 Residential Ventilating Fans

Circulation of fresh air in the home is not the major problem it becomes in public buildings. Usually, the home is occupied by comparatively few people, doors are continually being opened and closed, and infiltration around windows furnishes natural ventilation. In public buildings, however, where many people congregate for extended periods, forced-air ventilating systems, usually designed by the same engineer who designs the heating–cooling systems, must be installed to provide a continual supply of fresh air.

Ventilation problems within the home consist mainly of eliminating excess moisture, odors, fumes, formaldehyde, and radon gas from specific areas such as kitchens, bathrooms, laundry rooms, basements, and attics. These areas should be serviced by locally placed exhaust fans, which are available in many models and sizes for almost any situation. Kitchen fans can be installed in ceilings or outside walls, incorporated in range hoods, or included within cabinetwork; if access to the exterior is difficult, forced-air fans with electronic filters are installed to clean the air without requiring an outside outlet. Bathroom fans for ceiling installation commonly combine the exhaust fan with a light fixture and a supplementary resistance-type heater. Any source of excess moisture should have direct exhaust vents to the outside.

Central ventilating fans are effective as well as economical for cooling purposes when air-conditioning equipment is not installed. In many regions, pulling cool evening air through the house helps to make the interior more comfortable by alleviating the effects of the sun's radiation (the heat retained by the roof and walls) on the structure. These quiet running fans can be located in central hallway ceilings or other appropriate locations to draw outside air through windows of the lower floors and discharge it through the attic. Fan sizes, based on air movement capacities, should be selected to provide at least one air change (volume of the house in cubic feet) every 3 minutes. Some types of fans are made to operate in a horizontal position and others in a vertical position.

The locations of attic fans are usually shown on floor plans by the use of broken lines, drawn to the approximate size; dimensions and type may be inserted with a note or included in the set of specifications. Manufacturers' catalogues must be consulted for detailed information about fans, which, like other types of equipment installed in a building, should be identified with model numbers and relevant size descriptions.

12.6 Load Calculation and Sizing of Heating Equipment

To maintain a satisfactory air temperature within the home, the heating plant must be large enough to replace the heat loss of the house during average exterior temperatures; yet it should not be oversized if it is to operate efficiently and provide balanced heating. First, the *design temperature difference* must be established. Outside design temperature varies with the climate and can be determined for a given locality from tables compiled by the American Society of Heating, Refrigerating, and Air Conditioning Engineers (A.S.H.R.A.E.), *Heating, Ventilating, Air-conditioning Guide*, and other books on heating design. Usually 72°F is taken as a comfortable inside temperature in the winter. If the recommended outside temperature is, say, 5°F for a given area, then the design temperature difference for the heating system would be 67°F. If an outside design temperature is 20°F, then the design temperature difference would be 52°F. A correctly designed heating system would be able to furnish enough heat to the interior to maintain the 72°F inside temperature. Only after the rate at which the building loses heat during average extreme temperatures is calculated can the heating plant size be determined.

The next step is to find the entire heat loss of the building. This is done by individually computing the heat loss of each room to be heated. The number of square feet of cold partitions, cold ceilings, exposed walls, cold floors, windows, and exterior doors is calculated for each room. Then each surface area is multiplied by its *U factor*. Several different factors dealing with heat loss calculation are found in this information and various A.S.H.R.A.E. and N.E.S.C.A. tables available on home heating and cooling. The following definitions of the major ones encountered may clarify their meanings:

U FACTOR Coefficient of heat transmission through a combination of materials commonly found in walls, floors, and ceilings. It is the Btus flowing from air surface to air surface through 1 square foot of structure for each degree (F) difference in temperature between the two surfaces.

k FACTOR Unit conductivity. The rate of heat flow in Btuh through 1 square foot of a homogeneous material 1″ thick per degree (F) difference in temperature between its two surfaces.

R FACTOR Thermal resistance of materials. It is obtained from the reciprocal of U factors and is expressed in degrees (F) per Btuh per square foot. For example, a ceiling with a U factor of 0.20 would have an R factor of $1/0.20 = 5.0$. The larger the R value, the more resistance to heat flow and therefore the better heat barrier material.

HTM FACTOR Heat transfer multiplier as used in the N.E.S.C.A. *J-Manual* method of heat loss calculation. It is similar to a U factor except that HTM factors are shown in their tables already multiplied by specific design temperatures and are used with the calculation forms shown in Appendix D. Window and door HTM factors also are modified to include infiltration heat losses, which simplifies the total calculation.

The larger U factors in the tables indicate comparatively poorer insulators. Heat transfer characteristics of the different materials and types of construction, as found in A.S.H.R.A.E. tables, have been established under controlled laboratory conditions.

The rate at which a building loses heat depends directly on the heat loss characteristics of its structural components and on the temperature gradient (difference between inside and outside air temperatures). Remember that the areas of doors and windows in outside walls must be subtracted from the gross wall areas, and, usually, different U factors must be used for their calculations. The tables will show that windows and exterior doors have rather high transmission factors.

In heated basements, the masonry walls above grade have a different U factor from that of the walls below grade, since the ground absorbs very little heat compared to outside air. Partitions between heated rooms are not considered in heat loss calculations; one balances the other when uniform inside temperatures are maintained.

To sum up, heat loss by *transmission* will vary in proportion to the area in sq ft (A) of the ceiling and the outside wall areas, to the coefficients of their transmission values (U), and to the difference between the required inside temperature (t_i) and to the outside design temperature (t_o). Thus the formula:

$$H = AU(t_i - t_o)$$

H = British thermal units per hour where, after the heat loss of each different exposed surface of a room is determined, the result will be the heat loss of the room if it were airtight and doors were never opened. But cracks around doors and windows allow heat to escape by what is called *infiltration* and must be considered in an accurate heat-loss calculation.

The amount of heat loss by infiltration varies directly with the wind pressure against the structure and the temperature difference between inside and outside air. In cold, windy climates heat loss is considerable, especially if no weather stripping is used around loose-fitting windows and doors. Naturally, tight construction reduces infiltration. One method of determining heat loss by infiltration is by measuring the length of the cracks around all windows and doors in feet and multiplying the totals by the appropriate infiltration factors, which also can be found in the previously mentioned heating manuals. This method is preferred for accurate calculations, especially in commercial building design.

An approximate, *air change* method is satisfactory for residential heating systems. With this method, the number of air changes within a room per hour has been found by experience to vary from $1/2$ to 2 changes. Under ordinary conditions, then, one air change per hour can be assumed. Therefore, a roomful of air must be reheated every hour to allow for infiltration loss, and the volume of the room in cubic feet is conveniently used. The density of air is taken to be 0.075 lb per cu ft. The specific heat of air is 0.24 Btu (the heat needed to raise the temperature of one lb of air 1°F). Therefore, $0.075 \times 0.24 = 0.018$ gives the Btu of heat necessary to raise one cu ft of air 1°F. The infiltration heat loss can then be stated by the following formula:

$$H = V(.018)(t_i - t_o)$$

in which V = volume of air in room, t_i = inside design temperature, and t_o = outside design temperature.

Totals of infiltration heat losses are combined with the transmission heat losses through walls, ceilings, floors, etc.

In calculating the heat loss of concrete slabs on grade, usually only a 10′ wide area around the perimeter of the slab is considered (see the discussion on slab insulation in Section 7.3-Pages 155–56). The heat loss to the ground within the interior of the slab is negligible. Transmission factors are available for both heated and unheated slabs.

After heat loss totals by both transmission and infiltration are determined for each room, the grand total provides the heat loss for the structure. It must be remembered that, since U factors are given for a 1° difference in inside and outside air, room heat-loss calculations must include multiplication by the design temperature difference. The grand total Btu per hour heat loss is the basis for sizing the heating unit after several points have been taken into account. Usually, it is considered good practice to add 20 percent capacity to the unit to compensate for morning pickup when nighttime heating is allowed to drop as low as 55°F. Also, if plenum systems are placed in unheated crawl spaces or attics, the design temperature difference should be 30° greater than when ducts pass only through heated portions of the building. Heat loss in ductwork must also be considered in sizing individual room ducts as well as in sizing the central unit. Heat loss of ducts passing through heated areas is not considered.

At present, the majority of all residential heating–cooling contractors throughout this country and Canada use the N.E.S.C.A. *J Manual* method of load calculation. Their tables and calculation forms have been devised from A.S.H.R.A.E. *U* factors and engineering information. Various shortcuts, such as infiltration factors included with door and window factors and specific design temperatures included with the factors, simplify either heating or cooling load calculation for residential buildings. The form in Appendix D shows the calculation for the heat losses in the one-story house given in Appendix F. A thorough study of the step by step procedures given in the *J Manual* must be made before attempting the calculations. Those students wishing to pursue this area of work would be advised to take one of the short courses offered by N.E.S.C.A. several times each year in various metropolitan and university centers throughout the nation. Write to N.E.S.C.A., 1501 Wilson Blvd., Arlington, VA 22209, for further details.

Heating calculations and system design for commercial buildings are required by law to be done by registered engineers engaged in this specialized field.

Hot-water boiler sizes must be taken from design tables distributed by the Institute of Boiler and Radiator Manufacturers (I.B.R.), after total heatloss calculations have been made. Sizes are usually indicated in Btu per hour output and are determined after the following requirements have been considered:

1. Maximum heat necessary for all the connected radiator or convector units
2. Heat necessary for domestic hot water, if combined in the boiler

3. Heat loss in piping (piping factor)
4. Heat necessary for warming up the radiators or convectors and piping system after starting (picking factor)

Items 3 and 4 are often overlooked, inasmuch as the average boiler possesses enough reserve capacity to overcome the extra load, and in modern residences piping and equipment are usually installed within insulated areas.

Boiler manufacturers' catalogues give boiler dimensions and vent pipe and flue sizes, according to rated outputs.

Room convectors or radiator sizes and capacities are based on individual room heat losses as well as their distance from central boilers.

In hot-water radiant systems, the lineal feet and size of pipe that must be embedded in floors or ceilings are based on emission factors and individual room heat losses. Tables must be consulted for the emission rates in Btu per hour per foot of piping in order to determine the amount and size of piping necessary to satisfy each room's heat loss. Water design temperatures adopted for the system must also be considered.

12.7 Sizing Cooling Equipment

In heating, the major problem is the addition of heat and moisture to the interior; in cooling during the summer, on the other hand, the problem becomes just the reverse, the *removal of heat and moisture*.

Many factors, both internal and external, affect the cooling load and become part of the cooling calculations. Appliances, such as exhaust fans, for example, which remove heat and moisture from kitchen and baths, aid in reducing the cooling load. However, despite such reductions, the heat gain in the residential kitchen is rather large, so it is common practice to compensate for it by adding 1200 Btu to the kitchen heat gain calculations. Another source of internal heat is that given off by the occupants. For this, 300 Btu is usually allowed for each person living in the home. Larger factors up to 1400 Btuh per person are used for calculations for commercial installations.

The major source of residential heat gain, however, is due to external factors: outside air temperature and the sun shining on glass, roof, and walls. Sun shining on fixed-glass units and windows contributes considerably to cooling loads and should be avoided if possible during early planning, as previously discussed. Also, the radiant heat of the sun, although not considered in heating loads, must be dealt with in air conditioning. Remember that heat has a natural tendency to travel from warm to cold temperatures.

All these heat sources contribute to the cooling load, and the size of the cooling equipment is based on its capacity (Btu per hour) to remove this heat.

To arrive at the correct cooling load for air systems, design temperatures must be taken from tables similar to those used for heating design. Usually, 78°F (50 percent humidity) is used for the desirable inside temperature during the summer. The outside design temperature, including factors for daily temperature range, is taken from regional cooling tables. The design temperature difference between inside and outside air will then reveal the temperature reduction necessary for inside comfort.

Finally, the total heat gain within the structure must be calculated. Total exposed areas of walls, warm floors, warm ceilings, windows, and doors are multiplied by the heat gain factors. Heat gain by air leakage is found by applying the correct factors from tables. Sizes of windows receiving direct sun are multiplied by their factors. To the total heat gain through the structural components (external heat) is added the internal heat produced by people and appliances. Because moisture removal is part of comfort cooling, factors are used also for determining the heat gain from dehumidification (latent heat), which changes the moisture from a vapor to a liquid. Heat gain to ductwork in noncooled areas and other special heat sources are found with the use of factors from tables. All these sources require attention in arriving at a heat gain total for each room. To determine the total for sizing the central cooling unit, all the calculated room Btu per hour are added together.

Load calculations, design data, and code requirements for air systems can be taken from *Manual J* and *Manual 9* published by the N.E.S.C.A. Work sheets for job design and installation are also available (see Appendix D).

Cooling loads can also be calculated by a method developed by the I.B.R. Although basically similar to the N.E.S.C.A. method, the I.B.R. method bases its tables for determining regional design temperatures on latitude. The I.B.R. has also formulated its own factors for calculating sensible heat gains through walls, roofs, floors, windows, and doors. This method requires that shade lines be determined on walls and glass receiving direct sunlight and that different factors be used for shaded and sunlit portions. In addition, like the N.W.A.H.A.C.A. methods, similar calculations must be made for infiltration around doors and windows, internal heat gains, and the latent heat gain (usually taken as one-third of the sensible heat gain).

Cooling units have been rated in tons of refrigeration capacity, 1 ton of refrigeration being the amount of cooling necessary to melt 1 ton of 32°F ice at 32°F in 24 hours. The latent heat of ice is 144 Btu per pound; then 1 ton (2000 pounds) of ice absorbs 144 × 2000 or 288,000 Btu per 24 hour in changing ice to water. The heat gain in buildings is calculated in Btu per hour; therefore, 288,000 ÷ 24 = 12,000 Btu per hour, which is the capacity of 1 ton of refrigeration. *Total heat gains are simply divided by 12,000 to find the tonnage required.* A ton of refrigeration does not necessarily equal 1 horsepower, although some units are rated in horsepower. Most manufacturers now rate their equipment in Btu per hour, including both input and output.

It must be remembered that if a water chiller is added to an existing hot-water system, new convectors must be installed in the rooms. Combination convectors, having fan, filter, condensate drains, and heating–cooling coils, as well as individual room thermostats, provide a more positive distribution of cooled air. Compared to residential cooling with air, hydronic systems have not become as universally popular.

Duct sizes for air distribution of combination heating–cooling systems are usually based on the total cubic feet of air per minute (CFM) necessary for the cooling. Total CFM circulating through a system is based on unit manufacturers' recommendations, usually from 300 CFM to 420 CFM per ton. (Heating ductwork need not be as large.) Tables indicate duct sizes for both main trunk and individual room ducts, based on total and room Btu heat gains. Minor factors such as register distance from the central unit, duct offsets, and risers, are also considered. Ducts passing through unheated and uncooled spaces or outside walls must be insulated. Filters are installed in the return duct side of the system.

12.8 Location of Outlets in Rooms

Placement of registers and heat outlets in rooms requires careful consideration if the ultimate in comfort is to be attained from the system, especially in areas of extreme outside temperatures. Generally, it becomes advisable to place outlets in or near outside walls where the greatest amount of heat loss or heat gain occurs. To counteract cold downdrafts below windows, often uncomfortable in winter, low wall or floor outlets that blow the air up along the wall and windows are effective. However, when covered with floor-length window drapes, their maximum efficiency is decreased. Registers can also be placed in partitions near the outside walls to blow the air along the exterior wall and thereby reduce downdrafts. Concrete floor slabs, utilizing the perimeter loop system, should have their registers in the slab. Sheet-metal boots for bringing the ductwork into wall registers placed near the floor may also be used. Generally, in northern regions where heating seasons are comparatively long, registers and heat outlets are located in the floor or low sidewall; in southern areas where cooling seasons are longer, air is dispersed better with high sidewall or ceiling outlets. Aside from these considerations, outlets should be so placed that air distribution is not noticeable to the occupants, no drafts are created, and the conditioned air will not have a tendency to stratify. Registers should be unobstructive and fit into the decorative scheme of the interior, and they should not restrict the placement of furniture. Since many types are available, it is possible to choose registers that fill the requirements of any situation.

Convectors for hot-water systems are mainly the baseboard type or wall units placed low near the floor.

Proper placement of return air grilles contributes to the dispersion of the conditioned air. In small homes, if centrally located returns are used, air will generally find its way through doorways, halls, and stairwells. Doors normally left closed are usually specified to be undercut 3/4" for an economical method of air return; or a grille may be installed in the door. Returns, however, must be large enough to prevent noise in the ductwork, and their sizes should be based on the volume of air delivered to the supply outlets. Properly sized and placed returns aid considerably in maintaining comfort throughout the building.

After studying the problems involved in providing comfort within a building during all seasons of the year, it is evident that each installation requires an individual application during planning. Selection of the most satisfactory equipment must necessarily follow a thorough analysis of all the conditions involved. Heat loss factors of the various building materials and their combinations deserve attention. Initial costs of insulation should be compared in terms of fuel cost savings over the life span of the building. Of course, early costs of equipment and insulation generally will vary directly with the degree of comfort required.

12.9 Solar Equipment

Because of the extensive solar equipment now available to homebuilders, properly designed and integrated solar systems for homes can provide a large percentage of the energy needed for heating and cooling and domestic hot-water systems. When combining both passive and active features, solar systems can realistically and economically realize about 70 percent of space heating needs and about 90 percent of domestic hot-water needs. Mechanical solar cooling, on the other hand, while technically feasible at this time, requires additional research and development to achieve the same levels of efficiency and practical economy. This material will discuss mainly solar heating and solar domestic hot-water system equipment that is useful to students of residential construction. Manufacturers of equipment are continually improving the efficiency of their products and introducing new components, including more efficient heat pumps, new and more efficient furnaces, automatic dampers, and controls that will make solar and backup equipment energy efficient without sacrificing comfort. New components should be evaluated on the basis of energy performance (EER

FIGURE 12-20 Solar collectors can be placed on south facing roofs and made to contribute to the design of the exterior. An RFT, Inc., mobil home design.

rating), installed cost, reliability, maintenance costs, and warranties provided.

Passive solar planning is discussed in Chapter 6 and should be an important aspect of systems that include any of the active solar equipment.

There are several properties that apply to all solar heating–cooling and domestic hot-water systems, whether they are simple or relatively complex. Each

system includes these components: collector, storage, and distribution. It may also include transport, auxiliary energy system, and controls. These components can vary widely in design and function, depending on needs and climate.

Solar radiation reaches the earth's surface by two methods: by direct (parallel) rays and by diffuse (non-parallel) sky radiation, which is reflected from clouds

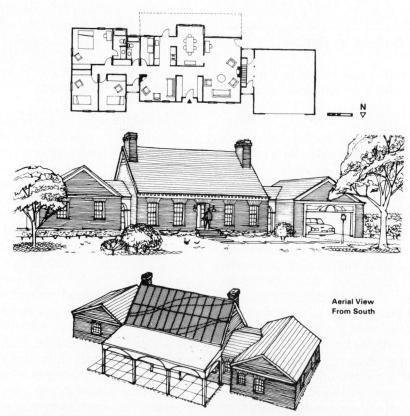

Aerial View
From South

FIGURE 12-21 Use of solar panels on a traditional style house with a back-to-south orientation.

and atmospheric dust. The solar energy that reaches the surface of buildings includes not only direct and diffused rays but also radiation reflected from adjacent ground or building material surfaces. The amount of total radiation from these various sources varies widely according to climate, from hot, dry climates where clear skies enable a large amount of direct radiation to strike a building, to temperate and humid climates where up to 40 percent of the total radiation may be dispersed, to northern climates where snow reflection from the low winter sun may result in a greater amount of incident radiation than in warmer but cloudier climates. As a result of the wide variation of solar availability in different locations, the design as well as need for solar systems varies widely as well. Selecting the most effective solar system and equipment begins with an analysis of local climatic conditions to determine the solar energy available. Before designing a solar house, take the time to review the subject further in several specialized texts and government publications.

12.9.1 Collectors

As the name implies, collectors convert incident solar radiation into useful thermal energy. Transparent cover plates of glass or plastic are used to reduce convective and radiative cooling of the absorber. That is, they tend to trap more of the heat that is reemitted from the absorbing surface. An efficient absorbing surface, usually dark, will have a high solar absorbance and low emittance quality so that the maximum amount of energy will be conducted to the gas or liquid transporting medium.

The ideal slope of a collector is perpendicular to the sun's rays acting on it. This ideal situation is ordinarily not feasible since the sun's relationship changes throughout the days and seasons; a stationary mounting is the most economical. Some mountings are flexible so that the most ideal angle can be variable, yet the majority of collectors are mounted directly to the roof for the best appearance, which requires some consideration in new construction on the selection of the most appropriate roof slope. Collectors may also be mounted on the ground near the building or mounted to appear as awnings above windows. Sun angle charts are available for determining the most desirable collector tilt in local areas. A rule of thumb tilt is the local latitude plus 15° (plus or minus 5° tolerance).

Experimental models of focusing collectors are made to focus the solar radiation to a concentrating point or area. Some are even made to follow the sun throughout the day. These are comparatively more efficient, requiring an automatic tracking mechanism, than the fixed flat-plate type, yet their cost usually prohibits their use in residential systems.

12.9.2 Flat-Plate Collectors

This relatively simple type of collector (see Fig. 12-22) has now found the widest application. Possibly the reason for the popularity is economy of fabrication, installation, and maintenance. Of equal importance from an architectural standpoint is the fact that flat-plate collectors can be made to look well on gable roofs and be made an integral part of the total design, rather than an unrelated appendage of the building. Usually, they are placed on the rear of the house if possible, however, regardless of type.

Flat-plate collectors utilize both direct and diffuse solar radiation. Temperatures up to 250°F (121°C) can be attained if correctly designed and oriented. This is well above the moderate temperatures needed for space heating and domestic water heating. The collectors generally consist of an absorbing plate, usually metal, which can be flat, grooved, or corrugated and painted black (or chemically treated) to increase absorption. To minimize loss of heat, the backside is well insulated (with a type of insulation that is unaffected by intense heat), and the front is covered with a transparent cover sheet to trap heat and minimize convective cooling, as we mentioned earlier (see Fig. 12-23).

The captured solar heat is removed from the absorber by a working medium, usually air or treated water, which becomes heated as it passes through or near the absorbing plate. Water must be an anti-freeze solution to prevent freezing. The heated medium must then be transported to the interior of the house or to storage, depending upon energy demand.

In selecting solar collectors, consider their thermal efficiency, the total area and orientation required, durability of the materials, and of course the initial cost. There are innumerable variations, but the three basic types are:

Open Water Collector (see Fig. 12-24) This type has water entering at the top, high side, which trickles down over the corrugated absorbing plate. The heated water collects in a gutter on the lower side and is transported to interior storage. Some models have two corrugated plates spaced apart to allow the water to flow between, which tends to reduce evaporation of the water and increase efficiency. Condensation forming on the inside of the cover plate reduces solar absorption, and therefore open water collectors should be carefully evaluated before being used in cold climates.

Factory-produced collectors have steadily improved in efficiency, yet on-site collectors are less expensive and have proved to be adequate if carefully constructed.

Air-cooled Collector (see Fig. 12-25) This type receives direct air through ducts from the building. The

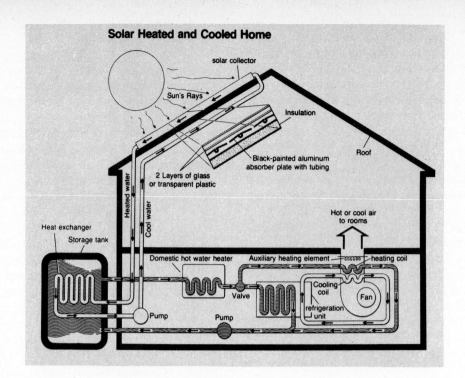

Solar Heated and Cooled Home

solar collector

Sun's Rays

Insulation

Roof

Black-painted aluminum
absorber plate with tubing

2 Layers of glass
or transparent plastic

Heated water

Cool water

Hot or cool air
to rooms

Heat exchanger
Storage tank

Domestic hot water heater

Auxiliary heating element

heating coil

Cooling
coil

Fan

refrigeration
unit

Pump

Valve

Pump

FIGURE **12-22** Solar heated and cooled home. Solar heated water heats storage tank water, which (a) heats domestic water, (b) heats water flowing through solar heating coil, and (c) drives refrigeration unit that chills water for air-conditioning cooling coil.

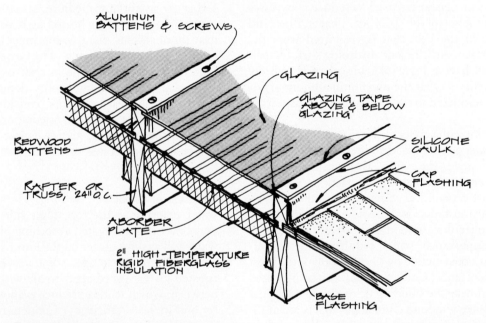

ALUMINUM
BATTENS & SCREWS

GLAZING

GLAZING TAPE
ABOVE & BELOW
GLAZING

REDWOOD
BATTENS

SILICONE
CAULK

RAFTER OR
TRUSS, 24" O.C.

CAP
FLASHING

ABSORBER
PLATE

2" HIGH-TEMPERATURE
RIGID FIBERGLASS
INSULATION

BASE
FLASHING

FIGURE **12-23** Site-built solar collector detail.

air is heated within the covered collector and forced back into the building or heat storage compartment. Low maintenance and freedom from freezing problems are the major advantages. Disadvantages include the need for relatively large ducts, electrical power for transport of the air, and the inefficiency of transfer of heat from air to domestic hot water. It is felt that air-cooled collectors will increase in use in the future.

Liquid-cooled Collector (see Fig. 12-26) Water or an antifreeze solution is usually the liquid maintained within the piping of this type of collector. The liquid is

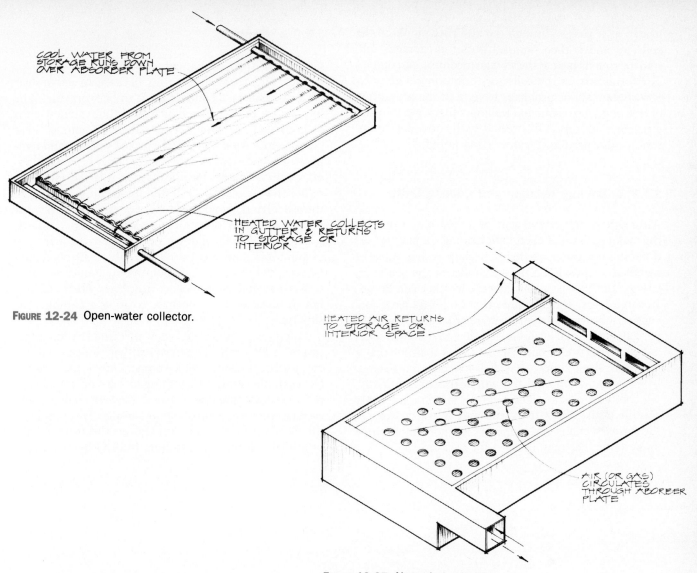

COOL WATER FROM
STORAGE RUNS DOWN
OVER ABSORBER PLATE

HEATED WATER COLLECTS
IN GUTTER & RETURNS
TO STORAGE OR
INTERIOR

FIGURE 12-24 Open-water collector.

HEATED AIR RETURNS
TO STORAGE OR
INTERIOR SPACE

AIR (OR GAS)
CIRCULATES
THROUGH ABSORBER
PLATE

FIGURE 12-25 Air-cooled collector.

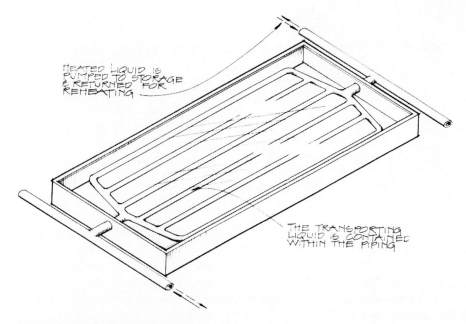

HEATED LIQUID IS
PUMPED TO STORAGE
& RETURNED FOR
REHEATING

THE TRANSPORTING
LIQUID IS CONTAINED
WITHIN THE PIPING

FIGURE 12-26 Liquid-cooled collector.

Sec. 12.9   solar equipment   **353**

heated as it passes through the absorber piping in the collector and is then pumped back to a storage tank, transferring its heat to the storage medium. No condensate forms within the collector to interfere with solar absorption. Major problems have been the prevention of freezing, corrosion, and leaking; otherwise, they are efficient collectors. Oil, treated with corrosion inhibitors, is also used as a transporting liquid.

12.9.3 Backup Heating and Cooling Units

Although solar systems can be relied on to provide the major amount of energy for heating a home and the domestic hot water needed, a backup system must be installed for providing the remainder of the necessary energy and provision for extreme weather conditions. In some areas, codes require that buildings have conventional heating systems that are sized to provide 100 percent of the total load. Usually, it is advisable to select a system that is low in initial cost rather than one that is less expensive to operate (such as a electrical resistance baseboard), assuming that it will be used infrequently. All components should be carefully sized to meet only specific loads, rather than randomly selected. Refer to the earlier sections in this chapter for more information on systems that may be used for backup.

12.9.4 Controls

Controls on solar equipment are important, not only for comfort and safety, but mainly because an active solar system must have controls for it to be workable. The best advice about controls as well as the system itself is to keep them as simple as possible. Of course, solar components are subjected to extreme weather and temperature conditions and therefore should be of the highest quality—made specifically for solar installations rather than run of the mill plumbing components. On the other hand, avoid hard to find or exotic controls that may cause time delays before replacements can be found should a breakdown occur. Controls make the system work, and only the most reliable controls should be accepted to avoid disappointment. Remember that collectors continue to collect heat even when controls fail to dispose of the energy, creating a troublesome situation.

Much solar equipment is now furnished by manufacturers in kit form. This ensures that the controls are compatible with the other components of the system. For example, some air handling kits are preengineered packages that include sensors, blowers, valves, and even ductwork to control the air completely throughout the system. These kits with less on-site fittings have proved to be the most trouble free. Other manufac-

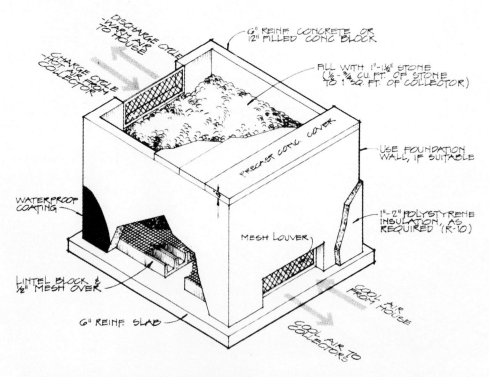

Figure 12-27 Suggested stone storage bin for air-collector system. Rock storage requires two and one-half times as much volume as compared to water to store the same amount of heat over the same temperature rise.

turers recommend the exact type of controls that must be used with their components to have them function satisfactorily. Heretofore, the most trouble in active solar systems has been the electrical controls and electrically operated valves. Manufacturers are now using solid-state technology and more innovation in their designing, which should result in more reliability.

Controls include thermostats, collector sensors, storage sensors, controllers, on–off switches, mixing valves, backflow stopping valves, circulators, and others.

12.9.5 Domestic Hot-Water Units

Various manufacturers now furnish domestic hot-water kits that are made to be installed during new construction or may be installed in existing houses as retrofit applications. Even units that are made up of components furnished by different manufacturers can be satisfactory if installed by competent mechanics; many of the components can be site constructed, such as collectors or piping. Many units are combined as part of the space heating system. The basic types of solar water heaters are closed loop, thermosiphoning, recirculating, drain back, and batch heaters. The majority of units now in use are closed loop, mechanically circulated types that include roof-mounted flat-plate collectors and covers, insulated piping, individual controls, with various adaptations to satisfy local codes and weather conditions.

The closed-loop unit is controlled by a differential thermostat, one sensor at the collector, and one sensor on the side of the water heater (see Fig. 12-28). As the early morning sun warms the collector sensor to a temperature of 15°F warmer than the tank sensor, the controller starts the circulator. On cloudy days or in the evening when the sun goes down, the collector quickly cools. When it reaches a temperature that is only 5°F warmer than the tank sensor, the controller turns off the circulator. Subsequent hot-water needs are automatically provided by the backup heater until the sun warms the collectors again. Many systems have high-limit controls that automatically stop the operation when the domestic water reaches 180°F to protect the tanks from overheating.

The other types of water heaters mentioned operate slightly differently, as their names imply, relating mainly to their method of freeze protection. Various conditions, such as availability, hot-water demand, architectural limitations, and type of backup unit, may restrict the selection.

Solar equipment may be combined with either gas-fired or electrical resistance-type water heaters for backup. Select units that are capable of furnishing 100 percent of domestic hot-water needs. In Fig. 12-28 the

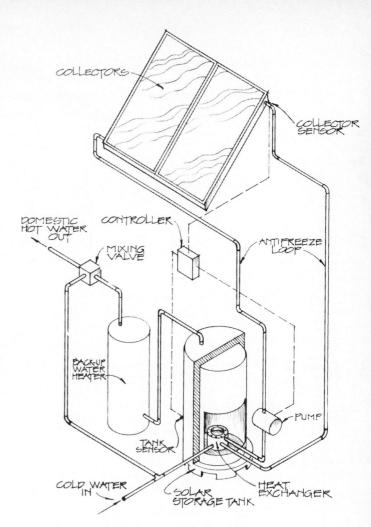

FIGURE 12-28 Closed-loop solar water heater.

transport liquid in the closed loop could be water, propylene glycol, glycerin, Freon, or silicone oil. A nonfreezing liquid must be used in colder climates. Notice in Fig. 12-29 that the closed loop also includes a line through the wood-burning fireplace grate, which can be used to reclaim some of its heat for the central heating system. Otherwise, the figure shows a typical space heating system with a water storage tank in the basement combined with a domestic hot-water unit. The stored solar heat is supplied to a conventional forced-air system trunk duct with a water to air heat exchanger.

12.10 Drawing the Heating and/or Cooling Plan

The "Heating and Air-conditioning Plan" is basically a floor plan showing walls and structural features of the building with the layout of the central unit, the distri-

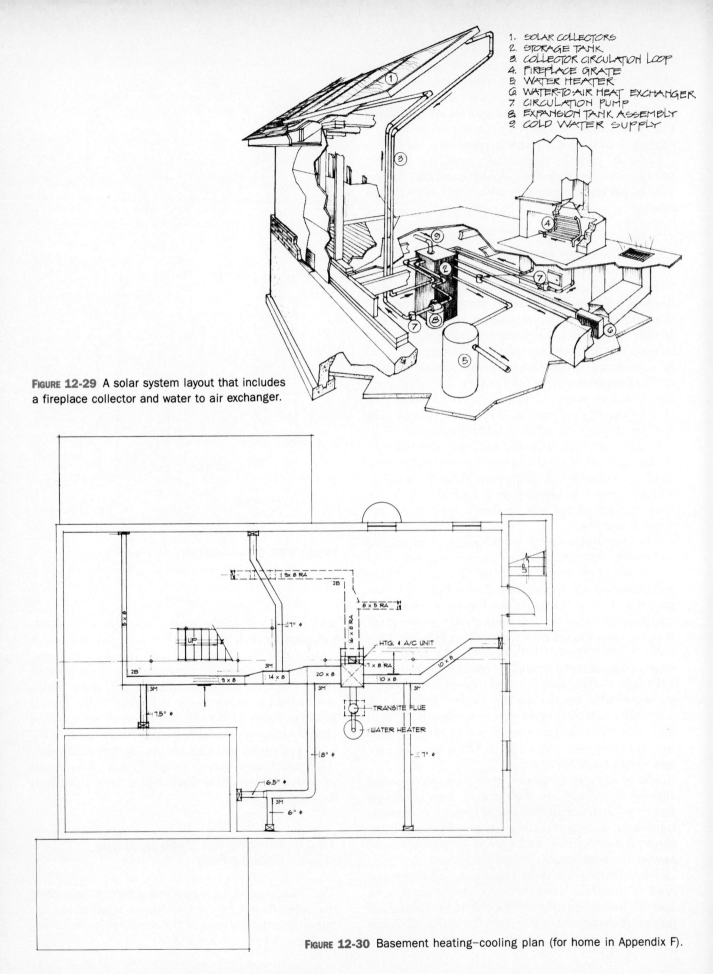

1. SOLAR COLLECTORS
2. STORAGE TANK
3. COLLECTOR CIRCULATION LOOP
4. FIREPLACE GRATE
5. WATER HEATER
6. WATER-TO-AIR HEAT EXCHANGER
7. CIRCULATION PUMP
8. EXPANSION TANK ASSEMBLY
9. COLD WATER SUPPLY

FIGURE 12-29 A solar system layout that includes a fireplace collector and water to air exchanger.

FIGURE 12-30 Basement heating–cooling plan (for home in Appendix F).

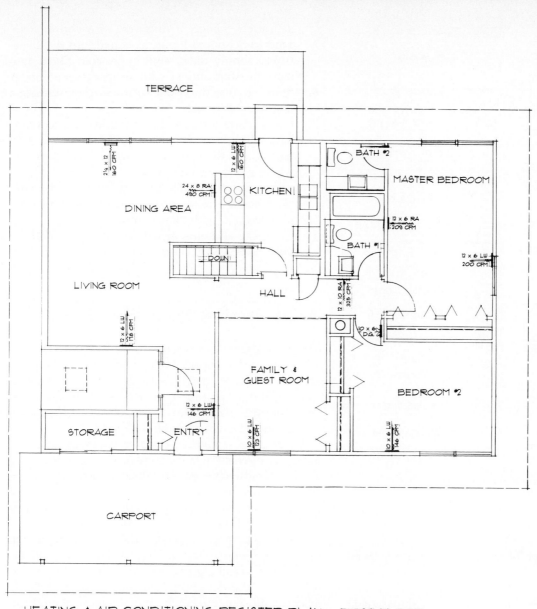

HEATING & AIR CONDITIONING REGISTER PLAN - FIRST FLOOR

SCALE : 1/4" = 1'-0"

FIGURE 12-31 First-floor heating-cooling plan showing the layout of room registers (for home in Appendix F).

bution system, and the room outlets in their correct position (see Figs. 12-30 and 12-31). A plan of each floor involved is usually sufficient to show the important information, supplemented by several small details, if necessary. Information about simple heating or heating–cooling installations could be incorporated into the regular floor plan, but with more complex systems it is usual practice to put the information on a separate plan for easier identification. Use the heating and piping symbols (Fig. 12-32) adopted by the American Standards Association, Inc. (A.S.A.), which have been standardized and are universally recognized. Large ductwork is scaled to show its horizontal dimension,

and notes are added to indicate their cross-sectional sizes. In residential ductwork it is standard procedure to use only 8″ vertical-duct depths with increased widths for increased air capacities. For example, a smaller duct might be 10″ × 8″ and a larger one may be 16″ × 8″. Notice that the horizontal dimension is given first in the specification. Piping is shown by single lines.

After heat loss calculations and design information are determined, start the plan with a freehand sketch of the entire layout. Add all pertinent sizes and information to the sketch. When ready to do the instrument drawing, fasten a clean sheet of tracing paper directly

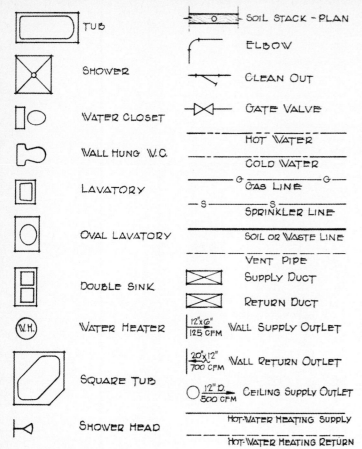

TUB

SHOWER

WATER CLOSET

WALL HUNG W.C.

LAVATORY

OVAL LAVATORY

DOUBLE SINK

WATER HEATER

SQUARE TUB

SHOWER HEAD

SOIL STACK - PLAN

ELBOW

CLEAN OUT

GATE VALVE

HOT WATER

COLD WATER

GAS LINE

SPRINKLER LINE

SOIL OR WASTE LINE

VENT PIPE

SUPPLY DUCT

RETURN DUCT

12"x6"
125 CFM WALL SUPPLY OUTLET

20"x12"
700 CFM WALL RETURN OUTLET

12" D.
500 CFM CEILING SUPPLY OUTLET

HOT-WATER HEATING SUPPLY

HOT-WATER HEATING RETURN

FIGURE 12-32 Plumbing and heating symbols.

over the regular floor plan and follow these general steps:

1. Trace the structural features (start with basement plan, if applicable) using rather light linework. The linework of the heating or cooling equipment and symbols, drawn later, should dominate the structural features.
2. Scale the floor size of the central unit and locate it where planned; show vent pipe to chimney or vent. Unit output rating in Btu per hour and manufacturers' catalogue numbers may be added later.
3. Using their correct symbols, locate all room outlets and indicate their sizes and capacities. Locate return outlets with their capacities.
4. If ceiling outlets are indicated, coordinate them with ceiling electrical outlets. Care must be taken near structural girders and plumbing piping.
5. If rectangular ductwork is to be drawn, lay out duct sizes to satisfy room Btu per hour requirements by starting with the outlet farthest from the plenum. In general, one register will handle about 8000 Btu heat loss in heating; for cooling, one register will handle only 4000 Btu heat gain. Indi-

cate each change of ductwork size with a note. Ductwork should be incorporated into the structure as simply and directly as possible. Show standard ductwork fittings with identification numbers.

6. Show circular ductwork with a single line, with a note giving its size.
7. Locate risers for second-story outlets, if necessary. Riser duct sizes are made to pass through stud partitions. Be sure second-floor partitions fall where risers are indicated.
8. In hot-water systems, use a single line for feeder pipes and a broken line for returns. Draw fittings, if necessary, with simple symbols.
9. Complete all notes, schedules, and structural details necessary to accommodate the system.

12.11 Plumbing Systems and Drawings

Plumbing drawings are mainly concerned with the piping systems that supply hot and cold water, the pipes that carry waste materials to the sewer or disposal system, and the plumbing fixtures. With the exception of the fixtures, the systems are largely concealed within the structural cavities of the building.

For complex structures, the plumbing system design, like other mechanical or electrical design work, is usually done by registered engineers. Because these systems are often complicated, involving the action and control of water and air within pipes, engineers must be well qualified in the fields of hydraulics and pneumatics.

Small home systems, on the other hand, even though they involve similar basic principles, seldom require the services of plumbing engineers. Usually, the responsibility for the design of residential systems falls on licensed subcontractors who are familiar with local and national plumbing codes. Much of residential plumbing is standardized, requiring little more than the location of plumbing fixtures on the working drawings. Simple structures do not always warrant separate plumbing plans, whereas complex commercial buildings may require a number of individual drawings devoted entirely to plumbing information.

Strict compliance with local plumbing codes is mandatory, regardless of the type of building. Plumbing codes, which may vary slightly from area to area, serve to ensure a sanitation standard to protect the health of the community. Students must understand the principles underlying good plumbing practices (Fig. 12-33) and be acquainted with local code restrictions. The most up to date requirements can be found in the *National Plumbing Code* published by the American Society of Mechanical Engineers. Many of these recommendations have become part of local plumbing codes throughout the country. Some of the more common terms found in codes are illustrated in Fig. 12-34.

The drainage system combines the use of TRAPS, VENTS, WASTE LINES, and SOIL STACKS

VENTS protect the water seals in traps and permit them to operate effectively. By admitting air to the system, vents permit atomspheric pressure on both sides of the trap seal to be maintained, and permit air to enter at the same time as gases escape the drainage system.

TRAPS permit waste and waste water to enter the drainage system and prevent any sewer gases from entering the house. The water seal utilizes a portion of the waste water to act as the barrier.

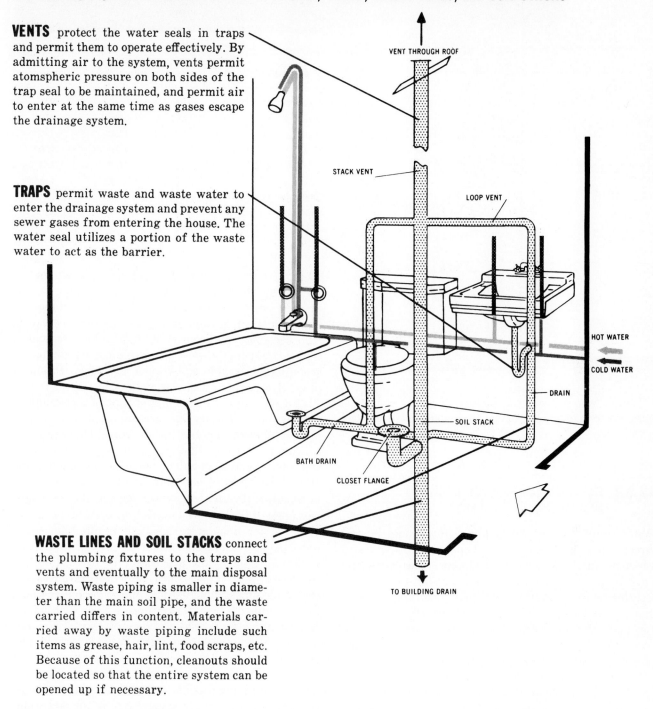

WASTE LINES AND SOIL STACKS connect the plumbing fixtures to the traps and vents and eventually to the main disposal system. Waste piping is smaller in diameter than the main soil pipe, and the waste carried differs in content. Materials carried away by waste piping include such items as grease, hair, lint, food scraps, etc. Because of this function, cleanouts should be located so that the entire system can be opened up if necessary.

FIGURE 12-33 The basic parts of a bath plumbing system without reference to code or engineering limitations.

Economy in plumbing costs is the direct result of careful planning when arranging the placement of rooms and fixtures requiring water outlets. Simplification of arrangement and the clustering of plumbing fixtures, usually into one wet-wall, should be the designer's objective in low-cost construction. In multis-

tory construction, definite savings ensue if fixtures are located above each other to benefit from the use of common vents and soil stacks. However, in planning better-class homes, the workability of a good floor plan should not be sacrificed merely because extended plumbing lines constitute an added expense.

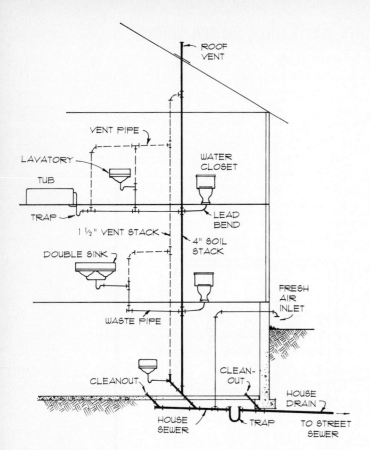

Figure 12-34 A drainage diagram for a multistory residence.

Table 12-1
Fixture minimum pipe sizes (FHA)

Fixture	Branch hot water	Branch cold water	Soil or waste connections	Vent connections
Water closet		1/2″	3″ × 4″	2″
Lavatory	1/2″	1/2″	1¼″	1¼″
Bathtub	1/2″	1/2″	1½″	1¼″
Sink	1/2″	1/2″	1½″	1¼″
Laundry tray	1/2″	1/2″	1½″	1¼″
Sink and tray combination	1/2″	1/2″	1½″	1¼″
Shower	1/2″	1/2″	2″	1¼″

12.12 Basic Requirements of the Water Supply System

Water supply piping within the home should be as direct as possible and sized large enough to provide an adequate supply at each outlet. The entrance main pipe must be placed low enough below ground to prevent freezing or mechanical damage. Frequently, a copper pipe is used; a ³/₄″ or 1″ pipe is satisfactory. A shutoff valve near the entry of the line into the house is often a requirement, as is a pressure reducing valve, backflow preventer, and pressure relief valve.

One important consideration in water supply is the choice of piping material. Two types are commonly used today in residences: copper and plastic. Galvanized steel with its standard tapered pipe thread was used for many years. Although structurally rigid, steel pipe will eventually become corroded from oxygen in the water, reducing the capacity of the pipe sufficiently to eventually require replacement. Plastic pipe is now gaining in popularity. A flexible butyl pipe with compression fittings has been approved by many building codes for water supply. Plastic pipe (PVC) is used for the water supply from the street main to the house. Wrought-iron pipe, though more expensive than steel, has less tendency to corrode. Copper pipe, often called

tubing, eliminates the problem of corrosion altogether and is very durable. The diameter of the pipe can be smaller, simple no-lead antimony–tin solder joints are easy to make, and minimum water friction is created. Aboveground, in exposed locations, hard-tempered copper produces the most acceptable installation; below ground, the flexible soft-copper tubing is simple to place. Because of its desirable attributes, architects usually specify copper for the better type of construction.

Hot- and cold-water lines are commonly run parallel to each other throughout the structure. However, care is taken to keep the pipes at least 6″ apart, so that the water temperature in either pipe is not affected by the other. Insulating of hot-water lines is recommended, especially if the lines are long. Even cold-water lines in basements may require covering to prevent sweating. When water lines approach each fixture, hot water must be on the left, cold water on the right. Another important point is the provision for "air cushions" in the water lines. These short, sealed-off extensions of the water pipes, attached just above the outlet in the lines, eliminate hammering noises when faucets are quickly turned off. Other types of shock-relief and expansion chambers are available for incorporating into the lines. Much of the noise in plumbing walls can be isolated by having closets or storage rooms adjacent to baths; if this is not feasible, sound-deadening insulation or offset studding may be necessary in the wet-walls. Pipes should be sized for flow rates of 8 feet per second or less to avoid noise from rushing water in pipes.

12.13 Basic Requirements of the Discharge System

Whereas water is supplied into plumbing lines under pressure, drainage lines work on an entirely different principle—gravity. This must be fully understood to ensure their functioning properly. Compared to the water lines, then, the piping for waste discharge must be larger, and branches that carry the wastes horizontally into vertical stacks must be properly sloped ($1/8''$ to $1/2''$ per ft) to ensure complete and free drainage. Sewage lines produce offensive and harmful gases that would permeate the entire structure unless *traps* forming offsets in the pipe to retain a water seal are installed near each fixture. Water closets have a built-in trap. Vent stacks through the roof discharge sewer gases to the outside air. These vent stacks and their branch vents have other important functions. They allow a continuous atmospheric pressure to exist within the sewage system, which prevents the siphonage of water from fixture traps and reduces the decay action of bacteria on the sewage while it is in the piping. Sewer gases may possibly emerge through trap seals unless the vents allow the gases to pass readily to the open air. Vent stacks should be installed at least $6''$ and not exceed code distances from the traps and should extend at least $12''$ above the roof. Although minor variations in practice exist, local codes carefully regulate methods of venting fixture traps and drainage lines. Some new types of air relief vents used inside the dwelling are approved for use by local code officials.

Soil and vent pipe sizes vary according to the number of fixtures they serve. In residential systems the main soil stack and house drain are usually $4''$ cast-iron soil pipe; waste branches and minor vent stacks generally are $1 1/2''$ or $2''$ in diameter. The minimum size permitted for a soil stack pipe serving one water closet is $3''$; the pipe for stacks handling two water closets must be at least $4''$. Vent stacks that run parallel to soil stacks can be half as large as the soil stacks.

The majority of sewage line pipe used today is PVC plastic pipe, type DWV (drain, waster and vent). Cast-iron soil pipe is still used in some situations, but plumbers can install the plastic pipe easier and quicker. Other types of drainage pipe are also used: copper, galvanized steel and wrought iron, brass, or lead. The sewer pipe running below ground from the house to the public sewer may be cast iron, vitrified tile, concrete, or PVC plastic pipe; but codes usually require at least $5'$ of the piping used within the building to extend beyond the foundation wall (house sewer). Most pipe exposed near fixtures is chrome-plated brass or flexible plastic. Pipe connections at fixtures allow slight flexibility in case of shrinkage or movement of wood framing without putting strain on the connected piping. Plumbing fixtures must be solidly supported by the structure. All drainage pipe should be as straight and direct as possible, fittings made to minimize friction, and cleanouts inserted at critical points of the system to allow unclogging if this becomes necessary.

12.14 Domestic Water Heaters

To furnish a continual supply of hot water throughout the year, modern homes must be equipped with some type of automatic hot-water heater. The heater and storage tank combination unit is the most satisfactory, although heaters that supply hot water instantaneously as it is needed are available. Sizes of heaters and their tanks are based on the number of occupants. Figures show that the average residential occupant uses about 40 gallons of hot water per day. This estimate includes consumption for laundry and bath facilities, based on water heated to 140°F. Although tanks holding the minimum of 20 gallons are available, a 30-gallon tank is more satisfactory for the average family, and one holding 50 gallons is necessary for a larger family using automatic laundry equipment. Heaters with slow recovery rates require proportionately larger storage tanks. If a unit has a slow recovery rate, such as an electric water heater, then an 80-gallon tank unit would be necessary to furnish hot water at about the same rate as would a 30-gallon gas- or oil-fired unit.

In commercial buildings having many hot-water outlets, the consumption per fixture is usually not as great as in residences. However, the demands of the building and the consumption rate during peak hours must be known before the size and type of hot-water heater can be indicated. Because hot-water lines tend to corrode more than cold-water lines, piping from hot-water heaters should be thick-wall copper. Heaters should be located near their principal outlets, and heaters having adjustable temperature settings are appropriate for such installations.

Indicate hot-water heaters on working drawings with a circle symbol and a W.H. note. Tank size can also be noted, if necessary. Also note the minimum efficiency desired.

12.15 Private Disposal Systems

In most urban areas, buildings are serviced by public sewage lines that run along street thoroughfares. The house sewer connection is made by merely tapping the public sewer line. But in outlying areas where no public sewage facilities exist, provision must be made for satisfactory disposal of the sewage on the owner's property. The designs of individual disposal systems are closely regulated by local codes, and a number of conditions pertaining to the property must be analyzed before a permit is granted. Conditions affecting the disposal system design are number of occupants of the house, permeability of the soil, groundwater level in the area, size of the property, and the relative location of wells or streams that may be affected by the sewage disposal.

The simplest system (often prohibited by local codes) is a cesspool. This is an underground cylindrical pit with porous walls built of stone or masonry to allow seepage of the discharge into the surrounding ground. The sewage is deposited directly into the pit. If the

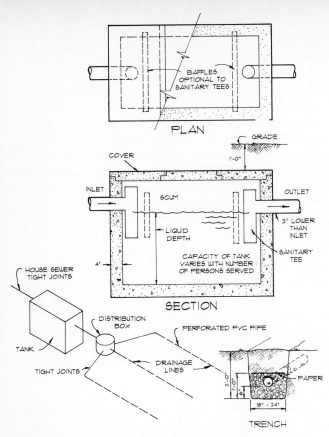

PLAN

SECTION

TRENCH

FIGURE 12-35 Septic tank details and a disposal field layout used on level ground. Perforated fiber or plastic pipe is commonly used for field lines.

surrounding soil is permeable enough to carry off the liquid and the underground water table is low enough to prevent contamination, the system may be adequate for retaining a small amount of solid matter. However, experience has shown that cesspools become troublesome when the apertures of the masonry become clogged and the surrounding ground becomes saturated. Secondary cesspools may then be necessary.

Probably the best solution for individual sewage disposal on property having sufficient amount of space is a *septic tank and tile drain field* (see Fig. 12-35). The sewage empties from the house sewer into a watertight concrete, fiberglass, or steel tank placed below ground. Cast-iron tees or wood baffles at the entrance and discharge end of the tank prevent disruption of the surface scum within the tank and direct the solids to the bottom. Bacteria act on the sewage to break down the solids into a compact sludge, which needs removal only after several years' use. Only after the sewage is about 70 percent purified will the effluent liquid leave the tank and flow through the seepage drains, thus eliminating the possibility of contaminating surrounding water tables.

Seepage lines consist of 4″ diameter perforated plastic pipe (PVC) placed in trenches filled with coarse gravel to allow positive drainage into the surrounding soil. Clay agricultural tile with open joints can also be used. The lines are placed about 16″ below ground level and sloped from 4″ to 6″ per 100′ to keep the drainage near the surface and yet maintain a gradual outflow. Much of the moisture near the surface evaporates into the air. Different arrangements of the tile lines are possible in restricted space and to accommodate various contours; if steep slopes are encountered, line drops to different levels are made with tight pipe. Lengths of drainage tile lines and sizes of gravel trenches are determined by local codes according to the size of the dwelling and the number of occupants, as well as the absorption rate of the soil. Usually, 100′ to 300′ of drainage line is required for the average residence. Tests should be made to determine the rate of water absorption in the disposal area before reliable disposal fields can be designed. Sewage disposal systems should be installed by competent and reliable contractors. Because detergents interfere with the bacterial action in septic tanks, wastes from automatic laundry equipment should be emptied into isolated drainage lines. Also, storm drains should not empty into the septic tank.

Some local codes allow a *seepage pit*, similar in construction to a cesspool, to take the discharge from a septic tank and allow it to release the effluent liquid into the surrounding soil instead of drainage lines. Low underground water tables permit the use of a seepage-pit system.

12.16 Drawing the Plumbing Plan

On drawings of simple, noncomplex buildings, show the plumbing fixtures to scale and locate any other water outlets on the regular floor plan. Usually, this is all the plumbing information that is necessary. Include all exterior hose bibbs and automatic washer outlets from which piping lines can be planned. Use plumbing templates, if available, or simply scale the symbols with instruments. List fixture sizes and manufacturers' catalogue numbers in the specifications, or list them in a plumbing fixture schedule. Public sewer lines and septic tank systems should be located on site plans.

If the plumbing information is more extensive, draw a separate floor plan showing the walls and main structural features, traced from the regular plan (see Fig. 12-36). In general, follow these steps in completing the plumbing plan:

1. Draw all plumbing fixture symbols to scale (see Fig. 12-36).
2. Locate the cold-water supply line from the street and lay out all cold-water lines to each outlet. Indicate valve, fitting, and pipe sizes.
3. Locate the water heating equipment and lay out the hot-water lines to all fixtures requiring hot water. Use a hot-water pipe symbol and label pipe sizes and fittings.
4. Locate the house drain according to public sewer connections or location of the septic tank.

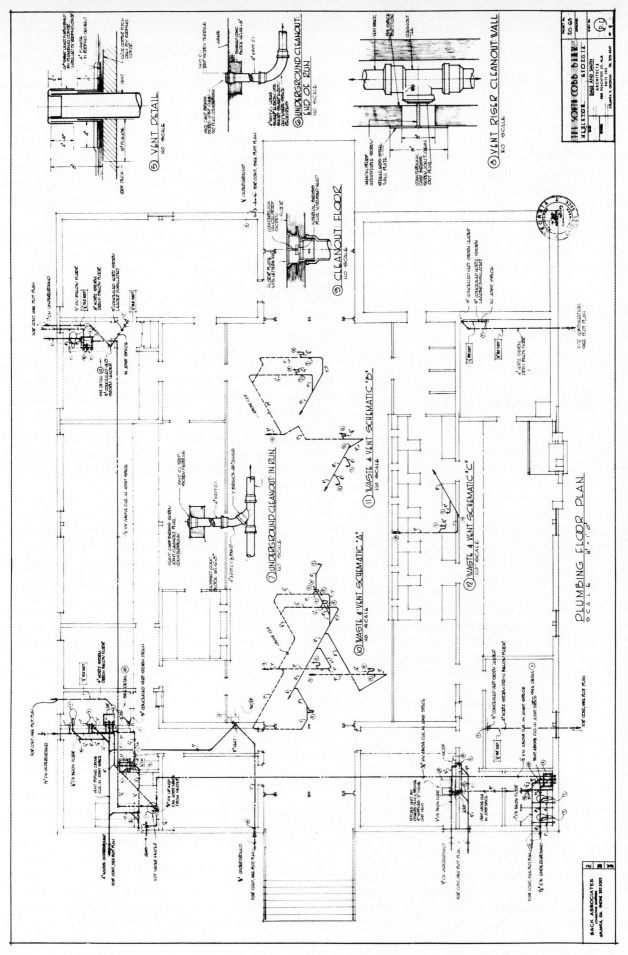

FIGURE 12-36 A typical plumbing drawing for a small commercial building (Chapter 15).

5. With heavy lines, lay out the soil lines after consulting local plumbing codes for pipe sizes and number of fixtures on each line. Show cleanout symbols and vents according to code. Make soil lines as short and direct as possible. Indicate size and description of pipe and fittings.

6. Locate gas line entrance and show pipeline to outlets. Give the pipe size.

7. Draw a vertical section through the stack and vent lines on drawings of multistory buildings. To show complex piping arrangements, use a single-line isometric layout without standard fitting and fixture symbols.

8. Darken all plumbing information to make it more prominent than the structural outlines.

9. Add appropriate notes and titles.

12.17 Home Electrical Systems

To represent electrical systems on the drawing board, the student should have a rudimentary knowledge of the principles of electrical distribution so that he or she may provide adequate wiring and lighting, not only to meet present demands, but also to anticipate future needs.

In planning an electrical wiring system, safety must be the primary consideration. Electricity passing through a conductor creates heat. Overtaxed wiring is not only inefficient, but dangerous as well. If the conductor is too small to accommodate the amount of current passing through it, the overload results in a breakdown and the melting of the protective insulation of the wiring, thus creating a hazard. Considerable destruction may be caused by fire due to outmoded electrical wiring. Minimum requirements for safety standards found in many local codes have been established by the *National Electrical Code*. Compliance with all applicable codes is the first requisite of the electrical system. A copy of the local electrical code should be studied for requirements of local construction.

Like the design of mechanical equipment systems, the design of electrical systems in large buildings requires the services of engineering firms specializing in such work; whereas residential systems of a less complex nature are usually designed and installed by licensed electrical contractors who are familiar with the limitations and requirements of local and national codes. Proper planning for home electrical needs, however, must be done on paper when the total concept is conceived and the major planning is undertaken.

ELECTRICAL TERMINOLOGY

AMPERE   The unit of current used to measure the amount of electricity passing through a conductor per unit of time. (Can be compared to the flow of water in gallons per second.)

CIRCUIT   Two or more conductors through which electricity flows from a source to one or more outlets and then returns.

CIRCUIT BREAKER   A device which breaks the flow of electricity in a circuit automatically, and which performs the same safety function as does a fuse.

CONDUCTORS   Common term for wires that carry the electricity.

FUSE   A safety device containing a conductor that melts when the circuit is overloaded, and thus interrupts the flow of electricity.

GROUND   A connection between the electrical system and the earth—it minimizes the damage from lightning and injury from shocks.

HORSEPOWER   A unit of work. One hp = 746 watts. (The term is diminishing in use.)

OUTLET   A point in a circuit that allows electricity to serve lights, appliances and equipment.

RECEPTACLE   A contact device to receive the plugs of electrical cords or portable lighting equipment and appliances.

SERVICE ENTRANCE CONDUCTORS   The conductors that connect the service equipment to the service drop (overhead) or service lateral (underground).

SERVICE EQUIPMENT   The associated equipment including switches or overcurrent devices that make up the main control of the power supply.

SHORT CIRCUIT   A condition resulting from the unintentional connection between two ungrounded (hot) conductors or between an ungrounded conductor and a grounded conductor (neutral).

VOLT   The unit used to measure the electrical potential difference.

VOLTAGE DROP   The loss of voltage caused by the resistance in conductors or equipment too small to produce overloading.

WATT   The practical unit of electrical power. (Amperes times volts.) Most appliances are rated in watts to indicate their rate of electrical consumption. Both voltage and amperage are considered.

> 1 ampere with pressure of 1 volt = 1 watt
> 1 watt consumed for 1 hour = 1 watt hour
> 1000 watt hours = 1 kilowatt hour (kwh)

12.17.1 The Service Entrance

Electricity is furnished to the home by a 3-wire service drop, installed by the local power company. This 3-wire service supplies $^{120}/_{240}$ volt single-phase 60-Hz alternating current to the house, now considered standard procedure in most localities. Several methods of firmly anchoring service drops are shown in Figs. 12-37 and 12-38. If the service is to be attached to a low roof, a masthead (or weatherhead) installation prevents the service conductors from being attached too near the ground. The service drop conductors should be at least 10' above the final grade. A rigid support for the service conductors must be furnished by the home owner. Locating the point of attachment should be governed largely by the location of the service equipment. Minimum distances between the entrance and the service equipment result in wiring economy, less voltage drop, and more electrical efficiency. Generally, the entrance is made near the kitchen or utility area to provide short runs for the important energy outlets.

In some areas, service conductors are brought to the house below ground. This method conceals the conductors and fittings that would otherwise be unsightly. Electric meters installed on the exterior of the house are more convenient for both the power company and the home owner. A protective device must be installed at the meter if the service conductors are extended more than 2 feet into the building.

The size of the service entrance conductors and conduit is determined by the capacity of the service equipment (see the next section). A minimum 60-ampere service requires No. 6 THW conductors and 1" conduit; 100-ampere service requires No. 3 THW conductors and 1¼" conduit; 150- or 200-ampere service requires No. 1/0 or No. 3/0 (type THW insulation) and 2" conduit.

12.17.2 Service Equipment

The service equipment (distribution panel) is the heart of the electrical system. Encased within a metal box, the equipment contains main disconnect switches, fuses or circuit breakers, and terminals for attaching the distribution circuit conductors. Panels can be either flush or surface mounted. Fuses in the panel are the protective devices in case of overloading or accidental short circuits and are sized according to each circuit capacity (replacements must be no larger than the original fuses). In place of fuses, similar protection may be provided by more expensive circuit breakers that automatically break the circuit when overloaded. No replacement is necessary when cut off; a tripped circuit breaker is merely switched back to its closed position. Show the location of the service panel on the floor plan.

Every electrical system must be grounded to moist earth with the use of a conductor from the ground terminal in the service panel to a metal ground rod or a metallic cold-water pipe.

The size of the service panel is determined by the estimated load requirements of the building, combined with the anticipated future needs. Lighting and appliance loads can be taken from the following wattage table and converted into amperes. For example, if a total of 30,000 watts was found to be needed in the home, the minimum service would then be 125 amperes (30,000 ÷ 240 = 125).

$$\frac{\text{watts}}{\text{volts}} = \text{amperes}$$

A 150-ampere service would be the logical selection to take care of future needs. A 20 percent additional capacity is commonly added for these contingencies.

Although a *60-ampere service* is the minimum acceptable by the National Electric Code for houses under 1000 square feet, a *100-ampere service* is recommended as the minimum for all new homes up to 3000 square feet in size. This service will be adequate for lighting and appliances requiring up to about 24,000 watts total load (see the wattage table). If an electric range, water heater, electric dryer, central air conditioning, along with lighting and the usual small appliances are included, a *150-ampere service* will be needed. If electric resistance heating or other unusual loads are to be included with the above loads, a *200-ampere service* should be selected. Large homes of 5000 square feet and over should have at least the 200-ampere service. Larger services are also available for commercial installations. Panels should be sized in accordance with N.E.C. standards so as not to oversize or undersize the building requirements.

Wattage table	
Home appliances	**Watts**
Automatic dryer (regular)	4500
Automatic dryer (high speed)	8700
Automatic washer	700
Bathroom heater	1500–2500
Dishwasher and waste disposal	1500
Exhaust fan	300
Fuel-fired heating system	800
Hand iron	1000
Home freezer	350
Ironer	1650
Microwave oven	1500
Personal computer	250
Range	8000–13,500
Refrigerator	300
Roaster–broiler	1500
Room air conditioner (1 ton)	1500
Stereo	450
Television	300

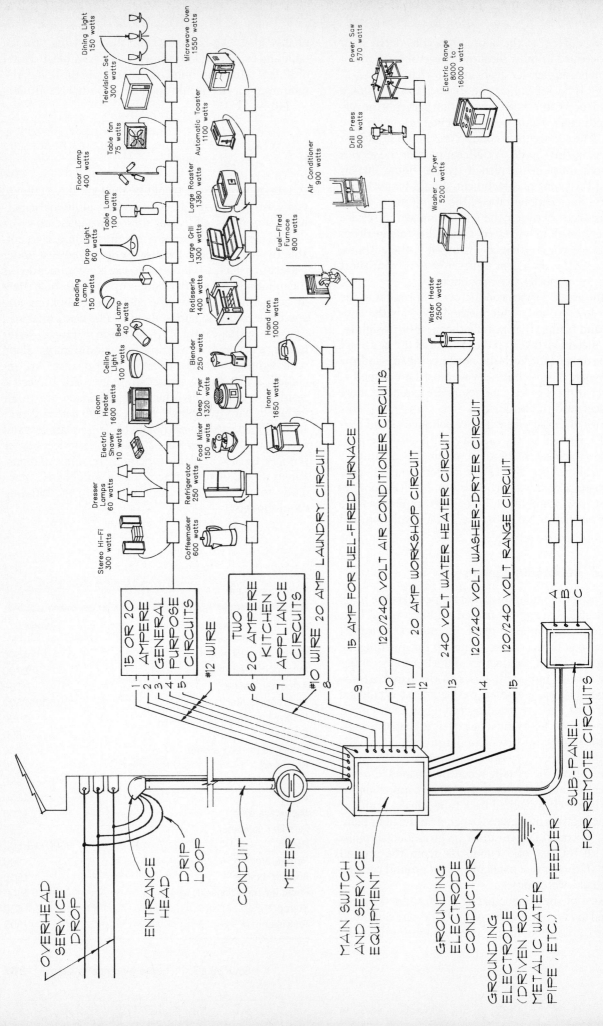

Figure 12-37 Wiring diagram of a residential electrical system.

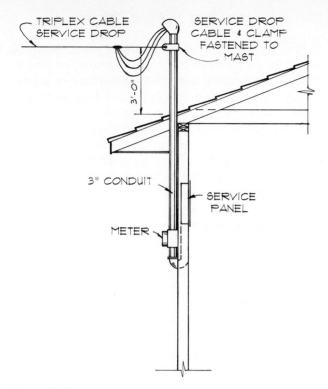

FIGURE 12-38 Entrance mast for low roofs.

12.17.3 Branch Circuits

Branch circuits have various capacities (15, 20, 30, 40, and 50 amperes), depending on their use. Both 240- and 120-volt circuits are furnished by the service panel. Depending on local codes, one of the following types of wiring is used in modern construction.

Nonmetallic-Sheathed Cable is inexpensive and easy to install. It is a flexible conductor that is encased with a plastic, moisture resistant, flame retardant, non-metallic covering over individually insulated copper or aluminum wires. Either two- or three-wire cable is available to be used only in dry locations. For damp locations or underground, a special plastic-covered cable is used instead of the standard plastic-covered kind. Either type is available in sizes from No. 14 to No. 6 wire.

Metal-Armored Cable (AC) is covered with a spiral, flexible metal sheathing that gives the wiring more protection from physical damage, yet it is unsuitable for damp locations.

Metal Conduit is more expensive and offers still more protection for the wiring. The conduit is installed with the boxes and the receptacles during construction; then the conductors are pulled through and connected. All splices must be made in junction boxes.

GENERAL-PURPOSE CIRCUITS (120 volts, 15 or 20 amperes) serve the lighting and general convenience outlets. Good circuitry layout provides several circuits in rooms or wings so that partial lighting will always be available in case of a blown fuse. Receptacle outlets are required in every kitchen, family room, sun room, bedroom, recreation room and the like so that no point along a wall shall be more than six feet from an outlet. Number 12 AWG electrical conductors should be used, which will allow a maximum of 2400 watts in circuits up to 75′ in length; longer circuits require larger conductors.

APPLIANCE CIRCUITS (120/240 volts, three-wire, 20 amperes) should be provided in kitchens, dining areas, and laundries to serve appliances requiring heavier loads.

INDIVIDUAL-EQUIPMENT CIRCUITS are needed to service each of the following permanently installed equipment: electric range, washer–dryer, fuel-fired furnace, dishwasher, electric water heater, central air conditioning, bath heaters, and other similar equipment. The capacity of each circuit must be sufficient for the needs of each piece of equipment.

FEEDER CIRCUITS with subdistribution panel equipment are sometimes used for remote areas. A four-wire feeder is run from the main panel to a subpanel, and two-wire branch circuits are extended from the subpanel with a minimum of voltage drop.

GROUND FAULT CIRCUIT INTERRUPTERS All 125 volt single phase 15 ampere and 20 ampere receptacles installed in bathrooms, garages with exceptions, outdoors with grade level access, one basement receptacle, kitchens within six feet of a sink above counter top surfaces, and boat houses must have ground fault circuit interrupter protection.

12.17.4 Low-Voltage Switching

Another variation of the conventional wiring system is the low-voltage switching system. With this system, wall switches control a low-voltage circuit (6 to 24 volts) through a relay that activates the line voltage at the outlet. Savings can be realized on the low-voltage wiring, since light bell wire can be used. There is no danger of shock at the switch, and any or all of the outlets can be controlled at a central station. Slightly different types of equipment are available for low-voltage systems.

12.17.5 Location of Outlets

For maximum convenience, the probable placement of furniture in each room should be considered before locating outlets. For instance, in a bedroom the outlets would best be on each side of the bed. Since bedrooms and living rooms rely primarily on movable lamps for general lighting, one or two of the outlets should be connected to wall switches. Outlets should generally be placed near the corners of rooms, where they are easily accessible and there is less chance of their being obstructed by furniture. In living areas, no point along a wall should be farther than 6' from an outlet. Small habitable rooms should have at least three receptacle outlets; in larger rooms they should be spaced about 8' apart along each wall. The conventional height for outlets is 12" above the floor except in kitchens and dining areas. In kitchens they are placed just above the countertops at 4' intervals, convenient for work centers; in dining areas they should be located near and just above table surfaces. Baths need an outlet near the lavatory or vanity and one on an opposite wall. Keep all outlets away from tubs or shower stalls, unless they are waterproof. All stationary appliances in kitchens, laundries, and utility rooms require an outlet near their place of installation. Remember to include sufficient outlets in garages, workshops and recreation rooms, as well as waterproof outlets near terraces for outdoor living, and one near the front entrance. Ground fault receptacles are required in baths, kitchens, and all outside areas.

12.17.6 Location of Lighting Fixtures

Interior lighting must be adequate for the activities of each area, yet subtle variations in the amount of general light and the careful use of supplementary or accent lighting give the overall lighting a less monotonous quality. Unusual architectural features must be given special consideration. Well-lighted interiors are often decidedly more interesting in the evening than during the daylight. Artificial light must be regarded as a definite part of the total design of the building.

Although fluorescent lighting is more efficient than incandescent, interiors of living areas will usually be more flattering in the warmer light of incandescent lamps. In bedrooms, also, such lamps are frequently used with or without the addition of a ceiling fixture. In work areas where abundant lighting is necessary for specific tasks, fluorescent-type light may be found more acceptable. However, glare and harsh light levels should be avoided. For example, a luminous suspended ceiling with uniformly spaced fluorescent tubes above produces a very pleasing method of lighting a kitchen. Fluorescent indirect lighting is also suitable for cove installations (see Fig. 12-39). Work counters in kitchens can often be provided with indirect lighting placed beneath wall cabinets. Other than the general lighting of each room, provision must be made for supplementary activity lighting with outlets and/or fixtures properly placed. Unusual architectural features can be given added interest by the use of recessed spots or other types of isolated lighting; be sure any special lighting has an outlet symbol indication.

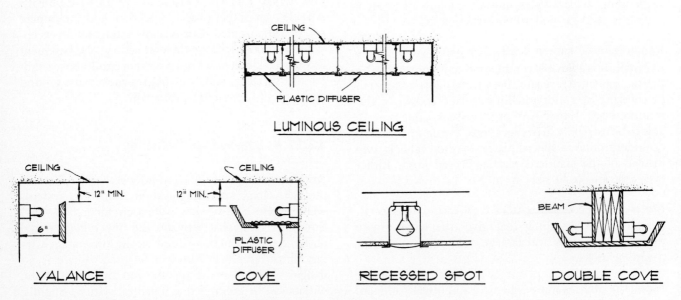

FIGURE 12-39 Methods for providing indirect lighting in living areas.

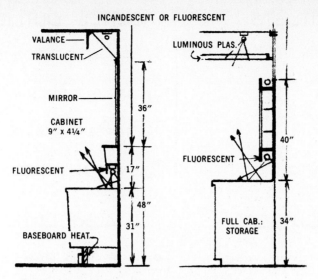

FIGURE 12-40 Indirect lighting in bathrooms.

Usually, small rooms have one centrally located ceiling fixture. Larger rooms and long hallways have several fixtures so arranged that uniform lighting is provided throughout. In bathrooms, light should fall on the face of the persons using mirrors and vanities (see Fig. 12-40). In dining rooms, the ceiling fixture should be located directly above the table placement. Closets can be lighted with door-operated or chain-pull outlets, or they may receive sufficient light from adjacent fixtures placed in front of their door openings. Surface-mounted light fixtures must meet the minimum clearance requirements as specified in the N.E.C.

All entrances and outdoor living areas should have provision for lighting with outlets operated from inside wall switches.

Students should acquaint themselves with the many types of lighting fixtures now available and with the energy codes that specify the maximum allowable wattage per square foot in each room. Each lighting situation has a variety of workable solutions; only experience can produce the most dramatic results.

12.17.7 Location of Light Switches

Wall switches are generally placed 4′ above the floor and should be located near the latch side of door openings for easy access. Switch placement must conform to the traffic patterns within the house. Switches should be located so that, in going from one room to another, lights can be switched on before entering or upon leaving. Rooms with several exits and stairways should be provided with a three-way switch at each exit so that the lighting can be turned on or off from all exits, or in the case of stairs, from each level. Lighting can be operated from two stations by the use of *two three-way switches* (Fig. 12-41). Usually, low-voltage switching is used when it becomes necessary to control the lighting from three or more stations. Low-voltage switches are indicated on the drawing with the same symbols as other switches. Silent mercury switches are recommended in and near bedrooms. In living rooms where variations of light intensity may be useful in creating different moods, dimmer switches can be indicated. Other types of switches are available for providing convenient lighting outlet control.

12.17.8 Special Outlets

The following special outlets are usually indicated on the electrical plan with appropriate symbols:

1. *Entrance signals* (bell or chimes) are best located in central locations such as hallways. Low-voltage current is provided by a transformer located near the service panel. Circuits to entrance-door push buttons utilize No. 18 AWG bell wire.
2. Locate *telephone outlets* in convenient locations.
3. *Intercom systems* become practical in rambling-type homes; panels and stations are indicated on the plan.
4. *Television antenna outlets* can be provided in new home construction for connection to C.A.T.V. service.
5. *Automatic fire- and/or burglar-alarm systems* are available for home protection. Locate alarm bells in the master bedroom.

GENERAL OUTLETS

⊗ CEILING OUTLET

⊖ WALL OUTLET

⊗F FAN OUTLET

⊖L LAMP & PULL SWITCH
  P.S.

SWITCH OUTLETS

⊢S SINGLE POLE SWITCH

⊢S₂ DOUBLE POLE SWITCH

⊢S₃ THREE-WAY SWITCH

⊢S₄ FOUR-WAY SWITCH

CONVENIENCE OUTLETS

⊖ DUPLEX RECEPTACLE

⊖ WATERPROOF RECEPTACLE
  W.P

◐ RANGE RECEPTACLE

⊖S SWITCH & DUPLEX RECEPTACLE

⊖₃ TRIPLEX RECEPTACLE

◓ SPECIAL PURPOSE RECEPTACLE

⊙ FLOOR RECEPTACLE

AUXILIARY

▣ PUSH BUTTON

☐ BUZZER

☐○ BELL

◀ OUTSIDE TELEPHONE

◁ INTERCONNECTING TEL.

Ⓜ MOTOR OUTLET

▬ LIGHTING PANEL

SWITCHING ARRANGEMENTS

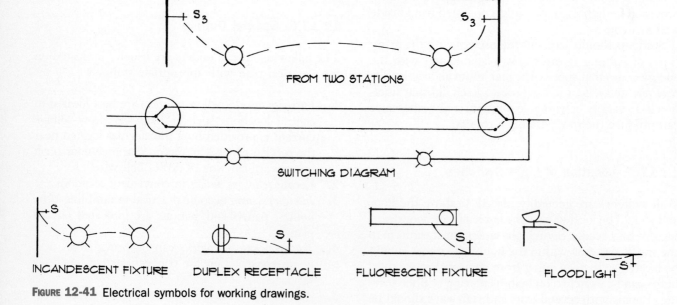

FROM TWO STATIONS

SWITCHING DIAGRAM

INCANDESCENT FIXTURE   DUPLEX RECEPTACLE   FLUORESCENT FIXTURE   FLOODLIGHT

Figure 12-41 Electrical symbols for working drawings.

6. *Built-in-hi-fi or stereo systems* can be shown with built-in main and remote speakers located in various living areas.

12.18 Drawing the Electrical Plan

The electrical information on residential working drawings is usually shown on the regular floor plan, as was mentioned earlier. However, if excessive information requires a separate drawing, as is often needed with complex homes and commercial buildings, use a separate floor plan (see Fig. 12-42). Follow these general steps in drawing the electrical plan:

1. Locate the service panel, show the symbol, and indicate its amperage information.
2. Show all receptable outlet symbols; use three-wire symbols for all outlets requiring 240 voltage such as range, dryer, and air conditioner.
3. Show all ceiling and wall lighting outlets.
4. Show all special outlets such as telephone and door bell.
5. Show all switches and their outlet connections (use an irregular curve).
6. If necessary, complete an electrical fixture schedule and symbol legend.
7. Complete titles and necessary notes.

REVIEW QUESTIONS

1. In planning a satisfactory residential heating system, what basic factors must be considered?

2. How can the architecture contribute to the efficiency of the heating and/or cooling system?

3. What is meant by *degree of comfort* in reference to heating–cooling systems?

4. What are the advantages of the forced warm air heating systems? The hydronic systems? The radiant systems?

5. Would a heat-pump system be efficient for heating a home in your locality?

6. Why are filters placed in the return duct side of a warm air heating system?

7. What type of warm air furnace must be used with heat ducts embedded in a concrete slab on ground floor?

8. How is the air that is removed by kitchen and bath exhaust fans usually replaced in a well-designed system?

9. What three controls are necessary in making a warm-air system fully automatic?

10. Why has electricity become popular as a home heating energy source?

11. Why would the two-pipe hot-water system be more satisfactory than the one-pipe system in home heating?

12. What general type of insulation is the most efficient with radiant heating systems?

13. What two methods of home heating commonly employ baseboard registers?

14. Which type of heating system is most easily combined with conventional cooling equipment?

15. If a room has a calculated heat loss of 3200 Btu per hour, what wattage resistance wire would be needed to satisfy the heat?

16. In heat-pump installations, what is the primary source of heat supplied to the rooms?

17. What mechanism reverses the cycles from heating to cooling in the heat pump?

18. What is the purpose of an outside thermostat?

19. What are the disadvantages of water chillers in residential cooling?

20. Are partitions between heated rooms considered when calculating heat losses?

21. Which part of a residential plumbing system operates by gravity? Which part by pressure?

22. How can initial plumbing costs be reduced when designing a home?

23. What is the purpose of a soil trap in plumbing fixtures?

24. What size hot-water heater would be sufficient for a family of three if the home contains automatic laundry equipment?

25. What factors determine the correct size septic tank and the length of tile drainage lines?

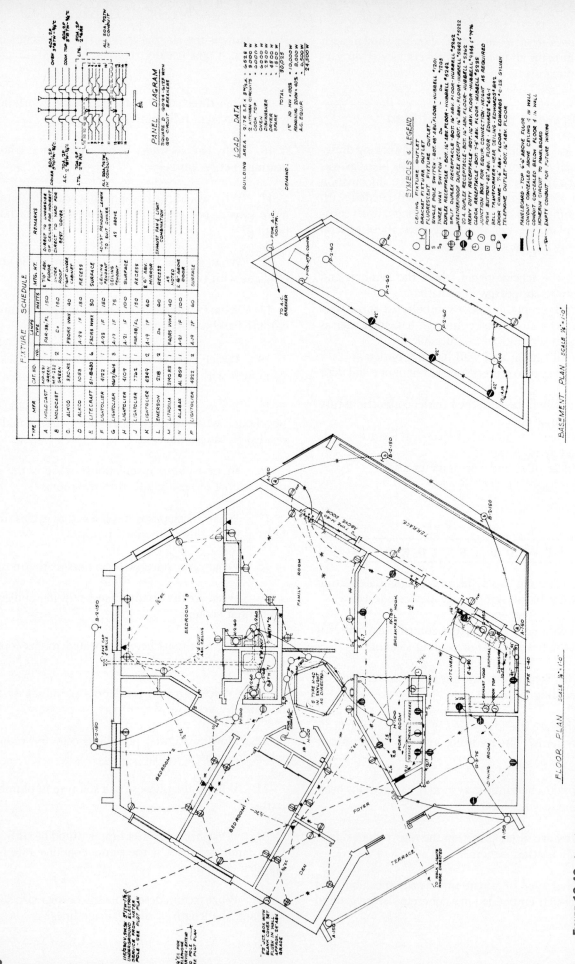

FIGURE 12-42 An electrical plan for a residence.

26. What size electrical service panel should be selected for a home of 2000 square feet?

27. What is a *feeder* circuit?

28. What should be analyzed to determine the location of wall switches?

29. What types of switches are needed to operate an outlet from three locations?

30. Why must lighting be considered in the total concept of a home?

PERSPECTIVE DRAWINGS, SHADES, AND SHADOWS

"Thus shadow owes its birth to light."

—JOHN GAY

13

It is of great advantage for the architectural drafter to be able to draw objects as they appear to the casual observer. A realistic representation is still the most effective way of showing a client, who may have a minimal knowledge of graphics, the appearance of a proposed structure. Through the years, architects have used perspectives in presentation drawings and also for preliminary planning sketches. Unquestionably, the value of perspective drawings is in the fact that architectural designs are shown in the most natural way. Drafters with a working knowledge of perspective will be better prepared for presentation work and, equally important, will find themselves with a keener sense of three-dimensional space visualization. To the beginner, perspective may seem difficult, but after careful study of the principles, even the novice with comparatively little experience will be able to do surprisingly well.

This chapter is not an exhaustive study of the theory of perspective; rather, it is meant to show the beginner the fundamentals and the methods commonly employed in drawing perspectives with the least difficulty and in the most practical way. We will concern ourselves mainly with the how rather than the why by the use of step by step illustrated instructions.

13.1 Theory and Nomenclature

Perspective drawing is a pictorial method of representing a building or object, very much as the lens of a camera records an image on film. We can say that a perspective is the projection of an object onto a fixed plane as seen from a fixed point. Remember that a view we observe with our eyes is actually two coordinated views from two points, usually not fixed as we move our

heads about, producing three-dimensional realism difficult to obtain on a drawing. The drawing can only show the image as it will appear from one point of view, and that point is fixed. This is a limitation inherent in every perspective drawing. Occasionally, even with the most accurate projection, an entirely unrealistic representation will result. For that reason, slight modifications of points and geometric arrangement in drawing may be necessary before arriving at a satisfactory picture. The student must be willing to make several trials, if need be, for the sake of appearance and true architectural proportions.

The basic theory of perspective drawing assumes that the image is produced on a transparent vertical plane called the *picture plane* (Fig. 13-1), very much as orthographic views (discussed in Chapter 3) are formed on transparent planes—the only difference being that the orthographic have parallel projectors, whereas the perspective views have projectors radiating from a single point, similar to the visual lines of sight from a person's eye (see Fig. 13-1). The outline of these projection points, as they pierce the picture plane, forms the perspective drawing. For comparison, we could produce a perspective on a window glass if we were looking through it at a building across the street and drew the exact outlines as we see them through the glass. On our paper, however, we will plot all the points of the perspective with projection lines from the orthographic plan and elevation view, thereby eliminating any guesswork. A pictorial representation of the planes and points necessary to draw a typical perspective is shown in Fig. 13-2. Later, we will discuss how each is laid out on paper to produce the finished perspective.

Down through the years, many artists and drafters have contributed to the system of perspective projection as we know it today. The accompanying woodcut,

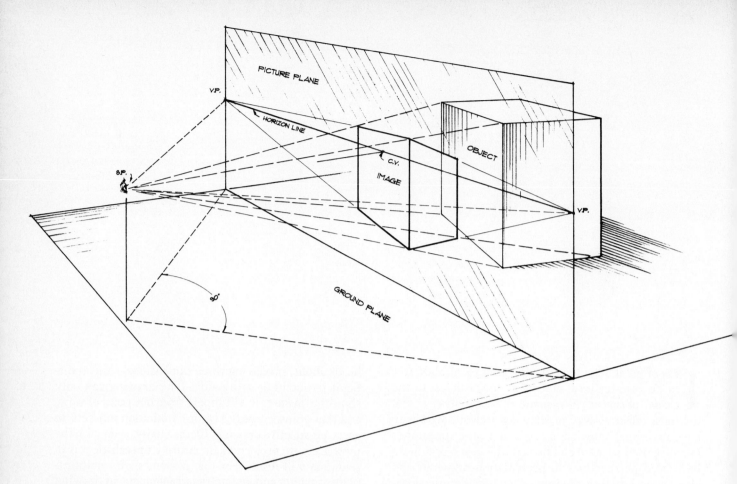

PICTURE PLANE

V.P.

HORIZON LINE

C.V.

IMAGE

OBJECT

S.P.

V.P.

80°

GROUND PLANE

FIGURE 13-1 In perspective drawing, the image of an object is produced on a theoretical, transparent plane called the picture plane as we look through the plane at the object.

"Demonstration of Perspective," by Albrecht Dürer, is from the artist's treatise on geometry, written in 1525. It illustrates a rather crude yet effective early attempt to prove the principle of projectors forming a true image as they pierce a vertical plane (Fig. 13-3).

To interpret both the drawings and written material, we must have an acquaintance with perspective terms. It would be wise at this point to study the drawings in this chapter and observe the significance of each of the following terms:

Picture Plane (P.P.)   As we mentioned, the picture plane is conveniently thought of as a transparent, vertical plane upon which the perspective is drawn. The lower edge of the plane intersects the ground plane. On the plan view of the layout, it appears as a simple, straight line parallel to the ground plane and usually is placed between the station point and the object (see Fig. 13-2). All horizontal measurements are marked on the picture-plane line and then projected to the perspective. Any part of an object touching the picture plane will have true-height characteristics, and these heights can be projected directly from an elevation of the object

or measured directly as long as the feature touches the picture plane. You will notice in the different drawings that the farther back from the picture plane the features fall, the smaller they will appear on the perspective. On the lower portion of our perspective construction layout, the surface of the paper becomes the picture plane. For convenience, we will label the picture-plane line P.P. on the drawings; the other terms will also be designated by their initial capital letters.

Ground Plane (G.P.)   The ground plane must be horizontal and is represented with a line on the elevation portion of our layout. If the object touches the picture plane on the plan, it must also touch the groundline in a similar manner on the perspective (see Fig. 13-2). If the object is placed in back of the picture plane in plan, it will appear above and back of the groundline on the elevation. The groundline is always parallel to the horizon line and represents the intersection of the picture plane and the ground.

Station Point (S.P.)   The station point is the origination of the observer's lines of sight as the object is seen

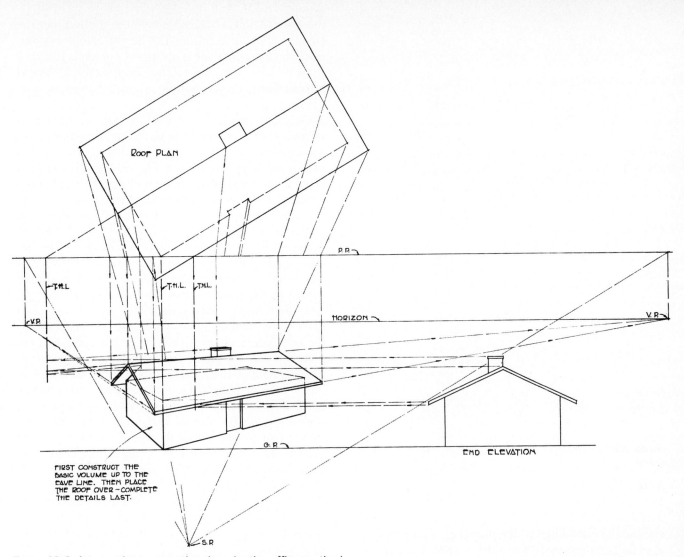

FIGURE 13-2 A two-point perspective done by the office method.

through the picture plane. It will appear as a point on both the plan and elevation construction. However, it is usually not obvious in elevation, because it falls on the horizon line. The placement of the point on the plan view obviously determines the view of the building. And this choice of placement would be very much like actually walking around the building to determine the most favorable position for observation. (Generally, it is most expedient to choose the front view showing the entrance.) It also becomes evident that the distance between the station point and the picture plane affects the sense of distance in the perspective (see Fig. 13-7).

In early attempts, students often make the mistake of placing the station point too near the picture plane. In general, the station point should be placed about twice as far away from the picture plane as the length of the building being drawn. Another method of determining the proper distance for a pleasing perspective is with the use of a 30° triangle. Place the triangle so that its sides

FIGURE 13-3 A woodcut by Albrecht Durer in 1525 verifying the principles of perspective. The string passing through the picture plane locates points to form the image.

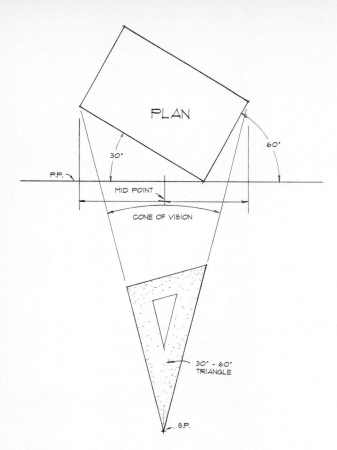

PLAN

30°

60°

P.P.

MID POINT

CONE OF VISION

30° - 60°
TRIANGLE

S.P.

Figure 13-4 A convenient method for locating the station point.

the horizon line is placed above the groundline; the amount above determines the height of observation, since the horizon plane is always at eye level. If a view from 30' high were desired, for example, the 30' would be scaled from the groundline to locate the horizon line.

Vanishing Points (V.P.) Vanishing points for horizontal lines always fall on the horizon line. Receding, horizontal lines that are not parallel to the picture plane vanish at these points (see Fig. 13-5). On the plan portion, perpendicular lines parallel to the sides of the building are projected from the station point to locate the vanishing points on the picture plane; to bring the points to the elevation portion of the setup, they are projected down to the horizon line (see Fig. 13-2). This is the method for a two-point, angular perspective. In a one-point perspective, the vanishing point is simply placed in the most favorable position on the horizon line. In drawing perspectives, the vanishing points make convenient terminations for the horizontal receding lines, and as long as the proper lines vanish at the correct point, the picture will develop with little trouble. Remember that parallel lines vanish at the same point. Sloping (non horizontal) surfaces, which will be discussed later, have vanishing points lying on a vertical trace through the original vanishing points. Unless a three-point perspective is drawn, all vertical lines are drawn vertically. Very few architectural delineators have found use for the three-point type of perspective. In reality, the sides of tall buildings would converge vertically as we look up at them. But the distortion does not lend itself to accurate presentation; therefore, we will not concern ourselves with three-point perspective in this material.

Occasionally, when working on large drawings, the vanishing point falls a considerable distance from the paper. If a large board is not available to overcome this problem, some method must be employed to vanish lines at the distant points. Often an adjacent table can be used, and a thumbtack in the vanishing point will aid in aligning an especially long straight-edge. Another method is shown in Fig. 13-6 with the use of an offset-head T square and a curved template fastened to the board.

enclose the extremities of the plan (Fig. 13-4), and the apex will locate a satisfactory station point. Usually, the point is located in the center of vision (see Fig. 13-7B), rather than off to one side. The most desirable placement of station points comes only after experience is gained in dealing with the correct appearances of the many architectural forms and features that are generally encountered.

Horizon Line (H.L.) The horizon line represents the height of the observer's eye and therefore is only represented on the elevation portion of the drawing. Usually,

VERTICAL

V.P.   V.P.
HORIZON

Figure 13-5 Photograph of a house with major lines extended to locate the vanishing points.

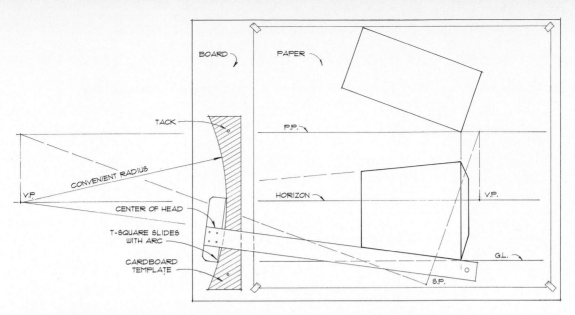

Figure 13-6 Handy method of drawing lines when their vanishing points fall off the drawing board.

True-Height Line (T.H.L.) If a vertical line of the object touches the picture plane in plan view, the line will appear at the same scale on the finished perspective, thus providing a convenient method for projecting true heights—from an elevation view or by measurement directly on the true-height line, if necessary (see Fig. 13-2). If difficulty is encountered in establishing heights for a certain feature of the floor plan with the use of only one true-height line, the problem can be solved by projecting the feature to the picture plane. Wherever the projection intersects the picture plane, a new true-height line can be drawn for measuring the height of that feature only. Remember that height measurements can be made on only those features that touch the picture plane.

13.2 Perspective Variables

Briefly, the variables in perspective construction, other than the actual scale change of the orthographic views, are the relationships between the station point, picture plane, and object (see Fig. 13-7). Naturally, there can be an infinite number of relationships, and the drafter should know the various ways in which these variables can be manipulated for the most desirable pictorial appearance.

Relationship of the Object to the Picture Plane (Fig. 13-7) First, a decision must be made as to which sides of the building should appear on the perspective. Ordinarily, the front is shown and given the most emphasis;

occasionally, an interesting feature in the rear will call for a view from that side. Emphasis is attained by placing the important side at a small angle from the picture plane—the larger the angle, the less the emphasis. Usually, the 30°–60° angles are convenient for laying out the plan in relation to the picture plane, with the 30° angle given to the more important side. A 45° angle produces equal emphasis on the two observable sides of a building. The perspective view may be more interesting if a 30°-60° angle is used.

It is worth remarking that without changing the scale of the orthographic views the size of the finished perspective can be controlled to a certain extent by merely changing the relationship of the plan to the picture plane (Fig. 13-7G, H, and I). Usually, the front corner of the plan is placed on the picture plane; but by bringing the plan *down*, with more of it (or all of it) in front of the picture plane, a larger perspective will result. Conversely, if a smaller perspective is desired, the plan can be placed in back of the picture plane.

Distance from the Station Point to the Picture Plane After observing the drawings, it will be seen that the closer the station point is to the picture plane, the smaller the perspective becomes. Also, close station points produce images with sharp angles on their forecorners, resulting in distorted and displeasing perspectives. On the other hand, if the station point is placed too far from the picture plane, it will usually fall off the paper and therefore become troublesome. Under ordinary conditions, a station point placed to produce a 30° angle of vision with respect to the extremities of the plan

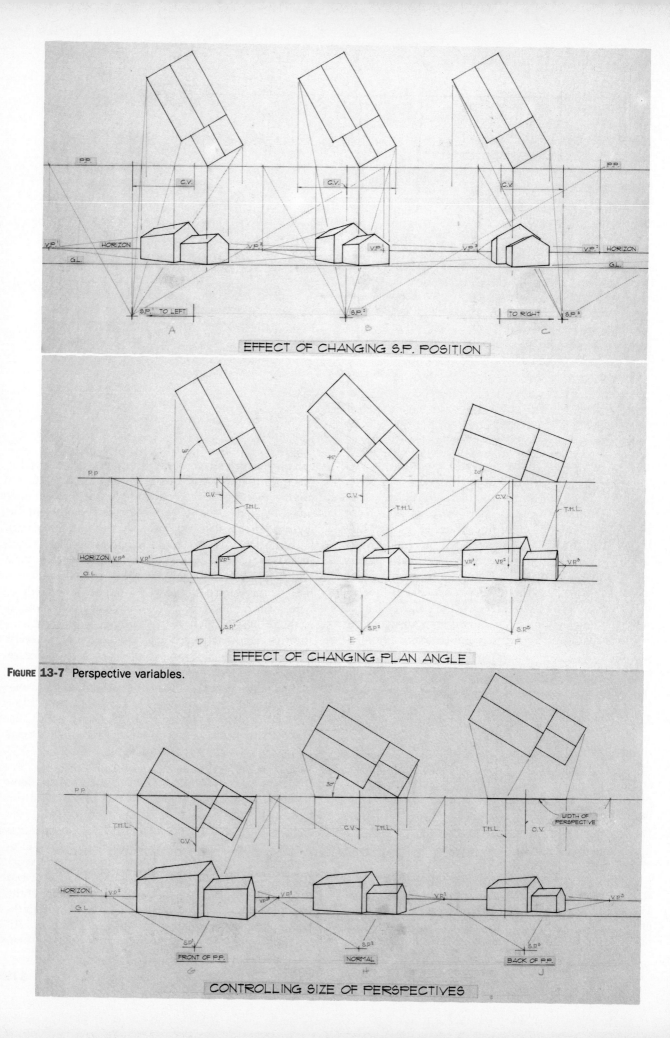

EFFECT OF CHANGING S.P. POSITION

EFFECT OF CHANGING PLAN ANGLE

FIGURE 13-7 Perspective variables.

CONTROLLING SIZE OF PERSPECTIVES

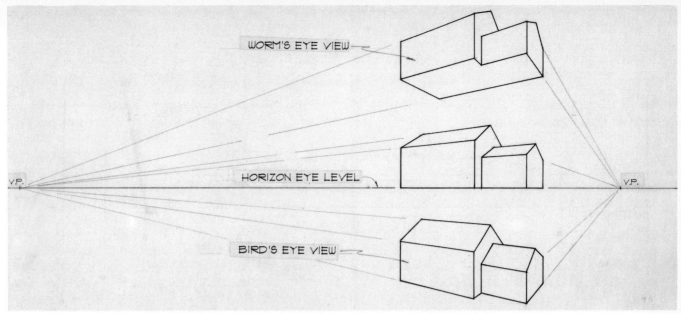

Figure 13-8 Effect of viewing a building from different heights.

produces satisfactory images (see Fig. 13-4). The cone of vision should not be more than 45° in width.

The station point can also be moved to the right or left of the center of vision (Fig. 13-7A, B, and C), but its placement too far either way will produce distortion. Similar effects can be gained by changing the angle of the plan in relation to the picture plane, as previously mentioned. The latter method is advisable since it keeps the station point and the center of vision in a perpendicular relationship to the picture plane, eliminating unnecessary distortion.

Height of the Horizon from the Ground Plane The placement of the horizon line in respect to the groundline determines the eye-level height in observing the building (see Fig. 13-8). The horizon represents eye level. If it is placed above the height of the roof, a bird's-eye view will result; if it is placed below the foundation of the building, the perspective will give one the impression of looking up at the building from a low position, such as a valley. The normal position of the horizon is 5'-6" or 6'-0" above the groundline; this distance represents the eye-level height of the average person standing on level ground. Care should be taken not to place the horizon line at the same height as a dominant horizontal feature on the building, such as a strong roof line. The feature will then coincide with the horizon line and thereby lose much of its interest and importance. Low buildings, such as houses with flat roofs, are usually given more interest if the horizon line is placed 25' or 30' high. Although this placement gives prominence to the roof, it nevertheless reduces strong, nearly horizontal roof lines (see Figs. 13-2 and 13-9).

We see that the variables that exist in the setting up of a perspective layout make it possible for the drafter to adapt a mechanical projection method to a variety of perspective situations. With experience, the modifications can be made to give variety to the perspectives, which will be limited only by a drafter's reluctance to experiment and improve the quality of her or his work. Do not forget, however, that interest is important on a drawing, but not at the expense of misrepresenting true architectural conditions.

13.3 Types of Perspectives

All linear perspectives (those defining outlines) used by delineators can be classified as either two-point or one-point perspectives (as we stated, three-point perspective is not effective in architectural presentation). The two-point angular perspective (Fig. 13-2) is the most popular type for showing the exteriors of buildings. Two sides of the building are seen, and the angular nature of these sides reveals the important information without excessive distortion. Two methods of construction have been developed:

1. The common or office method (direct projection)
2. The perspective-plan method

The office method is of particular importance to the beginner; it is widely used and most often the simplest method for orientation. Although more complex, the perspective-plan method has more versatility and drawings can be completed quicker once the principles

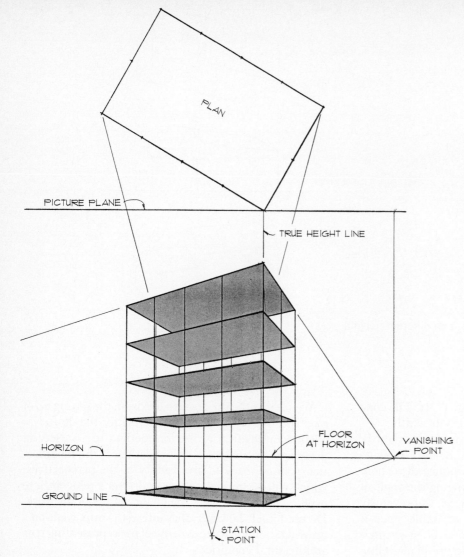

Figure 13-9 Appearance of floor levels at various heights.

have been mastered. The knowledge of these two methods will be sufficient for any perspective work encountered and will be discussed in what follows.

The one-point perspective (Fig. 13-18) depicts a building or interior with one side parallel to the picture plane. It will be seen that the horizontal lines of the parallel side are drawn horizontally, producing a true orthographic shape of the side. The receding, parallel sides are formed by lines converging to a single point, the *vanishing point*, usually placed within the view. Interior views of rooms are often drawn with the one-point method; it presents an accurate description of the facing wall, combined with observation of both receding sidewalls. Another typical application for one-point perspective is a street flanked by buildings. Looking directly down the street, the vanishing point falls at the end of the street. The receding building and street lines are then conveniently drawn to the one vanishing point (see Fig. 13-19). Other dramatic applications can be found for the one-point method, especially when for-

mal architectural arrangements are involved. Many of the principles of two-point perspective apply equally to the one-point, with only minor variations in setting up the perspective change.

13.4 To Draw a Two-point Angular Perspective of an Exterior (Office Method)

Figures 13-10 through 13-12 show the step by step sequence usually employed.

STEP A: THE PLAN VIEW

1. Draw the floor plan, or roof plan as shown, on a 30°–60° relationship with the horizontal. Or a separate plan can be taped down in a similar position.

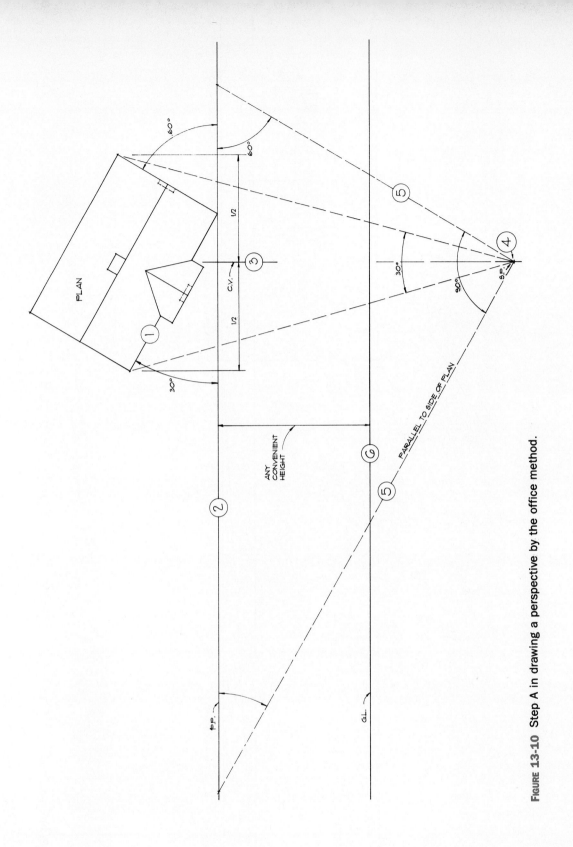

FIGURE 13-10 Step A in drawing a perspective by the office method.

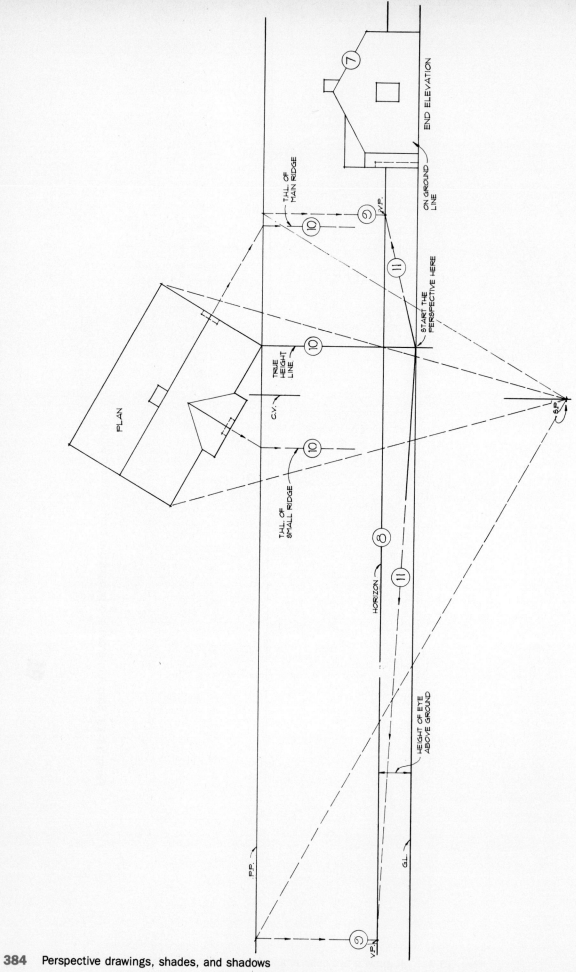

FIGURE 13-11 Step B: office method.

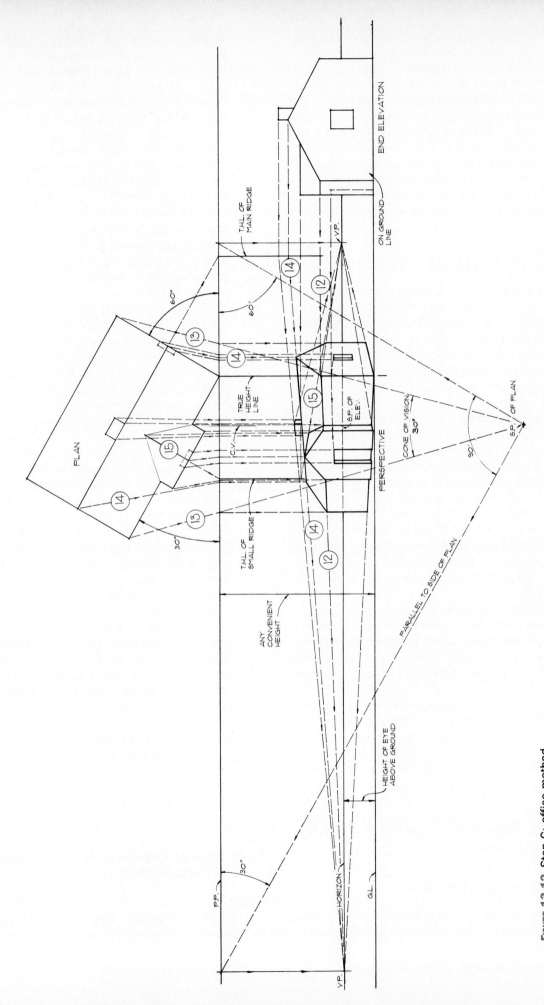

Figure 13-12 Step C: office method.

2. Draw the horizontal picture-plane line touching the lower corner of the plan. (Other relationships can be used later, if desired.)

3. Locate the center of vision (C.V.) midway on the horizontal width of the inclined plan.

4. Establish the station point on the center of vision far enough from the picture plane to produce a 30° cone of vision (refer to Fig. 13-4).

5. From the station point, draw projectors, parallel to the sides of the plan, to the picture plane. These points represent the vanishing points as seen in the plan view and are often called *distance points*.

STEP B: THE PERSPECTIVE SETUP

6. Draw a horizontal groundline a convenient distance below the plan view far enough from the picture plane to allow sufficient space for the perspective layout.

7. Draw the elevation view on the groundline. Place it off to the side of the perspective area; even if projection lines run through the elevation view, no harm will result. This view supplies the heights; therefore, it must be drawn to the same scale as the plan. Usually, the end elevation is sufficient if the major heights are shown. (If a perspective is being drawn from a separate set of plans, the elevation, like the plan, can merely be taped on the ground plane in a convenient position.)

8. Draw the horizon line as shown. The heights of the elevation view will aid in determining the most effective eye-level height. Usually, if a level view is desired, the horizon line is scaled 6'-0" above the ground-plane line. This distance is optional.

9. Drop vertical projectors from the picture-plane distance points in the plan view (found in step 5) to the horizon line. These points on the horizon line are the vanishing points of the perspective and should be made prominent to avoid mistaken identity.

10. Draw vertical true-height lines from the corner of the plan that touches the picture plane and the extension of the two roof ridges as they intersect the picture plane. Unless they are boxed in, ridgelines of gable roofs should be brought to the picture plane, where a true-height line can be established. Usually, this is the simplest method of plotting their heights; from the true-height line, the ridge height is vanished to the proper vanishing point.

STEP C: PERSPECTIVE VIEW

11. Now we are ready to start the perspective itself. From the intersection of the main true-height line

at the corner of the building and the ground plane, construct the bottom of the building by projecting the point toward both vanishing points. All perspectives should start at this point.

12. Next, continue developing the main block mass of the building. Mark the height of the basic block by projecting it from the elevation view to the true-height line. Again, project this point (on the true-height line) to both vanishing points.

13. To find the width of the basic block, we must go to the plan. With a straightedge, project both extreme corners of the plan toward the station point. Where these projectors pierce the picture plane, drop verticals to the perspective. This establishes the basic-block width; the back corner can be located, if desired, by vanishing the outer corners to the correct vanishing points.

14. Next, plot the main ridge so that the roof shape can be completed. Project the height of the ridge from the elevation view to the main ridge true-height line. Vanish this point to the left vanishing point. The ends of the ridge must be taken again from the plan view. Project both ends of the ridge on the plan toward the station point; where the projectors pierce the picture plane, drop verticals to the vanished ridgeline. This defines the main ridge, and the edges of the roof can then be drawn to the corners of the main block.

15. The small ridge of the front gable roof can be established by the same method as above. Because this ridge is perpendicular to the main ridge, the small ridge is vanished to the right vanishing point. The remaining corners and features of the gable extension in front of the main block can be taken from the plan by the method previously mentioned and vanished to the correct vanishing point.

16. Continue plotting the remaining lines and features on the perspective by locating each from the plan as usual and projecting their heights from the elevation view. After heights are brought to the true-height line, they must usually be projected around the walls of the building to bring them to their position. Remember that true heights are first established *on the picture plane* and then vanished along the walls of the building to where they are needed. Drawing a horizontal circle in two-point perspective by the office method is shown in Figure 13-21.

13.5 Interior Two-point Angular Perspective (Office Method)

Figure 13-13 illustrates the method of drawing an interior view with two-point perspective. The principles are the same as for exterior views. However, notice that

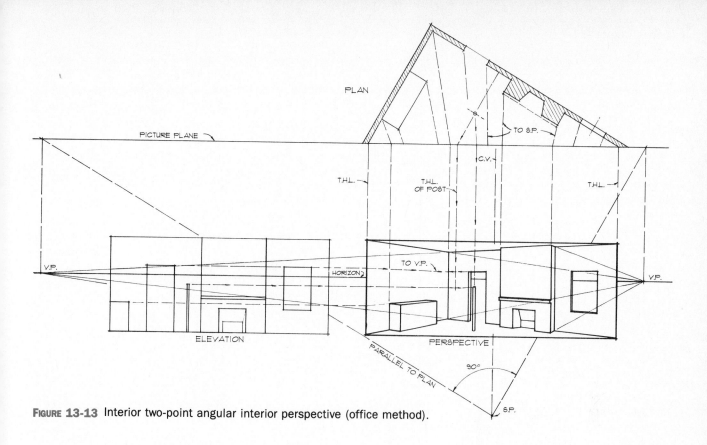

FIGURE 13-13 Interior two-point angular interior perspective (office method).

only a partial plan is drawn, and the rectangular shape of the interior touching the picture plane is drawn on the perspective. The view forms within this rectangle; later, the rectangle can be removed if a feathered out drawing is desired.

A pole has been placed in the room to indicate the method of plotting any point in space; other points can be located in a similar manner. Heights of features on the walls are projected to the true-height line and carried along the walls to their correct position, which is located from the plan. When setting up the perspective, keep the station point about twice as far from the picture plane as the greatest width of the plan being drawn; this effects a desirable appearance. Coordinates can be laid off on the floor, resembling square tile, if odd locations or shapes are required within the room.

The picture plane can be placed in other positions than shown on the figure; regardless, projectors locating the features must be brought to the picture plane before they are dropped to the perspective.

13.6 The Perspective-plan Method and Measuring Lines

Comparison will show that the perspective-plan method requires less space on the drawing board, has more versatility, and is obviously more sophisticated than the office method. Many professional architec-

tural delineators use the perspective-plan method exclusively. Although several new variations in procedure are encountered, the basic principles of the office method are still applicable.

The plan method requires no orthographic plan from which projections are taken. Rather, the perspective plan is drawn from measurements laid off on a horizontal measuring line. From this plan, vertical projectors establish widths and feature locations on the finished perspective. Heights are measured on a true-height line rather than projected.

It is usual practice to draw a perspective from a set of working drawings. The site plan serves as a guide for correctly orienting the station point. The plan and elevation views furnish all the measurements for drawing the perspective. Here lies one of the advantages of this method; when transferring the dimensions from the working drawings to the perspective layout, the size of the perspective can be controlled by changing the scale of the dimensions during transfer. Also, the method allows trials of various horizon heights without a major amount of reconstruction. With the use of tracing paper over the original perspective plan, experimentation becomes a simple matter.

Figures 13-14, 13-15, and 13-16 illustrate the three major steps necessary in completing a simple perspective by the plan method. The given conditions and dimensions, similar to a typical problem, are shown in Fig. 13-14.

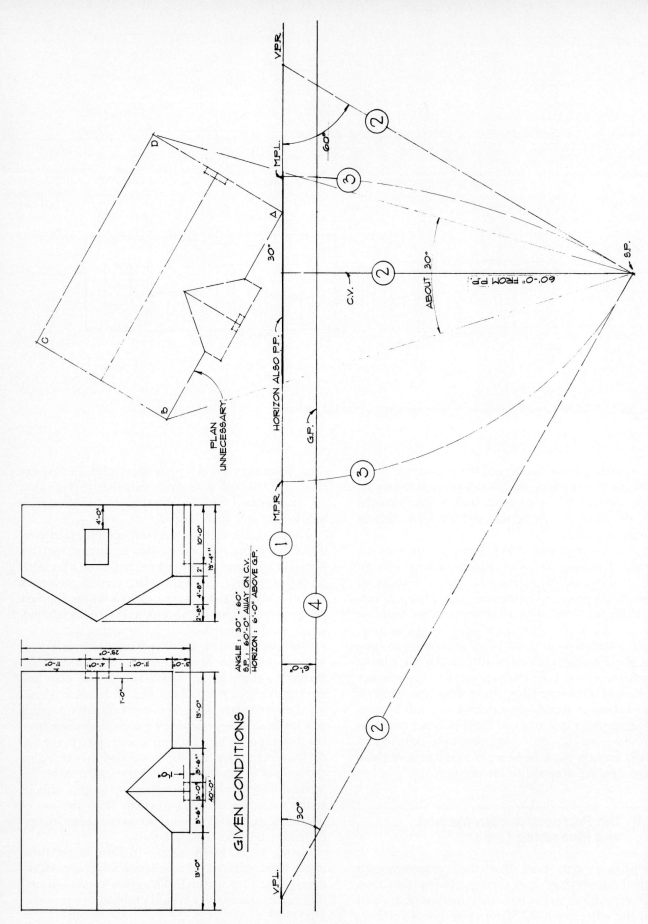

FIGURE 13-14 Step A in drawing a perspective by the perspective-plan method.

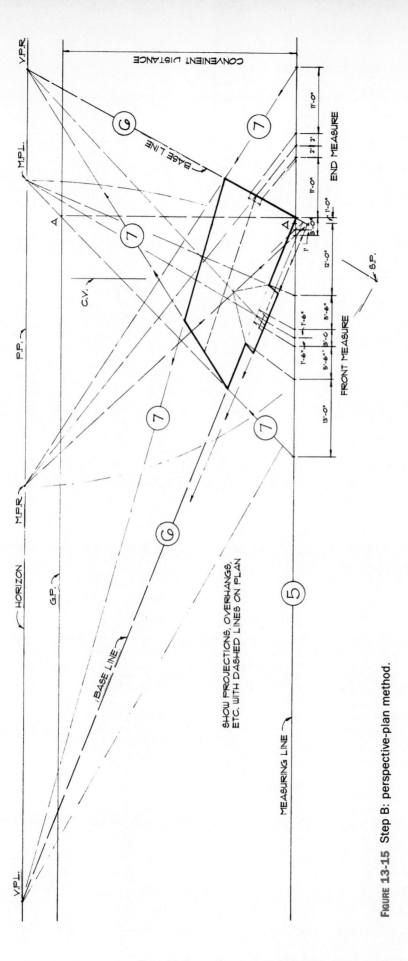

FIGURE 13-15 Step B: perspective-plan method.

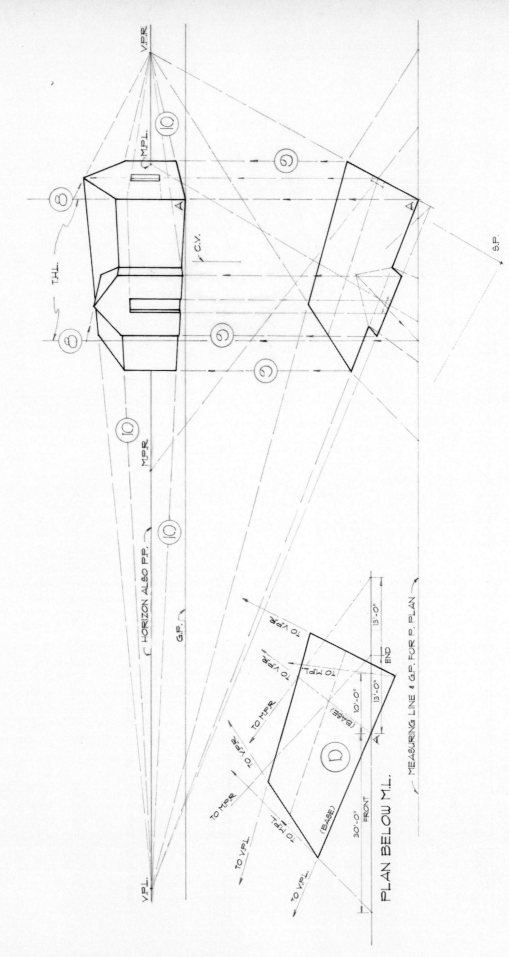

Figure 13-16 Step C: perspective-plan method.

STEP A: LOCATING THE PRELIMINARY POINTS

1. Start with the horizon line and draw it near the upper part of the paper. For convenience, this line also may be used as the picture plane in plan.
2. Establish the station point at the given distance on the center of vision (to scale) and draw the 30°–60° projectors to the picture plane. This locates the left and right vanishing points.
3. Construct the left and right measuring points (M.P.) on the picture plane. To locate the left measuring point, bring the distance between the left vanishing point and the station point to the picture plane with the use of an arc swung from the left vanishing point. From the right vanishing point, scribe the radius (right vanishing point to station point) to the picture plane; this point becomes the right measuring point. These measuring points will be vanishing points for the horizontal measurements we will use in our next step.
4. Draw the ground-plane line 6′-0″ (scaled) below the horizon line. This establishes our eye level.

The orthographic floor plan shown with dashed lines in the figure is unnecessary in an actual layout; it is added merely to give the beginner a visualization of the plan and picture-plane relationship, which, to the more experienced, would be indicated by the points just established on the horizon line.

STEP B: DRAWING THE PERSPECTIVE PLAN

5. At an arbitrary location below the horizon, draw a horizontal measuring line (H.M.L.). The plan in perspective will develop from this line, making it actually a groundline for the plan only, as well as a line upon which horizontal measurements of the building are laid off. It is helpful to know that projections from the plan to the finished perspective will be more accurate if the measuring line is placed well below the horizon; the exaggerated shape of the resulting plan will not adversely affect the perspective and, also, sufficient space will be gained for the development of the picture. Transfer the corner of the building touching the picture plane to the measuring line (point A).
6. From point A, draw lines to both the left and right vanishing points. These lines are the left and right edges of the plan and are referred to as *base lines*. Measurements laid off on the measuring line, when projected to the measuring point, will terminate at these base lines. To lay out the dimensions of the plan on the measuring line, start at point A. All the dimensions of the front side of the building (A–B), starting at the forecorner, are

stepped off to the left of point A, and those for the right end of the building (A–D) are stepped off to the right of point A. The depth of the small front entrance projection would necessarily extend in front of point A, and therefore its depth measurement would be laid off *to the left of point A* instead of to the right.

When a part of a plan falls in front of the measuring line (see Fig. 13-16D), the base line must continue through point A below the measuring line; and the measurements also must be laid off in continuity through point A. If the left side is in reference, the measurements of the features extending in front of the measuring line would be laid off *to the right of point A*, and the projection line to the left measuring point would therefore extend below the measuring line to locate the features on the base line. The opposite construction would be needed for similar right-side measurements.

7. To complete the plan, draw lines toward the correct vanishing point from the foreshortened measurements on the base lines.

STEP C: COMPLETING THE FINISHED PERSPECTIVE

8. Lay out a true-height line, projected from point A on the picture plane. Establish the bottom of the line on the ground plane, which has been scaled 6′-0″ below the horizon. This line represents the corner of the building on the picture plane, and all scale heights are measured on it.
9. Transfer corners and features from the plan to the perspective with vertical projectors.
10. Project heights of the building to the vanishing points as discussed in the office-method construction. Complete the perspective as shown by first blocking in the major forms and then adding the projections, openings, and other minor features after the general shape is found to be satisfactory.

When a number of similar-sloped features are needed on a perspective and the amount of slope or pitch is given, it may be advisable to locate the vanishing points of the sloping planes (see Fig. 13-17). Slope vanishing points must lie on traces (vertical lines) that pass through the vanishing points located for horizontal surfaces, V.P.L. and V.P.R. Notice that the V.P. for the 30° inclined roof plane, labeled No. 1, is located on the right trace *above* V.P.R. If a V.P. for a horizontal surface is located on the horizon line, then the V.P. for an inclined surface must be located *above* or *below* the horizon.

To locate the V.P. for slope No. 1, start at M.P.R. and lay out the given slope (30° in this case) from the

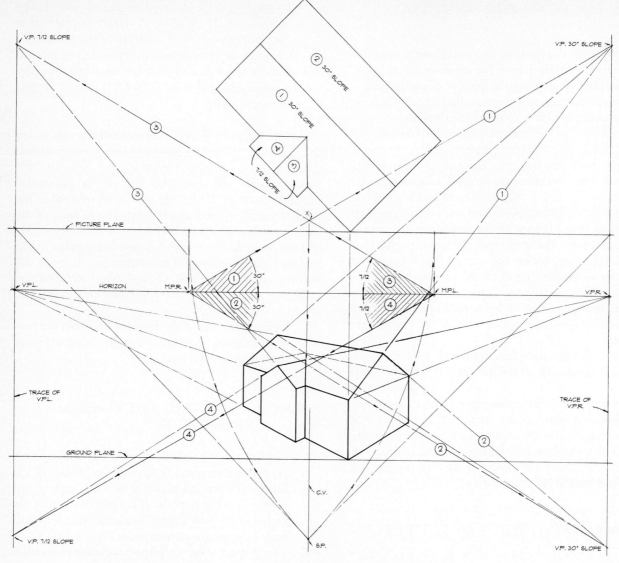

Figure 13-17 Vanishing points of slopes. Similar numbers indicate relative lines and angles.

horizontal, as shown by the shaded area, and extend the line to the right trace. This locates the V.P. of the inclined roof. The V.P. for the declining roof plane on the back part of the house is located from the same M.P.R., and the slope is layed out *below* the horizon and extended to the right trace *below* the V.P.R.

Opposite-slope V.P.s are located in a similar manner as shown by the shaded areas Nos. 3 and 4 and their related projection lines.

13.7 One-point Parallel Perspective (Office Method)

The one-point perspective has several typical applications, such as interiors, street scenes, and exterior details of entrances or other special features. Sometimes

the one-point method is the only effective way to represent buildings of unusual shape. For example, a U-shaped house being observed toward the U is most faithfully represented with a one-point perspective. This method is usually easier to draw than the two-point, angular perspective, and it is the only type that reveals three wall planes. All receding horizontal lines converge at only one vanishing point, and lines parallel to the picture plane in plan are parallel to the horizon in the perspective. Usually, less board space is needed.

Figure 13-18 shows a simple room interior drawn with the one-point method. Notice that many of the perspective principles previously discussed are applicable. All the variations in respect to the placement of the picture plane, station point, and horizon equally affect the finished one-point perspective drawing.

To construct a one-point parallel perspective (Fig. 13-18),

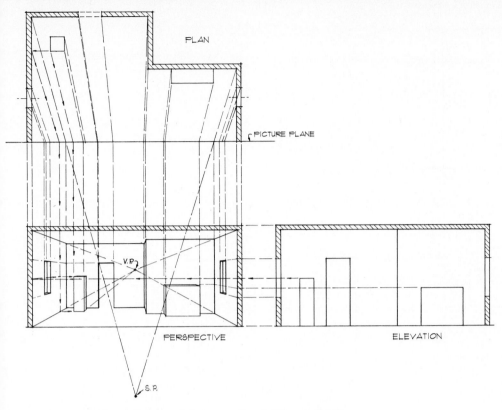

FIGURE 13-18 One-point parallel perspective (office method).

start by drawing the plan and elevation views as shown. Establish the picture plane at the lower part of the plan (it may be placed in front, in back, or at an intermediate area of the plan). On the center of vision below the plan, locate the station point, about the width of the plan away from the picture plane, or a 60° maximum cone of vision in this case will satisfactorily locate the station point. The elevation view can be placed on either side of the area reserved for the perspective drawing. From the plan and elevation views, project the frame of the perspective representing the picture plane in elevation. Locate the one vanishing point within the frame at the desired distance above the groundline (bottom of frame). No horizon line is needed. If other than a room interior is to be drawn, start the perspective by drawing the features touching the picture plane; project their lines from both the plan and elevation views. Project interior wall lines toward the vanishing point. Locate the horizontal spacing of points and vertical lines by projecting the features from the plan toward the station point; at the intersection of the projectors and the picture plane, drop verticals to the perspective in the same manner as described in two-point perspective (Section 13.4, Step C-13). Project heights from the elevation view to the true-height line. Notice how heights are carried along the walls, floors, or ceilings to where they are needed. Heights for objects away from the walls can be located by first establishing their heights on the nearest wall; then, after projecting the objects horizontally to the same wall on the plan view, their heights and locations can be easily brought down to the perspective view. This procedure is indicated by the arrowheads on projectors from the tall box in the room.

The perspective-plan method can also be adapted to one-point perspective construction, yet the office method is usually less time consuming.

Figure 13-19 shows the construction of a simple *exterior* perspective using the one-point method. Notice that the street lines converge at the vanishing point in the center of the drawing and that the buildings have one wall parallel to the frontal picture plane.

When drawing one-point perspectives of room interiors (frequently used by interior designers), the student often finds it difficult to place furniture in its desired position within the floor area. One method that will simplify the location of objects is with the use of grid lines (see Fig. 13-20). Notice that a scaled orthographic plan is first needed with the furniture layed out in its correct position. Convenient grid lines, similar in appearance to large, square floor tile, are lightly drawn on the plan and numbered consecutively if necessary both ways. The same grid lines are then drawn in perspective on the perspective drawing floor area.

Locate all the furniture outlines in perspective from the plan diagram using the correct grids for placement. Next, build up the heights of the furniture with mea-

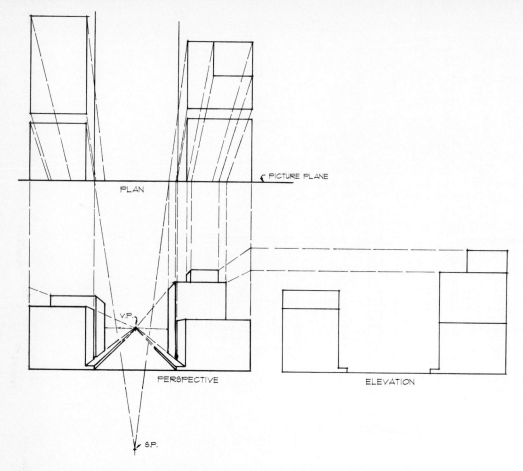

PLAN

PICTURE PLANE

V.P.

PERSPECTIVE

ELEVATION

S.P.

Figure 13-19 One-point parallel perspective (office method).

surements as previously mentioned to have correctly blocked in forms. To complete the actual appearance of the furniture, add the details last.

13.8 A Professional Method of Drawing Perspectives

As we have already seen, setting up the perspective construction for the average building is time consuming for the drafter. The professional delineator, who is continually concerned with architectural perspective, must adopt a rapid yet versatile system that consistently produces satisfying and faithful drawings. One method having these characteristics combines the perspective-plan and measuring-point principles with a simple way of modifying and controlling the setup during construction. It begins with a pictorial plan of very small scale, drawn by the perspective-plan method, mainly for the purpose of early study before the finish perspective is started. This small, preliminary layout is called a *diagram* and is the secret of good perspectives without unnecessary, large-scale, trial and error construction. After a small diagram is perfected as

to angle of observance, distance to station point, height of horizon, and the like, only the necessary lines and points are enlarged to scale for the final perspective. Several drawings employing this system will convince the student that it is as effective in the classroom as it is in an architectural office. Follow the sequence of the numbers shown in the accompanying drawings and in the written instructions that follow.

Before beginning to draw, study the site plan, if available, or proposed site arrangement. Determine which angle of observation will show the important elements of the building. Draw a line on the site plan indicating the line of sight you have chosen. On this line, establish the station point by laying a 30° triangle on the line so that the angle represents the angle of vision. The apex of the 30° angle, as previously indicated, locates a satisfactory station point when the length across the building forms the length of the side opposite the 30° angle of the triangle. This point will help you visualize the tentative picture and orient you to the problem at hand. Study the elevation views, which will then be visible, and concern yourself only with them; if you are using a set of working drawings, lay the other drawings aside.

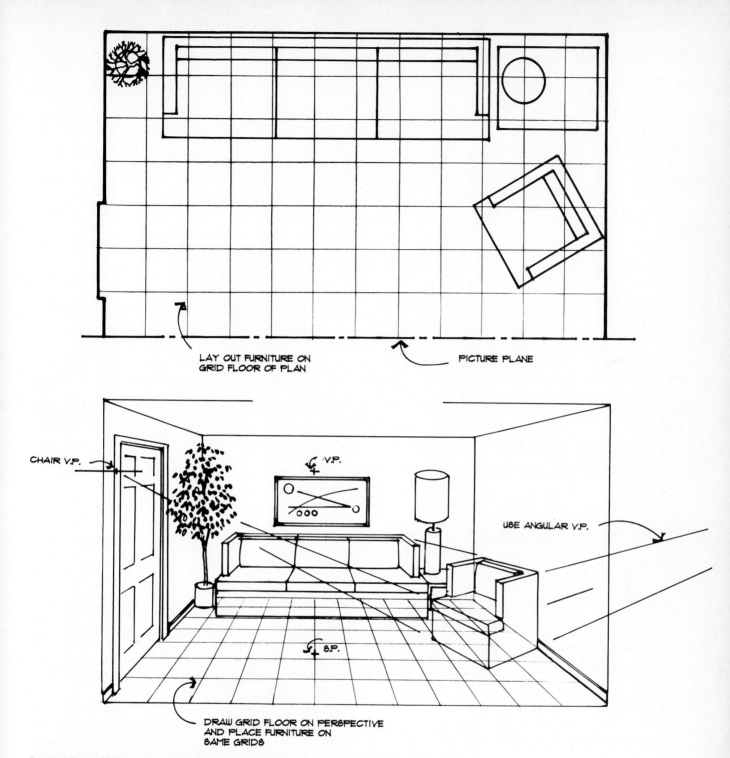

LAY OUT FURNITURE ON
GRID FLOOR OF PLAN

PICTURE PLANE

CHAIR V.P.

V.P.

USE ANGULAR V.P.

S.P.

DRAW GRID FLOOR ON PERSPECTIVE
AND PLACE FURNITURE ON
SAME GRIDS

FIGURE 13-20 Using a floor grid field on a one-point interior perspective to position furniture correctly.

STEP A (FIGS. 13-22 AND 13-23)

1. Draw the horizon line as shown.
2. Construct a vertical center of vision line. It will also serve as a true-height line later.
3. Establish the station point on the center of vision by scaling the distance you indicated on the site plan. Use a small scale. The civil engineer's scale

can be used for enlargements of scale, if desired; it provides convenient multiples of ten.

4. Through the station point, draw a horizontal line; this will be the picture plane in plan upon which all horizontal measurements of the building can be made. Occasionally, it may be necessary to construct an auxiliary picture plane for measuring; this will be discussed later.

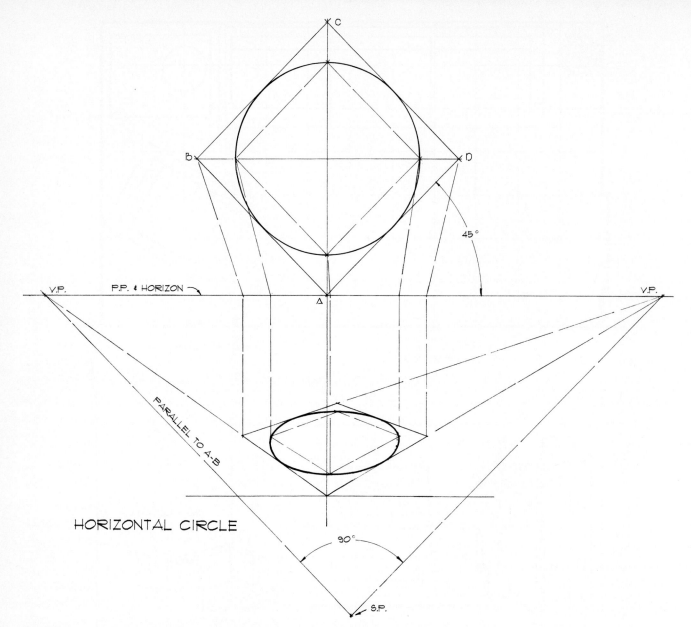

C

B   D

45°

V.P.   P.P. & HORIZON →   V.P.

A

PARALLEL TO A-B

HORIZONTAL CIRCLE

90°

S.P.

Figure 13-21 A method of drawing circular shapes in perspective.

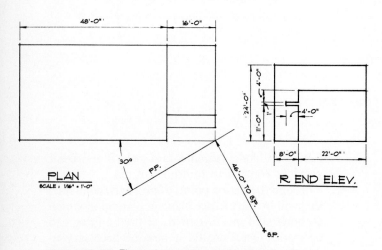

48'-0"   16'-0"

4'-0"
24'-0"   11'-0"   4'-0"
8'-0"   22'-0"

PLAN
SCALE : 1/16" = 1'-0"
30°   P.P.
46'-0" TO S.P.

R END ELEV.

S.P.

Figure 13-22 Floor plan and end elevation for the professional diagram perspective.

STEP B (FIG. 13-23)

5. Locate the right and left vanishing points on the horizon line by projecting from the station point as shown (if a 30°–60° angle of observance is satisfactory). Any angle can be used as long as the included angle between the two projectors is 90°. (These projectors can serve as base lines of the perspective plan if the drawing is small and space is not critical.)

6. Next, locate the left and right measuring points on the horizon line. With a compass, swing the distance between the station point and the right vanishing point to the horizon line, using the right vanishing point as a center, to locate the right measuring point. This point will be the vanishing

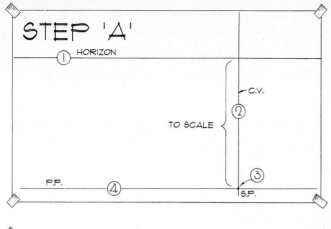

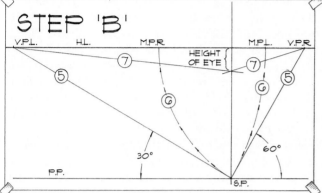

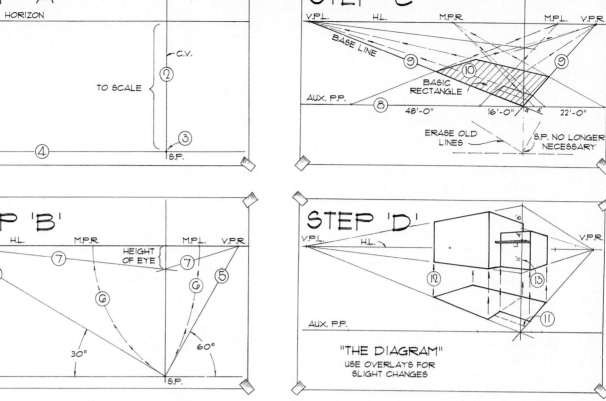

Figure 13-23 Preliminary steps for the professional diagram perspective.

Figure 13-24 Steps in drawing the diagram.

point of all parallel measuring lines laid off to the right station point. Follow the same procedure for bringing the distance between the station point and the left vanishing point to the horizon line and locate the left measuring point.

7. Establish the desired eye level of the perspective by measuring down (in scale) from the horizon on the center of vision to locate the corner of the building on grade. From this point, construct lines to both the left and right vanishing points. These lines become the base legs of our basic rectangle in perspective.

STEP C (FIG. 13-24)

In this step it may be advisable to construct a new picture plane in order to keep the drawing lower on the paper when working with larger buildings and scales. On small preliminary diagrams, the picture plane indicated in step B will usually serve the purpose without being cumbersome. It will be found satisfactory for laying off measurements and constructing the perspective plan. However, if a large building is drawn, re-

quiring a large piece of paper and considerable space on the board, when enlarging the diagram, an auxiliary picture plane will be found more convenient. This new picture plane will replace the original for measurements and is arbitrarily placed between the station point and the ground corner of the perspective. After the vanishing points and measuring points are located on the horizon line, the station point is no longer necessary and can be removed.

8. Draw the auxiliary picture plane, as shown.
9. Draw the new base lines from the intersection of the picture plane and the center of vision to both vanishing points. Use the original vanishing points and extend the lines below the auxiliary picture plane to take care of overhangs and offsets of the plan that occasionally fall outside the basic rectangle.
10. Draw the basic rectangular shape of the plan as shown. Notice that measurements are taken from the working drawings, converted to the working scale, and laid out on the auxiliary picture plane, on both sides from the center of vision (see Section 13.6, Step B). Project right-side measure-

ments to the right measuring point and left-side measurements to the left measuring point. When they *intersect the base line*, vanish them toward the corresponding vanishing point.

STEP D (FIG. 13-24)

11. Lay off measurements and construct all projections, overhangs, and roof lines if necessary. Intersections of sloping roofs will be needed to complete the perspective on gable and hip roofs. To avoid confusion later, when projecting the plan up to eye level, roof intersections, overhangs, exterior stoops, and the like, should be drawn as broken lines on the plan.

12. Project all visible corners from the plan up to the perspective. This final step is generally done on a separate tracing paper *overlay;* only the perspective will then be on the clean sheet. All construction is made from points under the overlay. Of course, preliminary diagrams are done on the original sheet for study when only general shapes are necessary.

13. Take heights from the working drawings and convert to scale. Mark off the heights on the center of vision starting at ground level. The center of vision is on the elevation picture plane and therefore can be used for true-height measurements. If necessary, project heights around the walls of the building to where they are needed, as explained in previous methods. Block in basic shapes first and then make measurements and project details last to avoid confusion between numerous lines.

STEP E: ENLARGING TO DESIRED SIZE (FIG. 13-25)

After several diagrams are studied and one is found to be satisfactory, a larger perspective can easily be constructed at the desired size. Lay out the horizon line and transfer the center of vision and all points from the diagram to a new scale. The size of the finished perspective can be controlled by the scale selected; for example, if the finished perspective is to be four times the size of the diagram, use a scale four times as large as the diagram for the new measurements along the horizon line, center of vision, and auxiliary picture plane.

At larger scales, horizontal measurements for constructing the plan will occasionally fall beyond the paper. To overcome this difficulty, follow the procedure shown in Fig. 13-26. Draw a horizontal line to the edge of the paper from a point on the base line where the longest measurement has been made. Make the additional measurement from the center of vision, and, instead of projecting toward the measuring point, project to the vanishing point on the same side of the center of vision until it intersects the horizontal line. From this point it is treated as previously shown in step C. The construction merely brings the dimension back in perspective to the point of maximum measurement and lays it off on that plane, rather than on the original forward picture plane.

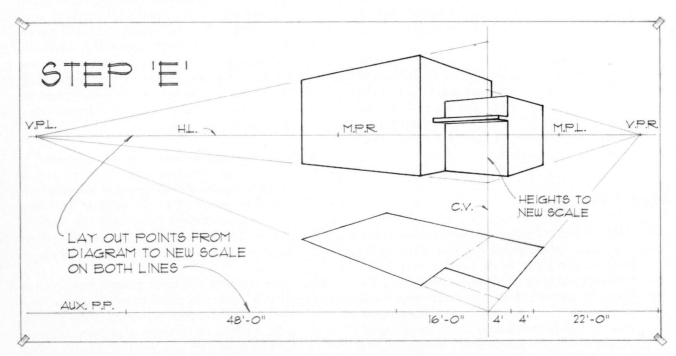

FIGURE 13-25 Laying out the perspective at a convenient scale from the diagram.

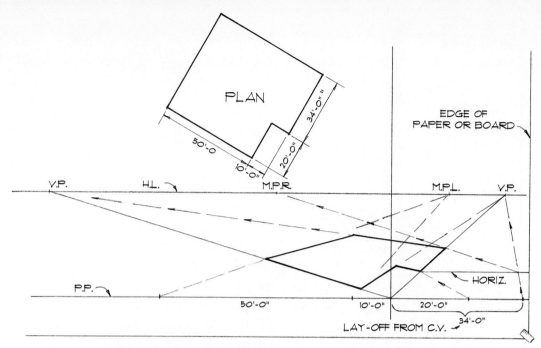

FIGURE 13-26 A method of making measurements that are too long for the drawing board.

After several drawings have been made, slight variations of the procedure may be found to save time and overcome minor difficulties, should they arise.

13.9 Time-saving Suggestions

Similar Perspectives   If a number of similar perspectives are to be drawn, use perspective grid charts as an underlay. Various charts are available at drafting supply stores (Fig. 13-27).

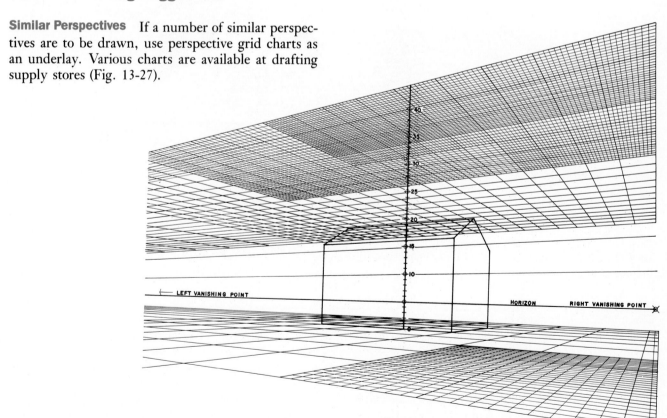

FIGURE 13-27 Perspective charts may be used by the drafter.

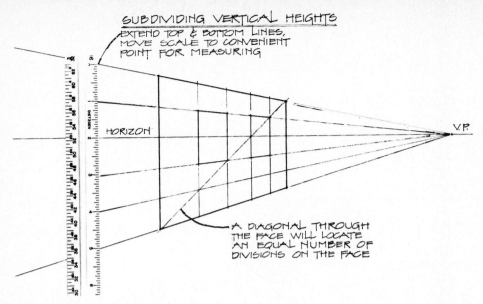

FIGURE 13-28 Subdividing perspective spaces.

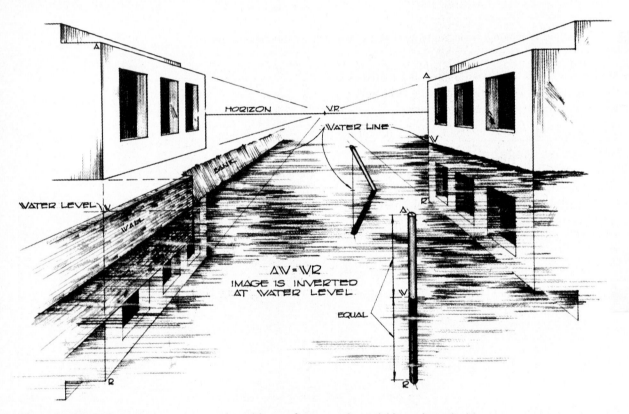

FIGURE 13-29 Reflections on water or other shiny surfaces can be quickly projected with the use of points as shown.

Diagonals Use diagonals of rectangular areas for quickly locating centers and for checking construction of the perspective as it develops (see Fig. 13-28).

Subdividing Vertical Heights When a vertical height must be divided into equal subdivisions, a scale can be positioned at a convenient point for measuring (see Fig. 13-28).

Reflections When showing the reflections of buildings in water or on other shiny surfaces, draw the reflections to the same vanishing point as the building. The water's edge is the dividing line between the reflections and the true images. Locate a reflected point as far below the shiny surface as the point is above (see Fig. 13-29).

Figure 13-30 A perspective rendering showing the use of shadows to reveal important architectural features.

13.10 Shades and Shadows

The geometric forms of light and shade produced by the action of the sun on architectural subjects are of particular interest to the architect and the drafter. Good architectural forms have the property of producing pleasing shadows regardless of the sun's position. To the observer, shadows are an integral part of an architectural composition, and their representation becomes almost as important as the building itself.

Linear perspective, as we mentioned earlier, produces only the outlines of objects. Realism is attained not by outlines, but by the sensitive selection of values of light and shade as well as texture to represent various surfaces. The effect of light on surfaces and materials produces the true image; often, outlines are almost entirely obscure. The study of shades and shadows is a further step in creating graphic realism. First the student must understand the action of light; then he or she must define it geometrically as it creates various patterns. These areas or patterns are then given the correct value or tone, in keeping with composition, contrast, and visual interest, to produce the desired pictorial effect.

On actual renderings, shadows can be overdone; if they are too mechanical and hard, much of their three-dimensional expression is lost. The uniformity of the shades and shadows on the illustrations in this material is for the introduction of principles only and should not be taken as the correct representation of shadow values. Other finished perspectives (see Fig. 13-30) should be observed for displaying this quality. It will be seen that shades and shadows of finished work seldom have uniform tones throughout; in fact, the interplay of re-

flected light usually produces a gradation of tone. Shadows on architectural subjects are generally most prominent close to the observer, near the center of interest, and those farther away from the center of interest become more neutral and indefinite as they recede. Contrast and intensity of shadows near the observer, then, should be given the most consideration by the drafter.

Light Source Usually, on elevation view shadowing, the light source is considered to be coming from the upper left. The conventional method illustrating light ray direction is by showing it passing through a cube diagonally, from upper left to lower right (see Fig. 13-31). Notice that it appears as a 45° line on both elevations and plan and can be easily drawn with the

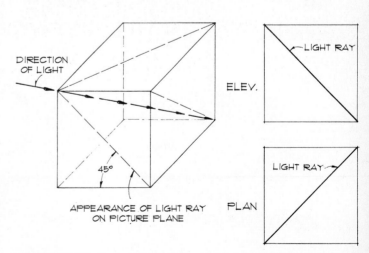

Figure 13-31 Conventional light source on orthographic views.

triangle. Another advantage of using the conventional 45° light source is that it conveniently reveals depth-dimensional characteristics. Shadows will fall to the right and below the object. The shadow of a point will be the same distance below as it is to the right of the original point. Therefore, the shadow clearly indicates the depth of recessed features. By its convenience for transferring distances from the horizontal to the vertical, and vice versa, the 45° triangle actually serves as a handy tool for measuring when plotting shadows. However, if a different shadow effect is desired, the 30°–60° triangle can also be used. In casting shadows, light rays are assumed to be parallel.

Orthographic Shadows As an introduction to the characteristics of shades and shadows, it would seem logical to begin with shadows produced on ortho-graphic views. You might ask, "Why learn to put shadows on orthographic views, which are commonly used only for working drawings?" It is true that ortho-graphic views are mainly for working drawings, and that they show depth information by association with related orthographic views. Yet many architectural offices have found that front elevations of buildings (as well as other elevations), with skillfully applied texture indications and shadows, make very adequate and often very attractive presentation drawings (see Figs. 13-32 and 13-33). Such drawings are used to show clients the tentative appearance of a building. The greatest advantage of shadowed elevations over perspectives is the tremendous saving in preparation time, and time and cost are usually important.

At the very outset, we can say that the casting of shadows is affected by three conditions:

FIGURE 13-32 An elevation rendering showing the use of shadows.

FIGURE 13-33 An elevation view rendering of a small commercial building showing the use of shadows.

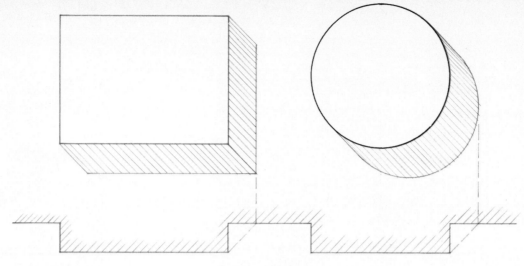

PLAN - SECTION

FIGURE 13-34 Plotting shadows of simple forms in orthographic views.

1. Direction of the light source
2. Shape of the object
3. Manner and shape of the surface on which the shadow falls

In analyzing the action of light, the student is encouraged to observe the shadows of buildings and different objects found in everyday life, even those of models in an artificial light source; the importance of astute observation of actual shadows cannot be overemphasized. After observing actual shadows and studying the accompanying shadow drawings, a number of *consistencies* become obvious. A few general ones are listed below and should be remembered:

1. Only an object in light casts a shadow.
2. A shadow is revealed only when it falls on a lighted surface.
3. The shadow of a point must lie on the light ray through that point.

4. On parallel surfaces, a shadow is parallel to the line that casts it.
5. The shadow of a plane figure will be identical to the outline of the figure if the shadow falls on a plane parallel to the outline of the figure.
6. The shadow of a line perpendicular to the picture plane will be inclined if it falls on a surface parallel to the picture plane.

In plotting orthographic shadows, usually two views are necessary for the projection (see Figs. 13-34 through 13-39). Sometimes it may be a plan and an elevation; other times it may be two elevations. The important view is the one having the surface that receives the majority of shadows. Plot each point or corner casting a

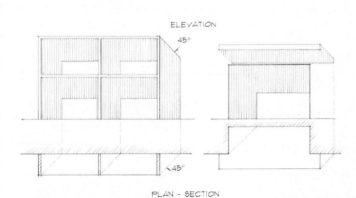

FIGURE 13-35 Plotting shadows to show relief in orthographic views.

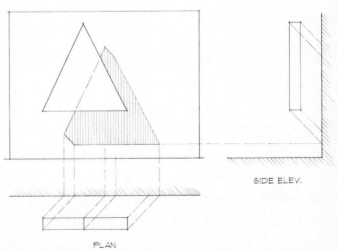

FIGURE 13-36 Plotting shadows on removed surfaces in orthographic views.

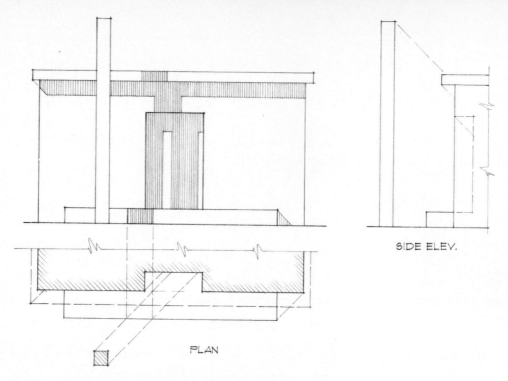

FIGURE 13-37 Plotting shadows on architectural features in orthographic views.

SIDE ELEV.

PLAN

shadow and complete the one shadow profile before going to the next. Check the resulting shadow to be sure each point is accounted for. If the result does not appear logical to the eye, the construction is usually faulty.

Perspective Shades and Shadows Similar principles to those we found in orthographic shadow casting are encountered in plotting shadows of pictorial subjects. On perspective drawings, often entire surfaces are on

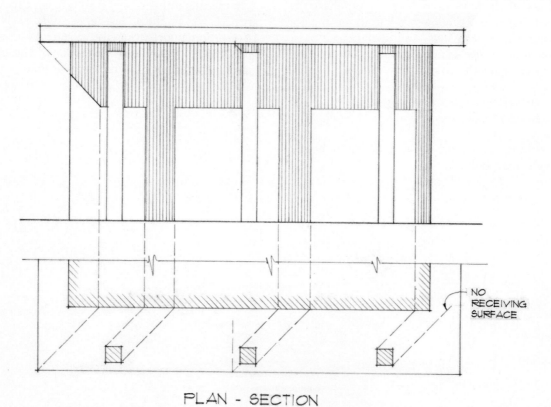

NO RECEIVING SURFACE

PLAN - SECTION

FIGURE 13-38 Shadows of columns in an orthographic view.

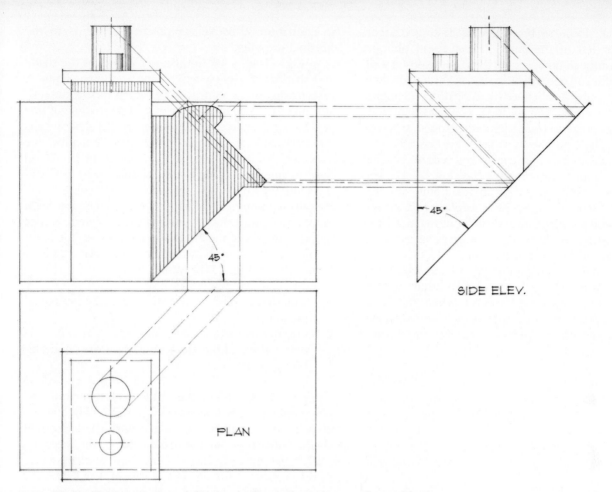

SIDE ELEV.

PLAN

FIGURE 13-39 Plotting shadows falling on inclined planes in an orthographic view.

the opposite side from the light source and therefore receive no light. These surfaces must be shown in darker tones; yet they are not shadows. We refer to the darker surfaces of the object not receiving light as *shades* (see Fig. 13-40). Determining the outlines of both shades and shadows (as well as occasional highlights) plays an important part in giving realism to perspective drawings.

Notice that the same vanishing points are used for both the shadows and the horizontal lines of the perspective itself (Fig. 13-40). If the light source is parallel to the picture plane, the shadows of horizontal lines will vanish at the same point as the object lines themselves. Also, the shadows of vertical lines will appear as horizontal shadows if they fall on a horizontal surface. Plotting shadows with a light source parallel to the

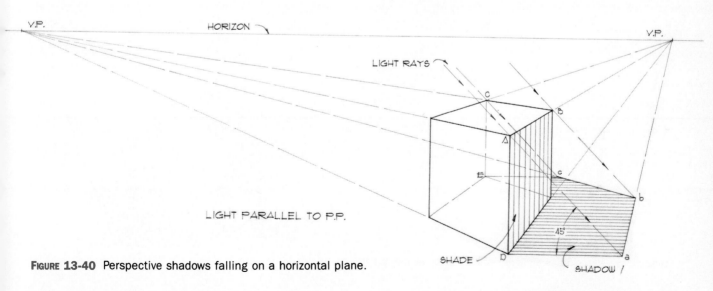

FIGURE 13-40 Perspective shadows falling on a horizontal plane.

picture plane, of course, limits shadow casting to either the right or left of the object, never in an oblique manner. In angular perspective, then, one exposed wall will be in light and one will be in shade. Various shadow characteristics can be obtained by using different angles of the light source. A high angle produces a narrow shadow on a horizontal plane such as the ground, whereas a low angle of light produces a wide shadow. Usually, 45°, 60°, or 30° angles are most convenient because of their construction with drafting triangles (see Fig. 13-41). For the student, casting shadows on two-point, angular perspectives with the *light source parallel to the picture plane* will produce adequate realism for most situations. For that reason, we will concern ourselves mainly with this method of shadow construction.

Actually, light striking an object such as a building that is drawn in an angular position produces rather interesting and revealing shadows when the light source is parallel to the picture plane. The shadows from overhangs, offsets, and other features can be made to contribute effective composition elements to the finished drawing.

In Fig. 13-40, a 45° light source produces the shade and shadow of a perspective cube as shown. Point A casts its shadow at point a, point B casts its shadow at b, and point C casts its shadow at c. The shadow of line A–D is drawn horizontal, inasmuch as the shadow falls on a horizontal plane. Line A–B creates the shadow line a–b, which must vanish at the same right vanishing point as line A–B. Line b–c is the shadow of B–C and therefore must vanish at the same left vanishing point. By plotting points and then the lines connecting these points, the entire shadow outline is completed. Notice that the shadow of the hidden corner C–E is plotted on the figure merely to show the horizontal relationship of E to c. From Fig. 13-40 we see that:

1. The shadow cast by a vertical line on a horizontal plane is horizontal.
2. On parallel surfaces, a shadow is parallel to the line that cast it and therefore vanishes at the same vanishing point.

Figure 13-42 shows the shadow of a vertical line being interrupted by a vertical wall plane. The shadow of point A cannot be established until the horizontal shadow line from point E is projected to the receiving wall. The remaining diagonal line above point a is a part of the shadow of line A–D and is completed after the horizontal shadow of line A–D is projected on the top of the small block (line x–y). Line a–x–y is the shadow of A–D falling on perpendicular surfaces. From Fig. 13-42 we see that:

1. The shadow of a vertical line is vertical if it falls on a vertical surface.
2. The shadow of a horizontal line is inclined if it falls on a vertical surface.

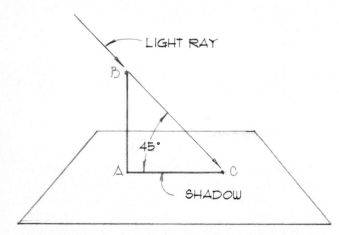

FIGURE 13-41 On perspective drawings, a light source parallel to the picture plane is convenient for casting shadows.

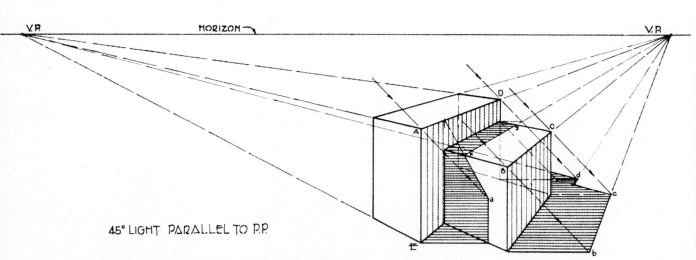

FIGURE 13-42 Perspective shadows falling on a vertical plane.

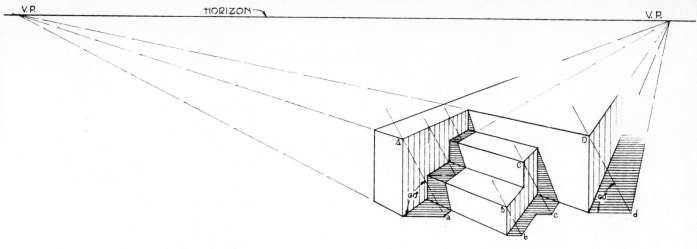

FIGURE 13-43 Perspective shadows on stairs.

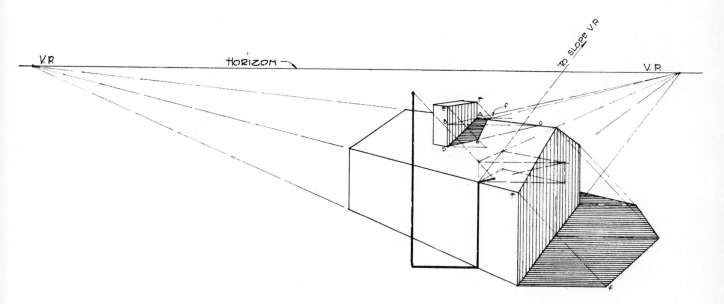

FIGURE 13-44 Perspective shadows falling on inclined surfaces.

We see in Fig. 13-43 the effects of a horizontal shadow cast on various levels of a simple stairs. The shadow is located on each level, vanished to the right vanishing point, and the shadows on the vertical risers merely connect the shadows falling on the treads. Notice the convenient points used to establish the width of each horizontal shadow.

Shadows falling on inclined surfaces (Fig. 13-44) present interesting projection problems. The shadow of the chimney is found by projecting the ridge at point A to point B on the forepart of the chimney. Point B is projected horizontally back to the ridge at point C. The line C–D will then be the shadow line of corner D–E; the 45° projection from corner E to e describes its length. To find the shadow of point F, we can consider a theoretical horizontal plane extending back from the ridge height. The shadow of F will fall at f on the

imaginary plane; by projecting f to the ridge, we have the shadow of line E–F on the inclined roof. A similar procedure is needed to plot the shadow of the flagpole after it reaches the incline of the roof. Notice that a line extending up the incline from the shadow at the eave produces a similar condition as the chimney provided. The shadow of the flagpole top is brought down to the vertical plane of the wall (just above the eave on a vertical line); from that point a theoretical horizontal plane is assumed that will intersect the roof, and a horizontal plane is assumed at the eave level. The diagonal connecting both planes will be the shadow of a vertical, such as the flagpole, as it falls on the inclined roof. This is plotted in the same manner as the shadow of vertical line D–E of the chimney. From Fig. 13-44, it can be deduced then that the shadows of vertical lines are inclined if they fall on inclined surfaces. From Fig.

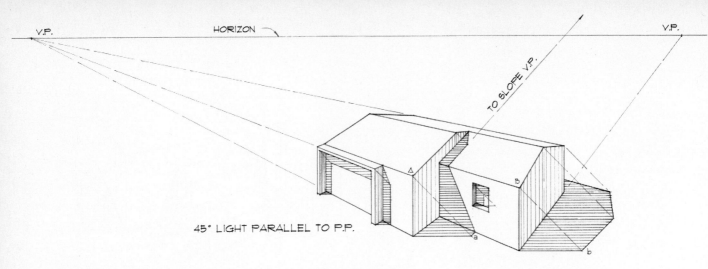

FIGURE 13-45 Various shadows showing the characteristics of buildings.

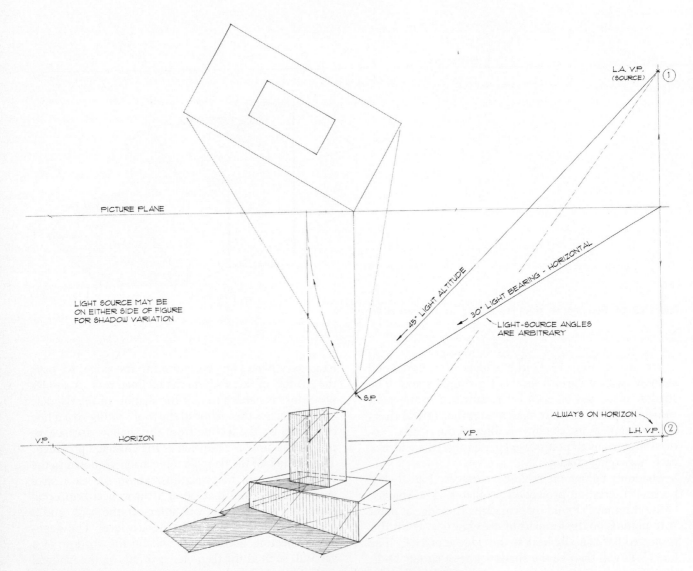

FIGURE 13-46 Perspective shadows with the light oblique to the picture plane. Notice that two shadow vanishing points are needed. They can be located at random or by bearing and altitude angles of a light source. The light-bearing V.P. is on the horizon and the altitude V.P. is on a trace through L.H.V.P.

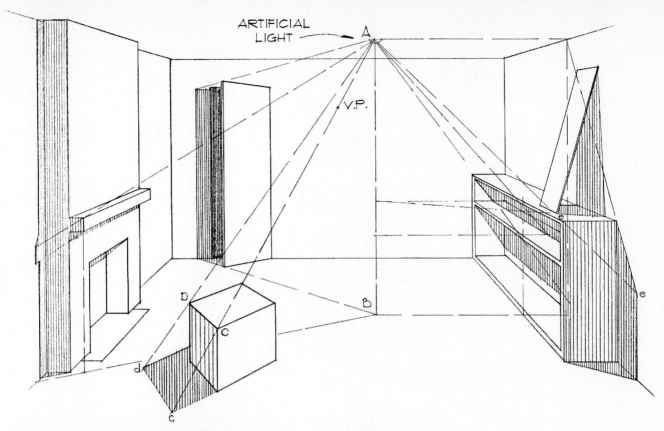

ARTIFICIAL
LIGHT

A

V.P.

FIGURE 13-47 Plotting shadows from a single light source on an interior perspective.

13-45 it will be seen that shadows from surfaces parallel to an incline will be parallel to the inclines.

Perspective shadows with the light source *oblique* to the picture plane can be projected if an actual exterior light condition is desired (see Fig. 13-46). Notice that two shadow vanishing points are needed. They can be located at random or by actual bearing and altitude angles of the light source. The light bearing V.P. is on the horizon and the altitude V.P. is on a trace through L.H.V.P.

Shadows from a single source such as a light fixture in an interior can be plotted as shown in Fig. 13-47.

EXERCISES

1. Using the office method, draw an angular perspective of Fig. 13-48A, B, and C.

2. Using the office method, draw an angular perspective of the interior views of Figs. 13-49 and 13-50.

3. Using the perspective-plan method, draw an angular perspective of Figs. 13-51, 13-52A–D, and 13-53.

4. Using the one-point perspective method, draw a parallel perspective of Figs. 13-49 and 13-54.

5. Construct the shadows on the orthographic views of Figs. 13-48B and C, 13-54, and 13-55.

6. Draw the angular perspective of Figs. 13-48A, B, and C, 13-52A-D, and 13-56, and complete their shades and shadows as indicated. Use a light source parallel to the picture plane. Make the shadows a darker tone than the shades.

7. Using the office method, draw an angular perspective of Fig. 13-57 on a 24″ by 36″ sheet with the 36″ dimension placed vertically on the drawing table. Draw the structure four times the size shown in the book. Locate the picture plane 9″ below the top edge of the sheet. Place the station point 9″ below the picture plane. Locate the ground line 11″ below the picture plane. The horizon line shall be 3″ above the ground line. Center line "A" on the sheet.

8. Draw a one-point perspective of the interior of the room in Fig. 13-58. Use a 12″ by 24″ sheet with the 24″ dimension placed vertically on the drawing table.

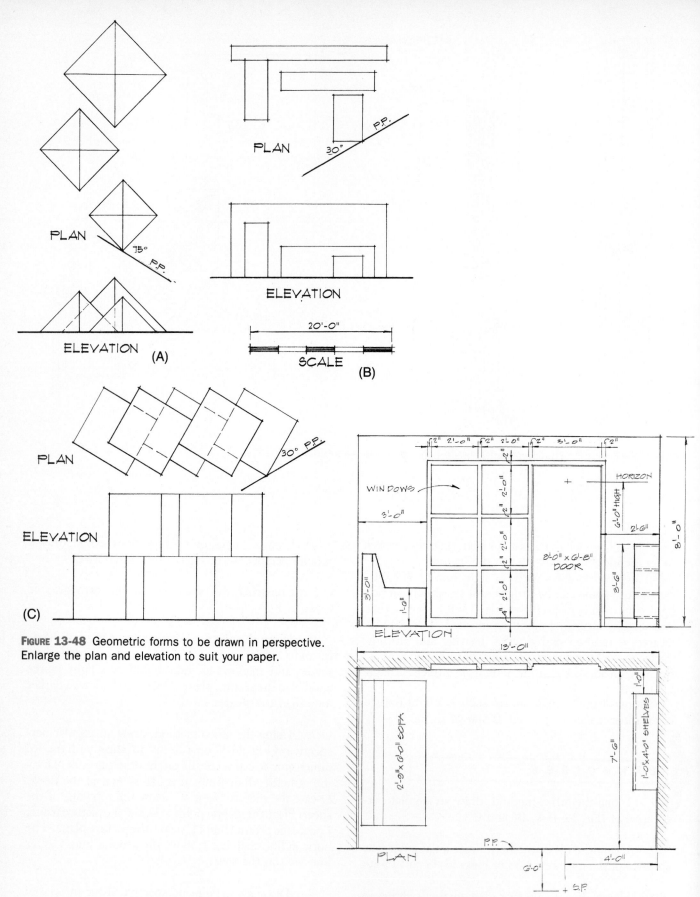

FIGURE 13-48 Geometric forms to be drawn in perspective. Enlarge the plan and elevation to suit your paper.

FIGURE 13-49 Problem for one-point and two-point interior perspective.

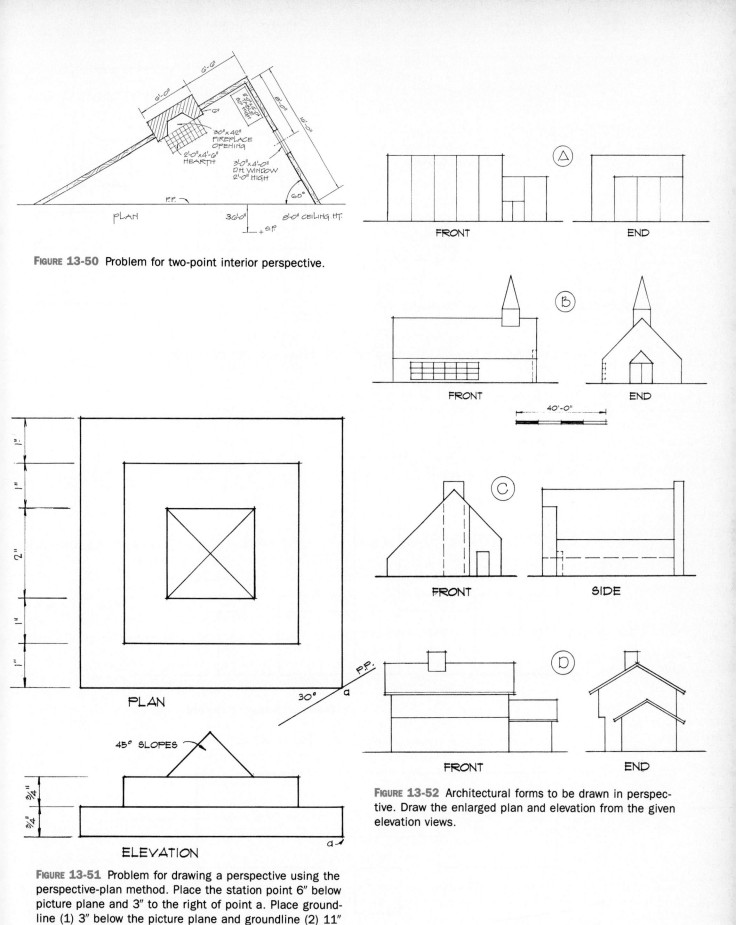

Figure 13-50 Problem for two-point interior perspective.

Figure 13-51 Problem for drawing a perspective using the perspective-plan method. Place the station point 6″ below picture plane and 3″ to the right of point a. Place groundline (1) 3″ below the picture plane and groundline (2) 11″ below the picture plane.

Figure 13-52 Architectural forms to be drawn in perspective. Draw the enlarged plan and elevation from the given elevation views.

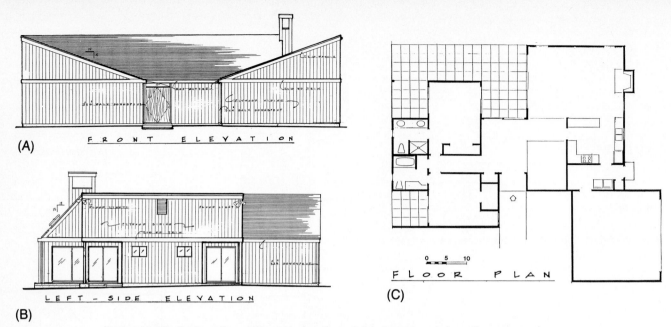

(A)

FRONT ELEVATION

(B)

LEFT - SIDE ELEVATION

(C)

FLOOR PLAN

0 5 10

FIGURE 13-53 Scale a floor plan and elevation of this house and draw the perspective.

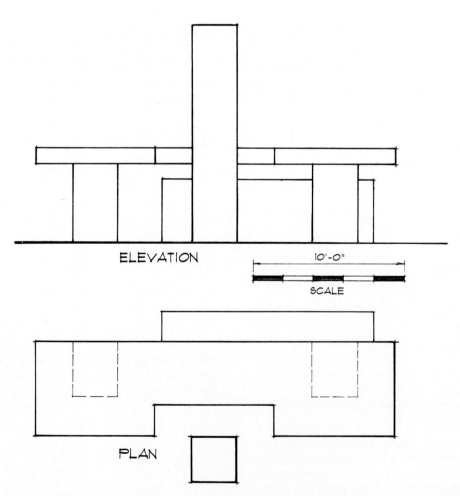

ELEVATION

10'-0"

SCALE

PLAN

FIGURE 13-54 A problem for plotting orthographic shadows or for drawing a perspective.

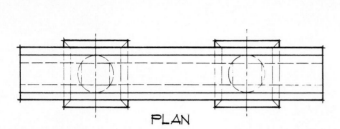

PLAN

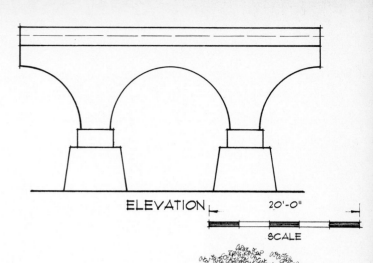

ELEVATION

20'-0"

SCALE

FIGURE 13-55 A problem for plotting orthographic shadows or for drawing a perspective.

46'-0"

52'-4"

TRAY CEILING

Master Suite
12⁰x14⁹

Vaulted
Dining Room

FPL.

Vaulted
Great Room
13¹⁰x18⁴

Bedroom 3
10¹x11¹

RANGE

Kitchen

8'-0" HIGH
WALL

PLANT
SHELF

REF

D.W.

VAULT

LINEN

TUB

Vaulted
M. Bath

K.S.

PANTRY

VAULT

COATS

COVERED
Porch

Bath

SHWR

W.i.c.

D.

W.

Breakfast
8⁷x9⁹

Bedroom 2
10¹x11⁶

OPT. STAIRS
TO BSMT.

OPT.
STORAGE

Garage

copyright © 1990 frank betz associates

FLOOR PLAN

FIGURE 13-56 Scale a floor plan and elevation of this house and draw the perspective.

Exercises 413

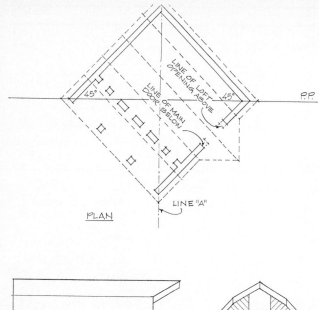

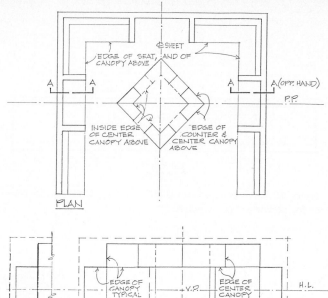

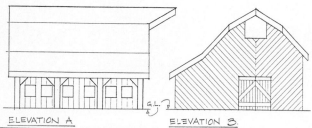

FIGURE 13-57

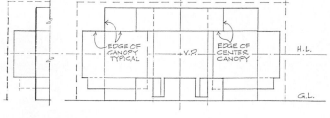

FIGURE 13-58

Draw the plan and elevations four times the size shown in the book. Locate the picture plane 6″ from the top edge of the sheet. Place the station point 14″ below the picture plane centered on the sheet. Locate the ground line 12″ below the picture plane. The horizon line shall be 2″ above the ground line. The vanishing point shall be placed on the horizon line and centered in the room.

9. Using the perspective-plan method draw an angular perspective including shades and shadows of Fig. 13-59 on a 24″ by 36″ sheet with the 36″ dimensions placed horizontally on the drawing table. Locate the picture plane 2″ below the top edge of the sheet. Place the station point 10″ below the picture plane and 10″ from the left edge of the sheet. Point "A" shall be placed 10″ from the left edge of the sheet. Locate the ground line 13″ below the picture plane. The horizontal measuring line shall be placed 5″ below the ground line. Locate the horizon line 3″ above the ground line. Draw the structure four times the size shown in the book. The light source is parallel to the picture plane and at 45° to the ground shining down from the left.

10. Using the office method draw an angular perspective including shades, shadows and reflections in

the pond of Fig. 13-60 on a 24″ by 36″ sheet with the 36″ dimensions placed vertically on the sheet. Locate the picture plane 15″ below the top edge of the sheet. Place the station point 10″ below the picture plane and centered on the sheet. The ground line shall be 9″ below the picture plane. Locate the horizon line ¾″ above the ground line. Point "B" shall be directly above the station point and centered on the sheet. Draw the structure four times the size shown in the book. The light source is parallel to the picture plane and at 60° to the ground shining down from the left.

R E V I E W   Q U E S T I O N S

1. What is meant by *linear perspective?*

2. How does the projection of a perspective view to the picture plane differ from the projection of an orthographic view?

3. What is the point called that approximates the eye when a person draws an object in perspective?

4. What effect is produced on a perspective when the horizon line is raised in relation to the groundline?

5. What effect is produced on a perspective when the object is placed farther away from the picture plane?

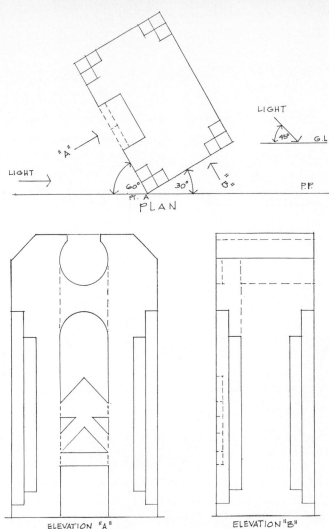

FIGURE 13-59

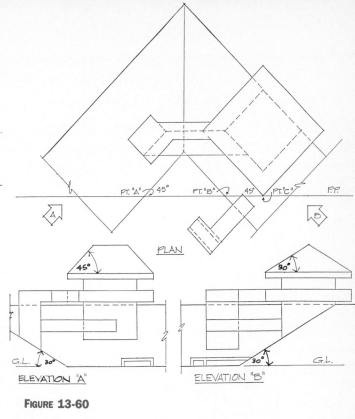

FIGURE 13-60

6. Why must true heights of an object be established only on the picture plane?

7. If an object is placed in an oblique position in relation to the picture plane, why are two vanishing points necessary?

8. What are the advantages of using the perspective-plan method for drawing a perspective?

9. In a one-point parallel perspective view of an interior, is the single vanishing point used to draw a piece of furniture that is in a diagonal position?

10. Why is the action of light on architectural subjects important to the designer?

11. Why is it convenient to use a 45° light source direction?

12. Explain the difference between a *shade* and a *shadow*.

13. What purpose do orthographic shadows serve?

14. When the light source is parallel to the picture plane, is the shadow of a vertical corner drawn vertically when it falls on a wall?

15. When would it be appropriate to use a three-point perspective?

16. Why are most two-point perspectives drawn with the horizon line located about 6' above the ground plane?

17. When drawing lines to represent shadows falling on a ground plane, would it be best to draw the lines vertically or horizontally?

18. Why is it important to limit the cone of vision from the station point to the picture plane to an angle of 30° to 45°?

19. When would it be appropriate to use a bird's-eye view perspective?

20. Describe a convenient method for drawing a circle in a two-point perspective?

PRESENTATION DRAWINGS AND RENDERING

"Good painting is like good cooking: it can be tasted, but not explained."

—*VALAMINCK*

14

14.1 Types of Presentation Drawings

Before working drawings can be started, it is generally necessary to prepare a presentation drawing of the tentative structure. This is done for several reasons. First, it combines the efforts of preliminary planning into a tangible proposal for a client's approval, making the presentation an actual marketing instrument. Second, it offers a means for careful study of the structure's appearance, by all concerned, upon which improvements or changes for final development can be based.

The presentation is the designer's graphic concept of a building, in its natural setting, made to represent the structure honestly, realistically, artistically, and in a manner easily understood by the layman. A great deal of unnecessary technical information is avoided to make the general concept more pronounced. Rendered perspective or elevation views showing the realism of light and shade, landscaping, and textures are usually the most effective elements of successful presentation drawings. However, considerable latitude in the selection of views is possible, depending on the nature of the proposal and the time allowed for its completion. Student projects usually include a perspective, a floor plan, several elevations, and a site plan. The duplication of similar information on the various selected views should be avoided so an attractive yet uncluttered graphic proposal results.

14.1 Types of Presentation Drawings

Many presentations consist of a perspective only. In fact, an architectural office will often give presentation work of complex buildings to professional delineators, specialists in this type of work, for elaborate perspective renderings—frequently in color. Many such presentations have

sufficient artistic merit to be used for promotional work, in brochures, and even in national publications.

If time is limited, effective presentations can be made with only a floor plan and a rendered elevation. Others may include a transverse section view or an interior perspective, if such features seem worthy of special consideration. Often residential presentations include a site plan to show the proposed orientation of the home and grounds. In other situations a well-executed freehand sketch may be adequate in showing a client sufficient information about a structure. We see, then, that on presentation drawings drafters can give their creative abilities free rein in depicting the most interesting qualities of buildings.

Successful renderings and presentations are done in almost all of the different art media; the most frequently used are pencil, pen and ink, colored pencil, watercolor, tempera, acrylic, pastel, and charcoal pencil (see Figs. 14-1 through 14-8). Usually, the mastery of one medium or another is the deciding factor in making the choice. After experimentation the drafter will find that each medium has advantages as well as limitations. Pencil and pen and ink, for example, capable of executing sharp, fine lines, can be used to reveal small details and various textures. But they are time consuming when covering large areas. The pencil is comparatively easy to control, yet it should be selected as the medium for rather small drawings, as should pen and ink. The combining of pencil or ink linework with transparent watercolor wash for large areas overcomes this limitation and is often an intelligent choice of media for many architectural subjects. Although color commands attention and excites the viewer, it requires considerable skill in handling, especially in representing finer detail.

Beginning students would be wise in developing their ability in pencil work first before attempting other

(A)

(B)

FIGURE 14-1 (A) A pencil and ink sketch; (B) A pencil rendering.

media. After some degree of skill is acquired in representing values, textures, light and shade, trees, and shrubbery and after command of composition and balance is attained, facility in other media becomes only a matter of mechanics.

14.2 Presentation Paper or Board

Pencil drawings may be done on a good grade of tracing paper, for convenient reproduction, or they may be done on illustration board stock for more rigid display drawings. As mentioned earlier, tracing paper, because of its transparency, aids trial and error composition with little wasted effort. Elements can be taken from previous sketches, rearranged to suit the composition with the final tracing as an overlay, and even improved on when we do the finish work. Also, weak points of the composition, when viewed from the reverse side, can be quickly observed.

Frequently it is necessary to display a tracing paper drawing or a paper print in an upright position. Since

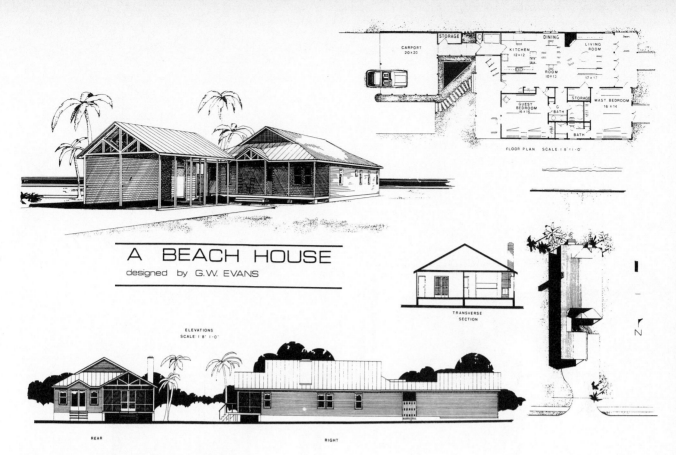

Figure 14-2 Residential presentation in ink.

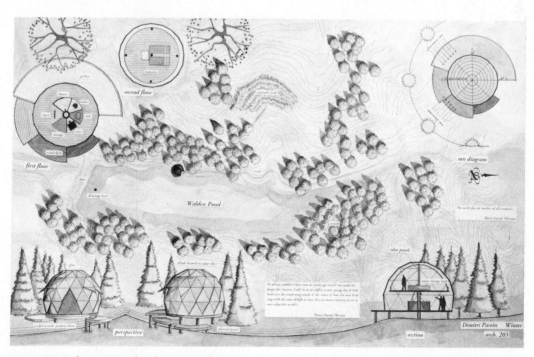

Figure 14-3 A presentation in watercolor.

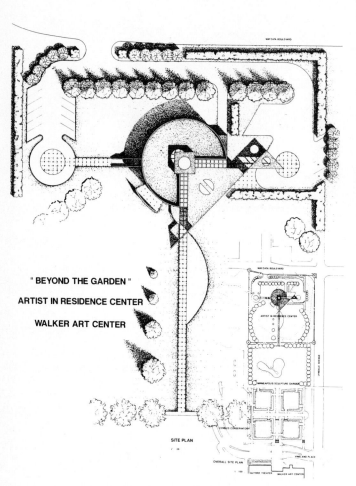

"BEYOND THE GARDEN"

ARTIST IN RESIDENCE CENTER

WALKER ART CENTER

SITE PLAN

OVERALL SITE PLAN

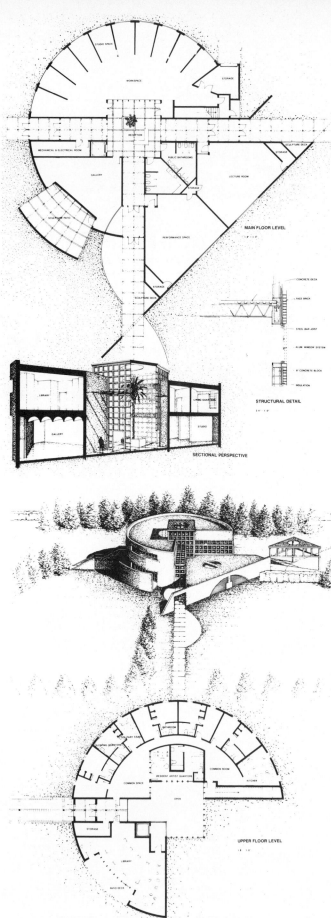

FIGURE 14-4 Presentation in ink.

Main Level

Upper Level

FIGURE 14-5 Residential presentation in ink and felt-tip markers.

tracing paper and print paper have little stiffness, it is desirable to attach drawings prepared on such media to a firm backing. These drawings may be merely taped to a suitable mounting board, and, if desired, surrounded with a neat frame cut from mat board stock (see Fig.

5-44). If permanent mounting is required, drawings on tracing paper or print paper may be mounted on illustration board or polystyrene core board that is commonly known as *foam core board*. A contact cement glue is used to attach the paper to the board backing; care

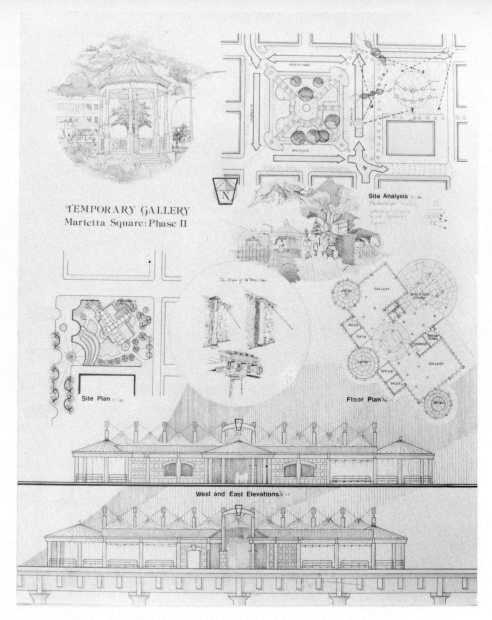

TEMPORARY GALLERY
Marietta Square: Phase II

Site Analysis

Site Plan

Floor Plan

West and East Elevations

Figure 14-6 Commercial presentation in watercolor and ink.

should be taken to eliminate air pockets between the drawing and the backing. Many print shops offer vacuum frame mounting. This professional mounting process usually guarantees a perfectly smooth surface and permanent bonding.

When preparing a presentation on heavy illustration board, first draw each drawing on tracing paper. This is especially important when a number of views or drawings must be arranged into a pleasing composition. Cut out all views so that they are individual units. Next, arrange the views on the board for balance and interest. Do not hesitate to try two or three completely different arrangements before you are satisfied that you have the best possible one. To transfer drawings from tracing paper to the board, scrub each drawing on its reverse side with a soft pencil to act as a carbon, making sure there is sufficient graphite in back of each line. Then

tape each view in place and go over the linework with a 2H pencil to transfer the drawings to the board. The illustration board is then ready for final rendering.

14.3 Composition

Composition is the art of arranging lines, values, spaces, masses, and other elements into a thing of beauty. Whether rendering a single perspective or a presentation drawing having a number of views, the principles of composition are equally important. Often a well-designed building will appear rather mediocre if the presentation is poorly planned. Thorough study of professional work will indicate the careful attention given to composition, which to the layperson is not readily apparent. To a fortunate few, pleasing composi-

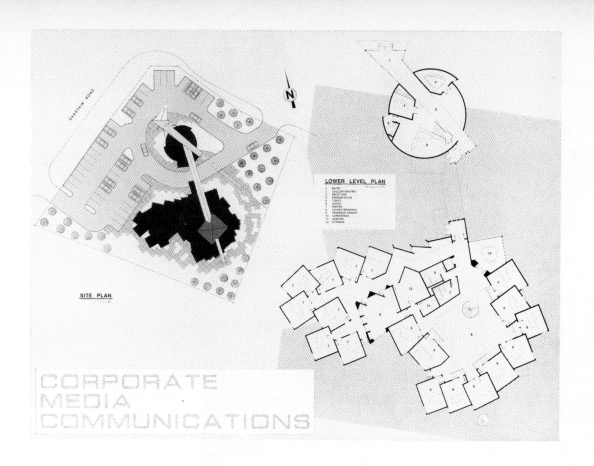

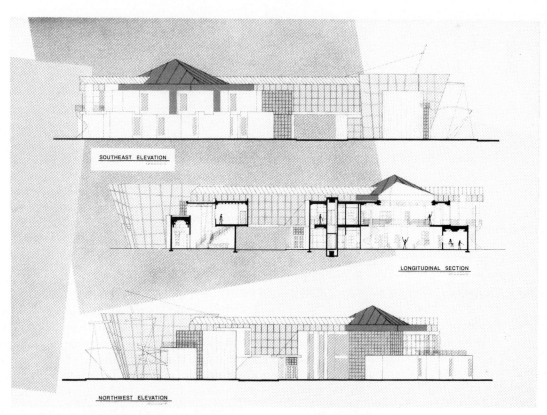

FIGURE 14-7 Presentation made with ink and pressure-sensitive transfers.

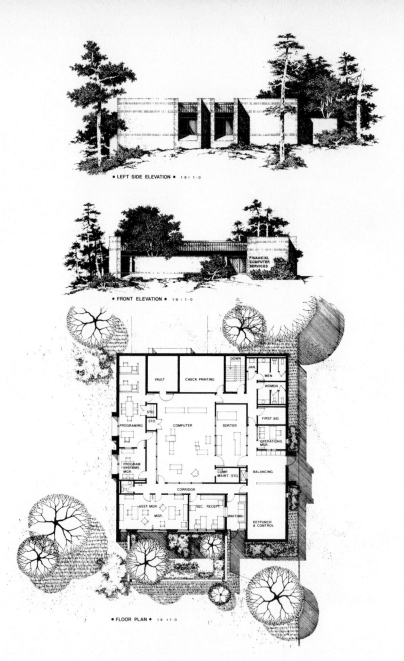

FIGURE 14-8 Presentation made with ink and watercolor.

tion comes easily and may require little more than a chance to experiment. To others, it means acquiring a thorough knowledge of composition by repeated applications in an effort to improve. Even if beginning work seems disappointing, composition can be mastered and the following suggestions may be of help.

Begin with Pleasing Forms Study the basic geometric shapes involved in the layout. Be sure the simple forms, both in themselves and in the surrounding spaces, are harmonious and attractive. There must be variety. Avoid mechanical and uniform patterns, unless minor repetition is necessary for harmony. Avoid strong lines near and parallel to the edges of the paper; an outline of

distant trees should not parallel a strong roof line (see Fig. 14-9). Avoid two or three strong elements in a straight line.

Provide Optical Balance in the Composition (Fig. 14-10)   Each element is affected by a feeling of gravitational pull and therefore has optical weight. Larger elements have more weight than smaller, darker elements more weight than lighter, and intense colors more effect than pale colors. These graphic weights must balance, and they must be placed to prevent the composition from appearing bottom heavy. Make the building the dominating element or one view the dominating view; the other elements should be subordinate

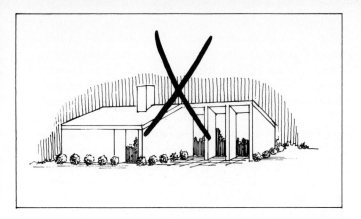

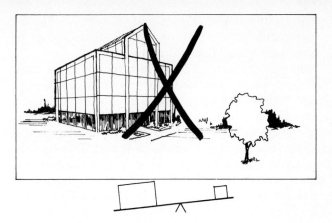

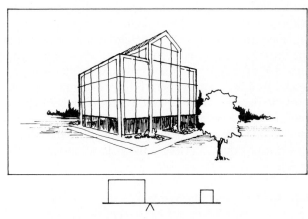

FIGURE 14-9 Avoid uniform foilage shape around the building.

FIGURE 14-10 Keep the composition balanced.

to it. Provide a center of interest, usually an entrance on a perspective, which acts as an optical fulcrum from which the various other elements are balanced. Avoid a static balance, yet combine features and spaces to appear restful and to retain attention without carrying the eye off the paper. Avoid placing the building or other prominent element in the dead center of the paper.

Use Contrast for Producing Emphasis Contrast in a composition is achieved by adjoining entirely different elements. They may be contrasting in value, size, shape, texture, or a combination of either. An important architectural feature, for example, shown in a very light tone can be given emphasis by surrounding it with a dark background of tree forms or a dark shadow nearby. Conversely, a light background can be made to emphasize a dark feature. Usually, the building is shown bathed in warm sunlight, and subordinate areas, whether shadows, foilage, sky, or similar elements, are shown in various darker tones to lend emphasis as well as relief to the building (see Fig. 14-11). Also, occasional strong contrasts create interest. *Remember that carefully drawn shadows help explain the surfaces on which they fall.* In planning contrasts and values, one of the very first decisions that must be made is the direction of light. This is very important. Even though you have certain liberties in this choice, adopt the most advan-

FIGURE 14-11 Use contrast for emphasis.

tageous direction from the standpoint of revealing the major architectural features as well as producing the most interesting shadow patterns.

In general, features in the foreground can be made darkest, features in mid-distance intermediate, and distant features the lightest. Other value arrangements may also be found satisfactory. Usually, a dark shadow falling across the foreground in front of a building is effective in creating a feeling of depth. Make sure the structure appears firmly attached to the ground and has space around, behind, and in front of it. Temper hard architectural lines with planting. Planting is also helpful in emphasizing an important entrance, by leading the eye to it with a hedgerow or a similar strong contrast along a walkway. The strong outline created by extreme contrasts, however, must be interesting.

When using color, we may achieve emphasis by making important features bright and subordinate elements subdued or grayed. On line drawings, emphasis is produced by line weights. Heavy lines become more important than thin, light lines. Give the center of interest the strongest lines and the various subordinate features weaker lines, often actually fading out near the edge of the composition. Variety holds the attention of the viewer.

Hold the Composition Together Avoid strong isolated elements that tend to fall away from the layout. To tie elements together, indicate trees, shrubs, or grass, but do not place a large tree in the foreground, which will detract or hide important information about the building. This problem can be eliminated, if need be, by making the tree in the foreground appear almost transparent, or several branches with foilage might be made to look as though they were part of a tree behind the viewer. Tree forms and planting indications must also be typical of the area where the building is to be built; palm trees around a New England residence would be ludicrous. Avoid strong indications of clouds or sky, birds, or smoke coming from a chimney; they are rarely needed on an architectural presentation.

Do Not Overburden the Composition with Too Much Detail Pick out essentials and leave some of the detail to the imagination. Carefully detail important features of the structure for interest and avoid details on subordinate elements. To create rhythm, however, some elements must reoccur throughout the composition. Too much of any one surface or texture representation will be found monotonous. On pencil drawings, you will find the eraser an important tool in composing. Erasing areas of superfluous detail can often add considerable interest to the finished drawing.

Keep All Elements of the Composition in Proportion To maintain reality, do not overscale a tree or other feature. Occasionally, a simple human figure or group of figures, if drawn the correct size, contributes an easily associated relative scale. The size of the building is then easily compared to the size of the figure. Sometimes a related object such as a vehicle can be shown to suggest the activity for which the building is designed. Keep these suggestions simple (see Figs. 14-1 through 14-7) and in the correct scale; avoid laborious, diligent studies. Also, consider the building itself in proportion to the size of the paper; the effect will not be pleasing if the building appears to be lost in the space or is so big as to appear overpowering. Beginning students often make the mistake of placing important elements of a composition too close to the outside edges of the paper or board. The finished drawing must give the impression of being tailor-made for the sheet on which it is placed.

Learn to Represent the Basic Architectural Textures Correct indications of the materials used in construction should be evident to the observer, especially in the foreground. In the distance, the various materials usually will appear only as values. The viewer should be able to distinguish between stone, brick, concrete masonry, wood, glass, roofing materials, and the like. Notice that some appear rough and others smooth, some dark and others light. In bright sunlight, even a rough texture is occasionally lost and therefore left completely white.

Study the Silhouettes and Character of Trees and Shrubs Get to know their forms, their trunk and branch structures, their foilage textures, and the manner in which they appear in groups. Notice the action of light and shade on the different types of foilage and on the bark, giving individuality to the representation of each species. Many drafters simplify and stylize their representations of trees and planting; this is advisable for students as long as they retain the basic natural characteristics of the subject. Study the planting on professional renderings and the way it relates to the total development. Sketch trees and outdoor scenes from nature to learn firsthand this necessary element of architectural presentation. Effective tree indications can be shown with only trunk and branch structures (as they would appear in winter) as long as their skeleton character is faithfully maintained.

14.4 Rendering in Pencil

For pencil rendering it is recommended to have available two each of the H, HB, 2B, 4B, and 6B drawing pencils. Sharpen one of each grade to a cone point (Fig. 5-1A) for outlines and fine detail work. Remove about 3/8″ of the wood on the other set and sharpen or wear down to a chisel point (Fig. 5-1B and C) for laying in various tones, often referred to as *pencil painting*. In beginning work, the pencil will be more expressive if both sharp and broad points are employed. Later, your individual style, developed after much experimentation and practice, dictates the use of either fine line or broad stroke linework.

Hold the pencil in a natural position, similar to writing, with the hand resting comfortably on the paper. (Always place a small sheet of paper under the hand to eliminate smudging the finished drawing.) Work in a restful, uncramped position. If you are working on thin paper, be sure you have several sheets of underlay paper underneath; this makes the drawing paper more responsive to pencil stroking. One of the secrets of velvety pencil tones is continual *extreme pressure* on the pencil, even on light tones. It makes the strokes more definite and minimizes grainy pencil work. Use harder pencils for lighter tones and softer ones for darker tones. If a tone seems to be too dark when pressure is applied, pick up a harder pencil, but always maintain firm pressure on the pencils if you want to develop interesting textures. Give each stroke identity, especially at its beginning and ending. Notice that occasional white areas left out between strokes contribute sparkle and variety. Artists develop individuality by going about a drawing in their own way; hence, students must feel free to develop drawings in their own way, as long as the results are satisfactory. Each person's work will differ, much like handwriting. Students will find it interesting and also very helpful to observe how professionals treat various features. In addition, it will be good experience—and many accomplished artists have profited by it—to reproduce some of the drawings of the old masters found in art museums.

One point students must remember is that they must exaggerate features such as contrast between light and dark areas in a composition occasionally, rather than try to make the rendering resemble a photograph (see Fig. 14-12). Plan a well-balanced tone arrangement (with values ranging from extreme darks to white, as shown in Figs. 14-14 and 14-15) before you start rendering. Have the main outlines carefully laid out with light lines, even major shadows, so that you will avoid mistakes and not lose control of your drawing. Fine detail such as window muntins can be omitted in the preliminary layout. Landscaping and tree studies are first done on tracing paper overlays. When their composition and general effect are satisfactory, they are transferred to the final drawing with light lines. While most of the strokes representing natural foliage and tone work are done freehand, strong roof lines and other architectural edges may be completed with the help of the straightedge.

Practice Strokes   With a grade B pencil sharpened to a conical point, practice the fine line strokes shown in Fig. 14-13A, B, E, F, and G. Try all these several times to develop discipline in pencil control. The exercises are

FIGURE 14-12 A pencil presentation and photograph of the finished building.

mainly for showing outline information and suggestions of surfaces and textures. Keep the pencil uniformly dressed throughout the exercises. With a softer pencil (2B or 3B) sharpened to a chisel point, and, using its flat surface, practice the broad stroke exercise shown in Fig. 14-13C, D, and N. These strokes become useful for pencil washes and various background tones throughout a drawing. Notice that definite pressure is required at the ends and beginnings of strokes. Try graduated

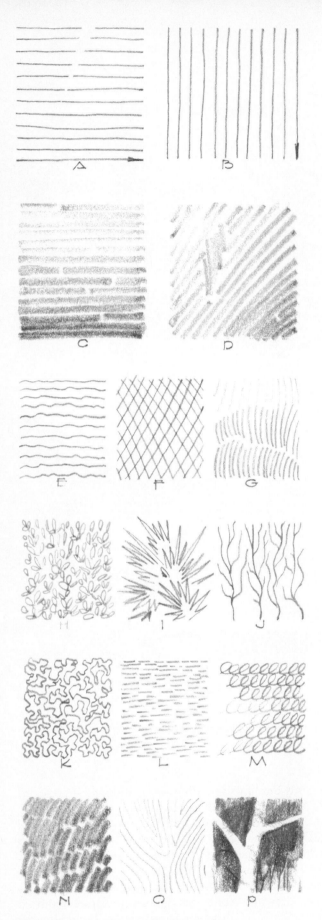

tone exercises, which will be continually useful in areas varying from a dark to a light value. Try the strokes in the full range of values, from darks to light. Experiment with other methods of your own for creating other tones, since there are unlimited ways of representing them with a pencil. Before applying pencil tones to a final rendering, evaluate their suitability first on practice paper.

For filling large areas, a broad sketching pencil, resembling a carpenter's pencil and available at art supply stores, can be useful, and a graphite stick may also be found appropriate for showing sharp edges and gradual, uniform tones. The wide pencil will save time in laying in larger backgrounds and in representing many other features. Observe the manner in which E. A. Moulthrop has so ably given a charming and casual quality to typical architectural subjects with the use of a broad sketching pencil (Figs. 14-12 and 14-21A). These drawings were originally done on tracing paper.

14.4.1 Pencil textures

Draw Brickwork Differently at Different Scales The need for rendering brick walls arises frequently in architectural subjects. For this, a pencil is especially suitable because it is a medium that lends itself well to soft, tonal variations. Care must be taken to plan the general tone of all the brick surfaces with respect to light and shade in the composition. In full sun, for instance, the tone value of brick will usually be very light, shown with generous areas of white, devoid of detail. In shade, the values become darker tones with more of the brick detail in evidence. Corners, where contrast is intense, must be carefully done to reveal the rough nature of the brick coursing joints. When drawing brick, first establish basic background values with the broad stroke; put in shade and shadow areas where they seem necessary. Change the intensity of some of the strokes to avoid monotony. Usually, shadow lines are suggested and allowances made for reflected light during this step. The representation of the actual brick is then applied over the tonework.

For drawing brick at a small scale, use a series of parallel wavy lines, broken occasionally, to produce a convincing texture (see Fig. 14-16A). It is important that the lines be in perspective and that their width and spacing be scaled properly. Remember that the height of one brick course with a mortar joint is only about 2½″. Although the linework is broken at irregular intervals, vertical joints of the brick are ignored. Do not try to indicate each brick. As suggested previously, let a bit of pure white show in a few areas. Be sure that shadows expressing the relief of corners, offsets, and reveals at window and door openings are carefully handled. Brick walls can often be a dark value at corners opposite the light, and as they recede, they can be made gradually

FIGURE 14-13 Practice strokes in pencil.

FIGURE 14-14 Rendering done in pencil.

FIGURE 14-15 Rendering showing various textures in pencil.

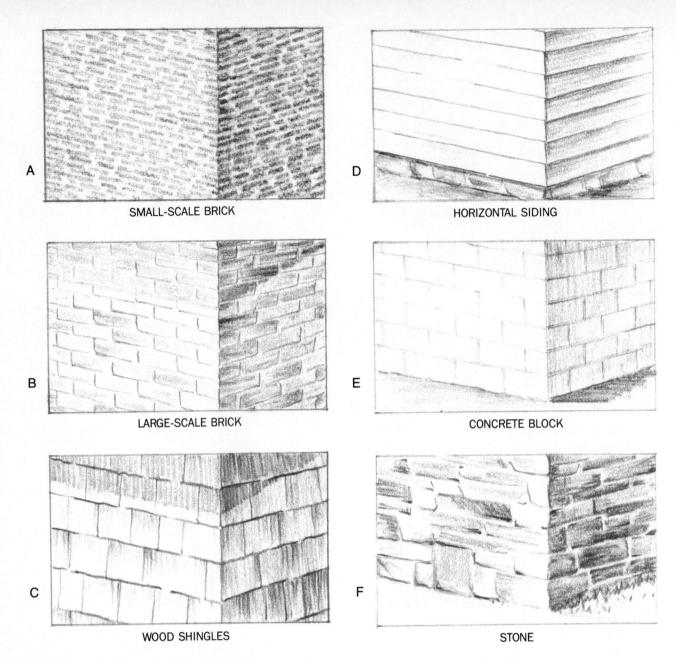

A   SMALL-SCALE BRICK

B   LARGE-SCALE BRICK

C   WOOD SHINGLES

D   HORIZONTAL SIDING

E   CONCRETE BLOCK

F   STONE

FIGURE 14-16 Architectural textures in pencil.

lighter, to where extremely dark tree backgrounds provide sharp contrast.

Brick surfaces near the viewer must be larger in scale and must therefore be given more individual brick detail (see Fig. 14-16B). For best results, use a pencil dressed to the proper brick width and show (with various short strokes) the brick and mortar joints between. Go over occasional strokes to bring out variations in color. Make bold, sharp-ending strokes. Fine line shadows along the lower edge and side of the individual brick, here and there, help emphasize the texture. Give brick in shadow a very dark value. Do not forget the shadows below brick windowsills. Shadows from

nearby foliage falling on a wall will help create interest; they are drawn with vertical strokes briskly applied over the finished brick.

Stonework Can Appear Smooth or Rough Much of the artistry of stonework is provided by the arrangement of the various unit sizes and the mortar joint pattern throughout the wall. The appearance of stone varies greatly, depending on coursing, unit sizes, and roughness. Cut stone usually has uniform coursing and a rather smooth texture, whereas field stone may have various unit sizes, and shadows indicate that the stones are rough and irregular. The rendering should capture the intended texture. The bold treatment of the stonework contributes to the rustic appearance of a building.

Begin stonework by lightly indicating the unit pattern throughout the wall, regardless of the desired texture. As a rule, patterns showing a dominance of horizontal courses are the most pleasing (see Fig. 14-16F). Place larger stones at corners for stability, and vary the sizes and shapes of the smaller ones in between to avoid regularity. Next, shade each stone with parallel broad strokes, making sure that the stones vary in value for interest and that the strokes change in direction occasionally. Leave generous amounts of white areas, especially if you plan dark features in back of the stone. Possibly, the suggestion of shadows, drawn in fine lines emanating from the lower edge of a few stones, may be all that need be shown in these areas. Let the mortar joints remain light and not very wide. As in brickwork, treat stone corners carefully, particularly where strong light and shade contrasts appear and where stone is bordered by sky. Emphasize stone textures near the center of interest where they should be darkest.

Use a dotted technique to represent stucco, a similar method can be used for concrete block by adding a few fine lines to suggest coursing (Fig. 14-16E).

Wood Siding is Drawn with Parallel Lines
The general tone of wood siding must be considered with respect to composition and light and shade—also to color, if painted. If it is painted white, only the shaded areas may require a background value. If, on the other hand, the wood is to be stained, more of the values will appear darker. However, use white highlights even on the darker wood surfaces to prevent monotony. Apply background values with the broad stroke mainly in the direction of the wood grain.

Show clapboard siding with fine horizontal lines (occasionally a few heavy lines may be needed), which represent the shadow below each board (see Fig. 14-16D). Spacing of the linework depends on the width of the boards exposed to the weather. Vary the weight of the lines, but in areas of a wall where light intensity is the strongest, omit them altogether. Be sure the lines are in perspective. Care must be taken to represent the sawtooth profile at corners or where the clapboards abut vertical wood trim. Show wood louvers in a similar way—with parallel lines and a sawtooth shade at the shadow side of the louver strips.

Represent board and batten siding by carefully drawing the edges of each vertical batten strip with light lines. Give the boards between the strips a light gray value and leave the strips white, except in shade. Accent the shadow side of the batten strips with a fine dark line. In shade, darken the boards rather than the battens (see Fig. 14-17A). Shadows falling across the wall must give evidence of the batten offsets.

Wood shingle siding is rendered by first drawing the horizontal coursing with freehand wavy lines to indicate the shadow at the butts. Break the lines frequently and vary their darkness to give the wall a weathered, rustic effect. Draw staggered vertical joints between shingles only here and there with the fine point (see Fig. 14-16C). Then apply broad strokes in slightly varying tones vertically throughout (to simulate the wood grain); the tone value of these strokes should create a pleasing overall value composition. Indicate shadows with dark, bold strokes.

Roofing shingles must be given an identification value in the composition; usually, it will vary throughout the roof surface. Coursing is drawn with wavy, horizontal lines, and very few vertical strokes are shown (see Fig. 7-92). Background tones are drawn down the slope of the roof to indicate a slight weathered effect. In some roofing materials the shingle coursing is not pronounced; the drawing must make this clear. Built-up roofing may be indicated with a dot technique in shadow and at important corners only.

Glass is Usually Dark
In general, glass appears dark unless there are drapes, blinds, or shades directly in back of it to receive the sunlight. Highlights on glass appear white. To indicate the dark areas, make definite broad strokes with a 3B or 4B pencil. The upper part of the shaded area is made the darkest. For highlighting, leave white openings that slope in the direction of the light; these will suggest the smoothness of the glass. Reflections of foliage or of surrounding features will add interest (see Fig. 14-12). In direct sunlight or on planes facing the viewer, windows are especially dark and more reflective on their shaded sides or on planes slanting away from the viewer. Leave muntins and mullions white if they are in direct sunlight. Large glassed areas may require suggestions of furniture within, since an expanse of glass admits a considerable amount of light to the interior.

The surface of glass is generally recessed several inches or more from the surface of the wall. This means that reveals and surrounding trim must be carefully drawn. When drawing window units such as double-hung or casement (or even entire glass walls), show drapery or curtains along the inside edges where they would ordinarily be seen. Indicate the folds of drapery with vertical light and dark areas, and show shadows from muntin bars as wavy lines across the drapery (see Fig. 14-17A). Curtains or other window treatment should look realistic. Remember that muntins and division bars, though white in sunlight, appear darker on the shadow side.

Trees Provide a Natural Setting
Trees, drawn in correct proportion to a building, establish the relative scale in the viewer's mind and add a note of softness and charm to the rendering. Often they are drawn in natural groupings as background, or a few may be shown in the foreground to achieve good composition. Earlier in this chapter we stressed the importance of direct obser-

(A)

(B)

Figure 14-17 (A) Pencil rendering showing reflections in glass. (B) Ink rendering showing reflections in glass.

vation from nature. This is particularly helpful in familiarizing the student with the individual characteristics of different tree species, and, before long, he or she will be able to draw trees from memory. Their silhouette, trunk and branch structure, bark texture, appearance at the base of the trunk, and foliage clusters and leaf forms all play a part in giving tree species identity.

Before drawing a tree, study its silhouette (Fig. 14-18) so that you get to know the character and form of the trunk and the angle of the branches in relation to it. Then lightly lay out the trunk and branch structure, which becomes the skeleton of the tree. Give the structure personality but do not overly distort it—this only detracts from the building; reserve slight distortions for needed interest in an otherwise weak composition. Notice that branches radiate in all directions (in front and back of the trunk, as well as the sides) and become consistently smaller toward the top. The pine tree, however, has a slightly different trunk system. The thickness of the trunk remains similar for most of its height and only near the top does it gradually diminish, where small branches radiate almost horizontally with needle clusters of various sizes. No two trees, even of the same species, are exactly alike; the drawing should

show slight variations, yet the identifying characteristics should be present.

After the basic structure is established, draw the clusters of foliage lightly (see Fig. 14-19B) with some darker areas to indicate shade; strive to make the general pattern a pleasing one. In the foreground, more detail must be shown on tree representations. Render the foliage with the broad stroke using a 4B pencil, starting with the darkest values. Have various tones throughout the foliage, using a fanlike series of continuous pencil strokes. Some foliage may be better represented by slightly different stroking, but accent the bottom edges of foliage clusters. Leave branches or parts of the trunk white where dark foliage falls in back of them. Remember as you work that highlights on leaf clusters appear white, similar to the highlight of a sphere, whereas shade appears dark below clusters. Treat the trunk as a

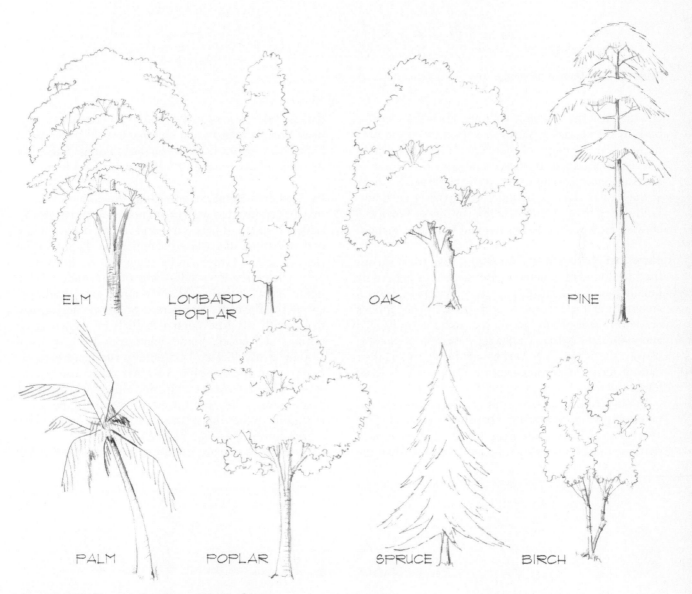

ELM

LOMBARDY POPLAR

OAK

PINE

PALM

POPLAR

SPRUCE

BIRCH

Figure 14-18 Shapes of various species of trees.

A SKELETON   B FOLIAGE   C VALUES

Figure 14-19 Steps in drawing a tree.

cylindrical form to give it volume. Then draw coarse bark, if the species requires it, with most of the bold dashes near the edges of the trunk to give it a rough, uneven appearance. In direct sunlight, leave some of the trunk entirely white. Soften any harsh vertical lines at the base of the tree by indicating grass or shadows. Undulating tree shadows falling on grass provide a convenient way of showing rise and fall of the terrain.

Show Shrubbery Near the Building Evergreen shrubs used for foundation planting and as accents help to tie building and ground together and eliminate hard, vertical architectural lines, especially at corners. Pleasing groups of various indigenous species contribute a landscaped appearance and help to emphasize the center of interest, usually the front door. Shrubs can be shown in their natural forms or trimmed into continuous geometric forms, such as a hedge along a walkway (see Fig. 14-20).

In rendering shrubbery, outline the groupings first before applying the broad stroke patterns shown in Fig. 14-13. Again, leave white areas. On some, show indications of the branch structure, and be sure that the darkest values are near the ground where shadows appear. Shrubs in front of a building should be rendered before drawing the linework on the building. This eliminates needless erasing of wall textures and lines.

Tie Elements Together with Grass Indications Grass may be represented with broad horizontal lines, drawn with a T square if necessary, and accented along edges of drives and walks. Make the indications lighter in sun than in shade. Grass can be suggested by drawing it only where shadows fall along the ground, leaving lighted areas entirely white; too much grass might deemphasize the center of interest. Short, vertical strokes made with the fine point can then be shown along borders and edges. Some delineators use a series of looping strokes drawn horizontally and close together to represent grass (see Fig. 14-13M); others use rows of short vertical strokes, varying in value, throughout the shaded areas. Be sure the edge of grass indications, extending to the edge of the rendering, forms an interesting outline (see Fig. 14-21A).

Clouds and sky are usually not indicated on pencil

Figure 14-20 Shrubbery suggestions.

(A)

(B)

(C)

FIGURE 14-21 Representing grass in foreground.

FIGURE 14-22 Indications of people must be drawn to the correct scale.

renderings. If they seem necessary for the composition, make clouds rather subdued and remember that sky appears lightest near the horizon and gradually darker above.

As we previously mentioned, trees and shrubbery on a rendering should be merely suggestive rather than too complex—subordinate to the architecture. For that reason, many renderings are shown with stylized indications. In this technique, trees and planting are simplified, often showing only outlines or branch structures; others show only flat tones of foliage masses. The treatment is effective if the natural forms and tree characteristics have been retained. Nature must be the source for ideas in arriving at authentic stylized treatments. Even the representation of people can be simplified (Fig. 14-22).

Use a Value Scale to Plan Values and Contrast   Nearly everything we see is made up of an almost unlimited number of shadings of colors or grays ranging from black to white. The variation of lightness or darkness of color or grays is known as *value*. To the beginner, most subjects appear to be muted in values that are difficult to distinguish. Early trials by students often result in dull gray renderings that are composed of nearly identical values. But this dullness must be avoided at all costs.

Contrast is defined as the striking difference in adjacent elements of a composition, whether by the use of color, value, texture, outline, or treatment. We know that the appearance of contrast is relative (Fig. 14-23). A black value next to a gray value will not appear as dark as a black value adjacent to a white area. Likewise, a relatively loud sound in a quiet bedroom may be very

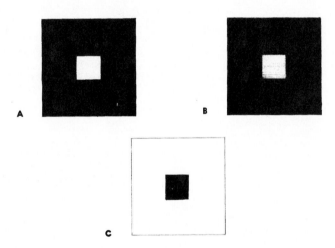

FIGURE 14-23 Contrast of values.

disturbing, whereas the same sound in a busy street may go unnoticed.

Before starting a drawing, develop a value scale that ranges from black to white similar to the one shown in Fig. 14-24. A value scale to the artist is similar to a score to the musician. Each produces a sense of order to the creation—the musician with sound value, the artist with color value. White and black with three or four intermediate grays between are satisfactory for the range of most drawings. Plan your drawings with the use of the value scale so that important features are accented with extreme contrasts (whites against blacks or blacks against whites), and make less important features or outlines with lesser amounts of contrast. Plan a

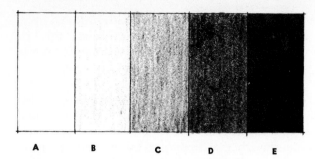

FIGURE 14-24 Use of a value scale to help you plan the light and dark areas.

FIGURE 14-25 Planning value layouts.

definite arrangement of the values. This is necessary even if reality is exaggerated to some degree. But if you want sparkle and interest in your pencil drawings, have light and dark values provide contrast where the dominance counts most. The size of the white or black areas also plays a part in developing brightness. Position the values in the composition so that they have variety yet balance (Fig. 14-25). Use dramatic profiles where the highest contrast occurs. This *shape accent* should be reserved for the dominating features only, since too many accents tend to cancel out each other. The pattern or repeating quality that holds the whole together is known as *matrix*.

14.5 Rendering in Ink

MATERIALS

1. Black waterproof India ink: the standard brands can be diluted with water for gray washes or gray ink linework

2. Technical drafting pen, points No. 0, No. 2: for lettering and other uniform linework
3. Technical drafting pens: for various-width ruled lines
4. Hunt's No. 102 Crow Quill pen: a fine, flexible point for delicate linework
5. Hunt's No. 99 pen: a nibbed point for general work
6. Speedball No. B6: a round nib pen for bold linework
7. Small pointed watercolor brush
8. Small bottle of white tempera color

Select a strong paper or board that will take ink well. A smooth surface is preferable, because a rough surface tends to interfere with fine pen stroking. Good grades of tracing paper and illustration board are satisfactory; plate-finish illustration board, if available, will be found very desirable.

Pen and ink drawing requires more care in planning than pencil. Pencil can be erased or darkened by repeated strokes until a desired value is attained; but ink work is difficult to remove or modify once it is put on paper. Successful pen renderings also require a carefully balanced composition of white, black, and intermediate values. Various line or dot techniques must be found to represent the intermediate values since the ink remains black unless, of course, it is diluted. Elements of the composition must therefore be reduced to their simplest expression to give the rendering a crisp yet delicate appearance.

Before you begin, a word of advice: do not make the mistake of using the same-width pen point throughout your entire drawing. Unless you are experienced in pen and ink technique, this is likely to make the drawing look monotonous and uninteresting. Use two or three points of different widths to give the lines character. If you want to soften the appearance of the ink rendering, do all the linework freehand; it is usually more appealing. To obtain a quality of perspective depth, draw tree and planting indications in the far background with a fine pen, the mid-distance trees with an intermediate point, and the foreground features with a broader pen.

Begin by practicing the various pen strokes shown in Fig. 14-26. Acquaint yourself with the capabilities of each pen; try each tone shown in the exercise. Experiment with the tone representations before you use them on your finished rendering. By all means, have the outlines and edges of all values laid out lightly in pencil (as well as other major linework), using care not to groove the paper, before you do any inking. Pencil lines can be easily erased when the ink is thoroughly dry. If you are not pressed for time, make a *value study* of the composition. After the perspective is completed in pencil, place a sheet of tracing paper over it and quickly establish the general value patterns rather roughly, using a soft pencil or charcoal. Avoid details on the study; instead, strive for pleasing value patterns that

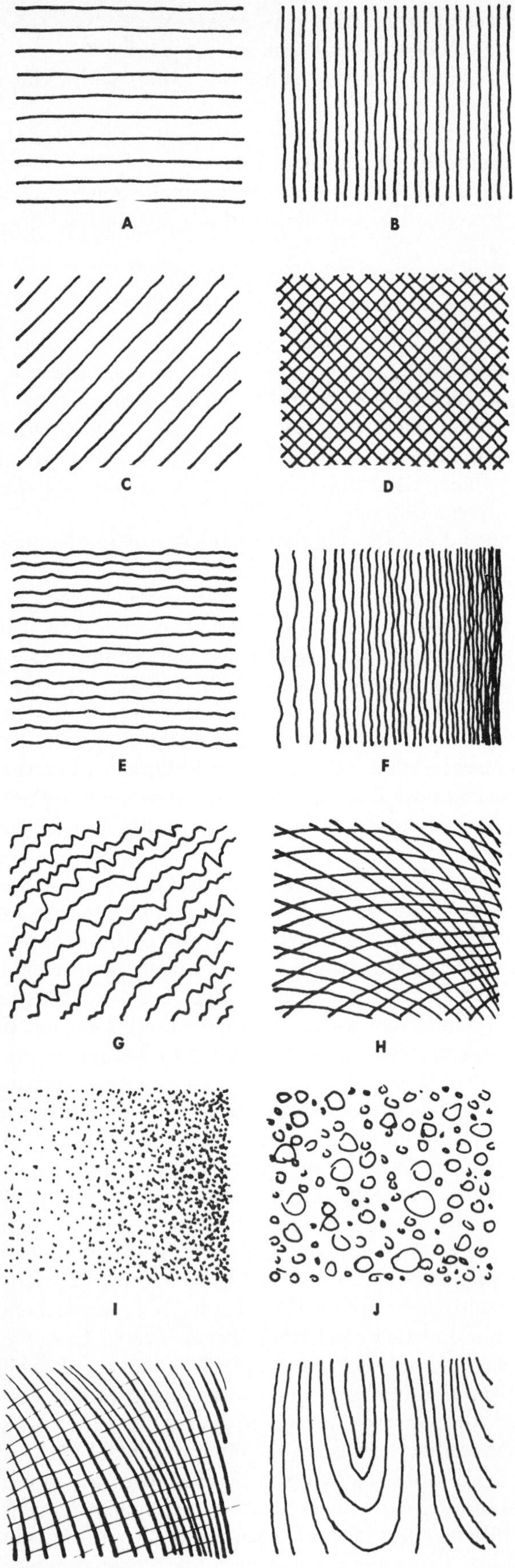

FIGURE 14-26 Practice strokes in pen and ink.

can be created by contrasts of light and shade and from the landscaping composition. When finished, this becomes your guide for choosing line technique, values, and landscaping on the final ink drawing (see Figs. 14-27 and 14-28).

To avoid smearing ink lines, start at the top of the drawing and work down. Remember that ink work cannot be rushed. To save time in filling large black areas, outline them with the pen and fill in the remainder with a small watercolor brush. Be sure there are sufficient areas left white to give the impression of strong light, as we mentioned earlier. If a minor mistake should occur in the linework, white tempera applied with a brush will cover it. Check the value study from time to time to see that the total desired effect is developing. The same basic principles of composition that were discussed in connection with pencil rendering apply equally to work done in ink.

14.6 Rendering with Color

After you have made a number of pencil and pen and ink renderings, you may have the urge to try working in color. There is something exciting about color work. It is dramatic and commands attention, and there is no question about its compelling qualities on architectural presentations if the color has been carefully handled. If, on the other hand, the coloring appears hard, unharmonious, and detracting, it would have been better if the presentation had been done in black and white. Color is a completely different graphic dimension requiring mental application not required in other work. The study of color is rather extensive, entailing scientific and psychological aspects, and there are many good books covering the subject. Here we can only discuss the major points, primarily to introduce the beginning student to the basic principles of color and to clear up any misconceptions he or she may have.

Let us start our study with an examination of the color wheel (inside the front cover) showing the interrelationship of basic colors. The color wheel, as you will notice, places colors in an organized position around the circle, relative to each other, for convenient reference by the student or color artist, and the wheel is the result of extensive study about color characteristics. It is handy for selecting actual color combinations or as an aid in mixing pigments to arrive at a desired color on the palette. Many of the rules governing the effective use of color are based on the relationship of the colors on the wheel. It does not solve all the problems concerning color, yet it can guide the bewildered novice in his or her early work; later these color characteristics will come automatically.

FIGURE 14-27 Perspective rendering in ink.

FIGURE 14-28 Elevation drawing in ink.

COLOR TERM DEFINITIONS

PRIMARY COLORS   Red, yellow, and blue, from which, theoretically, all other colors can be made.

SECONDARY COLORS   Orange, green, and purple, made by mixing adjacent primary colors on the color wheel.

TERTIARY COLORS   Colors located between primary and secondary colors on the color wheel and made by mixing adjacent colors.

HUE   The term used to designate the name of a color. Red, blue-green, orange, blue, and so on, are different hues.

VALUE   The lightness or darkness of the same hue, such as light red or dark red.

CHROMA   The intensity or purity of a color, that is, the degree to which it has been diluted or neutralized.

SHADE   A darkened value of a color.

TINT   A lightened value of a color, usually by the addition of white.

COMPLEMENTS   Colors located opposite each other on the color wheel and considered harmonious. Complements mixed together will produce a gray if the result ends midway between the two colors. A color can be darkened by adding a slight amount of its complement. Complements of equal chroma and value are usually not pleasing, but by varying their values or chromas in a subtle manner, for example, a dark green and a light red, a more pleasing color combination results.

MONOCHROMATIC   A color scheme using values of only one color. For instance, sepia produces a very artistic monochromatic color scheme.

ANALOGOUS   A color scheme employing two or three adjacent colors on the color wheel; usually, more interest is created if one of the colors predominates the scheme. For example, yellow, yellow-green, and green, with the yellow predominating.

WARM COLORS   Reds, oranges, and yellows, which seem to advance toward the viewer.

COLD COLORS   Blues, greens, or violets, which appear cool and seem to recede when seen from the same distance as warm colors. Gray can be either cold or warm.

Pure pigments, made from plants or minerals, reflect particular colored waves, while absorbing others. Pigments do this in varying degrees, so experimentation in mixing various colors is necessary; arriving at the desired colors is a matter of trial and error. When mixing colors it will become apparent that certain pigments have a greater affinity for one color than for another.

Colors on renderings, as we mentioned, should be kept soft and subdued, often grayed. Greens for foliage, for instance, should be yellowish green hues, rather than hard, high-intensity greens. If you will look about at the surrounding landscape you will notice that nature's colors are restful to the eye. Few abrupt, hard colors exist unless put there by people. Even the coloring on buildings should utilize soft, natural colorings of building materials to complement the landscape. Try to have three basic harmonious colors in your composition: one in the foreground, one in the mid-distance, and one in the background. In general, these three distinct planes can be treated in a monochromatic color scheme by using various values of one color for light and shade effects. Stay with simple, uncomplicated color combinations; usually, a few colors will be sufficient and more appropriate and also easier to handle than many colors. The choice of colors is personal, and you will find with experience that impressions created by color are affected by many things—light, adjacent colors, paper, patterns of the drawing, and so on. Make it a habit to "see" the colors around you and learn to identify them, and you have taken the first step in trying to master this troublesome technique.

Colored Pencils   One of the simplest methods of coloring a rendering is with colored pencils. Although many colors are available, they lack subtlety because a direct application is required. Some pencils, however, have water-soluble colors; the lines made by this type can be blended in with a wet brush to create a watercolor effect.

A rather effective color pencil rendering can be done on a dark black-line diazo print of an elevation view. The pencil or ink tracing is run through the machine so that the background of the print becomes gray rather than white, giving it an intermediate tone throughout the paper. Light pencil colors are used to bring out the architecture and to contrast the gray background. Major colored areas are filled in with close, parallel lines made with instruments, and the foliage indications are added in an abstract manner. A rendering, for example, can be done very quickly in this manner (see Fig. 14-29).

Watercolor   Down through the years, watercolor has been an important medium in architectural presentation. One distinguishes between two general types of watercolor work: transparent and opaque. As the name of the former implies, *transparent*-type watercolor pigments are used (see Fig. 14-30A). Thin washes are

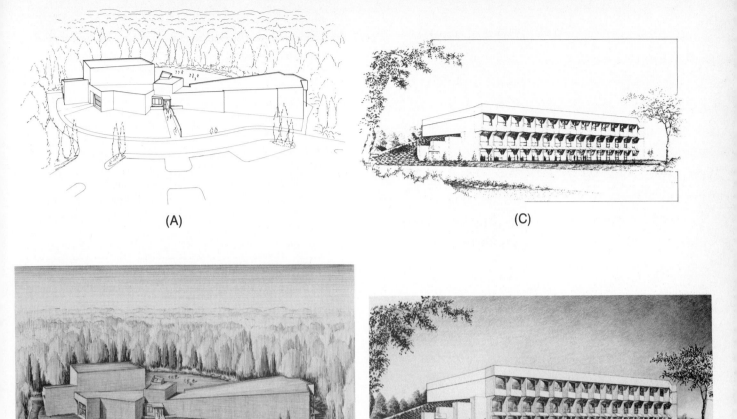

(A)

(C)

(B)

(D)

FIGURE 14-29 (A) Blackline diazo print; (B) Rendering with colored pencils; (C) Blackline diazo print; (D) Rendering with colored pencils.

spread over special paper stretched carefully on the drawing board or over commercially prepared watercolor board. In some cases the washes may have to be superimposed over each other to arrive at desired values and effects. *Opaque* watercolors, either tempera, acrylic, or casein, are slightly different in that they have the capacity of covering different colors beneath. They are applied in a creamy consistency rather than as a thin wash. Although the techniques of transparent and opaque watercolors are basically different, beautiful work can result by using both media, separately or in combination (see Fig. 14-30B).

Because tempera does not necessarily have to be diluted and because of its opaqueness, it is the ideal medium for the student's early work. Tempera can be put on regular inexpensive illustration board; and even though the paint is water soluble, it can easily be applied in successive layers, making it ideal for the beginner. Self-confidence will be gained when it is found that mistakes can be covered without much trouble or carefully sponged off with a damp sponge. However, tem-

pera colors possess strong, vivid qualities that require toning down, which is done by mixing with white or gray or with their complements. In mixing, as well as in method of application, tempera paints handle much like artist's oil colors (see Fig. 14-30C).

Colored Markers Felt-tip markers in a wide spectrum of colors and tip sizes are used over pencil and ink drawings. Different techniques can be accomplished with markers depending on the method of application. Colors may be dabbed or washed. Care must be taken to select less vivid colors. Colored markers are unforgiving; however, warm or cool tone grays can be placed over bright colors to subdue them. Practice on blueline or blackline prints before applying color on the original. Most media, such as illustration board, vellum and a variety of prints, are suitable for colored marker renderings (see Fig. 14-31).

Purchase the materials shown in the material list at your art or drafting supply store. You will find that the more expensive brands are more enjoyable to work

(A)

(B)

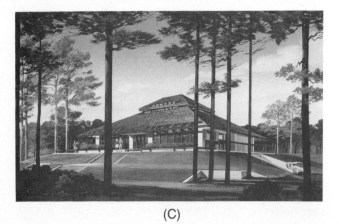

(C)

Figure 14-30 (A) Rendering in transparent watercolor; (B) Rendering in acrylics; (C) Rendering in tempera.

with. Brushes must be cleaned in water before the tempera dries; never allow brushes to rest on their bristles, since they would soon lose their shape and become worthless.

Materials for tempera, caesin, or acrylic rendering	
Colors (In tubes)	**Brushes**
Chinese white	1 No. 4 red sable, pointed watercolor brush
Alizarin crimson	
Cadmium red (medium)	
Cadmium yellow (pale)	1 No. 1 and 1 No. 4 red sable "Brights" flat-end brush
Yellow ochre	
Prussian blue	
Ultramarine blue	1 No. 5 flat bristle color brush
Viridian	
Ivory black	1 Regular painter's nylon bristle brush (1″)
Burnt sienna	
Burnt umber	

General

Muffin tin
Pint jar (for water)
Old dinner plate (for a palette)
Baby sponge

Painting a Color Wheel   To acquaint yourself with the tempera pigments, make your first color exercise the duplication of a color wheel. It will not only be a helpful exercise, but it will also become a serviceable reference when doing other color work. Lay out the wheel on illustration board using a 6″ outer and a 4″ inner diameter. Divide it into 12 equal 30° segments as shown. Allow a small amount of white space between each segment so that the colors do not run together. Paint the primary colors first, making sure that you have enough remaining pigment to mix the other colors. Use cadmium yellow (pale) for the yellow, alizarin crimson with a bit of cadmium red for the red, and Prussian blue mixed with a little ultramarine blue for the blue. In mixing the secondary colors, see if you can get them from the primaries; otherwise, you may have to draw on the other tube pigments. Viridian requires a touch of yellow for the proper green. Then mix and paint in the tertiary colors to complete the color wheel. Label all the colors correctly. (See inside of front cover of this book.)

Further experience will be gained by mixing various pigments and noting the results. See what happens when white is mixed with other colors. Try mixing a slight amount of black with the various colors as well. Try mixing complements. Be sure you feed small amounts of a strong color into a weaker color when mixing; otherwise, you may end up with more color than you need. All this experimentation will be helpful before attempting an actual rendering. Other exercises should include architectural textures such as stone, brick, and wood and the painting of trees, shrubs, and foliage. Study professional tempera renderings for ways of handling these features.

FIGURE 14-31 Rendering in felt-tip markers.

Helpful Hints Some artists cover the entire rendering with a thin sepia or pale yellow transparent wash before applying the tempera.

Do not overstroke the paint, let some of the brush work give character to the forms.

Blending can be done with a finger while the paint is wet. Blends can also be accomplished with a *drybrush* technique.

Avoid using too much white for light value tints. The overuse of white pigment results in a chalky painting, often appearing cold and lifeless.

Values in color rendering are just as important as they are in black and white renderings. Here, too, careful value studies are necessary in planning color renderings (see Figs. 14-30 and 14-31).

To create harmonious color combinations, the renderer does not have to stay with the colors found in nature—green grass, blue sky, and the like. Slight modifications of natural colors, as long as they are plausible and not extreme, create interest and a note of abstraction.

If the tempera painting is to occupy only a small rectangular area of a larger presentation, surround the area with masking tape before starting to paint so that it will stay within bounds.

Start the painting with flat tones in the major areas; then add the texture indications and the detail strokes in a systematic manner over the backgrounds.

When painting the landscaping, apply indications in the distance first, usually with flat tones along the horizon, then add the mid-distance foliage, and finally the trees and shrubs in the foreground. Paint any figures last.

If necessary, tempera can be reduced to a thin wash and brushed over underlying colors to soften their appearance and yet retain their identity.

Paint mullions over the general glass areas with a pointed brush or a ruling pen, or use a small (No. 1) flat-end brush if the mullions have more width. The flat brush is easier to control.

For painting straight lines on a building, use a bridge such as shown in Fig. 14-32 which can be made from an aluminum tube or wooden dowel (about 30″ long) with

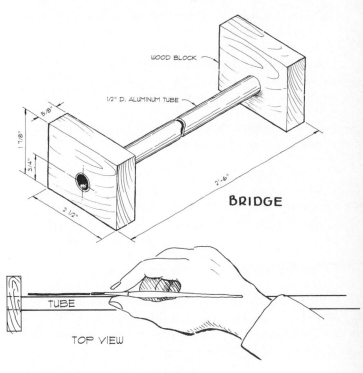

FIGURE 14-32 Convenient handrest for painting.

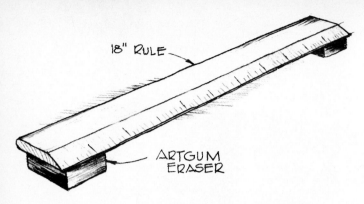

18" RULE

ARTGUM ERASER

FIGURE 14-33 An inexpensive bridge can be made by gluing art gum erasers to a brass-edged rule.

blocks of wood at each end. Have about ½″ clearance between the tube and the working surface. When using the bridge, rest several fingers and the thumb comfortably along the tube, with the brush held between the thumb and forefinger as you move the brush uniformly along the surface. For more versatility, make the clearance at the top of the blocks ⅞″ so that it can be turned over and used with larger brushes.

A more economical bridge can be made with an ordinary brass-edged ruler having art gum erasers (cubes) glued to each end (Fig. 14-33).

EXERCISES

1. On 8½″ × 11″ white drawing paper, lay out six equal rectangles with ½″ space between as shown in Fig. 14-16. Using a soft pencil, render the following material textures in the rectangles: brick, stone, horizontal siding, concrete block, board and batten wood siding, and wood shingle siding.

2. Draw a realistic deciduous tree; a coniferous tree; a group of evergreen shrubs—all in pencil.

3. Double the size of the plans, draw the elevation view shown in Fig. 14-5, and render it in pencil; add appropriate landscaping. Assume a vertical scale proportional to the horizontal scale and the perspective.

4. On 8½″ × 11″ white drawing paper, duplicate the ink textures shown in Fig. 14-26.

5. Using the scale ¼″ = 1′-0″, make an ink presentation drawing of a lakeside lodge. Use 20″ × 30″ illustration board and include a floor plan, two elevations, and perspective view.

6. Make an ink presentation drawing of an original home design using the scale ⅛″ = 1′-0″. Use 20″ × 30″ illustration board and include a site plan, floor plan, two elevations, and a perspective view.

7. Make an ink presentation drawing of a small commercial bank building; include a site plan, a floor plan, and four elevations using the scale ¼″ = 1′-0″.

8. With ink and colored pencils, render a perspective of a playground showing buildings in the background. Use either 20″ × 30″ illustration board or a black-line diazo print.

9. On 20″ × 30″ dark-tinted illustration boards, render a small two-story commercial building in white pencil. Show the site plan, floor plan, elevations, and perspective view.

10. Make an ink and felt-tip marker presentation drawing of a site plan. Draw a lake, amphitheatre, parking lot, and playground on the site plan. Use 20″ × 30″ white illustration board or apply colored marker to a diazo print that is reproduced from an ink tracing.

REVIEW QUESTIONS

1. What are the advantages, for client and architect, of preparing a presentation drawing of an architectural proposal?

2. For what reason are perspective views generally effective in presentation work?

3. What is meant by *optical balance?*

4. Why are plumbing fixtures and furniture usually shown on presentation plan views?

5. What media are appropriate for rendering small drawings?

6. On perspective renderings, why should the details nearest the observer be made more prominent than those in the distance?

7. What methods can the renderer employ to produce emphasis?

8. What do landscaping indications contribute to a perspective? Indications of people?

9. What is meant by a *value study?*

10. How are analogous colors related to each other on the color wheel?

11. When rendering sky, should the sky appear darker near the building or near the top edge of the rendering?

12. What is the most effective method for rendering glass?

13. What is the first step you should take in drawing a tree?

14. List three types of water-based paints frequently used in rendering.

15. Why is it important to draw people on a rendering of a building?

16. What drawing medium would be appropriate if a rendering must be prepared very quickly?

17. What is the best way to achieve contrast in a rendering?

18. Why are colored pencils a good media for the beginner?

19. Why is waterproof ink essential when it is combined with a wet medium?

20. What would be the advantage of preparing a pencil or ink rendering on vellum or Mylar instead of illustration board?

DRAWING A SMALL COMMERCIAL BUILDING

"Money is a good slave but a bad master."

—Horace

15

The planning of commercial buildings requires considerable research on the part of the designer or student. Each type of building presents problems that are unique—problems that must be resolved if the project is to be successful. Indeed, the success or failure of a commercial venture is frequently contingent on the qualities of the building itself. Because of the individual nature of each project, only general comments can be made about planning. For more specific information and to acquire a good background in this area of architecture, students must resort to personal observation, library references, and architectural magazines. Of course, in actual practice the designer would have to work closely with a client, who most likely would furnish definite requirements for a project. Designers nevertheless must thoroughly understand the activities for which a building is intended before they can do a creditable job of planning the project and completing the set of drawings. The following general factors are often essential in planning a small commercial building:

1. Zoning regulations
2. Code requirements
3. Site and contextual analysis
4. Land utilization plan
5. Vehicular and pedestrian traffic
6. Parking facilities
7. Erosion control
8. Landscaping
9. Building systems
10. Structural systems
11. Enclosure systems
12. Mass and form
13. Interior space requirements
14. Public space
15. Private space
16. Community space
17. Restrooms
18. Facilities for handicapped persons
19. Horizontal and vertical circulation (corridors, stairs, and the like)
20. Reception and receiving space
21. Administrative and clerical space
22. Sales space
23. Production and manufacturing space
24. Customer and client services space
25. Meeting and training space
26. Warehouse and storage space
27. Custodial space
28. Heating, ventilating, and air-conditioning (H.V.A.C.) space
29. Acoustical and noise control
30. Interior design and furnishings

Many small commercial buildings for offices and trade are constructed with load-bearing masonry walls, slab on grade floors, and steel bar joists for the roof structure (see Fig. 15-1). The joists rest on a reinforced bond beam formed with lintel block as the top course of the exterior walls. An acoustical ceiling is merely hung from the joists at the desired height with the use of wires and channel sections as shown on the detail. In this economical construction, the C.M.U. subwalls are frequently left exposed and painted with masonry paints to form the interior wall surfaces. With various modifications, interior partitions are commonly 4″ thick C.M.U. painted as well. Codes usually do not permit wood frame stud partitions in commercial areas. Vinyl tile set in mastic provides satisfactory finish floors over the slab unless subjected to unusual wearing conditions.

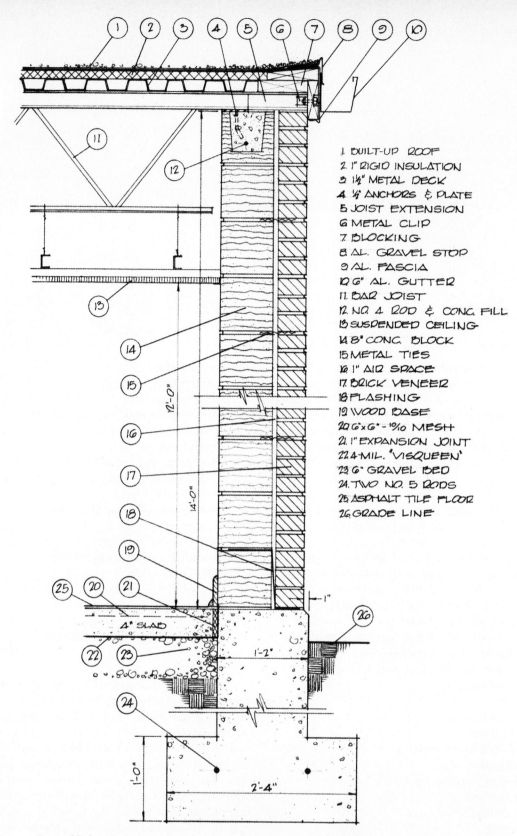

1. BUILT-UP ROOF
2. 1" RIGID INSULATION
3. 1½" METAL DECK
4. ½" ANCHORS & PLATE
5. JOIST EXTENSION
6. METAL CLIP
7. BLOCKING
8. AL. GRAVEL STOP
9. AL. FASCIA
10. 6" AL. GUTTER
11. BAR JOIST
12. NO. 4 ROD & CONC. FILL
13. SUSPENDED CEILING
14. 8" CONC. BLOCK
15. METAL TIES
16. 1" AIR SPACE
17. BRICK VENEER
18. FLASHING
19. WOOD BASE
20. 6"x6"-1%0 MESH
21. 1" EXPANSION JOINT
22. 4-MIL. 'VISQUEEN'
23. 6" GRAVEL BED
24. TWO NO. 5 RODS
25. ASPHALT TILE FLOOR
26. GRADE LINE

FIGURE 15-1 Typical wall section for a small commercial building.

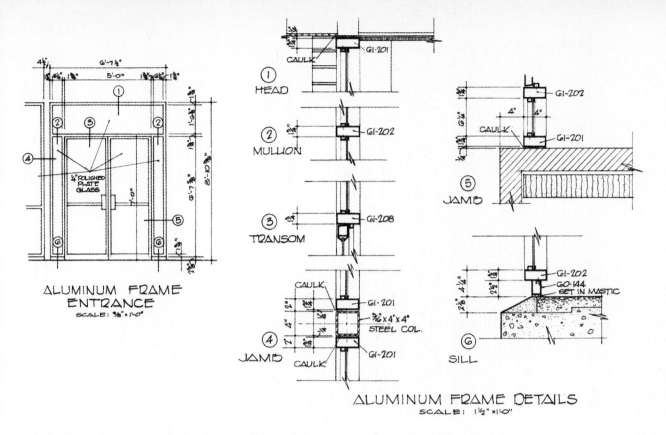

FIGURE 15-2 Entrance details for a small commercial building.

Front entrances and display windows are frequently constructed of stock aluminum tubing cut to size and fabricated according to dimensions shown on the drawings. Doors, plate glass, insulated glass or panels of prefinished materials can be inserted into the aluminum frames to form functional and attractive front wall units (see Fig. 15-2). Notice that manufacturers' stock numbers are shown on the drawings to indicate the correct frame profiles, and complete unit dimensions are given to provide a basis for fabrication. (Check *Sweet's Architectural File* for the various stock frame materials available for store fronts.)

Often landscape architects are employed to devise interesting settings for commercial buildings, which soften the architecture and provide a natural relationship to the land. An example of a typical landscape plan is shown in Fig. 15-3.

The following drawings (Figs. 15-4 through 15-25) are the major ones from a complete set for a small suburban health center; only some of the detail drawings have been omitted. They are reproductions of the actual architectural tracings originally drawn in plastic lead on 24″ × 36″ Mylar and reduced to page size. This completed project represents a typical solution to the needs of a client who desired an efficient yet pleasant appearing structure. The drafting technique is an example of professional work. On similar original proj-

ects, students will find that many of the features found on these drawings will be adaptable to theirs.

Like most architectural projects, this small building required numerous preliminary sketches before problems were resolved and before final working drawings could be started. All the needs and activities of a small health center had to be considered in refining the sketches. Locker rooms, showers, whirlpools, exercise rooms, counselling, snack bar, laboratory, private offices, customer service, storage spaces, rest rooms, and mechanical equipment had to be allotted their proportional amount of floor space after the general size of the building had been determined. Naturally, user traffic flow had to be considered and sufficient space provided for it.

The logical structural solution on a sloping site seemed to be a 2-story masonry and metal stud building with bearing walls supporting light steel bar joists and wood roof trusses. Concrete masonry units were selected as the exterior wall finish material. Interior walls were finished with gypsum wall board. Extruded aluminum window frames with fixed glass were placed in openings, which had concrete masonry unit lintels and sills. Entrance doors were glazed with tempered glass for safety and visibility. Gables at roof received an exterior metal siding. Elastomeric and composition shingle roofing was selected.

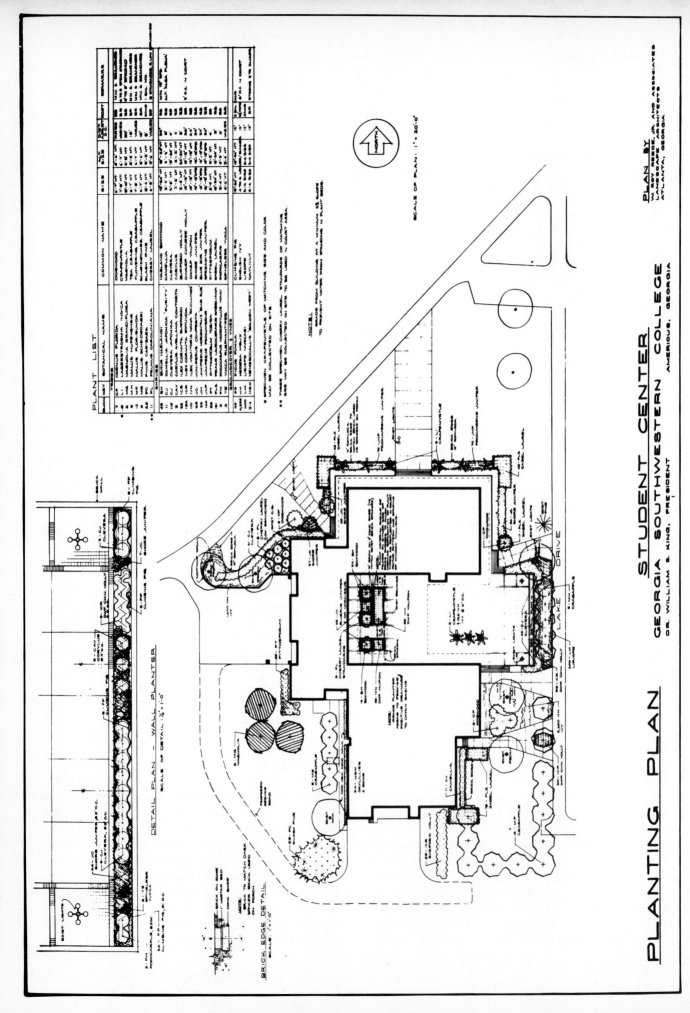

FIGURE 15-3 A landscaping plan.

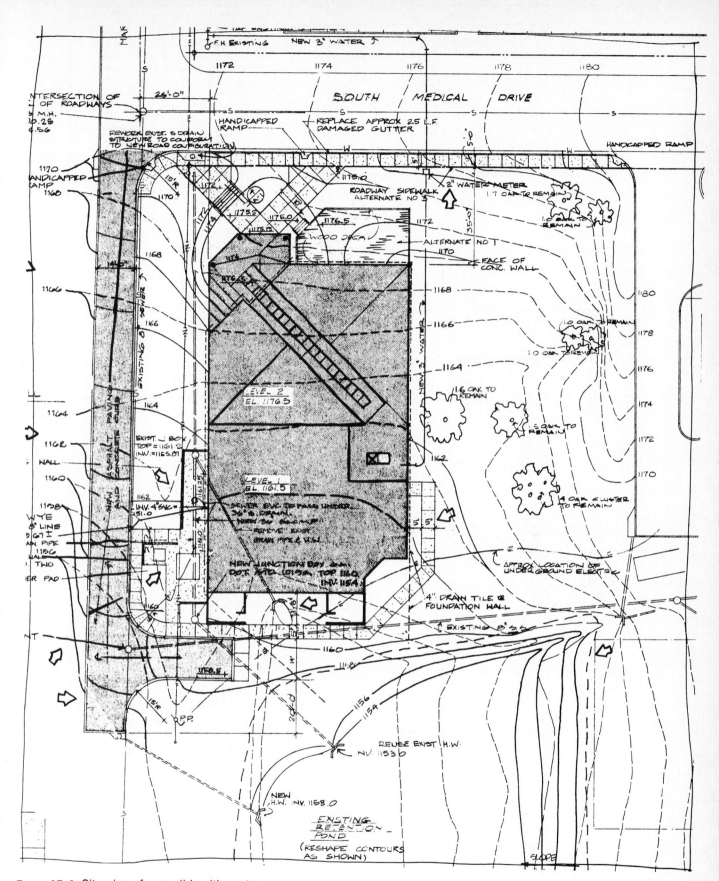

FIGURE 15-4 Site plan of a small health center.

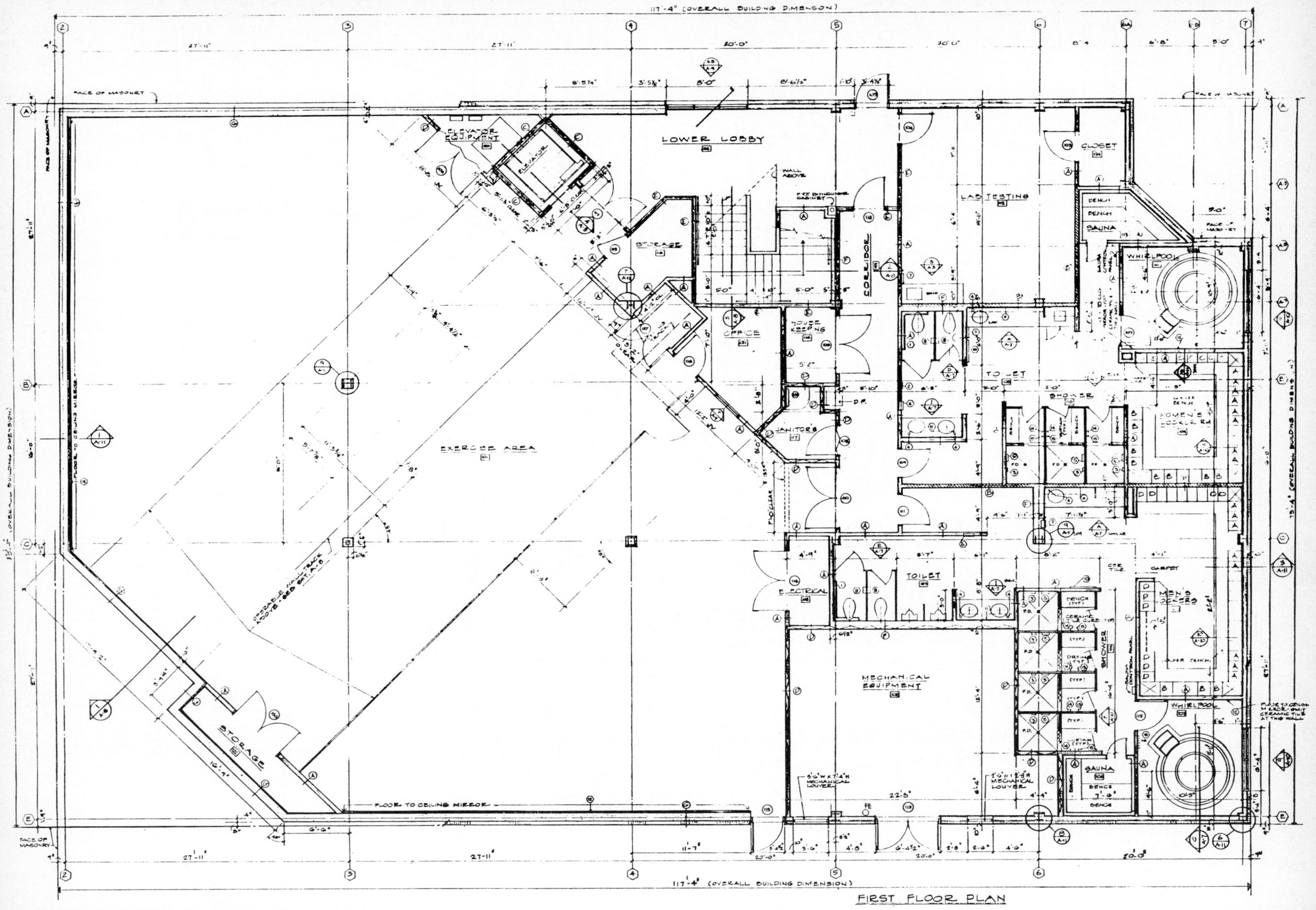

FIRST FLOOR PLAN

FIGURE 16-5 First floor plan of small health center

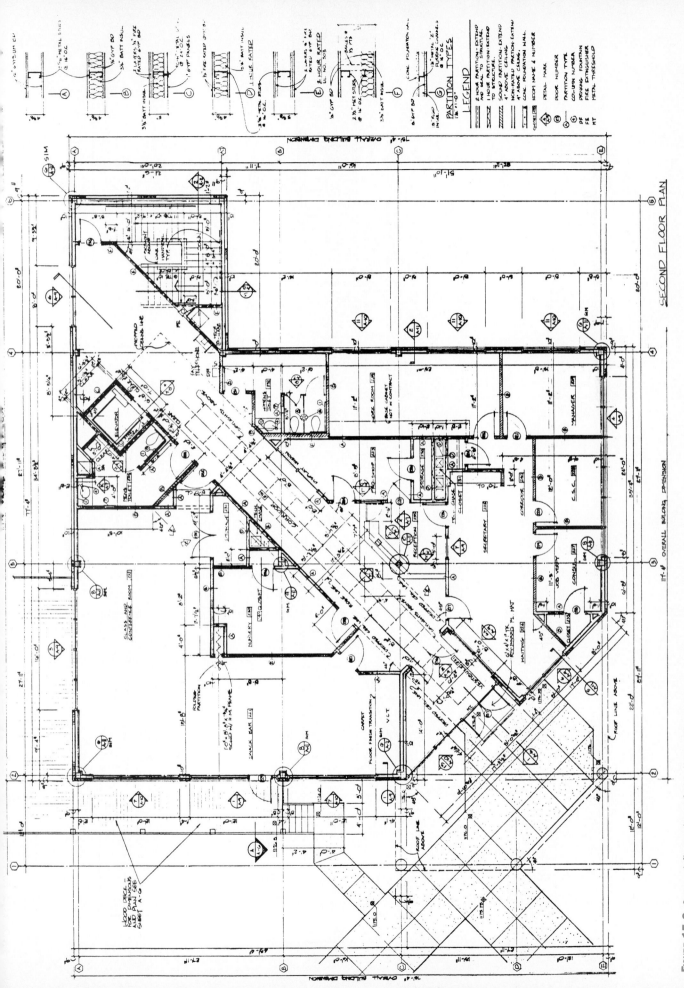

FIGURE 15-6 Second floor plan of small health center.

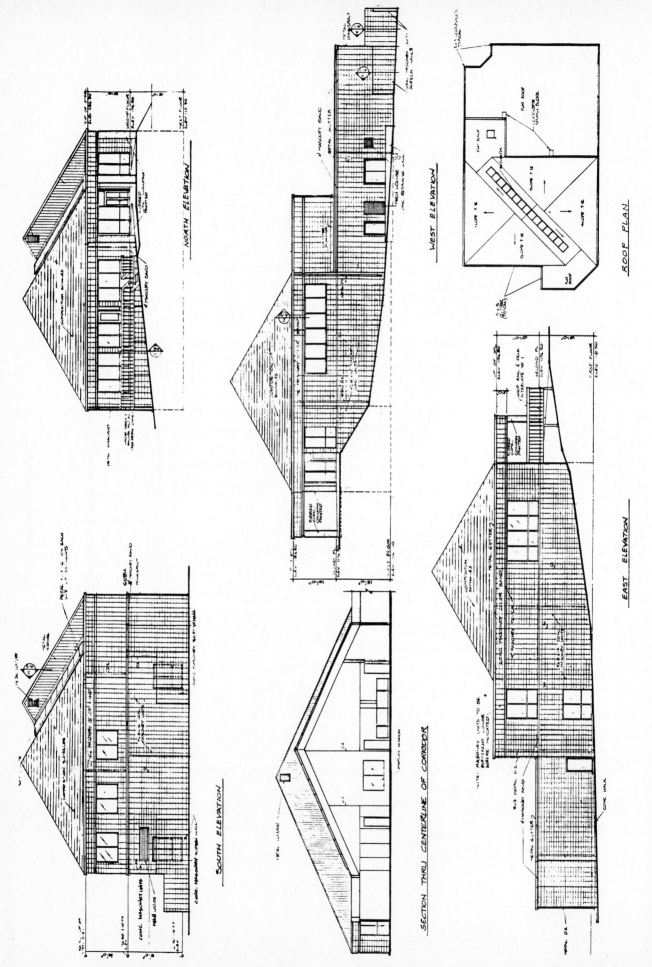

Figure 15-7 Elevations section and roof plan of small health center.

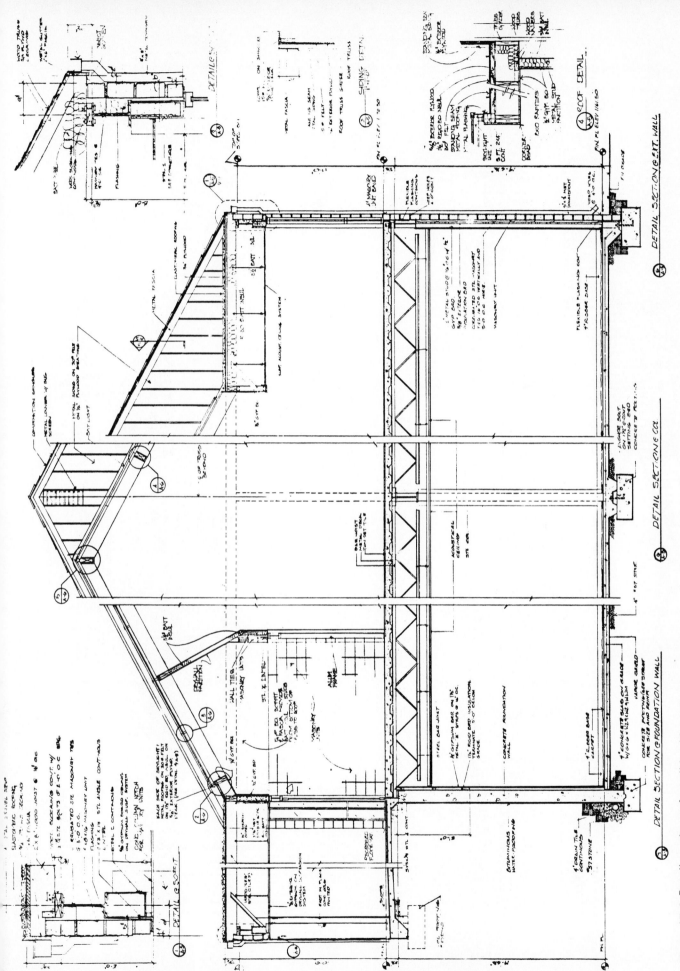

FIGURE 15-8 Detail sections of small health center.

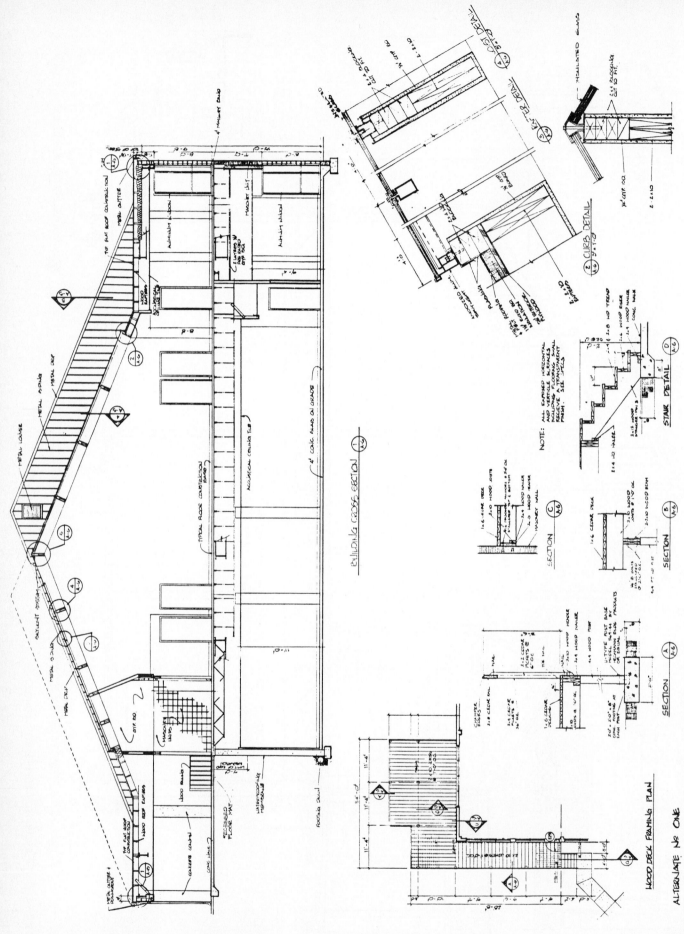

FIGURE 15-9 Building cross section of small health center.

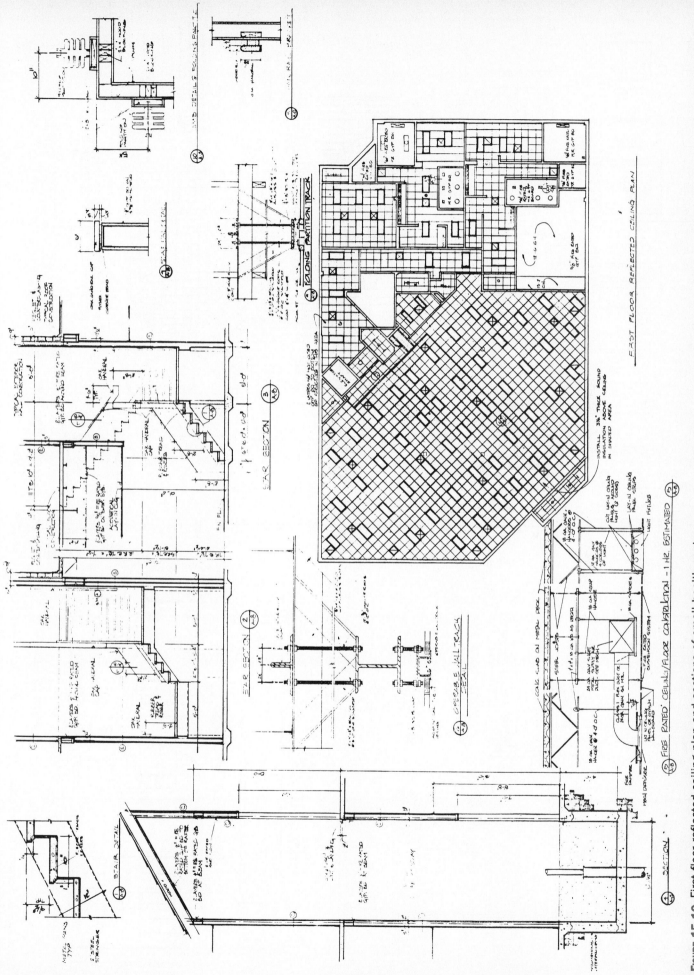

Figure 15-10 First floor reflected ceiling plan and sections of small health center.

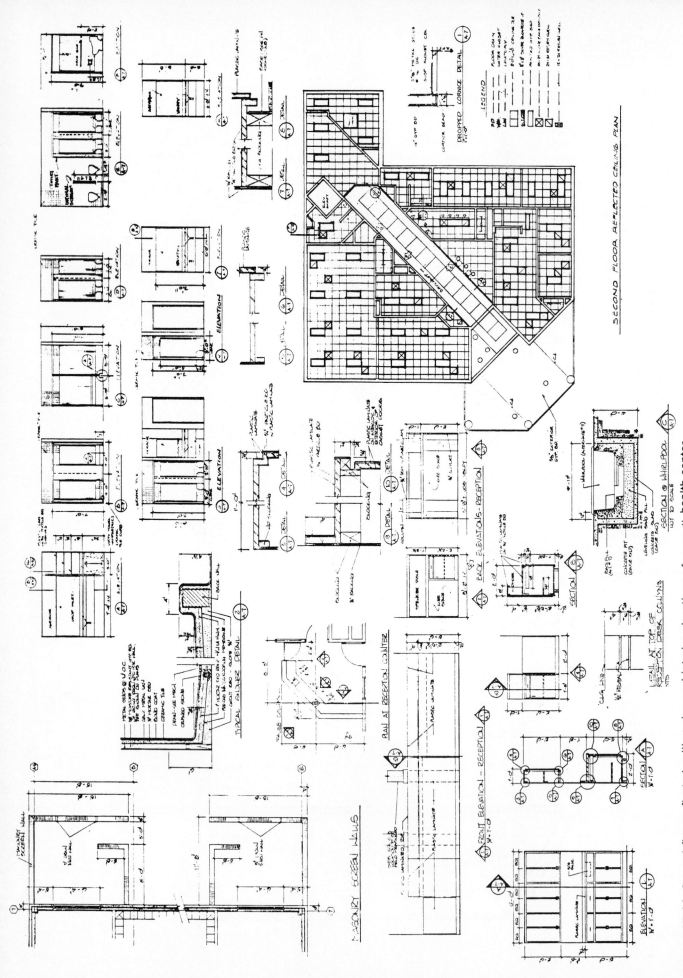

FIGURE 15-11 Second floor reflected ceiling plan and interior elevations of a small health center.

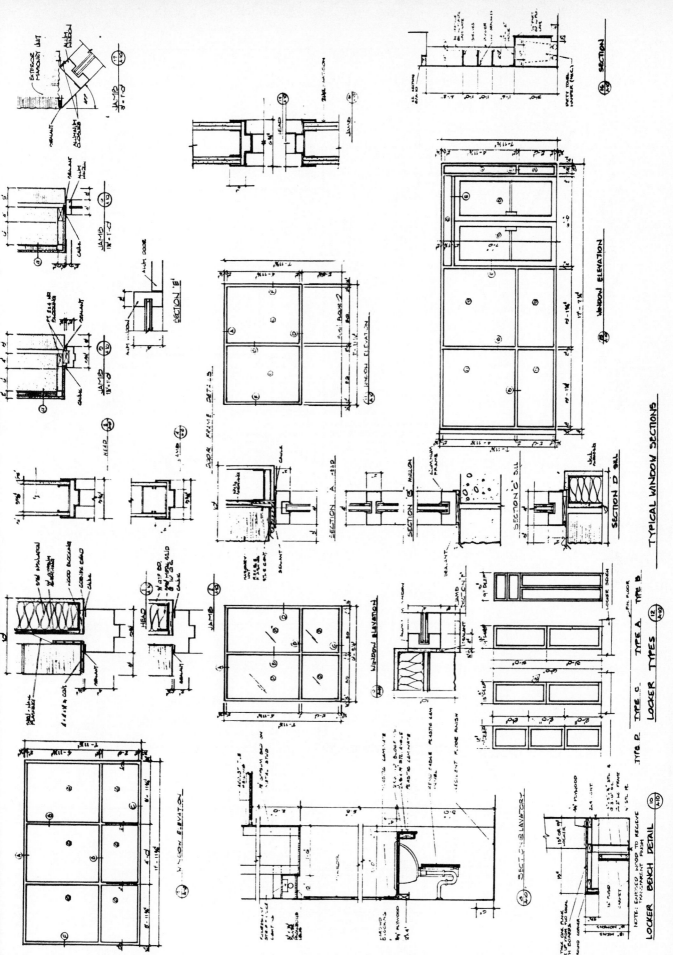

FIGURE 15-12 Window details of a small health center.

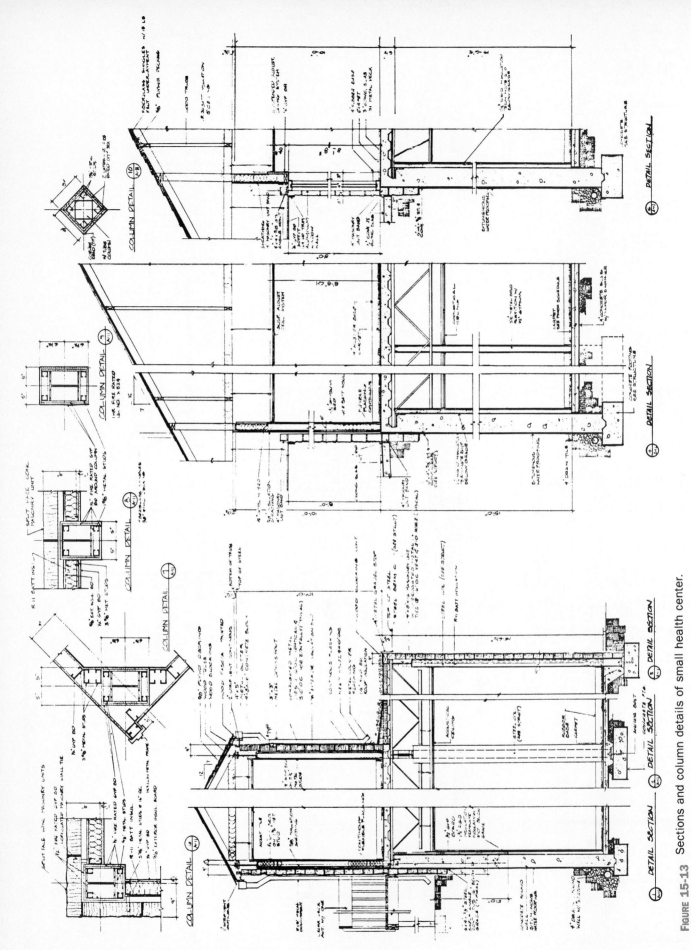

Figure 15-13 Sections and column details of small health center.

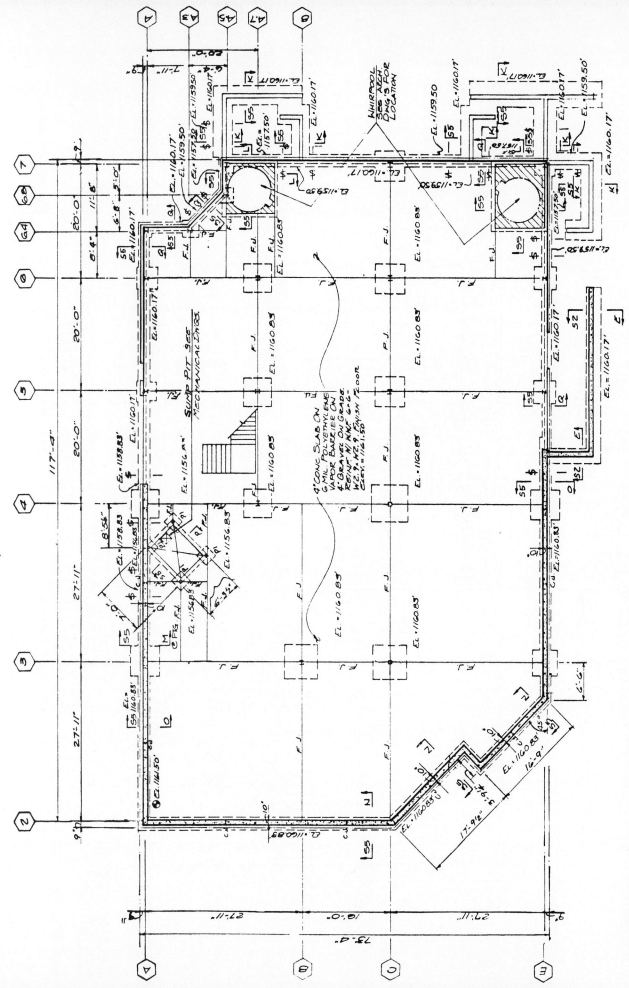

FIGURE 15-14 Foundation of a small health center.

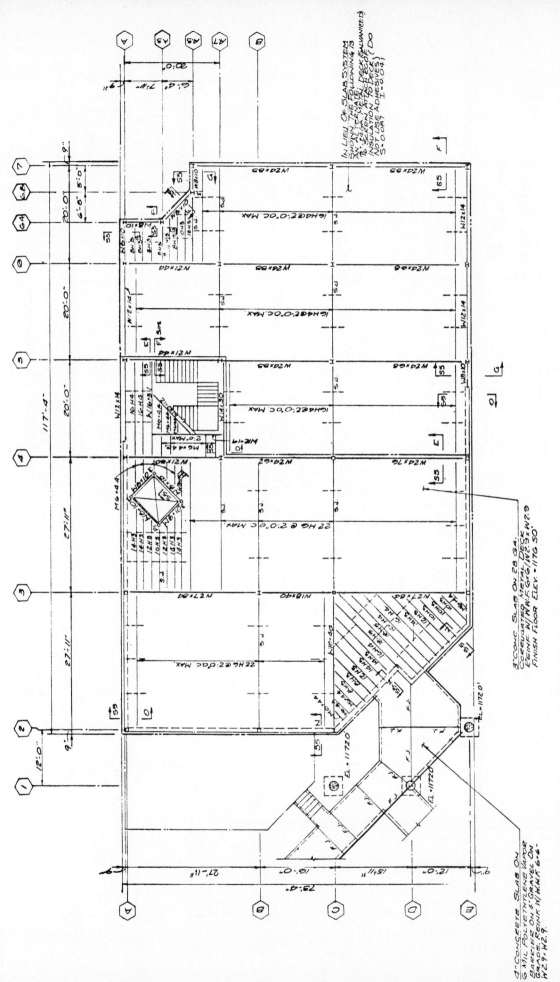

FIGURE 15-15 Structural second level and low roof framing plan of small health center.

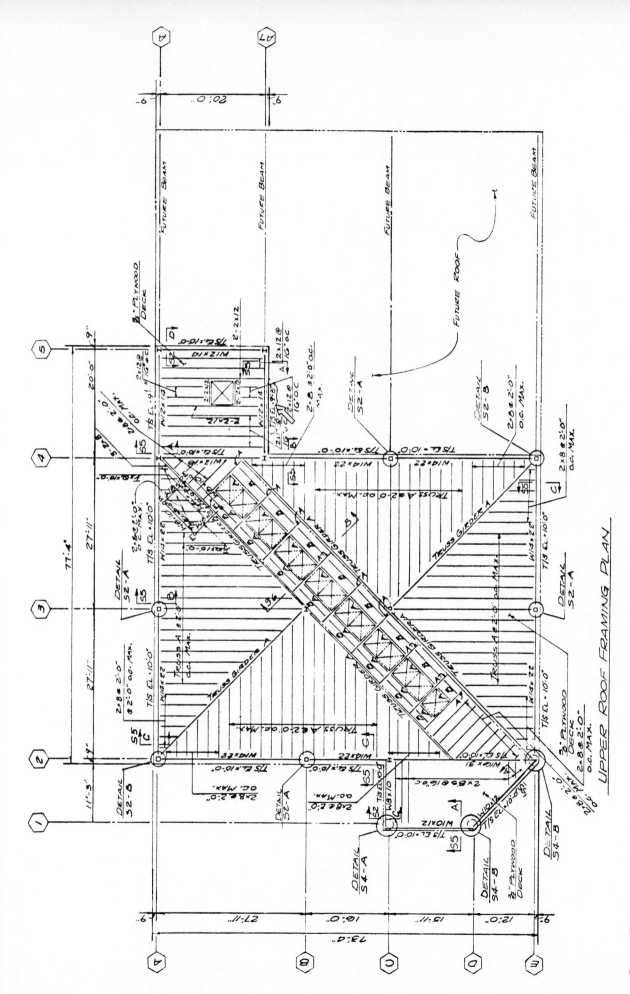

FIGURE 15-16 Structural upper roof framing plan of a small health center.

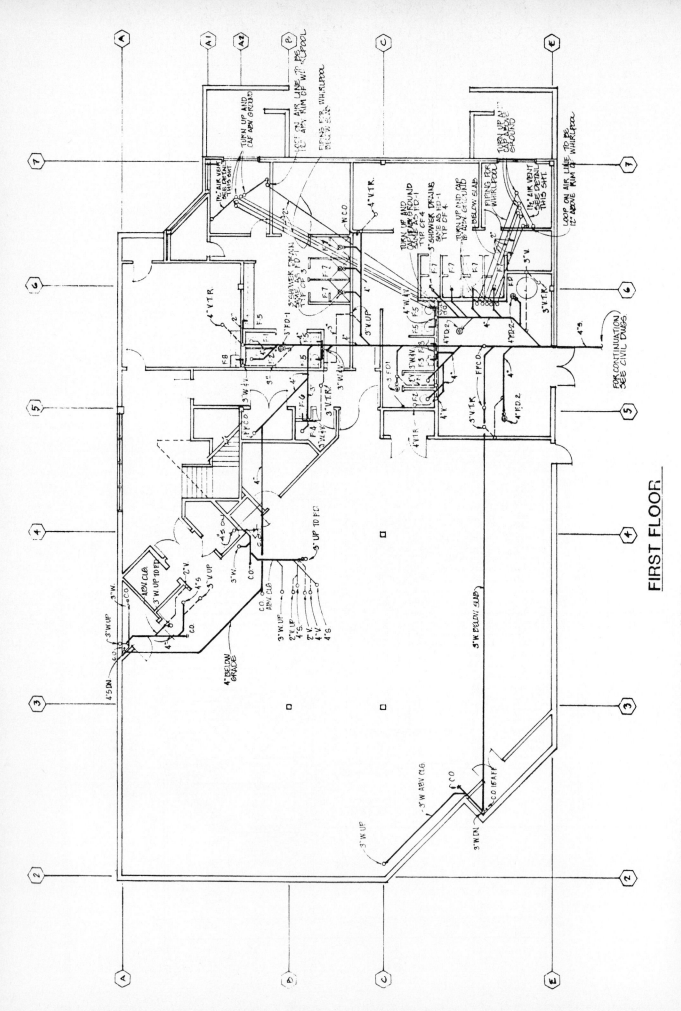

FIGURE 15-17 Plumbing first floor plan (sanitary drainage) of a small health center.

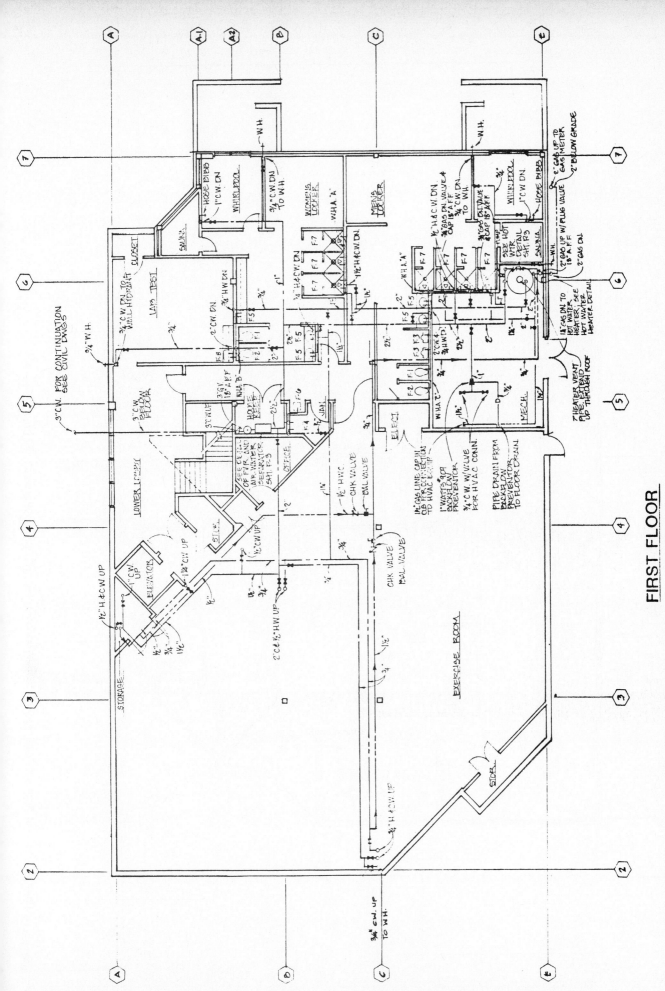

FIGURE 15-18 Plumbing first floor plan (hot and cold water supply) of a small health center.

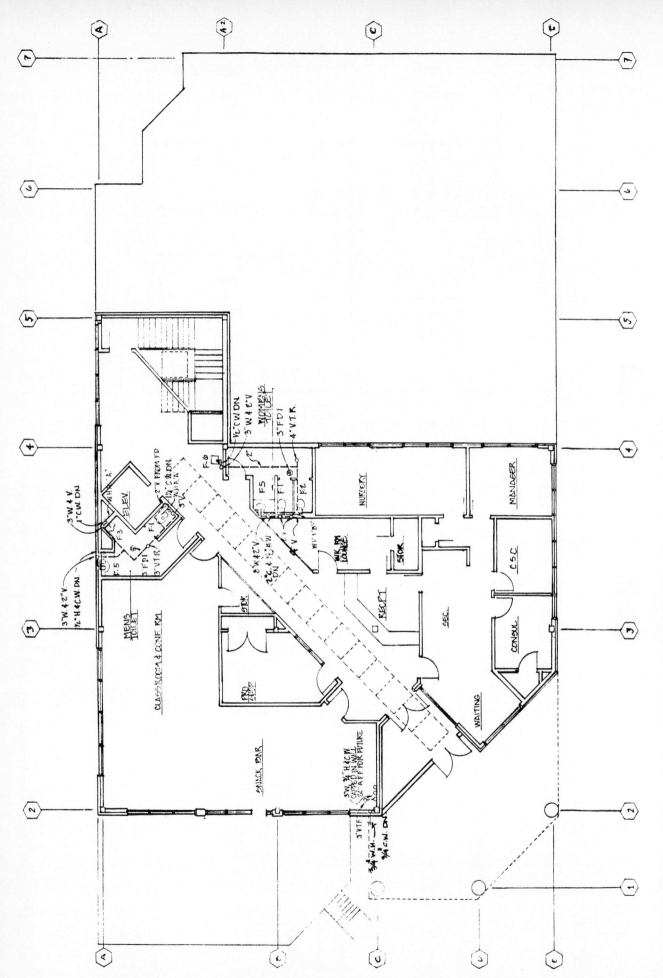

Figure 15-19 Plumbing second floor plan (sanitary drainage and water supply) of a small health center.

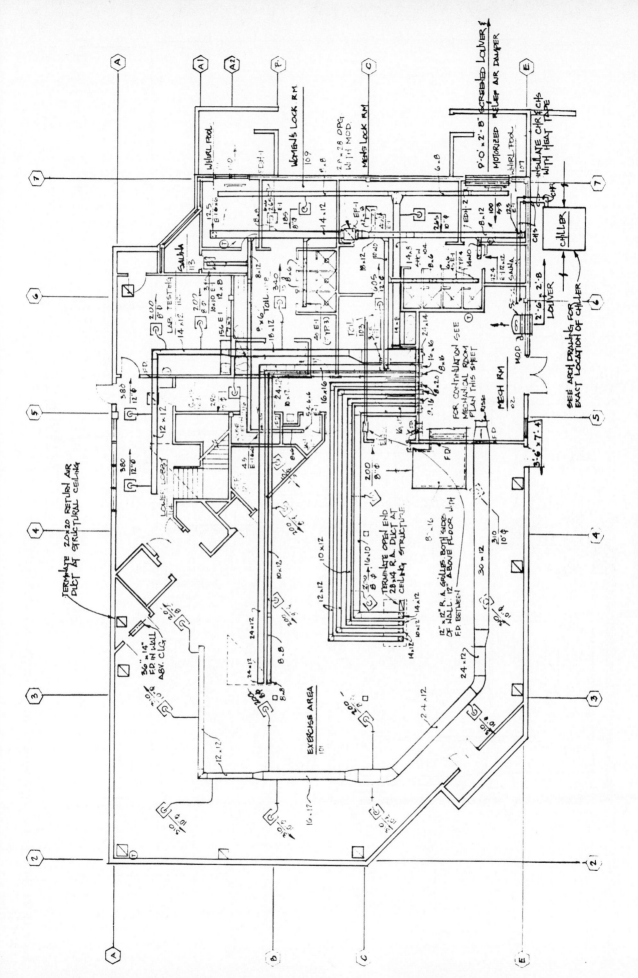

FIGURE **15-20** Heating, ventilation and air conditioning first floor plan of a small health center.

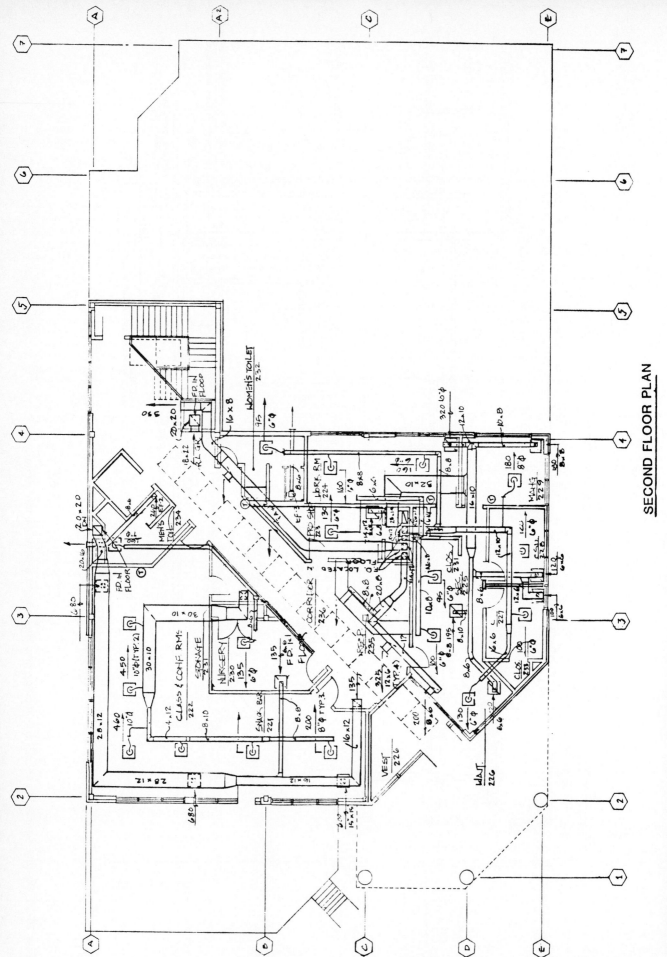

FIGURE 15-21 Heating, ventilation and air conditioning plan of a small health center.

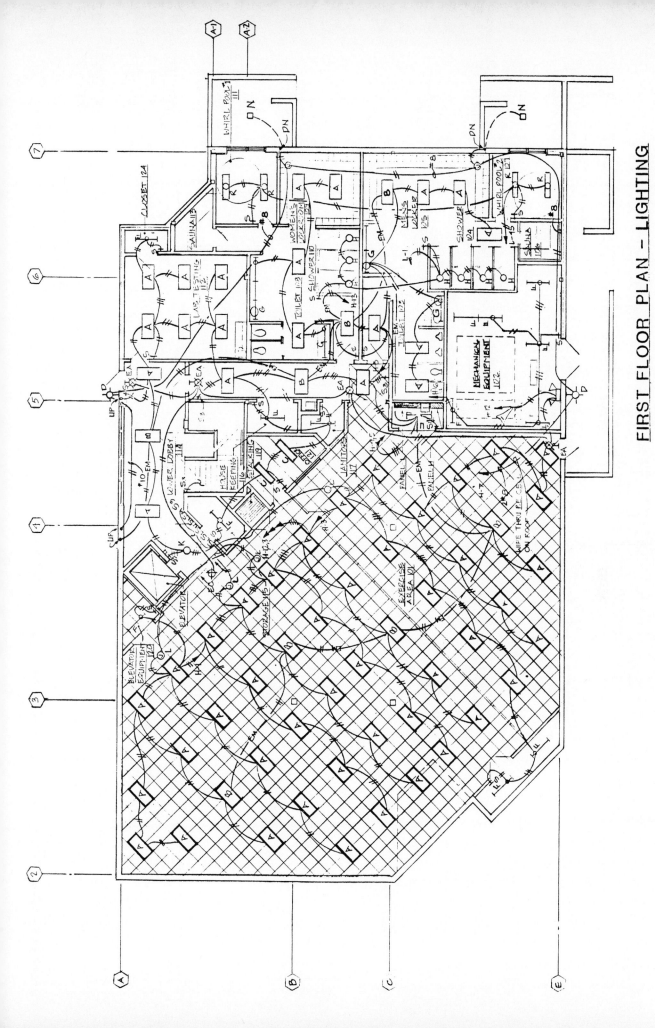

FIGURE 15-22 Electric first floor plan (lighting) of a small health center.

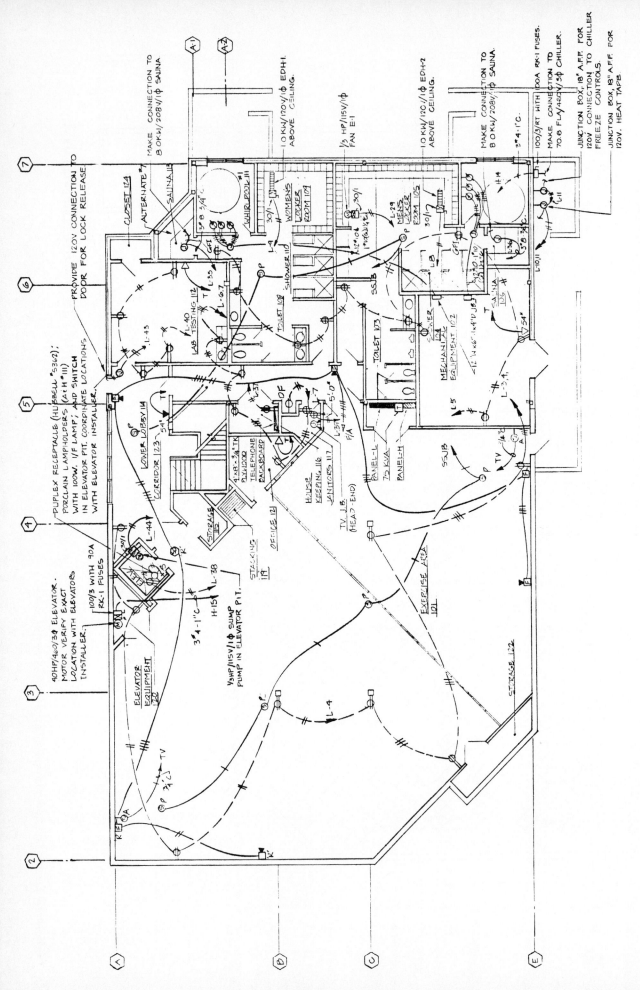

FIRST FLOOR PLAN–POWER & SYSTEMS

FIGURE 15-23 Electrical first floor plan (power and systems) of a small health center.

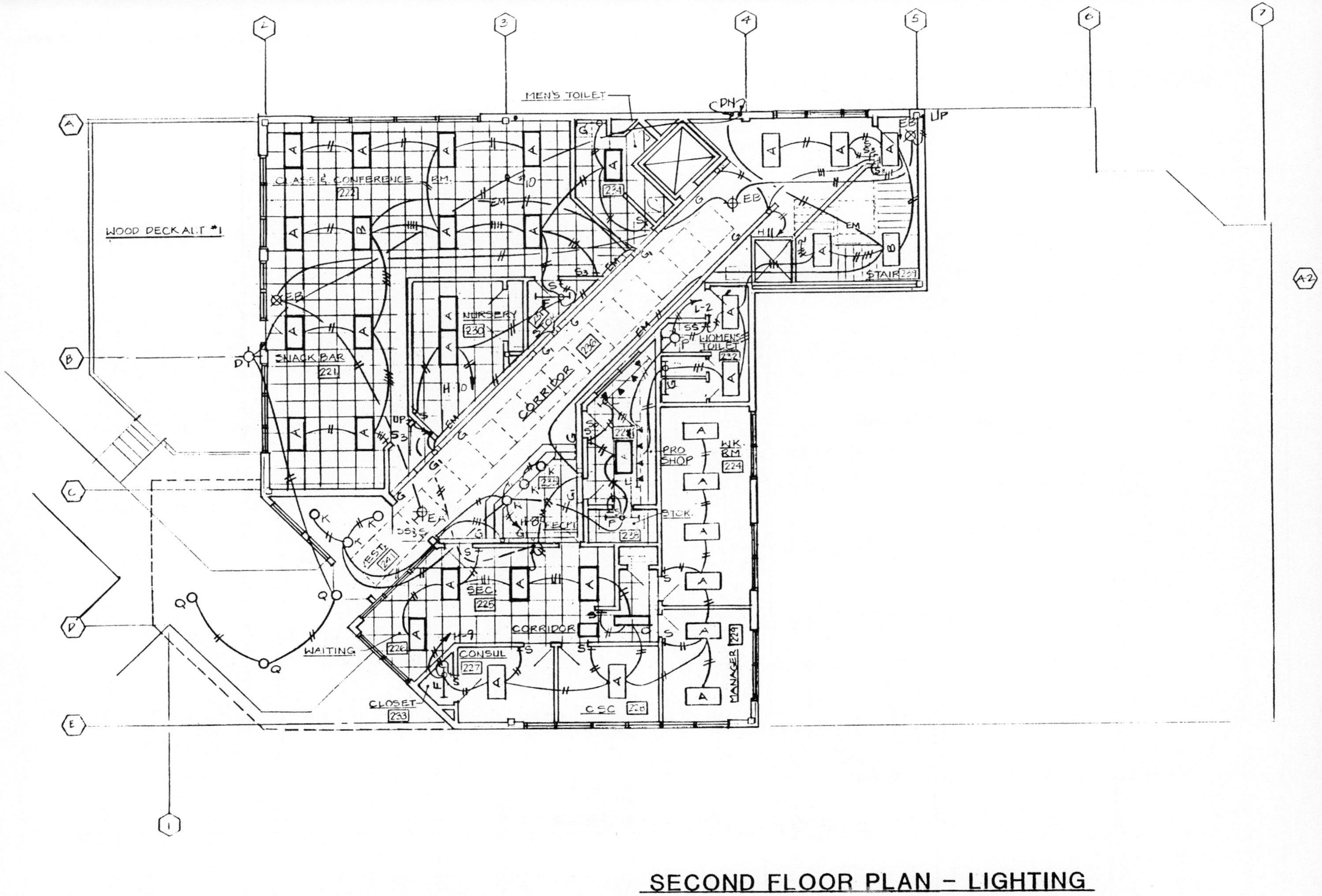

SECOND FLOOR PLAN – LIGHTING

FIGURE 15-24 Electrical second floor plan (lighting) of a small health center.

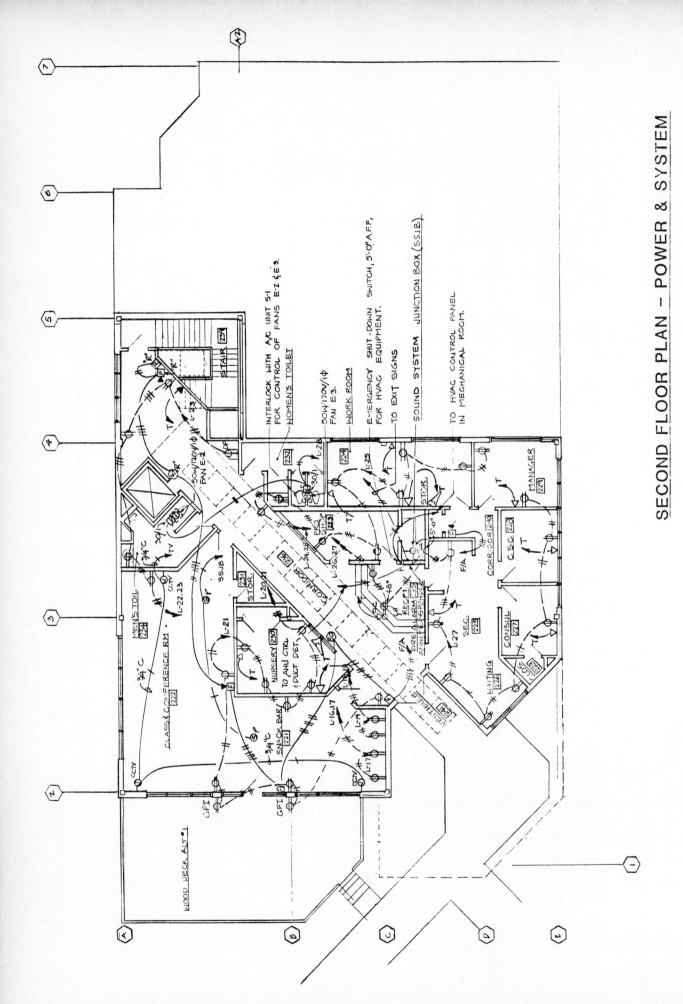

FIGURE 15-25 Electrical second floor plan (power and systems) of a small health center.

On the interior the raised ceiling was illuminated by skylights. In work spaces, suspended acoustical ceilings made room for H.V.A.C. duct and provided a grid for $2' \times 4'$ recessed light fixtures. Corridors and several other spaces were constructed with a 1-hour fire protection rating. A ramp to the front entrance, wide doors, elevator and toilet stalls were designed to make the building accessible to the physically handicapped.

To simplify the floor system, a slab on grade was used for the first floor. The second floor system has steel bar joists, metal decking and a concrete slab. Tile surfacing on the public lobby floor satisfied the demand for resistance to hard wear. The floor elevation was kept low eliminating the need for steps at the entrance; a ramp was provided for handicapped people. An optional wood deck was included on the plans as an alternate.

Reinforced concrete walls with waterproofing and foundation drains were placed below grade. Floor space was reserved for the mechanical equipment (heating and cooling). Notice that it was necessary to lower the ceiling in portions of the plan to accommodate the ductwork (see heating, ventilating, and air conditioning, Figs. 15-20 and 15-21). To reduce heating and cooling loads, double entrance doors were placed at the vestibule. Plumbing was kept near one end of the plan for additional economy.

Most of the interior gypsum board walls were left exposed and were painted or papered. Interior walls were arranged in such a way that construction was simple and neat. When laying out counters and other built-in cabinet work, sizes of standard furniture and fixtures had to be taken into consideration. The acoustical tile ceiling had to be suspended from the steel joists and wood trusses with a metal channel system, similar to systems currently popular in many commercial buildings.

15.1 Planning the Drawing Layout

Because of the size of the health center building, it became convenient to draw the floor plans to the $1/4'' = 1'-0''$ scale; larger buildings, naturally, may necessitate the use of the $1/8'' = 1'-0''$ scale, provided the corresponding size of tracing paper is used. Each plan view became suitable for placing on a single sheet. Four elevations a building section at $1/8'' = 1'-0''$ scale and a roof plan at $1/16'' = 1'-0''$ scale made the layout of the elevation sheet a simple procedure. The detail sheets required more careful planning. To show the many small members clearly, the soffit details were drawn to large scales and were therefore organized on a separate sheet. Various window and door details, requiring less space, were combined on another sheet.

15.2 Drawing the Plan

The first step in drawing a plan of this type is to lay out the exterior walls of the building. After the exact widths of the masonry veneer walls are determined, the outline of the plan is blocked in, and all partition walls are lightly drawn without regard for window and door openings. Then the door and window openings are located according to the scheme of the exterior and the traffic flow of the interior. Only construction lines are used up to this point. The walls are then darkened and refined, window and door symbols are drawn, and minor wall outlines are completed. Manufacturers' literature is consulted before drawing the doors and windows. Plumbing fixtures are drawn with the use of a template. In the public lobby area, the reception counter and other built-in cabinet work are located and drawn the correct size. Minor details are added throughout the plan. Exterior platform ramps and steps are drawn with the help of information from the site plan contour levels. Stair layouts are developed with the proper number of risers and treads between floors. Consult codes for acceptable riser heights and tread widths. Then door identification is shown, room titles are lettered, and all general call outs are added. Next, dimensions are inserted in positions where they do not interfere with linework. Notice that, along with important exterior dimensions placed around the periphery of the plan, a continuous line of dimensions is shown through the interior in each direction to locate all partitions accurately.

In some cases it is advisable to begin a project with a typical wall section rather than the plan. Much of the wall information must be known before the plan can be drawn.

15.3 Drawing the Elevations

Before starting the elevations, the sizes of the steel bar joists and wood roof trusses, both in the public reception ceiling and the lower surrounding ceilings on each floor, had to be designed, and with this information a typical wall section was drawn. In starting the elevations, the finish floor levels are drawn; then, after establishing the desired ceiling heights, the major horizontal lines are drawn from information taken from the preliminary section view. Lengths of the elevation view features, however, are projected directly from the plan, as in residential drawings. Windows, offsets, doors, and other features are drawn from preliminary sketches with the help of manufacturers' literature. Sizes of fixed-glass units are determined by their most pleasing proportions, which were developed on the sketches. It is necessary to space the battens on the metal siding by accurate measurement. Vertical center lines of the columns can be left on the plans to show their relative spacing. Where indicated, the trim members are completed, and the finish floor and roof level are added. To complete the drawing, the grade line, footings, stairs, ramps, railings, material symbols, notes, and titles are added as shown. For convenience in construction, the footing surfaces are labeled for their correct elevation below grade. To save time, portions of the symbols may be omitted.

15.4 Drawing the Full Sections

The longitudinal and transverse sections are drawn after all detail information has been completed on both the plan and elevations. These section views reveal all visible interior information on the cutting planes completely through the building. To conserve time, the longitudinal section is blocked in on the sheet placed directly over the left-side elevation drawing and the transverse section over the front elevation drawing. In both cases, the floor plan is oriented and attached to the board above the section view so that interior features can be easily projected. The center to center spacing of structural framing members is clearly evident on the building cross section, whereas the side view of the joists is visible on the detailed section. Dimensions of the doors and windows had to be verified for those views, and in completing the sections, it occasionally became necessary to duplicate information found on elevation views.

15.5 Drawing the Details

Although the drawing of details is a time-consuming part of the architectural routine, the drafter is required to draw all those necessary for each project. Details should be made consistent with each other, as well as with the general concept of the building. Major details have to be accurately drawn before portions of the plan or elevations can be completed; inaccuracies may result in costly building errors.

As stated previously, in drawing details, reference must continually be made to *Sweet's File* or manufacturers' catalogues for actual sizes and other information about pertinent materials. Measurements of masonry coursing must conform to the heights and widths of the individual units. Steel members are accurately scaled, and all wood members are drawn actual rather than nominal size. The relationship of members in details and especially the joining of different materials must be well thought out before the detail is drawn.

A detail may be typical in that it represents similar construction throughout the building, or it may be the construction of an individual feature; in either case, the title should correctly describe the application. Take, for example, the typical soffit detail. This detail shows the relationship of the roofing and the gutter and in turn shows the relationship of the gutter to the fascia and the fascia to the soffit. Note that the soffit contains a continuous vent that allows air to circulate through the attic space (see Fig. 15-8). Such details are essential since they describe a specific assembly of construction that is common at numerous locations throughout the building.

Various wall thicknesses throughout the building make it necessary to draw a number of doorframe details. In dimensioning detail drawings, important sizes are shown, and care must be taken to include dimensions that relate the detail to major dimensions shown on the plan or elevation. Titles and scale are shown on each detail drawing (scales have been deleted from the working drawings of the health center). Efficient organization of small details on a large sheet comes with drafting experience; neatness is the result of careful planning.

15.6 Integrating Drawings

Working drawings for most commercial buildings include drawings prepared by registered engineers. The engineering disciplines frequently involved in a commercial building project are civil, structural, mechanical, and electrical. It is important to coordinate the drawings prepared by the engineers with the architectural drawings. The engineers should be consulted during the development of the schematic drawings so that provisions for engineering concerns can be addressed at an early stage. The following sections of this chapter highlight activities performed by the various engineers and stress the importance of integrating engineering drawings with the architectural drawings.

15.7 Civil Drawings

The civil engineer usually prepares the property line survey and topographic map, gathers soil data, and locates existing utilities on a drawing before preliminary studies begin. In many instances the civil engineer is engaged to draw the site plan showing the building location, roads, pavements, utilities, topography, and site drainage. It is important that the building plan fit the site, complement the topography, and accommodate utility connections (see Fig. 15-4).

15.8 Structural Drawings

The foundation, floor and roof framing plans are developed by the structural engineer. Data concerning the soil conditions are important to the structural engineer for sizing the footings and to determine the proper foundation system for the building. The structural engineer gives valuable guidance to the designer regarding the location of columns, beams, bearing walls, and roof framing systems. The civil engineer, the designer, and the structural engineer must meet frequently to exchange information concerning the structural integrity of the building (see Figs. 15-14 through 15-16).

15.9 Mechanical Drawings

Plumbing and H.V.A.C. drawings are prepared by the mechanical engineer. Plumbing plans show plumbing fixtures, hot- and cold-water supply pipe, and sanitary drainage pipe (see Fig. 15-17 through 15-19). Existing utility information gathered by the civil engineer and the type, number, and location of plumbing fixtures determined by the designer are important to the mechanical engineer.

The mechanical engineer is frequently asked to prepare an analysis of the space conditioning needs for the building. Numerous types of heating and cooling systems are available. It is imperative that the proper type of system be selected. The designer, structural engineer, and mechanical engineer must carefully integrate the H.V.A.C. system into the design of the building (see Figs. 15-20 and 15-21). Adequate space for the mechanical equipment and sufficient structural supports for the system are essential.

Some buildings are required to have fire protection systems. The mechanical engineer usually develops a sprinkler system plan for fire protection for such buildings.

15.10 Electrical Drawings

The electrical engineer prepares the lighting plan and the power wiring plan for commercial buildings (see Figs. 15-22 through 15-25). In addition to the basic electrical plans, the electrical engineer is usually responsible for developing communications plans, which consist of telephone, intercom, fire detection, and alarm systems. Even some small buildings have massive amounts of electronic equipment. The designer and the electrical engineer must stay abreast of the users' needs and carefully coordinate the location of all the electrical features of the building.

15.11 Drawing the Reflected Ceiling Plan

Ceilings in many commercial buildings are quite complex. It is desirable to draw a reflected ceiling plan that shows the ceiling surface including the suspended ceiling grid system, lighting fixtures, H.V.A.C. diffusers, fire protection equipment (smoke detectors, sprinkler heads, and alarm devices), exit signs, sound and communications speakers, security equipment, walls, columns, skylights and openings in the ceiling (see Figs. 15-10 and 15-11). The reflected ceiling plan is drawn after the architectural, structural, mechanical and electrical plans are complete. Trace the floor plan walls. Do not show door or window openings. Lay the tracing over the mechanical and electrical plans and draw the equipment which is located on the ceiling.

15.12 Drawing the Roof Plan

Roofs on most commercial buildings vary in shape, height and materials. Using the floor plan and the structural roof framing plan, draw the outline of the roof edge. Draw ridges, valleys, stair towers, elevator penthouses, skylights and all other roof penetrations. Using mechanical plans as a reference locate and draw H.V.A.C. units, exhaust fans, plumbing vents, roof drains and the like on the roof plan. Arrows are used to indicate the direction of water flow on the roof surface. Like the reflected ceiling plan the roof plan is not drawn until the architectural, structural, mechanical and electrical plans are complete (see Fig. 15-7).

EXERCISES

Exercises in planning and drawing commercial buildings are best undertaken under the supervision of your instructor, who can check them occasionally and offer helpful criticism during their development. Start all exercises with sketches.

1. WAYSIDE REST STATION. Design and prepare the working drawings for a small restroom facility to be

located on a level, 1-acre lot along a federal highway. Provide for the following facilities:

a. Parking for 10 cars, one to be handicapped accessible
b. Parking for 3 semitrailer trucks
c. Rest rooms for men and women handicapped accessible
d. Trash receptacles
e. Water fountains
f. Two picnic tables and benches

Draw the plan, elevations, site plan, and necessary details.

2. SUBURBAN HARDWARE STORE. Design and make the working drawings for a small hardware store on a commercial lot 170′ wide and 290′ deep. Use C.M.U. bearing wall construction with a concrete slab on ground floor and a steel joist roof structure. Provide for the following facilities:

a. Floor area of 8000 square feet
b. Display windows across front
c. Storage space in rear with unloading doors
d. Private office, bookkeeping & lounge of 1000 square feet on the second floor above storage.
e. Rest rooms
f. Checkout counter and merchandise counters and racks
g. Parking spaces

3. SMALL CHAPEL. Design and draw the working drawings for a small chapel, 6,000 square feet, intended for people of all faiths. Use wood bearing walls and trusses. The lot is 5 acres. Provide for the following facilities:

a. The sanctuary to seat 250 people
b. Two private offices of 175 square feet each
c. Choir loft to seat 20 people
d. Rest rooms for men and women
e. Kitchen
f. Nursery
g. Three classrooms
h. Provision for mechanical equipment and janitorial care
i. Parking space for 70 cars

4. RETAIL SALES BUILDING. Design and draw the working drawings for a laundry and retail sales building 65′-0″ wide by 70′-0″ deep. The lot is 130′ wide by 200′ deep, and it slopes to the front. Use C.M.U. and brick veneer load-bearing construction with open web roof joists. Provide the following facilities:

a. Laundry 1300 square feet
b. Retail sales 2700 square feet
c. Canopy across front of bldg.
d. Toilets

e. Mechanical equipment room
f. Drive-up laundry pick-up
g. Parking for 23 cars

5. LIBRARY BUILDING. Prepare the working drawings for a suburban library building with two floor levels consisting of a ground floor and a mezzanine. Use C.M.U. and brick veneer walls. The floor is to be poured concrete and the roof is to be open web joist. The basic width is to be 54′-0″ and the length 91′-0″. The first floor to floor height is to be 11′-4″, and second floor to roof height is to be 12′-8″. Put columns on approximate 18′-0″ centers; use one elevator, two separate stairwells, toilets, and storage. Reserve space for air-conditioning equipment. Reserve the first floor level for an entry, checkout, conference, receiving, periodicals, reference area and audio-visuals. On the mezzanine level provide book stacks of various sizes with convenient circulation arrangements around the perimeter of the building.

Draw the following views, using the scale ¼″ = 1′-0″.

a. Two floor plans, first floor, and second floor (mezzanine) square feet
b. Two elevations
c. Site plan (convenient scale)
d. Transverse section

REVIEW QUESTIONS

1. Why must codes dealing with public buildings be carefully regulated?

2. List three general structural systems commonly used in commercial buildings.

3. Why are reflected ceiling plans commonly drawn for commercial buildings?

4. Why are enclosed vestibules often used in public entrances?

5. When laying out plan views of buildings with multiple floor levels, why is it important for the drafter to reserve suitable space for vertical plumbing and mechanical chases?

6. What detail is commonly drawn before starting the plans and elevations?

7. What factors must be considered in deciding on the spacing of modular columns in the planning of a commercial building?

8. In dimensioning, how are features in detail views made to relate to major features on plan and elevation views?

9. Why must masonry coursing sizes be accurately drawn on details?

10. What types of professional services are usually engaged by architectural firms to complete their sets of working drawings for commercial buildings?

BUILDING MODELS

"This modest charm of not too much, part seen, imagined part."

—*WORDSWORTH*

16

There are some who may contend that model building does not belong in a book on drawing—that the construction of a model house, for instance, like the building of model airplanes, is mainly for those who enjoy tinkering with miniature things. (Model building is one of the more pleasant aspects of architecture and it has become an important creative expression for professionals as well as students.) Many architects rely on three-dimensional models for final evaluations of their designs and sometimes reserve work space in their offices exclusively for this interesting phase of their activity. When the scope of a project justifies it, some offices engage the services of professional model builders to construct impressive and realistic models. If promotional methods have to be relied on to raise funds for a specific building project, executive boards or organization planning groups will find a model most advantageous. Lending institutions also will usually approve loans more readily when shown an impressive model of the projected structure.

Landscape architects find that models are the most expedient method for site planning and landscaping. City planners, plant layout experts, and safety engineers all make invaluable use of models.

To the layperson a model is usually the most honest means of visualizing all aspects of a building, including proportion and relationship of features, appearance of tentative materials, and its other three-dimensional qualities. Often the designer catches a feature on the model that may have been overlooked on the working drawings. The model, then, is visual proof that the spatial concepts of a design are workable and pleasing. Generally, the drafter is called on to construct a model after preliminary plans are drawn or occasionally after the final working drawings have been completed. Many architects rely on the professional model builders to construct elaborate models of the proposed project. Such models are expertly detailed and are frequently used as advertising tools by the client.

For the student, models are unquestionable learning instruments. In teaching architectural drawing, the authors have found model building to be one of the most convincing methods of helping students to determine, for example, the correct choice of details to be included in their final drawings or to discover why the choice of a roof slope was not complementary to the building. No other means, except perhaps working on an actual construction job, offers the student such an effective way of relating all the views of a drawing into a total building concept. Besides, the model has the advantage of small scale, which can be related to the drawing because of its similarity in size, and it allows the project to be viewed in its entirety.

16.1 Types of Models

Depending on their purpose, several types of models can be constructed.

Architectural Models (Figs. 16-1 and 16-2) Intended primarily to show the exterior appearance of the design only, this type of model is usually constructed of heavy illustration board, thin balsa wood panels, or, if need be, of hardboard, $1/8''$ thick, with surface textures applied directly to the board and scaled $1/4'' = 1'-0''$ ($1/8'' = 1'-0''$ for larger buildings). It is constructed directly from the drawings; and the elevations, roofs, walks, drives, landings, and so on, are cut out with a sharp model builder's knife and attached to the base (see Fig. 16-9). Contours are usually built up with layers of economical chip board; their edges are left to appear

FIGURE 16-1 Architectural model showing a building complex and built-up contour levels.

FIGURE 16-2 Student architectural model constructed of balsa wood and bass wood on a plywood base.

A

B

Figure 16-3 (A) Model of a contemporary residence; (B) photograph of the residence after construction.

very much like contour lines on a site plan (see Fig. 16-1). All exterior surfaces are neatly painted to represent the given materials; contours are made to look like grass or ground cover (see Fig 16-3A). Trees and shrubs of the same scale are carefully glued in place. In addition, many commercially printed papers are available that simulate various material textures. On smaller-scale city planning models, neatly painted solid wooden blocks may be used to show building masses.

Structural Models (Fig. 16-4)   For school projects or models requiring a visual analysis of their structural systems, larger-scale models (usually $1/2'' = 1'\text{-}0''$ or $3/4'' = 1'\text{-}0''$) are built to correspond exactly to the construction of the actual building. Framing members of either balsa, fir, or soft pine are cut to scale and assembled to represent the building's actual framing system. When assembling, quick-drying model builder's cement is used instead of nails or other fasteners. Considerable

A

B

FIGURE 16-4 Model of a contemporary residence showing structural framing.

amounts of the exterior surfacings, especially rear elevations, are omitted to allow full view of the structure as well as of the interior room arrangements. The termination of the wall and the roof are made to show the layers of materials within the actual construction. Usually, front elevations are completed in detail to reveal the important esthetic qualities of the design. Models of residences often include major interior cabinet work, plumbing fixtures, and even appliances or furniture. Leaving some areas open by omitting part of the roofing allows complete observation of these features. This type of model is the most rewarding for the student, since it requires solutions to structural problems that are not always evident on the drawings and that nev-

FIGURE 16-5 A model showing realistic building materials.

ertheless must be considered when the final drawings are done.

The qualities necessary for a successful model builder are patience, care in attention to detail, and the ability to track down simple, everyday items that will faithfully represent building materials at the small scale (see Fig. 16-5). Some items, such as sponges for shrubbery and small plastic figures and autos, are inexpensive; others, such as sandpaper, pins, bird gravel, and pieces of burlap or felt material, are common household items.

16.2 Model-Building Tools

The following list indicates the basic equipment needed for model building:

1. Model builder's knife (Stanley, Exacto)
2. Small framing square
3. Architect's scale
4. Metal straightedge
5. Tweezers
6. Small hammer
7. Handsaw
8. Several small paint brushes
9. Shears
10. Sandpaper and masking tape
11. Sturdy table
12. Hot glue gun

Although a minimum number of tools is generally required, supplementing these with other small hand tools facilitates working with diverse materials. If available, more elaborate tools can save time and produce more professional work. In constructing structural models, a miter box can be useful. Power shop tools can be very helpful, especially a power table saw for cutting structural lumber to scale, as we will discuss later; a power sander is also very useful.

16.3 Constructing Architectural Models

Working drawings, either preliminary or final, are necessary to construct a model, regardless of type. Dimensions must be taken from the drawings or prints of the drawings, and reference must be continually made to them throughout the model construction.

Start with a substantial base, either $1/2''$ or $3/4''$ plywood, upon which the model is to be attached. Use $1/4''$ thick plywood or hardboard, if the model will be rather small, and size the base to allow for sufficient landscaping without making it unwieldy. Cut the walls from heavy illustration board or balsa wood sheets of a thickness proportionate to the scaled-wall thickness. Work from the elevation views of your drawing and cut window and door openings to scale; allow for corner joints, either lapped or mitered. Avoid exposing the end grain of wood any more than necessary. If raised contours are to be applied to the base, allow for the height of the grade line above the base when cutting the wall pieces. It is best to glue the walls directly to the wood base, using triangles to keep them plumb. Occasionally, gluing small wooden blocks to the inside may be necessary to ensure a sturdy attachment to the base. If a detachable roof is planned, cut out partitions of a similar material and glue in place after exterior walls are finished and after the floor level has been constructed. The floor panel may have to be supported with blocking below. All work to be done on the interior should be completed before the roof is constructed.

Before gluing the exterior wall panels in place, apply the basic material texture to them. This is easier when the panels can be laid flat on the table.

Natural Wood finishes can be represented with balsa, placed with the wood grain in the proper direction, stained with a suitable color, and wiped with a cloth. Avoid getting glue on a wood surface that is to be stained; the stain will not penetrate evenly. Batten strips, for example, should be glued in place *after* the board surfaces have been stained. Uniform grooves to represent paneling are easily scored in the soft balsa with a stylus or empty ball-point pen.

Brickwork is simulated by painting the walls with a subtle variation of the basic brick color, usually earth colors, and occasional mortar joints drawn with white linework. Use white ink in a ruling pen.

Stonework can be represented in a similar manner. Paint subtle variations of the basic stone color—grays or dark ochres—with light-color mortar joints applied according to the desired stonework patterns, or actual small stones can be used (Fig. 16-6). Be sure to keep the textures in the same scale as the model.

Stucco and E.I.F.S. (Exterior Insulation Finish Systems) are shown by mixing sand and paint and applying this mixture as a final coat.

For the most part, use the subdued, opaque paints for model finishing. Tempera, acrylic, or casein colors are handy for color mixing, and latex-base wall paints are suitable for covering large areas. Avoid enamels and glossy paints, which are unsatisfactory because of light reflections. Because of its quick-drying qualities, lacquer is frequently used by professional model builders when spray painting is applicable.

After the walls have been fastened in place, the next step is the roof. Select a rigid material for roof panels to prevent warping. Work from a roof plan if necessary to ensure neat-fitting pieces; on complex roofs, such as hip roofs with offsets, it will be found simplest to project exact shapes carefully from roof drawings and lay them out on the material with drawing instruments before cutting. Use a sharp knife for clean, straight edges. Sloping roofs usually need several wood bracing members below, particularly on detachable roofs, if they are to remain rigid. Chimneys piercing the roof may be cut from wood blocks and merely glued to the roof.

To represent a built-up type of roofing, apply coarse sandpaper to the roof with contact cement applied to both surfaces. Asphalt-type shingles may be represented with strips of construction paper or fine sandpaper, cut to appear as strip shingles and painted the desired color if necessary.

Next, work on the construction of grade levels or site contours. If the model requires no contouring and is to be shown on a perfectly flat site, the base can be painted dark green and covered with flock (tinted fibers that adhere to the wet paint, giving the surface a velvety appearance), or it can be covered with model builder's

FIGURE 16-6 Student architectural model made with molding plaster.

simulated grass (sawdust dyed green). Use a thick, oil-base paint to hold the grass material securely. If suitable, apply a stippled surface of texture paint and finish it with green color.

Raised contours, if needed, are cut from heavy chip board and glued over each other to the correct heights. This stepped surface looks best if painted a dull green; walks, drives, and the like, are cut from separate pieces, painted, and glued over the contoured surface. The easiest way to make steep lot surfaces is to build them over wire screen or hardware cloth that has been blocked up to the correct height from below and covered with a layer of molding plaster or papier-mâché. After it has cured, paint and apply grass material as mentioned above (see Fig. 16-7).

Exterior details, such as window and door trim and cornice moldings, are applied after the contour levels are fixed. Cut the trim members from thin balsa sheets using the metal straightedge and sharp knife. Small dowels, toothpicks, and model builder's pieces may also be found appropriate. Paint the trim (usually white) before gluing it in place. This eliminates unsightly smearing and the running of paint on adjacent colors. Masking tape may be necessary in some situations. Cut doors from thicker balsa and add their trim details before gluing them in position; they can be left partially open rather than closed. Thin plastic may be fastened to the interior of window openings to represent glass, although windows are nearly as effective without it if the window trim has been carefully applied. On large glassed areas, muntin strips are usually glued directly to the plastic.

Complete the landscaping as the last step. Show fences, walls, terraces, swimming pools, and other outdoor features that will enhance the model. Water surfaces look realistic if represented with ripple window glass embedded in the surfacing material. Paint the area under the glass a light blue. For foundation planting, tear pieces of sponge (natural or synthetic) into various shrubbery shapes, dye them several shades of green, and glue them in natural appearing groups near the model corners and entrances. Green lichen is also available at model supply stores for this purpose and is similarly secured with glue. To simulate trees, take actual twigs or small branches having the proper scale and formation and glue pieces of the sponge or lichen throughout the small branches to shape the trees' foliage. Then drill a hole in the base and insert the tree trunk with glue.

Dress the edge of the base panel with suitable stock molding or trim; miter the molding neatly at the corners to give it a finished appearance. Incidental objects such as autos, people, furniture, and bath fixtures, if necessary to further elaborate the model, may be found generally at hobby shops or craft stores. Be sure they are the right scale. These items can also be carved from white or colored soap. However, avoid superfluous

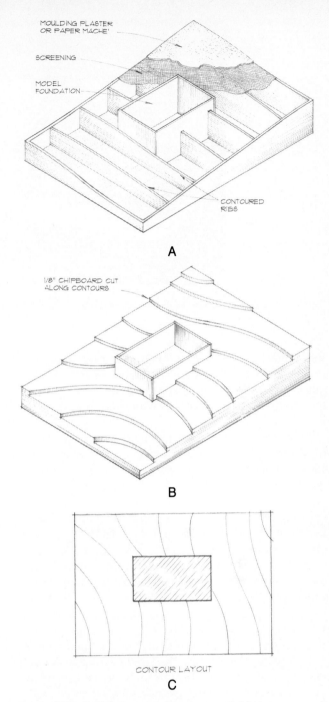

FIGURE 16-7 Building up contours on model bases.

items, which only clutter the model and detract from the architecture instead of supplementing it.

Many architectural offices use *chip board* or *foam core board* for the majority of their models. Chip board is a gray, economical paper board, about $1/16''$ to $3/32''$ thick, available at most drafting supply stores. All cuts are neatly made with a sharp knife, and pieces are glued together and held in place with straight pins, drafting tape, or rubber bands until the glue has set. The board has good stability, takes tempera, acrylic, or latex paint

FIGURE 16-8 Student architectural model made with chip board.

well, and does not seem to be greatly affected by humidity changes. Clean-cut appearing models can be quickly made with this versatile model material (see Fig. 16-8). Foam core board is white or gray and $1/16''$ to $1/14''$ thick.

In architectural planning, whether in an architectural office or for student projects, mass models are sometimes used to study space relationships, proportion, and general appearance of contemplated buildings. Only the general forms are needed. These can be cut from balsa blocks or Styrofoam and painted with a flat white latex to produce very effective planning models. Cut either of the materials with a sharpened putty knife or a slightly serrated bread knife after the scaled volumes have been laid out with pencil. Use a sturdy plywood base and glue the blocks directly to the base before paint is applied to ensure good adhesion. If thin sheets are needed in the model, use chip board or illustration board, carefully cut with the model knife.

For quick, less-definite mass models, use modeling clay pressed into the forms needed, or even soap bars cut into accurate shapes may be satisfactory.

Another material that should be investigated by the model builder is basswood. The wood possesses a fine, uniform grain and can be cut, glued, finished, and painted similar to other model materials. Textured basswood sheets representing many of the traditional architectural surfaces are available from many model supply stores and hobby centers. Polystyrene sheets, available from similar sources, are also used in model building. This clear, colorless plastic material can be scribed, tooled, sawed, scored, and textured, and bonds quickly with the model cements mentioned in the next section. Other preformed plastic features such as windows, doors, people, and autos are available in several scales from dealers, but generally those that are

custom made give the model a more professional appearance.

16.4 Constructing Structural Models

To build a model as a true miniature of the tentative building requires a working knowledge of the various framing systems (Chapter 7). Because of the many small pieces involved in a structural model, scales must necessarily be larger ($1/2'' = 1'\text{-}0''$ or $3/4'' = 1'\text{-}0''$) than architectural models, which are meant to show mainly exterior appearances. Small buildings such as residences, then, become the most practical projects when using these larger scales.

Structural models provide varied learning situations for students and lend themselves to classroom projects where groups can work together to solve the problems involved. The situations and problems encountered parallel actual construction jobs and offer interesting and informative experience to drawing students. A foreman, similar to an actual job superintendent, should be designated in the model crew to plan individual tasks of the construction and keep the model moving along smoothly. Considerable time and work are involved. If a student's original design is used, the model definitely creates added enthusiasm.

Framing lumber for structural models is best cut from ponderosa or sugar pine stock on a power table saw. Equip the saw with a *hollow-ground blade* to produce neat cuts and smooth surfaces requiring no sanding. When cutting the lumber, it is most convenient to scale it down to its *nominal* size rather than actual size. For example, $2''$ lumber would be scaled exactly $2''$ thick. Use convenient lengths (about $3'$) of the stock and cut the narrow dimension first. Although balsa wood is available for structural pieces, pine gives the model more stability.

Use model cement (Testor's, du Pont Duco) for most of your gluing work. When small pieces can be quickly assembled, use the *extra-fast-drying* type of cement to save time in setting. For stronger wood joints, use white wood glue (Elmer's) with pressure, if possible; on thin paper, use contact cement or a glue stick to prevent wrinkling.

Base for the Model   First, build a sturdy base for the model, making it large enough to accommodate the floor plan, and leave sufficient space around it to show exterior features and landscaping. Remember that if the base is built too large, the model will become difficult to display and move about. Usually, 1/4" plywood with 1" × 2" framework (set vertically) is satisfactory if securely nailed (see Fig. 16-9). Use diagonal bracing to ensure rigidity throughout the plywood.

Foundation Walls   Lay out the outline of the foundation on the base and proceed with the foundation walls. If a basement or site contours are planned, consideration must be given to floor-level heights, and the base surface as a reference level should be indicated on the typical wall section detail of the working drawings. Heights then can be quickly scaled from this reference point. If the house is to have a concrete slab floor, represent the slab with 1/4" plywood and, according to the drawings, fasten it directly to the base or block it up to the required height. Slabs may also be cast of molding plaster or spackling compound. Basements must have full-height foundation walls of the proper thickness with raised lot contours to be finished as a later step. Construct crawl space foundations according to the foundation plan and show walls and piers correctly placed. Build the foundation of wood, scaled to the correct thickness, and be sure it is built the same height above grade as indicated on the drawings. The foundation is a major step of the model construction and is important in getting it started correctly.

Wood Framing   Next, construct the wood framing (if applicable) according to the typical wall detail; follow good framing practice. Start with the sill plate and glue all members together in the same manner and sequence that carpenters would use on the full-size construction. If a wood floor is indicated, insert all wood built-up girders or steel beams to support the floor framing. Steel beams can be made from three strips of thin wood, glued together and painted orange to resemble structural steel. Space the floor joists, insert them in the direction shown on the drawings, and cover with the subflooring. To expose portions of the floor framing, cut circular free-form holes in the subflooring near the center of several rooms; then the flooring layers (sub-

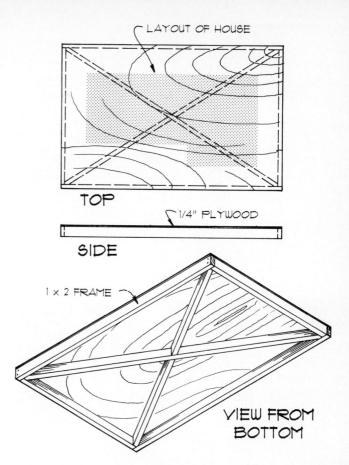

FIGURE 16-9   Details for constructing a satisfactory model base.

floors, underlayment, and finish floor) can be exposed by cutting similar holes just a little larger for each succeeding layer. Similar openings in ceilings and roofs are then planned directly above these floor openings so that the structure will be exposed completely through the model.

After the walls and partitions are laid out on the subfloor according to the plan, construct each wall section with the use of a jig on the table top. In gluing the studs and plates together to form the wall sections, remember to place the studs 16" on center (if conventional framing), insert the proper posts at corners (corner posts) and intersections of walls (T posts), provide double studs and lintels around window and door openings, cut the studs about 7'-9" long for 8' ceilings, build the sections with the sill and only *one* top plate (the other 2 × 4 plate should be attached after the wall sections are set in place), and allow enough plate length for corner joints (see Framing Details in Chapter 7). Be sure there will be nailing surfaces on both inside and outside wall corners. Glue the wall sections to the subfloor, using your triangles or tri-square to keep them plumb (see Fig. 16-10A). Now the second top plate is applied over

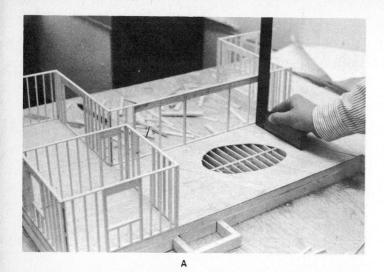

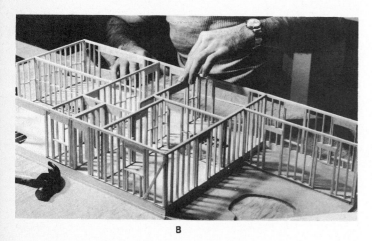

Figure 16-10 (A) Checking the plumb of wall framing; (B) applying the double plate on structural models.

the walls (see Fig. 16-10B), overlapping the other top plate at corners and at intersections to produce a rigid wall framework. Do not forget diagonal braces at outside corners.

Complete all work to be done within room interiors before applying ceiling joists. Show suggestions of major floor finishes, such as oak strip, parquet, tile, carpeting, ceramic, and flagstone. Usually, only portions of the various finishes need to be shown. Areas of the interior walls may be indicated with illustration board or wood paneling; however, avoid covering too much framing. Letter the room titles on small strips of white board and glue to the floor; place them so that they read from the front of the building.

While the interior is accessible, insert all permanent fixtures and built-in cabinet work. Bathroom fixtures may be carved from soap, as we mentioned earlier, and glued in place. Scaled fixtures of various types are available at hobby shops. Make cabinets from wood blocks. Cabinet doors may be made from thin balsa and

glued to the blocks. Paint or stain the cabinets before installing.

Next, attach ceiling joists to the wall framing according to the drawing (see Fig. 16-11A). On gable roofs, joists are usually parallel to the rafter direction and fastened to them above the plate. Cut common rafters from a pattern drawn out on paper, if need be. Hip and valley rafters may require projection layouts as well. Place the sloping rafters in pairs opposite each other and glue to the plate adjacent to the ceiling joists. This forms a strong framing arrangement. If feasible, temporarily fasten the ridgeboard in place before attaching the rafters. Keep the edges of the overhangs straight. If truss rafters are employed, set up a triangular jig on the table and build the identical trusses before setting them in place on the model.

In plank and beam framing, sand and stain ceiling beams *before* gluing them in place. Use cripples above top plates to bring partitions up to sloping plank and beam ceilings; or diagonal-top partitions may be built with full-height studs after the ceiling slopes have been established. Use double studs or 4 × 4's within the walls to support the ceiling beams. Treat the rafter or beam overhang as shown on the drawings, using thin balsa for soffit material if a boxed cornice is called for. After the framing is complete, reinforce major corners and roof joints with common pins, shortened if necessary, to prevent observers from accidentally damaging the structure.

Exterior Walls Apply exterior wall materials next; include subwall, building paper, and insulation, if applicable. Avoid covering walls around the entire building; usually the back walls can be left exposed so that the interior and structure are easily visible (see Fig. 16-11B). Complete the front in detail, on the other hand, to provide a basis for analyzing the design qualities (see Fig. 16-11C).

Make brick veneer of balsa sheets that have been sized to fit the framing, cut for door and window openings, and mitered at outside corners. Show brick sills extending out from the brick surface under windows with balsa strips glued in place. Before fastening the veneer in place, complete the brick texture by scoring the balsa with horizontal grooves to represent the brick coursing; do this with a blunt-tipped instrument such as a stylus. Provision must be made for the erection of the brick panels on the foundation. To paint the brick, first coat the entire surface with white color (tempera, acrylic, or latex works fine), making sure the grooves are filled. Then apply the basic brick color with a drybrush technique, covering mainly the brick surfaces and leaving the mortar grooves white. Use subtle color variations to give the brick a realistic appearance. If you want to represent older traditional brick, tone down the basic brick color by applying over it a wider variety of colors, primarily earthy reddish-brown shades. This is best

A

B

C

FIGURE 16-11 (A) Construction of the wood framing in a residential model; (B) completed view of model from rear showing interior space and framing; (C) completed view of model from front.

done in the drybrush technique also. Keep all the panels of similar value and check their development by viewing them at a little distance, rather than up close.

Stone textures are done in a similar manner; or relief is gained by cutting individual stones from thin balsa ($1/32''$ thick) and gluing them to the panels. Paint the panels white before applying the stones. Be sure the stone pattern is pleasing and the pieces are glued in place with their wood grain in the same direction, usually horizontal. The stones are then painted in slight variations of gray or earth colors.

It may be worth mentioning that very attractive masonry walls and textures can be produced with molding plaster or spackling compound, available at builder's supply stores. First, build a wooden mold or form for each masonry wall or unit required; then mix sufficient plaster and water in a container and carefully pour into one form at a time and level off. Add the plaster to the water when mixing; to prevent air bubbles, avoid vigorous mixing. You must work rather hurriedly, as the plaster sets quickly and cannot be left or worked too long. Avoid spilling the plaster, since it is difficult to remove from clothes and floor. After the plaster is sufficiently hard, remove it from the form without breaking. Repair any imperfections, and carve stone, brick, or other masonry textures on the surface with a suitable tool. The plaster carves easily if not entirely cured. When dry, coat with white shellac to seal the surface and paint the masonry units the desired colors, leaving the mortar joints white. Chimneys can be cast as a unit by this method, as well as replicas of many precast panels now in use in construction.

For even more textural stonework realism, small pea gravel or other aggregate can be placed in the bottom of forms to produce the face of the masonry panels, and a thick mixture of the molding plaster is poured over it. When these aggregate panels or units are cured and cleaned, they look very authentic and are extremely effective. Take precautions to construct the forms in the correct size and to scale. Join the panels at intersections with a thin mixture of the plaster as an adhesive, or use white wood glue.

Make the various types of wood siding from balsa wood. Whether painted or stained surfaces are required, balsa can be easily cut and finished to resemble many wood exterior finishes. Glue the siding to the exterior walls after the subwall materials have been applied. Before attaching siding to the walls, carefully cut the openings for doors and windows, groove if necessary, and paint or stain. As mentioned previously, be sure the wood grain runs in the same direction as it would on the actual building and that stain is applied before glue is used. To simulate horizontal clapboard siding, apply thin strips of balsa in a lapped fashion, allowing the correct amount of exposure to the weather. Paint after all the siding is in place. Make wood shingle siding from small balsa pieces, which are cut and glued in place individually.

Build landings, steps, planters, and the like, from wood blocks, and veneer with thin balsa if necessary for uniform masonry textures; paint off-white to represent concrete. Chimneys rising up through wood framing must be independent of the framing and may be made from cast molding plaster or constructed of soft wood and veneered with thin balsa to obtain horizontal wood grain completely around the unit. Show flue extensions and a sloping wash at the top. If needed, fireplace openings can be carved out with a chisel or a knife, and the cavity painted a dull black. When completed, fasten the chimney to the base before framing the roof structure around it.

Roofing Because of the comparatively small nature of models, their roofs are a predominant feature and therefore necessitate a great deal of care in finishing. Select a stable material such as balsa for the roof decking, rather than paper board, which has a tendency to warp when the roofing materials are glued on. At this point you should plan which parts of the roof surfaces are to be left exposed for viewing the framing members and the interior structure of the model. For this purpose, leave off most of the sloping surfaces in the rear. On gable or hip roofs, cover a considerable amount of the front slopes so that the front view gives the impression of completion. Roofing over important roof edges and ridges is necessary. On flat roofs, leave a large portion of the central area without covering, since it does not detract from the appearance of the elevations. Use black construction paper to represent roofing felt, usually cut to expose the multiple layers of a built-up roof. Fasten coarse sandpaper as the final aggregate surface to this type of roof or use sand or bird gravel glued to the felt. Various abrasive sheets can be fashioned into strip fiberglass shingles and glued to the roof, placing them so that they overlap. For realistic wood shingles, take actual cedar shingles and cut the miniatures from the thin ends or purchase them at a hobby shop. Copper foil (gasket stock) will be found attractive and easy to shape for metal roofs and flashing applications. Many similar materials can be found to simulate other types of roofing; some will require painting. Half the enjoyment of building models is the challenge offered in finding simple, inexpensive materials that will represent building textures at the correct scale.

Details Minor details should be one of the last operations in the construction of the model, even through it often becomes tempting to add a few during the construction to see how they will appear. By details we mean the small features such as doors, windows, cornice trim, and shutters that give the model its finished touch. When trim pieces are to be different in color from adjacent surfaces, paint the trim before attaching. Avoid using aluminum paint on models; it generally appears tacky. If an aluminum window is specified, paint the pieces white. Positioning small pieces may require the use of a pair of tweezers. Cut window members, surrounds, sills, muntins, and the like, from thin balsa, making sure that the type and scale of the window are accurately reproduced. Some of the muntin bars of a double-hung window, for instance, must be made very thin.

For exterior doors, cut each from balsa after the trim around their openings has been affixed and give them their correct detail according to the door schedule. To represent various treatments, you may score a balsa door with a stylus to show panels, glue stile and rail strips on the door, or glue small panels on the door. Flush doors are smooth except possibly for suggestions of the latch hardware. Take time to detail the front entrance carefully. Form wrought-iron work from soft wire, solder the joints, and spray a dull black. Other minor details may be added if they contribute additional character to the model.

Landscaping Landscaping on structural models is done in a similar manner as was suggested for smaller architectural models; the important thing is maintaining scale (see Fig. 16-1).

If necessary, build up the lot contours with wire screen and blocking, covering the surface grade with molding plaster, spackling compound, or papier-mâché. Papier-mâché may be made from shredded newspapers soaked in water until they become a fibrous mass. Drain and mix the fibers with wallpaper paste and sawdust to make a sticky, plastic material for covering the screen. Large areas of papier-mâché require considerable time in drying and may split when dry unless shrinkage joints are provided.

Paint the grass surfaces green and cover with model builder's grass material (green sawdust), or use green flocking over the paint. When painting drives, walks, and the like, use masking tape to maintain neat edges between the adjacent colors. Drives and walks may be edged with small balsa strips to make them definitive and give them a clean-cut appearance.

For the trees and shrubs, use green sponges or lichen, properly shaped and sized (see Fig. 16-2). For trees, cement the forms to the twigs or branches; to attach the trees, follow the same procedure as for architectural models. Fasten the shrubbery in interesting groups near corners of the model and in other areas where the architectural lines need to be softened. Also, use plantings to emphasize the front door, or place them as natural screens for privacy.

If edge grain shows around the periphery of the base, select a suitable molding or stock casing for covering the edge. Nail the trim about $1/8''$ above the surface of the grade line to prevent the grass material from dropping off. Miter the corners of the trim and either paint or stain with a suitable finish.

REVIEW QUESTIONS

1. What part does the model of a building play in architectural service?

2. What characteristics of an architectural proposal does a model most effectively show?

3. Why is balsa wood a favorite material for many model builders?

4. How are site contours usually represented on architectural models?

5. Why is the scale so important when selecting model-building materials?

6. Why must the model builder use particular care as to the direction in which wood grain is placed on exterior textures?

7. Why is soft pine recommended for structural lumber rather than balsa wood?

8. What is the disadvantage of using glossy enamels on model surfaces?

9. Name various materials convenient for representing roofing textures.

10. Why can landscaping problems be more easily solved on a model than on a landscaping plan?

WRITING SPECIFICATIONS

"Nothing is achieved before it is thoroughly attempted."
—Sir Phillip Sidney

17

In the light of what has been said about graphic description, it will be seen that working drawings, however well drawn, cannot be entirely adequate in completely revealing all aspects of a construction project. Many things cannot be shown graphically. For example, how would one show on a drawing the quality of workmanship required on a kitchen cabinet, except by an extensive hand-lettered note? It becomes standard procedure, then, to supplement working drawings with written specifications. Working drawings describe the construction quantitatively, that is *how much*, while the specifications describe the project qualitatively, or *how good*. Together, the working drawings and specifications communicate a complete picture of the construction.

This chapter examines the detailed instructions, often called *specs*, together with other written documents and shows their relationship to working drawings, the graphic portion of the contract documents.

17.1 Relationship of Drawings to the Specifications and Other Written Documents

We have seen the importance of architectural drawings in conveying the architect's intent. However, in the world of construction, several other written documents are just as important as the drawings in establishing the "contract between the owner and contractor." We must remember that the purpose of these documents is to provide communication that will allow the project to be constructed by the general contractor and the subcontractors in a fashion and to the quality intended by the architect and perceived by the owner, as indicated in the contract documents, and to meet building codes and other applicable laws.

The term *contract documents* is accepted as meaning those documents that taken together make up the contract between the owner and contractor for building construction. These documents are:

1. Working drawings
2. Specifications
3. Contract conditions (general and supplementary)
4. Addenda (changes made before contract signing)
5. Change orders (changes made after contract signing)
6. Agreement (or the contract between the owner and contractor)

In projects for which contracts are awarded through the bidding process, additional documents called *bidding requirements* must be added to the contract documents. These include the following:

1. Invitation to bid
2. Instructions to bidders
3. Bid form
4. Information available to bidders

Notice that bidding requirements are not contract documents and, since they are not, do not actually make up a part of the documents upon which a contract or agreement is signed between the owner and contractor.

In the past, there was a tendency to develop *precedence* of one document over another in case of dispute. Under that scenario, specifications usually had precedence over drawings, assuming that the written word was more correct than graphics. This proved not to be true, and it is recommended that precedence not be incorporated into documents. Discrepancies should be referred to the architect for clarification.

17.2 Types of Projects

There are a number of types of project delivery, depending on the conditions surrounding the project and, to a lesser extent, on project size. The most common form is the *bid* project, in which the bidding documents are distributed by the architect to several general contractors, called *bidders*. These contractors, along with their subcontractors, estimate the construction cost and bid for a project, with the contract award going to the bidder submitting the lowest-cost bid. This type of contract is used for most government and public projects where bidding is required by law. Many owners prefer this method as it assures them of the lowest initial construction cost.

Also in widespread use is the *negotiated* type of contract. A negotiated contract eliminates bidding and has the owner select a contractor with whom he or she negotiates the cost and time for construction. When using this type of contract, the contractor uses every effort to control costs and stay within the owner's budget and construction time frame as established before construction begins. Many owners protect themselves from cost overruns in negotiated projects by establishing a *guaranteed maximum cost* ceiling. This assures the owner that the contract amount cannot exceed this given amount unless the nature of work is changed. A private owner might select a negotiated contract to get a contractor on line who has experience with a particular type of construction or who has expertise in delivery of a project within a short period of time. Naturally, the architect and contractor work more closely together as a team during pricing and construction.

A variation of the negotiated type contract is the *fast track* type of delivery process. The procedure is much the same as in a negotiated-type contract, except that the contractor is involved much sooner in the process, advising the owner and architect of systems and products, costs, and methods during the development of the Contract Documents. Construction may actually start prior to completion of the working drawings and specifications to shorten the construction time. This may be important when an owner has a commitment to a tenant for an early move-in date or when construction financing costs make it advantageous to the owner to gamble in order to reduce this "soft cost." As with negotiated contracts, fast-track contracts usually have guaranteed maximum cost caps. The architect, contractor, and owner must work very closely in fast-track construction as decisions must be made quickly and can require input from all. Since construction may already be underway as documents are developed, it is incumbent on all that the proper decisions be made in a timely manner.

The *design–build* type of project delivery stipulates that one entity, the contractor, has a contract with the owner to perform design as well as construction. This is opposite to the normal process in which the architect has a separate design contract with the owner. In this case, the contractor has control of the design process and integrates it within his or her estimation, schedule, and construction processes to take total responsibility for design and construction.

17.3 The Project Manual Concept

The term *specifications*, used to describe the book often accompanying the working drawings, is actually a misnomer as the book called *Specifications* in most cases include documents, such as bidding requirements and Contract Conditions, that are not specifications. The American Institute of Architects (A.I.A.) developed the idea of the *Project Manual* in 1964, as the volume that would contain the specifications and any other data conveniently bound into one volume. Although slow to gain acceptance, the term Project Manual has now come into wide usage. This definition is even more important with the increased inclusion of such items as door and finish schedules, traditionally designated as drawing items, in the Project Manual.

17.4 Who Writes Specifications

Regardless of the form a firm uses to define its specification writing operation, the functions are essentially the same. The specifier has primary responsibility for producing the Project Manual, including performing product research and the evaluation necessary to specify the right material to perform the right purpose. The specifier will prepare this text from a master specification that he or she maintains and must write specification sections from scratch when no master section exists. The specifier sees product manufacturer's representatives who visit the office and discuss their products and the specifier's needs as they relate to the projects in the office. The specifier is generally the source for product and industry information for others in the office and in many cases handles the field problems. The specifier is responsible for seeing that information gained is incorporated back into the system. The specifications may be written by one of several people.

In small architectural offices, firm principals, who

have great experience and appreciation for the liabilities of poorly written specifications, may do the specifying. In others, project architects and construction administration personnel who have had experience with materials and construction frequently compile the specifications.

In larger architectural offices, designated *specification writers* or *specifiers* often prepare specifications and related documents. These are registered architects or architectural personnel who have extensive experience in material evaluation and selection and with field applications and problems. In addition, specifiers usually have acquired an ability to write in correct English grammar and agreement and to use accepted words, spellings, and abbreviations consistently within established office policy. Increasingly, as personal computers are being used for word processing, specifiers are becoming proficient in computer use.

Many multi-office firms maintain a central specification department in the home office, where specifications for projects the world over are prepared from the office's master specification system. Other firms prefer to keep specification personnel in various offices where they can be more conversant with local conditions, materials, and installations. At this time, there seems no clear-cut advantage to either system. Increasingly, specifiers are being assisted by office librarians, whose job it is to keep up with the building product catalogs and industry standards delivered to the office that arrive by mail and through manufacturer's representatives. It is virtually impossible for one person with several duties to be successful in maintaining a reference library used by an entire office.

In many firms, both large and small, the task of preparing project specifications from the firm's master system is the responsibility of the project architect. The master system is maintained by an in-house specification coordinator, who performs the duties of the specifier in a larger office, but leaves the preparation of the actual specification to the person who knows the most about the project—the project architect. This approach has grown greatly with the proliferation of commercially available master specification text and the personal computer.

The specification consultant specializes in the preparation of specifications and related documents for a number of architectural firms, while maintaining his or her independence as an outside consultant. The consultant's service makes expertly prepared specifications and related documents available to small- and medium-size firms without the cost of maintaining a full-time specification department. The specifier's expertise in material evaluation and selection as well as knowledge of contract forms makes him or her a valuable asset to firms not having or wanting in-house experience. Many specification consultants are members of an organiza-tion, Specification Consultants in Independent Practice (S.C.I.P.), that deals with the particular problems and concerns of the consultant.

17.5 Specification Material Sources

To write a completely new set of specifications for each job would be unnecessarily time consuming. Instead, specifiers rely on various sources for reference material and standard specifications from which they can compile a set for each new job. Specifications that have repeatedly proved satisfactory in the past are heavily relied on. Some may have to be modified to fit the conditions of a given job; many can be used word for word. Master specifications text such as A.I.A.'s Masterspec®, A.I.A.'s SPECSystem™, and C.S.I.'s Spec-Text® are often used to write new sections. These master systems contain guide specifications for many materials, allowing the specifier the luxury of editing out unnecessary text rather than generating new information each time. Master Specifications also incorporate correct specification language and format for ease of specification preparation. Most new specification sections are generated from master systems. Listed below are the major sources from which specification material is available:

1. City and national codes and ordinances
2. Manufactures' catalogues (Sweet's Catalog File, Man-U-Spec, Spec-data)
3. Manufactures' industry associations (Architectural Woodworking Institute, American Plywood Association, Door and Hardware Institute, Tile Council of America)
4. National standards organizations (American National Standards Institute, National Institute of Building Sciences)
5. Testing societies (American Society for Testing and Materials, Underwriters Laboratories)
6. Master specifications (Masterspec®, SPECsystem™, Spec-Text®)
7. Individual file of previously written specifications
8. Books on specifications
9. Federal specifications (Specs-In-Tact, G.S.A., N.A.S.A., N.A.F.V.A.C.)
10. Magazines and publications (*Construction Specifier*, *Architecture*, *Architectural Record*)

The specifier must not only be familiar with construction methods, new materials, and building techniques, but he or she must also be able to accumulate reference material and organize it for easy access when it is needed.

17.6 Specification Arrangement

The Construction Specifications Institute (C.S.I.) has for a number of years engaged in a program of standardizing specification format. The Institute concluded, after questioning its members, that a universal need exists for more uniformity in format arrangement and that a consistent national format would prove beneficial not only to the writers of specifications, but also to the contractors and material suppliers as well. After evaluating the various comments, the Institute has compiled a format that provides the advantages of standardization, yet has sufficient flexibility to allow writers throughout the country enough latitude in expression to accommodate local codes and trade practice variations. Only the arrangement in the format is restrictive, so that a set of specifications, like the alphabet, or numbering system, will be universally useful because of its consistency. The benefits of the format will be realized mainly from its widespread usage. Although nearly every set of specifications varies in content because of variations in circumstance, it has been found that arrangement of content can be identical.

The C.S.I. format consists of a universal numbering system applicable to all possible items of work, breakdowns for each technical item and group of related items, a three-part designation for each technical item, and a suggested page layout.

CSI breaks down construction into a group of *sections*, where each section is an item of work. Breakdown does not presume that the contractor will subcontract with regard to the section since the contractor has control over and charge of the construction, although the breakdown is so reasonable that in many cases this is possible. Each section can be either *broadscope*, *mediumscope*, or *narrowscope* in nature, depending on the complexity of the project and what the specifier chooses to include. An example would be a section for acoustical ceilings. As a broadscope section, the section entitled "Acoustical Ceilings" might include several types of lay-in ceiling panels, a concealed grid acoustical ceiling system, and metal suspension systems for all. In a mediumscope section, the specifier might specify only the lay-in ceiling panels and the related metal suspension system in a section entitled "Lay-in Acoustical Ceiling Systems." Another mediumscope section would specify the concealed grid system. Finally, a narrowscope section might be limited to only the metal suspension systems, entitled "Ceiling Suspension Systems," assuming related narrowscope sections would be written for the acoustical panels themselves.

The C.S.I. format groups sections of like construction into *divisions*. This format is often referred to as the 16-division format since there are 16 static divisions. Since these divisions are always the same, any person familiar with this format can easily find his or her way through the Project Manual. In the table of contents, divisions that are not applicable to the project in question are simply designated as "Not Used."

The specification user is further aided by the breakdown of each section into three *parts*. The three-part format locates data within each section with regard to its basic relationships. The parts are:

Part 1 General, or those items relating in general to an item, such as shop drawing requirements and delivery procedures.

Part 2 Products, relates to the material itself, including mixing and fabrication.

Part 3 Execution, relates to the installation of the material.

Breakdown of the section into these parts provides a skeleton for the specifier, thus making it simpler to prepare the specification in a consistent manner, and makes it easy for the user to find exactly what he or she is looking for without laboriously reading the entire section. See Fig. 17-1 for a suggestion of article titles within the parts.

C.S.I. further simplifies the use of the section by using the *page format*. This suggested layout provides article, paragraph, and subparagraph numbering, spacing, tabs and margins, and similar data necessary to create the most readable text.

The five-digit numbering system unifies the 16-division, three-part format. Under this system, broadscope and many mediumscope section titles are given static numbers. The first two digits represent the division, 1 through 16. The other three digits represent a somewhat arbitrary sequence of sections, although by being organized into standard order the sequencing promotes standardization. Creation of numbers for narrowscope sections rests with the specifier. The master list of titles and numbers is published by C.S.I. in conjunction with Construction Specifications Canada (C.S.C.) in *Masterformat*. See Fig. 17-2 for a list of divisions and broadscope section titles with appropriate five-digit numbers. Masterformat is available individually or as a part of the CSI *Manual of Practice*, which contains a great deal more information regarding specification preparation and use than can be included in this text. It is recommended that the C.S.I. Manual of Practice be used by those having a need for greater detail.

A sample specification section incorporating the C.S.I. division, section, and page format is shown in Fig. 17-3.

In addition to the format described above, specifiers realize the need for other, shorter formats to accommodate smaller commercial projects and residential projects. Outline specifications are often useful as communication tools for commercial projects and may be all that's necessary to construct simpler projects. A sample outline specification section is shown in Fig. 17-4.

ARTICLE TITLES BY PART

Part 1 GENERAL

1.01 SUMMARY
  A. Section includes.
  B. Products furnished but not installed under this section.
  C. Products installed but not furnished under this section.
  D. Related sections.
  E. Allowances.
  F. Unit prices.
  G. Alternates.
1.02 REFERENCES
1.03 DEFINITIONS
1.04 SYSTEM DESCRIPTION
  A. Design requirements.
  B. Performance requirements.
1.05 SUBMITTALS
  A. Product data, shop drawings, and samples.
  B. Quality control submittals.
  C. Design data, test reports, certificates, manufacturer's instructions, field reports.
  D. Contract closeout submittals.
  E. Project record documents, operation and maintenance data, warranty.
1.06 QUALITY ASSURANCE
  A. Qualifications.
  B. Regulatory requirements.
  C. Certifications.
  D. Field samples.
  E. Mock-ups.
  F. Preinstallation conference.
1.07 DELIVERY, STORAGE, AND HANDLING
  A. Packing and shipping.
  B. Acceptance at site.
  C. Storage and protection.
1.08 PROJECT/SITE CONDITIONS
  A. Environmental requirements.
  B. Existing conditions.
  C. Field measurements.
1.09 SCHEDULING AND SEQUENCING
1.10 WARRANTY
  A. Special warranty
1.11 MAINTENANCE
  A. Maintenance service.
  B. Extra materials.

PART 2 PRODUCTS

2.01 MANUFACTURERS
2.02 MATERIALS
2.03 MANUFACTURED UNITS
2.04 EQUIPMENT
2.05 COMPONENT
2.06 ACCESSORIES
2.07 MIXES
2.08 FABRICATION
  A. Shop assembly.
  B. Shop/factory finishing.
  C. Tolerances
2.09 SOURCE QUALITY CONTROL
  A. Tests, inspections.
  B. Verification of performance.

PART 3 EXECUTION

3.01 EXAMINATION
  A. Verification of conditions.
3.02 PREPARATION
  A. Protection.
  B. Surface protection.
3.03 ERECTION/INSTALLATION/APPLICATION
  A. Special techniques.
  B. Interface with other products.
  C. Tolerances.
3.04 FIELD QUALITY CONTROL
  A. Manufacturer's field service.
3.05 ADJUSTING/CLEANING
3.06 DEMONSTRATING
3.07 PROTECTION
3.08 SCHEDULES

FIGURE 17-1 Three-part format.

17.7 Division 1, General Requirements

In examining the breakdown of the 16 divisions, note that all divisions except division 1 relates to the construction itself. Division 1, General Requirements, applies to all other divisions and spans between the technical sections and other bidding and contract documents. Division 1 sections relate to administrative and procedural requirements and temporary facilities. Actual contract requirements might be specified by the agreement or contract conditions, but the rules for implementing would be specified in division 1.

17.8 General Points for Preparing Specifications

The following points should be kept in mind when writing specifications:

1. Use simple, direct language and accepted terminology, rather than abstract legal terminology.
2. Use brief sentences requiring only simple punctuation.
3. Specify standard items and alternates where possible, in the interest of economy, without sacrificing quality.
4. Avoid repetition; use cross-references if they apply and seem logical.
5. Avoid specifications that are impossible for the contractor to carry out; be fair in designating responsibility.
6. Avoid including specifications that are not to be part of the construction.
7. Clarify all terms that may be subject to more than one interpretation.
8. Be consistent in the use of terms, abbreviations, format, and arrangement of material.
9. Specify numbers, names, and descriptions of materials from the *latest editions* of manufacturers' catalogues.
10. Capitalize the following: major parties to the contract, such as Contractor, Owner, Designer, Architect; the contract documents, such as Specifications, Working Drawings, Contract, Supplementary Conditions; specific rooms within the building, such as Kitchen, Living Room, Office; grade of materials, such as No. 1 Douglas Fir, Clear Heart Redwood, FAS White Oak; and of course all proper names.
11. Differentiate between "shall" and "will"—"The Contractor shall, . . . " "The Owner or Architect will. . . . "
12. Avoid the term "a workmanlike job" or similar vague phrases; rather, describe the quality of workmanship or exact requirements to be expected;

BIDDING REQUIREMENTS, CONTRACT FORMS, AND CONDITIONS OF THE CONTRACT

00010	PREBID INFORMATION
00100	INSTRUCTIONS TO BIDDERS
00200	INFORMATION AVAILABLE TO BIDDERS
00300	BID FORMS
00400	SUPPLEMENTS TO BID FORMS
00500	AGREEMENT FORMS
00600	BONDS AND CERTIFICATES
00700	GENERAL CONDITIONS
00800	SUPPLEMENTARY CONDITIONS
00900	ADDENDA

Note: The items listed above are not specification sections and are referred to as "Documents" rather than "Sections" in the Master List of Section Titles, Numbers, and Broadscope Section Explanations.

SPECIFICATIONS

DIVISION 1—GENERAL REQUIREMENTS

01010	SUMMARY OF WORK
01020	ALLOWANCES
01025	MEASUREMENT AND PAYMENT
01030	ALTERNATES/ALTERNATIVES
01035	MODIFICATION PROCEDURES
01040	COORDINATION
01050	FIELD ENGINEERING
01060	REGULATORY REQUIREMENTS
01070	IDENTIFICATION SYSTEMS
01090	REFERENCES
01100	SPECIAL PROJECT PROCEDURES
01200	PROJECT MEETINGS
01300	SUBMITTALS
01400	QUALITY CONTROL
01500	CONSTRUCTION FACILITIES AND TEMPORARY CONTROLS
01600	MATERIAL AND EQUIPMENT
01650	FACILITY STARTUP/COMMISSIONING
01700	CONTRACT CLOSEOUT
01800	MAINTENANCE

DIVISION 2—SITEWORK

02010	SUBSURFACE INVESTIGATION
02050	DEMOLITION
02100	SITE PREPARATION
02140	DEWATERING
02150	SHORING AND UNDERPINNING
02160	EXCAVATION SUPPORT SYSTEMS
02170	COFFERDAMS
02200	EARTHWORK
02300	TUNNELING
02350	PILES AND CAISSONS
02450	RAILROAD WORK
02480	MARINE WORK
02500	PAVING AND SURFACING
02600	UTILITY PIPING MATERIALS
02660	WATER DISTRIBUTION
02680	FUEL AND STEAM DISTRIBUTION
02700	SEWERAGE AND DRAINAGE
02760	RESTORATION OF UNDERGROUND PIPE
02770	PONDS AND RESERVOIRS
02780	POWER AND COMMUNICATIONS
02800	SITE IMPROVEMENTS
02900	LANDSCAPING

DIVISION 3—CONCRETE

03100	CONCRETE FORMWORK
03200	CONCRETE REINFORCEMENT
03250	CONCRETE ACCESSORIES
03300	CAST-IN-PLACE CONCRETE
03370	CONCRETE CURING
03400	PRECAST CONCRETE
03500	CEMENTITIOUS DECKS AND TOPPINS
03600	GROUT
03700	CONCRETE RESTORATION AND CLEANING
03800	MASS CONCRETE

DIVISION 4—MASONRY

04100	MORTAR AND MASONRY GROUT
04150	MASONRY ACCESSORIES
04200	UNIT MASONRY
04400	STONE
04500	MASONRY RESTORATION AND CLEANING
04550	REFRACTORIES
04600	CORROSION RESISTANT MASONRY
04700	SIMULATED MASONRY

DIVISION 5—METALS

05010	METAL MATERIALS
05030	METAL COATINGS
05050	METAL FASTENING
05100	STRUCTURAL METAL FRAMING
05200	METAL JOISTS
05300	METAL DECKING
05400	COLD FORMED METAL FRAMING
05500	METAL FABRICATIONS
05580	SHEET METAL FABRICATIONS
05700	ORNAMENT METAL
05800	EXPANSION CONTROL
05900	HYDRAULIC STRUCTURES

DIVISION 6—WOOD AND PLASTICS

06050	FASTENERS AND ADHESIVES
06100	ROUGH CARPENTRY
06130	HEAVY TIMBER CONSTRUCTION
06150	WOOD AND METAL SYSTEMS
06170	PREFABRICATED STRUCTURAL WOOD
06200	FINISH CARPENTRY
06300	WOOD TREATMENT
06400	ARCHITECTURAL WOODWORK
06500	STRUCTURAL PLASTICS
06600	PLASTIC FABRICATIONS
06650	SOLID POLYMER FABRICATIONS

DIVISION 7—THERMAL AND MOISTURE PROTECTION

07100	WATERPROOFING
07150	DAMPPROOFING
07180	WATER REPELLENTS
07190	VAPOR RETARDERS
07195	AIR BARRIERS
07200	INSULATION
07240	EXTERIOR INSULATION AND FINISH SYSTEMS
07250	FIREPROOFING
07270	FIRESTOPPING
07300	SHINGLES AND ROOFING TILES
07400	MANUFACTURED ROOFING AND SIDING
07480	EXTERIOR WALL ASSEMBLIES
07500	MEMBRANE ROOFING
07570	TRAFFIC COATINGS
07600	FLASHING AND SHEET METAL
07700	ROOF SPECIALTIES AND ACCESSORIES
07800	SKYLIGHTS
07900	JOINT SEALERS

DIVISION 8—DOORS AND WINDOWS

08100	METAL DOORS AND FRAMES
08200	WOOD AND PLASTIC DOORS
08250	DOOR OPENING ASSEMBLIES
08300	SPECIAL DOORS
08400	ENTRANCES AND STOREFRONTS
08500	METAL WINDOWS
08600	WOOD AND PLASTIC WINDOWS
08650	SPECIAL WINDOWS
08700	HARDWARE
08800	GLAZING
08900	GLAZED CURTAIN WALLS

DIVISION 9—FINISHES

09100	METAL SUPPORT SYSTEMS
09200	LATH AND PLASTER
09250	GYPSUM BOARD
09300	TILE
09400	TERRAZZO
09450	STONE FACING
09500	ACOUSTICAL TREATMENT
09540	SPECIAL WALL SURFACES
09545	SPECIAL CEILING SURFACES
09550	WOOD FLOORING
09600	STONE FLOORING
09630	UNIT MASONRY FLOORING
09650	RESILENT FLOORING
09680	CARPETING
09700	SPECIAL FLOORING
09780	FLOOR TREATMENT
09800	SPECIAL COATINGS
09900	PAINTING
09950	WALL COVERINGS

DIVISION 10—SPECIALTIES

10100	VISUAL DISPLAY BOARDS
10150	COMPARTMENTS AND CUBICLES
10200	LOUVERS AND VENTS
10240	GRILLES AND SCREENS
10250	SERVICE WALL SYSTEMS
10260	WALL AND CORNER GUARDS
10270	ACCESS FLOORING
10290	PEST CONTROL
10300	FIREPLACES AND STOVES
10340	MANUFACTURED EXTERIOR SPECIALITIES
10350	FLAGPOLES
10400	IDENTIFYING DEVICES
10450	PEDESTRIAN CONTROL DEVICES
10500	LOCKERS
10520	FIRE PROTECTION SPECIALTIES
10530	PROTECTIVE COVERS
10550	POSTAL SPECIALTIES
10600	PARTITIONS
10650	OPERABLE PARTITIONS
10670	STORAGE SHELVING
10700	EXTERIOR PROTECTION DEVICES FOR OPENINGS
10750	TELEPHONE SPECIALTIES
10800	TOILET AND BATH ACCESSORIES
10880	SCALES
10900	WARDROBE AND CLOSET SPECIALTIES

DIVISION 11—EQUIPMENT

11010	MAINTENANCE EQUIPMENT
11020	SECURITY AND VAULT EQUIPMENT
11030	TELLER AND SERVICE EQUIPMENT
11040	ECCLESIASTICAL EQUIPMENT
11050	LIBRARY EQUIPMENT
11060	THEATER AND STAGE EQUIPMENT
11070	INSTRUMENTAL EQUIPMENT
11080	REGISTRATION EQUIPMENT
11090	CHECKROOM EQUIPMENT
11100	MERCANTILE EQUIPMENT
11110	COMMERCIAL LAUNDRY AND DRY CLEANING EQUIPMENT
11120	VENDING EQUIPMENT
11130	AUDIO-VISUAL EQUIPMENT
11140	VEHICLE SERVICE EQUIPMENT
11150	PARKING CONTROL EQUIPMENT
11160	LOADING DOCK EQUIPMENT
11170	SOLID WASTE HANDLING EQUIPMENT
11190	DETENTION EQUIPMENT
11200	WATER SUPPLY AND TREATMENT EQUIPMENT
11280	HYDRAULIC GATES AND VALVES
11300	FLUID WASTE TREATMENT AND DISPOSAL EQUIPMENT
11400	FOOD SERVICE EQUIPMENT
11450	RESIDENTIAL EQUIPMENT
11460	UNIT KITCHENS
11470	DARKROOM EQUIPMENT
11480	ATHLETIC, RECREATIONAL, AND THERAPEUTIC EQUIPMENT
11500	INDUSTRIAL AND PROCESS EQUIPMENT
11600	LABORATORY EQUIPMENT
11650	PLANETARIUM EQUIPMENT
11660	OBSERVATORY EQUIPMENT
11680	OFFICE EQUIPMENT
11700	MEDICAL EQUIPMENT
11780	MORTUARY EQUIPMENT
11850	NAVIGATION EQUIPMENT
11870	AGRICULTURAL EQUIPMENT

DIVISION 12—FURNISHINGS

12050	FABRICS
12100	ARTWORK
12300	MANUFACTURED CASEWORKS
12500	WINDOW TREATMENT
12600	FURNITURE AND ACESSORIES
12670	RUGS AND MATS
12700	MULTIPLE SEATING
12800	INTERIOR PLANTS AND PLANTERS

DIVISION 13—SPECIAL CONSTRUCTION

13010	AIR SUPPORTED STRUCTURES
13020	INTEGRATED ASSEMBLIES
13030	SPECIAL PURPOSE ROOMS
13080	SOUND, VIBRATION, AND SEISMIC CONTROL

THE C.S.I. FIVE-DIGIT BROADSCOPE FORMAT

13090	RADIATION PROTECTION		13900	FIRE SUPPRESSION AND SUPERVISORY SYSTEMS	15500	HEATING, VENTILATING, AND AIR CONDITIONING
13100	NUCLEAR REACTORS		13950	SPECIAL SECURITY CONSTRUCTION	15550	HEAT GENERATION
13120	PRE-ENGINEERED STRUCTURES				15650	REFRIGERATION
13150	AQUATIC FACILITIES				15750	HEAT TRANSFER
13175	ICE RINKS		**DIVISION 14—CONVEYING SYSTEMS**		15850	AIR HANDLING
13180	SITE CONSTRUCTED INCINERATORS		14100	DUMBWAITERS	15880	AIR DISTRIBUTION
13185	KENNELS AND ANIMAL SHELTERS		14200	ELEVATORS	15950	CONTROLS
13200	LIQUID AND GAS STORAGE TANKS		14300	ESCALATORS AND MOVING WALKS	15990	TESTING, ADJUSTING, AND BALANCING
13220	FILTER UNDERDRAINS AND MEDIA		14400	LIFTS		
13230	DIGESTER COVERS AND APPURTENANCES		14500	MATERIAL HANDLING SYSTEMS	**DIVISION 16—ELECTRICAL**	
13240	OXYGENATION SYSTEMS		14600	HOIST AND CRANES	16050	BASIC ELECTRICAL MATERIALS AND METHODS
13260	SLUDGE CONDITIONING SYSTEMS		14700	TURNTABLES	16200	POWER GENERATION-BUILT-UP SYSTEMS
13300	UTILITY CONTROL SYSTEMS		14800	SCAFFOLDING	16300	MEDIUM VOLTAGE DISTRIBUTION
13400	INDUSTRIAL AND PROCESS CONTROL SYSTEMS		14900	TRANSPORTATION SYSTEMS	16400	SERVICE AND DISTRIBUTION
13500	RECORDING INSTRUMENTATION				16500	LIGHTING
13550	TRANSPORTATION CONTROL INSTRUMENTATION		**DIVISION 15—MECHANICAL**		16600	SPECIAL SYSTEMS
13600	SOLAR ENERGY SYSTEMS		15050	BASIC MECHANICAL MATERIALS AND METHODS	16700	COMMUNICATIONS
13700	WIND ENERGY SYSTEMS		15250	MECHANICAL INSULATION	16850	ELECTRICAL RESISTANCE HEATING
13750	COGENERATION SYSTEMS		15300	FIRE PROTECTION	16900	CONTROLS
13800	BUILDING AUTOMATION SYSTEMS		15400	PLUMBING	16950	TESTING

FIGURE 17-2 The CSI five-digit broadscope format.

13. Use accepted standards when specifying quality of materials or workmanship required, such as "Lightweight concrete masonry units: A.S.T.M. C-90-85; Grade N, Type 1."

14. Number all pages within a section consecutively and include a table of contents.

15. Keep in mind that bidders and subcontractors of different trades will have to use the specifications to look up information in their respective areas and that the information dealing with their work should be stated in the logical section and not hidden throughout the various sections.

17.9 Methods of Specifying

One of the first things a specifier must do when writing a master specification section or an individual project section from scratch is to decide what method he or she will use to communicate with the contractor. There are four basic types of specifications that can be prepared, and most items can be specified by one or more methods.

The first and easiest method of specifying is the *proprietary* specification, which basically names the manufacturers or products acceptable to the architect. A proprietary specification may be written as a *closed* proprietary specification, in which only one product is acceptable and the contractor is so advised by the nature of the specification. The specification may also be written as an *open* proprietary section, in which multiple manufacturers or products are named or alternates solicited. Naturally, an open proprietary specification results in more competition among vendors and may result in a lower installed price. However, an open proprietary specification may not be applicable if one specific product is desired.

An example of a closed proprietary specification would be one for brick for an addition to an existing building, where the brick must match existing brick. Only one product is desired. By comparison, an open proprietary specification might be applicable for building sealants when multiple products with the same characteristics can be specified. The specifier should be sure that the product specified is equivalent, though, and avoid an "apples and oranges" specification.

A word of caution about proprietary specifications is due with regard to use of the term "or equal." Frequently used in the past to convey the concept that the architect would consider products other than those specified, which he or she considered "equal" in quality, the term is unclear and leads to disagreement as to what is equal and in whose eyes. Thankfully, the use of the "or equal" clause has almost disappeared from specification writing and is most often used by persons unwilling to do the research and product evaluation necessary to specify the desired products.

The second method of specifying is the *descriptive* specification, which describes the product in detail without providing the product name. Descriptive specifications can be used when it is not desirous to specify a particular product. Some government agencies require that specifications be written in descriptive form to allow the greatest competition among product manufacturers. Descriptive specifications are more difficult to write than proprietary ones since the specifier must indicate all product characteristics for which he or she has concern in the specification.

A third type of specification in prevalent use is the

SECTION 07310

SHINGLE ROOFING

PART 1 GENERAL

1.01 SUBMITTALS
A. Product data: Indicate material specifications and installation instructions.
B. Samples: Submit full-size samples of shingles in selected color for architect's approval.

1.02 DELIVERY, STORAGE, AND HANDLING
A. Stack bundles of shingles not more than 3'-0" high. Store roll goods on end.

1.03 QUALITY ASSURANCE
A. Application standards: Standards of the following as referenced herein:
1. American Society for Testing and Materials (ASTM).
2. Underwriters Laboratories, Inc. (UL)

PART 2 PRODUCTS

2.01 SHINGLES
A. Acceptable product: Celotex Corp. Presidential Shake.
B. Characteristics:
1. Type: Heavy-weight asphalt-saturated fiberglass laminate shingles meeting ASTM D3018-82 Type I and UL Class A rating for fire and wind resistance.
2. Shingles shall be curved, double-laminated tabs, self-sealing, random tab style.
3. Minimum weight: 365 lb./sq.
4, Color: As selected by Architect from manufacturer's standard colors.

2.02 ACCESSORY PRODUCTS
A. Roofing felts: Meeting ASTM D226-87, Type I, #15 felt, asphalt-saturated organic felt, 3'-0" width, unperforated.
B. Nails: Hot-dipped galvanized, 10 ga. screw threaded shank, 3/8" head, length as required to penetrate roof deck 1" minimum.
C. Underlayment, starter and ridge shingles: Types furnished by shingle manufacturer for use with specified shingles. Match color of selected shingle.

PART 3 EXECUTION

3.01 APPLICATION
A. Install felt layer over roof sheathing, lapping each course over lower course 2" minimum horizontally and 4" minimum side laps at end joints. Lap 6" from both sides at ridge.
B. Secure felt layer to deck with sufficient fasteners to hold in place until shingles are secured.
C. Apply shingles in straight, even courses, parallel to eave and ridge line, with four nails per shingle; nail heads concealed. Drive nails tight without cutting into shingles.
D. Apply a starter course using starter shingles in accordance with manufacturer's product data.
E. Install shingles with exposure recommended by manufacturer, in regular pattern, in accordance with shingle manufacturer's product data.
F. Construct ridges using two layers of ridge shingles.
G. Furnish two extra squares of roofing shingles for Owner's maintenance use. Store where directed.

END OF SECTION

Smith Residence 07310-1
Atlanta, GA
October 1, 1992

FIGURE 17-3 Typical specification section.

DIVISION 7-THERMAL AND MOISTURE PROTECTION

Section 07310—Shingle Roofing

1. General requirements: Submit product data and samples for shingles. Provide 30-year warranty.
2. Materials: Fiberglass shingles shall be Certainteed Hallmark Shangle or similar by Celotex, Elk, or Tamco. Shingles shall be minimum 300 lb./sq weight in color selected by Architect from manufacturer's standard colors. Provide roofing felt and roofing nails.
3. Execution: Install shingle roofing in accorance with manufacturer's product data, in straight, even courses, parallel to eaves. Install one layer of 15# felt, shingle fashion over sheathing prior to shingle application. Attach each shingle with three roofing nails.

Smith Residence 07310-1
Atlanta, GA
January 15, 1991

FIGURE 17-4 Typical outline specification.

reference standard. This simply references an accepted industry standard as the basis for the specification and is often used to specify generic materials such as Portland cement and clear glass. In using a reference standard, the specifier should have a copy of that standard, know what is required by the standard, including choices that may be contained therein, and enforce those requirements for all suppliers.

A fourth type of specification is the *performance specification*. The performance specification gives the greatest leeway to the contractor because it allows him or her to furnish any product that meets the performance criteria specified. It is the most difficult for the specifier to prepare since he or she must anticipate all products and systems that could be used and to specify only those characteristics he or she desires—specifically those related to test results. A performance specification must provide sufficient data to ensure that product characteristic can be demonstrated. Performance specifications have their greatest use in specifying complex systems, such as a curtain wall, which can be easily custom designed for a certain application and engineered to perform to required levels, say for wind loading and air infiltration. Testing for compliance is often required in performance specifications.

Most product specifications actually end up using a combination of methods to convey the architect's intent. A specification for brick masonry would use a proprietary specification to name the product or products selected by the architect, a descriptive specification to specify size and color, and a reference standard to specify the ASTM standard, grade, and type required.

17.10 Allowances, Alternates, and Unit Prices

No discussion of specification types is complete without mentioning three methods that the architect may need to use to delay making a product selection during bidding or early construction.

An *allowance* is an amount of money (cash allowance) or a quantity of material (quantity allowance) for which the quantity can be determined from the working drawings, but an actual decision as to material to be used has not been reached, or simply a lump sum for a system that will be required but has not been designed at the time bids are solicited. An example of a cash allowance is one for a building's carpet, where an allowance of X dollars per square yard is specified. The quantity required can be determined from the working drawings. Or there might be a lump sum cash allowance established for landscaping not yet designed. A quantity allowance could be used for tenant work, where historically a certain number of doors or linear footage of wall might be anticipated, but the space has not yet been designed.

Unlike allowances, *unit prices* are prices solicited from the contractor per unit of material when the system is defined but quantity is not. Requests for unit prices are often included in the bid form for such items as rock removal, where the soils report indicates the presence of rock to be removed, but the quantity is unknown until the rock is exposed.

Alternates are often included in the architect's bidding documents in order to get a price for an alternative system or material from the contractor. This stems from the fact that the architect does not do detailed estimates and depends on the contractor's estimating ability to determine the affordability of some items. The architect is in effect asking, "How much does X cost more or less than Y?" This demonstrates that the architect may be willing to compromise if the budget is exceeded. Alternates may also be suggested by the contractor, especially in negotiated contracts, as a means of cost reduction. Such suggestions should usually be *value engineering* items, meaning that systems or products of equivalent or better value can be substituted for less or the same cost. Value engineering is an important concept best practiced by someone experienced in that discipline.

17.11 Product Evaluation

Perhaps the most important part of specification writing is proper product evaluation, or the applicability of a particular system or product. Product evaluation takes into consideration items such as esthetics, acoustics, fire safety, life safety, stain resistance, interface, and replaceability. Other considerations include the desires of the owner, the manufacturer's reputation, initial and maintenance cost, and long-term maintenance and service requirements.

17.12 Master Specifications

As already discussed, master specification systems are one source of information for specifiers. Specification writing is not about creating original text; it is about using standardized text, combined with product and project knowledge, to communicate clearly, completely, concisely, and correctly with others who use the information created by the specifier. The use of master specification systems is not new. What is relatively new is the ability, through the personal computer, to utilize and manipulate master systems to a greater extent than ever before.

Many architectural firms maintain master systems of their own. These represent the attitudes of the firm principals, define the level of quality normally desired by that firm, and contain master specifications for systems and products normally specified by that firm. A firm that does low-rise hospital work would need a highly refined specification for hydraulic, hospital elevators, but probably would not spend the time to develop a master section for gearless elevators.

Many other firms, particularly smaller firms and firms doing a wide variety of work, normally rely on one of the several commercial master specification systems available. The A.I.A.'s *Masterspec* and SPEC-System C.S.I.'s *Spec-text* are two of the most successful. All are available in hard copy form as well as disks. These systems contain master sections for a myriad of products and are available for those who perform only interior design or those who practice mechanical and electrical engineering. Master systems usually come complete with drawing coordination checklists and explanation sheets for those uninitiated in a particular type of construction. The biggest disadvantage of these systems is that by their nature their scope is at least national. Some even try to anticipate construction in other parts of North America and other continents. Their biggest advantage is the uniformity that they bring to construction. In an effort to eliminate the disadvantage, some firms buy these master systems and custom tailor the sections to their own practice.

17.13 Today and Tomorrow

Specification production and reproduction have come a long way in just a few years, due to advances in technology. In the area of production, the norm today is for the specifier to edit his or her master system directly from the computer screen. The commercially available master systems are available in floppy disk form using a number of word processors. The specifier simply loads the master system onto his or her personal computer and he or she has instant access to the master system, complete with drawing checklist and explanation sheets. The master text itself will contain notes that explain certain articles and paragraphs. Once the specifier has edited the section, he or she can print out a draft copy complete with an audit trail. The audit trail tells what has been deleted or what decisions must be made. After reviewing sections for the entire project, making changes and spelling corrections, and perhaps inserting the current date on every page, the specifier can send the entire Project Manual to print at eight pages per minute on a laser jet printer. The printing can be done in a relatively short time period, eliminating the need to print until very late in document development. This allows changes to be made until the last minute. The entire Project Manual is printed, complete with the name of the project on every page, and the table of contents is self-generated. The quality of the copy is far better than previously available by typing.

Now the Project Manual is ready for copying and binding. Most copying is done today using high-speed copiers. The cost for reproduction in this manner has been reduced to the point that only the needed number of copies must be made, as opposed to previous methods in which economy was achieved only through making many copies at the same time. Now, other copies can be economically made later, if needed.

Most offices use an 8½″ by 11″ page size with printing on one or two sides as preferred. The C.S.I. page format accommodates either one- or two-sided printing. After copying, the Project Manual copies are bound, usually with a heavy stock cover bearing the firm's name or logo. The manner of binding is an individual preference, with several options that a printer can explain. The basic idea in binding text is to use a system that will hold up as the Project Manual is used in the field.

The state of the art in specification preparation technology is the CD ROM disk and reader. The disk, which looks the same as those that contain music, is a read-only memory (ROM), meaning that we cannot store data on the disk, but can take data off, transferring it to personal computer hard disks or floppy disks. Many manufacturers are experimenting with the transfer of information by these disks and even *Sweet's Catalog* has used CD ROM disks to supplement their hard-copy files. One master specification system, SPECSystem™, uses the CD disk as a vehicle for its master system; it does not allow the specifier to actually see the specification section he or she is writing, but through answers to questions about the product and project, the software generates the specification. The National Institute of Building Sciences (N.I.B.S.), a government agency, has a CD disk that contains the Masterspec and Specs-In-Tact master specification systems; many Navy, N.A.S.A. and Corp of Engineers design and maintenance manuals; and A.S.T.M. standards and standards from many other industry associations. This process is continuing as other manufacturers are providing master specification text as well as drawing details on disks to the design community.

As for future developments in the area of specification writing, as in the area of changes in the way we now design and draw, we cannot imagine the changes that will take place in just a few years. With CADD already in place in many architectural offices, the next step is to integrate specification production so that the first draft of the Project Manual is produced along with the drawings. Toward this end, we will see more sophisticated development of master specification systems.

REVIEW QUESTIONS

1. What qualifications are required of a construction specification writer?

2. Drawings depict the quantity of a certain material. What do specifications depict?

3. List five sources for specification reference material.

4. Why are construction material manufacturers' associations interested in furnishing material to specification writers?

5. Who requires a copy of the specifications? How are these copies usually made?

6. How is the information in the general conditions related to the other technical sections?

7. How do dimensions given in the specifications differ from the dimensions required on the working drawings?

8. Why must requirements in specifications be made fair and just to all parties of the contract?

9. List the three recommended parts of a typical technical section.

10. What are the major advantages in using the five-digit numbering system in spec writing?

11. Name several architectural or construction books that follow the five-digit numbering format.

12. What organization originated the 16-division *uniform* construction specification system?

13. Describe the difference between broadscope, mediumscope, and narrowscope?

14. List and describe the *three-part section* in specification writing.

15. What is a *master specification*?

16. Who generally writes specifications in a small architectural firm?

17. What is an *allowance* and why would it be used?

18. What is an *alternate* and why would it be used?

19. What is a *proprietary* specification?

20. How do computers aid the specification writer?

COMPUTER AIDED
DRAFTING AND DESIGN

"Would you tell me, please, which way I ought to go from here?"
"That depends a good deal on where you want to get to," said the Cat. "I don't much care where-" said Alice. "Then it doesn't matter which way you go," said the Cat.
THE CHESHIRE CAT IN ALICE'S ADVENTURES IN WONDERLAND
LEWIS CARROLL

18

18.1 Introduction

Although somewhat lighthearted, Lewis Carroll's point is important. If you don't know where you're going, then any road will get you there. This is important when learning about computers. Keep your needs and applications in mind so as not to be confused by the multitude of options available in hardware and software.

A basic understanding of graphic principles is also important before learning how to operate CAD equipment and software. A beginner should already know the meaning and use of lines, the various types of drawings, and the graphic symbols used in technical drawing. It is also very useful to have an understanding of three dimensional drawings such as axonometric and perspective drawings. CAD does not eliminate the need for knowledge of these principles. Sketching is still used by technicians and designers as a means of communicating preliminary ideas, basic design schemes and rough drawings of details.

18.2 Advantages of Computers for Architectural Drawing

18.2.1 Modeling

The underlying purpose of most technical drawing is the creation of a model of an object that one has conceived, prior to actual construction. According to Webster's dictionary, a model is "a miniature representation of something." It is impractical, particularly in the construction industry, to build a building without a thorough understanding of how it looks and functions, otherwise, a great deal of time and expense would be required for making changes and improvements during the process of construction. Therefore, scale drawings are made to identify the exact size and relationship of each component. Scale models are frequently built to further verify the appearance and function of the design idea. The construction industry, unlike the manufacturing industry rarely builds prototypes of its designs; therefore, it is very important that that the drawings accurately depict the intended final product.

Computer-aided drafting and design enables the designer to depict the model of the design in a relatively quick, convenient, and clean manner. Once entered, the description of the design can be changed easily and inexpensively. The computer not only produces drawings of the object, but also creates a three-dimensional computer representation of the object that can be viewed from any angle, thus verifying the design and saving time, money, and costly changes in the field.

18.2.2 Reduction of Workspace

The creation of paper drawings requires large sheets that are sometimes cumbersome to handle, are subject to damage, and require large areas for storage. Although paper is still used for architectural drawing extensively, CAD stores the information contained on drawings electronically, which requires less physical space. Paper drawings are retained only when necessary.

18.2.3 Increased Accuracy and Precision

Computers can store information about graphics in two ways. The most precise is known as vector format: lines and curves are stored according to their mathematical coordinates. The other is known as rastor format: graphic images are stored as a picture composed of a series of dots. Most full-featured CAD software packages use the vector format, but drawings are occasionally converted to rastor format during scanning, plotting, or printing.

As drawings are created in CAD, each item is given an exact mathematical description; therefore, it is more precise. In architectural drawing, the size of a component drawn can only be approximated to as close as the scale of the drawing will permit. For example, in a $\frac{1}{4}'' = 1' - 0''$ scale drawing, using a drafting scale, nothing smaller than 1 inch can be accurately drawn. With CAD, since every item is entered by its exact size, it is drawn exactly to size.

18.2.4 Scale

With CAD, objects are often drawn at full size. There is virtually an unlimited "electronic area" defined by the CAD package. A box 1 inch square and a box 1 mile square require the same amount of computer memory. Therefore, actual dimensions can be used to create the drawing instead of scaled dimensions. If one wants to view an object in the computer at a different size, the distance of the viewpoint is changed (things are larger when viewed closer). When the time comes to produce a scale drawing, the electronic version is easily reduced just before it is put on paper with a printer or plotter.

18.2.5 Flexibility

The images developed in a CAD system can be used in a variety of ways. Once drawn they can be easily changed. They can be viewed on a monitor, plotted, or printed to create hard copies. Drawings can easily be reused or copied into other drawings within the system itself or transferred into other CAD software systems through the use of widely accepted formats such as DXF (Drawing Exchange Format)[1] or IGES (International Graphic Exchange Specification). These features enable the operator to gain speed and efficiency because the amount of time spent copying, enlarging, and reducing is minimized.

The electronic format of CAD drawings enables them to be displayed in and combined with a variety of other electronic media. Electronic drawings can be stored on optical disks such as compact disks. They can be combined with text in word-processing systems, with typefaces in desktop publishing, or with photographs in digital photography and video. Paper drawings can even be converted into electronic drawings through a process known as scanning.

---

[1] Trademark of AutoDesk Inc.

Another advantage of CAD drawings is that they can be transmitted to distant sites over telephone lines and printed or plotted at their destination. Data networks are developing with which an architect in Atlanta, for example, can have his or her drawings sent to San Francisco in a matter of minutes. These networks often store the drawings for large projects for the architect and print sets as needed for clients, engineers, and contractors. Electronic data transmission reduces mailing costs and increases the speed of communication.

18.2.6 Creativity

Finally, and most importantly, CAD can expand creativity. The ease with which drawings can be changed allows for rapid trials of ideas. The more alternatives a designer can generate, the more likely he or she is to develop the best solution. Because CAD allows for accurate models to be created at lower costs, the quality of the design ideas can be tested thoroughly prior to construction.

18.3 System Components

Microcad systems are composed of several components; some involve hardware (electronic gear) and others involve software (programs). All the components are used together to make the whole system work, but each must be in its proper place and interconnected with the other parts to function correctly. Figure 18-3 is helpful in picturing how each system works with the others to produce electronic drawings. Each component will be discussed in detail in the following sections.

18.4 Hardware

The first application of computer graphics occurred in the early 1950s at the Massachusetts Institute of Technology (MIT), where a very large, complicated computer drew simple pictures on a screen. In the years that followed, business devoted little interest or money to computer graphics development; most work in that area took place at universities and military research facilities. Military research eventually resulted in the SAGE system, which allowed the air defense command to use a light pen to identify targets on a screen. The 1960s, however, brought a reevaluation of the concept of computers and graphics. Major corporations embraced the idea of people interacting with computers in a graphic environment. Some large corporations bought massive computers and commissioned programmers to

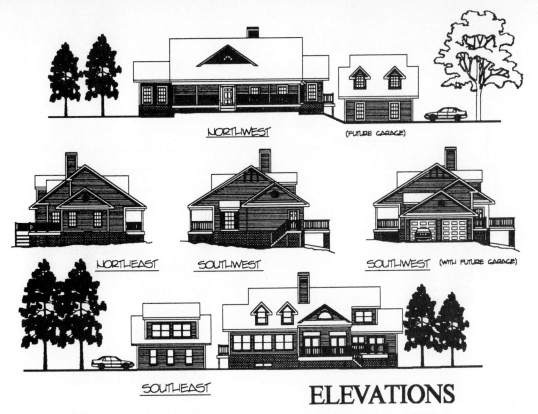

NORTHWEST

(FUTURE GARAGE)

NORTHEAST   SOUTHWEST   SOUTHWEST (WITH FUTURE GARAGE)

SOUTHEAST   ELEVATIONS

Figure 18-1 Computer-aided presentation elevations of a home for a young family.
(Paul M. Black AIA, architect)

develop CAD systems for their own use. Although creating these systems was extremely expensive and time-consuming, CAD soon proved cost effective because it allowed the computer to evaluate the reliability of a design.[2]

The January 1975 issue of *Popular Electronics* featured the worlds first minicomputer kit, the Altair 8800. Little was it known at the time that this was the beginning of a technology race roughly parallel to the space program. Personal computers, also known as microcomputers, have been through a remarkable evolution since then. The continued development of increased memory capacity and the speed at which data is manipulated has fueled the rapid rise in popularity of microcomputers for architectural drawing. With fast and powerful microcomputers, the CAD technology developed for larger computers has become affordable for more users and has resulted in widespread use of CAD among architects and engineers.

[2] Frank L., Conner, *The Student Edition of AutoSketch, User's Manual*, Addison Wesley Publishing Co., Inc., Reading, MA, The Benjamin/Cummings Publishing Co., Inc., Menlo Park, CA, 1991, p. 9.

18.4.1 Microcomputers

In August 1981, IBM announced its first Personal Computer, the IBM-XT. It had an 8088 microprocessor, 16K of standard memory, 160K diskette drives, and a text-only monochromatic display. Within a few short years, IBM took advantage of rapid developments in speed and memory and announced the IBM-AT. Its features included increased memory with a fixed disk and faster processing with a 80286 microprocessor. IBM encouraged other manufacturers to produce compatible hardware and software. Soon there was an entire industry producing IBM-AT-compatible components, not only for CAD but for many other applications.

On April 2, 1987, IBM made worldwide announcement of a new line of systems called IBM Personal System/2. This was the second generation of small computer systems. With this system, IBM ceased manufacture of IBM-AT-compatible hardware and developed a complete line of components based on an exclusive system called Micro Channel.[3] This system is manufactured only by IBM. Although the IBM-AT-compat-

[3] Trademark of IBM Corporation.

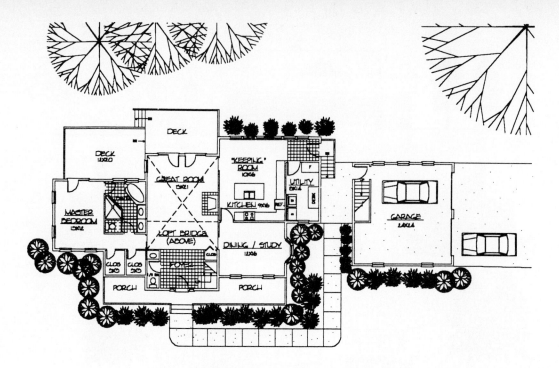

MAIN LEVEL

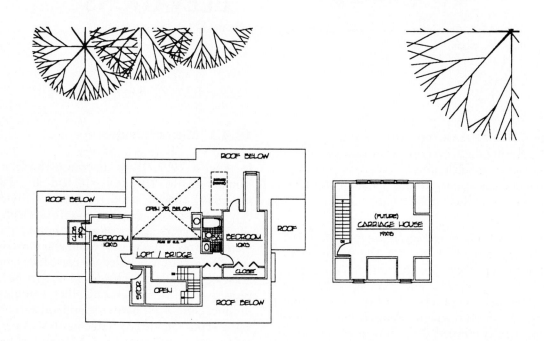

UPPER LEVEL

FIGURE 18-2 Computer-aided presentation floor plans of a home for a young family.

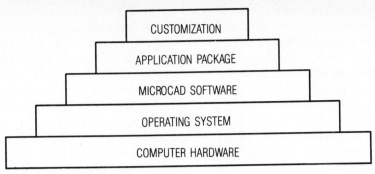

FIGURE 18-3 Components of a Microcad system.

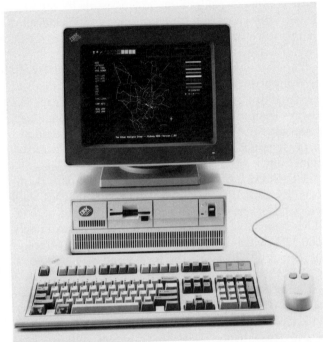

FIGURE 18-4 An IBM PS/2® computer. (Courtesy IBM Corp.)

ible industry remains strong, healthy, and extremely cost competitive, it continues to produce products based on the IBM-AT standard. Some IBM-AT-compatible manufacturer's equipment will work only with that manufacturer's components.

IBM continues to improve the PS/2 system (Figure 18-5) and reduce its cost. Both the IBM PS/2 and the IBM-AT use the same operating system, which means they can operate with much of the same software. It is important when purchasing equipment and software that claims to be IBM-AT compatible that both the software and hardware compatibility are verified by the manufacturers.

18.4.2 Hardware Components of Microcomputer Systems

The *microcomputer* is the cabinet where the disk drives are located on most machines and houses the system board, additional circuit boards, fixed disk, and central processing unit. The system board is the main circuit board for the computer, and it usually includes the microprocessor, numeric coprocessor, clock, and calender. It also includes connections (expansion slots) for additional circuit boards (cards). Typically, additional cards are added to CAD workstations to improve the appearance of the screen display (graphics) and to add connections (communications ports) to the additional equipment required for CAD.

The *microprocessor*, sometimes called the central processing unit, is typically the most important item in a computer system because it is the control center for information flow inside the computer. It is a single computer chip containing thousands of microscopic circuits that work together to execute computer programs. The microprocessor handles the data manipulation necessary to perform tasks for the user. The speed of the microprocessor has a significant effect on the performance of the computer. The internal structure or architecture of the microprocessor also determines the inherent capabilities of the personal computer in which it is used.[4]

Numeric coprocessor CAD programs usually store information about the drawings in a numerical format, as numbers; it takes a lot of numbers to describe many of the complex objects drawn in CAD. Therefore, it is advisable when setting up a microcad system to add another chip, known as a numeric math coprocessor, to supplement the microprocessor exclusively for numbers. Note, however, later-model microprocessors (80486 and above) have the numeric coprocessor built in, thereby eliminating the need to install one separately.

---

[4] Jim Hoskins, *IBM Personal System/2, A Business Perspective*, John Wiley & Sons, Inc., New York, 1987, p. 18.

The quality of the **monitor** is very important in CAD work. First, it should be large enough to view the drawing with minimum eye strain. Computer operators often spend long hours at their workstations. A monitor is usually measured diagonally across the screen; 13 inches is the minimum size recommended, 15 inches is preferred, and 19 inches is ideal. Second, although not absolutely necessary, color is very important. It helps the operator distinguish between objects on the screen. Although as many as 256 colors can be displayed, 16 are usually sufficient. Third, but no less important, is resolution. Resolution describes the fineness of the image displayed on the monitor. Monitors display images as a series of small dots on the screen. These are known as pixels, short for picture elements. The more pixels there are, the finer the image. Several standards have evolved with microcomputers for graphic display, but the most popular is VGA, which stands for video graphics array. Its display is accomplished by a field of 640×480 pixels. On the IBM PS/2 system and most other computers, VGA is provided as standard equipment.

Microcomputers have two types of *memory*. Read-only memory (ROM) contains permanent housekeeping programs used to manage the internal operation of the computer. This memory cannot be added to or altered. ROM memory is not lost when the computer is turned off. ROM also refers to any memory storage device that cannot be changed, only read. Random-access memory (RAM) is a temporary area of memory in which the current project is held while being worked on. The amount of RAM memory available on the microcomputer determines the size of the project upon which one can work and also the number of different projects upon which one can work simultaneously using a multitasking program like Windows. Early microcomputers had 512 KB of RAM, but 8MB is currently recommended for CAD. Generally, the more RAM a computer has, the better.

Programs and files are often very large. Most CAD programs are larger than the amount of RAM memory on many computers. To operate the program, a microcad computer should have a *fixed disk*, sometimes known as a hard disk. It consists of a drive mechanism with permanently installed metallic disks coated with a magnetic material. A fixed disk can store a tremendous amount of data. Microcomputers for CAD are often equipped with 10 to 250 megabytes of hard disk storage.

Diskettes are portable magnetic storage media. They can be used to record and retrieve computer information with a diskette drive. The magnetic coating is generally applied to a flexible material, thus the name floppy disk. Early diskettes were $5\frac{1}{4}''$ in diameter. Advances in technology have enabled manufacturers to increase the storage capacity of $5\frac{1}{4}''$ diskettes from 360K to 1.2 MB in a few short years. Thus $5\frac{1}{4}''$ diskettes remain widely used.

Rapidly increasing in popularity are $3\frac{1}{2}''$ diskettes enclosed in stiff plastic cases. They have a metal sleeve that slides over the magnetic material when not in use and thus are much more secure. They hold more data than $5\frac{1}{4}''$ diskettes, (up to 2 MB) and can be carried in a shirt pocket or briefcase. They are conveniently write-protected by a small switch on the case of the diskette.

Both types of diskettes require care in handling. Because they are sensitive to electromagnetic fields, they should be kept away from magnets. Magnets are often found in electric motors, speakers, televisions, and telephones. They should also be kept away from most computer equipment, except in their intended drive. They should be stored in rooms with a constant temperature and the exposed portion of the media should not be touched by hands.

Tape is another form of storage. Microcomputers can be equipped with a tape drive that allows the data from the fixed drive to be copied to magnetic tape. Tape has always been used on large mainframe systems and is a very quick and effective means to store large amounts of data. It is not common on individual CAD workstations, but is often used on networks.

CD-ROM stands for compact disk-read only memory. By utilizing laser disks much like musical and video CDs, one can store tremendous amounts of data. The capacity of a typical CD-ROM is approximately 680 MB, which is roughly equivalent to 225,000 pages of text. A CD-ROM reader is required in order to read CD-ROM disks.

Input devices are required to operate a CAD workstation. The keyboard is the most basic, but still very effective means of providing instructions to the software. An enhanced keyboard contains function keys and a calculator pad. Most CAD software will respond to instructions from the keyboard. Therefore, training in basic typing skills is highly recommended to anyone working with computers, particularly CAD.

A *mouse* (Figure 18-5) is a small device that fits into the palm of the hand and is moved horizontally across a surface. The motion is recorded on the screen of the monitor. When the operator has positioned the arrow or cursor on the screen, a button is pushed on the mouse to select that item. This is known as *clicking on* an item. The second button, if available, is usually equivalent to pressing the Enter key on the keyboard. There are two varieties; an optical mouse, which requires a reflective surface, and a mechanical mouse, which can be used on any flat surface.

The **digitizing tablet** is an electronically sensitized surface upon which a pen, puck, stylus or cursor can be used to interact with the CAD software (Figure 18-6). It can be used in three ways: (1) to point at a tablet menu to select commands, (2) to move the crosshairs in the coordinates in the CAD software. Most CAD software and applications packages utilize tablet menus, which are displayed on a digitizing tablet. They add speed and efficiency to CAD drawing.

18.4.3 Peripheral Devices and Connectivity

Printers are a form of output device that produces a paper drawing, or *hard copy* (Figure 18-7). Generally the term printer describes devices used primarily for printing text or small-scale graphics. There are two types, impact and nonimpact printers. Impact printers utilize a ribbon with either a dot-matrix or a daisywheel print head. Their quality is, at best, suitable for text, but rarely for drawings. They are helpful for running an occasional check-print.

Nonimpact printers include thermal, ink-jet, or electrostatic devices. "The best quality image comes from the laser printer. A laser draws a line on a revolving plate that is charged with a high voltage. The laser light causes the plate to discharge. An ink toner then adheres to the laser drawn images. The ink is then bonded to the paper by pressure or heat."[5]

A **pen plotter** is essentially a mechanical arm equipped with a pen. The arm moves in response to

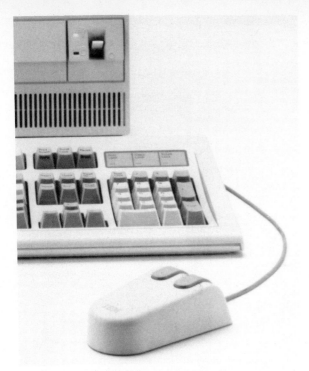

FIGURE 18-5 A two-button mouse. (Courtesy IBM Corp.)

CAD program and select the location for the work, and (3) to manually input paper drawings into CAD. It does this by converting the position of the cursor to X, Y

[5] Alan Jeffris and David Madsen, *Architectural Drafting and Design*, 2nd Ed., Delmar Publishers, Albany, N. Y., 1991, p. 102.

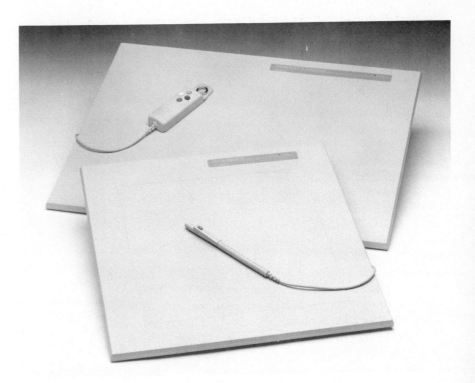

FIGURE 18-6 Digitizing tablets. (Courtesy Summagraphics Corp.)

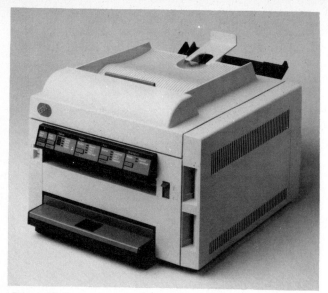

FIGURE 18-7 A compact office laser printer. (Courtesy IBM Corp.)

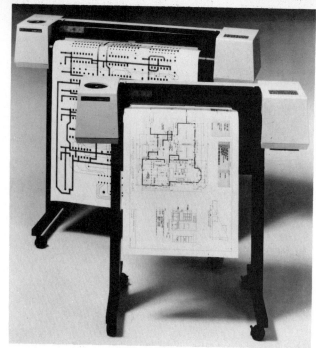

FIGURE 18-8 Roller-bed pen plotter. (Courtesy Hewlett Packard Company)

instructions from the computer and software. Plotters draw lines, curves, and characters by using a combination of side-to-side and up-and-down movements. Every plotter has a motor to move either the pen or the piece of paper up and down. A solenoid raises and lowers the pen in response to instructions from the software. The pen traces an image on paper, vellum, or polyester film. Most pen plotters have the capacity to change pens. Some stop and require the pen to be changed manually; others automatically change pens from a preloaded cartridge.

Flatbed plotters hold paper in place in a stationary position on a fixed, flat surface. Because the paper does not move, the plotter's mechanical arm moves a pen up and down and sideways to complete a drawing. Sometimes called *X-Y* plotters, these machines generally place limitations on paper size.

Roller-bed plotters (Figure 18-8) are generally more useful for engineering or architectural drawings. These devices have rollers that move the paper back and forth along a flat surface, providing up and down movement, while a pen moves horizontally along a fixed rod to make side-to-side shifts. Thus *X* motion is drawn by moving the pen and *Y* motion is drawn by moving the media.[6]

Electrostatic plotters (Figure 18-9) are reliable, because they draw without a moving mass. They draw without moving pens, hammers, inks, or ribbons. They are versatile, because they can dissect any picture, drawing, map, or text into a series of dots. This means they can handle extremely complex, high-den-

FIGURE 18-9 Electrostatic plotter. (Courtesy Hewlett Packard Company)

sity drawings and shaded areas that cannot be drawn with pen plotters. Electrostatic plotters are fast because they are not limited by the mechanical speed of pens.

[6] Roger Hart, "Plotters, Teaming up Your Compaq with the Right One," *PAQ Review*, Summer 1988, pp. 44–45.

They can operate unattended at remote sites because they do not require frequent adjustments, such as replacing dry pens or torn paper.[7]

To control plotting, a computer program dissects pictures or drawings into a matrix of dots and then selectively turns on the appropriate electrodes of the plotter to make those dots visible. The principle is similar to that of a television display, where the scanning beam is turned on and off to form a series of raster points. By selectively placing the dots of contrasting color on a substrate, any information can be displayed.

Thermal transfer plotters can be multicolor and produce a plot continuously, like an electrostatic plotter, except that in thermal transfer models an ink donor roll is coated with a wax-based ink. As the donor roll and plotting media pass over a thermal print head, small dots of ink are melted and transferred to the media. Generally, three primary colors, magenta (red), cyan (blue), and yellow are used, and each color is applied in a single pass. Thermal transfer plotters boast quiet operation, bright colors, and very good quality. Many print at the same resolution as most office laser printers, 300 dots per inch (dpi).[8]

Scanning is the process of converting paper drawings to an electronic format that is readable by the computer. A scanner "takes a picture" of a paper drawing and stores it as a series of dots known as a raster format. The more dots used, the higher is the resolution or quality of the image. As previously discussed, the raster format is not as accurate as the vector format, so the drawings must be converted manually to the vector format if a high degree of accuracy is required. Software programs are available to make the conversion, but their accuracy must still be checked and the images "cleaned up."

A *modem* is a device that allows for the transmission of computer data over telephone lines. With a modem, the user can connect to other computers and their resources. The speed at which a modem transmits and receives data is known as its *baud rate*. Commonly, modems transmit at 1200, 2400 or 9600 bps (bits per second), although higher speeds are available. Large networks have been developed, such as CompuServe,[9] that allow users to communicate with one another and access large databases of information.

Networks containing electronic versions of architectural drawings and specifications are being developed for the construction industry. Architects, engineers, and contractors can subscribe to these services for a fee. Drawings can be transmitted over a modem to the service where it can be transmitted to other consultants, plotted, printed, or filed for use by contractors in bid preparation

18.5 Operating Systems

An operating system helps coordinate computer components and performs basic housekeeping tasks. There are several different operating systems in the marketplace, but DOS (for disk operating system) is widely used for microcad systems.

18.5.1 DOS

DOS provides the foundation for a CAD software package. When the computer is first turned on, it helps set it up to operate the desired program. It acts as a translator, converting the commands the operator issues into commands the computer understands. It also translates messages from the computer into text that one can read on the screen. It also helps to organize the vast electronic memory and storage areas now available with microcomputers by creating a directory structure for the storage of files.

It is useful to think of your microcomputer workstation as a an office. The top surface of your desk, where you do your work, is like RAM memory. Your file cabinets are like directories. Each file drawer is analogous to a subdirectory. The files in the drawers are like files in DOS. With few exceptions, files are the smallest unit of information handled by DOS. Files are created in the CAD software package and they contain all the data that describe the drawings contained in them.

To perform various housekeeping tasks within the computer DOS contains 40 to 50 *commands*. These allow the user to set up the electronic office, copy files, delete files, and make back-up copies. They also allow the user to link directories together so that they can be used concurrently, with a minimum number of keystrokes.

18.5.2 Windows[10]

Introduced in 1985 as an easy to understand graphical environment, Windows allows the user to easily move back and forth from task to task. The screen displays pictures (icons), instead of words, arranged like papers on a desk. With Windows, many of the cryptic, awkward word commands of DOS can be used by pointing at a picture instead. Windows allows the user to open several files on the electronic desktop at once. As Windows becomes more widely adopted, more software products are being developed to run under DOS/Windows.

18.6 Microcad Software

Many microcad graphics software packages are available in the marketplace. A full-featured architecture

---

[7] Bill Lloyd, "Technical Notes, Note 102, Electrostatic Technology," Versatec, Inc., 1989.

[8] Hart, op. cit., p. 47–48.

[9] Trademark of CompuServe, Inc.

[10] Trademark of Microsoft Corporation.

and engineering software package provides a vector format for the storage of data and the means to create, change (edit), combine, and print drawings. Some packages contain features that allow for the drawing of three-dimensional objects (solids modeling), the addition of shade and color to the drawings, and even to create moving pictures of the objects described in the database.

Although advanced, the microcad software industry is still comparatively young and literally hundreds of software packages are available, each with its own distinct advantages. AutoCAD[11] is a widely used, general-purpose microcad package that can be combined with many special-purpose programs to accomplish a variety of tasks. MicroStation[12] is another general-purpose microcad package that also can be combined with special-purpose programs. MicroStation is compatible with Integraph's larger systems. DataCAD[13], written primarily for architects, features commands and procedures commonly used by architects in manual drafting.

It is important, however, to architects, engineers and clients for their electronic drawings to be compatible so that they can check and consult with one another. The DXF and IGES standards have been developed to allow a drawing created in one package to be displayed in another, but they are not always accurate. Therefore, many governmental agencies, A/E firms and clients require that their drawings be created or readable in AutoCAD. It has become so common that as of this writing seven out of ten microCAD workstations use AutoCAD, and the next most widely used CAD package comprises less that one in ten workstations.

18.7 Key Graphic Principles for CAD

18.7.1 Cartesian Coordinate System

In a full-featured microcad software package, all objects are stored by their mathematical coordinates in a coordinate system. Long the basis for analytic geometry, the Cartesian coordinate system is the basis for describing objects in AutoCAD. In its two-dimensional form, it contains an X and Y axes projecting vertically and horizontally from a point known as the origin (Figure 18-10). Positive numbers are indicated on the top and right quadrants. Negative numbers are indicated in the left and bottom quadrants. Motion to the left or down is indicated by a negative number, and motion to the right or up is indicated by a positive number.

Each point in the description of an object is indicated by an X and Y value, usually displayed as (X, Y). Because a line is defined by two points, lines in microcad are defined by two points, each with an X and Y

[11] Trademark of AutoDesk, Inc.
[12] Trademark of Integraph, Inc.
[13] Trademark of CADKEY, Inc.

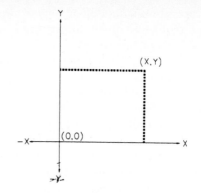

FIGURE 18-10 Cartesian Coordinate System.

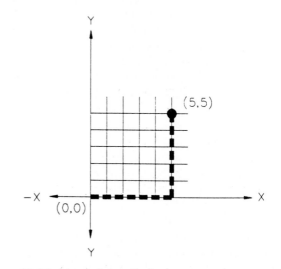

FIGURE 18-11 Linear point displacement.

coordinate on the coordinate system. "Displacements," in CAD terminology, are the distance one wishes to move along an axis (X, Y, Z) described in terms of points on the coordinate system.

18.7.2 Linear Displacement

Linear displacement is motion along an axis from point to point (Figure 18-11). It is the most fundamental method of drawing. At the keyboard one would draw from point (X, Y) to point (new X, new Y). There are two types of linear displacements. One is by absolute coordinates, which measure the location of all points from the origin. With other types, relative coordinates allow the user to reset the origin temporarily to the last point entered so that the new distances can be entered relative to the last point. Relative coordinates are frequently used because they are quicker.

18.7.3 Angular Displacement

Angular displacement (Figure 18-12) is motion from a known (X, Y) point with a distance and an angle. This is

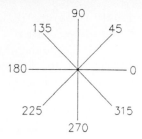

FIGURE 18-12 Angular displacement.

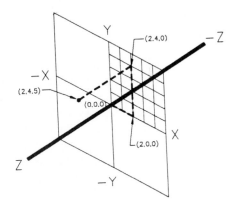

FIGURE 18-13 Three dimensional coordinate system.

ON/OFF/<Lower left corner> <0'-0",0'-0">:
Upper right corner <1'-0",0'-9">:
Command:

FIGURE 18-14 AutoCAD® screen menu.

called drawing with polar coordinates. Angles in the electronic drawing area in CAD are generally measured from east. North, then, represents 90 degrees, west; 180 degrees, and so on. Angles measured counterclockwise have a positive number, clockwise, they have a negative number.

18.7.4 Database

All the points and lines that define the objects in the drawings, taken together, represent the database of that drawing. Each time the drawing is added to or changed, the database is updated. As you might imagine, it takes many numbers to define the complex objects often depicted in CAD drawings; therefore, CAD requires special equipment and software and large amounts of computer memory.

18.7.5 Three-Dimensional Space (X, Y, Z Coordinates)

Even though we have only discussed the *X* and *Y* axes so far, the third coordinate, Z, has been there all along (Figure 18-13). The third axis helps to describe three-dimensional objects. In three-dimensional CAD, a 3D model is being created, not just a drawing. Therefore,

the model can be rotated and viewed from any direction. Most CAD packages display 3D drawings as axonometric drawings, but a few, including AutoCAD, can create perspective views that make attractive presentations. Once the model is created, it can be shaded. Moving pictures or "animations" can be made to simulate a walk-through or fly-over, making truly dynamic presentations.

18.8 BASIC Computer-Aided Drafting with AutoCAD

Once loaded onto a computer, most CAD packages can be started with a short keyword. This word is recognized by DOS and the program begins. Sometimes an instructor or CAD manager will set up a DOS screen menu, allowing the student to choose a CAD program. Once begun, there are often several ways to drive the program, including typing from the keyboard, pointing with a mouse or digitizing tablet, and interacting with items as they appear on the screen. In AutoCAD the following devices will appear on the screen as one works.

18.8.1 Menus

When the drawing editor is active, a *screen menu* can be displayed on the right edge of the graphics screen. This menu lets you enter a command by simply pointing to the command on the screen with a pointing device or by using the keyboard's arrow keys. The AutoCAD screen menu is illustrated in Figure 18-14.

Computers with advanced graphics support **pull-down menus**, which you pull down from the menu bar at the top of the screen (Figure 18-15).

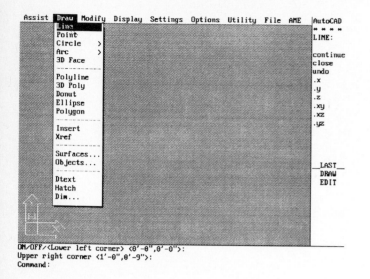

FIGURE 18-15 AutoCAD® pull-down menu.

Tablet menus (Figure 18-16) are stiff cards attached to the digitizing tablet. They contain a pointing area that equates to the screen on the monitor for drawing and illustrations of the commands that allow the user to quickly select an operation with the cursor, while drawing.

Dialogue boxes (Figure 18-17) are screens that appear when you need to make changes in values and it would be advantageous to review the current settings of those values. They provide a quick visual means of viewing the current setup and making changes.

18.8.2 Commands

The work in CAD is created primarily by a series of operations known as *commands*. Each allows for the creation or change of entities within the drawing. In AutoCAD, the prompt "command:" appears at the bottom left of the screen when the software is ready to receive instructions. Once started, a command may have several steps to define what is to be done before it can be executed. Commands can be invoked from the

FIGURE 18-15 AutoCAD® pull-down menu.

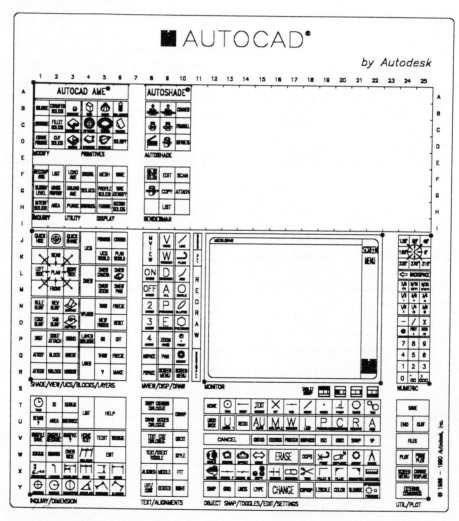

FIGURE 18-16 AutoCAD® tablet menu.

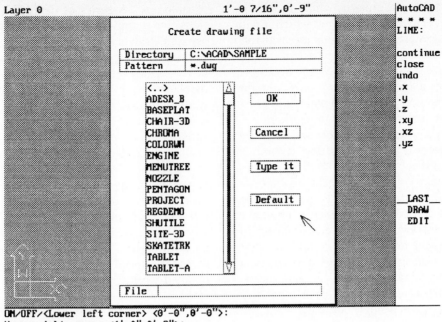

Create drawing file

Directory	C:\ACAD\SAMPLE
Pattern	*.dwg

```
<..>
ADESK_B
BASEPLAT
CHAIR-3D
CHROMA
COLORWH
ENGINE
MENUTREE
NOZZLE
PENTAGON
PROJECT
REGDEMO
SHUTTLE
SITE-3D
SKATETRK
TABLET
TABLET-A
```

OK

Cancel

Type it

Default

File

```
* * * *
LINE:

continue
close
undo
.x
.y
.z
.xy
.xz
.yz


__LAST__
DRAW
EDIT
```

ON/OFF/<Lower left corner> <0'-0",0'-0">:
Upper right corner <1'-0",0'-9">:
Command: save

FIGURE 18-17 AutoCAD® dialogue box.

keyboard, screen menus, pull-down menus, or the digitizing tablet with a tablet menu.

Draw commands take the user's input and create the geometric entities intended to be shown in CAD. Most systems have commands that will create points, lines, circles, polygons, ellipses, and the basic geometric shapes. Each shape is constructed by first establishing its location and then its size in accordance with its geometric properties. For example, a point must be defined by two coordinates, a line must be defined by two points, a circle by its centerpoint and radius, and a polygon by its number of sides. Beyond simple geometric entities, draw commands allow for more complex operations. Sketching consists of creating freehand lines with the cursor or arrow keys. Hatch patterns can be added to enclosed geometric shapes showing brick, concrete, steel, and much more. Annotating (lettering) drawings is simplified with CAD. One selects a typeface or font, size and location and then types the text from the keyboard. Notes can be easily changed and moved.

Edit commands are used to change and revise entities that have already been created within the program. This is where the power of CAD becomes obvious. Entities can be erased and then restored if necessary. Lines can be cut or trimmed to meet others. Items can be easily moved from place to place on the drawing. They can be enlarged and reduced in size and rotated a full (or any part of) 360 degrees. Entities can be stretched or enlarged in one direction, but not another. Through a process known as *mirroring*, upside-down or

reverse copies can be made, yet the writing on the drawing can stay "right reading." Probably the most powerful edit command, "array", allows for multiple copies of an entity in a circle or rectangular matrix.

Inquiry commands enable the user to get details from the database and the status of the drawing environment. They can provide a listing of the size and geometric description of the entities in the drawing and calculate the perimeter and area of shapes. One can use inquiry commands to identify the location in the Cartesian coordinate system of points, lines, and shapes.

18.8.3 The Drawing Environment

Recall the Cheshire Cat. Most CAD software packages offer so much flexibility that one can easily become confused. AutoCAD, like many CAD packages, can be used for a wide variety of applications. The drawing environment is extremely flexible in CAD and, when understood, this becomes another of its many advantages.

As our prime concern here is architectural drawing, think of the decisions that must be made before starting to draw with a pencil. How big a drawing table is necessary? What units will be used to draw? Architectural? Decimal-feet? Will a paper with a grid be used? Will the drawing be full size or scaled?

CAD programs have *settings* to control all of these factors and more. In AutoCAD these are known as "settings." They control the size of the area in which the objects will be drawn, the units in which it will be measured, and the relative size or scale at which it will be depicted. Furthermore, drawing aids are available that can set up a reference grid in the background to help keep one's place. Other drafting aids, impossible in manual drafting, allow one to draw only straight lines, draw only from grid point to grid point, and draw from one particular part of an object to another.

Layers in CAD drawings help to sort and organize data. They are derived from a drafting technique known as overlay drafting. In overlay drafting a series of translucent sheets were used to create a composite drawing. All the drawings were held in registration with a pin bar attached to the drawing board. The walls and doors would be drawn on one layer, the electrical plan, and HVAC plans on others. A composite print could be made by placing the drawings together on a flat-bed diazo machine and making a blue-line print.

CAD software packages offer the same capability and more. Using layers in a single "drawing," one can clearly organize the work and make it much easier to revise later. Each layer can have a separate name, color, and type of line (dashed, dotted, continuous, and so on). Each layer can be turned off, making it invisible on the screen, and then on again. Layers can also be temporarily excluded from the database (frozen) to save time. Items can be moved from layer to layer as desired. Only one layer can be edited at a time. Therefore, only the active layer can be changed.

Display is used to enlarge a portion of a drawing. If one is creating an object as large as an Olympic-sized (50 meters) swimming pool in CAD and looking through a 15-inch monitor, it will probably appear too small to work on, especially when drawing the pattern of the slots in the grid on the drain at the bottom. Although this example illustrates another advantage of CAD, the ability to draw infinite detail, there must be a way to move closer and farther away from our subject; and there is. In AutoCAD a group of **display commands** helps to control the point of view. The primary command for moving in or out on an object is "zoom" in AutoCAD. With this command, one can move in or out at specified increments. The primary way to move from side to side on an object in AutoCAD is "pan." A linear displacement is required for "pan." It can be either entered from the keyboard or graphically on the screen. When zooming and panning, it is important to remember that the object always remains the same; only the viewpoint changes.

18.8.4 Polylines

A complex CAD drawing can have a large database. It is not uncommon for a single architectural drawing to require more than one diskette. It is important, then, that drawings created on microcad, be kept to a man-ageable size. A series of detailed architectural elevations, for example, would best be stored as a series of separate drawings. They can be combined just prior to plotting or each plotted separately on the same sheet. CAD packages, however, are designed to minimize the database whenever possible. One way this is done is by putting related objects together as groups. In Auto-CAD a group is known as a *polyline*. For instance, a square can be stored in the database as four lines, each at an angle of 90 degrees and each with a beginning and ending point. Or it can be stored as a group known as a square with equal sides of N length, the latter being much more compact. However, if one wanted to remove one side of the square stored in this manner, it would be impossible without first breaking it down into its parts again. Therefore, polylines can greatly increase the speed of the CAD system, but can hinder detailed work.

18.8.5 Combining Drawings

Architectural drawings are often composed of symbols that are transferred from drawing to drawing. Sometimes they contain actual parts from other drawings. Draftspersons of the past laboriously copied drawings from one set to another or, more recently copied, cut and pasted them into new drawings. Just the ability to copy an entity in a single drawing would relieve this tedium, but there is even more.

"*Block*" allows the reuse of drawings and symbols within a drawing or from drawing to drawing. In some CAD systems they are called "*parts*". Whatever the name, it is one of the most powerful features of CAD. When the "Block" command is invoked in Autocad, the user is prompted to select the items to be included. After selection, the items are saved as a part of the drawing file. They can be recalled into the drawing with the "*insert*" command. If the user wishes to use those items in another drawing, then the block is converted into a drawing file with the "WBlock" (for Write BLOCK) command. The items contained in the block are now contained in a drawing file. When the items are needed again *in any drawing*, they can be recalled with the "insert" command. The beauty of this is that any drawing can be combined with any other drawing in CAD.

The power of blocks has two primary implications. First, drawing symbols that are frequently used, such as doors, windows, plumbing fixtures, and furniture, can be created just one time and reused. Symbol libraries are composed of these items. Second, parts of drawings can be combined with other drawings. For example, a title block can be created for a 24 × 36 sheet one time and then called into other drawings as required. With "attributes," another powerful CAD feature associated with "blocks," the user can be prompted

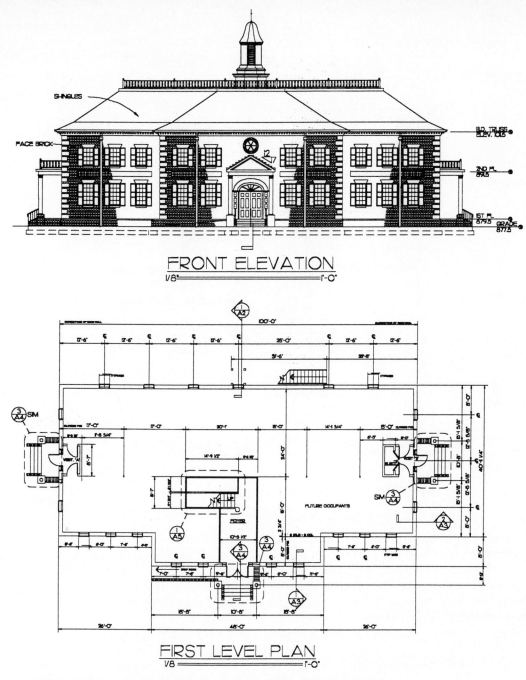

FRONT ELEVATION
1/8" = 1'-0"

FIRST LEVEL PLAN
1/8 = 1'-0"

Figure 18-18 Computer-aided drawing of an office building elevation and floor plan. (Robert Foreman Assoc., architect, Paul M. Black AIA, project manager)

to input the sheet number and date. Finally, details commonly used in an office can easily be reused on other projects.

18.8.6 Customization

The prototype drawing. CAD packages are very flexible, but they can also be customized for a particular use or user. Blocks are the first step in customization. The next step is automating the procedure by which the drawing environment is created. Normally, while booting up the CAD software looks for a seed drawing or *prototype*. Much as a word-processing system starts with an 8.5 × 11 sheet, CAD packages must have something from which to start; therefore, the manufacturer usually provides one with the package. In Auto-CAD, the exact information contained in the prototype drawing is normally duplicated in a new drawing. Therefore, one can duplicate the drawing environment of previous drawings with ease simply by changing the prototype drawing.

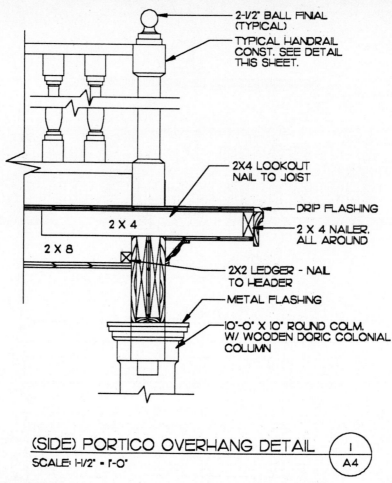

2-1/2" BALL FINIAL
(TYPICAL)

TYPICAL HANDRAIL
CONST. SEE DETAIL
THIS SHEET.

2X4 LOOKOUT
NAIL TO JOIST

DRIP FLASHING

2 X 4

2 X 4 NAILER,
ALL AROUND

2 X 8

2X2 LEDGER - NAL
TO HEADER

METAL FLASHING

10"-0" X 10" ROUND COLM.
W/ WOODEN DORIC COLONIAL
COLUMN

(SIDE) PORTICO OVERHANG DETAIL
SCALE: 1-1/2" = 1'-0"

I
A4

FIGURE 18-19 Computer-aided drawing of an office building detail.

In some applications, *other prototype drawings* are required. For example, title blocks for 18 × 24 sheets, 24 × 36 sheets and 30 × 42 sheets. In this case, not only the previous settings, but the previous drawing (the title block) should be duplicated. It is possible to set any one of these drawings as the pattern (prototype) for a new drawing, thus saving the time required to create again.

Macro is short for macro command, meaning a large or long command. Therefore, it is a series of commands attached together so as to perform a task. AutoCAD has several menus from which commands and tasks are selected. The menus actually consist of prewritten macros. An advanced user can rewrite these menus or add new ones to string together series of frequently used commands. Keyboard characters have special meanings in the AutoCAD menu, almost like a primitive programming language. The result is a customized menu. In the case of the tablet menu, blank spaces or cells are available that can be assigned to custom macros so that they can be activated with the cursor.[14] Macros can be written for the buttons on a cursor and the screen menu. An example of a simple two-step macro would be created to enter ZOOM Window in one step, thereby minimizing input from the user. ZOOM Window could then be included on and activated from a screen menu.[15]

LISP is a programming language that was derived from XLISP. AutoLISP[16] is a dialect of LISP and coexists with AutoCAD itself within the AutoCAD program.[17] LISP is short for list Processing. It can be used to create programs within AutoCAD using more than just the resident commands. "An example of an AutoLISP program would be one that would expedite creation of a staircase in a building. If properly written, the program would prompt you for the distance between the upper and lower floors, ask you for the size and/or number of steps (risers and treads), and automatically draw the detailed staircase for you."[18]

[14] D. Raker, and II. Rice, *Inside AutoCAD*, 5th ed. (New Riders Publishing, Thousand Oaks, Calif., 1989, p. 18-1-8.

[15] Wohlers, Terry, T., *Applying AutoCAD, Step by Step* (Glencoe Publishing) Mission Hills, Calif., 1989, p. 350.

[16] A registered trademark of Autodesk, Inc.

[17] Raker, and Rice, op cit., p. 20–1.

[18] Wohlers, op. cit., p. 380.

18.8.7 Third-Party Development

Many software packages including AutoCAD are general purpose, that is, intended for many different applications. Unfortunately, what is gained in flexibility is lost in utility. In other words, the basic package can be used for several different disciplines, but each discipline must adapt it for its particular way of drawing.

We have just had a brief overview of customization, in which new menu features and LISP routines can be added to increase speed and efficiency. Many users not proficient in customization and programming prefer to use customized features developed by others and incorporate them into their system. These include special type fonts, hatch patterns, text editors, macros, and LISP routines. Users sometimes share these add-ons through user's groups, bulletin boards, and personal contacts, taking care not to violate copyright law. Some items are available directly from the developer, such as text fonts. Macros and LISP routines are regularly published in customization books and CAD industry journals.

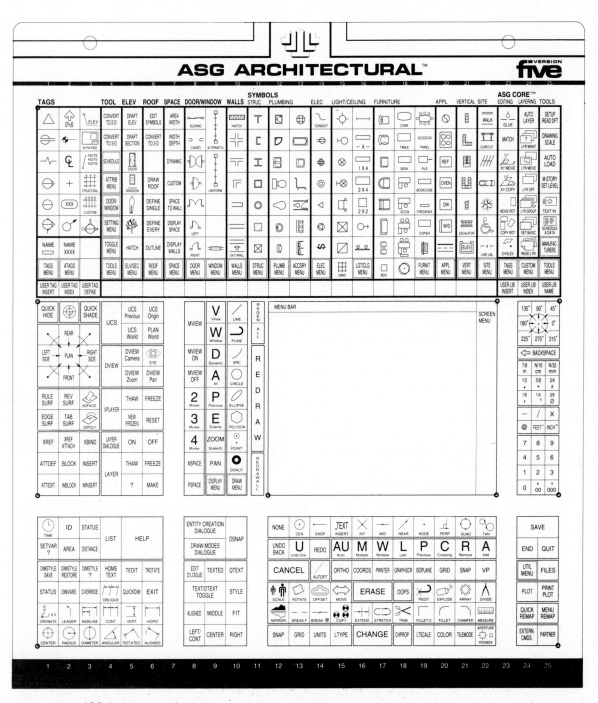

FIGURE 18-20 ASG Architectural® tablet menu. (Courtesy ASG, Inc.)

Some construction product manufacturers prepare details of their products in CAD and write custom programs to run within AutoCAD. These enable the user to select one of their products, including model, size, and features, and combine it with the working drawings. Such programs are now available from fireplace, window and plumbing fixture manufacturers.

Furthermore, packages that contain entire detail files are available that work within a CAD software package. Within these packages, the designer can choose among thousands of predrawn details, verify that they apply to the current project, change them if necessary, and then incorporate them into the working drawings. Currently, third-party software developers and construction product manufacturers are working together to combine their details into massive databases.

18.8.8 Applications Packages

A special type of software known as an applications package is available. Each is for use with specific microcad packages. In some cases they are developed by the primary CAD software company, but frequently they are produced by another company, a third party. They run within the primary CAD software and are a coordinated set of customized features, such as a drawing setup routine, layering schemes, drawing settings, menus, symbols, and macros.

Most application packages are developed in modular coordinated sets. They have the advantage of being integrated so that design professionals can easily exchange files and information. Softdesk, Inc., manufactures an integrated line of products to run within Auto-CAD: Civil/Surveying, Architectural, Facilities, and Structural. Within the architectural package, are programs such as Auto-Architect, HVAC, and Architectural Electric and Plumbing. Auto-Architect includes routines to draw double lines for walls; draw stairs, doors, and windows; and perform space planning. It also contains an extensive symbol library.

ASG[19] provides other integrated applications packages for use within AutoCAD. The heart of the system is called ASG Core. The Core software includes a facility for adding descriptive tags to any object. It also handles text generation, bills-of-materials and libraries of symbols and access to manufacturers' catalogs."[20] Layer Master, along with Core also allows management of layers through an advanced hierarchial system and provides AIA CAD layer guidelines. A dozen separate but integrated packages are available, including ASG Architectural.

[19] Trademark of Archsoft Group.

[20] "Autodesk AEC Architectural Is Now ASG Architectural," *Architectural Record*, July 1990, p. 105.

ASG Architectural contains a large library of predrawn symbols, including doors, windows, furniture, structural shapes, plumbing fixtures, electrical components, appliances, stairs, sitework, and landscaping. Given a space diagram, it can create a double-line wall drawing. Given a roof perimeter, slope, overhang, and elevation, it will automatically calculate the ridge, hip, and valley lines, even in 3-D if desired, and then construct the roof. Each package has a separate tablet menu (Figure 18-20), which is attached to a digitizing tablet. Selections are made by pointing at the tablet and from the screen.

18.8.9 Advanced CAD Concepts

Presently, many two-dimensional architectural drawings are produced with microcad. General-purpose microcad packages combined with an applications package and some customization are being used throughout the construction industry to create accurate working drawings with increased efficiency. Current estimates are that CAD drafters can increase their productivity three to twenty times, depending on the type of work.[21]

In the future, architectural drawing may be significantly different. CAD is used increasingly for conceptual design and architectural presentation. These presentations may become the basis for working drawings. Building forms may be initially conceived as three-dimensional objects in microcad software. In model form, surfaces may be shown as actual construction materials. The model can be rotated. The viewer can walk through or fly over the building with animation software. Plans, elevations and sections may then be derived directly from the three-dimensional model for working drawings.

Whatever the future holds, computers and microcad are likely to play a large part. But, even so, students who possess both an understanding of fundamental graphic principles and microcad systems are the most likely to find themselves working in the profession in the twenty-first century.

BIBLIOGRAPHY

Architectural Record, "Autodesk AEC Architectural IS Now ASG Architectural," McGraw-Hill, July 1990, p. 105.

Autodesk, Inc., *AutoCAD Release 11 Reference Manual*, 1990.

Conner, Frank L., *The Student Edition of AutoSketch*, User's Manual, Addison-Wesley Publishing Co., Inc., Reading, Mass., The Benjamin/Cummings Publishing Co., Inc. 1991.

[21] Jeffris, and Madsen, op. cit., p. 99.

Hart, Roger, "Plotters, Teaming up Your Compaq with the Right One," *PAQ Review*, Summer 1988.

Hoskins, Jim, *IBM Personal System/2, a Business Perspective*, John Wiley & Sons, New York, 1987.

Jeffris, Alan, and David Madsen, *Architectural Drafting and Design*, 2nd Ed., Delmar Publishers, Albany, N.Y., 1991.

Lloyd, Bill, *Technical Notes, Note 102, Electrostatic Technology*, Versatec, 1989.

Popular Electronics *"World's First Minicomputer Kit to Rival Commercial Models . . . "Altair 8800""*, January 1975.

Raker, Daniel, and Harbort, Rice, *Inside AutoCAD*, 5th Ed., New Riders Publishing Co., Thousand Oaks, Calif., 1989.

Sheldon, Thomas, *Hard Disk Management in the PC & MS DOS Environment*, McGraw-Hill Book Company, New York, 1988.

Wohlers, Terry T., *Applying AutoCAD, Step by Step*, Glencoe Publishing, Division of Macmillan, Inc., Mission Hills, Calif., 1989.

REVIEW QUESTIONS

1. Why doesn't learning to draw with a computer eliminate the need to learn to draw by hand?

2. What is meant by the term "model" in computer aided design?

3. In what ways can computer aided design aid creativity?

4. Which two major technological developments with computer hardware have fueled the rapid rise in popularity of micro computers?

5. What is the proper name of the main circuit board which contains the microprocessor numeric coprocessor and expansion slots?

6. How many pages of text can be stored on a typical CD-ROM disk?

7. Why is it important that CAD users develop good typing skills?

8. Discuss the advantages and disadvantages of pen and electrostatic plotters.

9. A device (other than a FAX) used to transmit files electronically over telephone lines.

10. What are the major purposes of an operating system?

11. Using AutoCAD conventions, give an example of each of the following:
    a. linear displacement by absolute coordinates
    b. linear displacement by relative coordinates
    c. angular displacement by polar coordinates

12. What are four different techniques to issue commands using AutoCAD?

13. In a typical CAD drawing session, which type of commands are used most frequently, draw or edit?

14. Why does a square one inch long on each side require the same amount of computer memory as a square one mile long on each side?

15. Points, lines, and circles are examples of *entities*. What is the name of a compact group of entities in AutoCAD?

16. Polylines can greatly increase the *speed* of CAD work, but can hinder *detailed work*. Why?

17. What are the advantages of combining drawings?

18. Explain how symbol libraries are created in CAD.

19. Explain the difference between graphic images stored in vector format and raster format.

20. When objects are drawn at full scale in CAD, how are scale drawings generally produced?

APPENDICES

Appendix A: Glossary of Construction Terms

Also see: Electrical Terms, p. 364
Stair Terms, p. 300
Typical Residential Terms, p. 152

A

ABUT   Joining the end of a construction member.

ACRE   A unit of land measurement having 43,560 sq ft.

ADHESIVE   A natural or synthetic material, usually in liquid form, used to fasten or adhere materials together.

ADOBE CONSTRUCTION   Construction using sun-dried units of adobe soil for walls; usually found in the southwestern United States.

AGGREGATE   Gravel (coarse) or sand (fine) used in concrete mixes.

AIR-DRIED LUMBER   Lumber that has been dried by unheated air to a moisture content of approximately 15 percent.

ANCHORS   Devices, usually metal, used in building construction to secure one material to another.

ANGLE   A piece of structural steel having an L-shaped cross section, with equal or unequal legs.

APRON   Inside window trim placed under the stool and against the wall.

ARCADE   An open passageway usually surrounded by a series of arches.

ARCH   A curved structure designed to support itself and the weight above.

AREAWAY   Recessed area below grade around the foundation to allow light and ventilation into basement window.

ARRIS   The sharp edge formed by two surfaces; usually on moldings.

ASBESTOS BOARD   A fire-resistant sheet made from asbestos fiber and portland cement.

ASH PIT   An enclosed opening below a fireplace to collect ashes.

ASPHALT SHINGLES   Composition roof shingles made from asphalt-impregnated felt covered with mineral granules.

ASTM   American Society for Testing and Materials.

ASTRAGAL   T-profiled molding usually used between meeting doors or casement windows.

ATRIUM   An open court within a building.

ATTIC   The space between the roof and the ceiling in a gable house.

AWNING WINDOW   An outswinging window hinged at the top of the sash.

AXIS   A line around which something rotates or is symmetrically arranged.

B

BACKFILL   Earth used to fill in areas around foundation walls.

BACKSPLASH   A protective strip attached to the wall at the back edge of a counter top.

BALCONY   A deck projecting from the wall of a building above ground level.

BALLOON FRAME   A type of wood framing in which the studs extend from sill to eaves without interruption.

BALUSTERS   Small, vertical supports for the railing of a stairs.

BALUSTRADE   A series of balusters supporting the railing of a stairs or balcony.

BANNISTER   A handrail with supporting posts on a stairway.

BARGEBOARD   The finish board covering the projecting portion of a gable roof.

BAR JOIST   A light steel structural member fabricated with a top chord, bottom chord and web members.

BASEBOARD   The finish trim board covering the interior wall where the wall and floor meet.

BATT   A type of insulation designed to be installed between framing members.

BATTEN   The narrow strips of wood nailed vertically over the joints of boards to form board-and-batten siding.

BATTER BOARDS   Horizontal boards at exact elevations nailed to posts just outside the corners of a proposed building. Strings are stretched across the boards to locate the outline of the foundation for workmen.

BAYS   Uniform compartments within a structure, usually within a series of beams, columns, etc.

BAY WINDOWS   A group of windows projecting from the wall of a building. The center is parallel to the wall, and the sides are angular. A bow window is circular.

BEAM   Horizontal structural member, usually heavier than joist.

BEARING PLATE   A metal plate that provides support for a structural member.

BEARING WALL   A wall that supports a weight above in addition to its own weight.

BENCH MARK   A mark on some permanent object fixed to the ground from which land measurements and elevations are taken.

BIDET   Low plumbing fixture in luxury bathrooms for bathing one's private parts.

BLIND NAILING   Method of nailing to conceal nails.

BLOCKING Small wood pieces in wood framing to anchor or support other major members.

BOARD MEASURE The system of lumber measurement. A unit is 1 board ft which is 1' sq by approximately 1" thick.

BONDS The arrangement of masonry units in a wall.

BOND BEAM Continuous, reinforced concrete block course around the top of masonry walls.

BRICK Small masonry units made from clay and baked in a kiln.

BRICK VENEER A facing of brick on the outer side of wood frame or masonry.

BRIDGING Thin wood or metal pieces fastened diagonally at midspan between floor joists to act as both tension and compression members for the purposes of stiffening and spreading concentrated loads.

BUCK Frame for a door, usually made of metal.

BUILDING LINE An imaginary line on a plot beyond which the building may not extend.

BUILT-UP ROOF A roofing composed of layers of felt impregnated with pitch, coal tar, or asphalt. The top is finished with crushed stone or minerals. It is used on flat or low-pitched roofs.

BULLNOSE Rounded edge units.

BUTT Type of joint having the pieces edge to edge or end to end. Also a type of door hinge allowing edge of door to butt into the jamb.

BUTTRESS Vertical masonry or concrete support, usually larger at the base, which projects from and strengthens a wall.

C

CALL OUT A note on a drawing with a leader to the feature.

CANTILEVER A projecting beam or structural member anchored at only one end.

CANT STRIP An angular board used to eliminate a sharp, right angle, usually on roof decks.

CAP Covering for a wall or post.

CARPORT A garage not fully enclosed.

CASEMENT WINDOW Window with one or two sash that hinge on their sides. They may open either in or out.

CASING Trim around a window or door opening.

CAULKING A soft, waterproof material used to fill open joints or cracks.

CAVITY WALL A masonry wall having a 2" air space between brick wythes.

CEMENT A fine, gray powder made from lime, silica, iron oxide, and alumina that when mixed with water and aggregate produces concrete.

CHAMFER The beveled edge formed by removing the sharp corner of a material.

CHANNEL A piece of structural steel having a C-shaped cross section.

CHASE A vertical space within a building for ducts, pipes, or wires.

CHORD The lower horizontal member of a truss.

CLEANOUT Accessible fitting on plumbing pipe which can be removed to clean sanitary drainage pipe.

CLEAT A small board fastened to another member to serve as a brace or support.

CLERESTORY A portion of an interior rising above adjacent roof tops and having windows.

COLLAR BEAM A horizontal member tying opposing rafters below the ridge in roof framing.

COLUMN Vertical supporting member.

CONCRETE A building material made from cement, aggregate and water.

CONCRETE MASONRY UNIT A concrete block extruded from cement, aggregate and water.

CONDUIT, ELECTRICAL A metal pipe in which wiring is installed.

CONTOUR A line on a map connecting all points with the same elevation.

COPING A cap or top course of masonry on a wall to prevent moisture penetration.

CORBEL A projection of masonry from the face of a wall, or a bracket used for support of weight above.

CORE The inner layer of plywood. It may be veneer, solid lumber, or fiberboard.

CORNER BOARD Vertical board forming the corner of a building.

CORNER BRACE Diagonal brace at the corner of a wood-frame wall to stiffen and prevent racking.

CORNICE The molded projection of the roof overhang at the top of a wall.

CORNICE RETURN The short portion of a molded cornice that returns on the gable end of a house.

COUNTER FLASHING Flashing used under cap flashing.

COVE A concave molding usually used on horizontal inside corners.

CRAWL SPACE The shallow space below the floor of a house built above the ground. Generally it is surrounded with the foundation wall.

CRICKET A device used at roof intersections to divert rain water.

CRIPPLE A structural member that is cut less than full

length, such as a studding piece above a window or door opening.

CROWN MOLDING   A molding used above eye level, usually the cornice molding under the roof overhang.

CUL-DE-SAC   A court or street with no outlet which provides a turnaround for vehicles.

CUPOLA   A small, decorative structure placed on a roof, usually a garage roof, and can be used as a ventilator.

CURTAIN WALL   An exterior wall that provides no structural support.

D

DADO JOINT   A recessed joint on the face of a board to receive the end of a perpendicular board.

DAMPER   A movable plate which regulates the draft through a flue or duct.

DAMPPROOFING   Material used to prevent passage of moisture.

DEAD LOAD   The weight of the structure itself and the permanent components fastened to it.

DECK   Exterior floor, usually extended from the outside wall.

DEFLECTION   The deviation of the central axis of a beam from normal when loaded.

DIMENSION LUMBER   Framing lumber which is 2″ thick and 4″–12″ wide.

DOME   A roof in the shape of a hemisphere used on a structure.

DOORJAMB   Two vertical pieces held together by a head jamb forming the inside lining of a door opening.

DOORSTOP   The strips on the doorjambs against which the door closes.

DORMER   A projection on a sloping roof framing a vertical window or vent.

DOUBLE GLAZING   Two pieces of glass with air between to provide insulation.

DOUBLE HUNG   A type of window having two sashes which can be operated vertically.

DOWNSPOUT   A pipe for carrying rainwater from the roof to the ground or sewer connection.

DRESSED SIZE   The actual finish size of lumber after surfacing.

DRIP   A projecting construction member or groove below the member to throw off rainwater.

DRY-WALL CONSTRUCTION   Interior wall covering with sheets of gypsum rather than traditional plaster.

DUCTS   Sheet-metal conductors for air distribution throughout a building.

DUPLEX OUTLET   Electrical wall outlet having two plug receptacles.

E

EARTH BERM   An area of raised earth.

EASEMENT   A right or privilege to a piece of property held by someone other than the owner. Usually the right to run utility lines, underground pipe, or passageways on property.

EAVES   The lower portion of the roof that overhangs the wall.

EFFLORESCENCE   The forming of white stains on masonry walls from moisture within the walls.

ELL   An extension or wing of a building at right angles to the main section.

ESCUTCHEON   The decorative metal plate used around the keyhole on doors or around a pipe extending through the wall.

EXCAVATION   A cavity or pit produced by digging the earth in preparation for construction.

EXPANSION JOINT   A flexible joint used to prevent cracking or breaking because of expansion and contraction due to temperature changes.

EXTERIOR INSULATION FINISH SYSTEM   An exterior wall finish made from styrofoam, cement, fiberglass and an acrylic coating.

F

FACADE   The face or front elevation of a building.

FACE BRICK   Brick of better quality used on the face of a wall.

FASCIA   The outside horizontal member on the edge of a roof or overhang.

FASTENERS   General term for metal devices, such as nails, bolts, screws, etc., used to secure structural members within a building.

FENESTRATION   The arrangement of window and door openings in a wall.

FIBERBOARD   Fabricated structural sheets made from wood fiber and adhesive under pressure.

FILL   Sand, gravel, or loose earth used to bring a subgrade up to a desired level around a building.

FIRECUT   An angular cut at the end of a floor joist resting on a masonry wall.

FIRE-RATING   A fire resistance classification assigned to a building material or assembly.

FIRE-STOP   A tight closure of a concealed space with incombustible material to prevent the spreading of fire.

FIRE WALL A fire-resistant masonry wall between sections of a building for the purpose of containing a fire.

FLAGSTONE Thin, flat stones used for floors, steps, walks, etc.

FLANGE The top or bottom pieces which project from a web of a structural steel member.

FLASHING Sheet metal or other material used in roof or wall construction to prevent water from seeping into the building.

FLAT-PLATE COLLECTOR A solar energy collector made from metal piping with glass over.

FLITCH BEAM A built-up beam formed by a metal plate sandwiched between two wood members and bolted together for additional strength.

FLOOR JOIST Structural member of a floor.

FLUE The passage in a chimney through which smoke, gases, and fumes escape to the outer air.

FOOTING Poured concrete base upon which the foundation wall rests.

FRIEZE The flat board of cornice trim which is fastened to the wall.

FROSTLINE The deepest level of frost penetration in soil. This depth varies in different climates. Footings must be placed below the frostline to prevent rupturing the foundation.

FURRING STRIPS Thin strips of wood fastened to walls or ceilings for leveling and for receiving the finish surface material.

G

GABLE The triangular end of a gable-roofed house.

GAMBREL ROOF A roof with two pitches, the lower slope steeper than the upper.

GIRDER Heavy structural member supporting lighter structural members of a floor or roof.

GLAZING Placing of glass in windows and doors.

GRADE BEAM A horizontal member between two supporting piers at or below grade that supports a wall or structure above.

GRADIENT The inclination of a road, piping, or the ground, expressed in percent.

GRAVEL STOP A strip of metal with a vertical lip used to retain the gravel around the edge of a built-up roof.

GROUNDS Wood strips fastened to walls before plastering to serve as screeds and nailing base for trim.

GROUT Thin cement mortar used for leveling and filling masonry cavities.

GUSSET A plywood or metal plate used to strengthen the joints of a truss.

GUTTER A metal or wood trough for carrying water from a roof.

GYP BOARD Gypsum sheets covered with paper that are fastened to walls and ceilings with nails or screws.

H

HANGER A metal strap used to support piping or the ends of joists.

HEADER In framing, the joists placed at the ends of a floor opening and attached to the trimmers. In masonry work, the small end of a masonry unit.

HEARTH The incombustible floor in front of and within the fireplace.

HEARTWOOD The central portion of wood within the tree, which is stronger and more decay-resistant than the surrounding sapwood.

HIP RAFTER The diagonal rafter that extends from the plate to the ridge to form the hip.

HIP ROOF A roof that rises by equally inclined planes from all four sides of a building.

HOSE BIBB A water faucet made for the threaded attachment of a hose.

HOUSE DRAIN Horizontal sewer piping within a building which carries the waste from the soil stacks.

HOUSE SEWER The watertight soil pipe extending from the exterior of the foundation wall to the public sewer.

HUMIDIFIER A device, generally attached to the furnace, which supplies or maintains correct humidity levels in a building.

I

I-BEAM A structural steel shape with a web and flange components, having an I-shaped cross section.

INCANDESCENT LAMP A lamp within which a filament gives off light when sufficiently heated by an electric current.

INSULATING CONCRETE Concrete with vermiculite added to produce lightweight, insulating concrete for subfloors and roofs.

INTERIOR TRIM General term for all the finish molding, casing, baseboard, etc., applied within the building by finish carpenters.

J

JACK RAFTER A rafter shorter than a common rafter; especially used in hip-roof framing.

JALOUSIE A type of window having a number of small, unframed yet movable pieces of glass.

JAMB The vertical members of a finished door opening.

JOINERY A general woodworking term used for all better-class wood-joint construction.

JOIST A horizontal structural member supported by bearing walls, beams, or girders in floor or ceiling framing.

JOIST HANGER A metal strap to carry the ends of floor joists.

K

KEYSTONE The wedged center stone at the crown of an arch.

KILN-DRIED LUMBER Lumber that has been properly dried and cured to produce a higher grade of lumber than that which has been air dried.

KING POST The center upright strut in a truss.

KIP A unit of 1000 pound load.

KNEE WALL A low wall resulting from 1½-story construction.

KNOCKED DOWN Unassembled; refers to construction units requiring assembly after being delivered to the job.

L

LAITANCE Undesirable surface water that forms on curing concrete.

LALLY COLUMN A steel column used in light construction.

LAMINATED BEAM A beam made of superimposed layers of similar materials by uniting them with glue and pressure.

LANDING A platform between flights of stairs or at the termination of stairs.

LAP JOINT A joint produced by lapping two similar pieces of material.

LATH Metal, wood, or gypsum base for plastering.

LATTICE Framework of crossed or interlaced wood or metal strips.

LEADER A vertical pipe or downspout that carries rainwater from the gutter to the ground or storm sewer.

LEDGER STRIP A strip of lumber fastened to the lower part of a beam or girder on which notched joists are attached.

LIGHT A single pane of glass in a window or door.

LINEAL FOOT A 1′ measurement along a straight line.

LINTEL A horizontal support member across the head of a door or window opening.

LIVE LOAD Loads other than *dead loads* on a building such as wind, snow, people.

LOAD-BEARING WALL A wall designed to support the weight imposed upon it from above.

LOOKOUT A short wooden framing member used to support an overhanging portion of a roof. It extends from the wall to the underside surfacing of the overhang.

LOT LINE The line forming the legal boundary of a piece of property.

LOUVER An opening or slatted grill allowing ventilation while providing protection from rain.

LUMINAIRE An electric lighting fixture used within a room.

M

MANSARD ROOF A hip-type roof having two slopes on each of the four sides.

MASONRY A general term for construction of brick, stone, concrete block, or similar materials.

MASTIC A flexible adhesive for adhering building materials.

MATTE FINISH A finish free from gloss or highlights.

MEMBRANE A thin layer of material used to prevent moisture penetration.

METAL WALL TIES Corrugated metal strips used to tie masonry veneer to wood walls.

MILLWORK A general term that includes all dressed lumber which has been molded, shaped, or preassembled at the mill.

MITER JOINT A joint made with ends or edges of two pieces of lumber cut at a 45° angle and fitted together.

MODULAR CONSTRUCTION Construction in which the size of all components has been based upon a standardized unit of measure.

MOISTURE BARRIER A sheet material that retards moisture penetration into walls, floors, ceilings, etc.

MONOLITHIC Term used for concrete construction poured and cast in one piece without joints.

MORTAR A mixture of cement, sand, lime, and water used to bond masonry units.

MORTICE A hole, slot, or recess cut into a piece of wood to receive a projecting part (tenon) made to fit.

MOSAIC Small colored tile, glass, stone, or similar material arranged to produce a decorative surface.

MULLION The structural member between a series of windows.

MUNTIN A small bar separating the glass lights in a window.

N

NEWEL POST   The main post supporting a handrail at the bottom or top of a stairs.

NOMINAL SIZE   The size of lumber before dressing, rather than its actual size.

NONBEARING WALL   A wall supporting no load other than its own weight.

NONFERROUS METAL   Metal containing no iron, such as copper, brass, or aluminum.

NOSING   The rounded edge of a stair tread.

O

ON CENTER   A method of indicating the spacing between framing members by stating the measurement from the center of one member to the center of the succeeding one.

OPEN WEB JOIST   See bar joists.

OUTLET   Any type of electrical box allowing current to be drawn from the electrical system for lighting or appliances.

OVERHANG   The projecting area of a roof or upper story beyond the wall of the lower part.

P

PALLET   A rugged wood skid used to stack and mechanically handle units of masonry.

PANEL   A flat, rectangular surface framed with a thicker material.

PARAPET   A low wall or railing; usually around the edge of a roof.

PARGE COAT   A thin coat of cement plaster applied to a masonry wall for refinement of the surface or for dampproofing.

PARQUET FLOORING   Flooring, usually of wood, laid in an alternating or inlaid pattern to form various designs.

PARTING STOP   Thin strips set into the vertical jambs of a double-hung window to separate the sash.

PARTITION   A wall that divides areas within a building.

PARTY WALL   A wall between two adjoining buildings in which both owners share, such as a common wall between row houses.

PASSIVE SOLAR SYSTEM   An integral energy system using only natural and architectural components to utilize solar energy.

PENNY   A term used to indicate the size of nails, abbreviated "d". Originally, it specified the price per hundred nails, (i.e., 6-penny nails cost 6¢ per hundred nails).

PERGOLA   An open, structural framework over an outdoor area usually covered with climbing shrubs or vines to form an arbor.

PERIPHERY   The entire outside edge of an object.

PIER   A masonry pillar usually below a building to support the floor framing.

PILASTER   A rectangular pier attached to a wall for the purpose of strengthening the wall. Also a decorative column attached to a wall.

PILES   A long shaft of wood, steel or concrete driven into the earth to support a building.

PITCH   The slope of a roof usually expressed as a ratio.

PLASTIC LAMINATE   A thin melamine surfaced sheet used to cover counter tops.

PLAT   A graphic description of a surveyed piece of land, indicating the boundaries, location, and dimensions. The plat, recorded in the appropriate county official's office, also contains information as to easements, restrictions, and lot numbers, if any.

PLATE   The top horizontal member of a row of studs in a frame wall.

PLUMB   Said of an object when it is in true vertical position as determined by a plumb bob or vertical level.

PLYWOOD   A relatively thin building material made by gluing layers of wood together.

POCHÉ   The darkening in of areas on a drawing to aid in readability.

POST-AND-BEAM CONSTRUCTION   A type of building frame in which roof and floor beams rest directly over wall posts.

PRECAST   Concrete units that are cast and finished at the plant rather than at the site of construction.

PRIME COAT   The first coat of paint that serves as a filler and sealer in preparation for finish coats.

PURLINS   Horizontal roof members laid over trusses to support rafters.

Q

QUARRY TILE   Unglazed, machine-made tile used for floors.

QUARTER ROUND   Small molding presenting the profile of a quarter circle.

QUARTER-SAWED OAK   Oak lumber, usually flooring, which has been sawed so that the medullary rays showing on end-grain are nearly perpendicular to the face of the lumber.

QUOINS   Large squared stones set in the corners of a masonry building for appearance's sake.

RABBET (or rebate)   A groove cut along the edge or end of a board to receive another board producing a rabbet joint.

RADIANT HEATING   A method of heating with the use of radiating heat rays.

RAFTER   A roof structural member running from the wall plate to the ridge. There are jack, hip, valley, and common rafters. The structural members of a flat roof are usually called roof joists.

RAKE JOINT   A mortar joint that has been recessed by tooling before it sets up.

RAKE MOLDING   Gable molding attached on the incline of the gable. The molding must be a different profile to match similar molding along the remaining horizontal portions of the roof.

RANDOM RUBBLE   Stonework having irregular shaped units and coursing.

REGISTER   Opening in air duct, usually covered with a grill.

REINFORCED CONCRETE   Concrete containing steel bars or wire mesh to increase its structural qualities.

RETAINING WALL   A heavy wall that supports an earth embankment.

REVEAL   The side of an opening for a window or door, between the frame and the outer surface of a wall.

RIBBON   A wood strip set into studs to support floor joists in balloon framing.

RIDGE   The top edge of a roof where two slopes meet.

RIDGEBOARD   The highest horizontal member in a gable roof; it is supported by the upper ends of the rafters.

RIPRAP   Irregular stones thrown together loosely to form a wall or soil cover.

RISE   The vertical height of a roof or stairs.

ROCKLATH   Paper covered gypsum sheets used as a plaster base.

ROUGH HARDWARE   All the concealed fasteners in a building such as nails, bolts, hangers, etc.

ROUGH OPENING   An unfinished opening in the framing into which doors, windows, and other units are placed.

ROWLOCK   A special brick coursing placed at the exterior window sill.

RUBBLE   Irregular broken stone.

RUN   The horizontal distance of a flight of stairs, or the horizontal distance from the outer wall to the ridge of a roof.

R VALUE   Unit of thermal resistance in rating insulating materials; higher values are better insulators.

SADDLE   A small gable roof placed in back of a chimney on a sloping roof to shed water and debris.

SANITARY SEWER   Drainage pipe which transports sewage from buildings.

SASH   An individual frame into which glass is set.

SCAB   A short piece of lumber fastened to a butt joint for strength.

SCHEDULE   A list of similar items and information about them, such as a window schedule.

SCRIBING   Marking and fitting a piece of lumber to an irregular surface such as masonry.

SCUTTLE   A small opening in a ceiling to provide access to an attic or roof.

SECTION   A unit of land measurement usually one mile square. A section contains approximately 640 acres, and there are 36 sections to a township. (Also a drawing showing the cut-open view of an object.)

SEPTIC TANK   A concrete or steel underground tank used to reduce sewage by bacterial action.

SHAKE   A handsplit wood shingle.

SHEATHING   The rough boarding or covering over the framing of a house.

SHIM   A thin piece of material used to true up or fill a space between two members.

SHOE MOLD   The small molding covering the joint between the flooring and the baseboard on the inside of a room.

SHORING   Planks or posts used to support walls or ceilings during construction.

SIDING   The outside finish covering on a frame wall.

SILL   The horizontal exterior member below a window or door opening. The wood member placed directly on to the foundation wall in wood frame construction.

SKYLIGHT   A window in a flat roof.

SLEEPERS   Wood strips placed over or in a concrete slab to receive a finish wood floor.

SMOKE CHAMBER   The enlarged portion of a chimney flue directly above the fireplace.

SOFFIT   The underside of an overhang such as a cornice or stairs.

SOIL STACK   The vertical pipe in a plumbing system that carries the sewage.

SOLAR COLLECTOR   A device used to collect the sun's heat.

SOLEPLATE   The horizontal member of a frame wall resting on the rough floor, to which the studs are nailed.

SPAN The horizontal distance between supports for joists, beams, or trusses.

SPECIFICATIONS The written instructions that accompany a set of working drawings.

SQUARE A unit of measure—100 sq ft. Commonly used in reference to the amount of roofing material to cover 100 sq ft.

STILE The vertical member on the door or panel.

STIRRUP A metal U-shaped strap used to support the end of a framing member.

STOOL Horizontal interior member of trim below a window.

STORY A complete horizontal portion of a building having a continuous floor.

STRETCHER COURSE A row of masonry in wall with the long side of the units exposed to the exterior.

STRINGER The inclined structural member supporting the treads and risers of a stairs; sometimes it is visible next to the profile of the stairs.

STUCCO A cement plaster finish applied to exterior walls.

STUDS The vertical framing members of a wall.

SUBFLOORING Any material nailed directly to floor joists. The finish floor is attached over the subflooring.

SUNSPACE Glassed-in area for the collection of solar heat.

SUSPENDED CEILING Finish ceiling hung below the underside of the building structure, either floor or roof.

T

TAIL JOIST A relatively shorter joist that joins against a header or trimmer in floor framing.

TENSILE STRENGTH The greatest longitudinal stress a structural member can bear without adverse effects (breaking or cracking).

TERMITE SHIELD Sheet metal placed over masonry to prevent the passage of termites into wood.

TERRA-COTTA Baked clay and sand formed into masonry units.

TERRAZZO FLOORING Wear-resistant flooring made of marble chips or small stones embedded in cement that has been polished smooth.

THERMAL CONDUCTOR A substance capable of transmitting heat.

THERMOSTAT An automatic device for controlling interior temperatures.

THRESHOLD The beveled metal, stone, or wood member directly under a door.

TITLE Legal evidence to the ownership of property.

TOE NAIL Nailing at an angle to the wood fiber.

TONGUE The narrower extension on the edge of a board that is received by the groove of an adjacent board.

T-POST A post built up of studs and blocking to form the intersection of the framing of perpendicular walls.

TRANSOM A hinged window over a door.

TRAP A U-shaped pipe below plumbing fixtures to create a water seal and prevent sewer odors and gases from being released into the habitable areas.

TREAD The horizontal surface member of a stairs upon which the foot is placed.

TREATED WOOD Wood which has been chemically treated to prevent decay and insect infestation.

TRIM A general term given to the moldings and finish members on a building. Its installation is called finish carpentry.

TRIMMER The longer floor framing member around a rectangular opening into which a header is joined.

TROMBE WALL A passive heating concept consisting of a south-facing masonry wall with glazing in front. Solar radiation is absorbed by the wall, converted to heat, and conducted and radiated into the building.

TRUSS Structural members arranged and fastened in triangular units to form a rigid framework for support of loads over a long span.

TRUSS JOISTS A structural framing member fabricated with a thin wood web and wood flanges.

V

VALLEY RAFTER The diagonal rafter at the intersection of two intersecting sloping roofs.

VAPOR BARRIER A watertight material used to prevent the passage of moisture or water vapor into and through walls.

VENEERED CONSTRUCTION Type of wall construction in which frame or masonry walls are faced with other exterior surfacing materials.

VENT STACK A vertical soil pipe connected to the drainage system to allow ventilation and pressure equalization.

VESTIBULE A small entrance room.

W

WAINSCOT The surfacing on the lower part of an interior wall when finished differently from the remainder of the wall.

WALLBOARD   Large sheets of gypsum or fiberboard that are usually nailed to framing to form interior walls.

WALL TIE   A small metal strip or steel wire used to bind tiers of masonry in cavity-wall construction, or to bind brick veneer to the wood-frame wall in veneer construction.

WATER CLOSET   A toilet.

WATER-TABLE   A horizontal member extending from the surface of an exterior wall so as to throw off rainwater from the wall. Water level below ground.

WEATHER STRIPPING   A strip of fabric or metal fastened around the edges of windows and doors to prevent air infiltration.

WEB   The member between the flanges of a steel beam or the vertical and diagonal members between the top and bottom chords of a truss or bar joist.

WEEP HOLE   Small holes in masonry cavity walls to release water accumulation to the exterior.

WIDE FLANGE   A structural steel beam with a web and top and bottom flanges.

WINDER   The radiating or wedge-shaped treads at the turns of some stairs.

WYTHE   Pertaining to a single-width masonry wall.

Appendix B: Abbreviations used in architectural drawings

Alternate	ALT
Aluminum	AL or ALUM
American Institute of Architects	A.I.A.
American Institute of Architecture Students	A.I.A.S.
American Institute of Electrical Engineers	A.I.E.E.
American Institute of Steel Construction	A.I.S.C.
American National Standards Institute	A.N.S.I.
American Plywood Assoc.	A.P.A.
American Society of Heating, Refrigerating, and Air-Conditioning Engineers	A.S.H.R.A.E.
American Society of Testing and Materials	A.S.T.M.
American Standards Association, Inc.	A.S.A.
American Wire Gauge	AWG
Americans With Disabilities Act	A.D.A.
Apartment	APT
Architectural	ARCH
Association of General Contractors	A.G.C.
Avenue	AVE
Basement	BSMT
Bathroom	B
Beam	BM
Bedroom	BR
Bench mark	BM
Better	BTR
Blocking	BLKG
Board	BD
Board feet	BD FT
Board measure	BM
Boulevard	BLVD
British thermal unit	BTU
Building	BLDG
Building line	BL
Cabinet	CAB
Cast iron	CI
Ceiling	CLG
Cement	CEM
Center line	CL or ℄
Center to center	C to C
Centimeter(s)	cm
Clean out	CO
Closet	CLO
Column	COL
Combination	COMB
Composition	COMP
Concrete	CONC
Construction	CONST
Construction Specifications Institute	C.S.I.
Countersink	CSK
Cubic feet of air per minute	CFM
Cubic foot (feet)	CU FT
Cubic inch (inches)	CU IN
Cubic yard (yards)	CU YD
Detail	DET
Diameter	DIA(M)
Diagonal	DIAG
Dimension	DIM
Dining room	DR
Dishwasher	DW
Ditto	DO or ”
Divided (division)	DIV
Door	DR
Double-hung window	DHW
Double-strength grade A glass	DSA
Double-strength grade B glass	DSB
Douglas fir	DOUG FIR
Down	DN
Downspout	DS
Dozen	DOZ
Drainage, waste & vent	DWV
Drawing	DWG
Dressed and matched (4 sides)	D4S
Duplicate	DUP

Each	EA	I beam	S or I (old designation)
East	E		
Elevation	ELEV	Inch(es)	IN or "
Enclosure	ENCL	Inside diameter	ID
Entrance	ENT	Institute of Boiler and Radiator Manufacturers	I.B.R.
Equipment	EQUIP	Insulate (insulation)	INS
Exterior	EXT	Interior	INT
Exterior insulation finish system	EIFS	Joint	JT
Fabricate	FAB	Joist and plank (lumber designation)	J&P
Fahrenheit	F	Kiln dried	KD
Federal Housing Authority	FHA	Kilowatt	kw
Feet per minute	FPM	Kitchen	K
Finish	FIN	Laminate	LAM
Finish all over	FAO	Landing	LDG
Flashing	FLG	Laundry	LAU
Floor	FL	Lavatory	LAV
Foot board measure	FBM	Left hand	LH
Footing	FTG	Length	L
Forest Products Association	F.P.A.	Light (pane of glass)	LT
Foundation	FDN	Linear feet	LIN FT
Furring	FUR	Linen closet	L CL
Gallon	GAL	Living room	LR
Galvanized	GALV	Louver	LVR
Galvanized iron	GI	Lumber	LBR
Gauge	GA	Manufacture(r)	MFR
General contractor	GC	Material(s)	MTL
Glass	GL	Maximum	MAX
Gypsum	GYP	Mechanical	MECH
Head	HD	Medicine cabinet	MC
Heat- and moisture-resistant rubber insulation	RHW	Medium	MED
Height	HGT	Meter(s)	m
Hemlock	HEM	Millimeter(s)	mm
Hexagonal	HEX	Minimum	MIN
Home Builders Association	H.B.A.	Miscellaneous	MISC
Horsepower	HP	Modular	MOD
Horizontal	HORZ	Molding	MLDG
Horizon line	HL	National Bureau of Standards	N.B.S.
Hose bibb	HB	National Environmental Systems Contractors Association	NESCA
Hundred	C		

National Housing Authority	NHA	Round	RD
National Lumber Manufacturer's Association	N.L.M.A.	Rubber base	RB
		Schedule	SCH
National Warm Air Heating and Air Conditioning Contractors Assoc.	N.W.A.H.A.C.C.A.	Second(s)	s
		Shower	SH
Nominal	NOM	Single-strength grade B glass	SSB
North	N	Sink	SK
Not in contract	NIC	South	S
Number	NO. or #	Southern Pine Inspection Bureau	S.P.I.B.
Office	OFF	Southern Yellow Pine	SYP
On center	OC	Specifications	SPEC
Opening	OPG	Square foot (feet)	SQ FT
Ounce(s)	OZ	Standard	STD
Overhead	OH	Station point	SP
Paint(ed)	PNT	Street	ST
Parallel	PAR or ‖	Surface 4 sides	S4S
Partition	PART	Telephone	TEL
Penny (nail)	d	Television	TV
Pi	π	Temperature	TEMP
Picture plane	PP	Terra-cotta	TC
Piece	PC	Terrazzo	TZ
Plaster	PLAS or PL	Thousand	M
Plate	PL or P_L	Thousand board feet	MBM
Plumbing	PLBG	Threshold	THR
Plywood	PWD	Tongue and groove	T & G
Pounds per cubic foot	PCF	Tread	T or TR
Pounds per square inch	PSI	Typical	TYP
Prefabricate(d)	PFB	Unexcavated	UNEX
Pressure treated	PT	Unfinished	UNFIN
Property line	PL	U.S. standard gauge	USG
Quart(s)	QT	Vanishing point	VP
Radiator	RAD	Ventilation	VENT
Radius	RA	Vertical	VERT
Receptacle	RECP	Volts	V
Refrigerator	REFR	Volume	VOL
Revolutions per minute	RPM	Water closet	WC
Riser	R	Water heater	WH
Road	RD	Waterproof(ing)	WP
Room	RM	Weight	WT
Rough opening	RO	Welded wire fabric	WWF

Welded wire mesh	WWM	Window	WDW
West Coast Lumber Inspection Bureau	W.C.L.I.B.	With	W/
Western Wood Products Assoc.	W.W.P.A.	Wood	WD
		Yard(s)	YD
Wide flange (steel)	W, WF (old designation)	Yellow pine	YP

Appendix C: Modular vertical brick coursing

Module	Course	Dim.	Module	Course	Dim.
	1C	2⅝″		37C	8′–2⅝″
	2C	5⅜″		38C	8′–5⅜″
1M	3C	8″	13M	39C	8′–8″
	4C	10⅝″		40C	8′–10⅝″
	5C	1′–1⅜″		41C	9′–1⅜″
2M	6C	1′–4″	14M	42C	9′–4″
	7C	1′–6⅝″		43C	9′–6⅝″
	8C	1′–9⅜″		44C	9′–9⅜″
3M	9C	2′–0″	15M	45C	10′–0″
	10C	2′–2⅝″		46C	10′–2⅝″
	11C	2′–5⅜″		47C	10′–5⅜″
4M	12C	2′–8″	16M	48C	10′–8″
	13C	2′–10⅝″		49C	10′–10⅝″
	14C	3′–1⅜″		50C	11′–1⅜″
5M	15C	3′–4″	17M	51C	11–′4″
	16C	3′–6⅝″		52C	11′–6⅝″
	17C	3′–9⅜″		53C	11′–9⅜″
6M	18C	4′–0″	18M	54C	12′–0″
	19C	4′–2⅝″		55C	12′–2⅝″
	20C	4′–5⅜″		56C	12′–5⅜″
7M	21C	4′–8″	19M	57C	12′–8″
	22C	4′–10⅝″		58C	12′–10⅝″
	23C	5′–1⅜″		59C	13′–1⅜″
8M	24C	5′–4″	20M	60C	13′–4″
	25C	5′–6⅝″		61C	13′–6⅝″
	26C	5′–9⅜″		62C	13′–9⅜″
9M	27C	6′–0″	21M	63C	14′–0″
	28C	6′–2⅝″		64C	14′–2⅝″
	29C	6′–5⅜″		65C	14′–5⅜″
10M	30C	6′–8″	22M	66C	14′–8″
	31C	6′–10⅝″		67C	14′–10⅝″
	32C	7′–1⅜″		68C	15′–1⅜″
11M	33C	7′–4″	23M	69C	15′–4″
	34C	7′–6⅝″		70C	15′–6⅝″
	35C	7′–9⅜″		71C	15′–9⅜″
12M	36C	8′–0″	24M	72C	16′–0″

[1] The module corresponds to 8″ concrete block course heights.

WORKSHEET FOR MANUAL J
LOAD CALCULATIONS FOR RESIDENTIAL AIR CONDITIONING

For: Name _____ MR. & MRS. JOHN DOE _____
    Address _____ 1918 PINEDALE AVE. _____
    City and State or Province _____ ATLANTA, GA. _____
By: Contractor _____
    Address _____
    City _____

Winter Design Conditions

Outside __10°__ F   Inside __75°__ F   Temperature Difference __65°__ Degrees

(Insert data below only after all heat loss calculations have been completed)

Total Heat Loss (Btuh) __66,535__ (From Line No. 15)   Model No. __LENOX G-8-110__
Serial No. _____   Manufactured by __LENOX__
Rating Data: Input __110,000__ Btuh   Output at Bonnet __88,000__ Btuh
Description of Controls _____

Summer Design Conditions

Outside __95°__ F   Outside Wet Bulb __76°__ F   Inside __75°__ F
North Latitude __35__ Degrees   Daily Range __MEDIUM__

(Insert data below only after all heat gain calculations have been completed)

Total Heat Gain (Btuh) __33,280__ (From Line No. 21 or 22, if used)
Equipment Capacity Multiplier __.89__   Model No. __COND. HSG-311V; Ev. CI-41-V__
Serial No. _____   Manufactured by __LENOX__
Rating Data: Cooling Capacity __30,000__ Btuh   Air Volume __1,125__ Cfm
Description of Controls _____

Winter Construction Data (See Table 2)	Summer Construction Data (See Table 14)
Walls and Partitions __7a & 8a__	Direction House Faces __SE__
	Windows and Doors __6a__
Windows and Doors __20a & 27a__	Walls and Partitions __7a & 8a__
Ceilings __11c__	Ceilings __11c__
Floors __15a__	Floors ___

FILE

#	TYPE OF EXPOSURE	Const. No.	HTM Htg	HTM Clg	Entire House Area/Crack	Htg	Clg	1 LIVING 19x16 (SE&SW) Area/Crack	Htg	Clg	2 DINING RM Area	Htg	Clg	3 KITCHEN 10 (S.W.) Area/Crack	Htg	Clg	4 FAMILY-GUEST (N.E.) Area/Crack	Htg	Clg	5 B.R. #2 (N.E.&N.W.) Area/Crack	Htg	Clg	6 MASTER B.R. (S.W.&N.W.) Area/Crack	Htg	Clg	7 ENTRANCE HALL 10 (S.E.&N.E.) Area/Crack	Htg	Clg	8 BASEMENT Area/Crack	Htg	Clg
1	Name of Room							1 LIVING 19x16			2 DINING RM			3 KITCHEN 10			4 FAMILY-GUEST			5 B.R. #2			6 MASTER B.R.			7 ENTRANCE HALL 10			8 BASEMENT		
2	Running Ft Exposed Wall							152 / 196						80			101			192			232			14 / 42					
3	Ceiling Ht, Ft.							8						8			8			8			8			8			8		
4	Room Compass Directions							S.E. & S.W.						S.W.			N.E.			N.E. & N.W.			S.W. & N.W.			S.E. & N.E.					
5a	Gross Exposed Walls and Partitions	8a						152						80			101			192			232			14					
5b		7a						196																		42					
5c																															
6a	Windows and Doors (Heating)	1a						76	5,550								32	2,300		35	2,550		56	4,080		14	1,020		25	1,830	
6b		6a																								42	1,390				
6c		1c												21	800																
7 SW	Windows and Doors (Cooling)		48					76		3,650																			12.5		580
7 NE			40																	35		1,400							12.5		480
7 SE			78													1,640	32		1,260				56		2,690	14		1,090			
8a	Net Exposed Walls and Partitions	8a	7.9					152	4,720	1,200				59	1,000	350	69	1,170	414	157	2,670	945	176	3,000	1,060	80	1,360	480	74 / 21	2,200	250 / 685
8b		7a	6.0					120	2,040	720																					
8c		8h																											91 / 6		3,660
9	Ceilings	11c	5.1					304	3,040	1,550				130	650	260	186	930	410	181	905	398	198	990	435	46 / 4	460 / 260	235 / 356	108		4,350
10a	Floors	15a																													
11a	Infiltration	27b						48	3,120					16	1,040		16	1,040		16	1,040		28	1,820		40	2,600		40 / 20	2,600 / 1,300	
11b		20b																													
12a	Infiltration or Ventilation (Heating)/(Cooling)	20	1.5					368	552					80	120		88	132		140	210		232	348		20	300		94		745
13	Sub Total Btuh Loss								18,470						2,450			5,440			7,165			9,890			7,090			16,030	
14	Duct Btuh Loss								—						2,450			544 0													
15	Total Btuh Loss					66,535			18,470						2,450			5,440			7,165			9,890			7,090			16,030	
16	People		@300						4						2																
17	Appliances		1200						1,200						2,370 / 1,200																
18	Sensible Btuh Gain (Structure)								7,672						3,570			2,816			2,953			4,533			2,995			2,040	
19	Duct Btuh Gain																														
20	Sum of Lines 18 and 19 (Cooling)								7,672						3,570			2,816			2,953			4,533			2,995			2,040	
21	Total Btuh Gain (Line 20 x 1.3)		1.3						8,872						4,650			3,670			3,840			5,900			3,900			2,450	
22	Btuh for Air Quantities				33,280				4,435		4,435																				

Appendix D   **541**

Modernized Metric System

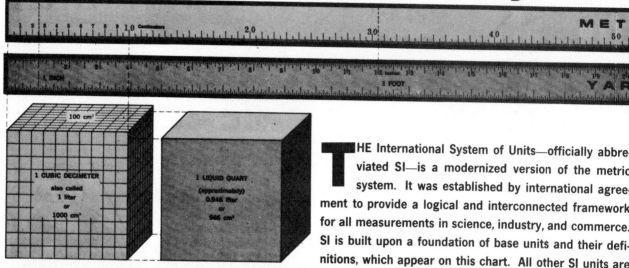

THE International System of Units—officially abbreviated SI—is a modernized version of the metric system. It was established by international agreement to provide a logical and interconnected framework for all measurements in science, industry, and commerce. SI is built upon a foundation of base units and their definitions, which appear on this chart. All other SI units are

The Six Base Units

Length METER—m

The meter is defined as 1 650 763.73 wavelengths in vacuum of the orange-red line of the spectrum of krypton-86.

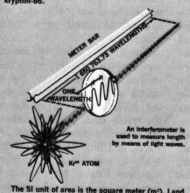

An interferometer is used to measure length by means of light waves.

Kr⁸⁶ ATOM

The SI unit of area is the square meter (m²). Land is often measured by the hectare (10 000 square meters, or approximately 2.5 acres).

The SI unit of volume is the cubic meter (m³). Fluid volume is often measured by the liter (0.001 cubic meter).

National Bureau of Standards Special Publication 304 A

For sale by the Superintendent of Documents, U.S. Government Printing Office, Washington, D.C. 20402 - Price 20 cents

References:

NBS Spec. Publ. 330, International System of Units (in press)
NBS Misc. Publ. 247, Weights and Measures Standards of the United States, A Brief History, 40 cents
NBS Misc. Publ. 286, Units of Weight and Measure, Definitions and Tables of Equivalents, $2.25

Time SECOND-s

The second is defined as the duration of 9 192 631 770 cycles of the radiation associated with a specified transition of the cesium atom. It is realized by tuning an oscillator to the resonance frequency of the cesium atoms as they pass through a system of magnets and a resonant cavity into a detector.

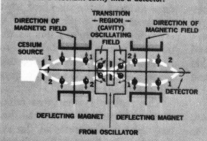

A schematic of an atomic beam spectrometer. The trajectories are drawn for those atoms whose magnetic moments are "flipped" in the transition region.

The number of periods or cycles per second is called frequency. The SI unit for frequency is the hertz (Hz). One hertz equals one cycle per second.

Standard frequencies and correct time are broadcast from NBS stations WWV, WWVB, WWVH, and WWVL, and stations of the U.S. Navy.

Many shortwave receivers pick up WWV on frequencies of 2.5, 5, 10, 15, 20, and 25 megahertz. The standard radio broadcast band extends from 535 to 1605 kilohertz.

Dividing distance by time gives speed. The SI unit for speed is the meter per second (m/s).

Rate of change in speed is called acceleration. The SI unit for acceleration is the meter per second per second (m/s²).

Mass KILOGRAM—kg

The standard for the unit of mass, the kilogram, is a cylinder of platinum-iridium alloy kept by the International Bureau of Weights and Measures at Paris. A duplicate in the custody of the National Bureau of Standards serves as the mass standard for the United States. This is the only base unit still defined by an artifact.

U.S. PROTOTYPE KILOGRAM NO. 20

Closely allied to the concept of mass is that of force. The SI unit of force is the newton (N). A force of 1 newton, when applied for 1 second, will give to a 1 kilogram mass a speed of 1 meter per second (an acceleration of 1 meter per second per second).

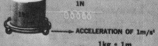

ACCELERATION OF 1m/s²

$$1N = \frac{1kg \cdot 1m}{1s^2}$$

One newton equals approximately two tenths of a pound of force.

The weight of an object is the force exerted on it by gravity. Gravity gives a mass a downward acceleration of about 9.8m/s².

The SI unit for work and energy of any kind is the joule (J).

$$1J = 1N \cdot 1m$$

The SI unit for power of any kind is the watt (W).

$$1W = \frac{1J}{1s}$$

he International System of Units (SI)
nd its relationship to U.S. customary units

6,0   7,0   8,0   9,0

2 FEET

...rived from these base units. Multiples and submultiples
...e expressed in a decimal system. Use of metric weights
...d measures was legalized in the United States in 1866,
...d our customary units of weights and measures are de-
...ed in terms of the meter and the kilogram. The
...gal units for electricity and illumination in the United
...ates are SI units.

The comparative dimensions of the meter and the yard, the liter and the quart, and the kilogram and the pound are shown.

1 pound = 0.453 592 37 kg

1 KILOGRAM   1 POUND

f Measurement
definitions, symbols, and some SI units derived from them

...emperature KELVIN—K

...thermodynamic or Kelvin scale of temperature
...d in SI has its origin or zero point at absolute zero
...has a fixed point at the triple point of water de-
...d as 273.16 kelvins. The Celsius scale is derived
...n the Kelvin scale. The triple point is defined as
...1 °C on the Celsius scale, which is approximately
...02 °F on the Fahrenheit scale. The relationship of
...Kelvin, Celsius, and Fahrenheit temperature
...les is shown below.

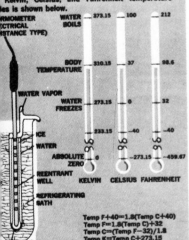

THERMOMETER (ELECTRICAL RESISTANCE TYPE)	WATER BOILS	273.15	100	212
	BODY TEMPERATURE	310.15	37	98.6
WATER VAPOR	WATER FREEZES	273.15	0	32
ICE		233.15	−40	−40
WATER				
REENTRANT WELL	ABSOLUTE ZERO	0	−273.15	−459.67
	KELVIN	CELSIUS	FAHRENHEIT	

REFRIGERATING BATH

Temp F+40=1.8(Temp C+40)
Temp F=1.8(Temp C)+32
Temp C=(Temp F−32)/1.8
Temp K=Temp C+273.15

...PLE POINT CELL

...The triple point cell, an evacuated glass cylinder
...d with pure water, is used to define a known fixed
...perature. When the cell is cooled until a mantle
...ce forms around the reentrant well, the tempera-
...e at the interface of solid, liquid, and vapor is
...1 °C. Thermometers to be calibrated are placed
...the reentrant well.

Electric Current AMPERE—A

The ampere is defined as the magnitude of the current that, when flowing through each of two long
parallel wires separated by one meter in free space,
results in a force between the two wires (due to their
magnetic fields) of 2×10^{-7} newton for each meter of
length.

1A
1m   FORCE = 2 x 10⁻⁷N
←1m→   1A

The SI unit of voltage is the volt (V).

$$1V = \frac{1W}{1A}$$

The SI unit of electrical resistance is the ohm (Ω).

$$1\Omega = \frac{1V}{1A}$$

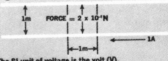

COMMON EQUIVALENTS AND CONVERSIONS

Approximate Common Equivalents		Conversions Accurate to Parts Per Million	
1 inch	=25 millimeters	inches x 25.4*	=millimeters
1 foot	=0.3 meter	feet x 0.3048*	=meters
1 yard	=0.9 meter	yards x 0.9144*	=meters
1 mile	=1.6 kilometers	miles x 1.609 34	=kilometers
1 square inch	=6.5 sq centimeters	square inches x 6.4516*	=sq centimeters
1 square foot	=0.09 square meter	square feet x 0.092 903 0	=square meters
1 square yard	=0.8 square meter	square yards x 0.836 127	=square meters
1 acre	=0.4 hectare †	acres x 0.404 686	=hectares
1 cubic inch	=16 cu centimeters	cubic inches x 16.3871	=cu centimeters
1 cubic foot	=0.03 cubic meter	cubic feet x 0.026 316 8	=cubic meters
1 cubic yard	=0.8 cubic meter	cubic yards x 0.764 555	=cubic meters
1 quart (liq)	=1 liter †	quarts (liq) x 0.946 353	=liters
1 gallon	=0.004 cubic meter	gallons x 0.003 785 41	=cubic meters
1 ounce (avdp)	=28 grams	ounces (avdp) x 28.3495	=grams
1 pound (avdp)	=0.45 kilogram	pounds (avdp) x 0.453 592	=kilograms
1 horsepower	=0.75 kilowatt	horsepower x 0.745 700	=kilowatts
1 millimeter	=0.04 inch	millimeters x 0.039 370 1	=inches
1 meter	=3.3 feet	meters x 3.280 84	=feet
1 meter	=1.1 yards	meters x 1.093 61	=yards
1 kilometer	=0.6 mile	kilometers x 0.621 371	=miles
1 sq centimeter	=0.16 square inch	sq centimeters x 0.155 000	=square inches
1 square meter	=11 square feet	square meters x 10.7639	=square feet
1 square meter	=1.2 square yards	square meters x 1.195 99	=square yards
1 hectare †	=2.5 acres	hectares x 2.471 05	=acres
1 cu centimeter	=0.06 cubic inch	cu centimeters x 0.061 023 7	=cubic inches
1 cubic meter	=35 cubic feet	cubic meters x 35.3147	=cubic feet
1 cubic meter	=1.3 cubic yards	cubic meters x 1.307 95	=cubic yards
1 liter †	=1 quart (liq)	liters x 1.056 69	=quarts (liq)
1 cubic meter	=250 gallons	cubic meters x 264.172	=gallons
1 gram	=0.035 ounces (avdp)	grams x 0.035 274 0	=ounces (avdp)
1 kilogram	=2.2 pounds (avdp)	kilograms x 2.204 62	=pounds (avdp)
1 kilowatt	=1.3 horsepower	kilowatts x 1.341 02	=horsepower

† common term not used in SI   * exact

Luminous Intensity CANDELA—cd

The candela is defined as the luminous intensity of
1/600 000 of a square meter of a radiating cavity
at the temperature of freezing platinum (2042 K).

LIGHT EMITTED HERE

CAVITY

FREEZING PLATINUM

INSULATING MATERIAL

The SI unit of light flux is the lumen (lm). A source
having an intensity of 1
candela in all directions
radiates a light flux of 4π
lumens.

A 100-watt light bulb emits about 1700 lumens

THESE PREFIXES MAY BE APPLIED TO ALL SI UNITS

Multiples and Submultiples	Prefixes	Symbols
1 000 000 000 000 = 10¹²	tera (tĕr'á)	T
1 000 000 000 = 10⁹	giga (jĭ'gá)	G
1 000 000 = 10⁶	mega (mĕg'á)	M *
1000 = 10³	kilo (kĭl'ō)	k *
100 = 10²	hecto (hĕk'tō)	h
10 = 10	deka (dĕk'á)	da
0.1 = 10⁻¹	deci (dĕs'ĭ)	d
0.01 = 10⁻²	centi (sĕn'tĭ)	c *
0.001 = 10⁻³	milli (mĭl'ĭ)	m *
0.000 001 = 10⁻⁶	micro (mī'krō)	μ *
0.000 000 001 = 10⁻⁹	nano (năn'ō)	n
0.000 000 000 001 = 10⁻¹²	pico (pē'kō)	p
0.000 000 000 000 001 = 10⁻¹⁵	femto (fĕm'tō)	f
0.000 000 000 000 000 001 = 10⁻¹⁸	atto (ăt'tō)	a

*Most commonly used

(See page 525 for the perspective view of this home.)

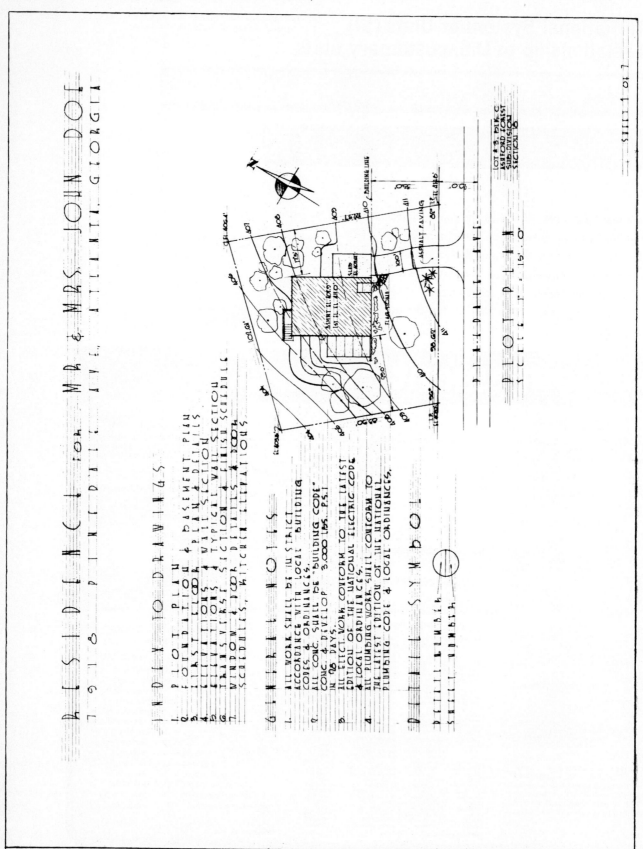

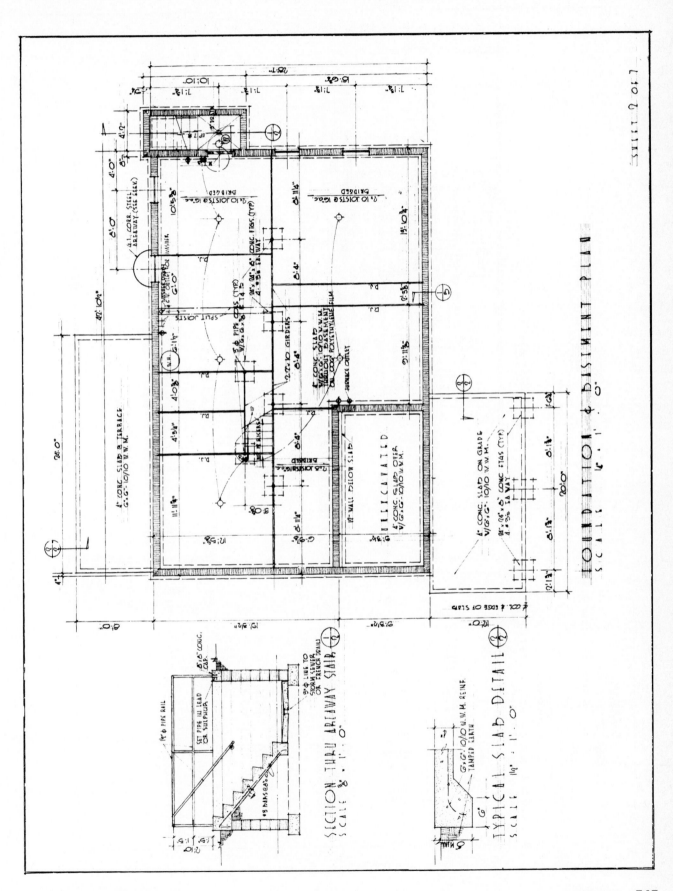

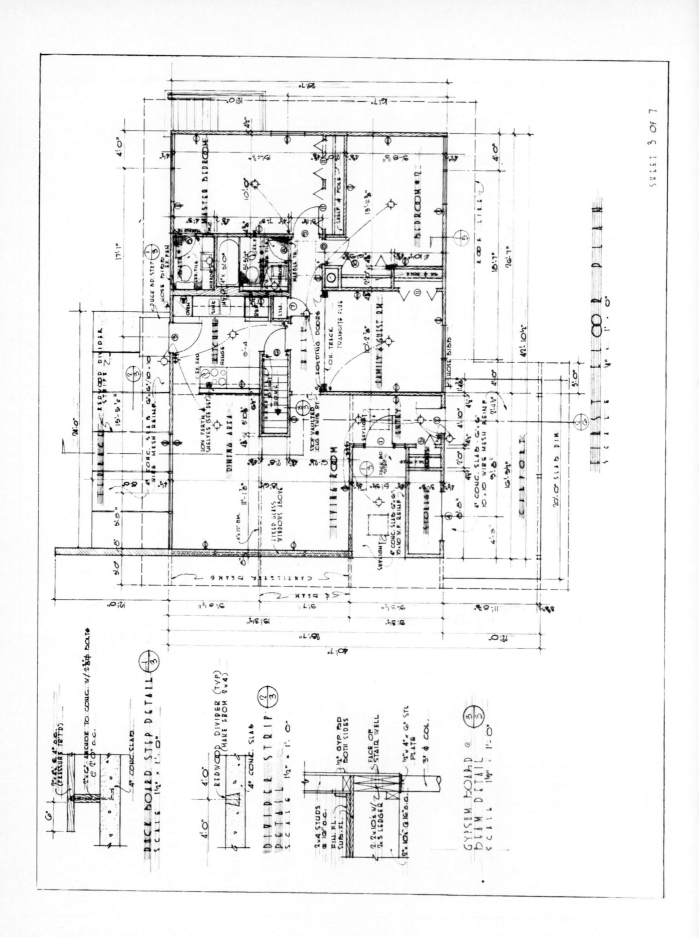

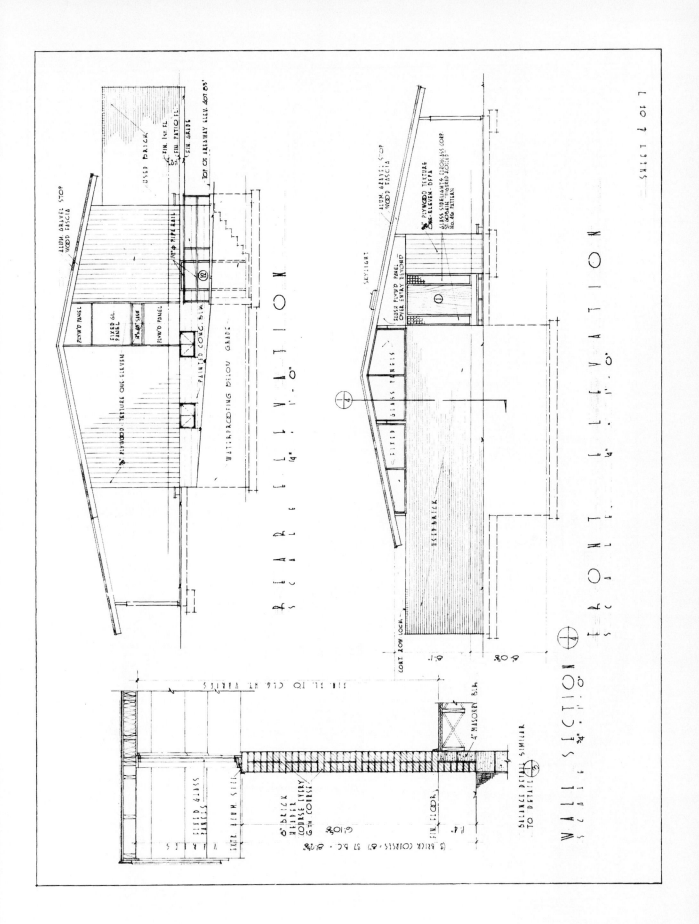

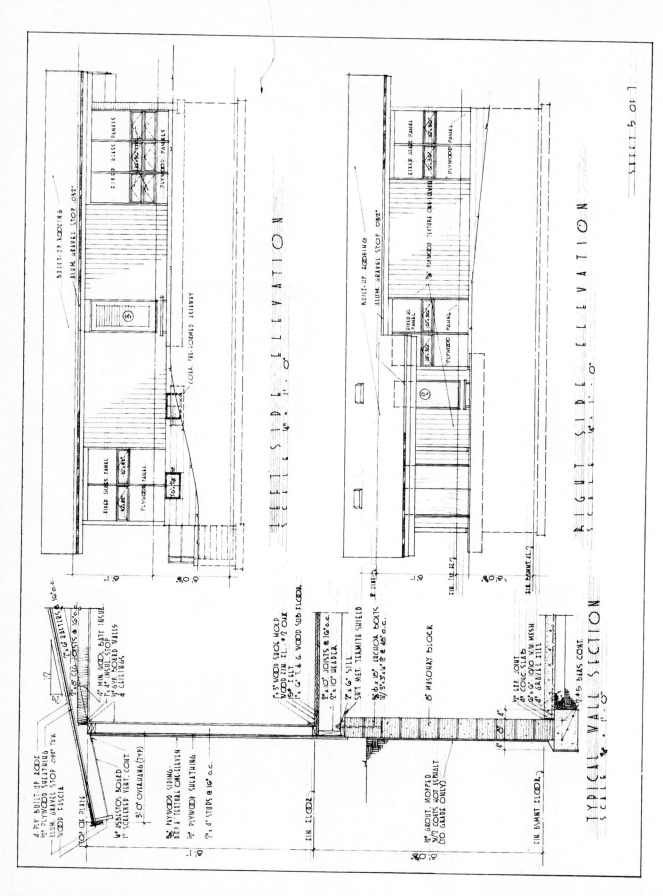

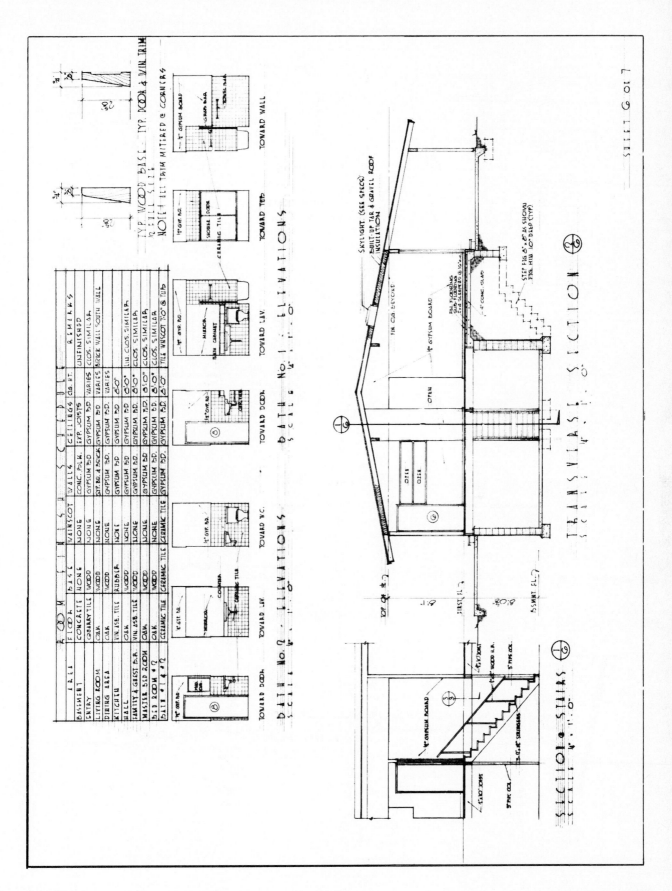

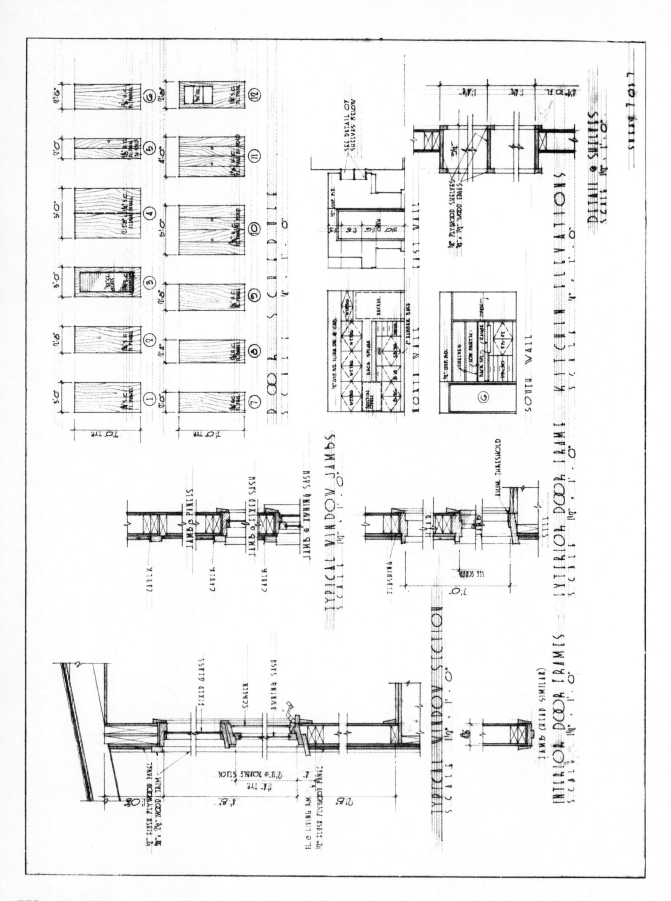

INDEX